to be returned on or befo

D1422686

PERSPECTIVES IN PSYCHIATRY VOLUME 6

Depression and Physical Illness

Edited by

M.M. Robertson

and

C.L.E. Katona

Department of Psychiatry and Behavioural Sciences,
University College London Medical School, London, UK

JOHN WILEY & SONS

Chichester · New York · Weinheim · Brisbane · Singapore · Toronto

Other Wiley Editorial Offices

John Wiley & Sons, Inc., 605 Third Avenue,
New York, NY 10158-0012, USA

VCH Verlagsgesellschaft mbH, Pappelallee 3,
D-69469 Weinheim, Germany

Jacaranda Wiley Ltd, 33 Park Road, Milton,
Queensland 4064, Australia

John Wiley & Sons (Canada) Ltd, 22 Worcester Road,
Rexdale, Ontario M9W 1L1, Canada

John Wiley & Sons (Asia) Pte Ltd, 2 Clementi Loop #02-01,
Jin Xing Distripark, Singapore 0512

Library of Congress Cataloging-in-Publication Data

Depression and physical illness / edited by M.M. Robertson and C.L.E.
Katona.
     p.   cm.—(Perspectives in psychiatry ; v. 6)
     Includes bibliographical references and index.
     ISBN 0-471-96148-5 (alk. paper)
     1. Depression, Mental.   2. Psychological manifestations of general
diseases.   3. Medicine, Psychosomatic.   I. Robertson, Mary M.
II. Katona, C. L. E. (Cornelius L. E.), 1954–   .   III. Series:
Perspectives in psychiatry (Chichester, England) ; v. 6.
     [DNLM: 1. Depression—complications.   2. Depression—etiology.
W1 PE871F v.6 1996 / WN 171 D424 1996]
RC537.D427527   1996
616.85'27—dc21
DNLM/DLC
for Library of Congress   96-37003
                                                                   CIP

British Library Cataloguing in Publication Data

A catalogue record for this book is available from the British Library

ISBN 0-471-96148-5

Typeset in 10/12pt Garamond by Acorn Bookwork, Salisbury, Wilts
Printed and bound in Great Britain by Biddles Ltd, Guildford
This book is printed on acid-free paper responsibly manufactured from sustainable forestation,
for which at least two trees are planted for each one used for paper production.

Contents

Contributors

T.J. Anfinson — *Emory University School of Medicine, PO Box AF, Atlanta, GA 30322, USA*

S. Barry — *Cluain Mhuire Service, Blackrock, Co. Dublin, Eire*

E.B. Boswell — *Emory University School of Medicine, PO Box AF, Atlanta, GA 30322, USA*

C.K. Bridgett — *Charing Cross and Westminster Medical School, London*

C.B. Bunker — *Charing Cross and Westminster Medical School, London*

R. Campos — *Hospital Clinico Universitario, Zaragoza 50009, Spain*

P.R. Casey — *University College Dublin, Mater Misericordiae Hospital, 62/63 Eccles Street, Dublin 7, Eire*

I. Collis — *St Luke's-Woodside Hospital, London N10 3HU*

S. Cox — *Middlesex Hospital, Riding House Street, London W1N 8AA*

F. Creed — *University of Manchester, Oxford Road, Manchester M13 9WL*

E. Finch — *The Institute of Psychiatry, De Crespigny Park, London SE5 8AF*

J. Firth-Cozens — *NHS Executive, Durham University Science Park, Durham DH1 3YG*

C. Gala — *University of Milan, Via Francesco Sforza 35, 20122, Milan, Italy*

F. Galetti — *University of Milan, Via Francesco Sforza 35, 20122, Milan, Italy*

R. George — *Camden and Islington Palliative Care Team, 26 Nassau Street, London W1N 7RF*

P. Hill — *St George's Hospital Medical School, Cranmer Terrace, Tooting, London SW17 0RE*

M. Hotopf — *Kings College School of Medicine and Dentistry and Institute of Psychiatry, 103 Denmark Hill, London SE5 8AZ*

G. Invernizzi — *University of Milan, Via Francesco Sforza 35, 20122, Milan, Italy*

G. Jackson — *Duke's Priory Hospital, Stump Lane, Springfield Green, Springfield, Chelmsford, Essex CM1 7SJ*

A. Jenaway — *University of Cambridge, Addenbrooke's Hospital, Cambridge CB2 2QQ*

C.L.E. Katona — *University College London Medical School, Wolfson Building, Middlesex Hospital Site, London W1N 8AA*

M.S. Keshavan — *University of Pittsburgh School of Medicine, Western Psychiatric Institute and Clinic, 3811 O'Hara Street, Pittsburgh, PA 15213, USA*

G.G. Lloyd — *Royal Free Hospital, Pond Street, London NW3 2QG*

A. Lobo — *Hospital Clinico Universitario, Zaragoza 50009, Spain*

P. Maguire — *CRC Psychological Medicine Group, Stanley House, Christie Hospital, Manchester M20 4BX*

M. Maj

Faculty of Medicine and Surgery, University of Naples, Largo Madonna della Grazie, 80138 Naples, Italy

R.A. Mayou

Warneford Hospital, Oxford OX3 7JX

C.B. Nemeroff

Emory University School of Medicine, PO Box AF, Atlanta, GA 30322, USA

P. Onghena

Faculty of Psychology and Educational Sciences, Katholieke Universiteit Leuven, Departement Pedagogische Wetenschappen, CMEPO, Vesaliusstraat 2, B-3000 Leuven, Belgium

J.C. Parker

Harry S Truman Memorial Veterans' Hospital, 800 Hospital Drive (116B), Columbia, MO 65201, USA

E.S. Paykel

University of Cambridge, Addenbrooke's Hospital, Cambridge CB2 2QQ

G.P. Prigatano

Barrow Neurological Institute, 350 West Thomas Road, Phoenix, AZ 85013, USA

M.M. Robertson

University College London Medical School, Middlesex Hospital Site, Mortimer Street, London W1N 8AA

T. Sensky

Charing Cross and Westminster Medical School, West Middlesex University Hospital, Isleworth, Middlesex TW7 6AF

J.D. Summers

Barrow Neurological Institute, St Joseph's Hospital and Medical Center, 350 West Thomas Road, Phoenix, AZ 85013, USA

N. Swire

Camden and Islington Palliative Care Team, 26 Nassau Street, London W1N 7RF

R.W. Taylor

Keld Head, Keld (near Shep), Penrith, Cumbria CA10 3QF

B. Van Houdenhove   *Faculty of Medicine, Katholieke Universiteit Leuven, Afdeling Psychosomatische Revalidatie, Universitair Ziekenhuis Pellenberg, Weligerveld 1, B-3212 Lubbeek Belgium*

Z. Walker   *University College London Medical School, Wolfson Building, Middlesex Site, London W1N 8AA*

S. Wessely   *Institute of Psychiatry, 103 Denmark Hill, London SE5 8AZ*

G.E. Wright   *University of Missouri-Columbia School of Medicine*

A. York   *St George's Hospital Medical School, Cranmer Terrace, Tooting, London SW17 0RE*

Preface

Depression all too frequently complicates physical illness. Such comorbid depression may adversely affect the outcome of the physical condition and, in turn, be perpetuated by it. Depression often goes undetected in physically ill people and, even where it is recognized, its treatment poses particular challenges.

We intend this book (which forms part of the *Perspectives in Psychiatry* series) to provide a comprehensive and scholarly account of depression in the context of physical illness as well as offering a practical approach to its management. With this in mind, considerable use is made of illustrative case vignettes. In addition, consistent reference is made to current diagnostic systems (ICD-10, DSM-IV).

The book has been compiled to address three main areas:

Part 1, Depression and Physical Illness: General Issues provides an overall framework and considers the general issues of detecting and managing comorbid depression in both the hospital and primary care context.

Part 2, Depression and Physical Illness in Relation to the Life Cycle, focuses on relationships between depression and physical illness in youth and old age, and in the context of female reproductive life.

Part 3, Depression and Specific Physical Conditions, is the largest section and explores the detection, management and prognosis of depression in the context of specific diseases. This section is organized mainly in terms of body systems with, in addition, chapters on depression in the context of malignant diseases, pain and dying. Within this section, each chapter offers a concise account of the physical condition(s) being discussed, followed by detailed consideration of the presentation, assessment (including diagnostic problems), aetiology, management and prognosis of the associated depressive disorders.

We have been fortunate in recruiting authors of considerable international eminence. As a result, the book should be of interest to a world-wide audience. In particular, it is aimed at trainees in psychiatry working towards specialist qualifications, as well as at established specialists with a particular interest in consulting and liaison psychiatry. In addition, it has much of interest to physicians and to family practitioners, as well as to professionals in allied disciplines including nursing, clinical psychology and health psychology.

Our thanks must go first to our authors for producing work of such high quality within considerable time constraints, and for their flexibility in response to our suggestions. We also owe a considerable debt of thanks to the staff at John Wiley & Sons, Ltd, and in particular to Elaine Hutton, for their patience and support as the book came together. Finally, we would like to thank Phillipa Katona and John Ludgate for tolerating the considerable toll of evenings spent on the project.

Mary Robertson and Cornelius Katona
London, December 1996

Part I

DEPRESSION AND PHYSICAL ILLNESS: GENERAL ISSUES

1

Assessing depression in the context of physical illness

Francis Creed

INTRODUCTION

There are many different aspects of assessing depression in the physically ill that have been discussed in a variety of papers and reviews (Mayou and Hawton, 1986; Meakin, 1992; McDaniel *et al.*, 1995; Rodin and Volshart, 1986; Rodin *et al.*, 1991; Jenkins and Jamel, 1994). Different reviews have made different points about depression in the physically ill.

Mayou and Hawton (1986) indicated the need for a new type of psychiatric classification for patients in the general hospital. They stated that a classification and set of measuring instruments which were primarily based on research with psychiatric inpatients can never be appropriate for the physically ill. They noted that the General Health Questionnaire is the best available self-administered questionnaire but felt that this had not been validated sufficiently in this population. They found the DSM-III definitions were not entirely satisfactory (definitions have been modified in the subsequent DSM-IIIR—see below). Mayou and Hawton also highlighted the importance of the relationship between demographic and social factors, which may influence the prevalence of depression in the physically ill to a greater extent than severity of physical illness. The fairly extensive literature concerning lack of recognition of psychiatric disorder by medical staff is based on seriously flawed evidence.

Depression and Physical Illness. Edited by M.M. Robertson and C.L.E. Katona
© 1997 John Wiley & Sons Ltd

Meakin (1992) is alone in suggesting that self-administered questionnaires can provide satisfactory screening of depression with the hope that this can lead to an indication of patients who require treatment. The suggestion comes from Snaith (1987) who developed the Hospital Anxiety and Depression Scale with the aim of indicating to physicians those patients who might require treatment with antidepressants.

In the most thorough review, House (1988) proposes that depression be regarded as a continuously distributed variable among the physically ill, as in the general population. Further research is required to determine the level of severity and symptom pattern which will define a "case"; this will be the cut-off point, which most closely relates to outcome and depression which is likely to merit specific treatment.

House reminds us that a definition of depression is purely descriptive and needs to be free of aetiological discussions; the latter relate to management, not case definition. House describes paper and pencil screening tests as "theoretically and practically undesirable" and suggests that the repeated demonstration of the existence of "psychiatric symptoms", without any demonstration that they can be treated psychiatrically, leads to alienation of our colleagues in other disciplines. House indicates that a test for psychiatric disorder in the physically ill needs to be sensitive at a low prevalence of psychiatric disorder and raises the possibility that persistence of mood disorder needs to be considered alongside its severity; chronic mild depression may be of particular significance. House advocated a population-based approach to depression in the physically ill rather than a preoccupation with identification of individual cases. Finally, House indicates that nondepressive phenomena, including denial, may be important in relation to the physically ill.

Rodin *et al.* (1991) state that the assessment of depression in the physically ill is especially difficult because clinicians are called upon to differentiate symptoms of depressive disorder, not only from those of less severe adjustment disorders but also from symptoms that are more direct manifestations of physical disease. They comment on the problems of somatic symptoms, which may lead to over-diagnosis of depression. These authors discuss depressive symptoms and depressive disorders separately. Their table (Rodin *et al.*, 1991, pp. 44–51) indicates that reported prevalence of depressive symptoms in general medical inpatients has varied between 10% and 50%. Such depressive symptoms were often associated with severity of physical illness, but also with demographic factors.

McDaniel *et al.* (1995) also noted that the reported prevalence of major depressive disorder, assessed by standardized diagnostic interview, ranged from 4.8% to 9.2% in medical outpatients, from 8% to 15% in medical inpatients and from 1.5% to 50% in cancer patients (mean 24%, median 22%). They also commented that there is an increased chance of depression with increased severity of the accompanying medical illness.

Jenkins and Jamil (1994) also support the latter view and suggest that the prevalence of depression is lower on surgical wards. They support the use of the "Endicott" criteria to diagnose depressive disorder in clinical practice. These criteria substitute the following four psychological symptoms of tearful/depressed appearance, social withdrawal/not talking, brooding/pessimism, and nonreactive mood instead of the four somatic symptoms of weight change, sleep disturbance, fatigue, and diminished concentration, as these may be caused by physical illness rather than depression.

These different reviews have highlighted the following aspects of depression in the physically ill.

1. The need for further research to clarify a "case" definition that is useful in predicting outcome and against which self-administered questionnaires can be validated.
2. Clarification of the relationship between depressive disorder and severity of physical illness.
3. The potential value of self-administered questionnaires in this field needs to be clarified; depressive disorder needs to be reliably distinguished from adjustment disorders and diagnosed independently of somatic symptoms which may result from physical illness rather than depressive disorder.

These principles will be discussed in this chapter and recommendations for routine practice will be made.

PREVALENCE OF DEPRESSION IN THE MEDICALLY ILL

The wide variation of the reported prevalence of depression in the physically ill has already been noted (McDaniel *et al.*, 1995). Meakin's review also indicated a variation in the prevalence of depression of between 8% and 60% in different populations using different self-administered questionnaires. Rodin *et al.* (1991) found similar variations both for depressive symptoms and depressive disorders (10.8–27%, median 22%, when standardized interviews were used). Rather higher figures were found for neurological patients.

The clearest impression one gains from the tables in these review articles is the fact that the prevalence of depression in the physically ill has been coming down with time. This is because early studies used self-administered questionnaires in a population for which they have not been standardized, whereas later studies used research interviews. One recent study indicated the different prevalence figures from such methods (Clarke *et al.*, 1991); the estimated prevalence of psychiatric morbidity using the General Hospital Questionnaire was 30% but only 12% of the population had major depressive disorder.

In addition, the enormous variation in the published literature reflects the following problems (Rodin and Voshart, 1986).

1. Lack of a clear definition of depressive disorder in the physically ill.
2. Use of different thresholds (major depression, dysthymia, minor depression, etc.).
3. The absence of specific assessment measures which have been validated in the physically ill.
4. Selection bias in the population of medically ill patients according to treatment centre.
5. Heterogeneity in terms of sociodemographic variation.
6. No appropriate control groups.

LACK OF A CLEAR DEFINITION OF DEPRESSIVE DISORDER IN THE PHYSICALLY ILL—THE NEED FOR DEFINITION OF A "CASE"

Somatic symptoms

One of the problems with the assessment of depression in the physically ill is the presence of somatic symptoms such as fatigue, sleep loss, anorexia and weight loss. These may be scored as symptoms of depression when, in fact, they may arise from the physical illness itself.

Several studies have compared the features of depression in patients with physical illness with nonphysically ill depressed patients. Moffic and Paykel (1975), Clarke et al. (1983), and Berrios and Samuel (1987) all found that medical depressives were older than depressed patients seen in a psychiatry department. The depression among the physically ill was less severe than that seen in a psychiatry department and there was less family history, less previous history and less female preponderance.

Attempts to define the symptoms that best discriminate between depressed and nondepressed patients in medical and psychiatric samples have not been entirely consistent in their results (Table 1).

It can be seen from the middle column of Table 1 that psychological symptoms discriminated better than somatic symptoms in the medically ill in the study by Clarke et al. (1983), but Moffic and Paykel (1985) found that somatic preoccupation, sleep disturbance and appetite loss, although common in medical patients in general, did help to distinguish the depressed medical inpatients from the nondepressed medical inpatients. Clarke et al. (1983) found that these somatic symptoms of depression gradually increase in severity as one moves from non-cases to cases; they do not appear as an "all or none" phenomenon as they do in psychiatric depressives.

Table 1. Symptoms that discriminate between depressed and nondepressed medical and psychiatric patients (Clarke *et al.*, 1983).

Symptom	Psychiatric versus normal	Medical sample versus nondepressed	Medical Depressed and nondepressed (Moffic and Paykel)
Sadness			+
Hopelessness	+		+
Sense of failure	+	+	
Dissatisfaction	+	+	
Guilt	+		+
Sense of punishment	+	+	
Self-hate	+		
Self-blame	+		
Suicidal thoughts	+	+	+
Crying		+	
Irritability	+		+
Loss of social interest	+	+	
Indecision	+		+
Poor body image	+		+
Work inhibition			
Sleep disturbance			+
Fatigue	+		
Loss of appetite			+
Weight loss			
Hypochondriasis			
Loss of general interest			

Berrios and Samuel (1987) reported that neurological depressed subjects suffered from significantly more depressed mood, psychomotor retardation, suicidal ideas and irritability than the nondepressed neurological subjects. These authors found that the following symptoms were less common in the depressed neurological subjects than in the psychiatric depressed sample: early morning wakening, guilt and suicidal ideas. However, irritability and headaches were more common in the depressed neurological subjects than in the psychiatric depressives.

Koenig *et al.* (1993) controlled for severity of medical illness, functional status and alcohol use before identifying the symptoms that discriminated manic depressive disorder among young male patients. These symptoms were loss of interest, feelings of guilt, being a burden, suicidal thoughts and depressed mood—primarily cognitive and affective symptoms. They found that fatigue, weight loss, genital symptoms and somatic anxiety (somatic symptoms)

Table 2. Symptoms of depression in the medically ill (includes Endicott's criteria, 1984).

---

*Tearful or depressed appearance
*Social withdrawal or decreased talkativeness
*Psychomotor retardation or agitation
*Depressed mood
*Mood that is nonreactive to environmental events
Morning depression
*Marked diminished interest or pleasure in most activities
*Brooding, self-pity or pessimism
*Feelings of worthlessness or excessive or inappropriate guilt
Feelings of helplessness
Feeling a burden
*Recurrent thoughts of death or suicide
Thoughts that the illness is a punishment
Frequent crying

---

*Endicott's criteria which should be present for at least two weeks for a diagnosis of depressive illness.

were not related to major depressive disorder. The number of somatic complaints (headache, dizziness, palpitations, sweating, dry mouth, etc.), however, did help differentiate patients with major depressive disorder from the remainder.

These authors noted that in older men there was a mixture of cognitive/affective and somatic symptoms which differentiated depressed from nondepressed medical patients, with loss of interest, insomnia, suicidal thoughts and hypochondriasis most strongly discriminating. Thus it seems likely that age differences may help to explain some of the differences spelled out above.

It has been suggested (Kathol and Petty, 1981; Cavanaugh, 1983) that understanding this area requires somatic symptoms (anorexia, weight loss, sleep disturbance, psychomotor changes, fatigue, loss of energy, decreased sexual drive and decreased concentration) and cognitive/affective symptoms (depressed mood, social withdrawal, restlessness or irritability, lack of self-worth, feelings of inadequacy or failure, self-blame, guilt, helplessness and suicidal thoughts) to be treated separately in diagnosing depression in the physically ill.

Two approaches are possible. Endicott (1984) suggested that the criteria for depression in the medically ill should have the somatic symptoms removed (weight loss, sleep disturbance, fatigue, difficulty in concentration/indecision), and/or cognitive/affective items inserted (see Table 2). An alternative approach (Spitzer et al., 1992; Robins et al., 1981) suggests that symptoms count towards the diagnosis of major depressive disorder if judged "not to be due primarily to the medical illness". This approach was taken by the Oxford group (Feldman et al., 1987) and the authors admitted the difficulty in discriminating between physical and psychological causes of symptoms and eventually scored somatic symptoms such as tiredness irrespective of the purported cause.

THE ABSENCE OF SPECIFIC ASSESSMENT MEASURES, WHICH HAVE BEEN VALIDATED IN THE PHYSICALLY ILL

Standardized interviews

Rodin *et al.* (1991) described the relevant structured diagnostic interviews to determine the prevalence of depressive disorders in medical samples. They comment that in the Present State Examination, symptoms apparently caused by physical illness should not be recorded as symptoms of depression (mentioned above—Feldman *et al.*, 1987). However, no guidance is given as to how this judgement can be made. By contrast, the Diagnostic Interview Schedule includes a decision-tree to help determine which symptoms are the result of the physical illness. This instrument was developed for lay interviewers. For this reason, it is specified that particular symptoms will not contribute to a diagnosis of depression if the patient was told by a physician that these symptoms are the result of a physical illness or medication. Rodin *et al.* suggest that such operationalized criteria add reliability to the decision-making process, although this could be debated.

The DSM-IIIR, but not DSM-III, includes a directive "to not include symptoms which are clearly due to a physical disorder", although this requires medical judgement. Rodin *et al.* (1991) have suggested that this approach is preferable to that of excluding all somatic symptoms as described above. They have criticized the elimination of somatic criteria from the diagnosis of mood disorders in the medically ill because the validity of standardized interviews and of the DSM-IIIR criteria is lost. It is also not clear how severe a medical illness must be to warrant use of the Endicott criteria; in psychiatric wards many patients also have physical illness. Elimination or replacement of somatic criteria would result in under-diagnosis of depression in the physically ill, especially those depressed patients who present with predominantly somatic symptoms.

Emmons *et al.* (1987) found the depression in the physically ill was characterized by worry and helplessness, loss of energy, insomnia and loss of appetite accompanied by weight loss. Based on the prominence of somatic symptoms in the depressed medical patients, these investigators also indicated that it would be inappropriate to abandon somatic items when diagnosing depression in the medically ill.

USE OF DIFFERENT THRESHOLDS (MAJOR DEPRESSION, DYSTHYMIA, MINOR DEPRESSION, ETC.)

The difficulty of establishing a clear definition of a "case" of depression in the physically ill is compounded by the fact that previous research has used different definitions—depressive symptoms, major depression, dysthymia and minor depression. It is not apparent which of these is of greatest interest, bearing in mind House's recommendation that we are concerned with a case definition that is related to outcome.

There is some evidence that depressive symptoms which may not amount to a diagnosis of major depression may be sufficient to interface with the course of a physical illness. Wells *et al.* (1989), in the medical outcomes study, found that the effects of depressive symptoms and medical conditions on functioning were additive; for example, the combination of current advanced coronary artery disease and depressive symptoms was associated with about twice the reduction in social functioning associated with either condition alone. This study indicated that depressive symptoms not amounting to major depressive disorder could have an effect on social functioning.

Frank *et al.* (1988) studied depression in rheumatoid arthritis (RA) patients and reported the prevalence of dysthymia as 41% and major depressive disorder as 17%. These authors considered the prevalence figure for major depressive disorder to be more accurate than that for dysthymic disorder as the symptoms of the latter (depression with chronic tiredness, decreased activity and social withdrawal) overlap greatly with those of RA. For example, 80% of the sample of RA patients recorded loss of energy and insomnia, suggesting that they are not specific for depression.

The differentiation of depressive disorder from adjustment disorder is very difficult in the medically ill. The DSM-IIIR definition of adjustment disorder requires a judgement that the distress is "in excess of what is expected". When an emotional response is in "excess of the expected" it may be difficult to determine. It is preferable to assume that the dimension of distress is a continuously distributed variable, as recommended by House, which indicates that, in the current state of knowledge, there is no clear cut-off between adjustment and depressive disorders.

Self-administered questionnaires

The self-administered questionnaires used to detect depression include many somatic symptoms. The General Health Questionnaire (GHQ) 28 includes the following somatic items on a subscale: feeling perfectly well and in good health, feeling in need of a good tonic, been feeling run down and out of sorts, felt that you are ill, been getting any pains in your head, been getting a feeling of tightness or pressure in your head, been having hot or cold spells, lost much sleep over worry, had difficulty in staying asleep once you were off, been taking longer over things you do. The Hamilton Rating Scale for Depression includes items on hypochondriasis (preoccupied by physical symptoms and a feeling of being physically ill), three items concerning insomnia, and gastrointestinal, general somatic, sexual and weight loss items.

The Beck Depression Inventory includes items concerning bodily change, difficulty with working, sleep problems, fatigue, appetite and weight loss, concerns about health, and change of interest in sex. Thus eight of the 21 items could be directly attributable to a physical illness.

The self-administered questionnaires reviewed by Meakin (1992) included the GHQ (60 and 28 question version), the Zung Depression Scale, the Beck Depression Inventory, the Geriatric Depression Scale and the Hospital Anxiety and Depression Scale. Of these, only the Hospital Anxiety and Depression Scale has been specifically designed for use in the medically ill (see below).

The Hospital Anxiety and Depression (HAD) Scale was specifically devised for detecting anxiety and depression in the physically ill and only includes psychological symptoms—somatic items which could be attributed to the physical illness have been omitted. The scoring system is also simple.

The HAD Scale has been compared with clinical rating scales (Zigmund and Sanith, 1983; Aylard *et al.*, 1987) and with standardized interviews. By using a "borderline" category, it is possible to achieve very low misclassification rates; but it is interesting that there is very little difference between the HAD Scale and GHQ in comparison with an observer-rated depression scale (Aylard *et al.*, 1987). Comparing the GHQ 12 and the HAD (with a raised HAD cut-off score of 10/11), Lewis and Wessley (1990) found the GHQ was marginally superior to the HAD Scale in categorizing patients, when caseness was defined by the Clinical Interview Schedule. In a genito-urinary clinic, a cut-off score of eight on the HAD Scale provided optimal sensitivity and specificity, but this was against the diagnoses of major depressive disorder (4% of patients) and dysthymic disorder (7% of patients).

The HAD Scale performed less well than the GHQ in stroke patients (Johnson *et al.*, 1995). However, this study also included dysthymia with major depression and this may be part of the reason for this result; had the results been published for major depression alone the overall result may have been different.

Adjustment of the threshold score of self-administered questionnaires

As mentioned above, the GHQ performs more accurately in distinguishing depressed from nondepressed medical patients when the threshold score is raised. Bridges and Goldberg (1986), in one of the few published studies demonstrating a receiver operating characteristic curve, reported a cut-off of 11/ 12 on the GHQ 28 in neurological patients. The threshold scores of other self-administered questionnaires have been modified to establish the appropriate cut-off threshold for the physically ill. Lewis and Wessley (mentioned above) used a cut-off of 10/11 on the HAD Scale in a dermatology clinic. Nielsen and Williams (1980) used the Beck Depression Inventory and suggested a cut-off score between 16 and 17 for moderate depression. Schwab *et al.* (1967) have used a similar recommendation. Cavanaugh (1983) published data for different cut-offs on the Beck Depression Inventory and at a cut-off of 18, for example, 18% of the patients had depression, compared to 32% at the conventional cut-off of 14.

Use of self-administered questionnaires

There are two reasons for using self-administered questionnaires: firstly, as an aid to detection of depression in clinical populations and, secondly, for research purposes, to determine the prevalence of depression or its correlates.

Clinical

The use of self-administered questionnaires to screen for depression in the medically ill has been reviewed by Meakin (1992). The justification, Meakin claims, is that this may aid detection and treatment of depression in general medical settings. He argues that the aim of self-administered questionnaires is to define a case which validates the need for treatment. In fact, there are several steps between detection of depression in a reliable way, to prescription of treatment.

One of the most widely used self-administered questionnaires is the General Health Questionnaire. Its author recommends that it should *not* be a substitute for a clinical interview (Goldberg, 1986). On the other hand, Goldberg (1986) suggests that screening may be useful as a trigger, to prompt the clinician to make a full assessment of the person's psychiatric status. This would seem a more realistic approach.

Prevalence

Self-administered questionnaires are particularly poorly suited to this population as they give very high rates of false-positive and false-negative results, they tend to measure nonspecific rather than depressive symptoms and may tend to include transient states as depression. Self-administered questionnaires cannot distinguish between short-lived and chronic depression; this is important as Koenig *et al.* (1993) reported chronic depressive disorder in physically ill patients (average 10 months for older men and 16 months for younger men).

In research, therefore, self-administered questionnaires should only be used as the first (screening) stage of a two-stage study, i.e. they should be followed up by a research interview.

Discriminating symptoms

Van Hemert *et al.* (1993) identified the symptoms on the Present State Examination which best discriminated 49 medical outpatients with anxiety/depression from 143 medical outpatients without psychiatric disorder. The seven symptoms were free-floating anxiety, panic, depressed mood, social withdrawal, lack of confidence, sleep delay and anergia. It can be noticed that the last two would be classified as somatic, rather than cognitive, affective symptoms.

The sensitivity and specificity of these symptoms were tested in a different sample of 74 general medical inpatients, of whom 37 were cases (Feldman *et al.*, 1987). The seven symptoms were able to discriminate between cases and non-cases with a sensitivity of 89% and a specificity of 97%.

This short list of symptoms was contrasted with those which had been identified as key symptoms in general practice, where the following symptoms were most discriminating: nervous tension, worry, irritability and muscular tension (for anxiety) and anergy, common loss of interest and hopelessness (for depression). The different lists clearly indicate that the key symptoms of anxiety or depression in medical patients are different from those established in primary care. It is therefore inappropriate to expect the screening instruments which have been developed in primary care to perform well in general hospital samples.

In another sample of medical inpatients (Hawton *et al.*, 1990), a study using similar instruments yielded somewhat different symptoms—depressed mood, morning depression and hopelessness contributed most to the discrimination of depressed and nondepressed medical inpatients. This illustrates the importance of repeating this work in different settings and in large samples.

Koenig *et al.* (1992) assumed that somatic symptoms should be excluded and devised a list of 11 symptoms which discriminated between depressed and nondepressed medical inpatients. The resulting list is similar to that in the Hospital Anxiety and Depression Scale, but it has not been widely validated.

Inclusive versus exclusive criteria

Cohen-Cole *et al.* (1993) proposed two systems for diagnosis of depression depending on whether the assessment is primarily for research (exclusive approach) or clinical (inclusive approach) purposes. The *exclusive* approach, which was initially proposed in relation to diagnosing depression in hospitalized cancer patients, maximizes specificity by eliminating anorexia and fatigue from the list of nine depressive criteria and requires four of the remaining symptoms for a diagnosis of major depression. Anorexia and fatigue are frequently elements of the cancer or side-effects of treatment.

However, for clinical purposes, the *inclusive* approach to diagnosing depression maximizes sensitivity and best protects the patient from the risk of undiagnosed depression. This approach recommends that clinicians count each relevant depressive symptom even if there is reason to believe the symptom may not be part of a depressive syndrome but may be secondary to the disease process or its treatment.

There is a danger that in clinical practice, depression might be under-diagnosed if symptoms are too readily attributed to physical illness. Clinicians should therefore have a lower threshold of suspicion for major depression in patients with physical illness than in the psychiatric population and err on the side of caution in interpreting persistent dysphoria, feelings of helplessness or hopelessness, loss of self-esteem, feelings of worthlessness and wishes to die as indicators of depression (Mermelstein and Lesko, 1992). Such symptoms are sometimes too readily dismissed by the patient, medical and nursing staff as "understandable" in the context of physical illness; in fact they may be part of a depressive syndrome.

Does it make a difference using different diagnostic criteria?

There have been several attempts to assess the difference when the modified diagnostic criteria are used. Rapp and Vrana (1989) used the Endicott criteria in 150 elderly male inpatients and found a surprisingly high correlation (0.44, $P <$ 0.0001) between the total score for somatic items (which were excluded) and the substituted, psychological symptoms. Indeed, the prevalence of depression was similar using Endicott criteria or traditional criteria—96% of their sample were classified similarly by the two systems.

Silverstone (1996) found the prevalence of major depressive disorder to be 7.7% of medical inpatients using the usual DSM-IV criteria; with the modified diagnostic criteria suggested by Endicott this prevalence fell to 5.1%. Further research would be required to explore which of these is the correct figure. Silverstone did draw attention to an important aspect of time course. Some patients who received a diagnosis of depression prior to admission had lost it one week after admission to the medical ward and others had developed depression during this time.

In addition, in the Silverstone study, a further 7% of patients received a DSM-IV diagnosis of adjustment disorder and nearly as many patients had symptoms of depression or anxiety not severe enough to reach diagnostic criteria for DSM-IV—this emphasizes the importance of viewing depressive symptoms on a continuum and taking into consideration their duration (see House, 1988).

Kathol et al. (1990) compared the diagnosis of major depression in cancer patients using different criteria. For DSM-III and Research Diagnostic Criteria (RDC) diagnosis symptoms were recorded if present, regardless of aetiology. For DSM-IIIR, somatic symptoms were not used in diagnosing depression if there was a definite relationship between the symptom and the physical condition. The study also used the Endicott criteria using substitute symptoms instead of somatic symptoms. The prevalence of depression varied: DSM-III 38%, Endicott criteria 36%, DSM-IIIR 30%, RDC 25%. The authors noted that the Beck Inventory and the Hamilton Scale both yielded higher scores for patients with major depression, whichever classification system was used. However, neither of these self-administered questionnaires could discriminate patients with major depression from patients with depressive symptoms until relatively high scores were achieved. They indicate that these should be used as screening instruments rather than for identifying specific cases. The authors comment, once again, that the possibility of accurate diagnosis of depression in the physically ill by using symptom checklist or scales score is not supported by their work. A good clinical history remains an essential part of the psychiatric evaluation of patients with physical illness in whom depression is a diagnostic consideration. They note the high number of somatic symptoms in the Beck Inventory and the Hamilton Scale.

Severity of physical illness

Rodin *et al.* (1991) commented that many of the studies cited in their review of studies using research interviews failed to find an association between major depression and increasing severity of illness, which is in distinct contrast to the studies using depressive symptoms inventories, in which the association between depression and illness severity was clear. They explain this discrepancy in the following ways.

1. The use of depressive symptom inventories includes a majority of patients with mild symptoms of depression, whereas the major depressive disorder demarcates a different group of patients.
2. Depressive symptom measures are more likely to include confounding somatic symptoms than DSM-III diagnostic criteria.
3. The diagnostic symptoms incorporate some directive about whether to include or exclude confounding somatic symptoms.

Diagnosis by different criteria—the example of rheumatoid arthritis

In order to reduce variation according to age, sex and type of medical condition, more may be learned by examining patients with a single diagnosis. Early studies in rheumatoid arthritis (RA) used the Minnesota Multiphase Personality Inventory (MMPI) and appeared to demonstrate a high prevalence of depression. However, a group of rheumatologists examined the items for depression and noted that a number could be answered simply on the basis of the underlying RA. The "disease-related" items were: "I am about as able to work as ever I was", "I am in just as good physical health as most of my friends", "During the past few years I have been well most of the time", "I do not tire quickly" and "I have few or no pains" (Pincus *et al.*, 1986). When these items were excluded from the MMPI scores in RA patients, the depression scores were found to be no different from those of other medically ill patients.

The prevalence of depression in RA when assessed by self-administered questionnaires has varied between 19% and 53%; studies which have used research interviews have indicated that the prevalence lies between 17% and 27% (Creed, 1990).

In a study of patients with RA, the Present State Examination (PSE) yielded 17 cases (21%) at ID (Index Definition) level 5 or above and 32 patients (40%) at ID level 4 or above (Creed et al., 1990). This emphasizes that there are a lot of patients who are just "sub-threshold", i.e. at PSE ID level 4.

Using the RDC in the same sample yielded a comparable figure of 19 cases (24%). The Clinical Interview Schedule (CIS), at a cut-off point of 13/14, yielded a prevalence figure of 36% but a revised CIS total score, derived by subcontracting the scores on the somatic items (fatigue, poor sleep, excessive concern and hypnotics), led to many patients being regarded as "non-cases".

It is not easy to remove somatic symptoms from the PSE in the same way but for the depressed patients in this study who scored at ID level 5, the diagnosis did not appear to rely on the somatic items.

This study also clarified the relationship between cases of psychiatric disorder and measures of severity of illness. Using a conservative criterion for diagnosis of psychiatric disorder (PSE ID level 5), there were few significant correlations between presence of psychiatric disorder and severity of RA. With lower thresholds (ID level 4 or CIS with 13/14 cut-off), there were numerous significant correlations with severity of physical disorder—the relationship would have been contaminated by the fact that somatic symptoms would be scored as both a psychiatric symptom and a symptom of the arthritis.

CONCLUSION

It is important to be clear why depression is being assessed in the physically ill. In the clinical setting, diagnosing depression in the individual patient is of great importance. It is essential to use the inclusive approach of Cohen-Cole, mentioned above. We have seen above, however, that restrictive criteria are preferable if one is assessing the prevalence of major depression in the physically ill as part of a research project. There are many ways in which the prevalence figure might be spuriously inflated, most notably by the presence of somatic symptoms and the use of self-administered questionnaires.

Adjustment disorders are very common in the physically ill. Deciding whether a depressive disorder is present follows the same lines as differentiating between a normal bereavement reaction and a diagnosis of depressive disorder—severity and duration of symptoms are important.

The psychiatrist must take a careful history of the development of depressive symptoms in terms of their severity and time course. It often becomes clear that the depressive symptoms became more pronounced when the illness became more severe or disabling and/or when a concomitant social stress occurred. Severity, whether criteria for major depressive disorder are reached, and duration, are best regarded as separate aspects of the assessment.

It is usually best to measure severity with a depression scale, e.g. the Beck Depression Inventory. This provides more details of cognitive symptoms and may indicate when cognitive therapy is helpful in addition to antidepressants.

The routine use of a depression scale such as the Beck Depression Inventory will allow the clinician to become familiar with how this behaves in a variety of different clinical situations.

The psychiatrist will also need to define the relationship between the depressive symptoms/disorder and the physical illness. Moffic and Paykel (1975) noted three patterns:

1. Depressive disorder that is a clear reaction to the physical illness and its treatment. Such depression occurs after the physical illness and will fluctuate according to the phase of severity of the physical illness.
2. Depression which precedes the onset of physical illness. Both the depression and the physical illness may start soon after a severe life event, such as bereavement (Murphy and Brown, 1980).
3. Depressive disorder which precedes the onset of the physical symptoms and may actually be responsible for them (somatization).

Further research clarifying the points in this chapter should enable liaison psychiatrists to develop a much clearer picture of the relationship between depression and physical illness with much clearer guidelines regarding when treatment for the depressive disorder is required.

REFERENCES

Aylard PR, Gooding JH, McKenna PJ *et al.* (1987) A validation study of three anxiety and depression self-assessment scales. *J Psychosom Res,* **31**, 261–268.

Berrios GE, Samuel C (1987) Affective disorder in the neurological patient. *J Nerv Ment Dis,* **173**, 173–176.

Bridges KW and Goldberg DP (1986) The validation of the GHQ-28 and the use of the MMSE in neurological inpatients. *Br J Psychiatry,* **148**, 548–553.

Cavanaugh SVA (1983) The prevalence of emotional and cognitive dysfunction in a general medical population: Using the MMSE, GHQ and BDI. *Gen Hosp Psychiatry,* **5**, 15–24.

Clarke DC, Cavanaugh SVA and Gibbons RD (1983) The core symptoms of depression in medical and psychiatric patients. *J Nerv Ment Dis,* **171**, 705–713.

Clarke DM, Minas IH and McKenzie DP (1991) Illness behaviour as a determinant of referral to a psychiatric consultation/liaison service. *Aust NZ J Psychiatry,* **25**, 330–337.

Cohen-Cole SA, Brown FW and McDaniel JS (1993) Diagnostic assessment of depression in the medically ill. In: Stoudemire A and Fogel B (eds) *Psychiatric Care of the Medical Patient.* New York: Oxford University Press, 55–70.

Creed F (1990) Psychological disorders in rheumatoid arthritis: A growing consensus? *Ann Rheum Dis*, **49**, 808–812.

Creed F, Murphy S and Jayson MV (1990) Measurement of psychiatric disorder in rheumatoid arthritis. *J Psychosom Res*, **34**, 79–87.

Emmons CA, Fetting JH and Zonderman AB (1987) A comparison of the symptoms of medical and psychiatric patients matched on the Beck Depression Inventory. *Gen Hosp Psychiatry*, **9**, 398–404.

Endicott J (1984) Measurement of depression in patients with cancer. *Cancer*, **53**, 2243–2249.

Feldman E, Mayou R, Hawton K, Ardern M and Smith EBO (1987) Psychiatric disorder in medical in-patients. *Q J Med*, **63**, 405–412.

Frank RG, Beck NC, Parker JC *et al.* (1988) Depression in rheumatoid arthritis. *J Rheumatol*, **15**, 920–925.

Goldberg D (1986) Use of the General Health Questionnaire in clinical work. *Br Med J*, **293**, 1188–1189.

Hawton K, Mayou R and Feldman E (1990) Significance of psychiatric symptoms in the general medical patient with mood disorder. *Gen Hosp Psychiatry*, **12**, 296–302.

House A (1988) Mood disorders in the physically ill—problems of definition and measurement. *J Psychosom Res*, **32**, 345–353.

Jenkins P and Jamil N (1994) The need for specialist services for mood disorders in the medically ill. In: Benjamin S, House A and Jenkins P (eds) *Liaison Psychiatry Defining Needs and Planning Services*. London: Gaskell Press.

Johnson G, Burvill PW, Anderson CS, Jamrozik K, Stewart-Wynne EG and Chakera TMH (1995) Screening instruments for depression and anxiety following stroke: experience in the Perth community stroke study. *Acta Psychiatr Scand*, **91**, 252–257.

Kathol RG and Petty F (1981) Relationship of depression to medical illness: A critical review. *J Affect Disord*, **3**, 111–121.

Kathol RG, Mutgi A, Williams J, Clamon G and Noyes R (1990) Diagnosis of major depression in cancer patients according to four sets of criteria. *Am J Psychiatry*, **147**, 1021–1024.

Koenig HG, Cohen HJ, Blazer DG, Meador KG and Westlund R (1992) A brief depression scale for use in the medically ill. *Int J Psychiatry Med*, **22**, 183–195.

Koenig HG, Cohen HJ, Blazer DG, Krishnan KRR and Sibert T (1993) Profile of depressive symptoms in younger and older medical inpatients with major depression. *J Am Geriatr Soc*, **41**, 1169–1176.

Lewis G and Wessley S (1990) Comparison of the General Health Questionnaire and the Hospital Anxiety and Depression Scale. *Br J Psychiatry*, **157**, 860–864.

McDaniel JS, Musselman DL, Porter MR, Reed DA and Nemeroff CB (1995) Depression with patients with cancer. Diagnosis, biology and treatment. *Arch Gen Psychiatry*, **52**, 89–99.

Mayou R and Hawton K (1986) Psychiatric disorder in the general hospital. *Br J Psychiatry*, **149**, 172–190.

Meakin CJ (1992) Screening for depression in the medically ill. *Br J Psychiatry*, **160**, 212–216.

Mermelstein HT and Lesko L (1992) Depression in patients with cancer. *Psychooncology*, **1**, 199–215.

Moffic HS and Paykel ES (1975) Depression in medical in-patients. *Br J Psychiatry*, **126**, 346–353.

Murphy E and Brown GW (1980) Life events, psychiatric disturbance and physical illness. *Br J Psychiatry*, **136**, 326–338.

Nielsen AC and Williams TA (1980) Depression in ambulatory medical patients. *Arch Gen Psychiatry*, **37**, 999–1004.

Pincus T, Callahan LF, Bradley LA, Vaughn WK and Wolfe F (1986) Elevated MMPI scores for hypochondriasis depression, and hysteria in patients with rheumatoid arthritis reflect disease rather than psychological status. *Arthritis Rheum*, **29**,1456–1466.

Rapp SR and Vrana S (1989) Substituting non-somatic for somatic symptoms in the diagnosis of depression in elderly male medical patients. *Am J Psychiatry*, **146**, 1197–1200.

Robins L, Helzer JE and Croughan J (1981) National Institute of Mental Health Diagnostic Interview Schedule: History, characteristics, validity. *Arch Gen Psychiatry*, **33**, 381–389.

Rodin G and Voshart K (1986) Depression in the medically ill: An overview. *Am J Psychiatry*, **143**, 696–705.

Rodin G, Craven J and Littlefield C (1991) *Depression in the Medically Ill—An Integrated Approach.* New York: Brunner/Mazel.

Schwab JJ, Bialow M, Brown JM and Holzer CE (1967) Diagnosing depression in medical inpatients. *Ann Intern Med*, **67**, 695–707.

Silverstone PH (1996) Prevalence of psychiatric disorders in medical inpatients. *J Nerv Ment Dis*, **184**, 43–51.

Snaith RP (1987) The concepts of mild depression. *Br J Psychiatry*, **150**, 387–393.

Spitzer R, Williams J, Gibbon M *et al.* (1992) Structured Clinical Interview for DSM-III-R (SODNP (Version 1.0)). *Arch Gen Psychiatry*, **49**, 624–636.

Van Hemert AM, Hengeveld MW, Bolk JH, Rooijmans HG and Vandenbroucke JP (1993) Psychiatric disorders in relation to medical illness among patients of a general medical outpatient clinic. *Psychol Med*, **23**, 167–173.

Wells KB, Golding JM and Burnam MA (1989) Chronic medical conditions in a sample of the general population with anxiety, affective, and substance use disorders. *Am J Psychiatry*, **46**, 1440–1446.

Zigmund AS and Snaith RP (1983) The Hospital Anxiety and Depression Scale. *Acta Psychiatr Scand*, **67**, 361–367.

2

Depression and types of physical disorder and treatment

Richard A. Mayou

INTRODUCTION

The majority of chapters in this book discuss the occurrence of depression in relation to specific medical disorders. This chapter takes a general overview of evidence and considers the general associations between depression and medical illness. However, it excludes all discussion of the role of depression in the aetiology and course of the many forms of functional somatic symptoms which are common in primary and general hospital medical care and have been reviewed elsewhere (Mayou *et al.*, 1995). It begins with a review of general conceptual and methodological issues and then considers the nature of the evidence on types of illness which are especially associated with depression. The argument is illustrated with discussion of specific examples, each of which is covered more fully elsewhere in this book.

Depression, both as a symptom and as a series of diagnostic categories, is common in the general population. It is especially common in the medically ill for two main groups of reasons, the nature of the physical disorder and its treatment, and the individual circumstances and psychological vulnerability of the patient (see Table 1). Whilst this chapter is primarily concerned with issues relating to types of illness and physical treatment and to depressive symptoms and disorder, it is essential to be aware of the very considerable significance of individual vulnerability. Whatever the physical disorder, most sufferers show

Depression and Physical Illness. Edited by M.M. Robertson and C.L.E. Katona
© 1997 John Wiley & Sons Ltd

Table 1. Factors associated with emotional disorder.

Nature of the physical disease
Biological factors: CNS disease, systemic disorder

Measuring the illness
Pathological diagnosis
Anatomical location
Course: acute, chronic, relapsing, progressive
Severity: threat to life, symptom severity, disability, disfigurement
Loss of function or self-esteem

Nature of treatment
Success
Quality of information and advice
Side-effects
Demands on patient (self-care)

Factors in the patient
Biological vulnerability
Personality
Psychological vulnerability
Social vulnerability and protective factors
Other life stresses

Social consequences of the illness
Work
Reactions of family and others

remarkable resilience and it is usually only a minority who report severe distress.

It is also important, in a book concentrating on depression, to keep in mind that other emotional symptoms and disorders are also common (either alone or comorbid with depression) in the medically ill, as are various types of cognitive disorder (Table 2). It is arguable that both in clinical practice and in the literature, depression has sometimes been overemphasized and anxiety and other symptoms have been relatively neglected.

This chapter covers the following issues.

1. Theoretical and methodological issues.
2. The nature of the association.
3. Mood disorder due to general medical conditions.
4. General population studies: (a) suicide; (b) depression and chronic physical illness.
5. Evidence from studies of specific disorders and treatments.

Table 2. The principal psychiatric illnesses (DSM-IV) which may be associated with physical illness in adults.

Cognitive disorders
  Dementia
  Delirium
  Amnesic disorders
Mental disorders due to a general medical condition not elsewhere classified
Substance-related disorders
Adjustment disorders
Mood disorders
  Dysthymia
  Major depression
  Bipolar disorder
Anxiety disorders
  Generalized
  Panic
  Acute stress disorder
  Post-traumatic stress disorder
  Specific phobias: hospitals, injections and venesection, chemotherapy, etc.
  Agoraphobia
Factitious disorders
Somatoform disorders
Eating disorders
Sleep disorders
Sexual and gender identity disorders
Psychological factors affecting medical conditions

THEORETICAL AND METHODOLOGICAL ISSUES

Discussion of the relationship between depression and medical illness depends on an understanding of the definition of these terms and of their clinical and research use, and of the nature and quality of the available evidence (Table 3).

Problems of comparison

In a large and rapidly increasing literature it remains difficult to make comparisons between studies of particular types of illness or treatment. Differences in the choice of patient samples, in patterns of medical care and in the measures used mean that it is rarely possible to make direct comparisons between studies of different medical groups, or even to draw clear conclusions about the relative risk as compared with general populations. As a result, reviewers and discussants have often been tempted to be somewhat selective in adducing evidence to support their preconceptions about the impact of different types of illness.

Table 3. The nature and quality of the evidence.

Problems in comparison of studies using different design and measures
Definition and assessment of the physical disease
Definition, type and assessment of the psychiatric illness
Timing during the course of the medical disease
Choice of the sample of the patient population
Types of available evidence

Physical disorder

Physical disorder can be defined in many ways and a number of aspects are relevant to the patient's psychiatric state. Classification may be in terms of the organ system (the way in which this book is organized), pathology, time course and severity. Even severity needs to be considered in terms of a variety of interventions, including the threat to life, the unpleasantness of the symptoms and functional limitation. To make matters more difficult, severity is not an objective concept; it must be considered in the light of the meaning to the patient. An apparently minor back injury may be no more than a nuisance to a sedentary psychiatrist but can be devastating to a football playing manual worker.

The conceptual problems of definition of the physical disorder are matched by the problems of objective measurement. It is essential to consider as many variables as possible, but it must be recognized that there are few satisfactory objective measures.

Psychiatric disorder

Categories and dimensions

This book restricts discussion to depression, but even so it refers to a very common and varied symptom complex which may be considered either in dimensional terms or in terms of the several categories in either DSM-IV or ICD-10. Much of the recent literature has concentrated on DSM Major Depression. The identification of severe depression is important not least because antidepressant medication is usually inappropriate and ineffective. However, it is also necessary to consider other categories of depression, including *dysthymia* and depression as part of *adjustment disorder* (see Table 4). Depression may also occur in the context of the syndrome of *emotionalism* seen following cerebrovascular accident or as a feature of anxiety and other disorders.

Sub-threshold distress

Depression of moderate severity insufficient to satisfy the criteria for mental disorder is common. It may be persistent, adversely affecting life over many

Table 4. Classification of depression.

Major depressive episode
Major mood disorder due to general medical conditions
Adjustment disorder with depressed mood
Dysthymic disorder
Depressive disorder not otherwise specified

---

years. In clinical practice this sub-threshold depression is often associated with other distressing psychological symptoms and with psychologically determined effects on everyday life. It may therefore be of considerable importance to the patient and to medical care. Over-preoccupation with DSM or ICD diagnostic categories can, therefore, be misleading.

Use of standard criteria

There are particular problems in the use of standard diagnostic categories of depression in the medically ill, a theme which runs throughout this book. The first main difficulty is that many of the symptoms which feature in the criteria for depression can also commonly be symptoms of physical disease. Four types of solution have been used to overcome this problem.

1. The psychiatric syndrome criteria are applied unmodified.
2. The syndrome criteria are modified to include symptoms that might be a reflection of physical disease.
3. The syndrome criteria are unmodified but judgement is made about the aetiology of individual symptoms and they are only counted towards a symptom if they are deemed not to be a direct manifestation of physical disease.
4. The criteria developed in psychiatric populations are redefined for use in the physically ill.

Experience suggests that the inclusion of somatic symptoms may not be as important as is often argued. It is almost certainly less important than the overall care with which criteria are used. Kathol and his colleagues (1990) concluded, after comparison of four sets of criteria in patients with cancer, that "there is no evidence that one is more valid than another in a medically ill population". Two analyses of symptom patterns among consecutive medical admissions with present state examination (PSE) psychiatric disorder suggest that the pattern of symptoms is in fact very similar to those reported in general populations (Hawton *et al.*, 1990; Van Hemert *et al.*, 1993). It may well be that in many instances this particular diagnostic problem is not as substantial as sometimes feared. The findings also suggest that specific issues in relation to some forms of severe medical illness (for example, cancer) should not be generalized to medical illness in general. Concern about the physical causes of somatic symptoms, which may be wrongly attributed to depression, should not obscure the clinical importance of the complainant's need to be aware that somatic symptoms may be a symptom of depression and are frequently overinvestigated and badly treated.

Research on biological markers of depression may eventually have practical relevance to the medically ill. Current knowledge has been recently reviewed in relation to cancer (McDaniel *et al.*, 1995). Whilst the theoretical issues are of considerable interest, clinical applications at present seem slight.

The difficulties in determining the presence and severity of psychiatric disorder in a patient with physical disease are important in assessing the individual patient and in understanding and judging research evidence. However, awareness of the difficulties should enable sensible conclusions to be drawn.

Timing during the course of the medical condition

Both the prevalence and severity of depressive symptoms are related to the course of the medical condition, being most conspicuous in acute physical illness, whether initial onset or relapse. Associations with psychological and social variables may therefore vary throughout the duration of an illness.

The patient population

It is clear from the very substantial and varied evidence presented in this book, that it is essential that the nature of research samples is specified. Inevitably, hospital inpatients are likely to report higher rates of psychiatric disorder than patients with the same medical problem seen in primary care. Many reports are flawed by being based on unrepresentative samples whose origins are not described and it is therefore impossible to compare these with other reports of the same condition, or with those of patients with other types of illness. Overall, there is a very marked bias towards highly selected samples of patients who are more likely to show psychiatric disturbance.

Types of available evidence

Questions about type of medical disorder and rates of depression can be answered by considering several types of information.

1. Population studies of rates of suicide (an indicator of the occurrence of major depression) associated with common physical conditions.
2. Studies of population samples including subjects with several types of chronic physical disorder.

3. Comparison of reports on patients with individual and clearly specified medical conditions.

The overwhelming bulk of evidence comes from the third category. Unfortunately, differences in methodologies and the lack of controls or comparison samples mean that it is necessary to be cautious about drawing conclusions about relative risk in different types of medical disorder as compared with the general population. Despite all these caveats, current evidence is entirely adequate for us to draw broad general conclusions.

THE NATURE OF THE ASSOCIATION

Mechanisms

The mechanisms of comorbidity of depression and physical illness are complex (Cohen and Rodriguez, 1995; Mayou and Sharpe, 1995), but four main categories are apparent:

Coincidence

In clinical practice it is common to see patients whose psychiatric disorder appears unrelated to the physical illness. Such disorders do, however, greatly complicate the management of the physical disease. Other disorders that may often be caused by physical disease (such as depression) may also be independent with an onset which preceded that of the physical illness. For example, Moffic and Paykel (1975) concluded that in one-quarter of depressed medical inpatients the depression predated the onset of the physical illness.

Common cause for both

Here either patient factors and/or nondisease factors may have given rise to both. For example, stressful life events in a vulnerable person may precipitate both a stroke (House *et al.*, 1991) and a depressive illness (Brown and Harris, 1978). Although it seems unlikely to be a major reason for the association of physical and emotional disorders, it is common in clinical practice to see patients for whom the independent life event is of much greater significance than the physical disease in determining their distress.

Psychiatric disorder may cause physical disease

Psychiatric disorder can certainly cause physical disease, for example, the numerous complications of chronic excessive alcohol consumption. Whether a psychiatric disorder (or even wider psychological factors) can make a person directly susceptible to disease is an intriguing but still controversial idea. One possible mechanism is by suppression of immune function. However, there is as yet little convincing evidence that depression is a major factor in the aetiology of physical disease although it may be a precipitant of onset and relapse, and may affect the course. For example, it seems probable that mood at the time of a myocardial infarct is a determinant of subsequent mortality (Frasure-Smith *et al.*, 1993).

DSM-IV includes a category of *psychological factors affecting medical condition*, which is intended to cover patients who have an Axis 3 general medical condition and in whom psychological factors adversely affect the course of treatment. The category is broadly defined and the psychological factors include not only mental disorder but also psychological symptoms, personality traits and maladaptive health behaviours. Previous formulations of this category were not widely used and its validity, reliability and clinical value remain uncertain.

Physical disease may cause psychiatric disorder

This type of association is our main focus. The physical disease may cause the predisposed individual to develop a psychiatric disorder, either by a biological mechanism or as a psychological reaction.

Nature of physical illness and type of psychiatric disorder

In addition to the issues about the general association between physical and psychiatric disorder, we must consider associations with particular types of psychiatric disorder. In general, it seems that threat (to life, of disability, of distress) is particularly likely to lead to anxiety, whilst loss (of function, role, hopes and ambitions) is more likely to result in depression (Lipowski, 1985). Whilst both clinical experience and research evidence support this generalization, it is also apparent that the interaction between the particular type of physical disorder and individual psychological vulnerability and circumstances results in wide individual variation in patterns of psychiatric response.

Nature of physical treatment and type of physical disorder

Acute major treatment, such as surgery, is likely to be associated with initial anxiety with possible depression during convalescence. More chronic treatment, for example treatment of renal failure or diabetes, is a common cause of mild, persistent depression. In other instances in which the treatment is unpleasant and threatening, as in chemotherapy for cancer, anxiety can be prominent.

Effects on quality of life

Psychiatrists naturally and appropriately are particularly concerned with psychological consequences of physical illness but they need also to be aware of effects on the various domains of quality of life. The clinical significance of psychiatric disorder depends not only on the severity of the symptoms, but also on the associated effects upon everyday life. Thus, following breast cancer surgery, depression is a frequent complication but it may, by itself, be less significant than effects on sexual function, on marital relationships and on everyday life, which may be of major importance for both patients and their families.

Assessment of quality of life, using both generic and disease-specific measures, is required in order to understand the clinical significance of depression and indeed the full psychosocial impact of the physical disorder. This should include considering the effects on close relatives who may also suffer depression and major changes in their everyday lives.

MOOD DISORDER DUE TO GENERAL MEDICAL CONDITIONS

It is generally accepted that some medical conditions may, by their nature, be biological risk factors for depression. The significance of such factors and their interrelationship with other aetiological variables remains uncertain.

A number of criteria have been suggested to determine whether psychiatric illness can be regarded as being biologically caused by the medical disorder.

1. The presence of organic cause (disease, physical treatment).
2. The organic cause being present before the psychiatric disorder.
3. The treatment of the organic cause resulting in relief of the psychiatric symptoms.
4. The absence of a family history of psychiatric disorder.

These criteria are clearly difficult to apply in the individual patient and caution is appropriate.

DSM-III and ICD-10 have seen biologically caused depression as a form of organic disorder. DSM-IV has recognized the difficulties in the use of the term organic and in the judgement as to whether biological processes are contributing to aetiology. Whilst it includes *mood disorder due to general medical conditions*, most comorbid depression can be classified by one of DSM-IV's most useful innovations, descriptive classification on the basis of the mood symptoms but with an extra code to indicate comorbid physical disorder. It is in this respect clearly superior to ICD-10. Even so, the importance of biological causation of depression is controversial and the interpretation of research findings is considerably hampered by the methodological problems discussed earlier.

Table 5 lists examples of mood disorder due to physical disease that are given in DSM-IV. The list appears to have been mainly derived from clinical impressions rather than convincing epidemiological or other evidence. However, a number of examples, all of which are discussed at greater length elsewhere in this book, are well established. They include:

1. *Endocrine disorders.* Depression is common in a number of endocrine abnormalities and the course of the mood disturbance appears to parallel that of the physical disorder.
2. *Puerperal major depression.* There is considerable and striking evidence that the relative risk of first onset and recurrent major depression is very substantially raised in the puerperium. This is especially striking for bipolar disorder. The precise mechanism is unclear but the very dramatic changes in endocrine levels following childbirth do seem to be remarkably potent precipitants of affective illness.
3. *Cerebrovascular accident.* A series of papers by Robinson and his colleagues (Robinson *et al.*, 1984; Starkstein and Robinson, 1993) have claimed that depression is not only common after stroke but also is associated with a particular lesion site. The precise importance of biological factors remains unclear in view of issues about the selection of subjects and interpretation of findings (House *et al.*, 1991). Whatever the biological factors, it is also apparent from all the studies that all the other factors are relevant to the aetiology of depression are also important following stroke. One should consider biological factors as an extra aetiological factor amongst several.
4. *Other neurological disorders.* Rates of depression during the course of Parkinson's disease, multiple sclerosis and other neurological disease are common and would appear to suggest that there are associations between course and severity of the physical disorder and the prevalence and course of mood symptoms (Starkstein and Robinson, 1993).

Prodromal symptoms

One further aspect of the biological aetiology of depression is the possibility that mood change may be a very early feature of illness. Affective disturbances often seem to precede major medical illness, or at least to occur before the underlying medical illness becomes clinically noticeable and important (Fava *et al.*, 1994). Literature on this association is unsatisfactory but it is reasonably convincing for a number of the neurological and endocrine conditions listed in Table 5.

Table 5. Examples of mood disorder due to physical disease in DSM-IV.

Cancer
   Carcinoma of the pancreas
Cerebrovascular disease
Degenerative myocardial conditions
   Parkinson's disease
   Huntington's disease
Endocrine conditions
   Thyroid disorder
   Adrenal disorder
Parathyroid disorder
Metabolic conditions
   B_{12} deficiencies
Viral and other infections
   Hepatitis
   Mononucleosis
   HIV
Autoimmune disease
   Systemic lupus erythematosus

EVIDENCE FROM GENERAL POPULATION STUDIES

Reports from general medical settings, specialist general medical populations, inpatient and secondary care outpatient clinics have consistently described a high incidence of depression. Selection factors make comparisons difficult and it is unsurprising that results are inconsistent. A small number of studies have been based on representative general population samples.

Suicide

One should be cautious of considering suicide rates as indicating rates of severe depression but it is likely that there is a close association. Suicide rates are generally higher in the physically ill than in the general population. Specific associations have been reported for cancer, multiple sclerosis and a number of other conditions.

Harris and Barraclough (1995) have recently discussed the literature on suicide and mental disorder on the basis of a systematic literature review. Increased risk was found for a number of disorders including human immunodeficiency virus (HIV) infection, malignant neoplasms in general, head and neck cancer, Huntington's disease, multiple sclerosis, peptic ulcer, renal disease, spinal cord injury and systemic lupus erythematosus. Inconclusive evidence was found for increased risk in relation to a number of other disorders, including major heart surgery, amputation, major bowel disorder and Parkinson's disease. Pregnancy in the puerperium had decreased risks and there was no evidence of either increased or decreased risk for any other of the disorders studied.

Depression and chronic illness

It is disappointing that, in studying the epidemiology of depression, many major projects have disregarded the presence of physical illness or have mentioned it without giving details of type or severity. Few physical illnesses are common enough in any general population sample for specific conclusions, but general categorizations of presence or absence of physical disorder and the severity of disability are possible.

Jorm (1995) has recently reviewed the epidemiology of depressive states in the elderly. He concludes that prospective studies of general population samples of the elderly have shown that ill health is a predictor of subsequent depressive symptoms, even when baseline symptoms are controlled. Ill health predicts onset and course in both community samples and hospital cases. There is also evidence that disability and activity limitation predict subsequent depressive symptoms when baseline symptoms are controlled. The relation is complex since although disability and physical health are highly related, physical disability predicts subsequent depressive symptoms even when physical health is statistically controlled.

A number of reports have provided findings about common chronic physical disorders but the findings are to some extent contradictory. Wells and his colleagues (1988) found at the Los Angeles centre of the Epidemiologic Catchment Area (ECA) study that there was a recurrent and lifetime prevalence of psychiatric disorder at 24.7% and 42% respectively, compared with 17.5% and 33%; a risk ratio of 1.41% overall and particularly strong associations with arthritis, chronic lung disease, and neurological and heart disease. They found no association between psychiatric disorder and high blood pressure or diabetes. They state that depression was one of the commonest diagnoses in the medically ill but do not give precise figures. Weyerer (1990) found an increased risk associated with chronic medical illness in a Bavarian study and again noted the association that diabetes was modest as compared with other chronic medical conditions. Palinkas and colleagues (1990) reported on findings in subjects aged over 65 in southern California. Depression was associated with a number of chronic medical conditions, self-perceived health status and medication.

A particularly interesting recent study by Penninx and others (1996) describes a Dutch community study of subjects aged 55 to 85. Depression was associated with a number of chronic conditions; there were particular associations with osteoarthritis, rheumatoid arthritis and stroke and less striking links with diabetes and cardiac disorders. Their findings suggest the particular importance of the degree of functional disability and illness controllability as factors associated with psychiatric disorder.

Other epidemiological evidence concerned the effect of comorbid physical illness on the course of depressive disorder. Several studies suggest that physical illness is associated with longer duration and poorer outcome of depression. For example, in the Medical Outcome Study it was found that depressed adult outpatients with a history of myocardial infarction had a particularly poor clinical prognosis. However, course of depression appeared to be unaffected by comorbid insulin-dependent diabetes or hypertension (Wells *et al.*, 1993).

EVIDENCE FROM STUDIES OF PARTICULAR CONDITIONS AND TREATMENTS

Systematic studies of the relation between disease and psychological status date from the work by Hackett and his colleagues at the Massachusetts General Hospital (Cassem and Hackett, 1977). They described initial anxiety and subsequent depression following myocardial infarction, with gradual adaptation and return to normal mood over days or weeks. Initial "denial" was conspicuous and was apparently usually a helpful defence, but was sometimes maladaptive. A minority of subjects were especially vulnerable to enduring psychiatric disorder.

Subsequent work has borne out this general pattern and has generally shown moderate levels of depression in chronic disorders and higher levels in progressive or relapsing conditions. Earlier research was ably summarized and effectively promoted in a series of papers in a book by Lipowski (1985). He, more than anyone else, was responsible for directing medical attention to the importance of depression and other psychological complications of physical illness and for clarifying our understanding of aetiology, course and implications for clinical management. The research summarized in this book is an indication of substantial recent success in establishing psychiatric research in this field and the clinical subspecialty of consultation–liaison psychiatry.

The nature of physical illness

A large number of factors may be important (Table 1). They include both the course of the physical disorder (acute, relapsing, chronic, progressive) and the type of treatment.

It is important not to make apparently common-sense assumptions about the *subjective severity of illness*, and the relative risk associated with different conditions may be surprising. For example, the prevalence of psychiatric disorder in those who have suffered major spinal injury is only moderately raised compared with the general population (Fuhrer *et al.*, 1993; Ditunno Jr and Formal, 1994), whereas the rate of psychiatric disorder immediately following a therapeutic or spontaneous abortion is higher than in the majority of acute major illnesses (Iles and Gath, 1993). Within any pathologically defined disease category, emotional symptoms are more likely in those with more *extensive and disabling disease*. For example, depression in survivors of stroke is strongly associated with disability (Sharpe *et al.*, 1993). As already mentioned, there are large differences between *chronic illness* and *acute illness*.

Acute onset of physical disease is associated with a higher rate of psychiatric illness than chronic illness. This is the case in stroke, for example (House *et al.*, 1991). In relapsing conditions, exacerbations of illness are associated with anxiety as well as depression. This pattern has been observed in patients with multiple sclerosis (Dalos *et al.*, 1982). In progressive conditions such as Parkinson's disease, deterioration is associated with depression (Starkstein and Mayberg, 1993).

The association of exacerbation of psychiatric illness with worsening of physical disease is likely to be largely a psychological reaction but in the case of disease of the central nervous system, a biological mechanism cannot be excluded. Medically stable chronic disease is not a major risk factor for anxiety and depression.

The nature of the medical care

Consultation and hospital admission can be distressing, and medical treatment can have a major effect on the patient's mental state. Examples include major investigations (Wilson-Barnett, 1992), procedures such as screening (Marteau, 1994), genetic counselling (Lernan and Croyle, 1994), surgery (Jacobsen and Holland, 1989; Riether and McDaniel, 1993), radiotherapy (Holland, 1989) and chemotherapy (Holland and Lesko, 1989). Many drug treatments are known to have neuropsychiatric side-effects; for example, beta-blockers are associated with depressive symptoms but less clearly with depressive illness, and steroids cause major psychiatric disorders (Kershner and Wang-Cheng, 1989). Some drugs, such as those used in chemotherapy of malignant diseases, have unpleasant physical side-effects which cause considerable distress (Holland and Lesko, 1989). A number of treatments, such as those for chronic renal failure and diabetes, not only have physical side-effects but also make considerable demands on self-care and require major modifications in everyday activities. The psychological impact of most surgical procedures is temporary but procedures resulting in impaired function, pain or mutilation are generally more likely to be associated with continuing psychological consequences. Radiotherapy is alarming to many patients, but the psychological impact is transient, and persistent consequences are unusual. Organ transplantation involving surgery and continuing investigations and drug treatment carries a particular risk of adverse psychological consequences (Craven and Rodin, 1992).

Other factors affecting the outcome of depression

For all physical diseases it is only a minority of patients who suffer severe persistent emotional distress. Most people confronted with severe physical disease are remarkably resilient and have a good psychological outcome. Several factors may increase an individual's vulnerability to psychiatric illness (see Table 1).

Biological vulnerability

The same constitutional factors predisposing to affective and other emotional disorders in the general population operate in the physically ill. However, the evidence is limited, partly because of the exclusion of the physically ill from most epidemiological, genetic and other research. In practice, patients with a previous history of psychiatric illness are more likely to suffer a recurrence when faced with disease than persons without any such history.

Psychological vulnerability

It is probable that the factors that increase vulnerability are the same as those in persons without physical disease. There is consistent evidence for many medical disorders that evidence of previous vulnerability to stress (neuroticism, poor copying style) is associated with both the occurrence and persistence of psychiatric disorder.

Social factors

The role of social factors in the genesis of psychiatric illness in people with physical disease also appears to be similar to that described in the general population. Social factors may decrease or increase vulnerability. Social support (especially marital and family) is of major importance in mitigating the impact of the diagnosis of disease (Dew *et al.*, 1990). Social factors in the form of life events may also be a potent cause of distress that may well overshadow the impact of the physical problems. In addition, some patients' occupations or interests make them particularly vulnerable to the consequences of physical illness, for example the effects of a stroke on a pilot or keen sportsman.

The importance of meaning

Review of evidence about a very wide range of types of medical disorder emphasizes the central significance of the *meaning* of the illness and its treatment to the individual patient (Lipowski, 1985). Psychiatric complications can only be understood if the significance of a particular type of medical problem is understood for an individual patient. Generalizations about the severity and course of illness and about disability are helpful, but in clinical practice, where doctors are concerned with the individual patient, there is no substitute for understanding the patient's particular viewpoint. It is only in this way that we can recognize that termination of pregnancy for medical reasons can be as upsetting in the first few weeks as major spinal cord injury. In both circumstances the loss of expectations and hope and the associated grief are likely to be severe. Inevitably, the subsequent course of depression is very different. Further research is required to identify and quantify beliefs and cognitions and their association with the occurrence, course and outcome of depression and other psychological symptoms.

CONCLUSIONS

The review of a wide range of evidence shows considerable similarities in psychological consequences of different types of major illness. The prevalence is high in acute physical illness and also in progressive or relapsing conditions. In chronic illness depression is more common than expected in the general population but is reported by only a minority of subjects. There are marked differences in the occurrence of severe depression in both acute and chronic illnesses which reflect the meaning to the individual patient in terms of threat, disability, pain and other symptoms. It is not uncommon for depressive symptoms to be accompanied by other comorbid psychiatric symptoms and disorder whose occurrence and pattern again relates to the type of illness.

As is evident from other chapters in this book, the occurrence of moderate and major depressive problems is generally underestimated in ordinary medical care and, even if recognized, frequently untreated. Recognition of the treatment of depression in relation to acute and chronic physical illness remains a major challenge for medicine and for those psychiatrists who work with medical patients.

REFERENCES

Brown G and Harris T (1978) *Social Origins of Depression*. London: Routledge.

Cassem NH and Hackett TP (1977) Psychological aspects of myocardial infarction. *Psychiatr Clin North Am*, **61**, 711–721.

Cohen S and Rodriguez MS (1995) Pathways linking affective disturbances and physical disorders. *Health Psychol*, **14**, 374–380.

Craven J and Rodin GM (1992) *Psychiatric Aspects of Organ Transplantation*. New York: Oxford University Press.

Dalos NP, Rabins PV, Brooks BR and O'Donnell P (1982) Disease activity and emotional state in multiple sclerosis. *Ann Neurol*, **13**, 573–577.

Dew MA, Ragi MV and Nimorwicz P (1990) Infection with human immunodeficiency virus and vulnerability to psychiatric distress. *Arch Gen Psychiatry*, **47**, 737–744.

Ditunno Jr JF and Formal C (1994) Chronic spinal cord injury. *N Engl J Med*, **330**, 550–556.

Fava GA, Morphy MA and Sonino N (1994) Affective prodromes of medical illness. *Psychother Psychosom*, **62**, 141–145.

Frasure-Smith N, Lesperance F and Talajic M (1993) Depression predicting death after myocardial infarction. *JAMA*, **270**, 1819–1825.

Fuhrer MJ, Rintala DH, Hart KA, Clearman R and Young ME (1993) Depressive symptomatology in persons with spinal cord injury who reside in the community. *Arch Phys Med Rehabil*, **74**, 255–260.

Harris EC and Barraclough BM (1995) Suicide as an outcome for medical disorders. *Medicine*, **73**, 281–296.

Hawton KE, Mayou RA and Feldman JE (1990) Significance of psychiatric symptoms in general medical patients with mood disorders. *Gen Hosp Psychiatry*, **12**, 296–302.

Holland JC (1989) Radiotherapy. In: JC Holland and JH Rowland (eds) *Handbook of Psychooncology*. New York: Oxford University Press, 131–145.

Holland JC and Lesko LM (1989) Chemotherapy, endocrine therapy, and immunotherapy. In: JC Holland and JH Rowland (eds) *Textbook of Psychooncology*. New York: Oxford University Press, 141–162.

House A, Dennis M, Mogridge L, Warlow C, Hawton K and Jones L (1991) Mood disorders in the year after first stroke. *Br J Psychiatry*, **158**, 83–92.

Iles S and Gath D (1993) Psychiatric outcome of termination of pregnancy for foetal abnormality. *Psychol Med*, **23**, 407–413.

Jacobsen P and Holland JC (1989) Psychological reactions to cancer surgery. In: JC Holland and JH Rowland (eds) *Handbook of Psychooncology*. New York: Oxford University Press, 117–133.

Jorm AF (1995) The epidemiology of depressive states in the elderly: implications for recognition, intervention and prevention. *Soc Psychiatry Psychiatr Epidemiol*, **30**, 53–59.

Kathol RG, Noyes R, Williams J, Mutgi A, Carroll B and Perry P (1990) Diagnosing depression in patients with medical illness. *Psychosomatics*, **31**, 434–440.

Kershner P and Wang-Cheng R (1989) Psychiatric side effects of steroid therapy. *Psychosomatics*, **30**, 135–139.

Lerman C and Croyle R (1994) Psychological issues in genetic testing for breast cancer susceptibility. *Arch Intern Med*, **154**, 609–616.

Lipowski ZJ (1985) *Psychosomatic Medicine and Liaison Psychiatry: Selected Papers.* New York: Plenum.

Marteau RM (1994) Psychology and screening: Narrowing the gap between efficacy and effectiveness. *Br J Clin Psychol*, **33**, 1–10.

Mayou RA and Sharpe M (1995) Psychiatric illnesses associated with physical disease. *Bailliere's Clin Psychiatry*, **1**, 2.

Mayou RA, Bass C and Sharpe M (1995) *Treatment of Functional Somatic Symptoms.* Oxford: Oxford University Press.

McDaniel JS, Musselman DL, Porter MR, Reed DA and Nemeroff CB (1995) Depression in patients with cancer. *Arch Gen Psychiatry*, **52**, 89–99.

Moffic HS and Paykel ES (1975) Depression in medical in-patients. *Br J Psychiatry*, **126**, 346–353.

Palinkas LA, Wingard DL and Barrett-Connor E (1990) Chronic illness and depressive symptoms in the elderly: a population-based study. *J Clin Epidemiol*, **43**, 1131–1141.

Penninx BW, Beekman AT, Ormel J, Kriegsman DM, Boeke AJ, van Eijk J and Deeg DJ

(1996) Psychological status among elderly people with chronic diseases: does type of disease play a part? *J Psychosom Res*, **40(5)**, 521–534.

Riether AM and McDaniel JS (1993) Surgery and trauma: General principles. In: A Stoudemire and BS Fogel (eds) *Psychiatric Care of the Medical Patient*. New York: Oxford University Press, 759–781.

Robinson RG, Kubos KL, Starr LB, Rao K and Price TR (1984) Mood disorders in stroke patients: importance of location of lesion. *Brain*, **107**, 81–93.

Sharpe M, Hawton KE, Seagroatt V, Bamford J, House A, Molyneux A, Sandercock P and Warlow C (1993) Depressive disorders in long-term survivors of stroke: associations with demographic and social factors, functional status and brain lesion volume. *Br J Psychiatry*, **164**, 380–386.

Starkstein SE and Mayberg HS (1993) Depression in Parkinson's disease. In: SE Starkstein and RG Robinson (eds) *Depression in Neurologic Disease*. Baltimore: The Johns Hopkins University Press, 97–116.

Starkstein SE and Robinson RG (1993) *Depression in Neurologic Disease*. Baltimore: The Johns Hopkins University Press.

Van Hemert AM, Hawton K, Bolk JH and Fagg J (1993) Key symptoms in the detection of affective disorders in medical patients. *J Psychosom Res*, **37**, 397–404.

Wells KB, Golding JM and Burnam MA (1988) Psychiatric disorder in a sample of the general population with and without chronic medical conditions. *Am J Psychiatry*, **145**, 976–981.

Wells KB, Rogers W and Burnam MA (1993) Course of depression in patients with hypertension, myocardial infarction, or insulin-dependent diabetes. *Am J Psychiatry*, **150**, 632–638.

Weyerer S (1990) Relationships between physical and psychological disorders. In: N Sartorius, D Goldberg, G De Girolamo, J Costa e Silva, Y Lecrubier and U Wittchen (eds) *Psychological Disorders in General Medical Settings*. Toronto: Hogrefe & Huber Publishers, 34–46.

Wilson-Barnett J (1992) Psychological reactions to medical procedures. *Psychother Psychosom*, **57**, 118–127.

3

Managing the psychiatry/primary care interface

Antonio Lobo and Ricardo Campos

INTRODUCTION

The crucial question is not how the general practitioner can fit into the mental health services but rather how the psychiatrist can collaborate most effectively with primary care medical services and reinforce the effectiveness of the primary physician as a member of the mental health team.

(World Health Organization, 1973)

Almost 30 years ago psychiatry started to look seriously at the morbidity seen in primary care (PC). The seminal work of Michael Shepherd *et al.* (1966) attracted the attention of clinicians and epidemiologists (Lobo, 1995). Very important work has been reported since then, particularly by European psychiatrists (Williams *et al.*, 1986; Jenkins *et al.*, 1988; Tansella and Williams, 1989; Vazquez-Barquero *et al.*, 1990; Ormel *et al.*, 1990, 1993b; Verhaak and Tijhuis, 1992). Among these, the publication of Goldberg and Huxley's pathway model (Goldberg and Huxley, 1980) made an enormous impact on psychiatrists over the world. More recently, American psychiatry has become particularly active in relation to PC (Von Korff *et al.*, 1987a; Barrett *et al.*, 1988; Wells *et al.*, 1989; Coulehan *et al.*, 1990; Katon *et al.*, 1990, 1992, 1994; Katon and Gonzales, 1994) and the managed care movement has influenced the new developments (Goldberg and Simundson, 1991; Gerarty, 1995; Summergrad *et al.*, 1995).

Depression and Physical Illness. Edited by M.M. Robertson and C.L.E. Katona
© 1997 John Wiley & Sons Ltd

Consultation–liaison (CL) psychiatry, traditionally hospital-based (Strain *et al.*, 1994), is at the crossroads of the new approaches. CL has also shifted towards PC (Lipsitt, 1995). This paradigm shift places primary care CL in a privileged position to develop new strategies of case identification, treatment and prevention (Goldberg and Stoudemire, 1995); it also attempts to optimize the management of health care delivery, assuring continuity of care for patients with psychiatric morbidity seen in the general hospital (Lefkovitz, 1995; Geraty, 1995).

It is now pertinent to discuss the bases of the interface between psychiatry, particularly CL and PC. We present a model which attempts to give specific and realistic solutions to the complex problems arising in the interface. Since the subject of this book is depression and physical illness, depression is the focus of our discussion.

PERSPECTIVES OF THE PSYCHIATRY/GENERAL PRACTICE INTERFACE

The role of general practice in relation to psychiatric morbidity has received considerable attention in recent years (Jenkins *et al.*, 1992; Eisenberg, 1992; Goldberg and Huxley, 1992; Crossley *et al.*, 1992; Corney, 1994; Schulberg and Burns, 1988). Some perspectives of the interface between general practitioners (GPs) and psychiatrists have also become classic (Williams and Clare, 1981; Mitchell, 1983; Tyrer, 1984; Strathdee and Williams, 1986). We believe, though, that the links between general hospital CL psychiatry and the GP have not yet been developed. We set up a Psychosomatic Medicine Service in our university hospital in Zaragoza in 1977 (Lobo and Seva, 1980a, b). While its main role was always the provision of service to general hospital patients, following the traditional lines of CL psychiatry (Lipowski, 1967a, b; Strain and Grossman, 1979), we made explicit from the beginning that attention to PC patients was of paramount importance. In recent years we have made specific moves to implement new links with PC, and depression is one of the main targets in this collaborative effort. Figure 1 shows the current Zaragoza model of interaction between psychiatry and general practice. An interpretation of the model in the specific case of depressed patients follows.

Links 1 to 6 in Figure 1 refer to traditional models of interaction. The high prevalence of psychiatric morbidity, and specifically depression, in PC, and the underdetection and undertreatment by GPs have been well documented (link 1). However, it is important to try to define when and how GPs should refer depressed patients for psychiatry (links 2 and 3). Some patients sent to psychiatrists are referred back to GPs with a treatment plan based on a careful assessment (link 4). On the other hand, severe or complex depression is treated and followed up by mental health (MH) specialists. Even in these cases,

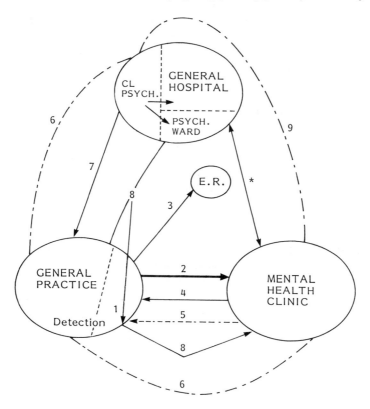

Figure 1. Links between psychiatry and GP, (1) psychiatric morbidity detected by GP, (2) referrals from GP to MH clinic, (3) referrals from GP to emergency room (ER), (4) MH clinic psychiatrist refers back to GP (with a report), (5) MH clinic psychiatrist reports to GP treatment plan on all patients treated in MH clinic, including patients temporarily admitted to psychiatric ward (Psych ward), (6) liaison meetings between psychiatrist and GP, (7) CL psychiatrist (CL Psych) refers patients to GP, with a treatment plan, (8) CL psychiatrist refers patients to MH clinic, but reports GP on the treatment plan, (9) liaison meetings CL psychiatrist/MH clinic psychiatrist.

we feel it is relevant to send a good report to the GP (link 5), who is also responsible for the general health of the patient. Finally, link 6 refers to classical liaison activities between the psychiatrist and the GP.

There is less experience in models or circumstances where the hospital-based CL psychiatrist makes special moves to link with the GP, to integrate psychological and psychiatric aspects in a comprehensive plan of care. Link 7 relates to depressed patients who may be followed up at discharge by the GP.

However, the CL psychiatrist should provide good diagnostic and treatment information. Severely ill or complex patients are referred to an MH clinic, but the GP should also be informed about crucial aspects of the CL intervention and recommendations (link 8). A direct and close liaison between the CL hospital-based psychiatrist and the GP is not currently feasible in our service. Therefore, link 9 refers to the interaction between the CL hospital-based psychiatrist and the MH clinic psychiatrist, since the latter has regular meetings with the GP. A more detailed explanation of each of these links follows.

PREVALENCE OF PSYCHIATRIC MORBIDITY (AND DEPRESSION) IN PRIMARY CARE

Some important and large studies recently completed in PC settings confirm previous classical reports (Shepherd et al., 1996; Goldberg and Blackwell, 1970; Regier et al., 1978; Schurman et al., 1985). By using standardized methods of assessment, a high rate of psychiatric morbidity has been documented (Table 1). All the studies reviewed in the table also document the prevalence of depression.

Major depression (MD) rates range from 4.8% to 13.5% and minor depression ranges from 3.4% to 6.4%. In the Zaragoza study, the rate of ICD-10 mixed depression–anxiety category is reported, while in most other studies this category is included in "sub-threshold" categories. The distribution of diagnostic categories in our study is presented in Figure 2. It shows that depression, in its different categories, affects almost one-half of all the detected psychiatric cases.

Different methods and strategies were used in all these studies. However, for the purpose of this chapter, the point to emphasize is that approximately one out of 10 patients seen by GPs has diagnosable and treatable depression. Unless there is good evidence that depression is adequately treated by the GP, such epidemiological findings give support to collaborative efforts by psychiatrists. In the next sections, we document the need for such efforts.

HIDDEN PSYCHIATRIC MORBIDITY IN PRIMARY CARE

Table 2 refers to the documented underdetection of psychiatric morbidity in primary care. It is suggested that depression, the most prevalent diagnostic category, is also one of the most frequently undetected categories. In fact, the American study by Coyne et al. (1995) refers specifically to depression. Recent studies, such as Ormel et al.'s (1993a) and Ustün's (1994), confirm the same problem, which has been known for some years.

Table 1. Psychiatric morbidity (and depression) in primary care

Authors	Site	Sample	Instruments	Prevalence	
Schulberg *et al.* (1985)	USA	1554	CES-D, DIS	31%	6.2% MD 3% Dys/AD
Ormel *et al.* (1990)	Holland	2237	GHQ, PSE	18%	5.6% MD 4.7% md
Kessler *et al.* (1987)	USA	1072	GHQ, SADS	35%	6.5% MD —
Von Korff *et al.* (1987a)	USA	1242	GHQ, DIS	25%	5% MD 3.7% Dys
Barrett *et al.* (1988)	USA	1055	SCL, SADS	27%	8.6% MD 3.6% md 2.1% Dys
Blacker and Clare (1988)	UK	2308	SADS, PSE	—	4.8% MD 3.4% md 5% Dys
Ustün and Sartorius (1995)	WHO 14 countries	25,916	GHQ CIDI	24%	10.4% MD 9% sub-threshold 2.1% Dys
Perez-Echeverría *et al.* (1993)	Zaragoza (Spain)	1559	GHQ/CAGE MMSE SPPI	27%	5% MD 4.4% mad 3.1% Dys 1.8% AD
Spitzer *et al.* (1994)	USA	1000	PRIME-MD	39%	12% MD 6.4% md 7.8% Dys 13% sub-threshold
Coyne *et al.* (1994)	USA	1928	CESD SCID	—	13.5% MD 9.1% dep NOS

MD, major depression; md, minor depression; Dys, dysthymia; AD, anxiety depression; mad, mixed anxiety depression; dep NOS, depression not otherwise specified

Some controversy has arisen in relation to the method of reporting under-detection (Kamerow, 1987; Campbell, 1987; Rand *et al.*, 1988). For example, the review of medical records may be insufficient, since some GPs may detect and treat patients although they do not document it in the medical chart (Jencks, 1985; Shapiro *et al.*, 1987; Ormel *et al.*, 1991). Furthermore, it has been reported that severe cases of depression, or depressions accompanied by anxiety, are better detected (Coyne *et al.*, 1995; Katon, 1995; Ormel *et al.*, 1991). While these critiques should be taken into consideration, the bulk of evidence suggests that the detection of general morbidity, and also depression, could be improved.

Table 3 presents some of the reasons for the nonrecognition of psychiatric morbidity, including depression. Goldberg and Blackwell (1970), Marks *et al.* (1979), Giel *et al.* (1990), and Ormel and Costa e Silva (1995) are among the

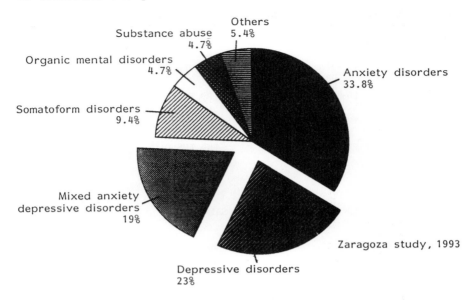

Figure 2. Psychiatric morbidity in primary care. Distribution by ICD-10 diagnostic groups.

Table 2. Detection of psychiatric morbidity by general practitioner.

Author	Site	Conspicuous morbidity %
Goldberg et al. (1976)	UK	36
Hoeper et al. (1984)	USA	16
Boardman (1987)	UK	21
Goldberg and Bridges (1987)	UK	28
Von Korff et al. (1987a)	USA	33
Rand et al. (1988)	USA	17
Ormel et al. (1989)	Holland	26
Ustün and Sartorius (1995)	WHO	23.4
Coyne et al. (1995)	USA	27.9

researchers who have carefully studied this subject. The reasons for under-detection may be related to the GP (Goldberg, 1990; Goldberg and Huxley, 1992; Freeling et al., 1985; Davenport et al., 1987; Verhaak, 1988; Wilmink et al., 1989; Freeling and Tylee, 1992; Robbins et al., 1994), or to the patients themselves (Olfson et al., 1995; Williams, 1986). Sometimes both doctors and patients take part in a collusive phenomenon: each one avoids his own

Table 3. Hidden psychiatric morbidity in primary care. Reasons for nonrecognition.

Related to the GP: "Collusion"
  Individual characteristics
    Less professional experience
    Lack of interest in psychological aspects
    Physicians burnt-out
  Lack of training: poor interviewing techniques
Related to the patient
  Demographic factors
    Old age
    Male sex
    Ethnic minorities
  Clinical determinants
    Perception of poor physical health
    Somatization
    Comorbid physical illness
    Chronic symptoms
    Depressive cues at the end of the interview
Related to the health care system
  Overburdened practices
  Shorter duration of visits
  Reimbursing policies unsensitive to psychological treatments
  No private and/or quiet facilities

responsibilities for eliciting, managing and facing up to psychological distress (Goldberg and Huxley, 1992). In relation to patients, we consider that both the presence of somatization and the presence of physical comorbidity are the most important determining factors. Finally, other reasons relate to the health care system. In Spain, we are painfully aware of the problems of overburdened practices in clinics supported by the national health system. This is among the main reasons for the resistance of GPs to be involved in liaison activities, although this might be counterbalanced if we were able to show some of the implications of underdetection.

IMPLICATIONS OF UNDERDETECTION OF PSYCHIATRIC MORBIDITY (AND DEPRESSION) IN PRIMARY CARE

The implications of psychiatric morbidity in patients attending primary care practices have been documented (Simon *et al.*, 1995). In a recent World Health Organization (WHO) cross-cultural study (Sartorius *et al.*, 1993), a clear dose–response relationship between severity of psychopathology and severity of disability, consistent across the 15 centres throughout the world, was reported.

Furthermore, using logistic regression models it was shown that occupational

Table 4. Hidden psychiatric morbidity in primary care: implications of underdetection.

Longer duration of symptoms
Higher number of unexplained medical symptoms
Higher use of health care resources
   (medical visits, repeated investigations,
   unnecessary symptomatic treatments including
   surgical procedures, etc.)
Increased healthcare costs
Lesser opportunity to receive psychological treatments
Worse prognosis and poorer quality of life (disability etc.)

---

disability was more related to mental disorder than to physical disorder (Ustün and Sartorius, 1995). The implications of the documented hidden psychiatric morbidity in this setting are partly related to the implications of the morbidity itself. Depression is one of the commonest syndromes where such implications have been reported (Ormel and Giel, 1990; Von Korff *et al.*, 1990). Table 4 summarizes some of the findings of different authors who studied the subject. Most research of this type was carried out in Anglo-Saxon countries, but the WHO has also completed an important cross-cultural investigation (Ustün and Sartorius, 1995).

It has been documented that undetected symptoms of depression tend to persist (Freeling *et al.*, 1985) and to cause a higher number of unexplained somatic symptoms (Mechanic *et al.*, 1982; Bridges and Goldberg, 1985). Patients with undetected psychopathological symptoms are more likely to generate more medical visits (Kamerow *et al.*, 1986; Manning and Wells, 1992), to require more diagnostic and treatment procedures (Mumford *et al.*, 1984; Katon *et al.*, 1986; Wells *et al.*, 1989), to have decrements in vocational and social functioning (Broadhead *et al.*, 1990; Johnson *et al.*, 1992; Wohlfarth *et al.*, 1993; Ormel and Costa e Silva, 1995) and to increase the costs of medical care (Jones and Vischi, 1979; Mumford *et al.*, 1984; Von Korff *et al.*, 1990; Lloyd and Jenkins, 1995). Indirect costs may also be noteworthy. For example, these patients have less opportunity to receive psychological treatment (Ormel *et al.*, 1989) and, probably in relation to this, their prognosis tends to be worse, their health perception becomes poorer and the disability becomes apparent (Ormel *et al.*, 1989, 1993b; Wells *et al.*, 1989; Von Korff *et al.*, 1990; Ormel and Costa e Silva, 1995).

The data reviewed here suggest immediately an area for the interaction between psychiatrists and GPs. However, before we discuss the specific models, it seems appropriate to refer to somatization and to somatized depression, since this is one of the main presentations of psychiatric morbidity and one of the main reasons for underdetection (Bridges and Goldberg, 1985).

Table 5. Somatized depression: Modified Bridges and Goldberg's diagnostic criteria.

Consulting behaviour
   The patient must seek medical help for somatic manifestation of depression
Attribution
   The patient considers at the time of consultation that somatic symptoms are caused
   by a physical illness
Psychiatric disorder
   Symptoms reported and/or observed in the examination justify diagnosis of
   depression according to research criteria
Expected response to treatment
   It seems reasonable to predict partial or complete response to conventional treatment
   for depression

SOMATIZED DEPRESSION

Somatization seems to be a world-wide phenomenon (Kleinman, 1977) and depression seems to be one of the main disturbances presented to the GP in a somatized form (Goldberg and Bridges, 1988; Kirmayer *et al.*, 1993). While depression presenting with somatic symptoms has frequently been referred to as "masked depression" (Stoudemire *et al.*, 1985), we prefer Bridges and Goldberg's more operational definition of "somatized depression" (Bridges and Goldberg, 1985) (Table 5). The patients have a diagnosable and treatable depression, but seek help because of somatic manifestations of depression and attribute the symptoms to a physical illness.

The Manchester group (Bridges *et al.*, 1991; Gask *et al.*, 1989; Creed *et al.*, 1992), and also some Canadian authors (Kirmayer and Robbins, 1991), have reported on the prevalence and some characteristics of this kind of morbidity. We have also shown that it is possible to use reliably Bridges and Goldberg's criteria in a cultural background different from that of the original authors (Lobo *et al.*, 1996; García-Campayo *et al.*, 1996). Following that, we were able to show in the Zaragoza study that approximately one-third of psychiatric cases in PC present to the GP in a somatized way (Figure 3). Furthermore, Table 6 compares somatizers and psychologizers in relation to DSM-IIIR/ICD-10 diagnostic distribution and shows that, among depressives, dysthymia is the category presenting more often in a somatized way.

The data reviewed until now suggest several points in relation to depression and the psychiatrist/general practice interface. First, this is an important area of collaboration, since the prevalence of depression is high and detection by GPs is rather low. Second, in support of the public health impact of the first point, the underdetection has implications for patients' quality of life, and economic implications. Third, in connection with this, somatized depression is probably a priority both for clinical practice and for teaching and research.

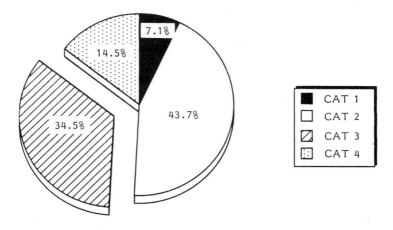

Figure 3. Distribution of psychiatric cases in primary care (Bridges and Goldberg's categories), Category 1 (CAT 1) physical illness and secondary psychiatric illness, Category 2 (CAT 2) physical illness and unrelated psychiatric illness, Category 3 (CAT 3) "somatized" psychiatric disorder ("somatizers"), Category 4 (CAT 4) entirely psychiatric illness ("psychologizers").

Table 6. ICD-10 diagnosis in somatizers and psychologizers.

Diagnosis (ICD-10)	Somatizers $N = 147$ (%)	Psychologizers $N = 46$ (%)
Generalized anxiety disorder	32 (21.7)	12 (26.0)
Mixed anxiety-depressive disorder	23 (15.6)	11 (23.9)
Major depression	22 (14.9)	13 (28.2)
Dysthymia	21 (14.2)	2 (4.3)
Somatization disorder	14 (9.5)	–
Adjustment disorder	12 (8.1)	5 (10.8)
Undifferentiated somatoform disorder	7 (4.7)	–
Panic disorder/agoraphobia	3 (2.0)	–
Others	13 (8.8)	3 (6.5)

REFERRALS OF DEPRESSED PATIENTS FROM GP TO PSYCHIATRY

The previous conclusions might indicate ways for the psychiatrist to proceed in relation to psychiatric morbidity and specifically to depression found in PC. However, a prescriptive case-finding might be unrealistic given the size of the problem (Coulehan et al., 1989; Brody et al., 1995). While some controversy has arisen in recent years (Rucker et al., 1986; Wright, 1994), the authors and

Table 7. Groups at high risk for depression.

Personal or family history of depressive episodes
Severe or chronically disabling physical illness
Recent psychosocial adversities
Lack of social support
Present or past history of substance abuse (including sedatives)
Frequent GP attendance
Ill-defined medical symptoms not explained by somatic diseases
Some demographic characteristics:
   Elderly
   Women (specially after childbirth)
   Ethnic minorities

---

some organizations (King M, 1993; Paykel and Priest, 1992; AHCPR, 1993; Zaragoza's Primary Care Agency, 1996) support a prescriptive approach only in patients considered to be at "high risk" for depression (Table 7).

Case-finding techniques are well known by many GPs and may be easily taught. The General Health Questionnaire (GHQ) (Goldberg, 1972), in its different versions, is among the best-known questionnaires and has been standardized in very different cultures. Depression scales, such as the Hamilton Rating Scale for Depression (Hamilton, 1960), Beck Depression Inventory (Beck *et al.*, 1961), Center for Epidemiological Studies—Depression Scale (Radloff, 1977), Zung Self-Rating Depression Scales (Zung, 1960) and Inventory to Diagnose Depression (Zimmerman and Coryell, 1988), have all been recommended in PC settings. The Hospital Anxiety and Depression Scale (Zigmond and Snaith, 1983) has the advantage that contamination by somatic symptoms of physical illnesses is less likely; while its main use may be in hospitalized patients, it also might be used here. Prime-MD (Spitzer *et al.*, 1994) and the Symptom-Driven Diagnostic System (Broadhead *et al.*, 1995) are two of the recently computerized devices developed for PC settings.

The new interview developed by Goldberg and colleagues (1988) and derived from latent trait analysis to screen for depression and anxiety may be promising. The standardization of the Spanish version during the Zaragoza study of psychiatric morbidity in PC supports the contention that it might be used cross-culturally (Lobo *et al.*, 1994). We have also found that GPs tend to favour its use, because it may be used as an interview guide in clinical practice (Monton *et al.*, 1993). This aspect is particularly important, because no questionnaire can be a substitute for the clinician's interview. Eventually, the GP has to decide whether or not the patient has treatable depression and whether or not he should be referred. In relation to this, Table 8 summarizes the criteria we recommend to GPs for referring depressed patients.

Severe depression is probably the main indication for referral, particularly when "endogenoform" and/or "psychotic" features are present and there is a

Table 8. GP's criteria for referring depressed patients to psychiatry.

Severe/recurrent depression and/or high suicidal risk
No/partial response to conventional treatments for depression
  Type of treatment with documented efficacy
  Adequate dose and duration of antidepressant
Diagnostic complexity
  Comorbidity (physical/psychiatric)
  Differential diagnosis
Patient's preference for psychiatric treatment in mental health clinic

---

high risk of suicide. Similarly, patients should be referred if there is no response to conventional treatment for depression. In our experience, inadequate doses of antidepressants and/or inadequate duration of treatment are often judged to be the reason for therapeutic failure. Diagnostic complexity is another reason for referral, often related to psychiatric or physical comorbidity. Finally, occasional patients insist on being referred to a psychiatrist.

The following factors tend to increase the referral rate from GPs to psychiatric departments: community-based mental health services (Jackson *et al.*, 1993), past psychiatric history, psychological presenting complaint, social problems, GP psychiatric diagnosis, younger age, male gender (the latter only in referrals to hospital mental health clinics) (Whitehouse, 1987; Verhaak, 1993; Wilkinson, 1989), living in an urban area (Goldberg and Huxley, 1980; Verhaak, (1993), scoring high in the GHQ, severe diagnosis, older GP, single-handed practice, doctor–patient relationship difficulty (Morgan, 1989), patient or relative request and ineffectiveness of previous treatment (Morgan, 1989; Robertson, 1979).

On the other hand, traditional hospital outpatient psychiatric departments (Kaeser and Cooper, 1971; Johnson, 1973), the presence of organic disease (Arreghini *et al.*, 1991), and GPs with interest in psychological issues (Creed *et al.*, 1990; Verhaak, 1993) have all been reported to be factors tending to decrease the referral rate. However, most of these situations might well be influenced by sociocultural factors, and the findings cannot be generalized. A recurrent theme in the literature is the need to negotiate the referral with the patient, since a considerable proportion of patients do not comply with GPs' recommendations (Carpenter *et al.*, 1981; Brown *et al.*, 1988). Therefore, new techniques might be important to improve compliance (Joint Report of the Royal College of Physicians and Psychiatrists, 1994).

Specific studies are needed to document with empirical data the best procedures to deal with depression found in PC. We have conducted a large epidemiological study in this setting and preliminary steps were taken to operationalize the referral criteria (Lobo *et al.*, 1993). We found that approximately one-third of the psychiatric cases identified among new inception episodes in a representative sample of primary care attenders might benefit from specialized assessment (Campos *et al.*, 1993). This number of referrals may well be unmanageable in practice. However, it should also be hypothesized that many such cases might be treated by the GP if good liaison with the psychiatric service is provided.

In relation to liaison procedures, the referral note from the GP has received some attention in the specialized literature (Pullen and Yellowlees, 1985; Creed *et al.*, 1990). Based on this and our clinical experience, we recommend that at least the following information should be included: specific reason for referral, physical illnesses and current somatic treatment; the experience of the GP with the particular patient in relation to previous and present episodes, including psychotropic medications prescribed and doses, duration of treatment and therapeutic response; and relevant psychosocial background known by the GP which might be difficult to elicit in the first interview.

REFERRAL FROM PSYCHIATRIST TO GP

A proportion of depressed patients (and other patients with psychiatric disturbances) may be referred to the GP after the psychiatric assessment has been completed. Meta-analysis studies have estimated specialist mental health treatment provided in PC to be only 10% more effective than the treatment provided by GPs (Balestrieri *et al.*, 1988). Most referred patients have probably been seen initially by the GP but pathways of care may vary considerably between countries. Similarly, the criteria for referral and the way to refer patients may vary according to local or national circumstances.

We follow considerations derived from the referral criteria listed in Table 8. When the patient is considered to have non-severe depression and there is no suicidal risk, the psychiatrist is more inclined to refer the patient back to the GP for maintenance treatment and follow up. Similarly, referral is appropriate once the patient's depression has been successfully treated and relapses are not expected; or, when the psychiatric assessment has eliminated any diagnostic complexity. In all cases, the referral is more justified when the patient agrees to follow up by the GP. In our experience, this acceptance varies considerably depending on how supportive the GP is of patients with psychological problems.

Referral to the GP is amenable to conclusions derived from some studies and/or the experiences of clinicians documented in specialized reports. Goldberg and Jackson (1992) emphasized the importance of continuing advice and the availability of resources after the initial one-off assessment. In our own experience, Strathdee's conclusion is highly relevant: four-fifths of the GPs surveyed valued as highly relevant the assessments by psychiatrists complemented with treatment conducted by GPs, or crisis intervention by psychiatrists

Table 9. GP's expectations of mental health teams.

Availability
   Crisis intervention
   24-hour service
   Short referral–appointment interval
   Home assessment (if needed)
   Joint visits (hands on learning)
Professional characteristics
   Seniority
   Continuity (follow up by the same MH professional)
   MH team involved in medical community
Improved communication
   Clearly written (computerized) reports
   Diagnostic formulation
   Competency/disability assessment
   Better treatment plans
      Specify medication (doses, duration, main side-effects, etc.)
      Type of psychosocial intervention (who is involved, number of sessions, etc.)
      Role of GP team (prescribing responsibilities, early intervention if relapse)
      Prognosis included
      Contingency plans (including decisions about hospitalization)
   Follow up information (reviews of plans in chronic patients)
   General information handouts

---

and follow up by GPs. In other words, GPs prefer easy access to MH clinics without losing clinical responsibility for their patient (Strathdee, 1987). Other GP requirements from MH teams, derived from different studies (Strathdee, 1992; Ferguson, 1987; Daniels and Linn, 1984), are summarized in Table 9.

The psychiatric report is crucial when referring patients back to the GP. Referral letters have often been described as ineffective, incomplete or deficient (De Alarcon and Hodson, 1964; Williams and Wallace, 1974; Pullen and Yellowlees, 1985). However, it is acknowledged that they remain the main way of communication.

Yellowlees and Pullen (1984) investigated the preferred format of a psychiatric report about new referrals to GPs: a one-page format, with two or three sub-headings was preferred. Similarly, the following were considered to be key items: diagnosis, treatment (including duration), follow up visits, prognosis and a brief explanation of the diagnosis (precipitants, and predisposing and perpetuating factors). Good letters promote a good therapeutic relationship but experience is needed; we consider that letter writing skills should be taught to under- or postgraduates.

Finally, respect for confidentiality is important, as is the avoidance of harmful labels. Legibility is of crucial relevance and that is one of the many reasons for the development of new CL psychiatry programmes providing computerized reports. Furthermore, joint audits using new microcomputerized databased information systems services will make possible a successful standard of consultation liaison in the future (Hammer *et al.*, 1995).

LIAISON MEETINGS BETWEEN THE PSYCHIATRIST AND GP

The general philosophy of liaison activities has been described mainly in the American literature (Von Korff and Myers, 1987; Schulberg, 1987). The peculiarities of liaison in PC have been described in recent years (Verhaak and Wennink, 1990; Dowrick, 1992; Strathdee, 1992; Horder, 1988; Gask and MacGrath, 1989; Ferguson and Varnam, 1994; Gonzales, 1994). One of the most important themes to consider is that "teaching" in this setting is usually two-way. GPs have a great deal of information about individual patients, their socio-cultural background and about where they live. Furthermore, their commitment to patients is often strong and long-lasting. Such attachments are usually highly therapeutic. The psychiatrist will be well received only when he/she respects what the GP is doing from the psychological point of view, when he/she is prepared to share experiences, tolerate difficulties and negotiate possible solutions. Important initiatives have been taken by several authors in this setting, although sometimes the movements were "silent" (Strathdee and Williams, 1984). Some authors (Strathdee *et al.*, 1992), however, have also made explicit plans to set up a new service in PC (Table 10).

Table 10 is self-explanatory and may be a good guide to new services. While each stage is not described in a rigid way, individual services may choose to follow a more flexible approach. Independently of this, several models of psychiatric interaction have been described. What model should be implemented is a key question to be included in the research agenda for the

Table 10. Stages to set up psychiatric attachment to general practice (Reproduced by permission of Strathdee *et al.*, 1992).

Rationale and objectives
   "What role will the primary care clinic serve within the existing or developing psychiatric service?"
Practice identification
   "In which practices can need and feasibility be accommodated?"
Negotiation of practicalities
   "When, where and how often?"
Model selection
   "Which model of interaction is best suited to the working practices of the psychiatrist and GP?"
Patient referral
   "Which patients will be seen?"
Patient management
   "Who does what?"

Table 11. The benefits of the psychiatric liaison–attachment scheme in primary care (modified from Creed and Marks, 1989).

For the patient
  Familiarity
  Accessibility
  Acceptability (less stigma)
  Less inappropriate admissions; shorter hospital length of stay
  Continuity of health care
For primary care services
  Better education on psychosocial aspects of health care
  Earlier intervention
  Joint assessments (therapeutic interviewing)
  More realistic expectations
  Better use of existing resources
  Shared and co-ordinated care
  More professional satisfaction
For CL psychiatric team
  Wider information on the patient's background
  Understanding of reasons for consultation: doctor–patient problems, etc.
  Modification of the referral process: more appropriate referrals
  Better use of service: fewer re-referrals, more new patients
  Less isolation. More professional satisfaction
  Larger scope of intervention: minor and major psychiatric disorders
  Cost-effectiveness

---

immediate future (Kamerow and Burns, 1987; Schulberg, 1991). Von Korff *et al.* (1987b) have reviewed, in an excellent article, how different variables may be measured to study outcomes regarding the patient (psychiatric symptomatic status, social dysfunction, illness behaviour, somatic status and quality of life), service (utilization pattern, costs and satisfaction) and physician capabilities (diagnostic and therapeutic skills, change of attitudes towards psychosocial aspects, etc.). Whenever possible a "generic psychiatric liaison team", including trainees, is recommended (Benjamin *et al.*, 1994).

We are now implementing in the University Hospital of Zaragoza a model inspired by Creed and Marks' liaison-attachment scheme (Creed and Marks, 1989). Our experience tends to support their conclusions about the potential advantages of the model for patients, for PC services and for the CL psychiatry team (Table 11).

NEW PERSPECTIVES: INTERFACE BETWEEN HOSPITAL-BASED CL PSYCHIATRY AND GP IN RELATION TO DEPRESSION

We believe there is an important, although not well-explored, place for interaction, in relation to depression, between hospital-based CL psychiatrists and GPs.

The rationale for this is as follows. First, there is abundant evidence suggesting that the prevalence of depression in specific medical illnesses such as cancer and in general medical patients is quite high, although the diagnosis is frequently overlooked (Lobo, 1986, 1989, 1990; Lobo *et al.*, 1986, 1988; Cohen-Cole *et al.*, 1993). Second, depression is one of the main reasons for referral to hospital-based CL services. This notion has recently been confirmed in a large, multicentre, multinational European study in close to 15 000 referred patients to CL services (Huyse *et al.*, 1993). Third, a proportion of depressed patients identified in medical wards is discharged when the depression has not yet disappeared (Pérez-Echeverría, 1985) and some of these remain depressed long after discharge (Hawton, 1981; Feldman *et al.*, 1987; Kathol and Wenzel, 1992). Fourth, while some patients still depressed at discharge require specialized follow up by the psychiatrist, clinical experience suggests that a considerable proportion of them might be managed by the GP. However, there is some evidence that few do so (Feldman *et al.*, 1987). In both cases, we would recommend that the GP is informed of the psychiatric opinion and of his role in the treatment. Fifth, the implications of undertreatment of depressed general hospital patients may be similar to the ones described in PC patients. Furthermore, some studies have also associated major depression in medical patients with higher morbidity and mortality (Frasure-Smith *et al.*, 1993; Hawton, 1981).

All these reasons justify a liaison attachment between hospital-based CL psychiatrists and GPs. Furthermore, some recent studies (Katon *et al.*, 1995; Sturm and Wells, 1995) document that multifaceted collaborative management of major depression in PC resulted in better outcomes in terms of patient satisfaction and compliance, and also in clinical outcome. It is apparent that new studies are needed to explore strategies for improvement of the liaison attachment in all cases but specifically in depressed medically ill patients after being discharged; the next generation of European Consultant–Liaison Workgroup (ECLW) research (Creed and Lobo, 1995) is focusing on this important issue. In the meantime, clinical and teaching experience indicate the practical approach. Table 12 includes some criteria we use to refer depressed hospital patients to the GP.

The psychiatric diagnosis should be clear and complicating psychiatric comorbidity should be ruled out first. Patients with severe depression, particularly if risk of suicide is evident, should be referred to an MH clinic. The type of depression is not included in the criteria: our experience suggests that in clinical practice, particularly in the mild severity cases, the distinction between "endogenous", dysthymia and adjustment disorder may be quite difficult. However, we would like to emphasize here that "organic" or secondary depression, for example post-stroke depression, may also be treated by the non-psychiatrist. The presence of severe social or personality problems, as well as abnormal illness behaviour such as noncompliance, may indicate a psychiatric referral. On the other hand, if the

Table 12. Hospital-based CL psychiatrist's criteria for referring depressed patients to GP.

Clear diagnosis, psychiatric comorbidity ruled out
Non-severe/non-psychotic depressions; not high suicidal risk
Absence of social and/or psychological problems with high potential to complicate the
  course of depression
Patient's preference for receiving treatment from GP
Compliance with treatment is expected
Clear guidelines about the type, duration and potential side-effects of pharmacological
  treatments when indicated

Table 13. Minimal standards for the liaison between hospital-based CL psychiatry and GP
for depressed patients (The Zaragoza model, Campos *et al.*, 1997).

Written report to GP, with patient consent, in all relevant patients:
  Patients to be managed by GP
  Patients to be managed by MH clinic psychiatrist
Telephone consultation available as requested
If poor compliance is anticipated:
  Call GP personally
  Call MH clinic psychiatrist personally when appropriate
  Social worker calls family to assure support from relatives
Liaison meetings with MH clinic psychiatrist attached to GP

patient is resistant to this referral, which is often the case in depressed patients with physical comorbidity, referral to the GP may be a good initial choice and clear suggestions should be given to the GP in relation to the specific treatment recommended. Finally, the suggestions discussed above in relation to reports to GPs should also be taken into consideration here.

LIAISON OF HOSPITAL-BASED CL PSYCHIATRY AND GP

Creed's plea for a more active approach by the psychiatrist to liaise with non-psychiatric colleagues should be remembered here (Creed, 1991). In addition to traditional models of liaison psychiatry (Torem *et al.*, 1979) we have always emphasized the need to link with GPs (Lobo and Seva, 1980b; Lobo, 1986; Lobo *et al.*, 1986), and the discussion above supports the decision to implement specific plans. The philosophy we favour for this particular liaison is inspired by the approach described for the link between MH clinic psychiatrists and GPs. However, logistical and staffing reasons may make the approach unrealistic; this is now the situation in our service. In the context of a quality improvement programme, under the auspices of a European study (Herzog *et al.*, 1995), we are now implementing a "minimal standards" programme for liaison with the GP. Table 13 describes the standards for depressed patients.

Some items in Table 13 are self-explanatory but liaison with the MH clinic psychiatrist needs discussion. In a busy CL/psychosomatic service (currently there is a 4% consultation rate for inpatients), with limited staff, a more intensive liaison programme seems unrealistic. However, it is possible to maintain a weekly meeting with the MH clinic psychiatrist attached to PC practices. In this meeting all relevant patients are discussed. Then the MH clinic psychiatrist transfers and discusses the information in his regularly scheduled meetings with GPs following the approach described above. While this model seems satisfactory, specific studies will be needed to assess the results.

CONCLUDING REMARKS

The described model of interaction between psychiatry and general practice is the product of immediate clinical needs. However, models of service provision in any medical field should ideally be research-based. Neither psychiatry nor PC are exceptions to this rule. In this respect, it seems appropriate to conclude this chapter by quoting the last report of a pioneer in this field, Professor Michael Shepherd, in the year of his death.

> The basic issues relating to scientific investigation in this context were addressed by Lord Platt 40 years ago in a paper on the theme of "Opportunities for research in general practice" that exposed the falsity of the division between mechanistic laboratory science and humanistic medicine (Platt, 1953). Two principal points were made. One was the close dependence of such research on medical statistics ... Platt's second point was to emphasize the need for GPs themselves to undertake research on the material arising from everyday clinical practice. The surface of investigative potential in this sphere has barely been scratched.
>
> (Shepherd, 1995)

REFERENCES

AHCPR (Agency for Health Care Policy and Research) (1993) *Depression in Primary Care: Vol 1. Detection and Diagnosis. Clinical Practice Guideline, No 5.* Rockville, MD: US Department of Health and Human Services, Public Health Service. Publication No. 93-0550.

Arreghini E, Agostini C and Wilkinson G (1991) General practitioner referral to specialist psychiatric services: a comparison of practices in north and south Verona. *Psychol Med*, **21**, 485–494.

Balestrieri M, Williams P and Wilkinson G (1988) Specialist mental health treatment in general practice: a meta-analysis. *Psychol Med*, **18**, 711–718.

Barrett JE, Barrett JA, Oxman TE and Gerber PD (1988) The prevalence of psychiatric disorders in a primary care practice. *Arch Gen Psychiatry*, **45**, 1100–1106.

Beck AT, Ward CH, Mendelson M, Mock J and Erbaugh J (1961) An inventory for measuring depression. *Arch Gen Psychiatry*, **4**, 561–571.

Benjamin S, House A and Jenkins P (1994) *Liaison Psychiatry: Defining Needs and Planning Services*. London: Gaskell.

Blacker CVR and Clare AW (1988) The prevalence and treatment of depression in general practice. *Psychopharmacology*, **95**, 514–517.

Bridges KW and Goldberg DP (1985) Somatic presentation of DSM-III psychiatric disorders in primary care. *J Psychosom Res*, **29**, 563–569.

Bridges KW, Goldberg DP, Evans B and Sharpe T (1991) Determinants of somatisation in primary care. *Psychol Med*, **21**, 473–483.

Boardman AP (1987) The General Health Questionnaire and the detection of emotional disorders. A replicated study. *Br J Psychiatry*, **151**, 373–381.

Broadhead WE, Blazer DG, George LK and Tse CK (1990) Depression, disability days, days lost from work in a prospective epidemiological survey. *JAMA*, **264**, 2524–2528.

Broadhead E, Leon A, Weissman M *et al.* (1995) Development and validation of the SDDS-PC screen for multiple mental disorders in primary care. *Arch Fam Med*, **4**, 211–229.

Brody DS, Thompson TL, Larson DB, Ford DE, Katon WJ and Magruder KM (1995) Recognizing and managing depressions in primary care. *Gen Hosp Psychiatry*, **17**, 93–107.

Brown RMA, Strathdee G, Christie-Brown JRW and Robinson PH (1988) A comparison of referrals to primary care and hospital outpatients clinics. *Br J Psychiatry*, **153**, 168–173.

Campbell TL (1987) Is screening for mental health problem worthwhile in family practice? An opposing view. *J Fam Pract*, **5**, 184–187.

Campos R (1993) Estudio de la morbilidad psiquica en el nivel de Atención Primaria de la Ciudad de Zaragoza. PhD Doctoral Thesis, University of Zaragoza.

Campos R, Lobo A, Martinez-Calvo A, Bellido M, Iglesias C and Carreras S (1997) Psiquiatria de interconsulta y enlace con atencion primaria desde el hospital general: El modelo Zaragoza. *Psiquis* (in press).

Campos R, Pérez-Echeverría MJ, García-Campayo JJ, Marcos G, Lobo A and GMPPZ (AP) (1993) *Psychosocial Treatment Needs in Primary Care*. Young Researcher's First Award of the Spanish Psychosomatic Medicine Society on Consultation–Liaison Psychiatry. Proceedings of XXIX National Meeting, 63.

Carpenter PJ, Morrow GR, Del Gaudio AC and Ritzel BA (1981) Who keeps the first outpatient appointment? *Am J Psychiatry*, **138**, 102–105.

Cohen-Cole SA, Brown FW and McDaniel JS (1993) Assessment of depression and grief reactions in the medically ill. In: A Stoudemire and BS Fogel (eds), *Psychiatric Care of the Medical Patient*. New York: Oxford University Press, 53–69.

Corney R (1994) Developing mental health services in the community: current evidence of the role of general practice teams. *J R Soc Medicine*, **87**, 408–411.

Coulehan JL, Schulberg HC and Block M (1989) The efficiency of depression questionnaires for case finding in primary medical care. *J Gen Intern Med*, **4**, 541–547.

Coulehan JL, Schulberg HC, Block M, Janosky JE and Arena VC (1990) Depressive symptomatology and medical co-morbidity in a primary care clinic. *Int J Psychiatry Med*, **20**, 335–347.

Coyne JC, Fechner-Bates S and Schwenk TL (1994) Prevalence, nature, and comorbidity of depressive disorders in primary care. *Gen Hosp Psychiatry*, **16**, 267–276.

Coyne JC, Schwenk TL and Fechner-Bates S (1995) Nondetection of depression by primary care physicians reconsidered. *Gen Hosp Psychiatry*, **17**, 3–12.

Creed F (1991) Liaison psychiatry for the 21st century: a review. *J R Soc Med*, **84**, 414–417.

Creed F and Lobo A (1995) The outcome of medical patients admitted to the general hospital: Psychiatric co-morbidity, subjective health, occupational difficulties, and the use of medical services. Paper read before the Joint Meeting of the BIOMED1 collaborative study group "Quality assurance in CL Psychiatry and Psychosomatics", Freiburg.

Creed F and Marks B (1989) Liaison psychiatry in general practice: a comparison of the liaison-attachment scheme and shifted outpatient clinic models. *J R Coll Gen Pract*, **39**, 514–517.

Creed F, Gowrisunkur J, Russel E and Kincey J (1990) General practitioner referral rates to district psychiatry and psychology services. *Br J Gen Pract*, **40**, 450–454.

Creed F, Mayou R and Hopkins A (eds) (1992) *Medical Symptoms not Explained by Organic Diseases*. London: Royal College of Physicians and Psychiatrists.

Crossley D, Myers MP and Wilkinson G (1992) Assessment of psychological care in general practice. *Br Med J*, **305**, 1333–1336.

Daniels ML and Linn LS (1984) Psychiatric consultation in a medical clinic: What do medical providers want? *Gen Hosp Psychiatry*, **6**, 196–202.

Davenport S, Goldberg DP and Millar T (1987) How psychiatric disorders are missed during medical consultations? *Lancet*, **3**, 439–442.

De Alarcon R and Hodson JM (1964) The value of general practitioners' letters. *Br Med J*, **2**, 435–438.

Dowrick, C (1992) Improving mental health through primary care. *Br J Gen Pract*, **42**, 382–386.

Einsenberg L (1992) Treating anxiety and depression in primary care: Closing the gap between knowledge and practice. *N Engl J Med*, **3**, 327, 731–732.

Feldman E, Mayou R, Hawton K, Ardern M and Smith EBO (1987) Psychiatric disorder in medical in-patients. *Q J Med*, **63**, 405–412.

Ferguson B (1987) Psychiatric clinics in general practices: an asset for primary care. *Health Trends*, **19**, 22–23.

Ferguson BG and Varnam MA (1994) The relationship between primary care and psychiatry: an opportunity for change. *Br J Gen Pract*, **44**, 527–530.

Frasure-Smith N, Lespéance F and Talajic M (1993) Depression following myocardial infarction. Impact on 6 month survival. *JAMA*, **270**, 1819–1825.

Freeling P and Tylee A (1992) Undiagnosed or mistreated depression in primary care. In: SA Montgomery and F Rouillon (eds) *Long-term Treatment of Depression*. Chichester: Wiley, 25–43.

Freeling P, Rao BM and Paykel ES (1985) Unrecognized depression in general practice. *Br Med J*, **287**, 535–537.

Garcia-Campayo JJ, Campos R, Marcos G, Pérez-Echeverría MJ, Lobo A and GMPPZ (AP) (1996) Somatization in primary care in Spain (II): Differences between somatizers and psychologizers. *Br J Psychiatry*, **168**, 348–353.

Gask L and McGrath G (1989) Psychotherapy and general practice. *Br J Psychiatry*, **154**, 445–453.

Gask L, Goldberg DP, Porter R and Creed F (1989) The treatment of somatisation: evaluation of a training package with general practice trainees. *J Psychosoc Res*, **33**, 697–703.

Gater R, Sousa BAE, Barrientos G *et al.* (1991) Pathways to psychiatric care: a cross-cultural study. *Psychol Med*, **21**, 761–774.

Geraty RD (1995) General hospital psychiatry and the new behavioral health care delivery system. *Gen Hosp Psychiatry*, **17**, 245–250.

Giel R, Koeter M and Ormel J (1990) Detection and referral of primary care patients with mental health problems. In: DP Goldberg and D Tantam (eds), *Social Psychiatry and Public Health*. Bern: Hoegrefe Huber, 25–34.

Goldberg DP (1972) *The Detection of Psychiatric Illness by Questionnaire*. Oxford: Oxford University Press.

Goldberg DP (1990) Reasons for misdiagnosis. In: N Sartorius, DP Goldberg, G de Girolamo, J Costa e Silva, Y Lecrubier and U Wittchen (eds), *Psychological Disorders in General Medical Settings*. Bern: Hoegrefe Huber, 139–145.

Goldberg DP and Blackwell B (1970) Psychiatric illness in general practice: a detailed study using a new method of case identification. *Br Med J*, **2**, 439–443.

Goldberg DP and Bridges KW (1987) Screening for psychiatric illness in general practice: the general practitioner versus the screening questionnaire. *J R Coll Gen Pract*, **37**, 15–18.

Goldberg DP and Bridges KW (1988) Somatic presentations of psychiatric illness in primary care settings. *J Psychosom Res*, **32**, 137–144.

Goldberg DP and Huxley P (1980) *Mental Illness in the Community: The Pathway to Psychiatric Care*. London: Tavistock.

Goldberg DP and Huxley P (1992) *Common Mental Disorders: A Bio-social Model*. London: Routledge.

Goldberg DP and Jackson G (1992) Interface between primary care and specialist mental health care. *Br J Gen Pract*, **42**, 267–268.

Goldberg RJ and Simundson S (1991) Managing Medicare reimbursement on medical-psychiatry unit. *Gen Hosp Psychiatry*, **13**, 313–318.

Goldberg RJ and Stoudemire A (1995) The future of consultation—liaison psychiatry and medical-psychiatric units in the era of managed care. *Gen Hosp Psychiatry*, **17**, 268–277.

Goldberg DP, Rickels K, Downing R and Hesbacher P (1976) A comparison of two psychiatric screening tests. *Br J Psychiatry*, **129**, 61–67.

Goldberg DP, Bridges KW, Duncan-Jones P and Grayson D (1988) Detecting anxiety and depression in general medical settings. *Br Med J*, **97**, 897–899.

Gonzales J (1994) Psychiatric problems in primary care: what are the problems, how will we recognize them, and how can we treat them? *Psychosom Med*, **56**, 94–96.

Hamilton M (1960) A rating scale for depression. *J Neurol Neurosurg Psychiatry*, **23**, 56–62.

Hammer JS, Strain JJ, Friedberg A and Fulop G (1995) Operationalizing a bedside pen entry notebook clinical database system in consultation–liaison psychiatry. *Gen Hosp Psychiatry*, **17**, 165–172.

Hawton K (1981) The long-term outcome of psychiatric morbidity detected in general medical patient. *J Psychosom Res*, **25**, 237–243.

Herzog T, Huyse FJ, Malt UF, Cardoso G, Creed F, Lobo A, Rigatelli M and ECLW (1995) *Quality Management in Consultation Liaison Psychiatry and Psychosomatics. Development and implementation of a European QM system*. Research proposal PL 931706 of the European Union Biomedical and Health Research Biomed 1 Program.

Hoeper EW, Nycz LG, Kessler JD, Burke JD and Pierce WE (1984) The usefulness of screening for mental illness. *Lancet*, **i**, 33–35.

Horder J (1988) Working with general practitioners. *Br J Psychiatry*, **153**, 513–520.

Huyse FJ, Herzog T, Malt U and Lobo A (1993) The effectiveness of mental health service delivery in the general hospital. In: GN Fracchia and M Theofilatou (eds), *Health Services Research*. Amsterdam: IOS Press, 227–242.

Jackson G, Gater R, Goldberg DP, Tamtam D, Loftus L and Taylor H (1993) A new community mental health team based in primary care: a description of the service and its effect on service use in the first year. *Br J Psychiatry*, **162**, 375–384.

Jencks S (1985) Recognition of mental distress and diagnosis of mental disorder in primary care. *JAMA*, **253**, 1903.

Jenkins R, Smeeton N and Shepherd M (1988) Classification of mental disorders in primary care. *Psychol Med* (monograph supplement 12). Cambridge: Cambridge University Press.

Jenkins R, Newton J and Young R (1992) *The prevention of depression and anxiety: The role of the primary care team.* London: HMSO.

Johnson DA (1973) An analysis of outpatient services. *Br J Psychiatry*, **122**, 301–306.

Johnson J, Weissman M and Klerman G (1992) Service utilization and social morbidity associated with depressive symptoms in the community. *JAMA*, **267**, 1478–1483.

Joint Report of the Royal College of Physicians and Psychiatrists (1994) *The Psychological Care of Medical Patients: Recognition of Need and Service Provision.* London: Royal College of Physicians and Psychiatrists.

Jones KR and Vischi TR (1979) Impact of alcohol, drug abuse and mental health treatment on medical care utilization: a review of the research literature. *Med Care*, **17**, 1–82.

Kaeser AC and Cooper B (1971) The psychiatric outpatient, the general practitioner and the outpatient clinic: an operational study and a review. *Psychol Med*, **1**, 312–325.

Kamerow D (1987) Is screening for mental health problems worthwhile in family practice? An affirmative view. *J Fam Pract*, **25**, 181–183.

Kamerow DB and Burns BJ (1987) The effectiveness of mental health consultation and referral in ambulatory primary care: a research lacuna. *Gen Hosp Psychiatry*, **9**, 111–117.

Kamerow D, Pincus H and Macdonald D (1986) Alcohol abuse, other drug abuse, and mental disorder in medical practice: prevalence, costs, recognition, and treatment. *JAMA*, **255**, 2054–2057.

Kathol RG and Wenzel RP (1992) Natural history of symptoms of depression and anxiety during inpatient treatment on general medicine wards. *J Gen Intern Med*, **7**, 287–293.

Katon W (1995) Will improving detection of depression in primary care lead to improved depressive outcomes? *Gen Hosp Psychiatry*, **17**, 1–2.

Katon W and Gonzales J (1994) A review of randomized trials of psychiatric consultation–liaison studies in primary care. *Psychosomatics*, **35**, 268–278.

Katon W and Schulberg H (1992) Epidemiology of depression in primary care. *Gen Hosp Psychiatry*, **14**, 237–247.

Katon W, Berg A, Robins AJ and Risse S (1986) Depression: medical utilization and somatization. *Western J Med*, **72**, 127–135.

Katon WJ, Von Korff M, Lin EH, Bush BT, Lipscomb P, Russo J, Wagner EH and Polk E (1990) Distressed high utilizers of medical care: DSMIII-R diagnoses and treatment needs. *Gen Hosp Psychiatry*, **12**, 355–362.

Katon W, Von Korff M, Lin E *et al.* (1992) Adequacy and duration of antidepressant treatment in primary care. *Med Care*, **30**, 67–76.

Katon W, Lin E, Von Korff M *et al.* (1994) The predictors of persistence of depression in primary care. *J Affect Disord*, **31**, 81–90.

Katon W, Von Korff M, Lin E *et al.* (1995) Collaborative management to achieve treatment guidelines: Impact on depression in primary care. *JAMA*, **273**, 1026–1031.

Kessler LG, Clearly PD and Burke JD (1987) Psychiatric diagnoses of medical service users: evidence from the Epidemiological Catchment Area Program. *Am J Public Health*, **77**, 18–24.

King M (1993) *Shared Care of Patients with Mental Health Problems: Joint Report of the Royal College of Psychiatrists and Royal College of General Practitioners.* Occasional paper 60. London: Royal College of General Practitioners.

Kirmayer LJ and Robbins JM (1991) Three forms of somatisation in primary care: prevalence, co-occurrence and sociodemographic characteristics. *J Nerv Ment Dis*, **179**, 647–655.

Kirmayer LJ, Robbins JM, Dworkind M *et al.* (1993) Somatisation and recognition of depression and anxiety in primary care. *Am J Psychiatry*, **150**, 734–741.

Kleinman A (1977) Depression, somatization and the "new crosscultural psychiatry". *Soc Sci Med*, **11**, 3–10.

Lefkovitz PM (1995) The continuum of care in a general hospital setting. *Gen Hosp Psychiatry*, **17**, 260–267.

Lipowski ZJ (1967a) Review of consultation psychiatry and psychosomatic medicine 1. General principles. *Psychosom Med*, **29**, 153–171.

Lipowski ZJ (1967b) Review of consultation psychiatry and psychosomatic medicine 2. Clinical aspects. *Psychosom Med*, **29**, 201–224.

Lipsitt DR (1995) Managed care: A catalyst for integrated medicine. *Gen Hosp Psychiatry*, **17**, 243–245.

Lloyd K and Jenkins R (1995) The economics of depression in primary care: Department of Health initiatives. *Br J Psychiatry*, **166** (suppl. 27), 60–62.

Lobo A (1986) Philosophical humanism and empirical science: Spanish perspectives on psychosomatics. *Advances, J Institute for the Advancement of Health, Int Issue*, **3**, 58–76.

Lobo A (1989) On multiaxial psychiatric diagnosis for general medical patients. *Br J Psychiatry*, **154** (suppl. 4), 38–41.

Lobo A (1990) Mental health in general medical clinics. In: DP Goldberg and D Tantam (eds) *The Public Health Impact of Mental Disorders*. Bern: Huber-Hoegrefe, 45–53.

Lobo A (1995) La contribución del Profesor Michael Shepherd a la Psiquiatría de Enlace y Medicina Psicosomática. *Cuadernos de Psicosomática y Psiquiatría de Enlace*, **36**, 61–73.

Lobo A and Seva A (1980a) Aportación psiquiátrica a una medicina "integral": un Servicio de Psicosomática y Psicoterapia I. Fundamentos empíricos y doctrinales II. *Actas Luso-Esp Neurol Psiquiat*, **5**, 347–358.

Lobo A and Seva A (1980b) Aportación psiquiátrica a una medicina "integral": un Servicio de Psicosomática y Psicoterapia II. La triple vertiente clínico-docente-investigadora. *Actas Luso-Esp Neurol Psiquiat*, **6**, 443–470.

Lobo A, Perez-Echeverría MJ, Artal J *et al.* (1986) Psychiatric morbidity among medical outpatients in Spain: A case for new methods of classification. *J Psychosom Res*, **33**, 697–703.

Lobo A, Folstein MF, Escolar MV, Morera B and Día JL (1988) Screening instruments and diagnostic criteria for psychiatric epidemiological studies in oncological patients. In: A Lobo and A Tres (eds) *Psicosomática y Cáncer* Madrid: Ministerío de Sanidad y Consumo, 456–458.

Lobo A, Campos R, Pérez-Echeverría MJ, Izuzquiza J, García-Campayo JJ, Saz P and Marcos G (1993) A new interview for the multiaxial assessment of psychiatric morbidity in medical settings. *Psychol Med*, **23**, 505–510.

Lobo A, Montón C, Campos R, García Campayo JJ, Pérez-Echeverría MJ and GMPPZ (AP) (1994) In: SA Luzan (ed) *Detección de Morbilidad Psíquica en la Práctica Médica: El Nuevo Instrumento E.A.D.G* España: Roche.

Lobo A, García-Campayo JJ, Campos R, Marcos G, Pérez-Echeverría MJ and GMPPZ (AP) (1996) Somatization in primary care in Spain (I): Estimates of prevalence and clinical characteristics. *Br J Psychiatry*, **168**, 344–348.

Manning WG and Wells KB (1992) The effects of psychological distress and psychological well-being on use of medical services. *Med Care*, **30**, 541–553.

Marks J, Goldberg DP and Hillier V (1979) Determinants of the ability of general practitioners to detect psychiatric illness. *Psychol Med*, **9**, 337–353.

Mechanic D, Clearly PD and Greenley JR (1982) Distress syndromes illness behavior, access to care and medical utilization in a defined population. *Med Care*, **20**, 361–372.

Mitchell ARK (1983) Psychiatrists in primary health care settings. *Br J Psychiatry*, **147**, 371–380.

Montón C, Pérez-Echeverría MJ, Campos R, García-Campayo JJ, Lobo A and GMPPZ (AP) (1993) Escalas de ansiedad depresión de Goldberg: una guía de entrevista eficaz para la detección del malestar psíquico. *Atención Primaria*, **12**, 345–349.

Morgan D (1989) Psychiatric cases: ethnography of the referral process. *Psychol Med*, **19**, 743–753.

Mumford E, Schlesinger HJ, Glass GV, Patrick C and Cuerdon T (1984) A new look at evidence about reduced cost of medical utilization following mental health treatment. *Am J Psychiatry*, **141**, 1145–1158.

Olfson M, Gilbert T, Weissman M, Blacklow RS and Broadhead WE (1995) Recognition of emotional distress in physically healthy primary care patients who perceive poor physical health. *Gen Hosp Psychiatry*, **17**, 173–180.

Ormel H and Giel R (1990) Medical effects of nonrecognition of affective disorders in primary care. In: N Sartorius, D Goldberg *et al.* (eds), *Psychological Disorders in General Medical Settings*. Bern: Hoegrefe Huber, 146–158.

Ormel J and Costa e Silva JA (1995) The impact of psychopathology on disability and health perceptions. In: BT Ustün and N Sartorius (eds), *Mental Illness in General Health Practice: An International Study*. Chichester: Wiley, 335–346.

Ormel J and Tiemens B (1995) Recognition and treatment of mental illness in primary care. Towards a better understanding of a multifaceted problem. *Gen Hosp Psychiatry*, **17**, 160–164.

Ormel J, Koeter MWJ, Brink W van den and Giel R (1989) Concurrent validity of GHQ and PSE as measure of change. *Psychol Med*, **19**, 1007–1013.

Ormel J, Brink W van den, Koeter M, Giel R, Meer K van den, Willige G van den and Wilmink FW (1990) Recognition, management and outcome of psychological disorders in primary care: a naturalistic follow-up study. *Psychol Med*, **20**, 909–923.

Ormel J, Koeter M, Brink M van den and Willige G van den (1991) Recognition, management and course of anxiety and depression in general practice. *Arch Gen Psychiatry*, **48**, 700–706.

Ormel J, Von Korff M, van der Brink W, Katon W, Brilman E and Oldehinkel T (1993a) Depression, anxiety and social disability show synchrony of change in primary care. *Am J Public Health*, **83**, 385–389.

Ormel J, Oldehinkel T, Brilman E and Brink W van der (1993b) Outcome of depression and anxiety in primary care: a three-wave three and a half-year study of psychopathology and disability. *Arch Gen Psychiatry*, **50**, 759–766.

Paykel E and Priest RG (1992) Recognition and management of depression in general practice: consensus statement. *Br Med J*, **305**, 1191–1202.

Perez-Echeverría MJ (1985) Correlaciones entre Tratornos Endocrinológicos, Niveless Hormonales en Sangre, Variables de Personalidad y Alteraciones Psicopatológicas. PhD Thesis, University of Zaragoza.

Perez-Echeverría MJ, Campos R, Garcia-Campayo JJ, Marcos G, Monton C, Lobo A and GMPPZ (AP) (1993) Multiaxial evaluation of primary care patients: The Zaragoza Study. Paper presented at the XXIX National Meeting of the Spanish Psychosomatic Medicine Society.

Platt R (1953) Opportunities for research in general practice. *Br Med J*, **i**, 577–580.

Pullen IM and Yellowlees AJ (1985) Is communication improving between general practitioners and psychiatrists? *Br Med J*, **290**, 31–33.

Radloff LS (1977) The CED-S scale: a self-report depression scale for research in the general population. *Appl Psychol Meas*, **1**, 385–401.

Rand EH, Badger LW and Coggings DR (1988) Towards a resolution of contradictions: utility of feedback from the GHQ. *Gen Hosp Psychiatry*, **10**, 189–196.

Regier DA, Goldberg ID and Traube CA (1978) The de facto U.S. Mental Health Service System: A public health perspective. *Arch Gen Psychiatry*, **35**, 685–693.

Robbins JM, Kirmayer LJ, Cathebras P, Yaffe MJ and Dworkind M (1994) Physicians characteristics and the recognition of depression and anxiety in primary care. *Med Care*, **32**, 796–812.

Robertson NC (1979) Variations in referrals patterns to the psychiatric services by general practitioners. *Psychol Med*, **9**, 355–364.

Rucker L, Frye E and Cygan R (1986) Feasibility and usefulness of depression screening in medical outpatients. *Arch Intern Med*, **146**, 729–731.

Sartorius N, Ustün BT, Costa e Silva JA, Goldberg D, Lecrubrier Y, Ormel J, Von Korff M and Wittchen HU (1993) An international study of psychological problems in primary care: Preliminary report from the WHO collaborative project on psychological problems in general health care. *Arch Gen Psychiatry*, **50**, 819–824.

Schulberg HC (1987) Ambulatory Mental Health Liaison Research: A review and a preview. *Gen Hosp Psychiatry*, **9**, 126–136.

Schulberg HC (1991) Mental disorders in the primary care settings: research priorities for the 1990s. *Gen Hosp Psychiatry*, **13**, 156–164.

Schulberg HC and Burns BJ (1988) Mental disorders in primary care: epidemiologic, diagnostic and treatment research directions. *Gen Hosp Psychiatry*, **10**, 79–87.

Schulberg HC, Saul M, McClelland M, Ganguli M, Christy W and Frank R (1985) Assessing depression in primary medical and psychiatric practices. *Arch Gen Psychiatry*, **42**, 1164–1170.

Schurman RA, Kramer PD and Mitchell JB (1985) The hidden mental health network. *Arch Gen Psychiatry*, **42**, 89–94.

Shapiro S, German PS, Skinner EA, Von Korff M, Turner RW, Klein LE, Teitelbaum ML, Kramer M, Burke JD and Burns BJ (1987) An experiment to change detection and management of mental morbidity in primary care. *Med Care*, **25**, 327–339.

Shepherd M (1995) Primary care psychiatry: Health services research is not enough. *Br J Psychiatry*, **166**, 1–3.

Shepherd M, Cooper B, Brown AC and Kalton G (1966) *Psychiatric Illness in General Practice*. Oxford: Oxford University Press.

Simon G, Von Korff M and Durham ML (1995) Predictors of outpatient mental health utilization by primary care patients in a health maintenance organization. *Am J Psychiatry*, **151**, 908–913.

Spitzer RL, Williams JBW, Kroenke K, Linzer M, De Gruy FV, Hanh SR, Brody D and Johnson JG (1994) Utility of a new procedure for diagnosing mental disorders in primary care: The PRIME-MD 1000 Study. *JAMA*, **272**, 1749–1756.

Stoudemire A, Kahn M, Brown JT, Linfors E and Houpt JL (1985) Masked depression in a combined medical psychiatric unit. *Psychosomatics*, **26**, 221–228.

Strain JJ and Grossman S (1979) *Psychological Care of the Medically Ill: A Primer in Liaison Psychiatry*. New York: Appleton-Century-Crofts.

Strain JJ, Hammer JS and Fulop G (1994) APM Task Force on psychosocial interventions in the general hospital setting. A review of cost-offset studies. *Psychosomatics*, **35**, 253–262.

Strathdee G (1987) Primary care–psychiatry interaction: a British perspective. *Gen Hosp Psychiatry*, **9**, 69–77.

Strathdee G (1992) Liaison between primary and secondary care towards early intervention. In: R Jenkins, J Newton and R Young (eds) *The Prevention of Depression and Anxiety: The Role of the Primary Care Team*. London: HMSO, 113–123.

Strathdee G and Williams P (1984) A survey of psychiatrist in primary care: the silent growth of a new service. *J R Coll Gen Pract*, **34**, 615–618.

Strathdee G and Williams P (1986) Patterns of collaboration. In: M Shepherd, G Wilkinson and P Williams (eds) *Mental Illness in Primary Care Settings*. London: Tavistock, 139–168.

Strathdee G, Fisher N and McDonald E (1992) Establishing psychiatric attachments to general practice. *Psychiatr Bull*, **16**, 284–286.

Sturm R and Wells K (1995) How can care for depression become more cost-effective? *JAMA*, **273**, 51–58.

Summergrad P, Herman JB, Weilburg JB and Jellinek M (1995) Wagons ho: forward on the managed care trail. *Gen Hosp Psychiatry*, **17**, 251–259.

Tansella M and Williams P (1989) The spectrum of psychiatric morbidity in a defined geographical area. *Psychol Med*, **19**, 765–770.

Torem M, Saravay SM and Steinberg H (1979) Psychiatric liaison: the benefit of active approach. *Psychosomatics*, **20**, 598–607.

Tyrer P (1984) Psychiatric clinics in general practice. An extension of the community. *Br J Psychiatry*, **145**, 9–14.

Ustün BT (1994) WHO Collaborative Study: an epidemiological survey of psychological problems in general health care in 15 centers worldwide. *Int J Psychiatry*, **6**, 357–363.

Ustün BT and Sartorius N (1995) *Mental Illness in General Health Practice: An International Study*. Chichester: Wiley.

Vazquez-Barquero JL, Wilkinson G, Williams P, Diez Manrique JF and Peña C (1990) Mental health and medical consultations in primary care settings. *Psychol Med*, **20**, 681–694.

Verhaak PFM (1988) Detection of psychological complaints in general practitioners. *Med Care*, **26**, 1009.

Verhaak PFM (1993) Analysis of referrals of mental health problems by general practitioners. *Br J Gen Pract*, **43**, 203–208.

Verhaak PFM and Tijhuis MAR (1992) Psychosocial problems in primary care: some results from the Dutch national study of morbidity and interventions in general practice. *Soc Sci Med*, **35**, 105–110.

Verhaak PFM and Wennink HJ (1990) What does a doctor do with psychosocial problems in primary care? *Int J Psychiatry in Medicine*, **20**, 151–162.

Von Korff M and Myers L (1987) The primary care and psychiatric services. *Gen Hosp Psychiatry*, **9**, 235–240.

Von Korff M, Shapiro S, Burke JDJ, Teitlebaum M, Skinner EA, German PS, Turner RW, Klein LE and Burns BJ (1987a) Anxiety, depression in a primary care clinic: comparison of Diagnostic Interview Schedule, General Health Questionnaire and practitioners assessments. *Arch Gen Psychiatry*, **44**, 152–156.

Von Korff M, Katon W, Lin EHB and Wagner EH (1987b) Evaluation of psychiatric consultation–liaison in primary care settings. *Gen Hosp Psychiatry*, **9**, 102–110.

Von Korff M, Katon W and Lin E (1990) Psychological distress, physical symptoms, utilization and the cost-offset effect. In: N Sartorius, D Goldberg, G de Girolamo, J Costa e Silva, Y Lecrubier and U Wittchen (eds) *Psychological Disorders in General Medical Settings*. Bern: Hoegrefe Huber, 159–169.

Wells KB, Stewart AL, Hays RD, Burnham MA, Rogers WH, Daniels M, Berry SD, Greenfield S and Ware JEJ (1989) The functioning and well-being of depressed patients. *JAMA*, **262**, 914–919.

Whitehouse CR (1987) A survey of the management of psychosocial illness in general practice in Manchester. *J R Coll Gen Pract*, **37**, 112–117.

Wilkinson G (1989) Referrals from general practitioners in psychiatrists and paramedical mental health professionals. *Br J Psychiatry*, **154**, 72–76.

Williams P (1986) Mental illness and primary care: screening. In: M Shepherd, G Wilkinson and P Williams (eds) *Mental Illness in Primary Care Settings*. London: Tavistock Publications, 63–65.

Williams P and Clare A (1981) Changing patterns of psychiatric care. *Br Med J*, **282**, 375–377.

Williams P and Wallace B (1974) General practitioner and psychiatrists—do they communicate? *Br Med J*, **1**, 505–507.

Williams P, Tarnopolsky A, Hand D and Shepherd M (1986) *Minor Psychiatric Morbidity and General Practice Consultations: The West London Survey*. Cambridge: Cambridge University Press.

Wilmink FW, Ormel J, Giel R, Krol B, Linderboom EG, Meer K van den and Soeteman JH (1989) General practitioners' characteristics and the assessment of psychiatric illness. *J Psychiatr Res*, **23**, 135–149.

Wohlfarth TD, Brink W van den, Ormel J, Koeter MWJ and Oldehinkel A (1993) The relationship between social dysfunctioning and psychopathology among primary care attenders. *Br J Psychiatry*, **163**, 37–44.

World Health Organization (1973) *Report of a Working Group: Psychiatry and Primary Medical Care*. Copenhagen: WHO.

Wright A (1994) Should general practitioners be testing for depression? *Br J Gen Pract*, **44**, 132–135.

Yellowlees A and Pullen IA (1984) Communication between psychiatrists and general practitioners. What sort of letters should psychiatrists write? *Health Bull*, **42**, 285–296.

Zaragoza's Primary Care Agency (Areas 2 and 5) (1996) *Clinical Guidelines for Depression and Anxiety in Primary Care Settings*. R Campos, C Montón and F Lorente (eds) Joint Report of Primary Care and Mental Health Workgroup.

Zigmond A and Snaith R (1983) The Hospital Anxiety and Depression Scale. *Act Psychiatr Scand*, **67**, 361–370.

Zimmerman M and Coryell W (1988) The validity of a self-report questionnaire for diagnosing major depressive disorder. *Arch Gen Psychiatry*, **45**, 738–740.

Zung WWK (1960) A self-rating depression scale. *Arch Gen Psychiatry*, **12**, 63–70.

4

Parasuicide in the general hospital setting

Patricia R. Casey

Parasuicide is a non-fatal act in which an individual deliberately causes self-injury or ingests a substance in excess of any prescribed or recognized therapeutic dosage (Kreitman, 1977). This is to distinguish the behaviour from attempted suicide in which suicide intent is high and from deliberate self-harm where physical harm occurs. Using this definition, it is apparent that parasuicide encompasses a broader spectrum of behaviours than do the other terms and makes no assumptions about motivation or severity of intent. To contend that parasuicide refers to low-intent self-harm, as some do, is erroneous since this is not the original definition. Moreover, there is no generally agreed level which distinguishes high from low intent—rather it is measured on a continuum.

PREVALENCE

The epidemiology of parasuicide is derived from attendances at accident and emergency departments. This in itself is unsatisfactory since those who are discharged from accident and emergency rather than admitted for medical reasons are not included. Neither are those who only attend the general practitioner (GP) or who choose to "sleep it off" without any medical contact. Thus a pyramid of decreasing prevalence is found from community-based studies to hospital studies analogous to the pyramid cited for depressive disorders.

Depression and Physical Illness. Edited by M.M. Robertson and C.L.E. Katona
© 1997 John Wiley & Sons Ltd

It is estimated that parasuicide is responsible for more than 100 000 admissions to hospital each year in England and Wales. On the basis of hospital admissions the parasuicide rate is about 300/100 000. However, rates derived from GPs would capture at least some of those lost in hospital-based data. This information is not available in the UK although a Belgium study using this approach obtained a prevalence lower even than the UK hospital-derived figure (Van Casteren *et al.*, 1993).

Figures from Oxford show that the decline in rates among women during the late 1970s and early 1980s has been reversed and the rate has crept up in recent years (Hawton and Fagg, 1992). Throughout this time, the rates among men were steady and the higher rate among women persists. The age-specific rates were somewhat different, with women in the 15–19 and men in the 20–34 age groups showing the highest rates. There is an inverse relationship with social class and an association with deprivation, leading to highest rates in inner cities (Daly *et al.*, 1986). The divorced have the highest rates and whose who are married the lowest rates (Platt *et al.*, 1988).

Although the seasonal variation in suicide has long been described, such variation in parasuicide has only recently been recognized. There is some evidence for a peak in late spring/early summer and a trough in late December/January (Masterson, 1991) in women only. A sociological explanation concerning the traditional role of women at Christmas and the sense of purpose accruing from that has been offered (Masterson, 1991) whilst the increased socialization which occurs in spring/summer with the attendant relationship problems may explain the peak at that time (Durkheim, 1897). An association between changing weather and extremes of temperature affecting thermoregulatory efficiency has also been postulated (Barker *et al.*, 1994).

About 20% of parasuicides repeat the episode in the subsequent year. The best predictor of repetition is previous psychiatric contact although not formal psychiatric illness. Other risk factors include sociopathy, male gender, low socioeconomic class, unemployment and divorce (Kreitman and Casey, 1988). In view of the high proportion of patients repeating parasuicide, techniques to improve prediction would be of benefit in prevention. These will be considered later. The number of people committing suicide within one year amounts to 1%.

METHODS

Overdosing still remains the most common method of parasuicide, accounting for over 90% of episodes among women and slightly less among men (Platt *et al.*, 1988). Nonopiate analgesics, minor tranquillizers and paracetamol are the drugs most often used in the UK and Ireland. Wrist cutting is next in frequency, accounting for about 10% of all deliberate self-harmers, and it is estimated that

1 in 600 adults deliberately wound themselves such as to require hospitalization (Kreitman, 1990).

RISK FACTORS

Social

The most common social risk factors are unemployment (Platt *et al.*, 1988) and social disintegration (Bille-Brahe and Wang, 1985), the latter derived from Durkheim's theory of anomie in relation to suicide and confirmed in many studies. Thus the rate of parasuicide would be highest in inner cities where the correlates of anomie (non-marital births, unemployment, divorce) are most prominent. More specific associations with social deprivation include overcrowding, marital difficulties, single parenthood, housing problems and child neglect (Daly *et al.*, 1986). Surprisingly the relationship to debt is unproven.

Psychiatric

The relationship between panic disorder and suicidal ideation or behaviour is uncertain. Weissman *et al.* (1989) suggested that panic disorder was as great a clinical risk as major depression. Others challenge this on the basis of detailed assessment of all diagnostic groups, including panic disorder patients (Beck *et al.*, 1991). Clearly further research is needed. One reason for this conflict may stem from the inclusion of those who were comorbid for other disorders whilst Beck only examined those with "pure" panic disorder. Some authors have also found a strong relationship between parasuicide and alcohol misuse (34% for men and 16% for women) (Merrill *et al.*, 1992) suggesting that treatment for alcohol abuse may be necessary in this group of patients, although others have found somewhat lower rates for alcohol abuse. Moreover, 40% of women and 50% of men used alcohol at the time of the act. The mechanisms by which alcohol abuse is associated with deliberate self-harm are several, including the simultaneous disinhibiting and depressing effects of alcohol, with the former giving a feeling of "Dutch courage", the likelihood that in some alcohol is used to relieve untreated depressive disorder, and finally the loss of social supports among alcohol abusers which at times of crisis are helpful in problem solving. A small but increasing proportion are dependent on drugs, especially male parasuicides (Platt *et al.*, 1988). The importance of other Axis 1 disorders such as depressive illness as a risk factor for deliberate self-harm is uncertain although assumed in view of the well-established risk of suicide. The frequency of parasuicide in the generality of those with Axis 1 disorders when compared to the general population is unknown. Similarly, there are few data on the relative risk of parasuicide in those with an Axis 2 disorder although it is likely to be high since this diagnosis is made in a significant proportion of patients (Ennis *et al.*, 1989; Casey, 1989). The mechanisms linking personality disorder and suicidal behaviour are unknown but studies of cognitive processes (see below) may in the future provide a clue.

Self-wounding, and its association with psychiatric disorder, is somewhat different from overdosing. It has occasionally been described in severely depressed or psychotic patients in whom the mutilation is a serious attempt at suicide. More usually the self-injury is repetitive and may be associated with other repetitive self-destructive behaviour such as problem drinking, eating disorders, violence and offending. Some believe that these activities constitute a unitary disorder termed "multi-impulsive personality disorder" (Lacey and Evans, 1986). Others have suggested a "wrist-cutter syndrome". The link between wrist cutting and sexual abuse and a diagnosis of personality disorder has been observed by others (Shapiro, 1987).

Physical illness

Although human immunodeficiency virus (HIV)-positive patients have been found in some studies to carry a somewhat higher risk of suicide, this has not been borne out by others. Perry *et al.* (1990) found that suicidal ideation did not increase at the time of testing, and in the immediate aftermath of testing there was no difference in ideation between sero-positive and sero-negative patients. This does not diminish the importance of pre- and post-test counselling, which can be used as an opportunity to identify those at risk of self-harm.

Biological

Biologically based research has largely focused on the role of serotonin in determining suicidal behaviour. A decrease in serotonin function has been demonstrated in some parasuicide patients (Marazziti *et al.*, 1989). However, research in this area is hampered by difficulties in defining suicidal behaviour, the lack of peripheral markers of central functioning and the problem of controlling for other variables such as depressive disorder.

Other neurotransmitters have also been investigated. Studies of the noradrenergic system in depressed suicidal patients have not shown any difference from non-suicidal depressed patients (Roy *et al.*, 1989), and there is no association with dexamethasone suppression although low levels of HVA (dopamine metabolite) have been found in depressed patients with a history of suicidal behaviour. Overall, the findings are inconclusive at present and do not as yet contribute to our clinical understanding or management of parasuicide. A link between suicidal behaviour and low serum cholesterol has been described, especially among men although the significance of this finding has yet to be elucidated (Lindberg *et al.*, 1992).

Psychological/psychodynamics

Some studies in this population have examined the role of locus of control and found that those in the external locus group are more likely to experience suicidal ideation than those with an internal locus (Pearce and Martin, 1993). A view which has won popular acclaim is the cry for help theory originally promulgated by Stengel and Cook (1958). This emphasized that "attempted suicide" was something other than incomplete suicide and focused on the social and communicational aspects of the behaviour. This view has found support in several quarters (Kreitman *et al.*, 1970; Sakinofsky and Roberts, 1990) as has the view that this behaviour is primarily cathartic (Sakinofsky and Roberts, 1990). Kreitman and colleagues (1970) found that parasuicide was concentrated in specific locations within a geographic area and hypothesized that the behaviour had a specific meaning within that subculture and was also receiving reinforcement from within that culture. Thus maladaptive learning is central to this behaviour.

The cognitive psychology of parasuicide is a developing field, stimulated by the increasing evidence for the effectiveness of cognitive therapy. Studies have so far focused on difficulties in problem solving (Schotte and Clum, 1987), particularly inflexible thinking leading to impairment in generating responses to stress (Patsiokas *et al.*, 1979). Other themes which have been described in the literature include "normalness" and powerlessness (Sakinofsky and Roberts, 1990). However, the most frequently cited cognition is that of hopelessness, which is believed to be the link between depressive affect and suicidal behaviour (Beck *et al.*, 1989; Dyer and Kreitman, 1984) and has been shown to predict suicide after a 10 year follow up period. Further study is undoubtedly indicated if the application of cognitive therapies to this group are to be refined and made more effective.

PRECIPITANTS

Studies of precipitants concern the immediate pre-parasuicide event which provoked the episode. There are few studies of this, epidemiologists instead focusing on risk factors as described above. In general, relationship difficulties such as marital discord, divorce and loneliness have been found to be the most commonly ascribed reasons although these are best considered as risk factors rather than precipitants.

WHO SHOULD ASSESS PARASUICIDE IN THE GENERAL HOSPITAL?

For many years all parasuicide patients were assessed by a psychiatrist although this practice changed in the 1980s. Part of the rationale for change lay in the cost-effectiveness of this approach. There has for some years been a recognition that nurses (Catalan *et al.*, 1980) and social workers (Newson-Smith and Hirsch, 1979) can assess parasuicide patients without any compromise on safety, although social workers recommended hospitalization more often than doctors. A caveat is that adequate training and supervision must be available and in recent years there has been an increase in the use of liaison psychiatry nurses for this purpose. Gardiner *et al.* (1978) found that non-psychiatrist doctors could also do this safely, although this has not been developed within general hospital, probably due to the competing demands on junior hospital doctors' time.

ASSESSMENT OF SUICIDE IDEATION/INTENT

Suicidal ideation should be assessed clinically in every person with an emotional disorder no matter how mild. Questions focus on the plans the patient has for the future, the presence or absence of hopelessness, and the frequency with which suicidal thoughts occur and their duration. Passive death wishes are relatively common in patients with psychiatric disorder and are usually described as a desire to "go to sleep forever" or to "escape the problems", but unlike active death or suicidal wishes these have not crystallized into a specific course of action to bring that about. They may be fleeting or of longer duration. As severity increases definite plans and methods are worked out culminating in an episode of parasuicide.

Following an episode of parasuicide the patient's current level of suicide intent is probably the most important measure to make since it will determine the immediate psychiatric management, e.g. whether hospitalization is necessary in order to protect the patient. Even when the act is apparently impulsive it is essential to make a thorough assessment especially of continuing suicidal intent. Indeed those with brittle moods, often associated with impulsive attempts, are particularly at risk of completed suicide, further confirming the importance of assessing suicide intent in all patients. The assessment of suicide intent and of the attempt itself has been well rehearsed in clinical practice. Direct questions are asked about the degree of planning, steps taken against being found, prior communication of intent either directly or indirectly, e.g. buying a grave plot, leaving a suicide note, the alleged purpose of the attempt and the patient's concept of the lethality of the method chosen. This latter is most important since there is little evidence for an association between the medical seriousness of the overdose and the degree of intent, except among those who have medical knowledge (Fox and Weissman, 1975) or among those using violent methods (Pierce, 1977) such as attempted hanging, drowning or jumping. Self-wounding, although violent, is often not associated with high intent except when it occurs in the context of severe depressive illness or schizophrenia.

Finally, the risk of completed suicide following an episode of parasuicide is 100 times greater than in the general population and about 1% of patients per year go on to commit suicide successfully. Short-term risk is determined by the level of suicide intent as described above. The risk is particularly high when intent is high, the chosen method is violent, and hopelessness and depressive illness are present although the latter is not always found and often acute stress reaction may be the more appropriate diagnostic label. Those possessing these characteristics should be hospitalized for assessment and treatment.

Long-term risk is more difficult to predict since suicide is a rare event and to date there is no evidence that it can be predicted in spite of numerous studies (see below). The procedure for attempting to predict suicide involves identifying the "at risk" group and delineating the features distinguishing the suicide completers from the non-completers. In general, the presence of psychiatric illness, older age, male sex, poor physical health, isolation, previous attempts, marital status, unemployment or retirement are all discriminators. However, attempts to develop a predictive scale using these characteristics have foundered because of the excessively large number of false-positives making any preventive intervention impossible (Hawton, 1987).

SCHEDULES FOR RESEARCH

Hopelessness has been shown to be an important contributor to future suicide risk and is more highly correlated with suicide intent than even depression (Dyer and Kreitman, 1984). The Hopelessness Scale of Beck *et al.* (1974) is the best-known measure of hopelessness used in research.

Suicidal phenomena can be divided into suicidal ideation, suicidal behaviour and completed suicide. Schedules to assess suicidal ideation have been developed, not to supplant the clinical method but to facilitate research in this field, and to supplement clinical assessment. A recently developed scale, the self-report Scale for Suicidal Ideation (Beck *et al.*, 1988), has been found to be as reliable as the original observer rating scale for assessing the severity of suicidal ideation and can be used in both inpatients and outpatients. It measures the intensity of suicidal thoughts, the patient's attitude to them, the extent to which the patient intends to make an attempt and possible deterrents such as courage.

The Suicidal Intent Scale (Beck *et al.*, 1974) measures the second aspect of suicidal phenomena. It is an interviewer-rated scale which assesses factual aspects of the parasuicide and the patient's thoughts and attitudes before and during the attempt. It is also useful clinically and can be incorporated into the routine assessment of parasuicide patients. There is no cut-off score above which the episode can definitively be said to be of high or low intent and its main role lies in examining relationships between intent and other measured variables.

An instrument which could be used as an ancillary when assessing the emotional balance between life and death in both ideators and parasuicides is the Reasons for Living Inventory (Linehan *et al.*, 1983). The inventory consists of 48 statements divided between six primary reasons for living which are scored according to their importance. The six areas are survival and coping beliefs, responsibility to family, child-related concerns, fear of suicide, fear of social disapproval and moral objections.

Scales to predict repetition have been derived from the known risk factors described above. One such scale is the Risk of Repetition Scale (Buglass and Horton, 1974). However, the problem of low sensitivity is pertinent and limits the use of this and other scales in clinical practice. A similar problem applies to attempts to identify parasuicide patients who will eventually complete suicide. The Tuckman and Youngman Scale (1968) scores a number of items considered to be risk factors for eventual suicide and includes such items as psychiatric disorder, age over 45, male gender and a number of established risk factors. Although valid, the level of prediction is low due to the large number of false-positives, a problem which bedevils the prediction of rare events.

DIAGNOSIS

Whilst most parasuicides meet criteria for Axis 2 disorders, Axis 1 disorders are less common. Ennis *et al.* (1989) found that whilst 80% were moderately or severely depressed when assessed using the Beck Depression Inventory, only 31% were found to have a DSM-111 diagnosis of major depression. Thus most of these patients are distressed but clinically would fall into the diagnostic categories of acute stress reaction or adjustment disorder. A different diagnostic picture is emerging in elderly parasuicides who are often widowed, living alone and suffering debilitating physical conditions (Nowers, 1993). Moreover, a diagnosis of depressive illness is made in about 60% and the proportion who complete suicide in the subsequent year is much higher than among young parasuicides. The profile which is found closely resembles that of the completed suicide population. Clinically, parasuicide in the elderly must therefore be regarded very seriously and with the appropriate service provision.

Axis 2 diagnoses are common in the parasuicide population. Up to 83% of patients have an Axis 2 diagnosis and this is found whether personality is assessed using a structured interview or using clinical assessment. Explosive (or borderline) is the most common category and overall personality disorder is more common in men than women (Casey, 1989). It is also a risk factor for repetition. Interestingly, the latter study, among others (Pierce, 1977), failed to find an association between personality status and suicide intent although other researchers have produced conflicting results, with Murthy (1969) describing an association with high suicide intent and obsessionality whilst Garvey and Spondon (1980) have demonstrated a relationship between antisocial personality disorder and low intent.

TREATMENT AND FOLLOW UP

A question which has continued to dominate research has been the usefulness or otherwise of admission for parasuicide patients. In general the consensus seems to be that there is no specific psychiatric benefit from medical admission followed by psychiatric assessment, in relation to repetition or symptoms (Waterhouse and Platt, 1990). However, for parasuicides of high lethality assessment by a psychiatrist has been shown to reduce the risk of eventual suicide (Suokas and Lonnquist, 1991). The latter may be explained by the clinical observation of an association between intent and lethality. Thus patients with the highest intent, e.g. those with depressive illness, can be identified and successfully treated after such an episode.

The role of specific treatments has received a lot of attention although until recently most has been disappointing. The goal of assessment and treatment can be delineated as follows:

1. The identification of those at risk of imminent suicide. The findings of Suokas and Lonnquist (1991) give some indication that this aim is being achieved.
2. The identification of those with treatable psychiatric disorders such as depressive illness, even where suicide is not imminent.
3. The prevention of repetition. This is one of the predominant aims of intervention since the cost of parasuicide is high and suicide risk increases with each parasuicide episode. Linehan *et al.* (1993) have developed a package of cognitive–behavioural therapy which is showing some promise in reducing repetition rate and improving social functioning although the numbers are small. The development of problem-solving skills has also received attention and there is some evidence that this also contributes significantly to reducing the repetition rate (McLeavy *et al.*, 1987; Salkovskis *et al.*, 1990). Physical treatment with flupenthixol decanoate has been shown by

Montgomery *et al.* (1983) to reduce the repetition of suicidal acts by stabilizing the mood changes in brief recurrent depression, although this finding has not been replicated.

4. The identification of those with social problems in order that they can be directed to appropriate agencies.

The self-wounding group pose a particular challenge as they tend to be repetitive. Treatment is generally long term (except when it occurs in the context of an Axis 1 diagnosis) and for this reason hospitalization is best avoided unless to a specialist unit with experienced staff. Moreover it removes responsibility from the patient and reinforces the perception of illness. Treatments are generally psychological and both cognitive and behavioural approaches have been used with some success. Analytic psychotherapy also has its proponents as have the SSRIs (selective serotonin reuptake inhibitors) suggesting a direct serotonergic effect on impulsivity. A comprehensive review of these approaches is provided by Tantam and Whittaker (1993).

ROYAL COLLEGE RECOMMENDATIONS

There is some evidence that both the non-psychiatric and psychiatric assessment of parasuicide patients is unsatisfactory. For example the attitudes of members of staff have been shown to be resentful. More worryingly, current suicide intent is often not mentioned in the case notes and in some cases, even where suicidal ideation is current, the patient is frequently discharged home (Ebbage *et al.*, 1994). The issue of whether or not routine psychiatric assessment by a psychiatrist is always necessary or desirable has also been debated on many occasions and until recently this was the practice. In response to these uncertainties and gaps in the service, the Royal College of Psychiatrists (1994) issued a consensus statement delineating the standards for facilities, training, supervision and assessment of parasuicide patients.

CONCLUSION

Parasuicide is a behaviour which affects women more than men and those from low socioeconomic groups. The importance of assessing these patients lies in identifying those at risk of suicide in the short term—the long-term prediction of suicide is difficult because of the high false-positive rate. There is some evidence for the benefit of cognitive–behaviour therapy in preventing repetition. Recent changes in the practice of parasuicide assessment have prompted the Royal College of Psychiatrists to issue guidelines.

REFERENCES

Barker A, Hawton K, Fagg J and Jennison C (1994) Seasonal and weather factors in parasuicide. *Br J Psychiatry*, **165**, 375–380.

Beck RW, Morris JB and Beck AT (1974) Cross-validation of the Suicidal Intent Scale. *Psychol Reprints*, **34**, 445–446.

Beck AT, Weissman A, Lester D and Trexler L (1974) The measurement of pessimism: The Hopelessness Scale. *J Consult Clin Psychol*, **41**, 861–865.

Beck AT, Steer RA and Ranieri WF (1988) Scale for Suicidal Ideation: psychometric properties of a self-report version. *J Clin Psychol*, **445**, 499–505.

Beck AT, Brown G and Steer RA (1989) Prediction of eventual suicide in psychiatric in-patients by clinical ratings of hopelessness. *J Consult Clin Psychol*, **57**, 309–310.

Beck AT, Steer RA, Sanderson WC and Skeie TM (1991) Panic disorder and suicidal ideation and behaviour: discrepant findings in psychiatric out-patients. *Am J Psychiatry*, **148**, 1195–1199.

Bille-Brahe U and Wang AG (1985) Attempted suicide in Denmark. 11. Social Integration. *Soc Psychiatry*, **20**, 163–170.

Buglass D and Horton J (1974) A scale for predicting subsequent suicidal behaviour. *Br J Psychiatry*, **124**, 573–578.

Casey P and Cole M (1992) Parasuicide and personality disorder. In: P Crepet, G Ferrari, S Platt and M Bellini (eds) *Suicidal Behaviour in Europe. Recent research findings*. Rome: John Libbey, 261–270.

Catalan J, Marsack P, Hawton KE, Whitwell D, Fagg J and Bancroft JHJ (1980) Comparison of doctors and nurses in the assessment of deliberate self-poisoning patients. *Psychol Med*, **10**, 483–491.

Daly M, Conway M and Kelleher MJ (1986) Social determinants of self-poisoning. *Br J Psychiatry*, **148**, 406–413.

Durkheim E (1897) *Le Suicide. Suicide: a Study in Sociology*. Translated by JA Spaulding and C Simpson. London: Routledge and Kegan Paul.

Dyer JAT and Kreitman N (1984) Hopelessness, depression and suicidal intent in parasuicide. *Br J Psychiatry*, **144**, 127–133.

Ebbage J, Farr C, Skinner DV and White PD (1994) The psychosocial assessment of patients discharged from Accident and Emergency departments after deliberate self-poisoning. *J R Soc Med*, **87**, 515–516.

Ennis J, Barnes RA, Kennedy S and Trachtenberg DD (1989) Depression in self-harm patients. *Br J Psychiatry*, **154**, 41–47.

Fox K and Weissman M (1975) Suicide attempts and drugs: Contradiction between method and intent. *Soc Psychiatry*, **10**, 31–38.

Gardner R, Hanka R, Evison B, Mountford PM, O'Brien VC and Roberts SJ (1978) Consultation–liaison scheme for self-poisoned patients in a general hospital. *Br Med J*, **2**, 1392–1394.

Garvey MJ and Spondon F (1980) Suicide attempts in antisocial personality disorder. *Compr Psychiatry*, **21**, 146–149.

Hawton K (1987) Assessment of suicide risk. *Br J Psychiatry*, **50**, 145–153.

Hawton K and Fagg J (1992) Trends in deliberate self-poisoning and self injury in Oxford 1976–90. *Br Med J*, **304**, 1409–1411.

Kreitman N (1977) *Parasuicide*. Chichester: Wiley.

Kreitman N (1990) Research issues in the epidemiological and public health aspects of parasuicide and suicide. In: D Goldberg and D Tantam (eds) *Public Health Impact of Mental Disorders*. Stuttgart: Hogrefe and Huber, 73–82.

Kreitman N and Casey P (1988) Repetition of parasuicide: an epidemiological and clinical study. *Br J Psychiatry*, **153**, 792–800.

Kreitman N, Smith P and Tan E (1970) Attempted suicide as language: an empirical study. *Br J Psychiatry*, **116**, 465–473.

Lacey JH and Evans CDH (1986) The impulsivist: a multi-impulsive personality disorder. *Br J Addict*, **81**, 641–649.

Lindberg G, Rastam L, Gullberg B and Eklund GA (1992) Low serum cholesterol concentration and short-term mortality from injuries in men and women. *Br Med J*, **305**, 277–279.

Linehan MM, Goodstein JL, Nielsen SL and Chiles JA (1983) Reasons for staying alive when you are thinking of killing yourself: The Reasons for Living Inventory. *J Consult Clin Psychol*, **51**, 276–286.

Linehan MM, Heard HL and Armstrong HE (1993) Naturalistic follow-up of behavioural treatment for chronically parasuicidal borderline patients. *Arch Gen Psychiatry*, **50**, 971–974.

Marazziti D, Deleo D and Conti L (1989) Further evidence supporting the role of the serotonin system in suicidal behaviour. A preliminary study of suicide attempters. *Acta Psychiatr Scand*, **80**, 322–324.

Masterson G (1991) Monthly and seasonal variation in parasuicide. *Br J Psychiatry*, **158**, 155–157.

McLeavy B, Daly RJ, Murray CM, O'Riordan J and Taylor M (1987) Interpersonal problem-solving deficits in self-poisoning patients. *Suicide Life Threat Behav*, **17**, 33–49.

Merrill J, Milner G, Owens J and Vale A (1992) Alcohol and attempted suicide. *Br J Addict*, **87**, 83–89.

Montgomery SA, Roy D and Montgomery DB (1983) The prevention of recurrent suicidal acts. *Br J Clin Pharmacol*, **15**, 183–185.

Murthy VN (1969) Personality and the nature of suicide attempts. *Br J Psychiatry*, **115**, 791–795.

Newson-Smith JGB and Hirsch SR (1979) A comparison of social workers and psychiatrists in evaluating parasuicide. *Br J Psychiatry*, **134**, 335–342.

Nowers M (1993) Deliberate self-harm in the elderly: a survey of one London borough. *Int J Geriatr Psychiatry*, **8**, 609–614.

Patsiokas AT, Clum GA and Luscomb RL (1979) Cognitive characteristics of suicide attempters. *J Consult Clin Psychol*, **47**, 478–484.

Pearce CM and Martin G (1993) Locus of control as an indicator of risk for suicidal behaviour among adolescents. *Acta Psychiatr Scand*, **88**, 409–414.

Perry S, Jacobsberg L and Fishman B (1990) Suicidal ideation and HIV testing. *JAMA*, **263**, 679–682.

Pierce DW (1977) Suicide intent in self-injury. *Br J Psychiatry*, **130**, 377–385.

Platt S, Hawton K, Kreitman N, Fagg J and Foster J (1988) Recent clinical and epidemiological trends in parasuicide in Edinburgh and Oxford: a tale of two cities. *Psychol Med*, **18**, 405–418.

Roy A, Pickar D, De Jong J, Karoum F and Linnoila M (1989) Suicidal behaviour in depression: relation to noradrenergic function. *Biol Psychiatry*, **25**, 341–350.

Royal College of Psychiatrists (1994) *The General Hospital Management of Adult Deliberate Self-harm. A Consensus Statement on Standards for Service Provision*. London: Royal College of Psychiatrists.

Safinofsky I and Roberts RS (1990) Why parasuicides repeat despite problem resolution. *Br J Psychiatry*, **156**, 399–405.

Salkovskis PM, Atha C and Storer D (1990). Cognitive–behavioural problem solving in the treatment of patients who repeatedly attempt suicide. A controlled trial. *Br J Psychiatry*, **157**, 871–876.

Schotte DE and Clum GA (1987) Problem solving skills in suicidal psychiatric patients. *J Consult Clin Psychol*, **55**, 49–54.

Shapiro S (1987) Self-mutilation and self-blame in incest victims. *Am J Psychother*, **41**, 46–54.

Stengel E and Cook N (1958) *Attempted Suicide*. London: Oxford University Press.

Suokas J and Lonnquist J (1991) Outcome of attempted suicide and psychiatric consultation: Risk factors and suicide mortality during a five year follow-up. *Acta Psychiatr Scand*, **84**, 545–549.

Tantam D and Whittaker J (1993) Self-wounding and personality disorder. In: P Tyrer and G Stein (eds) *Personality Disorder Reviewed*. London: Gaskell.

Tuckman J and Youngman WF (1968) A scale for assessing suicide risk of attempted suicide. *J Consult Clin Psychol*, **24**, 17–19.

Van Casteren V, Van der Veken J, Tafforeau J and Van Oyen H (1993) Suicide and attempted suicide reported by general practitioners in Belgium, 1990–1991. *Acta Psychiatr Scand*, **88**, 278–285.

Waterhouse J and Platt S (1990) General hospital admission in the management of parasuicide: a randomised controlled trial. *Br J Psychiatry*, **156**, 236–242.

Weissman MM, Klerman GL, Markowitz JS and Ouellette R (1989) Suicidal ideation and suicide attempts in panic disorder, *N Engl J Med*, **321**, 1209–1214.

5

Managing depression in the physically ill patient

Alison Jenaway and Eugene S. Paykel

DIAGNOSIS OF DEPRESSION IN THE MEDICAL PATIENT

This chapter reviews the management of patients suffering from a depressive disorder in the presence of additional physical illness. It is essential to make the correct diagnosis before embarking on treatment and, as this is not always straightforward in physically ill patients, we will address this problem first.

When considering the diagnosis of depression in the presence of physical illness, it is useful to be familiar with the concept of "major depression". This term has been developed over the last 10–15 years to describe a level of depression which is pathological and requires specific treatment. There are now several clear definitions of major depression which require certain criteria to be present to make the diagnosis. These include, most recently, the DSM-IV classification from the American Psychiatric Association (APA, 1994) and the ICD-10 classification from the World Health Organisation (WHO, 1992) which uses the term "depressive episode". These definitions generally require two weeks of pervasive low mood with a certain number of additional symptoms typically found in depressed patients (see Table 1). Although designed originally for research purposes, these criteria are also of considerable use in the clinical situation provided that they are not used too rigidly. When dealing with patients with physical illness it is often difficult to be sure whether a particular symptom is due to depression or the medical condition itself. This is particularly true of

---

Depression and Physical Illness. Edited by M.M. Robertson and C.L.E. Katona
© 1997 John Wiley & Sons Ltd

Table 1. Typical criteria for diagnosing major depression (based on DSM-III).

A two-week period during which the patient has either depressed mood or loss of enjoyment and interest in usual activities for most of the day, almost every day, as well as four additional symptoms from the list:
- Loss of interest and pleasure in usual activities
- Feelings of worthlessness or inappropriate guilt
- Recurrent thoughts of death or suicide
- Psychomotor retardation or agitation
- Decreased energy
- Change in appetite or weight (increase or decrease)
- Difficulty in concentrating
- Sleep disturbance (insomnia or hypersomnia)

the somatic symptoms such as lack of appetite, sleep disturbance and lack of energy which do not discriminate well between depressed and nondepressed medical patients (Fava, 1992). In ambulant patients with mild physical illness, it may be clear that the somatic disturbance is greater than one would expect, but this is less clear in those with severe illness. If too precise an interpretation of the definition of major depression is used, patients who would otherwise benefit from treatment may be left untreated and suffer unnecessarily. One study by Kathol, in cancer patients, found the prevalence of depression was 38% if all symptoms indicating depression were counted regardless of their aetiology, and only 30% if symptoms were not counted if they could be caused by the cancer itself (Kathol *et al.*, 1990). In general the symptoms of most use in diagnosing depression in the severely physically ill are those which relate to mood, thought content and suicidal feelings. An alternative set of diagnostic criteria has been proposed by Endicott, for use in cancer patients, in which somatic symptoms thought to be caused by the cancer are replaced by alternative psychological symptoms (see Table 2) (Endicott, 1984). This approach has not been widely used, although, in the study by Kathol mentioned above, the Endicott criteria resulted in a prevalence of depression of 36% which was similar to the 38% rate found when all symptoms were counted (Kathol *et al.*, 1990).

It is important not to assume that all patients with severe physical illness are, or should be, depressed and the fact that the depression is understandable should not be a criterion for withholding treatment once the diagnosis is made and the depression is persistent. In acute short-term crises such as bereavement or after receiving very bad news, it may be appropriate to delay treatment and review the patient in 2 or 3 weeks to see if the symptoms are improving spontaneously.

Clearly, as in physically healthy patients, other factors such as past history of depression, family history of affective disorder and previous response to

Table 2. Endicott criteria suggested as an alternative for diagnosing depression in the medically ill (modified from DSM-III).

A two-week period when the patient has depressed mood or loss of enjoyment and interest in usual activities for most of the day, almost every day, as well as four additional symptoms from the list:

- Loss of interest and pleasure in usual activities
- Feelings of worthlessness or inappropriate guilt
- Recurrent thoughts of death or suicide
- Psychomotor retardation or agitation
- Brooding, self-pity or pessimism (instead of loss of energy)
- Fearful or depressed appearance (instead of change in appetite or weight)
- Mood is nonreactive to environmental events (instead of lack of concentration)
- Social withdrawal or decreased talkativeness (instead of sleep disturbance)

---

treatment should also be taken into account when making decisions about diagnosis and management.

MANAGEMENT

There are three main ways in which depression and physical illness may be associated (Rodin and Voshart, 1986). In some patients the occurrence of depression may be merely a coincidence. In others it may be symptomatic, caused directly by the physical illness or by the drugs used to treat it. Thirdly, it may arise secondary to the pain, impairment or bad prognosis associated with the physical illness. Although, in practice, it is not always possible to disentangle these effects, it is important to make sure that everything possible has been done to treat the medical condition, reduce pain and correct any metabolic abnormality. In some cases this may be all that is needed to treat the depression. It is also important to be aware of any medication which patients are taking for their physical condition which could be aggravating the depression. Many case reports have been published reporting drugs which have apparently caused or worsened depression. However, where these are not reported by psychiatrists, it is often not clear whether it is nonspecific dysphoria of illness or drug toxicity which is being described rather than a true depressive episode. Even when depression is clearly present, these may be rare cases of unusual reactions in particularly vulnerable patients rather than a common adverse reaction. More detailed studies of the prevalence of depression in patients with the same medical condition but taking different medication would be useful as one would expect a certain proportion of any group of medical patients to be suffering from depression at a given time. In the absence of these studies it is often worth stopping a suspect drug for a trial period (long enough for plasma levels to be minimal for 2 or 3 weeks) to see if the depression improves. Drugs which have been reported to cause depression include methyldopa, reserpine, possibly beta-adrenergic blockers (Paykel *et al.*, 1982), corticosteroids, oral contraceptives (Ling *et al.*, 1981), H_2 antagonists (Billings and Stein, 1986), and non-steroidal anti-inflammatory drugs (Gyory *et al.*, 1972). This subject is discussed in more detail in Chapter 27. However, if a patient becomes depressed a few weeks after starting any new medication a possible adverse reaction should be considered. Close liaison between the psychiatrist and the medical team is essential as alternative treatments can then be discussed.

Once any direct causative factors have been excluded then all the usual methods of treating depression should be considered, with some awareness of specific problems encountered in those who are physically infirm.

PSYCHOTHERAPY

Supportive psychotherapy, allowing patients to talk about their problems and express how they feel without fear of being judged, is essential in the treatment of all psychological problems. In patients with physical illness the psychiatrist may again need to liaise with the treating physician or surgeon to ensure that the patient has taken in adequate information about his illness and the likely prognosis. Depressed patients are likely to have an unrealistically gloomy view of the future and may feel that further treatment is pointless. In the early stages of physical illness, patients and families require information and encouragement about their physical condition as well as an understanding of their psychological reaction. Later, they may need help to accept and adjust to any chronic disability or the diagnosis of a terminal illness.

The particular areas of importance for the clinician to enquire about when assessing the need for psychotherapy are the patient's reaction to the illness, its effect on his ability to fulfil his roles at work and within the family, and how it affects his view of himself or his body image. The use of more formal psychotherapy, either cognitive, interpersonal or psychodynamic, will depend on the patient's condition, his level of motivation and how psychologically minded he is. Psychotherapy is more likely to be effective in patients whose depression is brought on by the indirect effects of their illness, such as loss of self-esteem or difficulty in fulfilling important roles. Educational groups and supportive psychotherapy immediately after myocardial infarction have been shown to improve psychological and physical outcome in controlled trials (Perkins *et al.*, 1986). This has also been demonstrated in cancer patients (Worden and Weissman, 1984) although it is not clear how effective this approach would be after the onset of a major depressive illness.

Cognitive therapy has been shown to be as effective as antidepressants in milder depression (Dobson, 1989). It may be particularly useful for patients with medical illness who are likely to have severe side-effects of medication.

There are few controlled trials of cognitive therapy for depression in the medically ill. In one study, group cognitive therapy was shown to be more effective than remaining on a waiting list for depression in multiple sclerosis sufferers, although the number of patients included was small (Larcombe and Wilson, 1984). Pending further research, the specific indications for cognitive therapy in medically ill depressives remain uncertain.

ANTIDEPRESSANTS

Depression in the general hospital setting bears some resemblance to that seen in general practice. There is a range of severity and much of it is milder than the general psychiatrist normally sees, so that questions of the borderline between depression and the normal, understandable reaction to stress arise. There is good evidence from studies in psychiatric units and general practice that antidepressants are superior to placebo in the treatment of major depression, provided adequate doses are used. As a general rule, approximately 30% more people respond well to the active drug than to the placebo, and overall at least 70% recover. This appears to be true for tricyclic antidepressants (Morris and Beck, 1974), serotonin reuptake inhibitors (SSRIs) (Song *et al.*, 1993) and monoamine oxidase inhibitors (MAOIs) (Paykel, 1990). The studies in general practice have shown that antidepressants are more effective than placebo for patients whose symptoms meet the criteria for major depression and for those whose severity is just below this level but not for those with very mild depression (Paykel *et al.*, 1988). It is, therefore, probably worth treating physically ill patients with antidepressants if their symptoms approach the level of major depression even if not quite reaching it.

The specific research evidence on using antidepressants in medical patients is limited. There have been several double-blind, placebo-controlled studies of the treatment of depression in the physically ill and antidepressants do seem superior to placebo. However, it is not yet clear whether the difference is equivalent to that seen in healthy patients. In general the studies have used only small numbers of patients and have follow up periods of only a few weeks. This may be partly due to the difficulties posed by side-effects and drug interactions. In one study of antidepressant treatment prescribed by a liaison psychiatrist to medically ill patients, 32% of the courses had to be stopped because of side-effects, and in half of these cases the patient had developed delirium (Popkin *et al.*, 1985). Despite these problems, several controlled trials have been carried out, mostly using the older antidepressants. Those showing active medication to be more effective than placebo include: nortriptyline in patients suffering from Parkinson's disease (Anderson *et al.*, 1980), stroke (Lipsey *et al.*, 1984), severe tinnitus (Sullivan *et al.*, 1993) and chronic obstructive airways disease (Borson *et al.*, 1992); mianserin in cancer patients (Costa *et al.*, 1985);

trimipramine in a mixed group of medical outpatients (Rifkin *et al.*, 1985); and doxepin in elderly rehabilitation patients with various illnesses (Lakshmanan *et al.*, 1986). A trial of nomifensine and amitriptyline for depression in epileptic patients showed no benefit over placebo after 6 weeks of treatment (Robertson and Trimble, 1987). In most of these studies, outcome is measured using a rating scale, usually the Hamilton Depression Rating Scale (Hamilton, 1960), demonstrating significant reductions in the average score of the medication group. This does not necessarily mean that every patient has shown significant improvement in symptoms. In the study of antidepressants prescribed by a liaison psychiatrist (Popkin *et al.*, 1985) the response rate in medical patients was only 40% of the patients treated, which is less than that usually reported in healthy patients of around 70%. However, when the 32% who were unable to tolerate their medication were excluded, the response rate increased to 59%. Thus the apparent reduced efficacy in medical patients may be due to poor compliance and inadequate doses caused by difficulties of tolerability and drug interactions rather than intrinsic differences in response.

How to use antidepressants

The two most important issues in the use of antidepressants in clinical practice are how much to use and for how long. There are now clear guidelines on minimum doses of antidepressants which are necessary for a therapeutic effect. For older, tricyclic antidepressants these doses are the equivalent of 150 mg of amitriptyline or imipramine daily. For newer antidepressants, datasheet recommendations are usually based on the results of large controlled trials during development. Some caution is appropriate in medical patients because they may be particularly sensitive to side-effects, have pharmacokinetic changes because of their medical condition, or be taking other medication which may interact with the antidepressant. It is probably best to start with lower doses than usual (for example, using doses recommended for elderly patients) and increase at a slower rate than in healthy patients, aiming for standard doses provided that side-effects do not preclude this.

Relapse is common in most patients with depression when antidepressants are withdrawn early, and this probably also applies to physically ill patients with depression. Treatment should be continued for at least 4–6 months of complete remission and then gradually withdrawn. In patients who relapse, the medication should be restarted.

The choice of antidepressant

All antidepressants appear to be equally effective in uncomplicated depression. There is little clinical indication of who responds to one type of antidepressant better than another and it is worth trying the first drug at adequate doses for at least 2 months before considering an alternative or some additional treatment. For most patients the choice of drug will be either a tricyclic antidepressant, an SSRI or other newer antidepressant. Given equal efficacy, the particular first choice is still open to debate; the new drugs are generally more expensive but have greater specificity of receptor action, resulting in fewer side-effects. There are, however, some specific indications in particular medical conditions.

Specific conditions affecting choice of antidepressant

Cardiac disease

Tricyclic antidepressants cause slowing of intracardiac conduction. This is of particular concern in overdose but less of a problem at therapeutic levels and tricyclics cause few problems in most cardiac patients. However, the effects may be clinically significant for some patients and tricyclics should be used with caution in patients with a history of heart failure, conduction defects or arrhythmias. Serial ECGs (electrocardiograms) taken before and after starting the tricyclic should be compared for prolongation of the P–R, QRS, and Q–T intervals and the dose of tricyclic reduced if necessary. The commonest cardiovascular side-effect leading to discontinuation of tricyclics is postural hypotension. This is a particular problem in the elderly and, again, low doses and gradual increase should be the rule.

The newer SSRIs do not appear to have clinically significant effects on the ECG or on blood pressure. They are probably a safer choice as the first-line treatment in patients with cardiac problems.

MAOIs also cause postural hypotension although to a lesser degree than tricyclics. The main problem with these drugs is the possibility of a hypertensive crisis after ingestion of tyramine-containing food or sympathomimetic drugs. They should therefore be avoided in any patients who would be at risk if they became hypertensive, such as those on anticoagulants, who might be liable to cerebral haemorrhage. Moclobemide, the new reversible MAOI, is less likely to result in a hypertensive crisis and is safer in patients with cardiovascular disease.

Epilepsy

The tricyclics increase seizure frequency in those with a past history of fits, although this is probably only by a small amount. In a case note review of 400 patients it was estimated that tricyclics had caused spontaneous fits in 0.5% of those with no previous history and in 1% of those who had past history of seizure (Lowry and Dunner, 1980).

SSRIs also seem to have epileptogenic effects but probably less so than tricyclics.

MAOIs do not provoke fits and are therefore probably the safest drugs for those patients at high risk of seizures. There have been no reports so far that moclobemide causes problems in epilepsy.

Liver disease

The main factor to remember when treating patients with liver disease is that decreased metabolism may result in higher plasma levels. Tricyclics are reasonably safe, provided the dose is monitored closely. Similarly, SSRIs should be given at a reduced dose. Sertraline can cause reversible elevations in liver enzymes and should be avoided in patients with hepatic impairment (*ABPI Datasheet*, 1994–95). MAOIs can be hepatotoxic and should not be given to patients with liver disease unless it is essential, in which case very low doses should be started and liver function monitored closely (*ABPI Datasheet*, 1994–95). Moclobemide can be used in reduced doses although there have been reports of transient raised liver enzymes in patients taking it.

Renal failure

Tricyclics are generally safe in patients with renal disease. SSRIs are recommended in lower doses or alternate day dosing, especially fluoxetine which has a long half-life (*ABPI Datasheet*, 1994–95). MAOIs can generally be used in normal doses and moclobemide appears safe in renal disease.

Elderly patients with physical illness

Elderly patients are prone to develop side-effects on tricyclic antidepressants, particularly confusion and, if ambulant, falls due to postural hypotension. In patients over 70 the newer, more specific, antidepressants are probably preferable.

ADDITIONAL MEDICATION

Neuroleptics

These are used in clinical practice for patients with severe agitation or psychotic depression. In patients with physical illness, neuroleptics should be kept to low doses for short periods of time. Side-effects are likely to be worse than in healthy patients and there appears to be an increased risk of neuroleptic malignant syndrome in those with pre-existing physical problems, especially neurological disease (Rosebush and Stewart, 1989).

Lithium

The addition of lithium is the most commonly used adjunct to antidepressant therapy when antidepressants alone have failed to resolve the depression. There have been only a few controlled trials but these indicate a considerable improvement in mood for about 60% of depressed patients who are refractory to antidepressants alone (Katona, 1988). There have been no controlled trials of lithium in the medically ill. The main considerations for the use of lithium in the medical patient are renal function, since lithium is excreted unchanged by the kidney, and possible interactions with other drugs. It is essential to carry out the necessary screening procedures prior to starting lithium in a medically ill patient. These should certainly include measurement of renal function and thyroid function and an ECG. In addition, 24-hour creatinine clearance should be measured if renal function is impaired.

Lithium should be avoided in the presence of acute renal failure or severe renal impairment. In more chronic patients, whose renal function is stable and adequate, it can be introduced at low doses with close monitoring of plasma levels, if it is clearly necessary. Since there is a risk of further renal damage due to the use of lithium, renal function should be monitored more closely in these patients even after stabilization.

Drug interactions with lithium can result in unexpected changes in the plasma level of lithium and the patient's current drug regime should be scrutinized before lithium is added. In particular, thiazide diuretics and non-steroidal anti-inflammatory drugs can increase the lithium levels, while aminophylline and theophylline can decrease the lithium level (Stoudemire *et al.*, 1993).

Lithium can cause ECG changes, although these are rarely clinically significant at therapeutic levels, and lithium can be used with caution in patients with heart disease. Levels may be elevated where sodium retention is occurring and lithium should be avoided in patients who are in heart failure. It is probably safe to use lithium in patients with epilepsy but, since other mood stabilizers such as carbamazepine and sodium valproate have anticonvulsant effects, it is advisable to try these initially. Lithium is safe in liver disease as it is excreted unchanged by the kidneys. In patients with pre-existing hypothyroidism lithium can still be used provided the dose of thyroid replacement is monitored and increased if necessary.

ELECTROCONVULSIVE THERAPY

Electroconvulsive therapy (ECT) has been shown to be an effective treatment for depressive illness in controlled trials comparing real ECT with simulated treatment. It seems particularly effective in psychotic depression which responds less well to other treatments (Fink, 1992). In clinical practice it is generally used in severe depression when a rapid response is needed because of the risk of suicide or physical deterioration. ECT is also considered when depression has failed to respond to an adequate trial of antidepressant treatment or the patient is unable to tolerate such a trial. There are no absolute contraindications to the use of ECT and it should be considered in medical patients with a careful evaluation of the risks involved and the possible benefits to be gained. It is important to include the relevant physicians and the anaesthetist in the discussions. The anaesthetist may prefer the treatment to be given in the operating theatre where suitable staff and equipment are available should an emergency arise.

Both the Royal College of Psychiatrists in the UK (Freeman, 1989) and the American Psychiatric Association (APA, 1990) have issued recommendations about using ECT in those with medical illness. Relative contraindications noted by these organizations are space-occupying intracerebral lesion, recent (within 3 months) myocardial infarction, leaking aortic aneurysm, recent cerebrovascular accident, retinal detachment, pheochromocytoma and acute respiratory infection. Detailed practical information about giving ECT to high risk patients can be found elsewhere (Bidder, 1981; Knos and Sung, 1993).

There have been no controlled trials of ECT in the physically ill although comparisons have been made between the response rate in patients with primary depression and in those with secondary depression. This distinction was proposed by Woodruff (Woodruff *et al.*, 1967) to compare a primary depression arising in a previously healthy individual to that arising secondary to either a non-affective psychiatric illness or a physical illness. In a study by Rich, patients with secondary depression responded as well to ECT as those with primary depression (Rich *et al.*, 1984). This study included patients with depression secondary to either physical or psychiatric illness. However, in another study, patients with depression secondary only to psychiatric illness were compared with primary depressives and they responded less well than the primary depressives to ECT (Zorumski *et al.*, 1986).

After ECT the patient will usually need some kind of maintenance medication to prevent relapse, so it is often not a permanent solution for those who are unable to tolerate antidepressants.

PROGNOSIS

There are few long-term studies of depression in the physically ill. In the short term, the prognosis of depression in the context of acute, life-threatening illness seems to be good if the medical condition itself resolves (Moffic and Paykel, 1975). In one of the controlled trials mentioned above (Rifkin *et al.*, 1985) it was noted that, in the patients on placebo, improvement in depressive symptoms occurred mainly in those whose physical symptoms improved. In those on active medication, depressive symptoms improved even in those whose physical condition remained poor. If the physical illness is chronic and causes long-term disability, the depression is likely to be more persistent if untreated. Robinson (Robinson *et al.*, 1984, 1986) followed up patients after cerebrovascular accident and found that, at 6 months, 10 of the 13 who had been depressed immediately after the stroke were still depressed. Even 2 years after the stroke, the average Hamilton scores of the depressed patients had hardly changed. In a similar follow up study of patients after myocardial infarction, 70% of those who were depressed at 6 weeks were still depressed 1 year later, having had no specific treatment for depression (Stern *et al.*, 1977).

Follow up studies which have distinguished between primary and secondary depressives have generally found that patients with secondary depression have a lower recovery rate with treatment, and a higher relapse rate (Keller *et al.*, 1983, 1984). However, these studies have usually been confined to secondary depression superimposed on another psychiatric condition rather than a physical illness. Winokur (Winokur *et al.*, 1988) found that depression secondary to a physical illness had a better prognosis than that secondary to another psychiatric illness. In his follow up study, those with physical illness had a higher mortality rate due to their physical disease, but the survivors were more likely to be improved on follow up and to have only a single episode course. Unfortunately, there was no primary depression sample in this study but this pattern is similar to that described in the ECT studies mentioned above, where depression secondary to a psychiatric disorder has a worse prognosis than that secondary to a physical illness. It is not yet clear whether depression secondary to physical illness responds as well to treatment as primary depression.

Physical illness is one of the risk factors for completed suicide, particularly in older men (Dorpat and Ripley, 1960). The combination of chronic physical illness and depression should alert the clinician to this possibility and suicidal ideation should be enquired for and taken extremely seriously if present.

Finally, it is possible that treating depression in the physically ill improves the prognosis of the medical condition itself. This is a difficult hypothesis to test as the patients who become depressed may do so because their physical condition is in some way more severe and it may be this, rather than the depression, which results in a worse outcome. Certainly, the presence of depression early on in the follow up period is a predictor of poor prognosis. In a study of stroke patients (Robinson *et al.*, 1986) the presence of depression was predictive of poorer social functioning, but not physical disability, over the subsequent 2 years. Similarly, in the patients following myocardial infarction (Stern *et al.*, 1977), the presence of depression at 6 weeks predicted poor work and social functioning at 1 year and also a greater risk of readmission with physical illness during the year. Unfortunately, the patients were not treated for their depression in either of these studies, so it is not possible to say whether recovery from depression would have improved their physical prognosis. As mentioned before, in nondepressed patients, group therapy has been shown to improve physical outcome after myocardial infarction (Perkins *et al.*, 1986). It has also been shown to improve survival rates in nondepressed patients with cancer (McDaniel *et al.*, 1995). This is probably mediated by reduction in stress and improvement in immune function. It seems likely that the successful treatment of depressive illness would have similar results and would improve both prognosis and the quality of life for patients with physical illness but there is, as yet, little research evidence to support this.

REFERENCES

ABPI Data Sheet Compendium (1994–95) Datapharm Publications Limited: London.

Anderson J, Aabro E, Gulmann N, Hjelmsted A and Pedersen H (1980) Antidepressive treatment in Parkinson's disease: a controlled trial of the effect of nortriptyline in patients with Parkinson's disease treated with L-dopa. *Acta Neurol Scand*, **62**, 210–219.

American Psychiatric Association (1990) *The Practice of ECT: Recommendations for Training, Treatment and Privileging*. Washington DC: American Psychiatric Press.

American Psychiatric Association (1994) *Diagnostic and Statistical Manual of Mental Disorders*, 4th edition. Washington DC: American Psychiatric Press.

Bidder T (1981) Electroconvulsive therapy in the medically ill patient. *Psychiatr Clin North Am*, **4(2)**, 391–405.

Billings RF and Stein MB (1986) Depression associated with Ranitidine. *Am J Psychiatry*, **143**, 915–916.

Borson S, McDonald G, Gayle T, Deffebach M and Lakshminarayan S (1992) Improvement in mood, physical symptoms and function with nortriptyline for depression in patients with chronic obstructive pulmonary disease. *Psychosomatics*, **33**, 190–201.

Costa D, Mogos I and Toma T (1985) Efficacy and safety of mianserin in the treatment of depression of women with cancer. *Acta Psychiatr Scand*, **72**, 85–92.

Dobson KS (1989) A meta-analysis of the efficacy of cognitive therapy for depression. *J Consult Clin Psychol*, **57**, 414–419.

Dorpat T and Ripley H (1960) A study of suicide in the Seattle area. *Compr Psychiatry*, **1**, 349–359.

Endicott J (1984) Measurement of depression in outpatients with cancer. *Cancer*, **53**, 2243–2248.

Fava GA (1992) Depression in medical settings. In: ES Paykel (ed) *Handbook of Affective Disorders*, Edinburgh: Churchill Livingstone, 667–685.

Fink M (1992) Electroconvulsive therapy. In: ES Paykel (ed) *Handbook of Affective Disorders*, Edinburgh: Churchill Livingstone, 359–367.

Freeman C (1989) *The Practical Administration of Electroconvulsive Therapy (ECT)*. ECT Sub-Committee of the Research Committee, Royal College of Psychiatrists. Gaskell.

Gyory AN, Bloch HC, Burry HC and Grahame R (1972) Orudis in the management of rheumatoid arthritis and osteoarthritis of the hip: Comparison with indomethacin. *Br Med J*, **4**, 398–400.

Hamilton M (1960) A rating scale for depression. *J Neurol Neurosurg Psychiatr*, **23**, 56–61.

Kathol R, Mutgi A, Williams J, Clamon G and Noyes R (1990) Major depression diagnosed by DSM-III, DSM-IIIR, RDC and Endicott criteria in patients with cancer. *Am J Psychiatry*, **147**, 1021–1024.

Katona C (1988) Lithium augmentation in refractory depression. *Psychiatr Dev*, **2**, 153–171.

Keller MB, Lavori PW, Lewis CE and Klerman GL (1983) Predictors of relapse in major depressive disorder. *JAMA*, **250**, 3299–3304.

Keller MB, Klerman GL, Lavori PW, Coryell W, Endicott J and Taylor J (1984) Long-term outcome of episodes of major depression. *JAMA*, **252**, 788–792.

Knos G and Sung Y (1993) ECT anaesthesia strategies in the high risk medical patient. In: A Stoudemire and S Fogel (eds) *Psychiatric Care of the Medical Patient*, Oxford/New York: Oxford University Press: 225–240.

Lakshmanan M, Mion L and Frenglej J (1986) Effective low-dose tricyclic antidepressant treatment for depressed geriatric rehabilitation patients. *J Am Geriatr Soc*, **34**, 421–426.

Larcombe N and Wilson P (1984) An evaluation of cognitive behaviour therapy for depression in patients with multiple sclerosis. *Br J Psychiatry*, **145**, 366–371.

Ling MHM, Perry PJ and Tsuang MT (1981) Side effects of corticosteroid therapy. *Arch Gen Psychiatry*, **38**, 471–477.

Lipsey J, Robinson R, Parlson G, Rao K and Price T (1984) Nortriptyline treatment of post-stroke depression: a double blind study. *Lancet*, **i**, 297–300.

Lowry MR and Dunner FJ (1980) Seizures during tricyclic therapy. *Am J Psychiatry*, **137**, 1461–1462.

McDaniel J, Musselman D, Porter M, Reed D and Nemeroff C (1995) Depression in patients with cancer. *Arch Gen Psychiatry*, **52**, 89–99.

Moffic H and Paykel E (1975) Depression in medical inpatients. *Br J Psychiatry*, **126**, 346–353.

Morris J and Beck A (1974) The efficacy of antidepressant drugs: a review of research (1958–1972). *Arch Gen Psychiatry*, **30**, 667–674.

Paykel ES (1990) Monoamine oxidase inhibitors: when should they be used? In: K Hawton and P Cowan (eds) *Dilemmas and Difficulties in the Management of Psychiatric Patients*, Oxford: Oxford University Press, 17–30.

Paykel ES, Fleminger R and Watson J (1982) Psychiatric side effects of antihypertensive drugs other than reserpine. *J Clin Psychopharmacol*, **2**, 14–39.

Paykel E, Hollyman J, Freeling P and Sedgwick P (1988) Predictors of therapeutic benefit from amitriptyline in mild depression: a general practice, placebo controlled trial. *J Affect Disord*, **14**, 83–95.

Perkins R, Oldenburg B and Andrews G (1986) The role of psychological intervention in the management of patients after MI. *Med J Aust*, **144**, 358–360.

Popkin M, Callies A and Mackenzie T (1985) The outcome of antidepressant use in the medically ill. *Arch Gen Psychiatry*, **42**, 1160–1165.

Rich C, Spiker D, Jewell S and Neil J (1984) DSM-III, RDC and ECT: Depressive subtypes and immediate response. *J Clin Psychiatry*, **45**, 14–18.

Rifkin A, Reardon G, Siris S, Karagji B, Kim YS, Hackstaff L and Endicott N (1985) Trimipramine in physical illness with depression. *J Clin Psychiatry*, **46**, 4–8.

Robertson M and Trimble M (1987) The treatment of depression in patients with epilepsy. *J Affect Disord*, **9**, 127–136.

Robinson R, Starr L and Price T (1984) A two year longitudinal study of mood disorders following stroke. *Br J Psychiatry*, **144**, 256–262.

Robinson R, Lipsey J, Rao K and Price T (1986) Two year longitudinal study of post stroke mood disorders: comparison of acute onset with delayed onset depression. *Am J Psychiatry*, **143**, 1238–1244.

Rodin G and Voshart K (1986) Depression in the medically ill: An overview. *Am J Psychiatry*, **143**, 696–705.

Rosebush P and Stewart T (1989) A prospective analysis of 24 episodes of neuroleptic malignant syndrome. *Am J Psychiatry*, **146**, 717–725.

Song F, Freemantle N, Sheldon T, House A, Watson P, Long A and Mason J (1993) Selective serotonin reuptake inhibitors: meta-analysis of efficacy and acceptability. *Br Med J*, **306**, 683–687.

Stern M, Pascale L and Ackerman A (1977) Life adjustment post-myocardial infarction: Determining predictive variables. *Arch Intern Med*, **137**, 1680–1685.

Stoudemire A, Fogel BS, Gulley LR and Moran MG (1993) Psychopharmacology in the medical patient. In: A Stoudemire and BS Fogel (eds) *Psychiatric Care of the Medical Patient*, New York/Oxford: Oxford University Press, 155–206.

Sullivan M, Katon W, Russo J, Dobie R and Sakai C (1993) A randomised trial of nortriptyline for severe chronic tinnitus. *Arch Intern Med*, **153(9)**, 2251–2259.

The World Health Organisation (1992) *The ICD-10 Classification of Mental and Behavioural Disorders*. Geneva: WHO.

Winokur G, Black D and Nasrallah A (1988) Depressions secondary to other psychiatric disorders and medical illnesses. *Am J Psychiatry*, **145**, 233–237.

Woodruff R, Murphy G and Herjanic M (1967) The natural history of affective disorders I. Symptoms of 72 patients at the time of index hospital admission. *J Psychiatr Res*, **5**, 255–263.

Worden JW and Weissman AD (1984) Preventive psychosocial intervention with newly diagnosed cancer patients. *Gen Hosp Psychiatry*, **6**, 243–249.

Zorumski C, Rutherford J and Burke W (1986) ECT in primary and secondary depression. *Clin Psychiatry*, **47**, 298–307.

6

Depression in doctors

Jenny Firth-Cozens

The costs of depression are high—to organizations, to individuals, and to those involved with them, such as partners or patients. In terms of organizational costs, a recent survey at the First Chicago Corporation found that depression caused longer absence from work than any other medical disorder, and relapse was greater. Depressive disorders had the largest medical plan costs of all behavioural health diagnoses (Conti *et al.*, 1994). The impairment in role function suggested by this very much resembles that found in the Medical Outcomes Study (Wells *et al.*, 1989) which reported that the only chronic condition creating similar work-related impairment was advanced coronary artery disease. The costs to the individual employee that are implied by this level of impairment are of course equally significant. However, in the case of doctors, depression can also have repercussions in terms of impaired care to patients (Firth-Cozens, 1993), in particular because of the increased irritability, and decreased concentration, decision-making ability and memory involved in the disorder.

This chapter considers the levels of depression in doctors, and the possible causes, looking both at those concerned with the work situation, those intrinsic to the individual, and interactions between them. I use my own longitudinal study of doctors to explore these possible causes and interactions.

Depression and Physical Illness. Edited by M.M. Robertson and C.L.E. Katona
© 1997 John Wiley & Sons Ltd

THE PREVALENCE OF DEPRESSION IN DOCTORS

The perception that doctors might be prone to depression is borne out in various studies. For example, Rucinski and Cybulska (1985) reviewing psychiatric illness in doctors found the most common diagnoses to be alcoholism and drug addiction (which accounted for 51–57% of doctor's admissions to psychiatric hospitals) and affective disorders (which account for 21–64% depending on the study). Out of all the points of the medical career, the first postgraduate year has been most frequently studied, especially for depression, and has consistently shown itself to be a peak time for the disorder. For example, Valko and Clayton (1975) used a psychiatric interview to find that 30% of 53 first-year postgraduates had suffered clinical depression (defined by Research Diagnostic Criteria) during that year, four with suicidal ideation. More recently Reuben (1985) used the Center for Epidemiological Studies Depression Scale (CESDS) monthly during the first 3 years after graduation. He found a large peak between 3 and 6 months into the first year with up to 38% having scores within the depressed range at that time. When classified by year of training overall, responses indicative of depression occurred in 29% of first-year (remarkably similar to Valko and Clayton's findings), 22% of second-, and 10% of third-year postgraduates.

The same measure was used in a larger study by Hsu and Marshall (1987) who looked at scores from interns, residents and fellows at a number of hospitals. Overall, they found 415 (23%) of the 1805 respondents showing some degree of depression, with 72 of these categorized as severely depressed. As in Reuben's study, the first postgraduate year had the highest proportion of depressed respondents (31%). The CESDS used finds an average of 15% depression in community samples, indicating that these junior doctors have substantially higher levels of morbidity than the general population, despite the fact that, as professionals, they might be expected to have lower levels.

My own study was begun in 1983 with a cohort of 318 fourth-year medical undergraduates who were followed up in their first postgraduate year (Firth-Cozens, 1987) and again 8 years later (Firth-Cozens, 1994). Using the Symptom Check list–90 (SCL-90) 13-item depression scale (Derogatis *et al.*, 1973) and a cut-off of one standard deviation below the item mean of a sample diagnosed as having clinical depression using the Present State Examination (namely, 1.5), 28% scored above this level in their first postgraduate year. This reduced to 18% in 1993 when most were considerably more established in their careers.

These studies and others, taking place over two decades, appear to show consistently that around 30% of doctors in their first postgraduate year show symptom levels indicative of clinical depression, but that this falls as their career develops; still remaining higher, however, than community norms. Even as consultants, Caplan (1994) reported that 19% showed above threshold symptom levels, with 5% above the higher cut-off. In the same study 27% of general practitioners (GPs) met their criteria for depression, with 11% above the higher cut-off and 13% having suicidal thoughts.

Heavy use of alcohol is highly related to depression (Brooke *et al.*, 1993), and alcoholism is the other main psychological disorder for doctors (Rucinski and Cybulska, 1985). Use of alcohol as a coping mechanism was highly related to depression in my own study, and was a key predictor for women's depression levels. In fact there is growing evidence that women doctors' alcohol problems are equalling or surpassing those of men as they progress through medical training (Flaherty and Richman, 1993). Although excessive alcohol use is often seen as the result of depression, it may equally well be its cause. Bissell and Skorina (1987) interviewed 100 alcoholic women doctors (who had been sober for at least 1 year) and found that 73 had serious suicidal ideation prior to sobriety, with 38 making at least one overt suicide attempt.

Women doctors appear to be particularly prone to depression, showing rates higher than other professional women (Welner *et al.*, 1979), and higher than male doctors; for example, Hsu and Marshall (1987) found they were 1.5 times more likely to be depressed and eight times more likely to be severely depressed, while I found women doctors in their first postgraduate year were significantly more depressed than men, with 47% of them scoring above the cut-off on the SCL-90 (Firth-Cozens, 1990).

Other evidence for depression comes from what many studies have seen as elevated suicide rates in doctors. Ross (1971) estimated that every year in the USA a number of physicians equal to that of an average-sized final year of medical school took their own lives. Rose and Rosow (1973) reviewed death certificates and concluded that doctors and health care workers together are twice as suicide prone as the general population, perhaps partly as a result of their greater expertise and likelihood of success. Male doctors in the USA are said to commit suicide at a rate 1.15 times that of the overall male population, while the rate for women is three times that expected for the general female population (Steppacher and Mausner, 1974), or four times that for white American women of the same age (Pitts *et al.*, 1961). As with other measures of depression, it seems that women doctors have particularly high suicide rates. For example, Arnetz *et al.* (1987), looking at Swedish doctors and academics, showed that women doctors had higher suicide rates than either the general population or the academics, while male doctors had higher rates than academics, but close to those of the general population. British mortality statistics show that the suicide rate for women doctors has a predicted mortality rate of 391, compared with a corresponding standardized mortality rate for male doctors of 181 (Office of Population Censuses and Surveys, 1986).

The levels of depression in doctors have only rarely been compared to those in other occupational groups. When surveys of occupational distress of one type or another are carried out, the usual assessment of symptoms is by some type of general broad-based measure such as the General Health Questionnaire

(Goldberg, 1978). Although there is a version of this which provides us with an indication of clinical depression, it is much less often used. Because of this, estimates of depression in the workplace in most occupational groups are rare, especially when compared with the medical profession where studies of psychological problems frequently use clinical interviews, often by psychiatrists, or questionnaires such as those mentioned above which provide an indication of a clinical diagnosis of depression, rather than any general estimate of stress.

In the few studies which do compare doctors with other professions, Caplan's study (1994) found only 6% of managers to be above threshold, compared to 19% of consultants and 27% of GPs, and similar results were found by Rees and Cooper (1992) looking at mental ill health in general. This study showed no significant differences between the various professional groups involved in health care, with all staff showing above average levels of distress. Nursing, for example, has one of the highest rates of suicide among professional groups, and also one of the highest for psychiatric outpatient referrals (Gillespie and Gillespie, 1986). On the other hand, a comparison between GPs and teachers (Chambers and Belcher, 1993) found that only 13% of the doctors and 23% of the teachers reported "troublesome depression" in the preceding year. The lower rate for doctors in this study is, however, more likely to be to do with the methodology of simply asking doctors and teachers if they fitted the diagnosis rather than measuring symptoms as the other studies have done. In such a situation doctors may well under-diagnose themselves.

Taken together, these studies appear to demonstrate that doctors, and perhaps health care workers in general, are particularly prone to suffering from depression. Because of this and the repercussions it might have on patients, it is important to address the possible causes of depression found in this occupational group so that interventions might be targeted more success-fully.

THE CAUSES OF DEPRESSION IN DOCTORS

Within the applied psychology literature considerable research has been directed over the past 15 years to the relative strength of dispositional and environmental causes of general distress. It has been argued that a general negative affect, which is dispositional, will affect perceptions of general well-being and job satisfaction in ways which are consistent over time (Depue and Monroe, 1986; Ormel, 1983). Longitudinal studies demonstrate this quite convincingly (for example, Costa et al., 1987), but still "negative affectivity" explains only around 25% of the variance at best, and it is clear that other, contextual causes, such as those belonging to the workplace, are similarly influential.

Job-related causes of depression

One way to study the effects of work is through longitudinal studies of career paths or through intervention studies of organizations where changes have taken place. Like Reuben's longitudinal study (1985) and my own (Firth-Cozens, 1994), Girard *et al.* (1991) also showed that the high levels of stress and depression which occur in the first postgraduate year on the whole reduce with time, suggesting the possible role of context as hours reduce. They compared internship with the end of residency periods for those in internal medicine, and found significant improvements in emotions and attitudes over that 4 year period. Mosley *et al.* (1994) used the same instrument as Reuben on an undergraduate sample and found 23% of clinical students above threshold for depression, compared to Reuben's 38% peak on graduation, perhaps suggesting that individuals are reacting to changes in the work itself. Further on in the career path, very few studies have looked at more senior doctors, but Caplan's study (1994) again showed levels of depression in senior hospital doctors (19%) to be considerably lower than those found in juniors.

There is certainly evidence that purely work-related changes can increase stress and depression symptoms. Sutherland and Cooper (1992) reported increases in both types of symptoms in GPs after the introduction of their new contract in April 1990. The fact that the GPs in Caplan's sample showed such high levels (29%) again suggests that the job itself plays a role, unless there are characteristics of doctors entering general practice which predispose them to depression. Similarly, in Reuben's study, despite the fall in symptom levels over time, those in particular specialties such as intensive care had symptom levels as high as those in the first postgraduate year.

These changes in depression levels that occur over time and between specialties must at least in part be due to varying aspects of the work environment, although it may also reflect self-selection to particular jobs and fluctuations in confidence that make the initial responsibility of graduation less daunting.

One aspect of the work environment that doctors themselves see as increasing their general distress is the long hours and lack of sleep that their job often entails. Certainly the public, educated by a constant stream of television programmes on the dreadful conditions of medical training (Butler, 1995), would agree that these factors are potentially depressogenic. However, the evidence for this is much less conclusive than common sense might suggest (Harrington, 1994). For much of this century psychologists and others have studied the relationships between work overload, lack of sleep, symptoms of depression and decreased job performance, frequently finding small but significant correlations between the factors (Firth-Cozens, 1993). The relationship between overwork and lack of sleep and depression comes from findings that sleep loss in particular leads sometimes to anger and hostility (Ford and Wentz,

1986; Uliana *et al.*, 1984), and sometimes to lowered mood, sadness or inappropriate affect (Babkoff *et al.*, 1985; Friedman *et al.*, 1971). Hurwitz *et al.* (1987), using the Middlesex Health Questionnaire to identify what they called "demoralization" in doctors, found it was predicted best by an interaction between sleep deprivation and social deprivation, both of which are caused by overload.

My own study of doctors 8 years after graduation found that hours worked in the past week were significantly related (.14) to stress (as measured by the General Health Questionnaire) but not to depression. Concurrent workload was a small but significant predictor of male doctors' depression, but had considerably less impact than dispositional variables measured 10 years earlier (Brewin and Firth-Cozens, in press). In fact, the relationships between objective measures of workload (such as hours, bed responsibility, staffing numbers and patient attendances) and depressive symptoms are always small and often absent (Heyworth *et al.*, 1993), and wide individual differences in terms of reactions to these potential stressors are always apparent (for example, Deary and Tait, 1987).

It has been suggested that the emphasis made by doctors on the negative influence of workload on their mood might be a defence against recognizing less easily discussed issues such as the proximity to death and suffering, fears of failure, and humiliating experiences within medical training. The high levels of depression for those working in intensive care found in Reuben's (1985) study suggest, for example, that difficult aspects of that particular role, such as high levels of death and difficulties with patients' relatives, have a depressogenic effect in themselves. Nevertheless, it is likely, as one young doctor in my own study remarked after describing the death of a child, that most of the distressing incidents that occur in medicine would be coped with better if the individual were not exhausted. It may be that hours of work act more strongly upon symptom levels in indirect ways; for example, by sensitizing to events in the way described, or by affecting adversely social support networks (Butterfield, 1988), already under threat from poor living conditions (Hale and Hudson, 1992).

In my study (Firth-Cozens, 1994), a number of job factors were highly related to depression scores: conflict between career and personal life (.50), role responsibility (.39), making mistakes (.35), making decisions (.35), and litigation fears (.27). However, these relationships are as likely to reflect the consequences of the symptoms of depression as they are its causes. The conflict between career and personal life is a factor which has been shown on a number of occasions to be seen as the primary cause of distress by women doctors (Cartwright, 1987; Firth-Cozens, 1990) and it may at least partly explain why they show no differences in depression levels until graduation. However, in the most recent follow up of my sample, there were no differences between men and women on this item, either in the amount of distress it causes or the frequency. It seems that this somewhat traditional perception of women's difficulties may be due more to the fact that up until now the question has been asked only of them, while in fact men feel the dilemma just as strongly, although possibly in different ways. Perhaps women's higher depression levels, appearing as they do on graduation, come more from the higher levels of humiliating and discriminatory remarks and acts that they are subject to (Allen, 1994; Richman, 1992) which let them finally appreciate that the game they have joined has a playing-field that might be less than even (Walters, 1993; Dillner, 1993).

In recent years writers have increasingly pointed to these humiliating aspects of medical education, both at undergraduate (Richman, 1992; Wolf *et al.*, 1991) and postgraduate (Allen, 1994) levels, experienced by both men and women. Again, such experiences, although inexcusable, may be worsened by their interactions with various dispositions or resonate with particular early experiences in ways which may then result in depression (Blatt and Zuroff, 1992; Johnson, 1991). In addition, patients and their relatives appear to be becoming increasingly demanding and even harrassing and abusive (Hale and Hudson, 1992).

Other potential causes of depression certainly shown to cause general distress involve the experience of litigation, real or threatened. This is a relatively new stressor for British doctors, although those in the USA have described how potentially destructive it can be in terms of emotional distress (Scheiber, 1987; Martin *et al.*, 1991). Equally unstudied in this country is the experience of being suspended pending an enquiry, whether due to clinical or managerial matters. Individuals in this situation, whether in medicine or other professions, describe it in therapy as being "in limbo", "suspended", unable to control many aspects of their lives while they wait, sometimes for years, for a decision. For those who are particularly self-critical or whose self-esteem is built most firmly upon their jobs—and many doctors, whose careers have taken up so much of their lives, are among the latter—are seen clinically for depression and many of them contemplate suicide.

For all these potential job-related causes of depression, there is always wide variation. As with stress, there will be some aspects of the work role which help to create depression in some individuals but not in others (Firth-Cozens, 1992a). The next section considers the role that various individual characteristics and experiences might play in predisposing some doctors to depression.

Individual causes

Career choice

Fine and Wolf (1987) have suggested that career choice is a function of the life plan, and associated with the search for fulfilment of early need. More specifically, Malan has written of a "helping professionals syndrome" where the choice of occupation is indicative of earlier unresolved conflicts which may predispose a person to depression, namely, that the career is chosen as a way of making good earlier failures such as the resolution of parental conflict or depression (Malan, 1978). Certainly such an unconscious dynamic is seen within individual cases in psychotherapy (Firth, 1985; Sacks *et al.*, 1980), and Allen's (1988) interview study confirms that the choice of medicine as a career is often consciously recognized as fulfilling the aspirations of others. It is confirmed too by researchers such as Paris and Frank (1983) who asked medical and law students for the numbers of illnesses and legal problems in their families when they were young. Controlling for those with a medical parent, they found that medical students were more likely to have experienced illness in the family, and law students to have seen legal problems. Lief (1971) considered that 38% of the medical students he interviewed had conflicts which resulted, at least in part, from fantasies of omnipotence and "rescue". If some doctors have chosen their careers in reparation for earlier "wrongs" (Klein, 1957)—to rescue others where they failed to rescue their parents—then it is likely that the confrontation with failure that is inevitable after graduation might provoke depressive symptoms. This may too be a stronger dynamic in women than in men; Koestner *et al.* (1991) found that adult depressive tendencies were more strongly related to types of parenting for young women than they were for young men.

In my own study those who have chosen specialties which provide the most and least closeness to patients—psychiatry on the one hand, and pathology/ research on the other—on the latest follow up are the most depressed; surgeons are the least. Others have also noticed high depression levels in psychiatrists (Margison, 1987). Whilst it might be that there are aspects of the particular work which cause this, it is also true in my study that those who have chosen psychiatry were also significantly more depressed 10 years earlier when they were students, while surgeons were even then the least depressed. It is possible that for some psychiatrists, their specialty choice was more to do with a need to understand their own emotional state than simply the type of work involved.

It seems that in some cases predispositions to depression may predate career or specialty choice, perhaps acting through individual characteristics such as high self-criticism, or through early experiences such as parental loss or particular child–parent relationships.

Early experiences

Vaillant *et al.* (1972) found that physicians were especially likely to have aspects of psychopathology, including depression, if they had experienced an unhappy childhood. Like Malan's views on helping professionals as a whole, they considered that these disturbed physicians had attempted to redress their own unmet needs by becoming the caretakers of others, perhaps at the expense of themselves. Similarly, the Precursors Study, begun in the 1940s by Thomas (Thomas and Duszynski, 1974), reported that physicians who had subsequently committed suicide, suffered mental illness, or died from tumours, as students were more likely to describe their parents as lacking closeness. Although it might be thought that retrospective accounts of parenting would be biased by present mood, Brewin *et al.* (1993), after an extensive review of the literature, concluded that such accounts are reliable.

The results of the AMA–APA Physicians Mortality Project, Stage II (APA Council on Scientific Affairs, 1987) again confirmed the importance of early experience in finding that the parents of doctors who had killed themselves had a slightly higher incidence of suicide themselves than did parents of controls; for example, 6% compared with 3% for fathers and 10% compared with 2% for mothers. This may involve a genetic predisposition or perhaps be to do with the dynamic of reparation discussed above, but it might also be to do with loss more generally. I found that all but one of the five doctors in my sample whose mothers had died before they were age 10 showed severe symptom levels of depression in their first postgraduate year, although this had not been apparent when they were students, nor 10 years later when they were more advanced in their careers. This might have been to do with the sudden confrontation with death alongside responsibility which could have resonated with their earlier loss, or it might be, as suggested earlier, that they were sensitized by the long hours. There was no effect for fathers.

Within this study, various family relationship variables measured as students—in particular, guilty, anxious relationships towards mothers—were found to predict general distress in the first postgraduate year (Firth-Cozens, 1992b). The level of depressive symptoms was best predicted by a combination of older fathers ($P<.01$), higher self-criticism ($P<.001$), and poor current diet ($P<.05$), something which is a feature of hospitals where canteens shut at night. Previous depression scores and current hours were not significant predictors. Older fathers have been linked to depression in other studies; for example, Thomas and Duszynski (1974) and Paffenbarger and Asnes (1966) both found it to be a characteristic of those of their subjects who had committed suicide. It may be that older fathers show more characteristics of coldness and distance, also found in the Precursors Study to be important, than do younger ones.

Personality

There are various theories about which particular types of individuals are most likely to succumb to depression. In terms of doctors, this is an especially important question since it may be possible to predict depression early on in training and to intervene appropriately. The two areas which I consider here are Blatt's psychoanalytic perspective and Kohut's views from self-psychology, and I use the data from my own longitudinal study to begin to explore why self-criticism is such an important risk factor for doctors.

Blatt and his colleagues (Blatt and Zuroff, 1992) have distinguished two types of individuals at risk. The first group contains those who are prone to "anaclitic" or dependent forms of depression, perhaps because of earlier loss. This is characterized by feelings of loneliness, helplessness and weakness, where others are valued for the care they can provide: perhaps not the type of depression found in helpers. The second group are prone to "introjective" or self-critical depression and are those who are achievement-orientated and strive for perfection. This type of depression, we are told, is "characterized by self-criticism and feelings of unworthiness, inferiority, failure, and guilt. These individuals engage in constant harsh self-scrutiny and evaluation and have a chronic fear of being disapproved of and criticized ... They strive for excessive achievement and perfection, are often highly competitive and work hard ..." (Blatt and Zuroff, 1992, p.528).

Starting my longitudinal study in 1983, self-criticism seemed to me a particularly hazardous characteristic for doctors to have—both because of its frequent reinforcement by critical authority figures, and because the uncertainty of medical practice provides a constant opportunity for the phrase, "Could have done better". I used Blatt's measures of self-criticism and dependency for my sample when they were fourth-year medical students and again when they were house officers. We found that those individuals who, when asked to give an account of a recent stressful event, wrote about the mistakes that they had made were significantly more self-critical than those who wrote of other things (Firth-Cozens and Morrison, 1989), perhaps because they actually caused more accidents, or because they were more likely to see themselves being to blame. They were also those who showed above-threshold levels of stress both as students and as house officers. As mentioned earlier, the main predictor of depression in that first postgraduate year was the participants' self-criticism levels 2 years earlier as students ($T = 5.10$, $P < .001$). What is more, this measure remains the main predictor of depression 10 years later when they are established in their careers ($T = 2.96$, $P < .01$). Earlier depression was also a significant predictor ($T = 2.25$, $P < .05$), but not current workload (Brewin and Firth-Cozens, in press). Splitting the genders showed that these results were much stronger for men than for women who had no significant early predictors and, we suggested, this might indicate that their depression was more the result of context than of disposition, perhaps linked to the finding that they become significantly more depressed only when they graduate (Firth-Cozens, 1990). Nevertheless, they are significantly more self-critical on each testing. Self-criticism itself is predicted by early family relationships (Brewin *et al.*, 1992): for example, those high on self-criticism were significantly more likely to report poor maternal relationships and also to report below average relationships with both parents jointly, even after controlling for the possible confounding effects of current mood.

However, it cannot be said that very low self-criticism is necessarily healthy for individuals, and it may not be a particularly pleasant characteristic either for those with whom they interact. In fact, the doctors who wrote accounts of difficulties with patients were significantly less self-critical than others, while the main predictors of having problems with senior doctors were having low self-criticism and reporting, as students, having fathers who were strict, powerful and hard to please (Firth-Cozens, 1992a, 1995). It is possible that being loathe to consider one's own responsibility in events or relationships might be a defence against the acts of early authoritarian figures, while transference issues from these still affect these people in the workplace. The ideas of the psychoanalyst Heinz Kohut may help us to understand these aspects further.

Kohut's self-psychology (Kohut, 1971; Baker and Baker, 1987) is the other theoretical area of importance in exploring the individual characteristics which might, particularly in conjunction with the work involved, predispose doctors to depression. Out of all the psychoanalytical theorists, Kohut places greater emphasis on work being an integral part of mental health. He sees the self as a system which constantly compensates for early attacks in its struggle to achieve a healthy state. Normal and pathological development come from the presence or absence of appropriate empathic responses to the infant's exhibitionistic efforts. These involve (1) that a parent mirrors the infant's attempts to be creative or achieving, a mirroring which is ultimately internalized in the healthy child and central to the adult's ambition and pleasure at work; and (2) that the child idealizes the parent and that this idealized image is merged with its growing sense of self.

If a person has insufficient or inappropriate mirroring when young—and children of professional parents (Miller, 1987), and especially doctors (Gerber, 1983), may get less than most simply because of a lack of time—they are likely to use their work to replenish this through the obvious appreciations of others, but remaining subject to self-criticism. If they are sufficiently damaged, however, they may create a grandiose defence system which projects worthlessness on others (Czander, 1993), perhaps suggested by the findings on low self-criticism reported above. Within most work situations mirroring is provided by the appreciation of superiors and colleagues; however, the competitiveness of medicine may make this less likely, and theories on the cycle of abuse may explain the humiliation rather than appreciation that many young doctors experience. GPs, if they are successful, lose any form of superior and so any chance of mirroring from that source. The remaining source of mirroring therefore becomes the patients themselves, and certainly feeling helpful to and needed by them has been found to be a major source of satisfaction for doctors (Firth and Morrison, 1986; Mawardi, 1979). However, this makes self-worth dependent upon successful treatment and grateful patients, and so, in some specialties in particular, failure will appear common, and failure at work often precipitates depression (Czander, 1993). The specialties where patients are less likely to be appreciative are psychiatry and general practice (where depression levels among doctors are high), while in pathology and research (also with high levels) there are no patients to provide this admiration.

WHAT CAN BE DONE?

It is clear that depression in doctors results from a combination of factors—some to do with the individual and some concerning the work involved. In many people it will be the interaction of job characteristics, such as inadequate sleep or difficult colleagues, combined with particular dispositions such as high self-criticism or brittle grandiosity, or early family relationships characterized by disapproval or high, narrow expectations. Any attempt to intervene must be multifactorial rather than using simple goals to reduce hours or provide senior doctors with management training.

Nevertheless, the working patterns of junior doctors clearly affect their mood states, and the development of initiatives to tackle this must be helpful—not only to reduce hours but also, in particular, to create rotas which allow longer periods of uninterrupted sleep. Other aspects of working conditions which require attention are accommodation, the provision of a mess which is congenial (Hale and Hudson, 1993) and round-the-clock canteens.

Management education for consultants is naturally important too, especially in terms of team leadership skills. If we accept that high self-criticism and a lack of mirroring may play a role in the creation of depression for a proportion of young doctors, then there is a case for consultants to think in terms of re-parenting. This does not necessarily involve a large commitment: Moss (personal communication) has data which show that the main predictor of satisfaction in senior house officers is whether or not they were able to sit down at any stage with their consultant in order to discuss their work. Kohut's theories require therapy which produces a new kind of parenting experience, and it is possible for the workplace to provide some of that as well. Of course, consultants may find it hard to be appreciative of their juniors if they have not felt appreciated themselves, but insight and education are likely to make some inroads in this respect.

The importance of high self-criticism in predisposing doctors to depression is something which can be tackled throughout training, perhaps by teaching cognitive attributional restructuring (Jaycox *et al.*, 1994) alongside discussions of mistakes, difficult patients, etc. Effective coping styles (Quill and Williamson, 1990), including the problems of using alcohol to cope, can be taught formally alongside every clinical topic, and seminars can be introduced which specifically address realistic expectations and emotional reactions (Coombs *et al.*, 1990). The difficulty that doctors have in seeking help at all (Nuffield Provincial Hospitals Trust Report, 1994) needs to be addressed throughout their career, but especially in medical training by exploring their denial of illness in terms of what it means to be a doctor and to be a patient (Menzies Lyth, 1988).

Organizationally it is clear that help needs to be accessible, in a form that is acceptable, and that doctors, like other health workers, are encouraged to seek such help when they are depressed (Donaldson, 1994). Self-medication in particular requires tighter control. Although the Nuffield Provincial Hospital Report made it clear that occupational health services were seen by doctors as irrelevant, other initiatives appear to have been more successful; for example, a confidential "house call" scheme run by the local department of psychotherapy to provide confidential counselling and support when it is needed (Mushet, 1993), and the Sick Doctors' Scheme set up in Britain to provide confidential telephone advice and further counselling if needed both for the doctors and for concerned colleagues.

CONCLUSION

It is clear that depression in doctors requires tackling on a number of fronts. First and foremost comes the need to address denial and refusal to seek help which is characteristic of doctors. This may require a more proactive stand on the part of the profession, in particular of psychiatry, to promote acceptance of depression and to make confidential help-seeking as easy as possible. Beyond this there needs to be a range of organizational changes, conventional treatments and training initiatives such as those described above. These are much more likely to be effective than trying to identify and select out any potential medical students who may be predisposed to depression. Patients require a range of clinical and interpersonal skills, and they may not all be provided by those least likely to become depressed. Survival of the fittest doctor may not always mean survival of the best.

REFERENCES

Allen I (1988) Doctors and their Careers. London: Policy Studies Institute.

Allen I (1994) *Doctors and their Careers: A New Generation*. London: Policy Studies Institute.

APA Council on Scientific Affairs (1987) Results and implications of the AMA–APA physician mortality project. Stage II. *JAMA*, **257**, 2949–2953.

Arnetz BB, Horte L and Hedberg A (1987) Suicide patterns among physicians related to other academics as well as to the general population. *Acta Psychiatr Scand*, **75**, 139–143.

Babkoff H, Genser SG, Sing HC and Thoirne DR (1985) The effects of progressive sleep loss on a lexical decision task: Response lapses and response accuracy. *Behav Res Methods, Instruments Computers*, **17**, 614–622.

Baker HS and Baker MN (1987) Heinz Kohut's self psychology: An overview. *Am J Psychiatry*, **144 (1)**, 1–9.

Bissel C and Skorina JK (1987) One hundred alcoholic women in medicine. *JAMA*, **257**, 2939–2944.

Blatt SJ and Zuroff DC (1992) Interpersonal relatedness and self-definition: Two prototypes for depression. *Clin Psychol Rev*, **12**, 527–562.

Brewin CR and Firth-Cozens J (in press) Dependency and self-criticism as predictors of depression in young doctors. *J Occupational Health Psychol.*

Brewin CR, Firth-Cozens J, Furnham A and McManus C (1992) Self criticism in adulthood and recalled childhood experience. *J Abnorm Psychol*, **101**, 56–566.

Brewin CR, Andrews B and Gotlib IH (1993) Psychopathology and early experience: A reappraisal of retrospective reports. *Psychol Bull*, **113(1)**, 82–89.

Brooke D, Edwards G and Andrews T (1993) Doctors and substance misuse: Types of doctors, types of problems. *Addiction*, **88**, 655–663.

Butler P (1995) Down the tube. *Health Serv J*, **10 Aug**, 10–11.

Butterfield PS (1988) Stress in residency: A review of the literature. *Arch Intern Med*, **148**, 1428–1435.

Caplan RP (1994) Stress, anxiety, and depression in hospital consultants, general practitioners, and senior health service managers. *Br Med J*, **309(6964)**, 1261–1263.

Cartwright LK (1987) Occupational stress in women physicians. In: RL Payne and J Firth-Cozens (eds). *Stress in Health Professionals*. Chichester: Wiley, 71–87.

Chambers R and Belcher J (1993) Comparison of the health and lifestyle of general practitioners and teachers. *Br J Gen Pract*, **43**, 378–382.

Conti DJ, Wayne N and Burton MD (1994) The economic impact of depression in the workplace. *J Occup Med*, **36(9)**, 983–988.

Coombs RH, Perell K and Ruckh JM (1990) Primary prevention of emotional impairment in medical training. *Acad Med*, **65**, 576–581.

Costa PT, McCrae RR and Zonderman AB (1987) Environmental and dispositional influences on well-being: Longitudinal follow up of an American national sample. *Br J Psychol*, **78**, 299–306.

Czander WM (1993) *The Psychodynamics of Work and Organization*. New York: Guilford Press.

Deary IJ and Tait R (1987) Effects of sleep disruption on cognitive performance and mood in medical house offices. *Br Med J*, **15**, 13–16.

Depue RA and Monroe SM (1986) Conceptualisation and measurement of human disorder in life stress research: The problem of chronic disturbance. *Psychol Bull*, **99**, 36–51.

Derogatis LR, Lipman RS and Covi MD (1973) SCI-90: An outpatient psychiatric rating scale—preliminary report. *Psychopharmacol Bull*, **9**, 13–20.

Dillner L (1993) Why are there not more women consultants? *Br Med*, **307**, 949–950.

Donaldson L (1994) Sick doctors: A responsibility to act. *Br Med J*, **309**, 557–558.

Fine M and Wolf ES (1987) Career choice: The dynamics of self expression. *Psychoanal Enq*, **7(1)**, 39–57.

Firth J (1985) Personal meanings of occupational stress: Cases from the clinic. *J Occupat Psychol*, **59**, 111–119.

Firth J and Morrison L (1986) What stresses health professionals? *Brit J Clin Psychol*, **25**, 309–310.

Firth-Cozens J (1987) Emotional distress in junior house officers. *Br Med J*, **295**, 533–536.

Firth-Cozens J (1990) Sources of stress in women junior house officers. *Br Med J*, **301**, 89–91.

Firth-Cozens J (1992a) Why me? A case study of the process of perceived occupational stress. *Hum Relat*, **45**, 131–141.

Firth-Cozens J (1992b) The role of early family experiences in the perception of organizational stress: Fusing clinical and organizational perspectives. *J Occupat Organiz Psychol*, **65**, 61–75.

Firth-Cozens J (1993) Stress, psychological problems and clinical performance. In: C Vincent, M Ennis and RJ Audley (eds). *Medical Accidents*. Oxford: Oxford University Press, 131–149.

Firth-Cozens J (1994) *Stress in Doctors: A Longitudinal Study*. Department of Health, Research and Development Initiative on Mental Health of the NHS Workforce.

Firth-Cozens J (1995) Sources of stress in junior doctors and general practitioners. *Yorkshire Med*, **7**, 10–13.

Firth-Cozens J and Morrison L (1989) Sources of stress and ways of coping in junior house officers. *Stress Med*, **5**, 121–126.

Flaherty JA and Richman JA (1993) Substance use and addiction among medical students, residents, and physicians. *Psychiatr Clin North Am*, **16(1)**, 189–197.

Ford GV and Wentz DK (1986) Internship: What is stressful? *Southern Med J*, **79**, 595–599.

Friedman RC, Bigger JT and Kornfield DS (1971) The intern and sleep loss—*N Engl J Med*, **285**, 201–203.

Gerber LA (1983) *Married to their Careers: Career and Family Dilemmas in Doctors' Lives*. New York: Tavistock.

Gillespie C and Gillespie V (1986) Reading the danger signs. *Nursing Times*, **30 July**, 24–27.

Girard DE, Hickman DH, Gordon GH and Robinson RO (1991) A prospective study of internal residents' emotions and attitudes throughout their training. *Acad Med*, **66(2)**, 111–114.

Goldberg DP (1978) *Manual of the General Health Questionnaire*. Windsor: NFER-Nelson.

Hale R and Hudson L (1992) The Tavistock study of young doctors: Report of the pilot phase. *Br J Hosp Med*, **47(6)**, 452–463.

Harrington JM (1994) Working long hours and health. *Br Med J*, **308**, 1581–1582.

Heyworth J, Whitley TW, Allison EJ Jr and Revicki DA (1993) Correlates of work-related stress among consultants and senior registrars in accident and emergency medicine. *Arch Emerg Med*, **10(4)**, 271–278.

Hsu K and Marshall V (1987) Prevalence of depression and distress in a large sample of Canadian residents, interns and fellows. *Am J Psychiatry*, **144**, 1561–1566.

Hurwitz TA, Beiser M, Nichol H, Patrick L and Kozak J (1987) Impaired interns and residents. *Can J Psychiatry*, **32**, 165–169.

Jaycox LH, Reivich KJ, Gillham J and Seligman MEP (1994) Prevention of depressive symptoms in school-children. *Behav Res Ther*, **32**, 801–816.

Johnson, WDK (1991) Predisposition to emotional distress and psychiatric illness amongst doctors: The role of unconscious and experiential factors. *Br J Med Psychol*, **64**, 317–329.

Klein M (1957) *Love, Hate and Reparation*. London: Tavistock.

Koestner R, Zuroff DC and Powers TA (1991) Family origins of adolescent self-criticism and its continuity into adulthood. *J Abnormal Psychol*. **100**, 191–197.

Kohut H (1971) *The Analysis of the Self: A Systematic Approach to the Psychoanalytic Treatment of Narcissistic Personality Disorders*. New York: International Universities Press.

Lief HI (1971) Personality characteristics of medical students. In: RH Coombs and CE Vincent (eds). *Psychosocial Aspects of Medical Training*. Springfield, IL: Thomas.

Malan DH (1978) *Individual Psychotherapy and the Science of Psycho-Dynamics*. London: Butterworths.

Margison FR (1987) Stress in psychiatrists. In: RL Payne and J Firth-Cozens (eds). *Stress in Health Professionals*. Chichester: Wiley, 107–124.

Martin CA, Wilson JF, Fiebelman ND, Gurley DN and Thomas WM (1991) Physicians' psychologic reactions to malpractice litigation. *Southern Med J*, **84(11)**, 1300–1304.

Mawardi BH (1979) Satisfactions, dissatisfactions and causes of stress in medical practice. *JAMA*, **241**, 1483–1486.

Menzies-Lyth I (1988) *Containing Anxiety in Institutions*. London: Free Association Press.

Miller A (1987) *The Drama of Being a Child*. London: Virago.

Mosley TH Jr, Perrin SG, Neral SM, Dubbert PM, Grothues CA and Pinto BM (1994) Stress coping and well-being among third year medical students. *Acad Med*, **69(9)**, 765–776.

Mushet G (1993) Breaking the silence. New deal news. London: NHS Management Executive.

Nuffield Provincial Hospitals Trust (1994) *The Provision of Medical Services to Sick Doctors: A Conspiracy of Friendliness?* London: NPHT.

Office of Population Censuses and Surveys (1986) *Occupational Mortality Decennial Supplement Great Britain, 1979–80, 1982–83*. London: HMSO.

Ormel J (1983) Neuroticism and well-being inventories: Measuring traits or states? *Psychol Med*, **13**, 165–176.

Paffenbarger RS and Asnes DP (1966) Chronic disease in former college students. III. Precursors of suicide in early and middle life. *Am J Public Health*, **56**, 1026–1030.

Paris J and Frank H (1983) Psychological determinants of a medical career. *Can J Psychiatry*, **28**, 354–357.

Pitts FN, Winokur G and Stewart MA (1961) Psychiatric syndromes, anxiety symptoms and response to stress in medical students. *Am J Psychiatry*, **118**, 333–340.

Quill TE and Williamson PR (1990) Healthy approaches to physician stress. *Arch Intern Med*, **150**, 1857–1861.

Rees D and Cooper CL (1992) Occupational stress in health services workers in the UK. *Stress Med*. **8**, 79–90.

Reuben DB (1985) Depressive symptoms in medical house officers. Effects of level of training and work rotation. *Arch Intern Med*, **145**, 286–288.

Richman JA (1992) Occupational stress, psychological vulnerability and alcohol related problems over time in future physicians. *Alcoholism: Clin Exp Res*, **16(2)**, 166–171.

Rose DH and Rosow I (1973) Physicians who kill themselves. *Arch Gen Psychiatry*, **29**, 800–805.

Ross M (1971) Suicide among physicians. *Psychiatr Med*, **2**, 189–198.

Rucinski J and Cybulska E (1985) Mentally ill doctors. *Br J Hosp Med*, **33**, 90–94.

Sacks MH, Frosch WA, Kesselman M and Parker L (1980) Psychiatric problems in third year medical students. *Am J Psychiatry*, **137**, 822–825.

Scheiber S (1987) Stress in physicians. In: RL Payne and J Firth-Cozens (eds). *Stress in Health Professionals*. Wiley: Chichester.

Steppacher RC and Mausner JS (1974) Suicide in male and female physicians. *JAMA*, **228**, 323–328.

Sutherland VJ and Cooper CL (1992) Job stress, satisfaction, and mental health among general practitioners before and after introduction of new contract. *Br Med J*, **304 (6841)**, 1545–1548.

Thomas CB and Duszynski KR (1974) Closeness to parents and the family constellation in a prospective study of five disease states: Suicide, mental illness, malignant tumour, hypertension and coronary heart disease. *Johns Hopkins Med J*, **134**, 251–270.

Uliana RL, Hubbel FA, Wyle RA and Gordon GH (1984) Mood changes during internship. *J Med Educat*, **59**, 118–123.

Vaillant G, Sobowale NC and McArthur C (1972) Some psychological vulnerabilities of physicians. *N Engl J Med*, **287**, 372–375.

Valko RJ and Clayton PJ (1975) Depression in the internship. *Dis Nerv Syst*, **36**, 26–29.

Walters BC (1993) Why don't more women choose surgery as a career? *Acad Med*, **68** **(5)**, 350–351.

Wells KB, Stewart A, Hays RD, Burnam A, Rogers W, Daniel M, Berry S, Greenfield S and Ware JE Jr (1989) The functioning and well being of depressed patients: Results from the Medical Outcomes Study. *JAMA*, **262**, 914–919.

Welner A, Marten S, Wochnick R *et al.* (1979) Psychiatric disorders among professional women. *Arch Gen Psychiatry*, **36**, 169–173.

Wolf TM, Randell HM, Von Almen K and Tynes LL (1991) Perceived mistreatment and attitude change by graduating medical students: A retrospective study. *Med Educat*, **25**, 182–190.

Part II

DEPRESSION AND PHYSICAL ILLNESS IN RELATION TO THE LIFE CYCLE

7

Depression in pregnancy and childbirth

Siobhán Barry

INTRODUCTION

From the moment that conception occurs, relentless biological changes ensue for the pregnant woman. Becoming aware of being pregnant constitutes a defining moment psychologically, especially for first-time parents. Emotional difficulties can emerge for couples at this time, which have their origins at a much earlier point in their own lives, or in couples' relationships with their own parents. Temporary or permanent changes of career and of social role can be a direct consequence of pregnancy and are sometimes a source of major difficulty. Endocrine changes early on in pregnancy could be as important as those following childbirth in precipitating depression in vulnerable individuals, but this has not been an area which has been widely researched. Surprisingly, severe psychiatric disturbance is relatively uncommon in pregnant women despite the degree of psychological and physiological upheaval.

The arrival of a baby can give rise to a degree of stress between couples, as they adjust to the changes in their lives and attempt to attend to the considerable new physical and mental demands made upon them. Although the bulk of literature on perinatal psychiatry has tended to concentrate on mothers or their offspring, the emotional impact of childbearing on fathers has become the subject of recent interest (Ballard *et al.,* 1994; Lovestone and Kumar, 1993). The fact that new fathers can also become depressed (Atkinson and Rickel,

Depression and Physical Illness. Edited by M.M. Robertson and C.L.E. Katona
© 1997 John Wiley & Sons Ltd

1984) and emotionally upset (Quadagno *et al.*, 1986) suggests that the social and psychological fact of having to care for a child could, in some cases, be as important in the genesis of depression as the biological aspects of reproduction (Romito, 1989).

Three subgroups of women with mental disturbance are recognized in the context of pregnancy and childbirth (Melhuish *et al.*, 1988).

1. Women with pre-existing psychiatric illness who become pregnant, with consequences for their mental health, or leading to alterations in existing treatment regimes.
2. Women may develop psychiatric illness *de novo* during pregnancy which may or may not persist into the puerperium.
3. Mothers whose psychiatric disorders arise after childbirth.

This chapter will principally refer to the latter two groups.

Historical perspectives

Dating back to antiquity, Hippocrates, Celsus and Galen have described women who developed extreme mental disturbance in the aftermath of childbirth (Boyd, 1942). The most comprehensive and intellectually dominant 19th century description of postpartum psychosis was provided by Louis Victor Marcé who published a treatise in 1858 in which he regarded postpartum psychiatric illness as a distinct nosological group with unique psychopathology and outcome (Dinan, 1990).

At the beginning of the 20th century, Bleuler and Kraepelin independently contended that postpartum psychosis was simply an affective disorder precipitated by childbirth and that it did not possess characteristics which differentiated it from other forms of psychosis. Their influence still overshadows present nomenclature.

Although the DSM-II (American Psychiatric Association, 1968) contained a section entitled "Psychosis with childbirth" (294.4), the subsequent edition, DSM-III (American Psychiatric Association, 1980), argued that "there is no compelling evidence that postpartum psychosis is a distinct entity". The Registrar General in the UK instructed doctors not to diagnose puerperal psychosis (Sub-Committee on Classification of Mental Disorder, 1968), as did ICD-9 (World Health Organisation, 1978).

Epidemiology

Globally, the lifetime prevalence rates for depression are twice as high for women as men (Weissman *et al.*, 1993). It has been suggested that this is likely to be environmental rather than endocrine or genetic (Jenkins and Clare, 1985).

There is also a higher incidence of depression in married women with children than in childless married women (Bebbington *et al.*, 1991), which is likewise in evidence when first admission rates for affective psychosis are examined (Gater *et al.*, 1989). The effect of parity, which doubles the relative risk of admission of females with affective psychosis, is manifest up to the age of 54, having begun at the age of 20. Consequently, it is not confined to the childbearing years but extends to the period when children are reaching or have reached adolescence. The reported excess of parous women might be due to a biological mechanism which comes into play during pregnancy or childbearing, or due to social adversity which specifically affects mothers.

It has long been recognized that women are more liable to become depressed during the postpartum period (Hamilton, 1962) or to have an increased need for psychiatric admission at this time (Kendell *et al.*, 1987). The incidence of hospital admission after childbirth is substantially above the expected rate for nonpuerperal women of the same age, although the duration of hospitalization does not differ when compared to nonpuerperal controls (Dean and Kendell, 1981).

Prospective studies have demonstrated that anxiety and depression are found in pregnancy although the prevalence and consequent importance attached to this varies from one study to another (Cox *et al.*, 1982; O'Hara *et al.*, 1990). Those suffering from anxiety or depression antenatally have been described as particularly vulnerable to developing postpartum depression by some researchers (Tod, 1964; O'Hara *et al.*, 1990), but this has not been a consistent finding (Cox *et al.*, 1982). Pregnant women suffering from anxiety have been found to focus their concerns on the impending delivery and their babies' health. Depression in pregnancy (4%) has been found to be less common and less intense than in the puerperium (13%) (Cox *et al.*, 1982). Other workers have found 16% of a married sample of primigravidae to be depressed in pregnancy (Kumar and Robson, 1979) and 50% of diagnosable postpartum depression to begin in pregnancy (Gotlib *et al.*, 1989).

AETIOLOGICAL FACTORS

Maternal psychological morbidity in pregnancy and following childbirth is likely to be affected by genetic (O'Hara *et al.*, 1991), nurturing (Gotlib *et al.*, 1991) and personality factors (Boyce *et al.*, 1991). Sociocultural elements (Stern and Kruckman, 1983) and the quality of the conjugal relationship (O'Hara, 1985) are also of importance. Social support in pregnancy has been described as having a beneficial effect on the mental health and welfare of mothers and infants (Collins *et al.*, 1993). Conversely, the absence or withdrawal of practical help has been found to increase the likelihood of mothers becoming depressed (Entwistle and Doering, 1981; Paykel *et al.*, 1980). The closer the onset of a postnatal mental disorder to delivery the greater the likelihood that biological factors are causative (General Psychiatry Section Working Party, 1992).

The health and viability of the baby will also influence the parental emotional well-being. Maternal, but not paternal, anxiety is heightened in a pregnancy subsequent to a perinatal loss (Theut *et al.,* 1988).

POSTPARTUM PSYCHIATRIC DISTURBANCE

There is widespread agreement among mental health professionals that, on empirical grounds, three different categories of postpartum psychiatric disturbance are found: maternity blues, puerperal psychosis and postnatal depression (Romito, 1989; O'Hara, 1991a). These differ in terms of frequency, severity and their temporal relationship to delivery.

Maternity blues

General features

This is a common, relatively mild, transient episode of dysphoria, emotional lability, mild memory disturbance and tearfulness which can affect from 26% (O'Hara *et al.,* 1990) to 85% (Stein *et al.,* 1981) of hospital-confined mothers in the first few days after delivery. The wide range in prevalence figures is probably due to the failure to establish universally agreed diagnostic criteria, although a valid questionnaire for detecting and measuring this has now been devised (Kennerley and Gath, 1989a). The maternity blues tend to peak within 3–5 days after delivery, at a time when women are often still confined to hospital. This condition is considered by most clinicians to be a brief and benign sequel of childbirth which does not pose serious problems in clinical practice although for unprepared mothers, it can cause a degree of personal distress. As the maternity blues could throw light on the aetiology of mood disorders, it is primarily of research interest.

Maternity blues is more common in those who suffer from premenstrual tension (Nott *et al.,* 1976) or those who have experienced prior gynaecological problems (Gard *et al.,* 1986). Mothers with the maternity blues are more likely to have high neuroticism scores (Kendell *et al.,* 1984), have had symptoms of depression in the last trimester of pregnancy and appear to be at greater risk for becoming depressed postnatally, particularly if their symptoms are intense (Harris *et al.,* 1994). It is not related to complications of labour, to the use of anaesthesia or to whether delivery has been vaginally or by caesarian section (Kendell *et al.* 1984). Neither does it distinguish breast feeding from bottle feeding mothers (Cox *et al.,* 1982). Factors which might also contribute to the maternity blues include lactation, pain and soreness, lack of sleep, and the effects of hospitalization. It has been described as less prominent in women who return home 48 hours after delivery (Kendell *et al.,* 1984), but a recent study from the Netherlands, where home confinements occur in 35% of cases (Kloosterman, 1984), found that women who give birth in hospital are no more prone to postpartum mood disturbances than women who give birth at home (Pop *et al.,* 1995). Poor social adjustment, both overall and within family relationships, has also been found (Kennerley and Gath, 1989b; O'Hara *et al.,* 1991).

Biological features

As the predictable timing of onset of the blues coincides with the major hormonal upheaval of the puerperium and other physiological changes, the possibility that declining levels of circulating oestradiol, progesterone and total tryptophan or fluctuations in prolactin levels might be causative has been extensively studied. Results have been inconclusive (George and Sandler, 1988) which could be due to differences in subject selection, sampling methods or to the possibility that there is not a single underlying biochemical cause for this condition. Work in this field continues, implicating levels of free and total oestriol (O'Hara *et al.,* 1991), and more recently, a modest association has been found between scores for maternity blues and marked changes in progesterone concentrations in the saliva from antenatal to early postnatal measures (Harris *et al.,* 1994) in those who develop the maternity blues.

Conclusions

It would appear that the characteristic maternity blues syndrome is a specific affective syndrome associated with childbirth, which may be due to a combination of physical and psychological components (Iles *et al.,* 1989; O'Hara *et al.,* 1991), although an opposite view maintains that a similar and indistinguishable dysphoric state occurs in postoperative women (Levy, 1987). It is thought likely that the maternity blues has a biological basis related to postpartum hormonal upheaval, although the precise nature of this is unclear. It is also likely that the manifestation of symptoms may be modified by neuroticism, social adjustment, life events and a personal and family history of depression (O'Hara *et al.,* 1991).

Treatment and prognosis

No treatment is required in the majority of cases and the condition resolves spontaneously within a few days. Severe maternity blues affects about one in 10 mothers and considerably increases the risk of postnatal depression at 6 weeks postpartum (Glover *et al.,* 1994).

Puerperal psychosis

General features

Puerperal psychosis is the least common but potentially most serious mental disorder arising in the context of childbirth. Although puerperal psychosis is not a distinct diagnostic entity in the ICD-10 (World Health Organisation, 1992) or the DSM-IV (American Psychiatric Association, 1994), many workers have differentiated puerperal psychotics from nonpuerperal controls on the basis of phenomenology (Dean and Kendell, 1981). The DSM-IV has, however, included the term *postpartum onset* under the mood disorders section, since a better long-term prognosis for bipolar disorders has been observed in those with their onset in the puerperium (Purdy and Frank, 1993).

Puerperal psychosis occurs following 0.1–0.2% deliveries, is unrelated to obstetric factors and typically begins within the first 4 weeks after delivery, usually after a lucid interval of relative well-being (Kendell, 1985), and often after mothers have been discharged from hospital. Prevalence rates are remarkably consistent from one study to another and have not altered a great deal in the past 150 years, despite the considerable advances in obstetric care in this time (Dinan, 1990). It has been found that affective syndromes occur in 80% of those with puerperal psychosis (Dean and Kendell, 1981), with a high proportion of manic or mixed affective states.

Clinical features

Insomnia and mild confusion frequently herald the onset of the psychotic phenomena. Symptoms tend to be extremely florid, with more patients having auditory hallucinations, lability of mood, agitation, delusions and disorientation when compared to nonpuerperal controls (Agrawal *et al.*, 1990). Impaired reality testing, thought disorder and/or severe depression, with significant risk to the mother and infant, are a central feature of this condition (Stowe and Nemeroff, 1995). Since the mental state can change quickly in puerperal psychosis, this needs to be reassessed frequently. Severely depressed mothers may have delusional beliefs concerning the baby which may lead to attempts to harm the child. The risk of infanticide is about 1 in 50 000 deliveries but this is less likely if the condition is diagnosed at an early stage (Rohde and Marneros, 1993).

In a majority of cases, the illness is unexpected and relatively sudden in onset (Kendell *et al.*, 1981) although a previous personal (Protheroe, 1969) or family history of manic depressive illness or schizophrenia increases the likelihood of developing a psychosis in the puerperium (Jansson, 1964). This condition is not believed to be socially determined (Dowlatshahi and Paykel, 1990) which is in sharp contrast with non-psychotic postnatal depression. Women suffering from puerperal psychosis are almost universally admitted to psychiatric care as it is impossible to ignore their acute distress, strange behaviour and need for help.

Puerperal psychosis is more likely to follow a first birth in single mothers and is slightly more common following a caesarian section (General Psychiatry Section Working Party, 1992). A significant relationship has been found by some workers between the birth of a female child and the development of puerperal psychosis (Kendell *et al.*, 1987; Agrawal *et al.*, 1990). In a longitudinal study investigating psychiatric illness among the children of mothers who developed puerperal psychosis, 47% were found to have received psychiatric treatment, increasing to 58% when grandchildren were included (Thuwe, 1974), which suggests genetic transmission.

Biological features

It is likely that the biological triggering mechanisms for puerperal psychosis are unique and that dynamic neuroendocrine challenge tests to study oestrogen and progesterone receptors may ultimately prove of greatest benefit. The relative rarity of puerperal psychosis and the high degree of disturbance which arises with the onset of the condition conspire to make it difficult to recruit the necessary medication-free subjects for this type of neuroendocrine investigation.

Oxytocin and its related neurophysin have also been implicated in the genesis of puerperal psychosis. The hypothalamic cells which produce these hormones have oestrogen receptors in their cell bodies. Oestrogen-sensitive neurophysin levels are high in pregnant women. Among women with a vulnerability to puerperal psychosis, those who went on to relapse had significantly elevated levels of oxytocin and oestrogen-sensitive neurophysin following delivery (Whalley, 1986). Preliminary work examining the sensitivity of hypothalamic oestrogen receptors using the release of oestrogen-sensitive neurophysin as a marker has also been reported (Bearn *et al.*, 1986).

In studies of central noradrenaline and serotonin receptors, the monoamines which have been implicated in the development of depression, receptor sensitivity is found to fluctuate according to the phase of the menstrual cycle (Matussek *et al.*, 1984; Yatham *et al.*, 1989). Oestrogen-sensitive abnormalities in hypothalamic dopaminergic systems have been demonstrated in women at high risk for developing puerperal psychosis (Wieck *et al.*, 1991). Women who subsequently had a recurrent episode of psychosis following childbirth had a significantly greater apomorphine-induced growth hormone response, indicative of hypersensitivity of dopaminergic neurones, than did control subjects or women who did not have a recurrence.

Treatment and prognosis

Treatment prescribed is the same as for nonpuerperal psychosis, and is given according to the clinical syndrome (Melhuish *et al.*, 1988). Neuroleptic and antidepressant drugs are used, as are mood stabilizing preparations such as lithium and carbamazepine. The clinical features of puerperal psychosis render breast feeding impossible. Consequently, pharmacological concerns about the safety of psychotropic preparations in nursing mothers do not arise. For mothers with predominantly depressive symptoms, ECT is usually the treatment of choice as it tends to be rapidly effective and enables the mother to resume the care of her baby quickly. The increase in ECT usage in women with puerperal psychosis appears to be the only treatment modality which distinguishes puerperal patients from controls (Katona, 1982).

For most mothers, the prognosis is good with most making good clinical recovery and returning to their family within 2–3 months (Melhuish *et al.,* 1988). There is a one in two to three chance of experiencing a further psychosis following childbirth, and 20% of women develop a nonpuerperal manic depressive illness at a future point in their life. Women at high risk for developing puerperal psychosis who are treated with prophylactic lithium have shown a decrease in the relapse rate, on this treatment (Steward *et al.,* 1991). Mothers who opted for lithium prophylaxis following a subsequent confinement could not breast feed because of the considerable dangers of lithium toxicity developing in their infants.

Postnatal depression

General features

Postnatal depression is intermediate in severity and incidence, between the maternity blues and puerperal psychosis. Traditionally, it has been described as beginning after the first 2 weeks of the puerperium, although mounting epidemiological evidence points to similar rates of psychiatric difficulty in pregnancy (Cutrona, 1983; O'Hara *et al.,* 1990). The presence of anxiety or depressive symptoms during pregnancy is increasingly considered to be one of the best predictors of postnatal depression (Gotlib *et al.,* 1989).

Notwithstanding the previously referred to difficulties of measuring instruments, diagnostic criteria and the time after delivery that assessment is carried out, mothers in the postnatal period stand a 10–15% risk of developing depression (Kendell, 1985). Using stringent DSM-IV (American Psychiatric Association, 1994) or Research Diagnostic Criteria (Spitzer *et al.,* 1978) formulations, postnatal depression rates are 8–12% during the first 9 weeks. The Edinburgh Postnatal Depression Scale (EPDS) has been devised as a self-report screening instrument to measure the presence and severity of depression in postnatal women (Cox *et al.,* 1987). This scale has also been used to screen women antenatally (Green and Murray, 1994). A three-fold increase in the development of new cases of depression has been found in women in the first 5 weeks after delivery when compared to matched nonpuerperal controls (Cox *et al.,* 1993).

A positive family history for depression has been reported as increasing the likelihood of postnatal depression (O'Hara *et al.,* 1991). Women who have experienced a previous episode of nonpregnancy-related depression have a 30% chance of developing postnatal depression (Marks *et al.*, 1992). Up to 50% of all cases go undetected (Ramsay, 1993).

The effects of breast feeding, parity and advanced maternal age on the development of postnatal depression have produced equivocal results. A failed attempt to breast feed has been described as being associated with an increased prevalence of depression (Romito, 1990). While maternal age has not been clearly associated with postnatal depression, up to 26% of teenage mothers were found to experience non-psychotic depression in the postpartum period (Troutman and Cutrona, 1990).

Clinical features

The typical clinical picture is one where tiredness, anxiety, a sense of inadequacy in her mothering role and marked irritability may predominate over depression (Pitt, 1968). As changes in sleep, energy, tiredness and libido occur as a normal consequence of childbirth, elements such as an inability to sleep *even when the opportunity to do so arises* is often a more clinically relevant defect, indicative of high anxiety levels. Anxieties may frequently centre on the baby, and mothers in this state may need constant reassurance that the baby is reaching his milestones. Occasionally, mothers develop preoccupations with their own physical health and become quite self-absorbed. On a spectrum of severity, symptoms can range from mild to severe, with the latter group experiencing classic vegetative symptoms.

About 10% of women show features of mild hypomania ("the highs"), beginning immediately after delivery and present for the first week or so. It may coincide with, but is independent of, the maternity blues, and can be detected using a self-rating scale (Glover *et al.*, 1994). An elevated score on this scale is significantly related to depression at 6 weeks and might represent a mild and common form of bipolar disorder.

Women who were partially breast feeding and not taking oral contraceptive preparations were found in one particular study which followed women for up to 18 months after delivery to have the lowest incidence of depression (Alder and Cox, 1983). This finding might relate to the fact that these women had the most normal levels of endogenous hormones and had returned to their normal menstrual cycle. On the other hand, women who were taking oral contraceptives or were fully breast feeding had an increased incidence of depression at 3–5 month follow up.

Sociocultural aspects

The work entailed in being a new parent is substantial. Normal 5-week-old babies have 4–10 feeds every 24 hours, each of which may last 5–90 minutes. Additionally, babies of this age cry for an average of 90 minutes a day (range

30–300 minutes), and in most instances, the appropriate care and attention is provided by the mother (Romito, 1990). It has also been estimated that each child requires about 4000–5000 nappy changes in total until continence is achieved (Oakley, 1976). Sometimes these tasks have to be accomplished in addition to housekeeping, possibly caring for other children and against a background of interrupted sleep.

In prospective investigations seeking to identify factors associated with the development of postnatal depression, high levels of marital dissatisfaction and child-related difficulties, e.g. feeding, sleeping, health problems and perceptions of infant temperamental problems (Gotlib *et al.*, 1991; O'Hara *et al.*, 1991), have been almost universally found. Social vulnerability in the form of a lack of social and spouse support and the occurrence of significant life events during the pregnancy also play an aetiological role (Whiffen, 1988; O'Hara *et al.*, 1991). From a practical point of view, the help that a mother receives following child-birth is likely to be the most important of all (Romito, 1989). Husbands tend to do less housework after the birth of a child than they did while their wife was pregnant (Oakley, 1980). When the effect of this was explored it was found that mothers were more likely to be depressed when no practical help was offered, especially when this coincided with some negative life event (Paykel *et al.*, 1980).

Little is known about the duration of postnatal depression as there have been few longitudinal studies. It has been variably described, ranging from a mean time of 3.3 weeks (O'Hara *et al.*, 1984) to 3 months (Cox *et al.*, 1984) and even 14 months (Wolkind *et al.*, 1990), with retrospective data suggesting that duration is related to severity (Stowe and Nemeroff, 1995). Eight per cent of mothers were found to be still depressed 4 years after childbirth (Cogill *et al.*, 1986). In a prospective study of 247 primiparae from a working-class area of London, a subgroup of women were found who suffered from depression which antedated their pregnancy, and who remained depressed during their first years of motherhood (Wolkind and Zajicek, 1981). These were joined by another group of mothers who had their first experience of depression after the birth of their child. During follow up, an overall figure of 10% of new mothers were found to be depressed throughout the first 3½ years of their child's life. These findings would suggest that mothers are depressed at different times and/or for periods of longer duration than the first 6–8 weeks postpartum, which has been the time limit of many studies in this area (Watson *et al.*, 1984). Studies of the maternal mental health of mothers with two young children (Richman, 1974), or of mothers with children under the age of 6 (Brown and Harris, 1978) found significant rates of psychiatric illness, principally depression, in excess of one in five. Depression in women with older children is more closely linked to longer-term social adversity and deprivation, whereas recent findings implicate acute biopsychosocial stresses caused by the arrival of a baby in postnatal depression.

In many nonindustrialized societies, there is a recognition that a new mother is vulnerable and a proscribed seclusion, protection and rest period for mother and baby after childbirth is the norm (Stern and Kruckman, 1983). There appears to be little evidence of postnatal depression in these cultures, which has lead to the interpretation that a mandatory rest period to recover from parturition might contribute to postpartum well-being. However, there has not been any systematic investigation of postnatal depression in non-Western cultures, and were this to be undertaken, the indigenous belief systems of the people under investigation regarding childbirth and its consequences for both mother and baby would need to be taken into account (Leff, 1990). To date, the Edinburgh postnatal depression scale (EPDS) has gained widespread acceptance in Britain, the Netherlands (Pop *et al.,* 1992), the USA (O'Hara, 1991b) and the Antipodes (Boyce, 1991). As this research is still at a preliminary stage, there is scope for ongoing work in this area.

Biological features

To date, many biochemical investigations examining hormonal relationships and postnatal depression have not yielded very useful results. This may be due to diagnostic imprecision regarding time of onset, duration and severity (Gelder, 1978). Levels of progesterone, oestrogen, and beta-endorphin undergo massive changes from the end of pregnancy to the early puerperium. Unbound cortisol, adrenocorticotrophic hormone and corticotrophin-releasing factor are all elevated in late pregnancy, the placenta being the probable source of the latter hormone. All of these hormones are potentially psychoactive, and they diminish significantly within the first 4 hours after delivery (Tuimala *et al.,* 1976). High cortisol levels in the third trimester of pregnancy are reported to be a good predictor of postnatal depression (Handley *et al.,* 1980), while elevated cortisol levels in the puerperium are associated with mood elation (Handley *et al.,* 1977). Attempts to replicate these results have not been successful (Feksi *et al.,* 1984). When salivary progesterone was measured in women 6–8 weeks after delivery, levels correlated positively in bottle feeding mothers and negatively in breast feeding mothers with a number of indices of depression (Harris *et al.,* 1989), indicating that both an excess and a scarcity of progesterone could be important. Studies on beta-endorphin suggest that those whose mood deteriorated on the second day after delivery had larger drops in hormone when compared to levels at 38 weeks gestation (Smith *et al.,* 1990). It has also been suggested that there is a possible link between thyroid dysfunction and postnatal depression (Parry, 1989). The prevalence rate for thyroid dysfunction postpartum is 6% (Walfish *et al.,* 1992), the peak occurrence of positive anti-thyroglobulin and antimicrosomal antibodies is 4–6 months after delivery. Further study is required to make meaningful connections between thyroid defects and postnatal depression.

Treatment and prognosis

There is a place for psychological and psychiatric treatment of depression in women which arises in the context of childbearing. That mothers are prone to depression is something the public and professionals alike need to be informed of and educated about. Where possible, preventative interventions need to be established, and should depression arise, it needs to be identified early, either antenatally or postnatally, using a valid instrument, such as the EPDS.

Supportive therapy, e.g. health visitor counselling, and/or joint matrimonial work, is essential, and where the severity of depressive symptoms dictates, antidepressant medication needs to be prescribed as an adjunct. As yet, the safety of the selective serotonin reuptake inhibitor drugs in nursing mother needs to be proven, and for mothers who breast feed, tricyclic antidepressants appear to have an acceptable safety profile (Buist and Janson, 1995). As no long-term outcome studies have been carried out on the duration of pharmacological treatment, it is customary to continue medication for 9–12 months after symptom remission, and finally taper the treatment over 1–2 months (Stowe and Nemeroff, 1995). The recurrence rate of depression in a subsequent confinement is one in seven.

Conclusions

Postnatal depression is a condition with multifactorial contributions to its evolution. Whether this is a discrete and distinct entity is as yet unresolved, the evidence that mothers of young children are often depressed, and for long periods of time, being very powerful. It has been argued that the solution could lie in social change, leading to changes in society's expectations of new mothers, and a more realistic sense of the experience of pregnancy, childbirth and childrearing. However, the necessary supportive indication from other cultures, that this is the case, is not yet available.

While postnatal depression *per se* is not a major psychiatric condition, the repercussions on the family, particularly on the mother–child relationship, are likely to be far-reaching.

Preventive strategies

It is ironic that women's contact with health care professionals is at its height during the time of childbirth, yet emotional well-being often plummets. Depression arising at this time is often unexpected, unrecognized and untreated. Early studies into depression associated with childbearing demonstrated a decrease in the depressive symptoms in the postpartum period with *education* and *support* (Gordon and Gordon, 1960). Nearly four decades later, this remains a solid principle of prevention.

Education needs to stress the realities of parenthood, so that failure to live up to an impossibly high standard of mothering is realistically dealt with. Professionals also need to be educated to elicit early signs of depression, so that the necessary treatment can be promptly instituted, thereby reducing the likelihood of a chronic problem arising. In the case of previous puerperal psychosis, or recurrent postnatal depression, prophylactic mood stabilizing preparations or antidepressant treatment is essential.

RESEARCH INITIATIVES

The failure in most contemporary diagnostic manuals officially to recognize mental disorders related to childbirth or to define the term *postpartum* has had a consequent detrimental effect on research in this area (Stowe and Nemeroff, 1995). The current version of the *International Classification of Diseases* (ICD-10; WHO, 1992) has included mental disorders occurring in the puerperium, but only if they cannot be otherwise classified (F53). A further factor which has hampered research has been a lack of valid rating scales for use postnatally, but developments within the past decade have set out to remedy this (Cox *et al.*, 1987; Murray and Carothers, 1990).

The rarity of puerperal psychosis and the difficulty in securing drug-free psychotic subjects for biological studies has also restricted research endeavours. From a biological point of view, studies which examine the relationship between perinatal hormonal fluctuations and the onset of maternal psychopathology are unlikely to yield useful information if single daily samples of sex hormones or gonadotrophins are the only measurements taken. The pulsatile pattern of hormone release, often with cycles of only a few hours' duration, needs to be taken into account. The use of dynamic neuroendocrine challenge tests will probably ultimately add most to our current state of knowledge of both puerperal psychosis and postnatal depression (Dinan, 1990). Prospective follow up of women in high risk categories offers the best hope of early detection and investigation.

Research into postnatal depression needs to be multicentred, using common validated rating scales, with long follow-up periods.

REFERENCES

Agrawal P, Bhatia MS and Malik SC (1990) Postpartum psychosis: a study of indoor cases in a general hospital psychiatric clinic. *Acta Psychiatr Scand,* **81**, 571–575.

Alder E and Cox JL (1983) Breast feeding and postnatal depression. *J Psychosom Res,* **27**, 139–144.

American Psychiatric Association (1968) *Diagnostic and Statistical Manual of Mental Disorders,* 2nd edn. Washington, DC: American Psychiatric Association.

American Psychiatric Association (1980) *Diagnostic and Statistical Manual of Mental Disorders*, 3rd edn. Washington, DC: American Psychiatric Association.

American Psychiatric Association (1994) *Diagnostic and Statistical Manual of Mental Disorders*, 4th edn. Washington, DC: American Psychiatric Association.

Atkinson A and Rickel A (1984) Postpartum depression in primiparous parents. *J Abnorm Psychol*, **93**, 115–119.

Ballard CG, Davis R, Cullen PC *et al.* (1994) Prevalence of postnatal psychiatric morbidity in mothers and fathers. *Br J Psychiatry*, **164**, 782–788.

Bearn J, Fairhall K and Checkley SA (1986) A new marker of oestrogen receptor sensitivity with potential application to postpartum depression. Paper presented at meeting of the Marcé Society, Nottingham, August.

Bebbington PE, Dean C, Der G *et al.* (1991) Gender, parity and the prevalence of minor affective disorder. *Br J Psychiatry*, **158**, 40–45.

Boyce P (1991) Limitations in the use of the Edinburgh Postnatal Depression Scale and the Beck Depression Inventory in Postnatal Depression. Paper presented at the conference on Prevention of Depression After Childbirth: Use and Misuse of the Edinburgh Postnatal Depression Scale, University of Keele, Staffordshire, England.

Boyce P, Hickie I and Parker G (1991) Parents, partners or personality? Risk factors for post-natal depression. *J Affect Dis*, **21(4)**, 245–255.

Boyd DA (1942) Mental disorders associated with child-bearing. *Am J Obstet Gynecol*, **43**, 148–163 and 335–349.

Brown GW and Harris T (1978) *Social Origins of Depression: A Study of Psychiatric Disorder in Women*. London: Tavistock.

Buist A and Janson H (1995) Effect of exposure to dothiepin and northiaden in breast milk on child development. *Br J Psychiatry*, **167**, 370–373.

Cogill SR, Caplan HL, Alexandra H *et al.* (1986) Impact of maternal postnatal depression on cognitive development in young children. *Br Med J*, **292**, 1165–1167.

Collins NL, Dunkel-Schetter C, Lobel M *et al.* (1993) Social support in pregnancy: Psychosocial correlates of birth outcomes and postpartum depression. *J Pers Soc Psychol*, **65(6)**, 1243–1258.

Cox JL, Connor Y and Kendell RE (1982) Prospective study of the psychiatric disorders of childbirth. *Br J Psychiatry*, **140**, 111–117.

Cox JL, Rooney A and Thomas PF (1984) How accurately do mothers recall postnatal depression? Further data from a 3-year follow-up study. *J Psychosom Obstet Gynaecol*, **3**, 185–187.

Cox JL, Holden JM and Sagovsky R (1987) Detection of postnatal depression: Development of the 10-item Edinburgh Postnatal Depression Scale. *B J Psychiatry*, **150**, 782–786.

Cox JL, Murray D and Chapman G (1993) A controlled study of the onset, duration and prevalence of postnatal depression. *Br J Psychiatry*, **163**, 27–31.

Cutrona CE (1983) Causal attributes and perinatal depression. *J Abnorm Psychol*, **92**, 161–172.

Dean C and Kendell RE (1981) The symptomatology of puerperal illness. *Br J Psychiatry*, **139**, 128–133.

Dinan TG (1990) Post partum mental illness. In: TG Dinan (ed) *Principles and Practice of Biological Psychiatry*, Volume 2, London: CNS, 239–253.

Dowlatshahi D and Paykel ES (1990) Life events and social stress in puerperal psychoses: absence of effect. *Psychol Med*, **20**, 655–662.

Entwistle D and Doering G (1981) *The First Birth*. Baltimore: Johns Hopkins University Press.

Feksi A, Harris B, Walker RF *et al.* (1984) Maternity blues and hormone levels in saliva. *J Affect Disord*, **6**, 351–355.

Gard PR, Handley SL, Parsons AD and Waldron G (1986) A multivariate investigation of postpartum mood disturbance. *Br J Psychiatry*, **148**, 567–575.

Gater RA, Dean C and Morris J (1989) The contribution of childbearing to the sex difference in first admission rates for effective psychosis. *Psychol Med*, **19**, 719–724.

Gelder M (1978) Hormones and post-partum depression. In: M Sandler (ed) *Mental Illness in Pregnancy and the Puerperium*, Oxford: Oxford University Press, 80–90.

General Psychiatry Section Working Party (1992) Report on postnatal mental illness. *Psychiatr Bull*, **16**, 519–522.

George AJ and Sandler M (1988) Endocrine and biochemical studies in puerperal mental disorders. In: R Kumar and IF Brockington (eds) *Motherhood and Mental Illness 2: Causes and Consequences*, London: Wright, 78–112.

Glover V, Liddle P, Taylor A *et al.* (1994) Mild hypomania (the highs) can be a feature of the first postpartum week. *Br J Psychiatry*, **164**, 517–521.

Gordon RE and Gordon KK (1960) Social factors in the prevention of social problems. *Obstet Gynecol*, **15**, 433–437.

Gotlib IH, Whiffen VE, Mount JH *et al.* (1989) Prevalence rates and demographic characteristics associated with depression in pregnancy and the postpartum. *J Cons Clin Psychol*, **57**, 269–274.

Gotlib IH, Whiffen VE, Wallace PM and Mount JH (1991) Prospective investigation of postpartum depression: Factors involved in onset and recovery. *J Abnorm Psychol*, **100(2)**, 122–132.

Green JM and Murray D (1994) The use of the Edinburgh Postnatal Depression Scale in research to explore the relationship between antenatal and postnatal dysphoria. In: J Cox and J Holden (eds) *Perinatal Psychiatry*, London: Gaskell, 180–198.

Hamilton JA (1962) *Post-partum Psychiatric Problems*. St. Louis: Mosby.

Handley SL, Dunn TL, Baker JM *et al.* (1977) Mood changes in puerperium and plasma tryptophan and cortisol concentrations. *Br Med J*, **ii**, 18–22.

Handley SL, Dunn TL, Waldron G and Baker JM (1980) Tryptophan, cortisol and puerperal mood. *Br J Psychiatry*, **136**, 498–508.

Harris B, Johns S, Fung H *et al.* (1989) The hormonal environment of postnatal depression. *Br J Psychiatry*, **154**, 660–667.

Harris B, Lovett L, Newcombe RG *et al.* (1994) Maternity blues and major endocrine changes: Cardiff Puerperal mood and hormone study II. *Br Med J*, **308**, 949–953.

Iles S, Gath D and Kennerly H (1989) Maternity blues. 11. A comparison between post-operative women and post-natal women. *Br J Psychiatry*, **155**, 363–366.

Jansson B (1964) Psychic insufficiencies associated with childbearing. *Acta Psych Scand*, *Suppl*, 172.

Jenkins R and Clare AW (1985) Women and mental illness. *Br Med J*, **291**, 1521–1522.

Katona CLE (1982) Puerperal mental illness: comparison with nonpuerperal controls. *Br J Psychiatry*, **141**, 447–452.

Kendell RE (1985) Emotional and physical factors in the genesis of puerperal mental disorders. *J Psychosom Res*, **29**, 3–11.

Kendell RE, McGuire RJ, Connor Y and Cox JL (1981) Mood changes in the first three weeks after childbirth. *J Affect Disord*, **3**, 317–326.

Kendell RE, Mackenzie WE, West C *et al.* (1984) Day-to-day mood changes after childbirth: Further data. *Br J Psychiatry*, **145**, 620–625.

Kendell RE, Chalmers JC and Platz C (1987) Epidemiology of puerperal psychoses. *Br J Psychiatry*, **150**, 662–673.

Kennerley H and Gath D (1989a) Maternity blues. 1. Detection and measurement by questionnaire. *Br J Psychiatry,* **155**, 356–362.

Kennerley H and Gath D (1989b) Maternity blues. 111. Associations with obstetric, psychological, and psychiatric factors. *Br J Psychiatry,* **155**, 367–373.

Kloosterman GJ (1984) The Dutch experience of domiciliary confinements. In: LG Zander and G Chamberlain (eds) *Pregnancy Care for the 1980s.* London: Royal Society of Medicine, 115–125.

Kumar R and Robson K (1979) Neurotic disturbance during pregnancy and the puerperium: Preliminary report of a prospective study of 119 primigravida. In: M Sandler (ed) *Mental Illness in Pregnancy and the Puerperium*, Oxford: Oxford University Press, 40–51.

Leff J (1990) The new "cross-cultural psychiatry": A case of the baby and the bathwater. *Br J Psychiatry,* **156**, 305–307.

Levy V (1987) The maternity blues in post-partum and post-operative women. *Br J Psychiatry,* **151**, 368–372.

Lovestone S and Kumar R (1993) Postnatal psychiatric illness: The impact on partners. *Br J Psychiatry,* **163**, 210–216.

Marks MN, Wieck A, Checkley SA and Kumar R (1992) Contributions of psychological and social factors to psychotic and non-psychotic relapse after childbirth in women with previous histories of affective disorder. *J Affect Disord,* **24**, 253–263.

Maatussek N, Ackenhail M and Herz M (1984) The dependence of the clonidine growth hormone test on alcohol drinking habits and the menstrual cycle. *Psychoneuro-endocrinology,* **9**, 173–178.

Melhuish EC, Gamble C and Kumar R (1988) Maternal mental illness and the mother–infant relationship. In: R Kumar and IF Brockington (eds) *Motherhood and Mental Illness* 2, London: Wright, 191–211.

Murray L and Carothers AD (1990) The validation of the Edinburgh postnatal depression scale on a community sample. *Br J Psychiatry,* **157**, 288–290.

Nott PN, Franklin M, Armitage C and Gelder MG (1976) Hormonal changes and mood in the puerperium. *Br J Psychiatry,* **128**, 379–383.

Oakley A (1976) *Housewife*. Middlesex: Pelican Books.

Oakley A (1980) *Becoming a Mother.* Oxford: Martin Robertson.

O'Hara MW (1985) Depression and marital adjustment during pregnancy and after delivery. *Am J Fam Ther,* **13(4)**, 49–55.

O'Hara MW (1991a) Postpartum mental disorders. In JJ Sciarra (ed) *Gynaecology and Obstetrics* (Vol 6), Philadelphia: Harper & Row, 1–17.

O'Hara MW (1991b) The use of the Edinburgh Postnatal Depression Scale with a US sample. Paper presented at the conference on Prevention of Depression After Childbirth: Use and Misuse of the Edinburgh Postnatal Depression Scale, University of Keele, Staffordshire, England.

O'Hara MW, Neunaber DJ and Zekoski EM (1984) Prospective study of postpartum depression: Prevalence, course and predictive factors. *J Abnorm Psychol,* **93(2)**, 158–171.

O'Hara MW, Zekoski EM, Phillips LH *et al.* (1990) Controlled prospective study of postpartum mood disorders: comparison of childbearing and nonchildbearing women. *J Abnorm Psychol,* **99**, 3–15.

O'Hara MW, Schlechte JA, Lewis DA and Wright EJ (1991) Prospective study of postpartum blues. *Arch Gen Psychiatry,* **48**, 801–806.

Parry BL (1989) Reproductive factors affecting the course of affective illness in women. *Psychiatr Clin. North Am,* **12**, 207–220.

Paykel ES, Emms EM, Fletcher J and Rassaby ES (1980) Life events and social support in puerperal depression. *Br J Psychiatry,* **136**, 339–346.

Pitt B (1968) "typical" depression following childbirth. *Br J Psychiatry,* **114**, 1325–1335.

Pop VJ, Komproe IH and van Son MJ (1992) Characteristics of the Edinburgh Postnatal Depression Scale in the Nederlands. *J Affect Dis,* **26**, 105–110.

Pop VJ, Wijen HA, van Montfort M *et al.* (1995) Blues and depression during early puerperium: home versus hospital deliveries. *Br J Obstet Gynaecol,* **102**, 701–706.

Protheroe C (1969) Puerperal psychoses: a long-term study, 1927–1961. *Br J Psychiatry,* **115**, 9–30.

Purdy D and Frank E (1993) Should postpartum mood disorders be given a more prominent or distinct place in the DSM-IV? *Depression,* **1**, 59–70.

Quadagno D, Dixon L, Denney N and Buck H (1986) Postpartum moods in men and women. *Am J Obstet Gynecol,* **154**, 1018–1023.

Ramsay R (1993) Postnatal depression. *Lancet,* **341**, 1358.

Richman N (1974) The effects of housing on pre-school children and their mothers. *Dev Med Child Neurol,* **16**, 53–58.

Rohde A and Marneros A (1993) Postpartum psychoses: Onset and long-term course. *Psychopathology,* **26**, 203–209.

Romito P (1989) Unhappiness after childbirth. In: I Chalmers, M Enkin and MJNC Keirse (eds) *Effective Care in Pregnancy and Childbirth,* Volume 2: *Childbirth,* Oxford: Oxford University Press, 1433–1446.

Romito P (1990) Postpartum depression and the experience of motherhood. *Acta Obstet Gynaecol Scand,* **69(suppl 154)**, 1–37.

Smith R, Cubis J, Brinsmead M *et al.* (1990) Mood changes, obstetric experience and alterations in plasma cortisol, beta-endorphin and corticotrophin-releasing hormone during pregnancy and the puerperium. *J Psychosom Res,* **34**, 53–69.

Spitzer RL, Endicott J and Robins E (1978) Research diagnostic criteria: rationale and reliability. *Arch Gen Psychiatry,* **35**, 773–782.

Stein G, Marsh A and Morton J (1981) Mental symptoms, weight changes, and electrolyte excretion in the first postpartum week. *J Psychosom Res,* **25**, 395–408.

Stern S and Kruckman L (1983) Multi-disciplinary perspectives on post-partum depression: An anthropological critique. *Soc Sci Med,* **17**, 1027–1041.

Steward DE, Klompenhower JL, Kendell RE and van Hulst AM (1991) Prophylactic lithium in puerperal psychosis—the experience of three centres. *Br J Psychiatry,* **158**, 393–397.

Stowe ZN and Nemeroff CB (1995) Women at risk for postpartum-onset major depression. *Am J Obstet Gynecol,* **173**, 639–645.

Sub-Committee on Classification of Mental Disorders (1968) *A Glossary of Mental Disorders.* General Register Office Studies on Medical and Population Subjects, No. 22. London: HMSO.

Theut SK, Pederson FA, Zaslow MJ *et al.* (1988) Pregnancy subsequent to perinatal loss: Parental anxiety and depression. *J Am Acad Child Adolesc Psychiatry,* **27(3)**, 289–292.

Thuwe I (1974) Genetic factors in puerperal psychosis. *Br J Psychiatry,* **125**, 378–385.

Tod EDM (1964) Puerperal depression: A prospective epidemiological study. *Lancet,* **ii**, 1264–1266.

Troutman B and Cutrona C (1990) Nonpsychotic postpartum depression among adolescent mothers. *J Abnorm Psychol,* **99**, 69.

Tuimala R, Kaupilla A, Ronnberg L *et al.* (1976) The effect of labour on ACTH and cortisol levels in amniotic fluid and maternal blood. *Br J Obstet Gynaecol,* **83**, 707–710.

Walfish PG, Meyerson J, Provias JP *et al.* (1992) Prevalence and characteristics of postpartum thyroid dysfunction: results of a survey from Toronto, Canada. *J Endocrinol Invest,* **15**, 265–272.

Watson JP, Elliot SA, Rugg AJ and Brough OI (1984) Psychiatric disorder in pregnancy and the first postnatal year. *Br J Psychiatry,* **144**, 453–462.

Weissman MM, Bland R, Joyce PR *et al.* (1993) Sex differences in rates of depression: cross-national perspectives. *J Affect Disord,* **29**, 77–84.

Whalley LJ (1986) Putative role of oxytocin and its neurophysin in the pathogenesis of postpartum affective psychosis. Paper presented at meeting of the Marcé Society, Nottingham August.

Whiffen VE (1988) Vulnerability to postpartum depression: a prospective multivariant study. *J Abnorm Psychol,* **97**, 467–474.

Wieck A, Kumar R, Kirst AD *et al.* (1991) Increased sensitivity of dopamine receptors and recurrence of affective psychosis after childbirth. *Br Med J,* **303**, 613–616.

Wolkind S and Zajicek E (1981) *Pregnancy: A Psychological and Social Study.* London: Academic Press.

Wolkind S, Zajicek E and Ghodsian J (1990) Continuities in maternal depression. *Int J Fam Psychiatry,* **1**, 167.

World Health Organisation (1978) *The ICD-9 Classification of Mental and Behavioural Disorders.* Geneva: WHO.

World Health Organisation (1992) *The ICD-10 Classification of Mental and Behavioural Disorders.* Geneva: WHO.

Yatham LN, Barry S and Dinan TG (1989) Serotonin receptors, buspirone and the premenstrual syndrome. *Lancet,* **1**, 1447–1448.

8

Depression and gynaecological disorders

Ronald Taylor

There are several aspects of depression in women which justify special consideration. They are related to reproductive function and can either be sources of depression or influence the course of depression that has some other root. One group of problems relates to natural hormone changes at the menarche or during the normal menstrual cycle or the menopause, a second relates to the volume of blood loss with menstruation and any associated pain, and a third relates to gynaecological surgery.

THE EFFECT OF HORMONE CHANGES

The menarche

The menarche, like the menopause, is a time of great physical change but it is also a time of social turmoil, changing personal relationships and changing views on an individual's role. Not surprisingly, some girls have difficulty in coping with these things. However, there is no evidence that oestrogen, which is produced in increasing amounts in the 2 years or so prior to the first menstrual period, is depressing in itself and the moodiness that is sometimes troublesome to girls and to their families at this time is probably due to an

Depression and Physical Illness. Edited by M.M. Robertson and C.L.E. Katona
© 1997 John Wiley & Sons Ltd

awareness of the bodily changes which herald a change in status that will have consequences that are uncertain.

The first "periods" are commonly anovulatory, there is no progestational phase to the menstrual cycle and dysmenorrhoea is rare. However, after a variable time, ranging from 1 to 2 months to 1 to 2 years, ovulation begins, the menstrual cycle becomes biphasic and girls who are destined to suffer from primary dysmenorrhoea begin to do so.

With the advent of a progestational phase, the possibility of a girl developing the symptoms characterized as the "premenstrual syndrome" is realized although it is uncommon at this time in a woman's life. Progesterone is a hormone with many effects but it is mildly depressive and when given experimentally in very large amounts it has anaesthetic properties.

The premenstrual syndrome (PMS)

This is a condition about which medical opinion generally remains confused (Bancroft, 1993). Attempts to define it closely have not been very successful and the precise aetiology is still unknown (Severino and Moline, 1995). It can most easily be characterized as the cyclical recurrence of physical, mental and behavioural symptoms occurring in the luteal phase of the menstrual cycle and disappearing within 1–2 days of the menstrual flow being established. About two-thirds of women are able to identify changes which tell them that menstruation is approaching but only about one in 10 are ever sufficiently troubled by symptoms to seek medical advice or treatment (Taylor and James, 1979).

Although the search for an identifiable hormonal abnormality to account for PMS has long been a target for investigators, the evidence for the existence of such abnormality is unconvincing (Casper *et al.*, 1989; Rubinow *et al.*, 1995) and it seems increasingly likely that it is an individual woman's sensitivity to hormone change that causes the problems. This allows for the possibility that general stresses in a woman's life might alter the threshold at which symptoms become intolerable and the recognition of this has, I believe, led to a more satisfactory holistic approach to treatment.

The symptoms most easy to identify and check are the physical ones of breast discomfort and enlargement, fluid retention and abdominal bloating. Rare but well-documented physical symptoms include premenstrual migraine, premenstrual epilepsy and even premenstrual angina pectoris.

The common psychiatric problems associated with the premenstruum are uncharacteristic mood changes and aggression, but periods of severe depression or worsening of a pre-existing depressed state is well recognized as a premenstrual event. These are frequently more worrying to the woman than other emotional changes (Endicott, 1993).

The diagnosis of PMS depends on obtaining a reliable history over at least 3 months when there is daily recording of symptoms and signs which can then be checked for their relationship to the menstrual cycle. It is helpful but not essential to the diagnosis to have the symptoms rated both in the order of severity and in terms of the distress caused to the individual concerned. In some women, occasional cycles are trouble free and it is useful, then, to check on the regularity of ovulation. Cycles in which there are no untoward symptoms or signs are often found to be anovulatory.

A relationship between PMS and depression is suggested by the increased prevalence of prior depressive episodes in women with PMS, including postnatal depression, common neurotransmitter and chronobiological abnormalities and the fact that premenstrual syndrome can be successfully treated with some therapies used in depression (Pearlstein, 1995).

The treatment of the PMS *per se* remains as controversial as its aetiology (Rubinow and Schmidt, 1995). In practice, many women can be successfully treated by alleviating some of the symptoms that trouble them most, and the standard treatments for depression can form a part of this approach. However, when the woman is most severely troubled, this may not be sufficient. This is also true when a problem such as depression is adequately controlled except for the premenstrual phase of the cycle. Pregnancy is a time of relief but this is almost always temporary and not always an appropriate treatment to recommend. The suppression of ovulation is also effective and the period of relief obtained can be used to try to relieve other stresses which bear on the woman.

Inducing anovulation by the continuous administration of an oestrogen/progestational combination such as the oral contraceptive pill might be tried but the steroids commonly induce symptoms that are similar to those the woman is suffering, although the cyclical element may be abolished. Similarly, the administration of oral oestrogen on a regular, daily basis or by means of implants of oestrogen pellets can suppress ovulation and minimize symptoms. However, the fact that progestational agents have to be given to bring about periodic shedding of the endometrium in those women who have an intact uterus (see below) usually makes this approach unsatisfactory because the symptoms of PMS commonly occur during the time that the progestational agent is being administered.

Although some women obtain relief from PMS by having a simple hysterectomy, the majority of those whose ovaries are left intact to function normally will continue to experience cyclical symptoms, although the loss of menstruation might make their cyclical nature difficult to detect. In these patients, the implantation of oestradiol pellets at about 6 monthly intervals to suppress ovarian function is a very successful therapy.

An alternative approach for women with an intact uterus is to suppress ovulation by interfering with the pituitary production of gonadotrophins. This can be achieved by the use of the weakly androgenic compound, danazol. This has many effects but the most noticeable one is the inhibition of the mid-cyclical surge of gonadotrophins. The extent to which this occurs is dose-related and the hormone flux can often be reduced without suppressing menstruation. High doses do generally produce amenorrhea. By experimenting with dosage in individual women, therefore, premenstrual symptoms can be reduced or eliminated in many cases without always suppressing menstruation (Sarno *et al.*, 1987). In some cases, the androgenic side-effects of the danazol, such as acne, fluid retention and generalized weight gain, prove to be unacceptable and these side-effects can cause depression in themselves.

Another way of achieving a similar suppression of gonadotrophins is by the regular administration of gonadotrophin releasing factor (GnRF) analogue (Muse *et al.*, 1984). This also alters the normal pulsatile production of gonadotrophins, suppresses ovulation and produces amenorrhoea. The side-effects of the GnRF analogue are minimal but when it is used continually over a long period, it can result eventually in signs of oestrogen deficiency. Vaginal dryness and atrophic changes in the vaginal epithelium are usually the first symptoms and the easiest to identify. They commonly cause dyspareunia and so long-term treatment on these lines cannot be recommended. However, I have never had a patient who had significant problems within 6 months of starting treatment and such a period of relief from PMS is well worthwhile. My clinical experience has been that breaking the cycle for a time enables background stresses to be lessened and other treatments for the relief of symptoms, including depression, to become effective.

The menopause

The menopause is clearly a time of hormonal change but it also tends to occur at a time when there are social, physical and emotional pressures associated with ageing, the loss of fertility and perhaps a perceived loss of attractiveness, concerns about troublesome adolescent children or the loss of children from the immediate family circle. The loss of ovarian hormones has traditionally been blamed for emotional problems at this time but modern research has largely failed to substantiate the view that they could be affected significantly by hormone replacement therapy (HRT) in spite of the fact that this does relieve many of the physical symptoms (Studd *et al.*, 1985).

However, by relieving symptoms of hot flushes which can be associated with troublesome insomnia, regulating and limiting menstrual loss and preventing vaginal dryness and atrophy which frequently cause dyspareunia, hormone replacement therapy can alleviate many of the natural stresses that occur about this time and which can trigger depressive episodes in women who are prone to them. For this reason, hormone replacement therapy might well be of benefit to women who are depressed and careful thought should be given to this in women who appear to be approaching the menopause. Age itself is not necessarily a good guide to this stage in a woman's life but the occurrence of "hot flushes" and perhaps an altered menstrual pattern is strongly suggestive and justifies investigation of gonadotrophin levels.

One of the problems associated with hormone replacement therapy in women who have not had a hysterectomy is that although they need only oestrogen to relieve symptoms, they do require the periodic administration of progestogens to bring about shedding of the endometrium stimulated by oestrogen. This can result in problems indistinguishable from PMS. With skill in manipulating the dosage of oestrogen and the progestational agents, the problems can usually be minimized although I have experience of women in whom this was not possible and who eventually elected to forego the benefits of HRT.

In women who have had a hysterectomy, it is not usually considered necessary to use cyclical progestational agents and this problem does not occur.

Conclusion

It is reasonable to say that with the possible exception of a mildly depressing effect associated with progesterone, the female sex hormones do not cause depression. However, the cyclical changes normally seen during the menstrual cycle and perhaps some abnormal hormone patterns about the time of the menopause can add to stress. In a woman prone to depression they might trigger clinical deterioration. Relief of the problems known to be associated with hormone change or hormone abnormality can materially improve the woman's sense of well-being and thereby contribute to the effectiveness of more specific antidepressant therapy.

MENSTRUAL PROBLEMS

Menorrhagia

Heavy menstrual loss can be debilitating, even when it does not cause a significant reduction in the haemoglobin level. Feelings of lethargy in these circumstances usually respond promptly to oral iron therapy. In some women, very serious reduction of the haemoglobin levels occurs as a consequence of persistent heavy blood loss, even to the extent of causing cardiac embarrassment. When haemoglobin levels are seriously low it is not unreasonable to expect that chronic problems including some forms of depression will be made worse but subsequently relieved when the anaemia is corrected.

Not all women referred for medical advice because of menorrhagia have obvious gynaecological pathology and there is some evidence that the complaint can be a manifestation of psychological abnormality (Iles and Gath, 1989).

Greenberg (1983) found that 62% of women referred to a gynaecological clinic because of menorrhagia had mild to moderate depression. However, he also concluded that depressed women who were said to have menorrhagia probably bled less than those without depression which suggests that it is the depressed woman's tolerance of blood loss which is reduced rather than her absolute loss that is increased.

The condition of "intolerable menstruation" is well recognized clinically and it is a common reason for hysterectomy in spite of the fact that there is frequently no organic abnormality to be found. Among women who have completed their families, and particularly among those who have been sterilized, toleration of menstrual abnormalities tends to be lower than in those who still wish to bear children.

Dysmenorrhoea

In spite of the oft-repeated assertion that a woman's attitude to menstruation influences her experience of painful periods, there is now abundant evidence that it is hypercontractability of the myometrium leading to temporary ischaemia of the uterus which is responsible for the pain. These spasmodic contractions are hormonally induced and depend on the presence of progesterone as well as oestrogen because they are not present in anovular cycles. Our present understanding is that they are probably mediated by the local release of prostaglandins (Rees, 1988). There is no evidence that depression causes dysmenorrhoea but the regular anticipation of what can be a very debilitating pain might be depressing in itself and in women who are depressed, the experience of pain might be heightened.

In depression, therefore, it might be helpful in individual cases to try to alleviate the dysmenorrhoea. Cyclo-oxygenase inhibitors such as naproxen sodium and mefenamic acid are more effective than simple analgesics such as paracetamol but undoubtedly the most efficient means of relieving the pain of primary dysmenorrhoea is by the inhibition of ovulation. The oral contraceptive pill will bring significant and in some cases complete relief from pain but it can have the side-effect of causing or worsening depression so it must be used with care and proper supervision.

Conclusion

Menorrhagia and dysmenorrhoea are potentially debilitating conditions and, for this reason, can cause or aggravate depression in women who are prone to it. Relief of both problems might form a part of the total management of a woman who is suffering from depression.

GYNAECOLOGICAL SURGERY

In trying to assess the psychological effects of gynaecological surgery it is necessary to exclude surgery undertaken because of malignant disease because this diagnosis in itself is associated with a high incidence of anxiety and depression (Corney *et al.*, 1992). In many such cases psychiatric problems persist for years (Corney *et al.*, 1992a,b) although this long-standing effect is sometimes associated with the physical effects of the operation and loss of hormonal support, particularly on sexual function, rather than with the nature of the original disease (Gleeson *et al.*, 1994).

It is also important to remember that women attending gynaecological clinics have higher levels of psychiatric disorders than women of comparable age and situation (Byrne, 1984; Worsley *et al.*, 1977). Furthermore, women with psychiatric problems are more likely to undergo hysterectomy for what are sometimes termed "functional disorders" where there is no obvious pathological explanation for symptoms (Waldemar *et al.*, 1987). Many studies have shown that postoperative psychiatric morbidity was most frequent among patients in whom no significant pelvic pathology was demonstrated at the time of operation (Barker, 1968; Richards, 1973).

Hysterectomy

Simple hysterectomy for non-malignant disease, with or without oophorectomy, is one of the most common operations performed by gynaecological surgeons. It has long had a reputation for causing psychiatric morbidity and psychological stress (Richards, 1973) and this belief is remarkably persistent in the thinking of patients. However, modern prospective studies using standardized psychiatric assessments suggest that this reputation is largely unjustified (Coppen *et al.*, 1981; Gath *et al.*, 1981). Indeed, both of these studies found that the incidence of psychiatric morbidity, while remaining high, was reduced after hysterectomy.

The most important single determinant of postoperative psychiatric disorder is preoperative psychiatric disorder. Martin *et al.* (1980) found that almost all patients having psychiatric treatment after hysterectomy had had treatment for similar problems before the hysterectomy. The clear conclusion is that hysterectomy in itself seldom leads to psychiatric morbidity and for many women it leads to an improvement in their psychological functioning (Oates and Gath, 1989).

Gath *et al.* (1981) found no evidence of any different effect on the psychiatric outcome from using a vaginal approach to hysterectomy as distinct from the more common abdominal approach. This and other similar studies are difficult to interpret because the abdominal approach is most commonly used when there is some evidence of gynaecological disease, while the vaginal approach is most frequently used when there is a uterovaginal prolapse. In these cases it is combined with a pelvic floor repair which can itself cause problems.

The most recent and best studies in this area make use of preoperative psychiatric assessment and this presupposes good counselling beforehand. Some of the most devastating psychological consequences that I have seen after hysterectomy have been in women who have had a hysterectomy unexpectedly after some surgical or obstetric mishap and both of these things underline the importance of preoperative counselling (Taylor, 1992).

Hysterectomy with oophorectomy

Studies comparing hysterectomy alone with hysterectomy and bilateral oophorectomy have found no difference in the incidence of adverse psychiatric outcome and there appears to be no difference in the psychiatric outcome in those women who receive hormone replacement therapy after oophorectomy (Martin *et al.*, 1980; Gath *et al.*, 1981). However, this is not to say that, in practice, the longer-term physical effects of oestrogen deprivation such as atrophic vaginitis, which can disturb sexual function, will not have an adverse effect on a woman's general well-being.

Modern, prospective studies have failed to confirm the still commonly held belief that hysterectomy in itself, as distinct from hysterectomy with removal of the ovaries, has a negative impact on sexual intercourse (Martin, 1980; Gath *et al.*, 1981) although surgery itself is liable to have the effect of depressing libido for a time.

In cases where an oophorectomy is performed in premenopausal women without giving HRT, symptoms of oestrogen deprivation are common but variable in nature and degree. Vaginal atrophy leading to dyspareunia is a common problem although it usually occurs only 2–3 years after the surgery. In these cases there may be a secondary loss of libido and depression. These problems will usually be resolved by HRT if this is feasible. When there is a relative contraindication to general oestrogen therapy, low dose oestrogens applied vaginally might be helpful without taking the risks associated with full replacement. Where the surgery has been performed because of an oestrogen-dependent malignancy this will probably be considered unsafe and then symptomatic treatment with vaginal lubricants can be helpful. In some cases vaginal surgery can be helpful (Glesson *et al.*, 1994).

With this exception, modern studies have failed to show any psychiatric morbidity associated with the removal of the ovaries at the time of hysterectomy (Martin *et al.*, 1980).

Sterilization

Like hysterectomy, sterilization is commonly believed to lead to psychiatric problems and a loss of libido in many women. Like the studies on the effect of hysterectomy, reviews such as those of Enoch and Jones (1975) were flawed in a number of ways. For example, being retrospective, it is not possible to determine the quality of counselling received by the women concerned. Many operations 30 years ago were performed as a result of medical suggestion rather than at the woman's request and they were frequently done immediately after pregnancy or abortion. Further, they involved a variety of medical and social reasons for sterilization and the forms of assessment of the outcome were not standardized.

It is generally accepted that sterilization decided upon at times of emotional crises, including recent childbirth or abortion, is more likely to be regretted than interval procedures (WHO Collaborative Study, 1985) and today it is usual for the operation to be carried out at an interval of 3 months or more from the end of pregnancy. The older studies also are outdated in the sense that the general acceptability of sterilization in Western society has changed dramatically and so attitudes to the operation and to those who have been sterilized have also changed.

More recent prospective studies of women awaiting sterilization have suggested that the psychiatric morbidity is no higher in this group than in the general population (Smith, 1979; Cooper *et al.*, 1982).

A further study assessed women who had been sterilized at 6 and 12 months postoperatively (Cooper *et al.*, 1985) and it led to the conclusion that psychiatric morbidity was more than halved during this time. Furthermore, the incidence of new psychiatric problems was no higher than one would have anticipated in such a population.

As the commonest reason for requesting sterilization in this group was that the women had completed their families, it is reasonable to assume that the removal of the fear of an unplanned pregnancy was an important contributory factor in any improvement.

As might have been anticipated, this study, along with other relatively recent prospective studies, shows that there are consistent risk factors for an adverse psychiatric outcome after sterilization. As with hysterectomy, these include preoperative psychiatric morbidity and a history of previous psychiatric illness.

Repair of vaginal prolapse and urinary incontinence

Uterovaginal prolapse can be a debilitating condition, interfering with everyday activities and impairing sexual function. Pelvic floor repair, with or without a vaginal hysterectomy, is a highly successful operation in general, particularly when the cause of the prolapse has been the trauma of repeated vaginal deliveries. In such cases the normal anatomy can be restored with careful surgery and postoperative problems with sexual intercourse are rare. However, in cases where the prolapse has arisen because of inherently weak pelvic musculature, the form of the surgery required to relieve symptoms can impair intercourse and this is a potential problem that should be discussed with both partners in advance of surgery.

Repair of a posterior wall prolapse with reconstruction of the perineum can have an adverse effect on intercourse by the restriction of vaginal capacity and the development of painful scars. Both physical problems are usually temporary but they can lead to secondary vaginismus if a pattern of painful intercourse is allowed to persist for an undue length of time.

Urinary incontinence, whether it is associated with the stress of raised intra-abdominal pressure or urgency of micturition associated with bladder instability, both of which are most commonly seen in association with anterior vaginal wall prolapse, is socially embarrassing and can lead to women becoming increasingly reclusive and consequently seriously depressed.

Successful treatment by surgical means depends upon accurate diagnosis, but there are a number of pitfalls. The repair of a vaginal wall prolapse can reduce the capacity of the vagina and create physical impediments to intercourse. True stress incontinence can only be corrected by surgery while the unstable bladder is unlikely to be improved by surgery alone.

In carrying out any pelvic floor repair it is clearly necessary to recognize these potential physical problems which might have psychiatric repercussions. However, the benefits of relief from distressing symptoms can have considerable psychiatric benefit. One of my greatest professional successes was the cure of a woman who had been referred to a psychiatrist for treatment of severe depression. She had not been outside her own home for 3 years because of severe and acutely embarrassing stress incontinence of urine. When we had cured this symptom, it was clear that she did not require treatment for depression.

In general terms, the results of gynaecological surgery for non-malignant disease are good. However, when there are operative complications surgery can lead to impaired sexual function if there is appreciable vaginal or pelvic scarring, and the function of both bowel and bladder can be impaired. For a woman who had thought she was embarking on a straightforward hysterectomy but found herself with urinary or faecal incontinence, for example, the psychiatric consequences might be immense.

Conclusion

There is no evidence that gynaecological surgery in itself is a cause of depression although good preoperative counselling is important to achieve the most satisfactory outcome. Complications of such surgery can have psychiatric as well as physical sequelae, especially if they affect sexual, bladder or bowel function. Some women who undergo gynaecological surgery will have a pre-existing psychiatric disorder and in some cases, surgery might prove ultimately to have been the wrong choice of treatment. Gynaecologists should be aware of this and be prepared to have a proper psychiatric assessment in such patients before embarking on procedures that they, as well as their patients, might regret.

REFERENCES

Bancroft J (1993) The pre-menstrual syndrome—a reappraisal of the concept and the evidence. *Psychol* Med, **Suppl 24**, 1–47.

Byrne P (1984) Psychiatric morbidity in a gynaecological clinic: An epidemiological survey. *Br J Psychiatry*, **144**, 28–34.

Casper PF, Patel-Christopher A and Powell A (1989) Thyrotrophin and prolactin responses to thyrotrophin-releasing hormone in premenstrual syndrome. *J Clin Endocrinol Metab*, **68**, 608–612.

Cooper JE, Bledin KD, Brice B and Mackensie S (1985) Effects of female sterilisation: One year follow-up in a prospective controlled study of psychological and psychiatric outcome. *J Psychosom Res*, **29**, 13–22.

Cooper P, Gath D, Rose N and Fieldsend R (1982) Psychological sequelae to elective sterilisation in women: A prospective study. *Br Med J*, **82**, 461–464.

Coppen A, Bishop M, Beard RJ, Barnard GJ and Collins WP (1981) Hysterectomy, hormones and behaviour: A prospective study. *Lancet*, **i**, 126–128.

Corney RH, Everett H, Howells A and Crowther ME (1992a) Psychological adjustment following major gynaecological surgery for carcinoma of the cervix and vulva. *J Psychosom Res*, **36(6)**, 561–568.

Corney RH, Everett H, Howells A and Crowther ME (1992b) The care of patients undergoing surgery for gynaecological cancer: The need for information, emotional support and counselling. *J Adv Nursing*, **17(6)**, 667–671.

Endicott J (1993) The menstrual cycle and mood disorders. *J Affect Disord*, **29(2–3)**, 193–200.

Enoch MD and Jones K (1975) Sterilisation: a review of 98 sterilised women. *Br J Psychiatry*, **127**, 583–587.

Gath D, Cooper P and Day A (1981) Hysterectomy and psychiatric disorder: Levels of psychiatric morbidity before and after hysterectomy. *Br J Psychiatry*, **140**, 335–342.

Gleeson N, Baile W, Roberts WS, Hoffman M, Fiorica JV, Barton D and Cavanagh D (1994) Surgical and psychosexual outcome following vaginal reconstruction with pelvic excenteration. *Eur J Gynecol Oncol*, **15(2)**, 89–95.

Greenberg M (1983) The meaning of menorrhagia. *J Psychosom Res*, **27**, 209–214.

Iles S and Gath D (1989) Psychological problems and uterine bleeding. *Clin Obstet Gynaecol*, **3(2)**, 375–389.

Martin RL (1980) Psychiatric status after hysterectomy; a one year prospective follow up. *JAMA*, **244**, 350–353.

Martin RL, Roberts WV and Clayton PJ (1980) Psychiatric status after hysterectomy—a one year prospective follow-up. *JAMA*, **244**, 350–353.

Muse KN, Cetel NS and Futterman LA (1984) The premenstrual syndrome effects of "medical ovariectomy". *N Eng J Med*, **311**, 1345–1349.

Oates M and Gath D (1989) Psychological aspects of gynaecological surgery. *Clin Obstet Gynecol*, **3(4)**, 729–774.

Pearlstein TB (1995) Hormones and depression: What are the facts about premenstrual syndrome, menopause, and hormone replacement therapy? *Am J Obstet Gynecol*, **173(2)**, 646–653.

Rees M (1988) Dysmenorrhoea. *Br J Obstet Gynaecol*, **95**, 833–835.

Richards DH (1973) Depression after hysterectomy. *Lancet*, **ii**, 430–432.

Rubinow DR and Schmidt PJ (1995) The treatment of pre-menstrual syndrome—forward into the past. (Editorial: comment). *N Engl J Med*, **332(23)**, 1574–1575.

Rubinow DR, Hoban MC, Grover GN, Galloway DS, Roy-Byrne P, Anderson R and Merriam GR (1988) Changes in plasma hormones across the menstrual cycle in patients with menstrually related mood disorder and in control subjects. *Am J Obstet Gynecol*, **158**, 5–11.

Sarno AP Jr, Miller EJ Jr and Lundblad EG (1987) Pre-menstrual syndrome: Beneficial effects of periodic, low dose danazol. *Obstet Gynecol*, **70**, 33–39.

Severino SK and Moline ML (1995) Pre-menstrual syndrome. Identification and management. *Drugs*, **1**, 71–82.

Smith AHW (1979) Psychiatric aspects of sterilisation: A prospective study. *Br J Psychiatry*, **135**, 304–309.

Studd J, Chakravarti S and Oram D (1985) Practical aspects of hormone replacement therapy. *Curr Med Res Opin*, **3(3)**, 56–64.

Taylor RW (1992) Foreword. In: S Hasleff and M Jennings (eds) *Hysterectomy and Vaginal Repair*. Beaconsfield.

Taylor RW and James CE (1979) The clinician's view of patients with premenstrual syndrome. *Curr Med Res*, **6(5)**, 46–51.

Waldemar G, Werdelin L and Boysen G (1987) Neurologic symptoms and hysterectomy: A retrospective survey of the prevalence of hysterectomy in neurologic patients. *Obstet Gynaecol*, **70(4)**, 559–563.

WHO Collaborative Prospective Study Report (1985) Mental health and female sterilisation. *J Biosocial Sci*, **17**, 1–18.

Worsley A, Walters WAW and Wood EC (1977) Screening for psychological disturbance amongst gynaecological patients. *Aus NZ J Obstet Gynecol*, **17**, 214–219.

9

Depression and physical illness in childhood and adolescence

Ann York and Peter Hill

Prevalence studies show that between 5% and 15% of youngsters at any one time suffer from a chronic physical illness such as asthma or diabetes mellitus (Rutter *et al.*, 1970; Pless and Roughman, 1971; Cadman *et al.*, 1987) and many more from acute illnesses. One in 10 children will have had one or more chronic illnesses by the time they reach the age of 15 (Pless and Roughman, 1971). Children with a chronic physical disease are two to three times more likely to develop a psychiatric disorder compared to their healthy peers (Rutter *et al.*, 1970; Pless and Roughman, 1971; Cadman *et al.*, 1987).

Over recent years there has been increasing interest in children's adjustment to physical illness, not only in terms of identifying the sorts of difficulties they encounter but also whether disease-specific problems occur. The development of operational diagnostic criteria for psychiatric illness in childhood has facilitated the move from descriptive reports to controlled studies using standardized assessments. Models of coping with chronic illness have begun to generate hypotheses about the complexities of why and how some children adjust well whilst others do not.

Concern about depression, particularly in the context of self-harm, is the most frequent reason for referral to paediatric child psychiatry liaison teams, with poor adjustment to chronic illness coming a close second (Olsen *et al.*, 1988). It is now appreciated that children can and do become depressed and although the origins of this may seem understandable in the context of illness

Depression and Physical Illness. Edited by M.M. Robertson and C.L.E. Katona
© 1997 John Wiley & Sons Ltd

or disability, the degree of suffering, and impairment of functioning and development which result from depression are beyond understandable unhappiness. Child psychiatrists or psychologists working in liaison teams therefore require a working knowledge of paediatric illness and treatments to ensure diagnostic accuracy and formulation of psychiatric problems in sick children.

This chapter looks at depression in children and adolescents who have a chronic physical illness. Illness in this context will exclude congenital malformations or those due to injury.

PSYCHIATRIC DISORDERS IN CHILDREN WITH CHRONIC ILLNESS

The classic total population survey of 10- and 11-year-olds carried out on the Isle of Wight reported an overall prevalence rate of psychiatric disorder of 6.8% (Rutter *et al.*, 1970). For children with a physical disease not affecting the brain (e.g. asthma) the rate increased to 10.4%. For those in whom the brain was affected (e.g. cerebral palsy) the rate soared to 38.9%. This increased rate associated with physical illness was subsequently shown to be an independent consequence of brain injury *per se* and not simply the result of low IQ or the effects of visible crippling (Seidel *et al.*, 1975). These increased rates have continued to be described in more recent surveys. Cadman *et al.* (1987) in their population-based survey of 3294 children aged 4–16 years found chronic physical disease in 14%. Those with chronic disease were at twice the risk of developing a psychiatric disorder compared to healthy children. Additionally, children who suffered from a physical disability were three times more likely to develop a psychiatric disorder.

DEPRESSION IN CHILDREN AND ADOLESCENTS

The idea that children could become depressed was controversial until relatively recently. Depression was considered to be "masked" or only experienced in adolescence. The clarification of depression in adults and the development of standardized assessment methods led to increased research activity aimed at identification and description of psychiatric disorders in childhood and adolescence. The current view is that youngsters can suffer from adult-like affective disorders, although symptomatology may vary with developmental stage (Kazdin, 1990; Harrington, 1992). Preadolescents are especially likely to suffer somatic complaints. In a study comparing 100 11- and 12-year-olds meeting DSM-III criteria with 38 nondepressed controls it was found that 70% of children with major depressive disorder had significant somatic complaints compared to 34% of controls, independent of anxiety levels. The frequency of somatic symptoms also increased as the severity of depression increased

(McCauley *et al.*, 1991). The physical symptoms of depression can thus add to the symptoms of physical disease.

PREVALENCE OF DEPRESSION

Childhood and adolescence

Among healthy preadolescent children, rates of depression as a disorder vary from 0.6% to 2.5% (Kashani and Simmonds, 1979; Kashani *et al.*, 1983; Anderson *et al.*, 1987; Velez *et al.*, 1989; Fleming *et al.*, 1989). For adolescents, rates are consistently higher at 2.5% to 8.0% (Kashani *et al.*, 1987; Velez *et al.*, 1989; Whitaker *et al.*, 1990; McGee *et al.*, 1992). Rates vary according to diagnostic criteria used.

Physically ill children and adolescents

Again, rates vary according to diagnostic criteria used but, as a group, children suffering from a physical illness have somewhat elevated rates of depression. A recent meta-analysis of 60 studies that used standardized measures of depression or depressive symptoms in 4–18-year-olds with a chronic medical illness found a median prevalence rate for depression of 9% (Bennett, 1994). However, there are variations in rates according to illness category, with some showing no increase or lower rates than healthy children (see below for more full discussion).

Methodological problems prevent direct comparison between studies which use different criteria or instruments, sampling from small highly specialized clinics and varying comparison groups.

DIAGNOSTIC INSTRUMENTS

Categorical (where a child does or does not meet criteria for depression as a disorder) and dimensional (a continuum based on measures of severity of depressive symptoms) tools have been developed for the assessment of depression in children and adolescents. The former take the form of standardized psychiatric diagnostic interviews which generate DSM or ICD diagnoses. The latter are based on self-report questionnaires. Parent, child and teacher versions are available for several measures. Table 1 describes those most commonly used.

These instruments report different aspects of depression. For instance, high scores on the Children's Depression Inventory (CDI) do not necessarily equate with meeting the diagnostic criteria for major depression or vice versa (Kazdin,

Table 1. The most commonly used diagnostic instruments for depression.

Measure	Age Range	Format	Reference
Self-report questionnaires			
Children's Depression Inventory (CDI)	7–17	27 items	Kovacs and Beck, 1977
Children's Depression Scale	9–16	66 items	Lang and Tisher, 1978
Self-rating Scale	7–13	18 items	Birleson, 1981
Reynolds Adolescent Depression Scale (RADS)	High School students	30 items	Reynolds and Coats, 1986
Beck Depression Inventory (BDI) (modified for adolescents)	13–15	33 items	Chiles et al, 1980
Interviews and clinical rating scales			
Bellevue Index of Depression (BID)	6–12	26 items Child, parent and other versions	Petti, 1978
Children's Depression Rating Scale (CDRS)	6–12	16 items Child, parent and others	Poznanski et al, 1979
Interview Schedule for Children (ISC)	8–13	Child and parent interviews Herjanic and Reich, 1982	Kovacs, 1978
Diagnostic Interview for Children and Adolescents (DICA)	>6		
Diagnostic Interview Schedule for Children (DISC)	6–18	DSM-III	Costello et al, 1985
Kiddie-Schedule for Affective Disorders for School-age Children (K-SADS)	6–16	RDC criteria Parent and child interviews	Chambers et al, 1985

1990). At present there is no single measure which provides a comprehensive assessment of all aspects of childhood depression. The decision on which to use will depend on the research question to be investigated and whether a dimensional or categorical view is being taken. In addition, information from different sources will lead to different conclusions. It has been consistently demonstrated that child, parent and teacher ratings of depression differ (Achenbach *et al.*, 1987; Worchel *et al.*, 1988; Harrington, 1993). Ideally, researchers and clinicians alike should obtain information from multiple sources and use complementary assessment tools.

ASSESSMENT OF DEPRESSION IN MEDICALLY ILL CHILDREN AND ADOLESCENTS

The diagnosis of depression in youngsters can be difficult at the best of times but if they are physically ill the task becomes even more complicated. Of particular relevance is the fact that many symptoms used to diagnose depression may be due to the illness itself, e.g. sleep disturbance, weight loss and fatigue. The Bellevue and CDI both contain somatic items, for instance. However, it is important to note that generally studies have shown that, although physically ill children have increased scores on somatic items, this does not account for the total increase in scores of depression (Tebbi *et al.*, 1988; Seigel *et al.*, 1990). In a study comparing total Beck Depression Inventory (BDI) scores in 43 acutely ill, 42 chronically ill, and 140 adolescents from the general population, scores on somatic items were greater in those who were physically unwell but there was no difference in total scores between the three groups (Kaplan *et al.*, 1986).

Canning and Kelleher (1994) assessed the performance of the CDI, Pediatric Symptom Checklist and Child Behavior Checklist (CBCL) using the Diagnostic Interview Schedule for Children (DISC) to generate DSM-IIIR (APA, 1987) criteria for emotional and behaviour disorders in 112 children and adolescents with chronic physical conditions. They concluded that all three were poor screening instruments because of the low sensitivity in children who are physically unwell and recommended that they should not be relied upon in this group.

The mental state of the mother has been shown to have a bearing on depression in sick children, particularly for children with cancer. It has been demonstrated that higher levels of self-reported depression in mothers of children with cancer correlate positively with child depression scores on both child and parent report measures (Mulhern *et al.*, 1992).

The literature therefore suggests that caution should be exercised in using diagnostic instruments with ill children, and that depression scores in particular should be analysed in detail to separate out somatic and psychological items. Instruments should not be allowed to override clinical judgement. Maternal mental state should be taken into account and information gathered from several sources. Disentanglement of which complaints are due to depression requires close liaison with the medical staff, and observation of the child by ward staff can be very helpful. Observations and ratings of nonverbal behaviour have been shown to be associated with accuracy of diagnosis and severity of depression in children (Poznanski *et al.*, 1985).

DEVELOPMENTAL VARIATIONS IN DEPRESSIVE SYMPTOMATOLOGY

Depressed preadolescents tend to report more somatic complaints and show more agitation and hallucinatory experiences compared to depressed adolescents. They also have a more obviously depressed appearance. Depressed adolescents show greater anhedonia and hopelessness, hypersomnia and weight change (Kazdin, 1990).

DIFFERENTIAL DIAGNOSIS

It is vitally important to make an accurate diagnosis when assessing depressed mental state in ill children. The clinician should be especially alert for organic affective disorders secondary to drugs (prescribed or illicit), metabolic abnormalities, infection (especially those involving the central nervous system) and other psychiatric disorders such as anxiety (e.g. separation anxiety and post-traumatic stress disorder), grief reactions and adjustment disorders. Inaccurate diagnosis can occur in situations where staff tend to want to normalize or justify depressive symptoms (Kashani and Breedlove, 1994).

MECHANISMS OF DEPRESSION

Two aspects will be considered here—general issues relating to depression in children and adolescents, and issues specific to those who are chronically ill. Emotional and behavioural disorders in children are always related to the psychosocial context and it is important to note that psychiatric disturbance and physical disease may not necessarily be functionally connected (Taylor and Eminson, 1994).

Biological models

Models based on those developed for adults have been applied with limited success to children. Tests of the amine hypothesis have shown developmental differences in amine systems compared to adults. The role of amine system abnormalities in depressed young people has yet to be confirmed as important (Harrington, 1993).

The search for a reliable biological marker for depression in children continues, as it does for adults. No specific biological test has yet been identified as useful in children although depressed children do show adult-like responses to the dexamethasone suppression test (Harrington, 1993).

Psychological mechanisms in depression

Again, models have been developed from those described for adults. In addition to classical psychoanalytical models, particular importance has been attached to the relevance of cognitive–behavioural, social skills and family interaction models to childhood depression. Studies show that Beck's cognitive theory can be applied to this group and that depressed children suffer from social skills and problem-solving deficits, have an externalized locus of control and an attributional style of helplessness and self-blame. Depressed children are often living in families where family interactions are disturbed for various reasons and they may also have an increased genetic loading for affective disorder. Adverse life events appear to be a risk factor for depression in young people, albeit nonspecific. (See Rutter *et al.*, 1986, Kazdin, 1990 and Harrington, 1993 for comprehensive reviews.)

Additional mechanisms in medically ill children

The above general issues are all relevant in sick children. Serious preschool illness has been shown to be an early risk factor for depressive symptoms at the age of 15, in conjunction with anxiety and death of a parent in girls. Mediating factors were found to be family cohesiveness, satisfactory social supports and adolescent positive self-perceptions of popularity, attractiveness and intellectual competence (Reinherz *et al.*, 1989). It might be expected that having a chronic illness will increase the risk of depression through mechanisms such as disability and handicap, effect on daily living and necessary frequent contact with medical services including hospital admissions, amongst others. It is interesting therefore to find that although sick children are at somewhat increased risk of depression, most are not depressed and disease-specific patterns are demonstrable. Most research has focused on maladjustment to illness. Much less is known about why and how most children adjust well (Eiser, 1990).

Developmental issues

The age and developmental stage reached at the time of becoming ill will have a significant effect on the sense the child makes of his experience, and the developmental tasks that may be disrupted. School-aged children who are capable of concrete operational thought may be able to understand their illness but find it hard to accept. They are at the stage of developing a sense of mastery of themselves and their world, peer relationships become increasingly important and moral attitudes and values develop. Social relationships are disrupted and limitations put on physical activities as a result of illness (Rodgers et al., 1981). It can be hypothesized that some children will react by becoming depressed and for some this will be severe. Illness may be interpreted as a punishment for sexual and aggressive feelings which may lead to the development of depression (Lipowski, 1971).

For adolescents who have developed formal operational thinking and are facing different life tasks of moving away from dependency on parents, medical illness can be particularly distressing, whether newly diagnosed or newly thought about as a result of development. Adolescents become increasingly able to think about other people's thinking and see themselves as others may see them. Other people are assumed to be as aware of the adolescent as the adolescent is of themself. This belief in being special may lead to a belief in being invincible and contribute to denial of illness and rejection of treatment. Disability may lead to a sense of loss of status in other people's eyes, particularly peers (Elkind, 1985).

Illness factors

In most studies, depression seems unrelated to the severity of the illness but, if it is, body image disturbance and impaired functioning in daily living are the most relevant factors. Similarly, most studies show that duration of illness is also unrelated to the risk of depression (Bennett, 1994).

Age and gender

As with physically healthy children, depression is equally as common in physically ill girls and boys before puberty but then rises to become more frequent in girls during adolescence (Kazdin, 1990; Bennett, 1994).

Knowledge of illness

In a study of 53 children with cancer, those who were better informed about their illness were described by the authors as less depressed, although "depression" was not defined (Kvist et al., 1991).

Family stress

Having a chronically ill child does not necessarily place a heavy burden on families although clearly it may do and this can, in turn, affect the child's emotional state (Walker et al., 1992). Several studies have looked at parental adaptation to having a chronically ill child. For example, in a study of 159 couples with a child with juvenile rheumatoid disease, mothers self-reported more depressive symptoms than did fathers (Timko *et al.*, 1992). Depressed mothers report more disturbance in their chronically sick children (Walker *et al.*, 1989; Brown *et al.*, 1993) and have children who report more depression themselves (Mulhern *et al.*, 1992). Perceived low levels of social support seem a particularly important factor (Speechley and Noh, 1992). A mother's perception of the severity of her child's illness is also important and mild to moderate illness is less likely to increase maternal distress (Berenbaum and Hatcher, 1992). Less is known about the effect of adjustment by fathers.

> A 12-year-old boy of Caribbean extraction presented with social withdrawal resulting in school refusal coupled with a morose and pessimistic state of mind, anhedonia, inertia, inappropriate guilt and poor concentration. He had sickle cell anaemia, relatively recently diagnosed. His lone mother had sickle cell trait and had become guilty and self-reproachful at having passed the genetic condition on to her son. She had told him this but his cognitive immaturity led him to blame himself for his mother's unhappiness.

Other psychological issues

Other mechanisms leading to depression in chronically ill children have been described as perceived inferiority, altered body image, low self-esteem, and "mourning" the absence of health (Solnit and Stark, 1961).

DEPRESSION PRESENTING AS PHYSICAL ILLNESS

Physical symptoms in depression are well recognized and if the mental state is not examined they can be wrongly assumed to be evidence of an organic disorder. These include headache, chest pain, appetite and weight change, lassitude, sleepiness and general inertia.

Even when a mental state examination is attempted, adolescents in particular may not be willing to disclose depressive thoughts and low mood, especially if their parents are present in the room. Self-report questionnaires are clinically useful in such cases.

Conversion syndromes, especially affecting the legs, can be precipitated by a depressive episode. Once again, a selective focus on the physical problem can lead to the primary depressive condition being missed.

DEPRESSION IN SPECIFIC DISEASES

Asthma

Studies have found self-report depression to be in the normal range (Bender *et al.*, 1991a,b; Gizynski and Shapiro, 1990; Sandler *et al.*, 1992), or to be only a little higher than in controls (Nelms, 1989; Seigel *et al.*, 1990; Austin, 1989; Furukawa *et al.*, 1988). Self-report depression, anxiety or hostility and irrational beliefs in the importance of approval and lack of control of emotions were found to be strongly associated with disease severity in a study comparing 129 adolescent asthmatics with each other and with healthy controls (Silverglade *et al.*, 1994).

The role of depression in children who die of asthma has also been studied. A retrospective comparison of 21 children who died with a matched control group who had equally severe asthma yet survived concluded that "depressive symptoms" was one of eight variables that discriminated between the two groups, the others being related to medical management (Strunk *et al.*, 1985). A review of three deaths from childhood asthma found that all the children had depressive disorder or prominent depressive symptoms, although diagnostic criteria were not given (Fritz *et al.*, 1987). Deaths may be a form of suicide by deliberate overdose of medication or induction of severe attacks by noncompliance (Lewiston and Rubinstein, 1986, 1987). It has also been postulated that depression increases cholinergic tone/activity which increases the risk of an acute attack of asthma (Miller, 1987; Fritz *et al.*, 1987).

Theophylline has been linked both to improvement (Buckley, 1980) and exacerbation of depression (Brumback *et al.*, 1984) and it is therefore recommended that there be careful monitoring of mental state (Weinberger *et al.*, 1987).

In summary, it is not clear whether asthmatic children are at increased risk of depression, but depressive symptomatology does seem to be an important contributory factor in asthmatic deaths. There is a paucity of research using diagnostic interviews in this group.

Cancer

With one exception (Kashani and Hakami, 1982) studies have shown that children with cancer report less depression compared to healthy controls (Kaplan *et al.*, 1987; Worchel *et al.*, 1988; Canning *et al.*, 1992) or show no difference compared to questionnaire norms (Kaplan *et al.*, 1987; Tebbi *et al.*, 1988). A study of 34 inpatient children aged 5–18 years with cancer, using psychiatric interviews, found six to fulfil criteria for major depressive disorder, this being said to be lower than expected (Dunitz *et al.*, 1991) but clearly higher than rates obtained from self-report measures.

Somatic items on the CDI have been found to be poor discriminators between depressed and nondepressed patients and low self-concept was fairly frequent in all cancer patients (compared to psychiatric inpatients and normal school children) regardless of the level of depressive symptoms (Worchel *et al.*, 1988). The level of depressive symptomatology reported by children with cancer or their mothers has also been shown to he dependent on levels of maternal self-reported depression (Mulhern *et al.*, 1992).

A study looking at 138 survivors of cancer aged 8–16 who were currently well, compared to a matched group with no chronic psychiatric or physical problems, found no significant difference in self-report depression scores between the survivor group and comparison groups. However, those with severe medical late effects, e.g. concerning physical appearance, reported more depressive symptoms than those with mild or moderate late effects (Greenberg *et al.*, 1989). Adult survivors of childhood cancer do not appear to be at increased risk of major depressive disorder. Teta *et al.* (1986) interviewed 450 survivors over the age of 21 and their siblings and found that survivors did not have higher rates of lifetime major depressive disorder compared to their siblings.

Many authors have postulated that low rates of depression in children with cancer are due to the use of denial (Kaplan *et al.*, 1987; Tebbi *et al.*, 1988; Worchel, 1989) and repressive adaptation (Canning *et al.*, 1992).

In summary, children with cancer report themselves to have fewer depressive symptoms than healthy children when asked to complete questionnaires and this may be due to their use of psychological denial as a coping strategy. Further studies are needed using diagnostic interviews to clarify true rates of depressive disorder. Survivors do not appear to be at increased risk of depression in adult life. Assessment of children with cancer should use multiple information sources and take into account maternal mental state.

Chronic fatigue syndrome

Major depression is found in 50% of adults with chronic fatigue syndrome (CFS) and it is not clear whether this is primary or secondary (Powell *et al.*, 1990; David *et al.*, 1991; Ray, 1991). Similarly increased rates of self-reported depression have been found in children with CFS. Walford *et al.* (1993) compared 12 children aged 8–16 suffering from CFS with a matched group who had cystic fibrosis, and healthy controls. Children with CFS reported significantly more symptoms of depression compared to both control groups and five (42%) were depressed on the CDI, i.e. a similar rate to that found in adults, although numbers were small. The authors concluded that the increased rate of depressive symptoms was unlikely to be due to a reaction to suffering from an illness since the group with cystic fibrosis did not show elevated rates. Similarly, another study found that five out of 15 children with CFS reached criteria for major depressive disorder and the rest showed many depressive symptoms (Smith *et al.*, 1991).

Such findings are not absolutely consistent and in a clinical report, Vereker (1992) described 10 children aged 10–17 with CFS and reported that none met full DSM-IIIR criteria for depressive disorders. Sampling and assessment differences probably account for the discrepancy.

Many symptoms of CFS are similar to those of depression, causing diagnostic difficulty, but symptom patterns have been shown to vary. In adolescents who were depressed, 92% reported depressed mood and 92% anhedonia compared to only 10% and 50% respectively of adolescents with CFS who were not depressed (Smith *et al.*, 1991).

It is sometimes asserted that particular viral infections such as infectious mononucleosis and hepatitis A can be followed by a pure depressive disorder (not CFS) but there are no hard data to support this.

In summary, rates of depression in children with CFS appear similar to those found in adults with CFS, although this is not true in all studies and the probability of referral bias remains. The nature of the relationship between depression and CFS remains unclear. Symptoms of depressed mood and anhedonia seem useful in making a diagnosis of depression in this group.

Cystic fibrosis

Most studies do not reveal increased rates of depressive disorder in this group (Burke *et al.*, 1989; Thompson *et al.*, 1990). However, older adolescents and adults report more depression and anxiety than younger children and adolescents, who report more eating disorders (Pearson *et al.*, 1991).

There are conflicting results concerning the role of maternal adjustment in this group. Maternal self-report depression has been described as not associated with child self-report depression (Mullins *et al.*, 1995) whereas poor maternal adjustment is related to poor psychosocial functioning in the child (Thompson *et al.*, 1992).

In summary, children with cystic fibrosis do not appear to be at increased risk of depression although it is possible that older adolescents are.

Diabetes mellitus

Children with insulin-dependent diabetes mellitus have not been shown to be at elevated risk of major depressive disorder in the long term (Kovacs *et al.*, 1990) but may show elevated rates of self-reported depressive symptoms (Seigel *et al.*, 1990) and depression following diagnosis (Kovacs *et al.*, 1985). Of 74 newly diagnosed diabetic children 4% had major depressive disorder post-diagnosis and most recovered within 9 months without treatment (Kovacs *et al.*, 1985). Follow up over the first 6 years of diabetes revealed a mild increase in self-reported depressive symptoms after the first year but scores were not clinically significant and were lower than general population norms. Increasing duration of diabetes was associated with increased symptoms of depression and anxiety for girls but not boys. Adjustment in terms of depressive symptoms, anxiety and self-esteem shortly after diagnosis predicted later adjustment (Kovacs *et al.*, 1990).

Depressive symptoms in adolescents may be associated with poorer adherence to treatment (Littlefield *et al.*, 1992).

A 14-year-old girl with previously good diabetic control began to develop frequent hypoglycaemic attacks which perplexed the paediatric staff. It became evident that she had become depressed and her food intake had reduced. Like many depressed teenagers she had concealed her depressive state of mind from her parents and staff. Not until her mental state was examined did her depressive disorder become recognized.

On the other hand, psychosocial variables were found to be more strongly related to noncompliance in one study (Eaton *et al.*, 1992). It has also been postulated that the effort to maintain good control may lead to depression (Close *et al.*, 1986). Suicide by insulin overdose is also a risk in adolescents (Kaminer and Robbins, 1988).

Developmental differences have also been described, with preadolescents describing significantly less depressive symptoms and fewer adjustment problems compared to adolescents (Grey *et al.*, 1991).

In a review of psychosocial issues in diabetes, Rodin concluded that depression and helplessness are more strongly related to inadequate treatment than to the diabetes itself (Rodin, 1983).

In summary, although some children develop depressive symptoms or even major depressive disorder following diagnosis, the majority recover within the first year. Depressive symptomatology during this period tends to be mild and not clinically significant but is one of several factors that predict later adjustment. The risk of suicide, particularly in adolescents, should be considered.

Epilepsy

Children with epilepsy are at increased risk of emotional and behavioural disorders with over twice the risk compared to children with physical disorders not involving the brain (Rutter *et al.*, 1970). There is a paucity of studies looking at depression in epileptic children. In an otherwise comprehensive review of psychological effects of chronic disease there was little mention of epilepsy (Eiser, 1990). In a meta-analysis of 60 studies looking at depression in children with chronic illnesses, Bennett (1994) found only one study dealing with epilepsy. This study, comparing asthma and epilepsy, found depressive symptoms to be more common in girls than boys in both illnesses (Austin, 1989). Depressive disorder in epilepsy may be due to the state of being chronically ill rather than epilepsy *per se* (Kaminer *et al.*, 1988).

Phenobarbitone treatment is associated with increased rates of depressive disorder, especially in those children with a positive personal or family history of affective disorder (Brent *et al.*, 1988, 1990).

In summary, no conclusions can be drawn with confidence and more research is needed concerning depression in children with epilepsy.

Haemophilia

Logan *et al.* (1990) compared 43 children aged 3–16 years with haemophilia with 46 matched diabetics and 42 healthy controls. The three groups did not differ in rates of self-reported depression, and neither did the nine haemophiliac children who were HIV-positive differ in their levels of psychiatric morbidity. It was hypothesized that this may have been due to the high levels of psychosocial support at the clinic. Social functioning and behaviour on parent and teacher ratings on the CBCL have also been reported as within the normal range (Colegrove and Huntzinger, 1994).

In summary, insufficient research is available on the risk of depression in children with haemophilia but the implication is that it is not increased.

Juvenile rheumatoid disease

Studies are hindered by the fact that questionnaire scores may be distorted due to questions reflecting disease severity rather than emotional or behaviour problems (Daltroy *et al.*, 1992). It has been shown that children who felt their disease limited their activities reported lower levels of self-worth, and felt physically less attractive, less popular than others in their peer group and poorer in terms of their athletic ability. Depression *per se* was not measured (Ennett *et al.*, 1991).

Organ transplantation

Windsorova *et al.* (1991) found that children who have had a liver transplant report fewer depressive symptoms on the CDI than norms and appear to be as well-adjusted as a comparison group of diabetic children. However, Rorschach tests were interpreted as indicating relatively more frequent depressive experiences in the transplant group suggesting that the children tended to self-report falsely low levels of depression.

Brownbridge and Fielding (1991) studied 73 children with end-stage renal failure and found that there was no overall difference in self-reported depression in children on dialysis compared to those who had a functioning transplant. Adaptation to dialysis may be particularly difficult for adolescents as this treatment requires them to become dependent just at the stage when developmentally they are beginning to separate from dependency objects (Viederman, 1974; Levy, 1981).

A study examining adult adjustment of 45 former paediatric renal patients (of whom 36 had a functioning transplant), compared to healthy controls, found no statistically significant difference in psychiatric morbidity between the two groups although there was a doubling of the rate of major depression in the renal group to 9%. It was noticed that the renal patients tended to attribute their psychological symptoms to their kidney disease. They had also had more psychiatric disturbance and treatment of psychological symptoms before the age of 17 (Morton *et al.*, 1994).

A recent study of 41 children who had heart and heart–lung transplants did not assess depression directly but found that 10 had significant problems, of which the majority were of the neurotic type (Wray *et al.*, 1994).

In summary, findings are sparse but renal transplantation may be associated with later depression, particularly in adult life, although the risk is small.

Sickle cell anaemia

Conflicting results have been described. Increased rates of self-reported depression, not accounted for by somatic items, have been found (Morgan and Jackson, 1986). In contrast, none of a sample of 50 7–17-year-olds met DSM-III criteria for major depressive disorder (Thompson *et al.*, 1993). However, this may in part be due to the average age in the former of 14 years 8 months and in the latter of 9 years. Seigel *et al.* (1990) also found increased rates of self-reported depression in adolescents compared to healthy controls but they did not differ from rates found in control groups with asthma or diabetes.

In summary, symptoms of depression appear to be more common in adolescents with sickle cell anaemia compared to younger children but to be similar to rates found in other chronic illnesses.

Conclusions

Interpretation of the literature is necessarily cautious due to the paucity of studies of depression in individual conditions. However, depressive symptomatology has been reported in asthma, sickle cell anaemia, cystic fibrosis and diabetes mellitus, most commonly during adolescence. Chronic fatigue syndrome appears to be particularly associated with depressive disorder. Adults who have had renal transplantation during childhood seem at slightly increased risk of major depression, even if the transplant was successful.

However, it is important to note that most children and adolescents who have a chronic physical illness are *not* depressed.

MANAGEMENT OF DEPRESSION IN SICK CHILDREN AND ADOLESCENTS

Management of depressed children and adolescents with a chronic medical illness is similar to that of those who are physically healthy, but particular attention needs to be given to exclusion of organic and iatrogenic causes of affective disturbance, to enhancement of adaptive coping mechanisms and informed prescribing if indicated. Close liaison with paediatric and nursing staff is vital.

History and examination

Assessment should involve obtaining information from the child, parents, teachers and significant others, including ward staff. Screening instruments may be helpful, but questionnaires cannot substitute for clinical judgement. Appreciation of parental adjustment and mental state, especially of the mother, is important. Mental state examination of the child must include assessment of suicidal ideation and risk. Physical examination will provide information about the severity of illness and disability, possible organic causes of mood disturbance and an understanding of the relevance of somatic complaints.

Depression should be considered in all youngsters presenting with noncompliance with treatment, especially in diabetes mellitus, asthma and epilepsy. Aggression, irritability, withdrawal from social activities, acts of self-harm (even if these appear to be accidental) and somatic complaints out of proportion to disease severity are also important.

Further information should be obtained about medication and whether or not pain control is adequate.

Psychological management of depression and depressive symptoms

If there are depressive symptoms which do not amount to a full depressive disorder, then all that may be required is sympathetic discussion with the child and family to encourage dialogue, understanding and support. Adolescents, and also sometimes younger children, should be given the opportunity to be seen on their own. This does not necessarily need to be offered by a psychiatrist or psychologist. Medical or nursing staff are well placed to provide such help and may have the advantage of an existing long-standing relationship with the family.

It is important that the needs of parents and siblings are also met. If the child is coping well it does not necessarily meant that the parents are (Mullins *et al.*, 1995).

Families should be encouraged to reinforce intact strengths and abilities of the sick child and organize events and tasks that the child can take part in successfully (Rodgers *et al.*, 1981).

Hospital staff can help adolescents by allowing them to have as much input into their care as possible to maintain their sense of autonomy, establishing peer groups on the ward and encouraging activities outside hospital if possible (Hofman, 1975).

Diabetic children can be encouraged to gain knowledge about their illness and show details of their diabetic management to their peers (e.g. blood testing) as these have been found to be helpful coping strategies (Kovacs *et al.*, 1986).

Depressive disorder will require more focused treatment. There is a paucity of studies evaluating different psychological treatments for depressed children, especially in those with a medical illness. Brief, structured interpersonal psychotherapy is one treatment that is showing promise (Harrington, 1993) and mild cases may respond to a cognitive approach (Wood *et al.*, 1996). Family work is frequently found to be helpful clinically since developmental issues may be avoided by the family by attempting to put all symptoms down to the illness (Strickland, 1991). The issues discussed above are also all relevant.

Pharmacological treatment

A recent meta-analysis of 12 randomized controlled trials comparing the efficacy of tricyclic antidepressants (TCAs) with placebo in depressed 6–18-year-olds concluded that they were no more effective than placebo for the treatment of depression in this group. A placebo response of up to 50% was found in some studies (Hazell *et al.*, 1995). They also found that many studies had poor randomization procedures and were not adequately blind. Hazell *et al.* discussed the fact that it is not clear why TCAs have not been shown to be effective in young people; however, rapid hepatic first-pass metabolism and the fact that the noradrenergic system is not fully developed until adulthood may be of importance. The hormonal milieu in adolescence is also thought by some to have an effect on neurotransmitter activity, although this is largely speculative. The paper has been criticized on a number of counts but it is still true that unequivocal evidence for TCA efficacy in childhood depression is lacking.

However, many clinicians still feel that it is worth a trial of antidepressant medication using a tricyclic or particularly a specific serotonin reuptake inhibitor, especially in severe depression in adolescents with pronounced biological symptoms (who would have been a small minority in the studies examined by Hazell *et al.*). TCAs are suitable for use in depressed children with renal disease as there in no major removal by the kidney and therefore they are not removed by dialysis (Levy, 1981). However, steady state fluctuations are common and may lead to poor clinical response (Dawlings *et al.*, 1982).

It is possible that small doses may be needed in children with cancer. Pfefferbaum-Levine *et al.* (1983) reported more rapid clinical and rating scale responses to TCA doses of under 2 mg per kg per day in eight terminal cancer patients aged 4–16 years compared to healthy children. However, they did acknowledge that it was unclear if the effect was a placebo response or due to sedative or anxiolytic effects.

Close liaison with medical staff will be required to avoid drug interactions and harmful effects on the child's medical condition. Full medical work-up will be needed, as will conservative starting doses and careful monitoring. Blood levels may be indicated to avoid toxicity.

Social interventions

Practical interventions should be considered such as ensuring adequate social and respite support for the family, accessibility to state financial benefits and introduction to support groups.

Integrated treatment

It is vital that all the management techniques described above are used in combination for maximum effectiveness. Multidisciplinary teamwork may be required in complex cases.

PROGNOSIS OF DEPRESSIVE DISORDER

Among healthy children, most recover from a major depression within 2 years and often much sooner. Unfortunately, children and adolescents who have suffered a major depressive episode are likely to experience a recurrence (Poznanski *et al.*, 1976; Harrington, 1993). On first principles, the chance of recurrence would depend on whether the depression was thought to be precipitated by aspects of physical illness or whether depression and illness coincide, the depression having other precipitants. Available data do not allow a firm view although survivors of childhood cancer do not have an increased risk of depression compared to their siblings (Teta *et al.*, 1989).

RESEARCH QUESTIONS

The scope for research into the field of depression in children and adolescents with a chronic medical illness is enormous. In addition to areas highlighted above, studies need to look at outpatient populations of sick children, discover why there are disease-specific difference in rates of depression and what protects children from depression, develop standardized measurements of depression in this group, and evaluate the use of antidepressant medication and the efficacy of different forms and combinations of psychosocial interventions.

REFERENCES

Achenbach TM, McConaughy SH and Howell CT (1987) Child/adolescent behavioral and emotional problems: Implications of cross-informant correlations of situational specificity. *Psychol Bull*, **101**, 213–232.

American Psychiatric Association (1987) *Diagnostic and Statistical Manual of Mental Disorders*. Washington, DC: APA.

Anderson JC, Williams S, McGee R and Silva PA (1987) DSM-III disorders in preadolescent children: Prevalence in a large sample from the general population. *Arch Gen Psychiatry*, **44**, 69–76.

Austin JK (1989) Comparison of child adaptation to epilepsy and asthma. *Child Adolesc Psychiatric Ment Health Nursing*, **2**, 139–144.

Bender BG,, Lerner JA, Ikle D, Comer C and Szefler S (1991a) Psychological change associated with theophylline treatment of asthmatic children: A 6-month study. *Pediatr Pulmonol*, **11**, 233–242.

Bender BG, Lerner JA and Poland JE (1991b) Association between corticosteroids and psychologic change in hospitalised asthmatic children. *Ann Allergy*, **66**, 414–419.

Bennett DS (1994) Depression among children with chronic medical problems: A meta-analysis. Special Issue: Chronic illness. *Pediatr Psychol*, **19(2)**, 149–169.

Berenbaum J and Hatcher J (1992) Emotional distress of mothers of hospitalized children. *Pediatr Psychol*, **17(3)**, 359–372.

Birleson P (1981) The validity of depressive disorder in childhood and the development of a self-rating scale: A research project. *J Child Psychol Psychiatry*, **22**, 73–88.

Brent DA, Crumrine PK, Varma RR, Allan M and Allman C (1988) Phenobarbital treatment and major depressive disorder in children with epilepsy. *Pediatrics*, **80(6)**, 909–917.

Brent DA, Crumrine PK, Varma R, Brown RV and Allan MJ (1990) Phenobarbital treatment and major depressive disorder in children with epilepsy: A naturalistic follow-up. *Pediatrics*, **85(6)**, 1086–1091.

Brown RT, Kaslow NF, Madan-Swain A, Doepkr KJ, Sexson SB and Hill LF (1993) Parental psychopathology and children's adjustment to leukemia. *J Am Acad Child Adolesc Psychiatry*, **32(3)**, 554–561.

Brownbridge G and Fielding DM (1991) Psychosocial adjustment to end-stage renal failure: Comparing haemodialysis, continuous ambulatory peritoneal dialysis and transplantation. *Pediatr Nephrol*, **5**, 612–616.

Brumback RA, Wilson H and Station RD (1984) Behaviour problems in children taking theophylline. *Lancet*, **1**, 958.

Buckley JM (1980) Asthma and depression. *Hosp Pract*, **15(4)**, 20–28.

Burke P, Meyer V, Kocoshis S, Orenstein DM, Chandra R and Nord DJ (1989) Depression and anxiety in pediatric inflammatory bowel disease and cystic fibrosis. *J Am Acad Child Adolesc Psychiatry*, **28(6)**, 948–951.

Cadman D, Boyle M, Szatmari P and Offord DR (1987) Chronic illness, disability, and mental and social well-being: Findings of the Ontario Child Health Study. *Pediatrics*, **79**, 805–812.

Canning EH and Kelleher K (1994) Performance of screening tools for mental health problems in chronically ill children. *Arch Pediatr Adolesc Med*, **148(3)**, 272–278.

Canning EH, Canning RD and Boyce WT (1992) Depressive symptoms and adaptive style in children with cancer. *J Am Acad Child Adolesc Psychiatry*, **31(6)**, 1120–1124.

Chambers W, Puig-Antich J, Hirsch M *et al.* (1985) The assessment of affective disorder to children and adolescents by semi-structured interview: Test–retest reliability of the K-SADS-P. *Arch Gen Psychiatry*, **42**, 696–702.

Chiles JA, Miller ML and Cox GB (1980) Depression in an adolescent delinquent population. *Arch Gen Psychiatry*, **37**, 1179–1184.

Close H, Davies AG, Price DA and Goodyer IM (1986) Emotional difficulties in diabetes mellitus. *Arch Dis Child*, **61(4)**, 337–340.

Colegrove RW Jr and Huntzinger RM (1994) Academic, behavioral, and social adaptation of boys with hemophilia/HIV disease. *J Pediatr Psychol*, **19(4)**, 457–473.

Costello EJ, Edelbrock CS and Costello AJ (1985) Validity of the NIMH Diagnostic Interview Schedule for Children: A comparison between psychiatric and pediatric referrals. *J Abnorm Child Psychol*, **13**, 579–595.

Daltroy LH, Larson MG, Eaton HM, Partridge AJ, Pless IB, Rogers MP and Liang MH (1992) Psychosocial adjustment in juvenile arthritis. *J Pediatr Psychol*, **17(3)**, 277–289.

David AS, Wessely S and Pelosi AJ (1991) Chronic fatigue syndrome: signs of a new approach. *Br J Hosp Med*, **45**, 158–163.

Dawlings S, Lynn K, Rosser R and Braithwaite R (1982) Nortryptyline metabolism in chronic renal failure: Metabolite elimination. *Clin Pharmacol Ther*, **32(3)**, 322–329.

Dunitz M, Scheer PJ, Wurst L, Grientschnigg G and Urban EC (1991) Depression in children with cancer. *Padiatrie Padologie*, **26(6)**, 267–270.

Eaton WW, Mengel M, Mengel L, Larson D, Campbell R and Motague RB (1992) Psychosocial and psychopathologic influences on management and control of insulin-dependent diabetes. *Int J Psychiatry Med*, **22(2)**, 105–117.

Eiser C (1990) Psychological effects of chronic disease. *J Child Psychol Psychiatry*, **31(1)**, 85–98.

Elkind D (1985) Cognitive development and adolescent disabilities. *J Adolesc Health Care*, **6(2)**, 84–89.

Ennett ST, DeVellis BM, Earp JA, Kredich D, Warren RA and Wilhelm CL (1991) Disease experience and psychosocial adjustment in children with juvenile rheumatoid arthritis: Children's versus mother's reports. *J Pediatr Psychol*, **16**, 557–568.

Fleming JE, Offord DR and Boyle MH (1989) Prevalence of childhood and adolescent depression in the community: Ontario child health study. *Br J Psychiatry*, **155**, 647–654.

Fritz GK, Rubinstein S and Lewiston NJ (1987) Psychological factors in fatal childhood asthma. *Am J Orthopsychiatry*, **57(2)**, 253–257.

Furukawa CT, DuHamel TR, Weimer L, Shapiro GG, Pierson WE and Bierman CW (1988) Cognitive and behavioral findings in children taking theophylline. *J Allergy Clin Immunol*, **81**, 83–88.

Gizynski M and Shapiro VB (1990) Depression and childhood illness. *Child Adolesc Soc Work*, **7**, 179–197.

Greenberg HS, Kazak AE and Meadows AT (1989) Psychologic functioning in 8 to 16-year-old cancer survivors and their parents. *J Pediatr*, **114**, 488–493.

Grey M, Cameron ME and Thurber FW (1991) Coping and adaptation in children with diabetes. *Nursing Res*, **40(3)**, 144–149.

Harrington RC (1992) Annotation: The natural history and treatment of child and adolescent affective disorders. *J Child Psychol Psychiatry*, **33(8)**, 1287–1302.

Harrington R (1993) *Depressive Disorder in Childhood and Adolescence*. Chichester: Wiley.

Hazell P, O'Connell D, Heathcote D, Robertson J and Henry D (1995) Efficacy of tricyclic drugs in treating child and adolescent depression: a meta-analysis. *Br Med J*, **310**, 897–901.

Herjanic B and Reich W (1982) Development of a structured psychiatric interview for children: Agreement between child and parent on individual symptoms. *J Abnorm Child Psychol*, **10**, 307–324.

Hofmann AD (1975) The impact of illness in adolescence and coping behavior. *Acta Paediatr Scand Supplement*, **256**, 29–33.

Kaminer Y and Robbins D (1988) Attempted suicide by insulin overdose in insulin-dependent diabetic adolescents. *Pediatrics*, **81**, 526–528.

Kaminer Y, Apter A, Aviv A, Lerman P and Tyano S (1988) Psychopathology and temporal lobe epilepsy in adolescents. *Acta Psychiatr Scand*, **77(6)**, 640–644.

Kaplan SL, Grossman P, Landa B, Shenker IR and Weinhold C (1986) Depressive symptoms and life events in physically ill hospitalized adolescents. *J Adolesc Health Care*, **7(2)**, 107–111.

Kaplan SL, Busner J, Weinhold C and Lenon P (1987) Depressive symptoms in children and adolescents with cancer: A longitudinal study. *J Am Acad Child Adolesc Psychiatry*, **26**, 782–787.

Kashani JH and Breedlove L (1994) Depression in medically ill youngsters. In: WM Reynolds and HF Johnston (eds) *Handbook of Depression in Children and Adolescents. Issues in Clinical Child Psychology.* New York: Plenum Press, 427–443.

Kashani J and Hakami N (1982) Depression in children and adolescents with malignancy. *Can J Psychiatry*, **27**, 474–477.

Kashani JH and Simmonds JF (1979) Incidence of depression in children. *Am J Psychiatry*, **136**, 1203–1205.

Kashani JH, McGee R, Clarkson S, Anderson J, Walton L, Williams S, Silva P, Robins A, Cytryn M and McKnew D (1983) Depression in a sample of 9-year-old children: Prevalence and associated characteristics. *Arch Gen Psychiatry*, **40**, 1217–1223.

Kashani JH, Beck NC, Hoeper EW, Fallahi C, Corcoran CM, McAllister JA, Rosenberg TK and Reid JC (1987) Psychiatric disorders in a community sample of adolescents. *Am J Psychiatry*, **144**, 584–589.

Kazdin AE (1990) Childhood depression. *J Child Psychol Psychiatry*, **31**, 121–160.

Kovacs M (1978) *Interview Schedule for Children (ISC)* (10th revision). Pittsburgh, PA: University of Pittsburgh School of Medicine.

Kovacs M and Beck AT (1977) An empirical clinical approach towards a definition of childhood depression. In: JG Schulterbrandt and A Raskin (eds) *Depression in Children: Diagnosis, Treatment, and Conceptual Models.* New York: Raven Press, 1–25.

Kovacs M, Feinberg TL, Paulauskas S, Finkelstein R, Pollock M and Crouse-Novak M (1985) Initial coping responses and psychosocial characteristics of children with insulin-dependent diabetes mellitus. *J Pediatr*, **106(5)**, 827–834.

Kovacs M, Brent D, Steinberg TF, Paulauskas S and Reid J (1986) Children's self-report of psychologic adjustment and coping strategies during the first year of insulin-dependent diabetes mellitus. *Diabetes Care*, **9**, 472–479.

Kovacs M, Iyengar S, Goldston D, Stewart J, Obrosky DS and Marsh J (1990) Psychological functioning of children with insulin-dependent diabetes mellitus: A longitudinal study. *J Pediatr Psychol*, **15**, 619–632.

Kvist SBM, Rajantie J, Kvist M and Simes MA (1991) Aggression: The dominant psychological response in children with malignant disease. *Psychol Rep*, **68**, 1139–1150.

Lang M and Tisher M (1978) *Children's Depression Scale.* Victoria, Australia: Australian Council for Educational Research.

Levy NB (1981) Psychological reactions to machine dependency: Hemodialysis. *Psychiatr Clin North Am*, **4(2)**, 351–363.

Lewiston NJ and Rubinstein S (1986) Sudden death in adolescent asthma. *N Engl Regional Allergy Proc*, **7(5)**, 448–453.

Lewiston NJ and Rubinstein S (1987) The young Damocles. The adolescent at a high risk for serious or fatal status asthmaticus. *Clin Rev Allergy*, **5(3)**, 273–284.

Lipowski ZJ (1971) Physical illness, the individual and the coping process. *Psychiatr Med*, **1**, 91–98.

Littlefield CH, Daneman D, Craven JL, Murray MA, Rodin GM and Rydall AC (1992) Relationship of self-efficacy and bingeing to adherence to diabetes regimen among adolescents. *Diabetes Care*, **15**, 90–94.

Logan FA, Maclean A, Howie CA, Gibson B, Hann IM and Parry-Jones WL (1990) Psychological disturbance in children with haemophilia. *Br Med J*, **301**, 1253–1256.

McCauley E, Carlson GA and Calderon R (1991) The role of somatic complaints in the diagnosis of depression in children and adolescents. *J Am Acad Child Adolesc Psychiatry*, **30**, 631–635.

McGee R, Feehan M, Williams S and Anderson J (1992) DSM-III disorders from age 11 to age 15 years. *J Am Acad Child Adolesc Psychiatry*, **31**, 50–59.

Miller BD (1987) Depression and asthma: a potentially lethal mixture. *J Allergy Clin Immunol*, **80**, 481–486.

Morgan SA and Jackson J (1986) Psychological and social concomitants of sickle cell anemia in adolescents. *J Pediatr Psychol*, **11**, 429–440.

Morton MJ, Reynolds JM, Garralda ME, Postlethwaite RJ and Goh D (1994) Psychiatric adjustment in end-stage renal disease: a follow up study of former paediatric patients. *J Psychosom Res*, **38(4)**, 293–303.

Mulhern RK, Fairclough DL, Smith B and Douglas SM (1992) Maternal depression, assessment methods, and physical symptoms affect estimates of depressive symptomatology among children with cancer. *J Pediatr Psychol*, **17(3)**, 313–326.

Mullins LL, Chaney JM, Hartman VL, Olson RA, Youll LK, Reyes S and Blackett P (1995) Child and maternal adaptation to cystic fibrosis and insulin-dependent diabetes mellitus: differential patterns across disease states. *J Pediatr Psychol*, **20(2)**, 173–186.

Nelms BC (1989) Emotional behaviors in chronically ill children. *J Abnorm Child Psychol*, **17(6)**, 657–668.

Olsen RA, Holden EW, Friedman A, Faust J, Kenning M and Mason PJ (1988) Psychological consultation in a children's hospital: An evaluation of services. *J Pediatr Psychol*, **13**, 479–492.

Pearson DA, Pumariega AJ and Seilheimer DK (1991) The development of psychiatric symptomatology in patients with cystic fibrosis. *J Am Acad Child Adolesc Psychiatry*, **30(2)**, 290–297.

Petti TA (1978) Depression in hospitalised child psychiatry patients: Approaches to measuring depression. *J Am Acad Child Psychiatry*, **17**, 49–59.

Pfefferbaum-Levine B, Kumor K, Cangir A, Choroszy M and Roseberry EA (1983) Tricyclic antidepressants for children with cancer. *Am J Psychiatry*, **140(8)**, 1074–1076.

Pless IB and Roghmann KJ (1971) Chronic illness and its consequences; observations based on three epidemiologic surveys. *J Pediatr*, **79**, 351–359.

Pless IB, Cripps HA, Davies JNC and Wadsworth MEJ (1989) Chronic physical illness in childhood: psychological and social effects in adolescence and adult life. *Dev Med Child Neurol*, **31**, 746–775.

Powell R, Dolan R and Wessely S (1990) Attributions and self-esteem in depression and chronic fatigue syndrome. *J Psychosom Res*, **34**, 665–673.

Poznanski E, Zrull JP and Krahenbuhl V (1976) Childhood depression. *J Am Acad Child Adolesc Psychiatry*, **15**, 491–501.

Poznanski EO, Cook SC and Carroll BJ (1979) A depression rating scale for children. *Pediatrics*, **64**, 442–450.

Poznanski EO, Mokros HD, Grossman J *et al.* (1985) Diagnostic criteria in childhood depression. *Am J Psychiatry*, **142**, 1168–1173.

Ray C (1991) Chronic fatigue syndrome and depression: conceptual and methodological difficulties. *Psychol Med*, **21**, 1–9.

Reinherz HZ, Stewart-Berghauer G, Pakiz B, Frost A, Moeykens B and Holmes W (1989) The relationship of early risk and current mediators to depressive symptomatology in adolescence. *J Am Acad Child Adolesc Psychiatry*, **28**, 942–947.

Reynolds WM and Coats KI (1986) A comparison of cognitive-behavioral therapy and relaxation training for the treatment of depression in adolescents. *J Consult Clin Psychol*, **54**, 653–660.

Rodgers BM, Hillemeier MM, O'Neill E and Slomin MB (1981) Depression in the chronically ill or handicapped school-aged child. *Am J Matern Child Nursing*, **6(4)**, 266–273.

Rodin GM (1983) Psychosocial aspects of diabetes mellitus. *Can J Psychiatry—Revue Canadienne de Psychiatrie*, **28(3)**, 219–223.

Rutter M, Tizard J and Whitmore K (1970) *Education, Health and Behaviour*. London: Longman.

Rutter M, Izard CE and Read PB (eds) (1986) *Depression in Young People: Developmental and Clinical Perspectives*. New York: Guilford Press, 491–519.

Sandler IN, Reynolds KD, Kliewer W and Ramirez R (1992) Specificity of the relation between life events and psychological symptomatology. *J Clin Child Psychol*, **21**, 240–248.

Seidel V, Chadwick O and Rutter M (1975) Psychological disorders in crippled children. *Dev Med Child Neurol*, **17**, 563–573.

Seigel WM, Golden NH, Gough JW, Lashley MS and Sacker IM (1990) Depression, self-esteem and life events in adolescents with chronic diseases. *J Adolesc Health Care*, **11(6)**, 501–504.

Silverglade L, Tosi DJ, Wise PS and D'Costa A (1994) Irrational beliefs and emotionality in adolescents with and without bronchial asthma. *J Gen Psychol*, **121(3)**, 199–207.

Smith MS, Mitchell J, Corey L *et al.* (1991) Chronic fatigue in adolescents. *Pediatrics*, **88**, 195–202.

Solnit A and Stark M (1961) Mourning and the birth of a defective child. In: R Eissler, M Kris and A Freud (eds) *An Anthology of the Psychoanalytic Study of the Child. Physical Illness and Handicap in Childhood*. **16**, 523–537.

Speechley KN and Noh S (1992) Surviving childhood cancer, social support and parent's psychological adjustment. *J Pediatr Psychol*, **17(1)**, 15–31.

Strickland MC (1991) Depression, chronic fatigue syndrome and the adolescent. *Primary Care*, **18(2)**, 259–271.

Strunk RC, Mrazek DA, Fuhrmann GS and LaBrecque JF (1985) Physiologic and psychological characteristics associated with deaths due to asthma in childhood. A case-controlled study. *JAMA*, **254(9)**, 1193–1198.

Taylor DC and Eminson DM (1994) Psychological aspects of chronic physical sickness. In: M Rutter, E Taylor and L Hersov (eds) *Child and Adolescent Psychiatry. Modern Approaches*. Third Edition. Oxford: Blackwell Scientific, 737–748.

Tebbi CK, Bromberg C and Mallon J (1988) Self-reported depression in adolescent cancer patients. *Am J Pediatr Hematol Oncol*, **10**, 185–190.

Teta MJ, Del Po MC, Kasl SV, Meigs JW, Meyers MH and Mulvihill JJ (1986) Psychosocial consequences of childhood and adolescent cancer survival. *J Chronic Dis*, **39**, 751–759.

Thompson RJ, Hodges K and Hamlett KW (1990) A matched comparison of adjustment in children with cystic fibrosis and psychiatrically referred and nonreferred children. *J Pediatr Psychol*, **15**, 745–759.

Thompson RJ, Gustafson KE, Hamlett KW and Spock A (1992) Psychological adjustment of children with cystic fibrosis: The role of child cognitive processes and maternal adjustment. *J Pediatr Psychol*, **17**, 741–755.

Thompson RJ Jr, Gil KM, Burbach DJ, Keith BR and Kinney TR (1993) Role of child and maternal processes in the psychological adjustment of children with sickle cell disease. *J Consult Clin Psychology*, **61(3)**, 468–474.

Timko C, Stovel KW and Moos RH (1992) Functioning among mothers and fathers of children with juvenile rheumatoid disease: A longitudinal study. *J Pediatr Psychol*, **17**, 705–724.

Velez CN, Johnson J and Cohen P (1989) A longitudinal analysis of selected risk factors for childhood psychopathology. *J Am Acad Child Adolesc Psychiatry*, **28**, 861–864.

Vereker MI (1992) Chronic fatigue syndrome: a joint paediatric–psychiatric approach. *Arch Dis Child*, **67(4)**, 550–555.

Viederman M (1974) Adaptive and maladaptive regression in haemodialysis. *Psychiatry*, **37**, 68–77.

Walford GA, Nelson WM and McCluskey DR (1993) Fatigue, depression, and social adjustment in chronic fatigue syndrome. *Arch Dis Child,* **68(3)**, 384–388.

Walker LS, Ortiz-Valdes JA and Newbrough JR (1989) The role of maternal employment and depression in the psychological adjustment of chronically ill, mentally retarded and well children. *J Pediatr Psychol*, **14(3)**, 357–370.

Walker LS, Van Slyke DA and Newbrough JR (1992) Family resources and stress: A comparison of families of children with cystic fibrosis, diabetes, and mental retardation. *J Pediatr Psychol*, **17(3)**, 327–343.

Weinberger M, Lindgren S, Bender B, Lerner JA and Szefler S (1987) Effects of theophylline on learning and behavior: Reasons for concern or concern without reason? *J Pediatr Psychol*, **111(3)**, 471–474.

Whitaker A, Johnson J, Shaffer D, Rapoport JL, Kalikow K, Walsh BT, Davies M, Braiman S and Dolinsky A (1990) Uncommon troubles in young people; prevalence estimates of selected psychiatric disorders in a nonreferred adolescent population. *Arch Gen Psychiatry*, **47**, 487–496.

Windsorova DM, Stewart SM, Lovitt R, Waller DA and Andrews WS (1991) Emotional adaptation in children after liver transplant. *J Pediatr*, **119(6)**, 880–887.

Wood A, Harrington R and Moore A (1996) Controlled trial of a brief cognitive-behavioural intervention in adolescent patients with depressive disorders. *J Child Psychol Psychiatry*, **37**, 737–746.

Worchel FF (1989) Denial of depression; adaptive coping in pediatric patients? *Newsletter Soc Pediatr Psychol*, **13**, 8–11.

Worchel FF, Nolan BF, Willson VL, Purser JS, Copeland DR and Pfefferbaum B (1988) Assessment of depression in children with cancer. *J Pediatr Psychol*, **13**, 101–112.

Worchel FF, Rae WA, Olsen TK and Crowley SL (1992) Selective responsiveness of chronically ill children to assessments of depression. *J Pers Assess*, **59(3)**, 605–615.

Wray J, Pot-Mees C, Zeitlin H, Radley-Smith R and Yacoub M (1994) Cognitive function and behavioural status in paediatric heart and heart-lung transplant recipients: The Harefield experience. *Br Med J*, **309**, 837–841.

10

Depression in elderly people with physical illness

Zuzana Walker and Cornelius L.E. Katona

INTRODUCTION

The association between physical illness and depression in older people is well recognized (Eastwood and Corbin, 1986). However, the causal relationships between the two are far from clear. There are several possibilities: the coexistence of depression and physical illness may be coincidental; depression may lead to physical illness; physical illness may lead to depression; or, most likely, there is a two-way interaction. Depressive symptoms may at times be appropriate to the context of physical illness and may require only supportive care. In many cases, however, symptoms persist for an extended period and interfere with recovery, rehabilitation, social functioning or even basic self-care. Recognizing depression in older people with physical illness and managing it effectively, although more difficult than in younger adults, may make a considerable contribution to improving patient care. Distinguishing between the mere presence of one or more depressive symptoms and clinical depression may be crucial.

PREVALENCE

Depression is consistently reported to occur more commonly in physically ill elderly subjects than in their healthy counterparts. This may be particularly true

Depression and Physical Illness. Edited by M.M. Robertson and C.L.E. Katona
© 1997 John Wiley & Sons Ltd

for some subgroups of the elderly. Beekman *et al.* (1995) studied a community sample of 224 subjects in the Netherlands and found that the association between poor physical health and depression was much stronger for the old-old (age > 75) and for men than for the young-old (55–64) and women. They also noted that more subjective measures of physical health (pain and self-rating of health) appeared to have a much stronger relation with depression than relatively objective measures (number of chronic diseases, degree of functional limitation). Kennedy *et al.* (1990) found that 30% of elderly subjects in the community with four or more medical conditions were depressed compared with only 5% of those with no medical illnesses. Similarly, Evans and Katona (1993) found that the prevalence of depression in elderly primary care attenders with poor physical health was double that in the physically healthy.

The prevalence of depression in physically ill elderly inpatients has been reported as being between 11% and 59%, depending on the instrument used, sex, age and type of ward (Mayou and Hawton, 1986; Katona, 1994). Overall, the prevalence of affective disorder in elderly medical inpatients appears to be similar to that in comparable younger groups. This was confirmed in a systematic comparison by Koenig *et al.* (1992a) between older (age > 70) and younger men admitted to the medical wards of a veterans' hospital using DSM-IIIR criteria (APA, 1987). In contrast, however, Feldman *et al.* (1987) carried out a systematic comparison of patients aged 17–54, 55–69 and > 70 and found a much *lower* prevalence of depression in the elderly patients.

The relationships between major depression and age and gender among medical inpatients over the age of 65 have been examined by Fenton *et al.* (1994), also using DSM-IIIR criteria. They reported that the point prevalence rates of major depression in three age groups were similar: 28% for patients aged 65–74 years, 28% for those aged 75–84 years and 24% for those aged 85 years and older. The prevalence in women was over twice as high as that in men in the first two age groups, but virtually identical among men and women aged 85 years and older.

CLINICAL PRESENTATION

One of the difficulties clinicians face in recognizing depression in medically ill elderly patients is that it may present covertly, in particular with psychosomatic symptoms or with hypochondriasis, which may lead to confusion with the coexisting physical illness. On the other hand, somatic symptoms may result from the physical illness itself, and on their own they are poor predictors of depressive illness (Cavanaugh *et al.*, 1983). Stewart (1993) suggests that, although elderly patients may deny depression or sadness, the diagnosis should be suspected when they complain of anxiety, somatic symptoms (pain, constipation, fatigue), loss of concentration and difficulty with memory. To test the hypothesis that older age is associated with a decrease in self-reported depressive symptoms, Lyness *et al.* (1995) administered the Beck Depression Inventory (BDI) as a measure of self-reported symptoms and the Hamilton Rating Scale (Ham-D) for depression as a measure of examiner-rated symptoms to 97 subjects with DSM-IIIR major depression. Age was not associated with examiner-rated symptoms (Ham-D), but it had a highly significant negative correlation with self-reported depressive symptoms (BDI), older patients having much lower rates of self-reported symptoms. When BDI scores were divided into somatic/neurovegetative and psychological/affective subtotals, only the psychological/affective subtotal continued to have a significantly negative correlation with age, confirming that the decrease in self-reported symptoms was due specifically to under-reporting of affective and psychological symptoms, and not due to differences in somatic/neurovegetative symptoms. In keeping with this, Cavanaugh *et al.* (1983) suggest that the diagnosis of depression should be considered particularly when there is dysphoria or anhedonia which does not respond to treatment of the associated medical condition.

Summarizing the above, the following clinical pointers should be of help when making the diagnosis of depression in a physically ill elderly patient:

1. Previous psychiatric history.
2. Marked anxiety, agitation, irritability.
3. Feelings of guilt, self-depreciation.
4. Wish to be dead.
5. Loss of concentration, difficulties with memory.
6. Psychomotor retardation.
7. Complaints of pain, constipation, fatigue.
8. Poor compliance with medication.
9. Unsatisfactory rehabilitation or no response to adequate treatment.

DETECTION OF DEPRESSION BY PHYSICIANS

In view of the difficulties encountered in recognizing depression in medically ill elderly patients, it is perhaps not surprising that the rate of detection of depression by hospital physicians is low. In our recent study (Walker *et al.*, 1995) examining the point prevalence of psychiatric morbidity in 109 elderly patients presenting with physical illness at an accident and emergency department, 27% were found to be depressed and 16% were demented. Despite the fact that the attending doctors were asked specifically to make a judgement on the patient's mental state, they recognized only a very small proportion of the psychiatric morbidity (10%). Similar observations were made by Rapp *et al.* (1988a) and by Koenig *et al.* (1988a, 1992b). In the study by Rapp *et al.*, only 8.6% (2/23) of depressed inpatients were correctly recognized by junior medical staff. Koenig *et* al. (1988a) reported that among 15 patients identified to have major depression by DSM-III criteria, only three (20%) had depressive symptoms documented in their case notes by junior medical staff. In the same study, even after the junior doctors were informed that major depression was a possible diagnosis in these patients, only 27% (4/15) of the patients eventually had a psychiatric consultation and 13% (2/15) were started on antidepressant medication.

Rapp and Davis (1989) attempted to identify the possible reasons for the poor detection rate of depression in hospital inpatients, and concluded that, whereas medical residents considered detection and treatment of comorbid depression to be important, they knew few of the diagnostic criteria and aetiological factors, rarely screened their patients and viewed current treatments as only marginally effective. Koenig et al. (1992b) explain the low detection rate of depression by physicians on the basis that the majority of the depressed patients had concomitant severe medical illness and the urgent need for the care of multiple, complex medical problems in these patients was the primary focus of their physicians. In addition they reported that most physicians felt unsure about the risk–benefit ratio of known therapies of depression.

DEPRESSION AND LENGTH OF HOSPITAL STAY

A number of investigators have studied the impact of psychiatric morbidity on length of hospital admission, but no consensus has emerged (Johnson et al., 1987; Fulop et al., 1987; Koenig et al., 1989a; Ramsay et al., 1991; Rapp et al., 1991; Verbosky et al., 1993; Ames and Tuckwell, 1994). Two of the studies did not control for severity of physical illness (Johnson et al., 1987; Fulop et al., 1987). The others took severity of physical illness into account but reached differing conclusions. Koenig et al. (1989a), Verbosky et al. (1993) and Ames and Tuckwell (1994) found a relationship between depression and the length of hospital stay. In our study (Walker et al., 1995) depressed patients who were sufficiently ill to warrant admission had significantly longer hospital stays than patients who were not depressed. However, Rapp et al. (1991) and Ramsay et al. (1991) found no such association between depression and length of hospital stay. Verbosky et al. (1993) also found that, while depressed patients as a whole had a mean length of stay 10 days longer than nondepressed controls, the subgroup of depressed patients who were treated with antidepressants and supportive therapy had a mean length of stay 32 days shorter than those whose depression was not treated.

RISK FACTORS

The main risk factors for depression in physically ill elderly patients appear to be positive psychiatric history (Koenig et al., 1992; Feldman et al., 1987; Fenton *et al.*, 1994) and severity of the physical illness (Rapp *et al.*, 1991; Koenig *et al.*, 1988b). Among elderly elective surgical patients, Millar (1981) noted developing or persisting depression to be associated with postoperative medical complications. Coexisting cognitive dysfunction (Koenig *et al.*, 1988b, 1992a), lack of a support system (Koenig *et al.*, 1991) and a degree of functional disability (Fenton *et al.*, 1994; Koenig *et al.*, 1991; Dunham and Sager, 1994) have also been reported to be associated with an increased risk of depression.

EFFECT OF DEPRESSION ON THE OUTCOME OF PHYSICAL ILLNESS

There is mounting evidence that depression in old age is linked to higher than expected morbidity, disability and mortality from natural causes, and that these associations appear particularly strong in elderly patients with physical illness. Koenig *et al.* (1989a) found that elderly medical inpatients with major depression consumed more health care resources and suffered greater mortality. Harris *et al.* (1988) studied the association between depression and physical dependency arising from a recent physical illness. All patients whose mood improved also improved in physical functioning, whereas 75% of those whose mood did not improve failed to make headway in physical functioning. Bruce *et al.* (1994) followed up a community-based cohort of over 1000 high-functioning adults aged 70–79 for 2½ years. They showed that depressive symptoms at baseline were associated with an increased risk of onset of disability in activities of daily living for both men and women, even after adjusting for baseline sociodemographic factors, physical health status, and cognitive functioning. Aromaa *et al.* (1994) carried out a large two-stage (6 year follow up) random community survey of 1544 subjects aged 65 years or over and found that the relative risk of all-cause mortality and cardiovascular disease mortality was highest in depressed patients with cardiovascular disease. The relative risk of cardiovascular and coronary death was elevated even in depressed persons free of cardiovascular disease at entry. Ahern *et al.* (1990) looked at the major predictors of cardiac mortality and sudden death in the year after acute myocardial infarction and found that depression was one of the main risk factors for death or cardiac arrest, even allowing for other known clinical predictors of disease severity. Similarly, Silverstone (1990) studied 211 consecutive patients who had been admitted following a life-threatening illness (myocardial infarction, subarachnoid haemorrhage, pulmonary embolism or acute upper gastrointestinal haemorrhage) and found that 34% were significantly depressed. Although the depressed group did not have more severe physical illnesses, they did have a significantly poorer outcome over the subsequent 28 days: 47% of the depressed group (compared with only 10% of the nondepressed group) died or had a life-threatening complication. In keeping with this, Shamash *et al.* (1992) showed that in elderly patients undergoing emergency hip surgery, the effect of depression on mortality was independent of concurrent physical illness. Mortality was particularly high in subjects with both depression and dementia.

EFFECT OF PHYSICAL ILLNESS ON THE OUTCOME OF DEPRESSION

The prognosis of depression appears particularly poor in elderly subjects with concurrent physical illness. Murphy (1983) studied a cohort of hospital-referred depressed patients and found that acute new physical illness and chronic health problems predicted persistence or recurrence of the depression. Baldwin and Jolley (1986) reported similar findings in a consecutive sample of elderly depressed inpatients. Whereas 91% of those experiencing a lasting recovery from depression had had no active physical pathology at initial presentation, 71% of those with persistent depression had had at least one active physical health problem at the time of admission. Green *et al.* (1994), however, in a 3 year follow up study of depressed patients, found no association between physical ill-health and incapacity and persistent or recurrent depression.

PHYSICAL ILLNESS AND MORTALITY IN OLDER DEPRESSED SUBJECTS

With few exceptions (Fredman *et al.*, 1989; Thomas *et al.*, 1992), studies investigating the prognosis of depression in the elderly have found a higher than expected mortality at follow up (Murphy, 1983; Murphy *et al.*, 1988; Bruce and Leaf, 1989; Ashby *et al.*, 1991; Dewey *et al.*, 1993; Burvill and Hall, 1994). This cannot be explained by an excess of suicides or by the higher baseline prevalence of physical illness among depressed patients. Although physical health contributes to the excess mortality, depression appears to have an independent effect. Carney *et al.* (1995) hypothethized that one of the mechanisms underlying the increase in mortality in elderly depressed medical patients might be their poor adherence to medical treatment regimes. They assessed medication compliance of 55 patients over the age of 65 with coronary artery disease who were prescribed low dose aspirin. Ten of the patients met the DSM-III criteria for major depression. Nondepressed patients adhered to the regime on 69% of days, but depressed patients on only 45%. Poor compliance with prescribed medication may indeed thus be one of the factors responsible for the higher rates of mortality in depressed medically ill patients.

Treatment of depression itself might have an adverse effect on morbidity and mortality. Pollock *et al.* (1994) studied the effect of long-term nortriptyline (within the therapeutic concentrations) on physiological functions in 26 depressed patients over the age of 60 and found that after approximately 6 months of treatment there was no significant change in cholesterol levels, but triglycerides and very-low-density lipoproteins (VLDL) were significantly increased. Heart rate was also elevated, and there were modest but significant changes in cardiac parameters and in creatinine clearance, which declined by 34%. Against this are the findings of Katz *et al.* (1994), who, in a retrospective case note study, explored the extent to which treatment of depression affected survival in elderly subjects in residential care. They found that there was no difference between the death rate of elderly residents taking antidepressants or any other psychotropic medication and the death rate of the rest of the residents. Interestingly, in a subsequent prospective phase of the same study, patients who were depressed but not able to tolerate antidepressants due to side-effects exhibited significantly higher mortality. This suggests that inability to tolerate treatment with antidepressants, rather than the treatment itself, may be associated with increased mortality.

TREATMENT

As the above evidence suggests, clinicians treating depressed elderly patients with concurrent physical illness should be alert to contraindications to antidepressants and to the development of side-effects. According to Katz *et al.* (1990, 1994), side-effects are more prevalent in the frail elderly and for this reason a lower dose of tricyclic antidepressants may be necessary. Most elderly physically ill patients take a number of therapeutic agents and there is the potential for drug interaction. Particular care is also needed because of the danger of toxic effects in overdose (Montgomery, 1990). The danger of such side-effects is easy to exaggerate and therapeutic nihilism is a trap in elderly medical patients with coexisting depression.

Undertaking controlled trials of antidepressant treatments in elderly patients presents formidable problems, as exemplified by the attrition rate experienced by Koenig *et al.* (1986), who attempted a trial of nortriptyline versus placebo in elderly patients admitted to the medical wards of a veterans' hospital. Although 964 patients were evaluated, only 773 had well enough preserved cognitive function to allow Geriatric Depression Scale (GDS) screening. Eighty-one patients scored positive for depression and 63 were further evaluated by a psychiatrist. Forty-one patients were found to have DSM-III major depressive episode, but 14 of them had already been treated with antidepressants, 15 had medical contraindications to their use and five refused. Of the remaining seven subjects who could be randomized, four dropped out. Thus, out of nearly 1000 potential subjects screened, only three completed the study. Two were on placebo and one on nortriptyline; all three improved!

A number of small trials, however, have been successfully completed. Lipsey *et al.* (1984) demonstrated the efficacy of nortriptyline in the treatment of poststroke depression in a double-blind study of 34 patients with a mean age of approximately 60 years. Patients who were successfully treated had serum nortriptyline levels in the conventional therapeutic range. It should be noted, however, that only 14 patients were on active treatment, and three of these developed antidepressant-related acute confusional states. Reding *et al.* (1986) reported that trazodone showed a nonsignificant trend towards benefit when compared with placebo in stroke patients. Their findings are however difficult to interpret since not all subjects entered into the trial were clinically depressed and the main outcome measure was change in level of dependency rather than alleviation of depression. Schifano *et al.* (1990) compared the efficacy of mianserin and maprotiline in 48 elderly physically ill subjects with DSM-IIIR major depression or dysthymia (four cases). Thirty-five patients completed the trial, with mianserin showing significant superiority in terms of GDS scores. Only 40% of subjects in each group, however, showed improvement in terms of clinical global impression. More recently, Tan *et al.* (1994) have reported a double-blind, randomized 28-day trial of low dose lofepramine (70 mg once daily) compared with placebo in 63 depressed elderly inpatients on medical wards. Forty-six patients completed the trial. Both groups showed similar improvement during the trial. Lofepramine tended to be more effective than placebo in those patients who were more severely depressed (GDS ≥ 18). However, in patients who were less severely depressed (GDS < 18), improvement was greater in those on placebo. Koenig *et al.* (1992b) followed up 53 elderly men with medical illness and DSM-IIIR major depression for a mean of 2.3 months and found that, of the 33 patients still alive at follow up, 64% had persistent depression, 18% had some improvement of depressive symptoms, and 18% were in complete remission. Psychiatric consultation or pharmacotherapy had little impact on outcome. However, the number of patients in each group was small and so the power of the study was limited.

Despite the relative lack of controlled trial evidence demonstrating the efficacy of specific treatments for depression in physically ill elderly patients, such treatment is often necessary in clinical practice. Close links between geriatrician and psychiatrist are important to ensure that the possibility of comorbid depression is considered in the initial assessment and subsequent care of elderly patients admitted to acute or chronic hospital beds. Treatment should be considered particularly for patients with prominent neurovegetative symptoms (especially retardation, poor appetite and poor food and fluid intake) unexplained by their physical condition. Other indicators for initiating treatment of depression include the expression of suicidal thoughts or intent, and depressive symptoms that are persistent, intense or which impair social functioning. Patients who become depressed while undergoing medical treatment may become intolerant of levels of pain or disability that they were previously able to withstand without complaint (Williamson and Schulz, 1992). The possibility of depression should also be considered in patients whose medical problems fail to respond to apparently appropriate and effective treatment.

Systematic trials of antidepressants with better side-effect profiles and fewer medical contraindications are clearly needed in this population. The newer second-generation antidepressants, especially the selective serotonin reuptake inhibitors and venlafaxine, appear to offer an advantage in terms of fewer side-effects, wider therapeutic index and fewer interactions with other drugs and are now a reasonable first choice. Paroxetine has been shown to have a particularly favourable side-effects profile in the elderly. However, all these drugs require further evaluation in terms of efficacy (Cunningham, 1994; Stewart, 1993). The only two studies to date which have attempted to address this issue are difficult to interpret. Evans (1993) evaluated 23 depressed patients admitted to a geriatric medical ward who were treated with fluoxetine while inpatients and found that at 3 month follow up 57% (8/14) of the survivors recovered from their depression. Of the six patients still depressed, two had not continued the treatment. They were restarted on fluoxetine and both recovered within the next 3 months. Although the response to fluoxetine was fairly high, it was an open study, the sample was very small and the main comparison was between compliers and noncompliers. Roose *et al.* (1994) compared the response to fluoxetine and nortriptyline in 64 hospitalized elderly patients (mean age 70 years) with severe depression and heart disease and found that fluoxetine was significantly less effective (intent-to-treat response rate 23%) than nortriptyline (intent-to-treat response rate 67%). Allocation to treatment groups was not however randomized (historical comparison of two separate treatment trials) and it is possible that there were differences between the two treatment groups.

Fogel and Kroessler (1987) suggested that monoamine oxidase inhibitors (MAOIs) may be a safer option than tricyclic antidepressants among elderly depressed patients and that many elderly patients who do not respond to tricyclics will respond favourably to an MAOI. A new reversible and selective inhibitor of monoamine oxidase A, moclobemide, has not yet been tested in the elderly medically ill. Lithium augmentation, despite the relatively high risk of toxicity it carries in the frail elderly, has been specifically reported to be beneficial in physically ill elderly patients with refractory depression (Kushnir, 1986).

Finally, psychological therapies may be particularly useful in elderly medically ill patients on their own or as an adjunct to pharmacotherapy. Unfortunately, no study to date has evaluated any of the psychological approaches in this group of patients.

CONCLUSIONS

The prevalence of depression in the physically ill elderly is clearly high. This is of considerable importance as there are strong suggestions that the coexistence of depression and physical morbidity in old age worsens the prognosis of both. Routine screening for depression in geriatric patients is feasible and offers significant improvement over relying on unsystematic detection by junior medical staff. There are, however, several questions which remain unanswered. The aetiology and mechanism of the association between physical illness and depression are unknown and there has been a dearth of studies assessing the feasibility and utility of specific treatments for depression in elderly physically ill patients.

REFERENCES

Ahern DK, Gorkin L, Anderson JL *et al*. (1990) Biobehavioral variables and mortality or cardiac arrest in the cardiac arrhythmia. Pilot study (CAPS). *Am Cardiol*, **66**, 59–62.

Ames D and Tuckwell V (1994) Psychiatric disorders among elderly patients in a general hospital. *Med Aust*, **160**, 671–675.

APA (1987) *Diagnostic and Statistical Manual of Mental Disorders* (3rd edition, revised). Washington: American Psychiatric Association.

Aromaa A, Raitasalo R, Reunanen A *et al*. (1994) Depression and cardiovascular diseases. *Acta Psychiatr Scand*, **377**, 77–82.

Ashby D, Ames D, West CR, MacDonald A, Graham N and Mann AH (1991) Psychiatric morbidity as predictor of mortality for residents of local authority homes for the elderly. *Int J Geriatr Psychiatry*, **6**, 567–575.

Baldwin RC and Jolley DJ (1986) The prognosis of depression in old age. *Br J Psychiatry*, **149**, 574–583.

Beekman ATF, Kriegsman DMW and Deeg DJH (1995) The association of physical health and depressive symptoms in the older population: age and sex difference. *Soc Psychiatry Psychiatr Epidemiol*, **30**, 32–38.

Bruce ML and Leaf PJ (1989) Psychiatric disorders and 15-month mortality in a community sample of older adults. *Am J Public Health*, **79**, 727–730.

Bruce ML, Seeman TE, Merrill S and Blazer DG (1994) The impact of depressive symptomatology on physical disability: MacArthur studies of successful aging. *Am Public Health*, **84**, 1796–1799.

Burvill PW and Hall WD (1994) Predictors of increased mortality in elderly depressed patients. *Int Geriatr Psychiatry*, **9**, 219–227.

Carney RM, Freedland KE, Eison SA, Rich MW and Jaffe AS (1995) Major depression and medication adherence in elderly patients with coronary artery disease. *Health Psychol*, **14**, 88–90.

Cavanaugh S, Clark DC and Gibbons RD (1983) Diagnosing depression in the hospitalized medically ill. *Psychosomatics*, **24**, 809–815.

Cunningham LA (1994) Depression in the medically ill: Choosing an antidepressant. *J Clin Psychiatry*, **55(9, Suppl A)**, 90–97.

Dewey ME, Davidson IA and Copeland JRM (1993) Expressed wish to die and mortality in older people: A community replication. *Age Ageing*, **22**, 109–113.

Dunham NC and Sager M (1994) Functional status, symptoms of depression, and the outcomes of hospitalization in community-dwelling elderly patients. *Arch Fam Med,* **3**, 676–681.

Eastwood MR and Corbin SL (1986) The relationship between physical illness and depression in old age. In: E Murphy (ed) *Affective Disorders in the Elderly.* London: Churchill Livingstone, 177–186.

Evans M (1993) Depression in elderly physically ill in-patients: A 12-month prospective study. *Int Clin Psychopharmacol,* **8**, 333–336.

Evans S and Katona CLE (1993) The epidemiology of depressive symptoms in elderly primary care attenders. *Dementia,* **4**, 327–333.

Feldman E, Mayou R, Hawton K, Ardern M and Smith EBO (1987) Psychiatric disorder in medical in-patients. *Q J Med,* **241**, 405–412.

Fenton FR, Cole MG, Engelsman F and Mansouri I (1994) Depression in older medical inpatients. *Int J Geriatr Psychiatry,* **9**, 279–284.

Fogel BS and Kroessler D (1987) Treating late-life depression on a medical-psychiatric unit. *Hosp Commun Psychiatry,* **38**, 829–831.

Fredman L, Schoenback VJ, Kaplan BH, Blazer DG, James SA, Kleinbaum DG and Yankaskas B (1989) The association between depressive symptoms and mortality among older participants in the epidemiologic catchment area—Piedmont health survey. *J Gerontol Soc Sci,* **44**, S149–156.

Fulop G, Strain JJ, Vita J, Lyons JS and Hammer JS (1987) Impact of psychiatric comorbidity on length of hospital stay for medical/surgical patients: A preliminary report. *Am J Psychiatry,* **144**, 878–882.

Green BH, Copeland JRM, Dewey ME, Sharma V and Davidson IA (1994) Factors associated with recovery and recurrence of depression in older people: A prospective study. *Int J Geriatr Psychiatr,,* **9**, 789–795.

Harris RE, Mion LC, Patterson MB and Frengley JD (1988) Severe illness in older patients: The association between depressive disorders and functional dependency during the recovery phase. *J Am Geriatr Soc,* **36**, 890–896.

Johnston M, Wakeling A, Graham N and Stokes F (1987) Cognitive impairment, emotional disorder and length of stay of elderly patients in a district general hospital. *Br J Med Psychol,* **60**, 133–139.

Katona CLE (1994) Depression and physical illness in old age. In CLE Katona (ed) *Depression in Old Age.* Chichester: Wiley, 63–77.

Katz IR, Simpson GM, Curlik SM *et al.* (1990) Pharmacologic treatment of major depression for elderly patients in residential care settings. *J Clin Psychiatry,* **51(7 suppl)**, 41–47.

Katz IR, Parmelee PA, Beaston-Wimmer P and Smith BD (1994) Association of antidepressants and other medications with mortality in the residential-care elderly. *J Geriatr Psychiatry Neurol,* **7**, 221–226.

Kennedy GJ, Kelman HR and Thomas C (1990) The emergence of depressive symptoms in late life: The importance of declining health and increasing disability. *J Community Health,* **15**, 93–104.

Koenig HG, Meador KG, Cohen HJ and Blazer DG (1988a) Detection and treatment of major depression in older medically ill hospitalised patients. *Int J Psychiatry Med,* **18**, 17–31.

Koenig HG, Meador KG, Cohen HJ and Blazer DG (1988b) Depression in elderly hospitalized patients with medical illness. *Arch Intern Med,* **148**, 1929–1936.

Koenig HG, Shelp F, Goli V *et al.* (1989a) Survival and health care utilization in elderly medical inpatients with major depression. *J Am Geriatr Soc,* **37**, 599–606.

Koenig HG, Goli V, Shelp F, Kudler HS, Cohen HJ, Meador KG and Blazer DG (1989b)

Antidepressant use in elderly medical inpatients: lessons from an attempted clinical trial. *J Gen Intern Med*, **4**, 498–505.

Koenig HG, Meador KG, Shelp F *et al.* (1991) Major depressive disorder in hospitalized medically ill patients: an examination of young and elderly male veterans. *J Am Geriatr Soc*, **39**, 881–890.

Koenig HG, Meador KG, Goli V, Shelp F, Cohen HJ and Blazer DG (1992a) Self-rated depressive symptoms in medical inpatients: Age and ratial differences. *Int J Psychiatry Med*, **22(1)**, 11–31.

Koenig HG, Goli V, Shelp F, Kudler HS, Cohen HJ and Blazer DG (1992b) Major depression in hospitalized medically ill older men: documentation, management, and outcome. *Int J Geriatr Psychiatry*, **7**, 25–34.

Kushnir SL (1986) Lithium-antidepressant combination in the treatment of depressed, physically ill geriatric patients. *Am J Psychiatry*, **143**, 378–379.

Lipsey JR, Robinson RG, Pearlson GD, Roa K and Price TR (1984) Nortriptyline treatment of post-stroke depression: a double-blind study. *Lancet*, **1**, 297–300.

Lyness JM, Cox C, Curry J, Conwell Y, King DA and Caine ED (1995) Older age and the underreporting of depressive symptoms. *J Am Geriatr Soc*, **43**, 216–221.

Mayou R and Hawton K (1986) Psychiatric morbidity in the general hospital. *Br J Psychiatry*, **149**, 172–190.

Millar HR (1981) Psychiatric morbidity in elderly surgical patients. *Br J Psychiatry*, **138**, 17–20.

Montgomery SA (1990) Depression in the elderly: pharmacokinetics and antidepressants and death from overdose. *Int Clin Psychopharmacol*, **Suppl 3**, 67–76.

Murphy E (1983) The prognosis of depression in old age. *Br J Psychiatry*, **142**, 111–119.

Murphy E, Smith R, Lindesay J and Slattery J (1988) Increased mortality rates in late-life depression. *Br J Psychiatry*, **152**, 347–353.

Pollock BG, Perel JM, Paradis CF, Fasiczka AL and Reynolds CF (1994) Metabolic and physiologic consequences of nortriptyline treatment in the elderly. *Psychopharmacol Bull*, **30(2)**, 145–150.

Ramsay R, Wright P, Katz A, Beilawska C and Katona C (1991) The detection of psychiatric morbidity and its effects on outcome in acute elderly medical admissions. *Int J Geriatr Psychiatry*, **6**, 861–866.

Rapp SR and Davis KM (1989) Geriatric depression: physicians' knowledge, perceptions, and diagnostic practices. *Gerontologist*, **29**, 252–257.

Rapp SR, Walsh DA, Parisi SA and Wallace CE (1988a) Detecting depression in elderly medical inpatients. *J Consult Clin Psychol*, **56**, 509–513.

Rapp SR, Parisi SA and Walsh DA (1988b) Psychological dysfunction and physical health among elderly medical inpatients. *J Consult Clin Psychol*, **56**, 851–855.

Rapp SR, Parisi SA and Wallace CE (1991) Comorbid psychiatric disorders in elderly medical patients: a 1-year prospective study. *J Am Geriatr Soc*, **39**, 124–131.

Reding MJ, Orto LA, Winter SW *et al.* (1986) Antidepressant therapy after stroke: a double-blind trial. *Arch Neurol*, **43**, 763–765.

Roose SP, Glassman AH, Attia E and Woodring S (1994) Comparative efficacy of selective serotonin reuptake inhibitors and tricyclics in the treatment of melancholia. *Am J Psychiatry*, **151**, 1735–1739.

Schifano F, Garbin A, Renesto V, De Dominicis MG, Trinciarelli G, Silvestri A and Magni G (1990) A double-blind comparison of mianserin and maprotiline in depressed medically ill elderly people. *Acta Psychiatr Scand*, **81**, 289–294.

Shamash K, O'Connell K, Lowy M and Katona CLE (1992) Psychiatric morbidity and outcome in elderly patients undergoing emergency hip surgery: A one-year follow-up study. *Int J Geriatr Psychiatry*, **7**, 505–509.

Silverstone PH (1990) Depression increases mortality and morbidity in acute life-threatening medical illness. *J Psychosom Res*, **34**, 651–657.

Stewart JT (1993) Advances in pharmacotherapy: depression in the elderly—issues and advances in treatment. *J Clin Pharm Ther*, **18**, 243–253.

Tan RSH, Barlow RJ, Abel C *et al.* (1994) The effect of low dose lofepramine in depressed elderly patients in general medical wards. *Br J Clin Pharmacol*, **37**, 321–324.

Thomas C, Kelman HR, Kennedy GJ, Ahn C and Yang C (1992) Depressive symptoms and mortality in elderly persons. *J Gerontol*, **47**, S80–S87.

Verbosky LA, Franco KN and Zrull JP (1993) The relationship between depression and length of stay in the general hospital patient. *J Clin Psychiatry*, **54**, 177–181.

Walker Z, Leek CA, D'Ath PJ and Katona CLE (1995) Psychiatric morbidity in elderly attenders of an Accident & Emergency department. *Int J Geriatr Psychiatry*, **10**, 951–957.

Williamson GM and Schulz R (1992) Pain, activity restriction, and symptoms of depression among community-residing elderly adults. *J Gerontol Psychol Sci*, **47**, P367–P372.

Part III

DEPRESSION AND SPECIFIC PHYSICAL CONDITIONS

11

Depression and AIDS

Mario Maj

BIOMEDICAL AND PSYCHOSOCIAL BACKGROUND

The acquired immune deficiency syndrome (AIDS) results from infection with the human immunodeficiency virus (HIV). HIV is a retrovirus (i.e. a virus which works backwards, since its genetic material is encoded in RNA, and is transcribed, by the enzyme reverse transcriptase, into DNA, which is incorporated in the host cell's genome). The devastating effects of HIV are mainly related to the infection of a subset of lymphocytes, known as CD4 or T4 cells, which cause a collapse of cell-mediated immunity and a general immune dysregulation, resulting in a range of infections and neoplasms. As for all retroviruses, the time from infection to clinical disease is lengthy (with a median duration, in Western countries, of approximately 10 years).

HIV may be transmitted in three ways: through sexual intercourse (either homosexual or heterosexual); through blood (as a result of exchange of contaminated injection equipment by intravenous (IV) drug users, or of the medical transfusion of infected blood or blood products, or of the use of non-sterilized skin-piercing instruments in health care settings); and from mother to child (during pregnancy or delivery, or through breast feeding). In Western countries, people predominantly affected so far have been homosexual or bisexual men and IV drug users. However, in sub-Saharan Africa, where about 70% of estimated AIDS cases have occurred up to now, hetero-

Depression and Physical Illness. Edited by M.M. Robertson and C.L.E. Katona
© 1997 John Wiley & Sons Ltd

Table 1. Staging of HIV infection according to CDC (1987).

Stage	Symptoms
Stage I	Acute infection (flu-like syndrome, sometimes accompanied by aseptic meningitis)
Stage II	Asymptomatic infection
Stage III	Persistent generalized lymphoadenopathy
Stage IV	Other disease
	A. Constitutional disease (fever of more than 1 month duration and/or diarrhoea of more than 1 month duration and/or weight loss of more than 10%)
	B. Dementia or HIV disease of spinal cord or peripheral nerves
	C1. Life-threatening opportunistic infections (e.g. Pneumocystis carinii pneumonia)
	C2. Non-life-threatening opportunistic infections (e.g. oral candidiasis)
	D. Cancer (e.g. Kaposi's sarcoma or primary lymphoma of the central nervous system)
	E. Other disorders indicating cell-mediated immunodeficiency

Stages IVC1 and IVD are classified as AIDS

sexual transmission is predominant, and infected women outnumber men by six to five (WHO, 1994).

In people with HIV infection, antibodies to the virus can usually be detected by 3 months after exposure. At the time of seroconversion, about 30% of subjects present a flu-like reaction, which can be accompanied by aseptic meningitis. In most cases, however, the infection remains completely asymptomatic for many years. Prior to the occurrence of AIDS-defining infections or neoplasms, many subjects develop a persistent generalized lymphoadenopathy. In Western countries, the most common conditions leading to a diagnosis of AIDS are Pneumocystis carinii pneumonia, tuberculosis, candidiasis, oral hairy leukoplakia and Kaposi's sarcoma. Once a patient develops an AIDS-defining condition, the average survival is between 1 and 3 years. The staging of HIV infection, as proposed by the Centers for Disease Control (CDC, 1987), is summarized in Table 1. Progression from HIV infection to frank AIDS can be slowed by treatment with zidovudine (azidothymidine, AZT), which interferes with viral replication.

HIV usually enters the brain shortly after the infection (it is uncertain whether as a free virus, or within infected macrophages or monocytes, or through primary infection of choroid plexus or meningeal cells). In a proportion of AIDS cases variously estimated between 8% and 16%, a syndrome consisting of cognitive dysfunction (mental slowing, memory and concentration impairment), usually accompanied by behavioural and motor symptoms and signs (HIV-associated dementia complex), develops (Navia *et al.*, 1986). Higher cortical functions are usually spared in this syndrome, which is consistent with the histopathological picture, marked by a predominant involvement of deep grey structures and central white matter (with two main lesion patterns: HIV encephalitis, multifocal and inflammatory, and HIV leukoencephalopathy, diffuse and noninflammatory) (Budka *et al.*, 1991). The pathogenesis of the syndrome is uncertain: the release of viral products interfering with neuronal functioning and the production of cytokines by infected macrophages are the most likely mechanisms (Price *et al.*, 1988). Mild cognitive impairment not amounting to frank dementia is common in physically symptomatic HIV infection. Whether the risk of this impairment is significantly increased in the physically asymptomatic stages of the infection is at present controversial (Maj, 1990a).

Psychological reactions to HIV infection and AIDS resemble in part those commonly observed in patients with cancer or other life-threatening diseases. However, they also reflect some specific psychosocial dimensions, such as the stigma associated with homosexuality and drug abuse, and society's fear of contagion (Maj, 1990b). Many subjects with HIV infection have to face familial, social and occupational rejection, and some may feel that they deserve the illness and that the current situation is evidence of their past misdeeds (Miller, 1987). The age at which the infection usually occurs is another traumatic factor: most subjects are aged 25–49, an age group which does not expect to develop a fatal illness (Christ *et al.*, 1988).

The first key-point in the course of the infection at which psychological reactions are likely to occur is discovery of seropositivity. Subjects receiving the diagnosis are suddenly confronted not only with the likelihood of developing a disease with a very poor prognosis and for which no effective therapy is available, but also with several other issues: revealing their homosexuality or drug abuse to family, friends and colleagues; dealing with the fears of partner, family, friends and public; avoiding transmission of infection to others, and protecting themselves from opportunistic infections. However, people usually come to terms with the situation of being seropositive. During the subsequent asymptomatic phase, they may hold onto the hope that they will be the "lucky ones" who will not progress to AIDS, or that effective therapies will be discovered in the meantime. The emergence of physical symptoms, however, calls these coping strategies into question, and represents a second key-point in the history of the infection at which psychological reactions are likely to occur (Hays *et al.*, 1992). Subsequently, any change in the individual's clinical state may cause psychological reactions, as may isolation and abandonment, loss of physical and financial independence, the perception of the inability by partner or family to cope with the situation, the possible difficulty in obtaining medical treatment, and the loss of close friends or partners due to AIDS.

DEPRESSION IN SUBJECTS WITH HIV INFECTION

Aetiology

From the above background section, two factors emerge which may explain the occurrence of depressive symptoms or syndromes in subjects with HIV infection: firstly, the psychological impact of the diagnosis of the infection, of the onset of physical symptoms, and of the progression of the disease and related disabilities, which is made even more powerful by the usually young age of the affected persons and by the frequent occurrence of familial, social and occupational rejection (Maj, 1990b); secondly, the neurotropism of the virus, which produces neuropathological changes in deep grey structures (basal ganglia, thalamus, brain stem nuclei) whose dysfunction is known to bring about mood and motivation disturbances (Price *et al.*, 1988).

Probably more important, however, is a third factor: the groups that in Western countries are at the highest risk for HIV infection (i.e. homosexuals/bisexuals and IV drug users) are also known to be at high risk for depressive symptoms and syndromes, independently of the occurrence of the infection (Grant and Atkinson, 1990).

Both zidovudine and the antineoplastic drugs used to treat Kaposi's sarcoma and other tumours in AIDS patients have been found to produce depression in individual cases (Chabner and Myers, 1985; Volberding *et al.*, 1985; Ostrow, 1987), but the overall impact of this aetiological factor is negligible.

Diagnosis

The ascertainment of depression in persons with HIV infection is difficult for the following reasons.

1. The possible confounding effect of the physical symptoms of the infection (fatigue, diminished appetite and sleep, and loss of weight may be physical symptoms of HIV infection as well as depressive symptoms).
2. The possible confounding effect of the cognitive impairment related to HIV infection of the brain (psychomotor slowing, forgetfulness, and difficulties in concentration may be early symptoms of this impairment).
3. The frequent occurrence of transient emotional and behavioural reactions in coincidence with the above-mentioned key-points in the course of the infection (losing interest in human contact, feeling guilty about previous at-risk behaviours, thinking of death, may all be part of these reactions) (Maj, 1996).

In order to make the diagnosis of "clinical" depression, the psychiatrist should ascertain that a depressive syndrome has persisted for at least 2 weeks, most of the day, nearly every day, including aspects such as prominent depressed mood, markedly reduced interest or pleasure in all or almost all activities, true sense of worthlessness, and recurrent suicidal ideation. The clinical significance of aspects such as psychomotor retardation or diminished ability to think or concentrate should be considered equivocal, unless detailed neuropsychological assessment demonstrates the absence of cognitive impairment. Analogously, the clinical meaning of manifestations such as reduced weight or appetite, fatigue or loss of energy, and insomnia remains uncertain if the subject has reached the symptomatic stages of the infection.

Prevalence

Among the currently available studies reporting the prevalence of syndromal depression and/or the global ratings for depressive symptoms in HIV-seropositive subjects, we will review here only those meeting the following set of methodological requirements: homogeneity of the HIV-seropositive group(s) with respect to the stage of the infection; use of a control group of HIV-seronegative subjects matched to HIV-seropositive probands on sex, age, and at-risk behaviour; and use of operational diagnostic criteria and of an appropriate structured diagnostic interview to make syndromal diagnoses, or of a validated rating instrument to assess depressive symptomatology.

The studies fulfilling the above-mentioned criteria which report the current prevalence of major depression in people with HIV infection are summarized in Tables 2 and 3. All the studies mentioned in Table 2 were carried out in the USA on samples of well-educated, middle-class, mostly white, homosexual or bisexual men, who had been recruited by newspaper advertisements or talks with specific community groups. None of these studies reported a significant difference, with respect to the current prevalence of major depression, between HIV-seropositive subjects and HIV-seronegative controls. In the three studies reporting 1-month rates, and therefore comparable with the Epidemiologic Catchment Area Study (ECA) (Regier *et al.*, 1988), the prevalence of the above-mentioned condition was two to four-fold higher than the one detected in the ECA among males aged 25–44 years. Overall, these data seem to indicate that the risk of major depression is increased in homosexual/bisexual men, and that HIV infection is not associated with a significant increase of that risk.

Table 3 reports the results of the World Health Organization (WHO) Neuropsychiatric AIDS Study, conducted in the five geographic areas predominantly affected by the HIV epidemic (i.e. sub-Saharan Africa, Latin America, North America, South-East Asia, and Western Europe), on subject samples representative of the broad population of HIV-seropositive people living in those areas, consecutively recruited from outpatient medical units, and on matched seronegative controls enrolled from the same units. Currently available data concern a total of 955 subjects, assessed at five centres (Bangkok,

Table 2. Current prevalence of major depression (MD) in persons with HIV infection: results of studies conducted in the USA.

Authors (year)	Diagnostic criteria (interview, reference period in months)	HIV-seropositives			HIV-seronegatives	
		CDC stage	N	%MD	N	%MD
Atkinson et al. (1988)	DSM-III (DIS, 6)	II	17	17.6	11	9.1
		III–IV A	13	7.7		
		IV C1–IV D	15	6.7		
Perry et al. (1990)	DSM-IIIR (SCID, 1)	II	31	6.5	103	4.9
Williams et al. (1991)	DSM-IIIR (SCID, 1)	II–III–IV A	124	4.0	84	4.0
Rosenberger et al. (1993)	DSM-IIIR (SCID, 2)	II–III	102	9.0	31	6.0
		IV	64	11.0		
Perkins et al. (1994)	DSM-IIIR (SCID, 1)	II	98	8.0	71	3.0

CDC = Centers for Disease Control; DIS = Diagnostic Interview Schedule; SCID = Structured Clinical Interview for DSM-IIIR.

Table 3. Current prevalence of DSM-IIIR major depression (MD) and ICD-10 depressive episode (DE) in persons with HIV infection: results of the WHO Neuropsychiatric AIDS Study (Maj et al., 1994a, Arch Gen Psychiatry; **51**, 39–49. Copyright 1994, American Medical Association).

Centre	Symptomatic HIV-seronegatives			Asymptomatic HIV-seronegatives			HIV-seronegatives		
	N	%MD	%DE	N	%MD	%DE	N	%MD	%DE
Bangkok	38	18.4**	21.0*	89	9.0	10.1	59	1.7	3.4
Kinshasa	68	4.4	4.4	52	0	0	85	0	0
Munich	74	4.0	4.0	42	4.8	4.8	67	0	0
Nairobi	72	5.5	5.5	66	3.0	3.0	65	0	0
Sao Paulo	46	17.4	19.6	55	10.9	10.9	77	7.8	7.8

Significant difference with respect to HIV-seronegative controls: $P<0.05$; ** $P<0.01$.

Thailand; Kinshasa, Zaire; Munich, Germany; Nairobi, Kenya; Sao Paulo, Brazil). Reflecting the epidemiology of HIV infection in the relevant geographic areas, the subjects enrolled in Kinshasa and Nairobi were almost exclusively hetero-sexuals without a history of IV drug use; those recruited in Bangkok were almost exclusively IV drug users; the sample enrolled in Munich was mixed (homosexuals/bisexuals, IV drug users, blood recipients); and that collected in Sao Paulo mostly consisted of homosexuals/bisexuals and IV drug users (see Maj et al., 1944a,b for details).

Bangkok and Sao Paulo were the centres in which the prevalence of major depression (diagnosed according to DSM-IIIR) and of depressive episode (diagnosed according to ICD-10) was the highest, within all the serogroups. There was a consistent trend for physically asymptomatic seropositives to have higher rates than seronegative controls, and an almost consistent trend (four out of five centres) for physically symptomatic seropositives to have higher rates than asymptomatic ones. At the Bangkok centre, the rate of major depression was significantly higher in physically symptomatic seropositives as compared with seronegatives. These results suggest that, in specific at-risk groups or in contexts where the spreading of the infection is more recent and the social rejection of HIV-seropositive subjects is harsher, physically symptomatic stages of HIV infection may be associated with an increased prevalence of a syndromal diagnosis of depression.

Consistent with the results of the WHO Neuropsychiatric AIDS Study are those of a recent investigation carried out in the USA on a sample of predomi-nantly African-American male and female IV drug users (Lipsitz et al., 1994). In this study, the prevalence of DSM-IIIR-diagnosed depressive disorders (major depression or dysthymia or both) was significantly higher among HIV-seroposi-tive men as compared to matched seronegative controls. Unfortunately, the HIV-seropositive sample included both physically asymptomatic subjects and indivi-duals with "mild to moderate physical symptoms", and the relative proportions were not specified.

The studies fulfilling the above-mentioned methodological requirements that reported the global scores on depression-rating instruments in people with HIV infection are summarized in Tables 4 and 5. All studies reported in Table 4 were carried out in Western countries (eight in the USA, one in Australia, and one in Greece), all but one on samples of well-educated, middle-class, mostly white, homosexual or bisexual men (the Greek study was conducted on a sample of haemophiliacs attending a regional transfusion centre). Inter-study comparison is hampered by the diversity of the assessment instruments and of the composition of HIV-seropositive samples as to the stage of infection. However, a consistent finding is the lack of significant differences between physically asymptomatic seropositives and seronegative controls.

Two of the studies reporting separate data for physically symptomatic seropositives found that these subjects had a significantly higher depression

Table 4. Mean global scores on depression rating scales in persons with HIV infection; results of studies conducted in Western countries.

Authors (year)	Assessment instrument	CDC stage	HIV-seropositives N	Mean score	HIV-seronegatives N	Mean score
Atkinson et al. (1988)	POMS-D	II	17	13.8	11	13.3
		III–IV A	13	17.6		
		IV C1–IV D	15	9.5		
Clifford et al. (1990)	BDI	II–III	33	7.5	50	8.5
Kokkevi et al. (1991)	BDI	II–III	46	6.5	29	6.3
		IV	14	5.5		
Krikorian and Wrobel (1991)	BDI	II	16	11.3	14	9.1
		III–IV A	18	13.8		
		IV C1–IV D	14	22.4*		
Miller et al. (1991)	CES-D	II–III	439	9.6	507	9.2
		IV	47	17.0**		
van Gorp et al. (1991)	CES-D	II–III	223	9.5	256	9.4
Williams et al. (1991)	HRS-D	II–III–IV A	124	4.3	84	3.3
Perdices et al. (1992)	CES-D	II	101	15.0	36	9.9
		III–IV A	72	15.0		
		IV C1–IV D	34	14.3		
Rosenberger et al. (1993)	SCL-90, D	II–III	102	10.9	31	9.3
		IV	64	11.6		
Perkins et al. (1994)	HRS-D	II	98	4.6	71	3.9
	POMS-D			11.3		10.7

Significant difference with respect to HIV-seronegative controls,* $P < 0.01$, ** $P < 0.001$. BDI = Beck Depression Inventory; CES-D = Centre for Epidemiological Studies—Depression; HRS-D = Hamilton Rating Scale for Depression; POMS-D = Profile of Mood States, Depression Scale; SCL-90, D = Symptom Checklist-90, Depression.

Table 5. Mean scores on the MADRS in persons with HIV infection: results of the WHO Neuropsychiatric AIDS Study (Maj *et al*, 1994a, *Arch Gen Psychiatry*, **51**, 39–49. Copyright 1994, American Medical Association).

	Bangkok			Sao Paulo		
	S/HIV+ (n=38)	A/HIV+ (n=89)	HIV− (N=59)	S/HIV+ (n=46)	A/HIV+ (n=55)	HIV− (N=77)
Apparent sadness	2.1**	1.4*	0.3	1.6*	0.9	0.7
Reported sadness	2.1**	1.3*	0.5	1.5	1.0	0.9
Inner tension	1.1*	0.5	0.5	1.4	1.1	0.9
Reduced sleep	2.9**	0.8	0.7	1.7*	0.8	0.7
Reduced appetite	1.5**	0.7	0.3	1.6**	0.7	0.5
Concentration difficulties	0.6	0.4	0.5	1.6	1.0	1.0
Lassitude	0.8	0.5	0.5	1.7**	0.6	0.7
Inability to feel	0.5	0.2	0.2	1.3*	0.9	0.7
Pessimistic thoughts	1.5*	0.5	0.2	1.6*	1.0	0.8
Suicidal thoughts	1.2*	0.4	0.4	0.8*	0.6	0.2
Global score	13.3**	6.8	4.1	14.9**	8.7	7.8

	Kinshasa			Munich			Nairobi		
	S/HIV+ (n=68)	A/HIV+ (n=52)	HIV− (n=85)	S/HIV+ (n=74)	A/HIV+ (n=42)	HIV− (n=67)	S/HIV+ (n=72)	A/HIV+ (n=66)	HIV− (n=65)
Apparent sadness	1.3*	0.5	0.3	1.3**	0.5	0.3	1.5**	0.7	0.3
Reported sadness	1.9**	0.9	0.5	1.6**	0.7	0.4	1.5**	0.7	0.3
Inner tension	0.3	0.1	0.1	0.8	0.5	0.4	0.8*	0.3	0.2
Reduced sleep	0.9*	0.1	0.2	1.3**	0.7	0.6	1.9**	1.1	0.6
Reduced appetite	1.8**	0.5	0.5	0.9**	0.4	0.3	1.7**	0.8	0.3
Concentration difficulties	1.2**	0.3	0.2	1.1**	0.5	0.4	1.2**	0.3	0.3
Lassitude	1.7**	0.6	0.2	0.9**	0.4	0.3	1.5**	0.6	0.3
Inability to feel	1.1**	0.4	0.2	1.2**	0.5	0.3	1.2**	0.5	0.4
Pessimistic thoughts	0.7*	0.5	0.1	0.7*	0.3	0.2	1.2**	0.3	0.2
Suicidal thoughts	0.3*	0.3	0.1	0.6*	0.2	0.1	0.7*	0.1	0.2
Global score	11.5**	4.3	2.4	10.3**	4.1	3.1	10.1	5.5	3.3

Significant difference with respect to HIV-seronegative controls: *$P<0.05$; **$P<0.01$. MADRS = Montgomery–Asberg Depression Rating Scale; S/HIV+ = symptomatic seropositives; A/HIV+ = asymptomatic seropositives; HIV− = seronegatives.

score than seronegative controls, but four did not detect this difference. This variability of findings in symptomatic seropositives may be at least in part related to the above mentioned confounding effect of physical symptoms of HIV infection. It is worth noting, in this connection, that no study reported the mean scores for the individual items of the assessment instruments (so that the contribution of physical, cognitive, emotional, and behavioural symptoms to the global depression score cannot be established).

In the WHO Neuropsychiatric AIDS Study, depressive symptoms were rated by the Montgomery–Asberg Depression Rating Scale (MADRS), which was selected for its limited loading with somatic items. As shown in Table 5, the mean global score and the mean scores on several items (including emotional, cognitive, behavioural and physical symptoms and signs) were significantly higher in symptomatic seropositives as compared with seronegative controls at all the centres, whereas the mean scores of asymptomatic seropositives were often higher than those of controls, but this difference was significant only for two items at the Bangkok centre. The mean MADRS global score was significantly higher in women that in men among symptomatic seropositives assessed in Kinshasa ($P < 0.05$) and Munich ($P < 0.001$). The effect of the sex × serogroup interaction on the MADRS global score was found to be significant in Munich ($P < 0.0001$).

These results suggest that the symptomatic stages of HIV infection are associated with an increased prevalence of depressive symptoms. The lack of significant differences between symptomatic seropositives and seronegative controls, reported in some recent studies conducted in the USA on samples of homosexual/bisexual men, may reflect the development of more effective coping strategies and social networks within the homosexual community. In those studies, however, the recruitment of subjects by talks to specific community groups and newspaper advertisements may have created a bias, selecting HIV-seropositive people mostly involved in formal or informal support groups.

Risk factors

Among the reported risk factors for the development of depressive symptoms or syndromes in subjects with HIV infection, those which are documented by at least one research paper (apart from anecdotal evidence or theoretical speculations) include past personal history of depression, presence of personality disorders, presence or severity of HIV-related physical symptoms, inadequacy of social support, and the use of specific coping strategies.

In the study by Perkins *et al.* (1994), conducted on homosexual men living in an area with a low prevalence of HIV infection in the USA, the personal history of a major depressive episode was found to be significantly associated with current major depression. In the study by Johnson *et al.* (1995), carried out on homosexual men in New York, HIV-seropositive subjects with personality disorders had a significantly higher global score on the Hamilton Rating Scale for Depression (HRS-D) than those without these disorders. Ostrow *et al.* (1989) and Hays *et al.* (1992) reported that the number of HIV-related physical symptoms was significantly correlated with the score on the Centre for Epidemiological Studies–Depression (CES-D) scale in samples of homosexual men, whereas Perry *et al.* (1992) found that the severity of HIV-related physical symptoms correlated significantly with the global scores on both the HRS-D and the Beck Depression Inventory (BDI). Hays *et al.* (1992) reported that HIV-seropositive homosexual men who were more satisfied with the social support they received were less likely to show increased CES-D scores 1 year later, and that satisfaction with informational support (receiving advice or information on HIV-related issues) was especially crucial in buffering the depression associated with experiencing HIV-related symptoms. Leserman *et al.* (1994) found that low social support and frequent social conflict were associated with higher scores on both the HRS-D and the Profile of Mood States, Depression Scale (POMS-D) in physically asymptomatic HIV-seropositive subjects, and that increased frequency of conflict in relationships was associated with greater increases of both HRS-D and POMS-D scores 1 year later. Folkman *et al.* (1993) found that "detachment" coping strategies (including distancing, self-controlling and cognitive escape–avoidance) were associated with high levels of depressed mood (rated by the six-item depression subscale from the Brief Symptom Inventory) in HIV-seropositive homosexual men living in San Francisco, whereas Commerford *et al.* (1994) reported that "emotion-focused coping strategies of self-blaming denial, emotional expression and wish-fulfilling phantasy" were significantly related to depression, rated by the Symptom Checklist–90, Depression (SCL-90, D), in a sample of HIV-seropositive women.

Notification of CD4 count has been found not to be associated with an increase of either HRS-D or BDI scores at 6 months or 1 year later (Perry *et al.*, 1992). On the other hand, the claim that depression may accelerate the progression of HIV infection has not been supported so far by the bulk of research evidence. Actually, several longitudinal studies have found that depressive symptomatology does not predict decrease of CD4 cell count or other enumerative lymphocyte measures of HIV infection (Kessler *et al.*, 1991; Rabkin *et al.*, 1991; Perry *et al.*, 1992; Lyketsos *et al.*, 1993). However, Burack *et al.* (1993) did find that baseline depression (a score of 16 or higher on the CES-D scale) predicted a more rapid decline of CD4 count in HIV-seropositive subjects, although it was not significantly associated with earlier AIDS diagnosis or earlier mortality.

Treatment

One published randomized double-blind study has compared imipramine with placebo in HIV-seropositive subjects with a depressive syndrome (Rabkin *et al.*,

1994a). This trial was conducted on 97 patients (almost all white homosexual men), fulfilling DSM-IIIR criteria for major depression or dysthymia or both, and having a score of at least 14 on the HRS-D. Imipramine was given at the initial dose of 50 mg/day, and raised up to 300 mg/day as tolerated. Eighty patients completed the 6 week trial; 46% of them were physically asymptomatic, 15% had HIV-related present or past physical symptoms but not an AIDS diagnosis, and 39% had AIDS. Of the 17 drop-outs, 11 interrupted treatment because of side-effects; 8 of them were receiving imipramine and complained of drowsiness, dizziness, headache or cognitive problems. Among the completers, 74% of those treated with imipramine and 26% of those receiving placebo were found to be responders (i.e. their HRS-D global score at week 6 was less than eight and was reduced more than 50% with respect to baseline, and they were rated as much or very much improved on the Clinical Global Impression Scale (CGI)), a statistically significant difference. Improvement of the global score of the HRS-D was significantly greater with imipramine than with placebo. The imipramine response rate was about the same in patients with CD4 count above versus below 200 cells/mm^3. The average final imipramine dose was 241 mg/day. The most frequent side-effects of imipramine were dry mouth (maximum frequency, 59%), constipation, sweating, tremors and sexual dysfunction. Three-quarters of the patients who had memory or concentration problems at baseline did not present them at the end of the trial. Patients taking imipramine (as well as those receiving placebo) did not show a decrease of CD4 count over time. Of the 27 responders who were offered to continue imipramine treatment after the double-blind trial, eight (30%) interrupted treatment before week 26 because of troublesome side-effects, of which sexual dysfunction was the most common. The conclusion of the authors was that imipramine is as effective in HIV-seropositive subjects as in physically healthy depressed patients, and is not immunosuppressive.

Similar findings have been reported in a congress abstract by Manning *et al.* (1990). A randomized double-blind trial of imipramine versus placebo was carried out on 56 patients (mostly white homosexual men) with a DSM-IIIR diagnosis of major depression and without dementia. Imipramine was started at 50 mg/day and raised up to 250 mg/day as tolerated. Forty patients completed the 6 week trial. Among completers, 67% of patients treated with imipramine and 47% of those receiving placebo responded (i.e. had a final HRS-D score which was decreased more than 50% with respect to baseline and had an absolute value of less than 10). The improvement of the HRS-D and BDI global scores was significantly greater in patients treated with imipramine than in those receiving placebo. The mean peak dosage of imipramine was 225 mg/day, and was reportedly well tolerated.

Finally, Fernandez *et al.* (1989) treated 28 homosexual men (19 with HIV-related physical symptoms and nine with AIDS), who met DSM-IIIR criteria for major depression, with either amitriptyline or desipramine in a 1 year randomized trial. Patients improved on both drug regimes, without significant differences with respect to side-effects, but those without AIDS had a better overall outcome on CGI than did those with AIDS.

Overall, the above studies, although carried out on non-representative samples, suggest that tricyclic antidepressants are effective in HIV-seropositive depressed subjects, and relatively well tolerated. In particular, there seems to be no support to early claims that these drugs are likely to precipitate delirium or exacerbate cognitive impairment.

With the exception of the structured group therapy/fluoxetine study that will be examined at the end of this section, no published double-blind trial of selective serotonin reuptake inhibitors (SSRIs) is as yet available in HIV-seropositive depressed patients. We report here on three open trials: two carried out with fluoxetine and one with sertraline. Rabkin *et al.* (1994b) treated 31 patients (30 homosexual men and one woman) with fluoxetine after the 6 week trial of imipramine described above. Subjects included seven imipramine nonresponders, seven patients who interrupted imipramine because of side-effects, four imipramine responders who disliked the drug because of side-effects, and 13 placebo nonresponders or responders who requested fluoxetine treatment. Patients with chronic diarrhoea were excluded from the trial. The starting dosage of fluoxetine was 20 mg/day, except for patients who had discontinued imipramine because of side-effects, in whom it was 10 mg/day. After 4 weeks of treatment, the possibility was given to increase fluoxetine up to 60 mg/day or to add dextroamphetamine (2.5 mg/day). Twenty-three patients received only fluoxetine for 12 weeks, and 83% of them responded to treatment. Seven patients received fluoxetine plus dextroamphetamine, and all responded. In general, side-effects were less frequent and milder than during the imipramine trial. The most common side-effects were sweating (33%) and sexual dysfunction (20%). There were no reports of weight loss, diminished appetite or diarrhoea. CD4 count was not influenced by treatment.

Levine *et al.* (1990) reported on a sample of eight physically asymptomatic HIV-seropositive subjects meeting DSM-IIIR criteria for major depression, who responded to an open trial of fluoxetine (20–40 mg/day) with a fall of average HRS-D global score from 23 at baseline to six after 1 month and to two after 3 months. Side-effects included mild anxiety, insomnia and gastrointestinal discomfort, whereas no weight loss was reported.

Rabkin *et al.* (1994c) conducted an open trial of sertraline on 28 HIV-seropositive subjects (27 homosexual men and one woman; 55% physically asymptomatic, 25% with HIV-related physical symptoms but not AIDS, and 30% with AIDS), fulfilling DSM-IIIR for major depression or dysthymia or both, and having an HRS-D global score of at least 14. The starting dosage was 50 mg/day and was raised up to 200 mg/day as required. Twenty patients completed an 8 week trial; 70% of them were responders. Five of the eight drop-outs discontinued treatment because of side-effects (gastrointestinal symptoms, agitation and sexual dysfunction). There was no case of weight loss; in one case decreased appetite, lasting only 1 week, was observed. Treatment did not affect CD4 count, and patients with a count of less than 200 cells/mm^3 responded as well as the others and did not present an increased rate of side-effects.

The reported trials suggest that SSRIs may be better tolerated than tricyclics in subjects with HIV infection (excluding those with chronic diarrhoea), but systematic studies involving direct comparisons are clearly warranted.

The efficacy of psychostimulants (dextroamphetamine 5–60 mg/day or methylphenidate 10–90 mg/day) in improving depressed mood and lethargy of AIDS patients has been repeatedly suggested by case reports or studies conducted on small patient groups (Fernandez *et al.*, 1988; Walling and Pfefferbaum, 1990; White *et al.*, 1992; Rabkin, 1993).

In a recent randomized, double-blind trial, Fernandez *et al.* (1995) treated with either methylphenidate (average dose 30 mg/day) or desipramine (average dose 150 mg/day) 20 HIV-seropositive homosexual men who met DSM-IIIR criteria for major depression had a score of at least 16 on the HRS-D, and scored at least 25 on the Mini Mental State Examination. The stage of the infection was not reported, but subjects with severe physical impairment were excluded. Fifteen patients completed the trial. Drop-outs were not due to side-effects of the drugs. At 6 weeks, the mean scores on the HRS-D and the POMS-D were significantly reduced in both patient groups. A reduction of more than 50% of the HRS-D global score was detected in 47% of patients receiving desipramine and in 43% of those treated with methylphenidate (a nonsignificant difference). Side-effects were significantly more frequent at 6 weeks in patients receiving desipramine. Dry mouth, anxiety/nervousness, tingling/itching and insomnia were the most frequent side-effects of desipramine, and shakiness/restlessness was the side-effect most commonly produced by methylphenidate.

The above evidence suggests that psychostimulants may be useful in HIV-seropositive subjects with depression and anergia, but concerns about the risk of tolerance and dependence, especially in patients with a present or current history of drug abuse, are clearly warranted.

The efficacy of individual and group psychotherapies in reducing distress in HIV-seropositive subjects has been frequently described (Nichols, 1986; Beckett and Rutan, 1990), but only a few systematic studies testing the efficacy of specific psychotherapies on depressed HIV-seropositive subjects are available. Perry *et al.* (1991) reported that a six-session individual stress-prevention training (SPT) programme was significantly more effective than standard counselling on the score of BDI cognitive items in physically asymptomatic HIV-seropositive subjects. Kelly *et al.* (1993) found that eight-session cognitive–behavioural and support group interventions were both significantly more effective than no group intervention in reducing CES-D scores in HIV-seropositive men (56% asymptomatic or with HIV-related physical symptoms but not AIDS, the remaining with AIDS), and that the improvement was maintained at 3 month follow up. Markowitz *et al.* (1995) reported that 16 weeks of individual interpersonal psychotherapy was significantly more effective than supportive psychotherapy in reducing HRS-D and BDI scores in mainly asymptomatic HIV-seropositive subjects with a clinical diagnosis of DSM-IIIR mood disorder.

Targ *et al.* (1994) carried out the only available study comparing psychotherapy (namely, structured group therapy emphasizing active skills in behavioural coping) combined with drug treatment (fluoxetine 20 mg/day) versus the same psychotherapy plus a placebo. This double-blind randomized trial was conducted on 20 physically asymptomatic HIV-seropositive homosexual men receiving AZT, who met unspecified criteria for major depression or adjustment disorder with depressed mood, and scored 16 or above on the HRS-D. Although the range of HRS-D global scores was not reported, the subjects' depression was qualified as "mild to moderate". Eighteen patients (nine treated with fluoxetine and nine receiving placebo) completed the 12 week trial. A significant improvement of the HRS-D and the POMS-D scores was found after treatment in both patient groups, and the difference between the changes in the two groups was not statistically significant. The side-effects of fluoxetine were reported as "few", and no interactive effect of fluoxetine on cellular immune variables was observed over the 12 week treatment interval.

Suicide

The occurrence of AIDS has been found to be associated with a high risk of suicide.

The first epidemiological evidence in this sense was provided by Marzuk *et al.* (1988), who examined all the cases of suicide certified by the Chief Medical Examiner among New York City residents in the period of January 1–December 31, 1985. There were 668 suicides in New York City residents (rate = 9.29/100 000 person-years), of which 12 had occurred in subjects with a diagnosis of AIDS (rate = 614.50/100 000 person-years). The relative risk (which is the ratio of the suicide rate of AIDS subjects to that of the general population) was 66.15. Considering that all the AIDS patients committing suicide were men aged 20–59 years, another comparison was made focusing on that specific age group: using this procedure, the relative risk was 36.30.

Psychiatric information on the 12 AIDS patients who committed suicide was obtained from medical records and police investigations. Five subjects had been referred to a psychiatrist within 4 days of the suicide: two of them had been admitted to psychiatric hospitals for a depressive condition; and two had already attempted suicide after the diagnosis of AIDS.

The authors emphasize that the suicide rate reported in the study may be an underestimate, since there may have been suicide victims in whom the diagnosis of AIDS was not reported or even not suspected, as well as AIDS patients in whom suicide was not recognized as the cause of death. They list a number of psychosocial factors which may precipitate suicide in AIDS patients, including the social stigma related to the illness, the withdrawal of family support, diminished or lost occupational functioning, long-term dependency, loss of friends or lovers (often due to AIDS), and the spectre of an inexorable terminal illness that may lead to pain, disfigurement and emaciation. They also point out that the presence of concomitant psychiatric syndromes, especially depression and delirium, may increase the rate of suicide in AIDS patients.

The same research group, in a subsequent paper, published data concerning New York City residents in 1986 and 1987 (Marzuk, 1991). Thirty suicides occurred during that period among people with AIDS, yielding a rate of 380/100 000 in men aged 20–59. The relative risk was approximately 20 times that of the general population in the same age group.

Using a similar methodology, Kizer *et al.* (1988) studied the suicide rates in persons with or without a diagnosis of AIDS in California. In 1986, 3960 suicides were reported (rate = 14.68/100 000 person-years); in 13 cases, AIDS was identified as "a significant condition contributing to death". The age-specific rates (age group 20–59 years) were 27.12/100 000 for the general population and 462.69/100 000 for persons with AIDS, giving a relative risk of suicide, for California men with AIDS, 17.02 times higher than that of men without AIDS. Data on psychiatric morbidity in suicide cases were not reported.

Plott *et al.* (1989), reviewing the register of the Texas Department of Health, Bureau of AIDS and Sexually Transmitted Disease Control, found that five of the 2255 AIDS patients committed suicide during the period January 1, 1986–August 31, 1987, giving a rate of 221.7/100 000 AIDS patients. The estimated rate for the general population in the same period was 13.6/100 000; the relative risk in subjects with AIDS was, therefore, 16.3 times' higher. Again, no data were reported on the prevalence of psychiatric conditions in subjects who committed suicide.

Coté *et al.* (1992) examined the US National Center for Health Statistics multiple-cause mortality data from 1987 to 1989, to look for the cases in which both AIDS and suicide were reported on the death certificate. A total of 165 cases were identified: all but one of the patients were male; 87% were white, 12% black and 1% other races; the median age was 35 years (range 20–69 years). Among males, the suicide rate was 165/100 000 person-years of observation, 7.4-fold higher than among men in the general population (when adjusted for age and race). Self-poisoning with drugs was the most commonly used method (35%). Suicide risk in AIDS patients decreased significantly from 1987 to 1989.

In examining the evidence provided by the above studies, it should be taken into account that the assessment of the relative risk for suicide in AIDS patients should ideally rest on comparisons to individuals from the same at-risk groups, not to the general population. In fact, Gala *et al.* (1989), exploring the prevalence of suicide attempts in 218 HIV-seropositive subjects and 60 seronegative controls belonging to the same at-risk groups (homosexual and drug addicts), found that it was 22% in the former population and 17% in the latter, whereas it was only 0.2% in a control group from the general population. Analogously, Atkinson *et al.* (1990) detected, using the Diagnostic Interview Schedule (DIS), a lifetime proportion of attempted suicide of 9.1% in 22 CDC stage IV subjects, 6.3% in 48 CDC stage II–III individuals, and 9.1% in 34 HIV-seronegative controls (all homosexual), whereas the rate was 1.4% in 294 socio-demographically matched heterosexual men.

CONCLUSIONS

In subjects with HIV infection, the boundary between "understandable" demor-alization and clinical depression is difficult to place. The psychological impact of the notification of seropositivity and of the progression of HIV disease, often worsened by familial, social and occupational rejection, is such that emotional and behavioural reactions may be expected to occur frequently. Currently available rating scales and operational diagnostic criteria may not be sufficiently explicit in specifying the minimum duration and severity that these reactions must have in order to be regarded as depressive symptoms. Depending on where the "threshold" is placed, the rates of depressive symptoms and of syndromal depression may or may not be found to be significantly increased with respect to control groups. In the AIDS long-term survivor study, carried out in New York (Rabkin *et al.*, 1993), 42% of subjects reported "transient sad feelings", 11% had depressive symptoms and 6% had current depressive disorders, but the reliability of such a distribution is very doubtful.

A further problem is represented by the overlap between depressive symptoms and physical and cognitive manifestations of symptomatic HIV infection. Actually, five out of nine symptoms listed in the DSM-IV criteria for major depression are equivocal in this respect. Not to take into account these symptoms, when trying to establish whether a physically symptomatic HIV-seropositive subject has or has not a syndromal depression, implies a reduction of the sensitivity of the DSM-IV symptomatological criterion, whereas to include them implies a decrease of the specificity of the criterion.

HIV infection usually affects, in Western countries, groups which are at high risk for depressive symptoms and syndromes, independently of the occurrence of the infection. Therefore, to compare depression or suicide rates of HIV-seropositive subjects with those of the general population is certainly misleading. In an HIV-seropositive subject who is currently depressed, attempts should be made to establish whether the first depressive episode occurred before or after seroconversion.

All the above factors must be kept in mind when examining the research evidence concerning the prevalence of depressive symptoms and syndromes in

HIV-seropositive subjects. On the basis of this evidence, it may be tentatively submitted that the physically symptomatic stages of HIV infection are associated with an increased risk of depressive symptoms, and that such a risk is higher if the subject has a past personal history of depression or a current diagnosis of personality disorder, if social support is inadequate or if his/her coping strategies are not effective. In the most unfavourable conditions, the risk of syndromal depression may also be significantly increased. The social contexts in which HIV-seropositive subjects are living are very diverse world-wide, and the quality and quantity of available social support is certainly not the same for homosexual men involved in formal support groups in San Francisco as for IV drug users in Bangkok or Sao Paulo. It may be hypothesized that in those geographic areas where the epidemic has reached its second decade, social tolerance towards HIV-seropositive subjects is increasing, and this is reducing the risk of depressive symptoms and signs. Data on the decreased frequency of suicide in AIDS patients from 1987 to 1989 in the USA represent a clue in this direction.

Distress associated with HIV infection is likely to be reduced by individual and group psychotherapy, but, when clinical depression is present, drug treatment is, at the current state of knowledge, the first therapeutic option. Systematic evidence that SSRIs are better tolerated than tricyclics in HIV-seropositive subjects is currently lacking. Clearly, the overall clinical picture should be considered in each individual case: in the presence of chronic diarrhoea SSRIs are contraindicated, whereas the peripheral anticholinergic effects of tricyclics may be useful. The results of American double-blind trials, showing tolerability of imipramine at average daily doses of more than 200 mg, may cause scepticism in European clinicians, but surely balance previous anecdotal reports of precipitation of delirium or exacerbation of cognitive impairment by tricyclics, which may have deprived several depressed HIV-seropositive subjects of effective treatment. On the other hand, the toxicity in overdose of tricyclics remains a serious concern, especially in the light of the evidence that self-poisoning with drugs is the most common method of suicide in AIDS patients.

In conclusion, currently available information on HIV-associated depressive symptoms and syndromes certainly presents several gaps. Only a few studies have been conducted on samples which are representative of the broad population of HIV-seropositive persons, and no long-term follow up study is available. Moreover, the boundary between demoralization and clinical depression is often uncertain, and the decision whether or not to use antidepressant drugs may be difficult in some cases. Nevertheless, clinicians should be aware that, when currently available operational diagnostic criteria are fulfilled, syndromal depression of HIV-seropositive subjects should be treated as such, whatever its determinants may be and independently of how "justified" it may appear.

ACKNOWLEDGEMENT

The author would like to thank Luca Bartoli, Department of Psychiatry, University of Naples, for his help in setting up the manuscript.

REFERENCES

Atkinson JH, Grant I, Kennedy CJ *et al*. (1988) Prevalence of psychiatric disorders among men infected with human immunodeficiency virus. A controlled study. *Arch Gen Psychiatry*, **45**, 859–864.

Atkinson H, Gutierrez R, Cottler L *et al*. (1990) Suicide ideation and attempts in HIV illness. *Abstracts VI International Conference on AIDS*, San Francisco, abstr. SB 384.

Beckett A and Rutan JS (1990) Treating persons with ARC and AIDS in group psychotherapy. *Int J Group Psychother*, **40**, 19–29.

Budka H, Wiley CA, Kleihues P *et al*. (1991) HIV-associated disease of the nervous system: Review of nomenclature and proposal for neuropathology-based terminology. *Brain Pathol*, **1**, 143–152.

Burack JH, Barrett DC, Stall RD *et al*. (1993) Depressive symptoms and CD4 lymphocyte decline among HIV-infected men. *JAMA*, **270**, 2568–2573.

Centres for Disease Control (1987) Revision of the CDC surveillance case definition for acquired immunodeficiency syndrome. *Morb Mortal Wly Rep*, **36 (suppl. 1S)**, 3–15.

Chabner BA and Myers CE (1985) Clinical pharmacology of cancer. In: VT De Vita, C Hellman and SA Rosenberg (eds) *Cancer: Principles and Practice of Oncology*. Philadelphia: Lippincott, 287–328.

Christ GH, Siegel K and Moynihan RT (1988) Psychosocial issues: prevention and treatment, In: VT De Vita, S Hellman and SA Rosenberg (eds) *AIDS: Etiology, Diagnosis, Treatment and Prevention*, 2nd edn., Philadelphia: Lippincott, 321–337.

Clifford DB, Jacoby RG, Miller JP *et al*. (1990) Neuropsychometric performance of asymptomatic HIV-infected subjects. *AIDS*, **4**, 767–774.

Commerford MC, Gular E, Orr DA *et al*. (1994) Coping and psychological distress in women with HIV/AIDS. *J Community Psychol*, **22**, 224–230.

Coté TR, Biggar RJ and Dannenberg AL (1992) Risk of suicide among persons with AIDS. A national assessment. *JAMA*, **268**, 2066–2068.

Fernandez F, Levy JK and Galizzi H (1988) Response of HIV-related depression to psychostimulants: Case reports. *Hosp Community Psychiatry*, **39**, 628–631.

Fernandez F, Levy JK and Mansell PWA (1989) Response to antidepressant therapy in depressed persons with advanced HIV infection. *Abstracts V International Conference on AIDS*, Montreal, abstr. WBP 191.

Fernandez F, Levy JK, Samley HR, Pirozzolo FJ, Lachar D, Crowley J, Adams S, Ross B and Ruiz P (1995) Effects of methylphenidate in HIV-related depression: A comparative trial with desipramine. *Int J Psychiatry*, **25**, 53–67.

Folkman S, Chesney M, Pollack L *et al*. (1993) Stress, control, and depressive mood in human immunodeficiency virus-positive and -negative gay men in San Francisco. *J Nerv Ment Dis*, **181**, 409–416.

Gala G, Martini S, Pergami A *et al*. (1989) Psychiatric history among homosexuals and drug-addicts infected with human immunodeficiency virus. *Abstracts V International Conference on AIDS*, Montreal, abstr. WBP 215.

Grant I and Atkinson JH (1990) The evolution of neurobehavioural complications of HIV infection. *Psychol Med*, **20**, 747–754.

Hays RB, Turner H and Coates TJ (1992) Social support, AIDS-related symptoms, and depression among gay men. *J Consult Clin Psychol*, **60**, 463–469.

Johnson JG, Williams JBW, Rabkin JG *et al*. (1995) Axis I psychiatric symptoms associated with HIV infection and personality disorder. *Am J Psychiatry*, **152**, 551–554.

Kelly JA, Murphy DA, Bahr GR *et al*. (1993) Outcome of cognitive-behavioral and support group brief therapies for depressed, HIV-infected persons. *Am J Psychiatry*, **150**, 1679–1686.

Kessler RC, Foster C, Joseph J *et al*. (1991) Stressful life events and symptom onset in HIV infection. *Am J Psychiatry*, **148**, 733–738.

Kizer KW, Green M, Perkins CI *et al*. (1988) AIDS and suicide in California. *JAMA*, **260**, 1881.

Kokkevi A, Hatzakis A, Maillis A *et al*. (1991) Neuropsychological assessment of HIV-seropositive haemophiliacs. *AIDS*, **5**, 1223–1229.

Krikorian R and Wrobel AJ (1991) Cognitive impairment in HIV infection. *AIDS*, **5**, 1501–1507.

Leserman J, DiSantostefano R, Perkins DO *et al*. (1994) Longitudinal study of social support and social conflict as predictors of depression and dysphoria among HIV-positive and HIV-negative gay men. *Depression*, **2**, 189–199.

Levine S, Anderson D, Bystritsky A *et al*. (1990) A report of eight HIV-seropositive patients with major depression responding to fluoxetine. *J Acquir Immune Depressive Syndr*, **3**, 1074–1077.

Lipsitz JD, Williams JBW, Rabkin JG *et al*. (1994) Psychopathology in male and female intravenous drug users with and without HIV infection. *Am J Psychiatry*, **151**, 1662–1668.

Lyketsos CG, Hoover DR, Guccione M *et al*. (1993) Depressive symptoms as predictors of medical outcomes in HIV infection. *JAMA*, **270**, 2563–2567.

Maj M (1990a) Organic mental disorders in HIV-1 infection. *AIDS*, **4**, 831–840.

Maj M (1990b) Psychiatric aspects of HIV-1 infection and AIDS. *Psychol Med*, **20**, 547–563.

Maj M (1996) Depressive syndromes and symptoms in subjects with human immunodeficiency (HIV) infection *Br J Psychiatry*, **168(Suppl 30)**, 117–122.

Maj M, Janssen R, Starace F *et al*. (1994a) WHO Neuropsychiatric AIDS Study, cross-sectional phase. II. Neuropsychological and neurological findings. *Arch Gen Psychiatry*, **51**, 39–49.

Maj M, Satz P, Janssen R *et al*. (1994b) WHO Neuropsychiatric AIDS Study, cross-sectional phase. II. Neuropsychological and neurological findings. *Arch Gen Psychiatry*, **51**, 51–61.

Manning D, Jacobsberg L, Erhart S *et al*. (1990) The efficacy of imipramine in the treatment of HIV-related depression. *Abstracts VI International Conference on AIDS*, San Francisco, abstr. ThB 32.

Markowitz JC, Klerman GL, Clougherty KF *et al*. (1995) Individual psychotherapies for depressed HIV-positive patients. *Am J Psychiatry*, **152**, 1504–1509.

Marzuk PM (1991) Suicidal behaviour among HIV-infected patients. A review of the American literature. In: JE Beskow, M Bellini, JG Sampaio Faria *et al*. (eds) *HIV and AIDS-related Suicidal Behaviour*. Report on a WHO consultation, Bologna: Monduzzi.

Marzuk PM, Tierney H, Tardiff K *et al*. (1988) Increased risk of suicide in persons with AIDS. *JAMA*, **259**, 1333–1337.

Miller D (1987) *Living with AIDS and HIV*. Houndmills: MacMillan.

Miller EN, Satz P and Visscher B (1991) Computerized and conventional neuropsychological assessment of HIV-1 infected homosexual men. *Neurology*, **41**, 1608–1616.

Navia BA, Jordan BD and Price RW (1986) The AIDS dementia complex: I. Clinical picture. *Ann Neurol*, **19**, 517–524.

Nichols SE (1986) Psychotherapy and AIDS. In: T Stein and C Cohen (eds) *Contemporary Perspectives on Psychotherapy with Lesbians and Gay Men*, New York: Plenum Press, 209–239.

Ostrow DG (1987) Psychiatric consequences of AIDS: an overview. *Int J Neurosci*, **32**, 647–659.

Ostrow DG, Monjan A, Joseph J *et al.* (1989) HIV-related symptoms and psychological functioning in a cohort of homosexual men. *Am J Psychiatry*, **146**, 737–742.

Perdices M, Dunbar N, Grunseit A *et al.* (1992) Anxiety, depression and HIV related symptomatology across the spectrum of HIV disease. *Aust NZ Psychiatry*, **26**, 560–566.

Perkins DO, Stern RA, Golden RN *et al.* (1994) Mood disorders in HIV infection: prevalence and risk factors in a non-epicenter of the AIDS epidemic. *Am J Psychiatry*, **151**, 233–236.

Perry S (1990) Organic mental disorders caused by HIV: update on early diagnosis and treatment. *Am J Psychiatry*, **147**, 696–710.

Perry S, Fishman B, Jacobsberg L *et al.* (1991) Effectiveness of psychoeducational interventions in reducing emotional distress after human immunodeficiency virus antibody testing. *Arch Gen Psychiatry*, **48**, 143–147.

Perry S, Fishman B, Jacobsberg L *et al.* (1992) Relationships over 1 year between lymphocyte subsets and psychosocial variables among adults with infection by human immunodeficiency virus. *Am J Psychiatry*, **49**, 396–401.

Perry S, Jacobsberg LB, Fishman B *et al.* (1990) Psychiatric diagnosis before serological testing for the human immunodeficiency virus. *Am J Psychiatry*, **147**, 89–93.

Plott RT, Benton SD and Winslade WK (1989) Suicide of AIDS patients in Texas: A preliminary report. *Texas Medicine*, **85**, 40–43.

Price RW, Brew B, Sidtis J *et al.* (1988) The brain in AIDS: central nervous system HIV-1 infection and AIDS dementia complex. *Science*, **239**, 586–592.

Rabkin JG (1993) Psychostimulant medication for depression and lethargy in HIV illness: A pilot study. *Am Soc Clin Psychopharmacol Prog*, **4**, 1.

Rabkin JG, Williams JBW, Remien RH *et al.* (1991) Depression, distress, lymphocyte subsets, and human immunodeficiency virus symptoms on two occasions in HIV-positive homosexual men. *Arch Gen Psychiatry*, **48**, 111–119.

Rabkin JG, Remien R, Katoff L *et al.* (1993) Resilience in adversity among long-term survivors of AIDS. *Hosp Community Psychiatry*, **44**, 162–167.

Rabkin JG, Rabkin R, Harrison W *et al.* (1994a) Effect of imipramine on mood and enumerative measures of immune status in depressed patients with HIV illness. *Am J Psychiatry*, **151**, 516–523.

Rabkin JG, Rabkin R and Wagner G (1994b) Fluoxetine effects on mood and immune status in depressed patients with HIV illness. *J Clin Psychiatry*, **55**, 92–97.

Rabkin JG, Wagner G and Rabkin R (1994c) Sertraline effects on mood and immune status in patients with major depression and HIV illness: an open trial. *J Clin Psychiatry*, **55**, 433–439.

Regier DA, Boyd JH, Burke JD Jr *et al.* (1988) One-month prevalence of mental disorders in the United States based on five Epidemiologic Catchment Area sites. *Arch Gen Psychiatry*, **45**, 977–986.

Rosenberger PH, Bornstein RA, Nasrallah HA *et al.* (1993) Psychopathology in human immunodeficiency virus infection: lifetime and current assessment. *Compr Psychiatry*, **34**, 150–158.

Targ EF, Karasic DH and Diefenbach PN (1994) Structured group therapy and fluoxetine to treat depression in HIV-positive persons. *Psychosomatics*, **35**, 132–137.

van Gorp WG, Satz P, Hinkin C *et al.* (1991) Metacognition in HIV-1 seropositive asymptomatic individuals: Self-ratings versus objective neuropsychological performance. *J Clin Exp Neuropsychol*, **13**, 812–819.

Volberding PA, Abrams DI and Conant M (1985) Vinblastin therapy for Kaposi's sarcoma in the acquired immunodeficiency syndrome. *Ann Intern Med*, **103**, 335–338.

Walling VR and Pfefferbaum B (1990) The use of methylphenidate in a depressed adolescent with AIDS. *J Dev Behav Pediatr*, **11**, 195–197.

White JC, Christensen JR and Singer CM (1992) Methylphenidate as a treatment for depression in acquired immunodeficiency syndrome: an n-of-1 trial. *J Clin Psychiatry*, **53**, 153–156.

Williams JBW, Rabkin JG, Remien RH *et al.* (1991) Multidisciplinary baseline assessment of homosexual men with and without human immunodeficiency virus infection. II. Standardized clinical assessment of current and lifetime psychopathology. *Arch Gen Psychiatry*, **48**, 124–130.

World Health Organisation (1994) *Global Programme on AIDS: The HIV/AIDS Pandemic: 1994 overview*. Geneva: World Health Organisation.

12

Depression and cardiovascular disease

C. Gala, F. Galletti and G. Invernizzi

INTRODUCTION

The various forms of cardiovascular disease taken together represent the main causes of morbidity and mortality in the USA and other industrialized countries of the West. Myocardial infarction (MI) affects about 1.5 million people per year in the USA, and is responsible for 40% of deaths in men and 10% in women in the 45–64 age range. In the USA 2.5% of the population (5.7 million) suffer from ischaemic heart disease, and 42% of these experience limitations in both social and working spheres (Kannel and Thom, 1989). In addition, hypertension, which constitutes one of the major risk factors of cardiovascular disease, stroke, renal insufficiency, and cardiac failure, is the third most common chronic disorder affecting the adult population of the USA, accounting for as many as 50 million cases of chronic illness (Blumenthal *et al.*, 1993). From a large number of studies, the prevalence of depressive symptoms (major depression and minor depressive syndromes), evaluated according to DSM-IIIR (American Psychiatric Association, 1987), in the first weeks after MI, has been found to be between 30% and 40%. The prevalence of major depression alone is between 15% and 30%.

A number of follow up studies that have examined the evolution of depression in the months following MI have revealed that such disorders persist in a similar percentage of patients for up to 3–6 months, and even as long as 1 year,

Depression and Physical Illness. Edited by M.M. Robertson and C.L.E. Katona
© 1997 John Wiley & Sons Ltd

from infarction. The significance of such data is underlined by the fact that the presence at 6 months of major depression in a sample of the general population, comparable in terms of age and sex, is approximately 3% (Kavanagh et al., 1975; Carney et al., 1987; Schleifer et al., 1989; Frasure-Smith, 1991; Griego, 1993; Ladwig et al., 1994).

DEPRESSION IN THE MULTIFACTORIAL AETIOPATHOGENESIS OF CARDIOVASCULAR DISORDERS

The intimate connections between mind and body, mediated by the neurovegetative and neuroendocrine systems, justify the interest shown by a large number of investigators in the possible role of psychopathological disorders in the onset of cardiovascular disease. One of the most classic studies in the area assessed the rates of mortality of patients admitted to the New York State Hospital for involutional melancholia between 1928 and 1931, and compared them with those for the general population of the same State over the same period (Malzberg, 1937). The two groups were divided into subgroups according to age in order to enable a comparison to be made between homogeneous populations. The rates of mortality among the subjects with involutional melancholia were six times higher than those found in the general population. In particular, cardiovascular disorders were responsible for 40% of deaths among depressed patients, and this mortality rate for cardiovascular disease was eight times higher than that found in the control population.

A number of more recent studies have confirmed the pioneering conclusions of Malzberg (e.g. Carney, et al., 1988a, 1990). In a study conducted on patients suffering from coronary artery disease (CAD), a higher prevalence of ventricular tachycardia was found (ventricular tachycardia constitutes a significant factor in the increase of the risk of infarction) among depressed patients, as compared to nondepressed patients suffering from CAD. This difference remained significant even after the possible influence of confounding factors, such as the administration of beta-blockers or compounds that might be associated with symptoms and signs of a depressive nature, had been ruled out (Carney et al., 1993). The presence of a medical history of depressive disorders in depressed post-MI patients proved also to be correlated to significant clinical and prognostic factors.

Lloyd and Cawley (1983) showed that depression in post-MI patients with previous psychopathological disorders and high neuroticism tends to persist longer than does that manifested by post-MI patients who do not have psychopathological precedents. Freedland et al. (1992) noted that, in the period following infarction, subjects with a medical history of depression presented a clinical picture that matched that of classic major depression, whilst patients who presented a first depressive episode following infarction had a clinical picture that was comparable to that of patients suffering from depression with late onset.

The hypotheses that have been formulated to explain the role of depression in the pathogenetic mechanisms of infarction vary in nature. The first of these correlates depression to the patient's habits and life-style, which constitute the major factors of risk of infarction, such as smoking, obesity, sedentary occupation, etc. (Glassman *et al.*, 1990; Kendler *et al.*, 1990; Littman, 1993). The presence of depression increases mortality from cardiovascular events in patients with high blood pressure (Friedman, 1984; Booth-Kewley and Friedman, 1987). However, the evidence for a direct aetiological correlation between depression, development of hypertension, and consequent increased risk of death from vascular causes is still scant (Mann, 1986). According to some authors (Simonsick *et al.*, 1995), the main mechanism of action of depression is of an indirect nature, i.e. its presence would appear to interfere with an adequate management of hypertension through factors linked both to the therapists (e.g. modification of therapy, reduction or suspension of antihypertensive treatment in the case of a possible iatrogenic depressive condition) and to the patients (reduced compliance), which thus intensify the potentially harmful effects of hypertension. On the other hand, a depressive state might simply be a "marker" of a more serious hypertensive disorder or of a higher medical comorbidity. Each of these factors may independently increase the risks of vascular-related deaths in hypertensive patients (Wells, 1995). Furthermore, psychosocial variables that are strongly associated with depression, such as personality traits and stressful life events, may play a role in increasing the vulnerability of the individual to cardiovascular disease through specific neuroendocrine mechanisms.

Personality

Among the psychological factors correlated with a higher risk of CAD, an important role is played by personality traits. As was initially observed by authors such as Dunbar (1948) and Alexander and French (1948), and subsequently by Friedman (1984), the individual at risk for CAD presents a feeling of insecurity and a depressive state masked by hyperactivity and aggression (type A behaviour). The presence of this type of personality reinforces the pathogenetic effects of other coronary risk factors (Blumenthal *et al.*, 1978). The subject with a type A personality is ambitious, overactive, presents marked traits of aggression and hostility, and has a strong need to control the world around him. He is simultaneously engaged in a number of activities, feels the constant urge to bring the things with which he is involved to fulfilment, even during his leisure time and holiday periods, and is incapable of relaxing and resting sufficiently. Inactivity is perceived as a "waste of time". Aggression and hostility, both direct and indirect, seem to represent the major elements of cardiovascular risk among the traits typical of the type A individual. In the development of this behavioural model, childhood affective experience and environmental variables play an important role. The child who has not received adequate support and affective backing from his parents tends to show a greater sense of insecurity and lack of self-esteem, which is accentuated if he is in a family environment that is particularly demanding on the level of physical or intellectual attainment. The child tends to seek love and the confirmation of his personal worth from his parents by increasing his performance, which, however, always falls short of the excessive expectations set by himself or by his parents. In this way, in adulthood, the development of type A behaviour will become functional in continuing this pursuit at a social level, as a means of hiding a fundamental depressive condition.

Although the type A individual appears to be a person who is sure of himself and assertive, in actual fact all his energy is spent seeking a confirmation from the world and a control over emotions and external situations. This precarious balance breaks down with serious biological repercussions when uncontrollable life situations arise, or situations that involve a loss on the affective or working planes. In this respect, the type A personality, whose mode of behaviour may be interpreted as a means of defence from a depressive experience, appears to constitute a risk factor both for the development of cardiovascular disorders and for the onset of depression (Shima and Kitagawa, 1994).

Stressful events

The psychological variable which presents the strongest correlation with the risk of developing a depressive condition, as well as MI, is represented by experiences of bereavement or loss, such as the death of someone close, or the loss of roles, of objects that carry a particular meaning, or health. In fact, stressful life events have been found to precede the onset of both depressive episodes and acute MI to a significant extent. The most important event studied and correlated with sudden cardiac death is bereavement or separation from an important person. It has been shown that the mortality rate among those who have suffered a loss of this sort increases significantly during the year that follows, and that the cause of death is most often linked to disease of the cardiovascular system (Post, 1992). The organic event, however, may even fail to appear with any direct and immediate link, but may be preceded by a period in which clear depressive signs appear subsequent to events which again may be of an affective nature, but above all may be associated with the person's working life.

In a large number of cases, prolonged stress at work, not followed by success or promotion, dissatisfaction at a career level, and early retirement all bring about a state of depression, which precedes an infarct by a few hours in certain cases, or by a few days or weeks in others. It has been shown that retirement increases the risk of death from CAD by 80% (Cascelles *et al.*, 1980). Subsequent prospective studies confirm these data but also indicate that, if the sense of loss is "compensated for" by rebuilding a valid affective relationship or by using a satisfactory network of affective and social supports, the risk of death decreases significantly (Helsing *et al.*, 1981).

Neuroendocrine correlations between depression and cardiovascular disease

Biological correlates of stressful and depressive experience determine an increased risk of cardiovascular illness.

It has now been adequately shown that psychological stresses are accompanied by measurable and quantifiable changes in heart rate, arterial pressure and cardiac output (Cinciripini and Galveston, 1986). Emotional stimulation, through the limbic system, the hypothalamus and the pituitary gland, acts directly on the cardiovascular system through the autonomic nervous system, which innervates the heart and blood vessels, and indirectly through the release of adrenaline, cortisol and neuropeptides (Schneiderman, 1983). Emotions have an effect on both the circulatory dynamics and the biohumoral parameters connected thereto.

The results of studies performed on the cardiovascular activity in animals subjected to stressful stimuli, though varying according to species, genetic characteristics and hierarchical role, have made it possible to delineate physiological models of cardiovascular reaction to stressful situations, which are associated with particular behaviours and are strictly correlated to the characteristics of the stimuli (novelty, foreseeableness, possibility of control). In the case of a subordinate animal, which is continuously exposed to the threat of attack from a dominant individual of the group without having any chance of flight, the phenomena that are noted are a constant increase in peripheral resistance, reflex bradycardia, and reduction in cardiac output and impairment of cardiovascular functional efficiency, which may even lead to cardiac arrest when stress is excessively prolonged. This physiological response, which is associated with behavioural aspects of a "depressive" type (immobility, inhibition of aggressive conduct, attitudes of submission, and flinching from combat), thus appears in all situations in which the animal has no chance of facing up to the stressful stimulus in an active and effective way. This phenomenon is defined as "learned helplessness". To this model of response to uncontrollable or unavoidable stressors there has been correlated a specific neurohormonal pattern characterized in particular by an increase in the plasma levels of cortisol (Henry *et al.*, 1972; Mason, 1975; Weiner, 1981; Weiss *et al.*, 1989).

Weiss *et al.* (1989) demonstrated that behavioural stress enhances serotoninergic sensitivity in an animal model of depression, which would suggest a neurochemical basis of stress-induced depression. It is interesting to note that this model of response of the animal and the response found in man present notable affinities.

1. An association between major depression and corticoadrenal hyperactivity has been demonstrated (Gold *et al.*, 1988).
2. Clinical studies in humans have suggested a role of emotionally distressing events (especially loss) in depression (Post, 1992).
3. A marked increase has been found in adrenal 17-OH-C, adrenaline and noradrenaline in people who are the object of repeated and humiliating reprimands from their superiors (Frankenhaeuser and Rissler, 1970).
4. A relationship has been established between aggression, degree of deactivation of the sympathetic nervous system and levels of noradrenaline and renin in circulation on the one hand, and the appearance of high blood pressure on the other (Esler *et al.*, 1977).
5. A trend has been revealed towards a higher excretion of catecholamines in the urine during execution of an activity which involves the attainment of a precise goal.
6. Activation of the sympathetic-adrenomedullary system has been demonstrated in men who have to make an effort to overcome a distressing situation. When the situation is not accompanied by the corresponding attempt to overcome it, or when the effort made does not lead to success, feelings of renunciation and passivity appear, and a corticoadrenal hypersecretion is instead observed (Frankenhaeuser *et al.*, 1980).

Catecholamines exert an action on the heart at the level of the conductive tissue and myocardial cells. They are able to influence the genesis and conduction of the electrical stimulus, and to determine an increase in excitability, with a consequent lowering of the triggering threshold of cardiac arrhythmias. For this reason, it has been suggested that stressful situations that are initially characterized by overexcitation of the sympathetic nervous system, followed by feelings of impotence, despair and renunciation, are the ones that most often predispose to MI and sudden cardiac death, since the heart muscle is exposed simultaneously to the action of high levels of catecholamine and corticosteroid (Engel, 1978). The state of vasoconstriction determines a hypertensive condition that brings about further damage to the vasal endothelium through increased vascular turbulence.

DEPRESSION ASSOCIATED WITH A CARDIOVASCULAR EVENT

Myocardial ischaemic disorders are diseases that arise suddenly and are life-threatening. Consequently, their very nature makes them stressful life events of particular seriousness that entail a significant impairment of global bodily function and impose the need for major modifications in the patient's way of life. Patients who survive MI must face up to a persistent preoccupation with possible relapse, which necessarily exposes then to limitations of both an objective and subjective nature. The patient must adjust to the adoption of certain new behaviour patterns (e.g. the taking of medication), to the abandonment of certain others (e.g. smoking), and to the modification of yet others (e.g. dietary and physical habits). The limitation of physical capacity may interfere adversely with the patient's functioning at work and socially, and also in his family life and sexual activities. All these factors of an existential and psychological nature contribute to the onset of depressive symptoms and, if not overcome, justify the persistence of such symptoms.

Cassem and Hackett (1973) have coined the term "home-coming depression" to define the depressive state that occurs in subjects who have to face up to the modifications in their family, social and working roles and to restrictions imposed during the period of convalescence. The extent and duration of this reaction, and hence its possible evolution in the direction of a real depressive disorder, will largely depend upon how the subject values the losses that he has suffered and their consequences (West, 1986).

DEPRESSION AND OUTCOME OF MI

The most important prognostic factors for mortality or relapse in the post-infarction period are those concerning the myocardial injury suffered (left ventricular ejection fraction, seriousness of the concomitant coronary heart and myocardial disorders, and possibility of malignant ventricular arrhythmias). The presence of postinfarction depression appears to constitute a factor predictive of mortality that is independent of the seriousness of the heart disease and hinders physical recovery, delaying return to a good level of functioning, and increasing the risk of cardiac complications and death (rehospitalization, surgery, significant ventricular arrhythmias, reinfarction, death) in the course of the year following diagnosis of MI (Carney *et al.*, 1988b; Schleifer *et al.*, 1989; Freedland *et al.*, 1992).

A study conducted on post-MI patients hospitalized with a diagnosis according to DSM-IIIR criteria of major depression found a risk of mortality in the 6 months following infarction three to four times higher than in non-depressed post-MI patients (Frasure-Smith *et al.*, 1993). In all the studies, such correlations were maintained even after allowing for the possible influence of other characteristic risk factors of the postinfarction period (prior MI, left ventricular ejection fraction).

A number of specific studies aimed at assessing the relationship between poverty of social support and incidence of MI or reinfarction have pointed to a significant correlation between the two variables. The absence of social support is acknowledged as a risk factor for MI and death due to cardiovascular disorders probably because an important "buffer" factor that could serve to cushion the impact of stressful events experienced by the individual is missing (Travella *et al.*, 1994; Garcia *et al.*, 1994).

Increase in prevalence or seriousness of ventricular arrhythmias

One plausible correlating mechanism is represented by an increase in the prevalence or seriousness of ventricular arrhythmias linked to an alteration of the sympathetic tone: physically healthy depressed patients have proved to have increased activity of the sympathetic nervous system and increased "cholinergic tone" (Esler *et al.*, 1982), increased plasma catecholamines, and increased heart rate at rest as compared with nondepressed controls (Roy *et al.*, 1985). A higher mortality amongst patients with MI has, on the other hand, been associated both with increased heart rate (Kannel, 1989) and with a diminished variability of heart rate (Kleiger *et al.*, 1987). Depressed patients with CAD present a diminished variability in heart rate (in particular as regards the high rates regulated by vagal mechanisms), which in turn is correlated to unfavourable prognoses in the postinfarction period (Carney *et al.*, 1988b; Dalack and Roose, 1990). The increased activity of the autonomic nervous system described in depression could therefore trigger ventricular arrhythmias, which are acknowledged as constituting a risk factor for mortality in the post-MI patient (Bigger *et al.*, 1984).

Modifications in platelet function/aggregation processes

In addition to being by now generally recognized as an important neurotransmitter involved in the neurobiological mechanisms of depression, serotonin exerts a significant action on thrombogenesis. The presence of a dysfunction of serotoninergic neurotransmission (in accordance with the serotoninergic model of depression) could thus be correlated also with alterations in blood platelet function. Serotonin is itself a weak thrombogenic agent and amplifies the platelet response to other thrombogenic agents. Some studies (Kusumi *et al.*, 1991; Mikuni *et al.*, 1992) have revealed that the thrombogenic response is in fact increased in depressed patients. The presence of depression could therefore expose individuals who have had an MI to a higher risk of thrombosis.

Behavioural mechanism

Depressed patients have a higher likelihood of noncompliance to medication and thus of remaining exposed to the risk of heart disease. The characteristic symptoms and signs of depression are all potentially disturbing to the process of postinfarction recovery. The somatic signs (low energy loss of appetite, weight loss) may further worsen the general physical condition of patients; cognitive disorders (difficulty in concentrating, psychomotor retardation or agitation) may lead to inadequate patient compliance with medication; and psychological disorders (depressed mood, feelings of loss of worth, suicidal ideation) may finally lead to a more or less deliberate resistance to measures aimed at prevention, treatment and rehabilitation that are necessary during the convalescent period (avoidance of risk factors, physical exercise, dietary limitations, etc.). All these elements can concur to develop "pathological patterns of behaviour" which interfere considerably with patient compliance and pose serious obstacles to rehabilitation.

PHARMACOLOGICAL TREATMENT

The rational treatment of depressive disorders constitutes one of the major factors responsible for the reduction in the risk of mortality of patients with MI (Littman, 1993). One of the main reasons for the inadequate treatment of depressed patients suffering from cardiovascular disorders is fear that the use of antidepressant drugs, and above all the tricyclic antidepressants (TCAs), may have harmful consequences on the patient's heart condition. The concerns are certainly well-founded; however, antidepressant drugs that are safe for the cardiovascular system are currently available.

Tricyclic antidepressants (TCAs)

Sinus tachycardia, postural hypotension and episodic hypertension are the side-effects most frequently observed in the course of treatment with TCAs. For example, increases of 15–20 beats per minute have been observed with nortriptyline and amitriptyline in depressed patients not suffering from cardiovascular disease. Alterations of such a degree in patients with coronary circulation deficits could have serious consequences (Levenson and Friedel, 1985). All these effects are largely due to the wide-ranging pharmacological action of TCAs that is not correlated to the recognized mechanisms of action on depression (Table 1). Also, asymptomatic ECG modifications are detectable, such as lengthening of the Q–T, P–R, and QRS intervals, which points to alterations in atrioventricular conduction and repolarization (Table 2). In healthy patients, such modifications are generally clinically unimportant, but in patients with pre-existing conduction disorders, in particular bundle branch block, treatment with TCAs may cause significant conduction disorders in approximately 20% of subjects. This action exerted by TCAs depends upon the anti-arrhythmic activity of these compounds, which is analogous to that of class 1 anti-arrhythmic compounds, such as quinidine and procainamide. On the basis of these obser-

Table 1. Pharmacological basis of TCA cardiotoxicity

Property	Effect on cardiovascular system
Anticholinergic (atropine-like)	Sinus tachycardia
Adrenoceptor (α-1) antagonism	Postural hypotension
"Sympathomimetic" (noradrenaline uptake inhibition and α-2 antagonism)	Atrial and ventricular arrhythmias, A–V dissociation, hypertension
Local anaesthetic (quinidine-like)	QRS, Q–T, ST–T changes, myocardial depression, anti-arrhythmic action
Effects on K^+ and Ca^{2+}	Conduction/repolarization changes

Table 2. Electrocardiographic effects of tricyclic antidepressants.

Observable ECG effects	Dose range (plasma level)	
	Therapeutic (<300 ng/ml)	Overdose (>1000 ng/ml)
Sinus tachycardia	+	+
Increased:		
P–R	+	+
QRS	+	+ +
Q–T	+	+
ST–T	+	+
Atrial arrhythmia	+	+
Anti-arrhythmic	+	–
Ventricular arrhythmic	–	+
A–V block	–	+

vations, up to a few years ago it was believed that in patients with depression and cardiac arrhythmias the use of TCAs was beneficial for both conditions. However, recent research into the effect of anti-arrhythmic compounds on the suppression of ventricular arrhythmic phenomena in postinfarction patients has revealed that the use of these drugs not only does not reduce mortality, but indeed, also determines its increase, and moreover that such effects are not limited to postinfarction patients. No data have emerged that suggest a better profile for any single TCA as against others as far as impairment of cardiac conduction is concerned (Cardiac Arrhythmia Suppression Trial, 1989). The incidence and seriousness of the effects are dose-dependent and above all dependent upon the pre-existence of heart disease. Depressed patients suffering from cardiovascular disorders have been found to have three to seven times more likelihood of presenting with serious postural hypotension than do depressed subjects without cardiovascular disorders (Glassman et al., 1983).

This fact determines the need to suspend treatment in 25–50% of patients with pre-existing cardiovascular disease (Glassman *et al.*, 1983). Another factor is the particular TCA used. The tertiary amine tricyclics (amitriptyline, imipramine, clomipramine) present more evident cardiovascular effects than do secondary amine tricyclics (nortriptyline, desipramine, etc.) on account of their greater anticholinergic, histaminergic and α-1 and β-2 adrenergic receptor affinity. The TCA that has proved to have a lesser orthostatic hypotensive effect is nortriptyline, which has consequently become the TCA of choice for the treatment of depression in patients suffering from cardiovascular disease, and above all in elderly patients, in whom the onset of postural hypotension may have disastrous effects (falls and consequent injuries). Other factors that have a significant bearing are patient age, the presence of other somatic diseases (e.g. liver disease) which may reduce metabolism of TCAs, and the simultaneous taking of other drugs having effects on the cardiovascular system (Glassman *et al.*, 1993; Glassman and Roose, 1994). The highest degrees of interaction are with α-methyldopa and clonidine, the antihypertensive effect of which is blocked. The introduction of TCA therapy may lead to imbalance of a situation of good compensation of blood pressure levels achieved thanks to maintenance antihypertensive therapy. Also, the suspension of TCA therapy must be approached with care, wherever the blood pressure levels are stabilized by it (Giardina *et al.*, 1982; Levenson and Friedel, 1985; Series, 1992). Overdosage of TCAs is associated with modifications in cardiac and cardiovascular dynamics that in a number of cases may even be fatal. In addition to a serious condition of hypotension, serious atrial and ventricular arrhythmias may arise even to the point of complete A–V block. For all these reasons, the use of TCAs must be considered unsafe in patients with angina pectoris, myocardial infarction, cardiac failure, and hypertension.

Other antidepressants

Among the antidepressant drugs, selective serotonin reuptake inhibitors (SSRIs), such as fluoxetine, fluvoxamine, paroxetine, sertraline, nefazodone, citalopram, etc., are devoid of antimuscarinic effects, do not appear to determine variations in the P–R or QRS intervals, or block the calcium fast channels, and it is therefore likely that SSRIs do not posses the pro-arrhythmic or anti-arrhythmic effects possessed by TCAs. These compounds moreover do not cause postural hypotension, or have a clinically significant effect on heart rate. There is not yet sufficient evidence in the literature on the use of SSRIs in patients suffering from cardiovascular disease to confirm them as a valid and safe alternative to TCAs in this type of patient. However, on the basis of data currently available, it is beyond any doubt that this class of drugs presents a profile of side-effects that is clearly more favourable than that presented by TCAs (Cooper, 1988; Kuhs and Rudolph, 1990; Stokes, 1993).

The situation is similar as regards the new selective monoamine oxidase inhibitors (MAOIs), such as moclobemide, which appear to be free from the adverse side-effects of TCAs, but the use of which is not yet supported by controlled clinical trials in patients with cardiovascular disease (Tiller, 1992).

Trazodone, which was initially believed to have a more benign effect than other antidepressants on the cardiovascular system, has been found to bring about postural hypotension, exacerbate pre-existing ventricular premature beats, and even precipitate a ventricular tachycardia in some patients (Janowsky *et al.*, 1983).

REFERENCES

Alexander F and French TM (1948) *Studies in Psychosomatic Medicine*. New York: Roland Press.

American Psychiatric Association (1987) *Diagnostic and Statistical Manual of Mental Disorders*. 3rd Edition, Revised. Washington, DC: American Psychiatric Press.

Bigger JT, Fleiss JL, Klieger R, Miller JP and Rolnitsky LM (1984) The Multicenter Post-Infarction Research Group. The relationships among ventricular arrhythmias, left ventricular dysfunction, and mortality in the 2 years after myocardial infarction. *Circulation*, **69**, 250–258.

Blumenthal JA, Williams RB, Kong Y, Schanberg SM and Thompson LW (1978) Type A behaviour pattern and coronary atherosclerosis. *Circulation*, **58**, 634–639.

Blumenthal JA, Madden DJ, Pierce TW, Siegel WC and Appelbaum M (1993) Hypertension affects neurobehavioural functioning. *Psychosom Med*, **55**, 44–50.

Booth-Kewley S and Friedman HS (1987) Psychological predictors of heart disease: a quantitative review. *Psychol Bull*, **101**, 343–362.

Cardiac Arrhythmia Suppression Trial (CAST) (1989) Preliminary report: effect of encainide and flecainide on mortality in a randomized trial of arrhythmia suppression after myocardial infarction. *N Engl J Med*, **321**, 406–412.

Carney RM, Rich MR, Te Velde A, Saini J, Clark K and Jaffe AS (1987) Major depressive disorder in coronary artery disease. *Am J Cardiol*, **60**, 1273–1275.

Carney RM, Rich MR, Freedland KE, Saini J, Te Velde A, Simeone C and Clark K (1988a) Major depressive disorder predicts cardiac events in patients with coronary artery disease. *Psychosom Med*, **50**, 627–633.

Carney RM, Rich M and Te Velde A (1988b) The relationship between heart rate, heart rate variability and depression in patients with coronary artery disease. *J Psychosom Res*, **32**, 159–164.

Carney RM, Freedland KE and Joffe AS (1990) Insomnia and depression prior to myocardial infarction. *Psychosom Med*, **52**, 603–609.

Carney RM, Freedland KE, Rich MW, Smith LJ and Jaffe AS (1993) Ventricular tachycardia and psychiatric depression in patients with coronary artery disease. *Am J Med*, **95**, 23–28.

Cascelles W, Hennekens CH and Evas D (1980) Retirement and coronary death. *Lancet*, **1**, 1288–1289.

Cassem NH and Hackett TP (1973) Psychological rehabilitation of myocardial infarction patients in the acute phase. *Heart Lung*, **2**, 382–388.

Cincipirini PM and Galveston PD (1986) Cognitive stress and cardiovascular reactivity. *Am Heart*, **5**, 1051–1065.

Cooper GL (1988) The safety of fluoxetine: an update. *Br J Psychiatry*, **153 (Suppl 3)**, 77–86.

Dalack GW and Roose SP (1990) Perspectives on the relationship between cardiovascular disease and affective disorder. *J Clin Psychiatry*, **Suppl 51**, 4–9.

Dunbar F (1948) *Psychosomatic Diagnosis*, New York: Hoeber.

Engel GL (1978) Psychological stress, vasopressor syncope and sudden death. *Ann Intern Med*, **89**, 403–412.

Esler M, Julius S and Zweifler A (1977) Mild high-renin essential hypertension: neurogenic human hypertension? *N Engl J Med*, **296**, 405–411.

Esler M, Turbott J and Schwarz R (1982) The peripheral kinetics of norepinephrine in depressive illness. *Arch Gen Psychiatry*, **39**, 295–300.

Frankenhaeuser M and Rissler A (1970) Effects of punishment or catecholamine release and efficiency of performance. *Psychopharmacologia*, **17**, 378–390.

Frankenhaeuser M, Lundberg U and Forsman L (1980) Dissociation between sympathetic-adrenal and pituitary-adrenal responses to an achievement situation characterized by high controllability. *Biol Psychol*, **10**, 79–91.

Frasure-Smith N (1991) In-hospital symptoms of psychological stress as predictors of long term outcome after acute myocardial infarction in men. *Am J Cardiol*, **67**, 121–127.

Frasure-Smith N, Lesperance F and Talajic M (1993) Depression following myocardial infarction. Impact on 6-months survival. *JAMA*, **270**, 1819–1825.

Frasure-Smith N, Lesperance F and Talajic M (1995) Depression and 18-month prognosis after myocardial infarction. *Circulation*, **91**, 999–1005.

Freedland KE, Carney RM, Lustman PJ, Rich MV and Jaffe AS (1992) Major depression in coronary artery disease patients with vs. without a prior history of depression. *Psychosom Med*, **54**, 416–421.

Friedman M (1984) *Treating Type A Behaviour and Your Heart*. New York: Fawcett Crest.

Garcia L, Valdes M, Jodar I, Riesco N and de Flores T (1994) Psychological factors and vulnerability to psychiatric morbidity after myocardial infarction. *Psychother Psychosom*, **61**, 187–194.

Giardina EGV, Bigger JT Jr and Glassman AH (1982) Antiarrhythmic effect of imipramine hydrochloride in patients with ventricular premature complexes without psychological depression. *Am J Cardiol*, **50**, 172–179.

Glassman AH and Roose SP (1994) Risks of antidepressants in the elderly: tricyclic antidepressants and arrhythmia-revising risks. *Gerontology*, **Suppl 1**, 15–20.

Glassman AH, Johnson LL and Giardina EGV (1983) The use of imipramine in depressed patients with congestive heart failure. *JAMA*, **250**, 1997–2001.

Glassman AH, Helzer JE, Covey LS, Cottler LB, Stetner F, Tipp JE and Johnson J (1990) Smoking, smoking cessation, and major depression. *JAMA*, **264**, 1546–1549.

Glassman AH, Roose SP and Bigger JT Jr (1993) The safety of tricyclic antidepressants in cardiac patients. Risk-benefit reconsidered. *JAMA*, **269**, 2673–2675.

Gold PW, Goodwin FK and Chrousos GP (1988) Clinical and biochemical manifestations of depression. *N Engl J Med*, **319**, 348–353.

Griego LC (1993) Physiologic and psychologic factors related to depression in patients after myocardial infarction: a pilot study. *Heart-Lung*, **22**, 392–400.

Hackett TP, Cassem NH and Wishnie HA (1968) The coronary-care unit: an appraisal of its psychological hazards. *N Engl J Med*, **25**, 1365–1370.

Helsing KJ, Szklo M and Comstock GW (1981) Factors associated with mortality after widowhood. *Am J Public Health*, **71**, 802–809.

Henry JP, Ely DL and Stephens PM (1972) Blood pressure, catecholamine and social role in relation to the development of cardiovascular disease in mice. *Psychosom Med*, **33**, 227–237.

Janowsky D, Curtis G and Zisook S (1983) Trazodone—aggravated ventricular arrhythmias. *J Clin Psychopharmacol*, **3**, 372–376.

Kannel WB and Thom TJ (1989) Incidence, prevalence, and mortality of cardiovascular diseases. In: JW Hurst (ed) *The Heart, Arteries and Veins*. New York: McGraw-Hill, 32–41.

Kavanagh T, Shepard RJ and Tuck JA (1975) Depression after myocardial infarction. *Can Med Assoc*, **113**, 23–27.

Kendler KS, Neale MC and MacLean CJ (1990) Smoking and major depression. *Arch Gen Psychiatry*, **50**, 36–43.

Kleiger RE, Miller JP, Bigger JT and Moss AJ (1987) Decreased heart rate variability and depression in patients with coronary artery disease. *J Psychosom Res*, **32**, 159–164.

Kuhs H and Rudolf GAE (1990) Cardiovascular effects of paroxetine. *Psychopharmacology*, **102**, 379–382.

Kusumi I, Koyama T and Yamashita I (1991) Serotonin stimulated Ca^{2+} response is increased in the blood platelets of depressed patients. *Biol Psychiatry*, **30**, 310–312.

Ladwig KH, Lehmacher W, Roth R, Breithardt G, Budde T and Borggrefe M (1992) Factors which provoke post-infarction depression: Results from the post infarction late potential study (PILP). *J Psychosom Res*, **36**, 723–729.

Ladwig KH, Roll G, Breithardt G, Budde T and Borggrefe M (1994) Post-infarction depression and incomplete recovery 6 months after acute myocardial infarction. *Lancet*, **343**, 20–23.

Levenson JL and Friedel RO (1985) Major depression in patients with cardiac disease: Diagnosis and somatic treatment. *Psychosomatics*, **26**, 91–102.

Littman AB (1993) Review of psychosomatic aspects of cardiovascular disease. *Psychother Psychosom*, **60**, 148–167.

Lloyd GG and Cawley RH (1983) Distress or illness? A study of psychological symptoms after myocardial infarction. *Br J Psychiatry*, **142**, 120–125.

Malzberg B (1937) Mortality among patients with involutional melancholia. *Am J Psychiatry*, **93**, 1231–1238.

Mann AH (1986) The psychological aspects of essential hypertension. *J Psychosom Res*, **30**, 527–541.

Mason JW (1975) Emotions as reflected in patterns of endocrine integration. In: L Levi (ed) *Emotions, their Parameters and Measurement*. New York: Raven Press, 143–181.

Mikuni M, Kagaya A, Takahashi K and Meltzer HY (1992) Serotonin but not epinephrine induced calcium mobilization of platelets is enhanced in affective disorders. *Psychopharmacology*, **106**, 311–314.

Post RM (1992) Transduction of psychosocial stress into neurobiology of recurrent affective disorder. *Am J Psychiatry*, **149**, 999–1010.

Roose SP and Glassman AH (1994) Antidepressant choice in the patient with cardiac disease: Lessons from the Cardiac Arrhythmia Suppression Trial (CAST) studies. *J Clin Psychiatry*, **55 (suppl A)**, 83–87.

Roy A, Pickar D, Linnoila M and Potter WZ (1985) Plasma norepinephrine levels in affective disorders: Relationship to melancholia. *Arch Gen Psychiatry*, **42**, 1181–1185.

Schleifer SJ, Macari-Hinson MM and Coyle DA (1989) The nature and course of depression following myocardial infarction. *Arch Intern Med*, **149**, 1785–1789.

Schneiderman N (1983) Behaviour, autonomic function and animal models of cardiovascular pathology. In: TM Dembroski, TH Schmidt and G Blumchen (eds) *Behavioural Bases of Coronary Heart Disease*. Basel: Karger.

Series HG (1992) Invited review: Drug treatment of depression in medically ill patients. *J Psychosom Res*, **36**, 1–16.

Shima S and Kitagawa Y (1994) Poststroke depression. *Gen Hosp Psychiatry*, **16**, 286–289.

Simonsick E, Wallace RB, Blazer DG and Berkman LF (1995) Depressive symptomatology and hypertension-associated morbidity and mortality in older adults. *Psychosom Med*, **57**, 427–435.

Stokes PE (1993) Fluoxetine: A five year review. *Clin Ther*, **15**, 216–243.

Tiller JWG (1992) Post stroke depression. *Psychopharmacology*, **106**, S130–S133.

Travella JI, Forrester AW, Schultz SK and Robinson RG (1994) Depression following myocardial infarction: one-year longitudinal study. *Int J Psychiatry Med*, **24**, 357–369.

Weiner H (1981) Behaviour and bodily disease: A summary. In: H Weiner, MA Hofer and AJ Stunkard (eds). *Brain Behaviour and Bodily Disease*. New York: Raven Press, 335–370.

Weiss JM, Simson PG and Simpson PE (1989) Neurochemical basis of stress-induced depression. In: H Weiner, I Florin, R Morison and D Hellhammer (eds) *Frontiers of Stress Research*. Toronto: Huber, 37–50.

Wells KB (1995) The role of depression in hypertension-related mortality. *Psychosom Med*, **57**, 436–438.

West CM (1986) Ischemia. In: VK Carrieri, AM Lindsey and CM West (eds) *Pathophysiological Phenomena in Nursing: Human Responses to Illness*. Philadelphia: WB Saunders.

13

Depression and the skin

Christopher Bunker and Christopher K. Bridgett

INTRODUCTION

Skin disease

Skin disease is very common. About 15% of consultations in general practice are related to skin problems and 20–25% of all outpatient visitors to an average district general hospital will be for dermatology appointments.

There are well over 1000 named skin diseases but the vast majority of patients have common problems: 25% of the population is atopic; 5% of people have hand eczema which accounts for 10–35% of all occupational diseases; 2% have psoriasis; 1% have vitiligo; one million people have chronic leg ulceration; acne affects about 20% of young adults and 5% of women and 1% of men still require treatment at the age of 40; 20–25% of all people have urticaria or angiopedema at some stage in their lives; skin cancer is the commonest of all cancers; benign lumps, bumps and blemishes are universal; 0.5% of neonates have a port-wine stain, and other forms of congenital deformity of the skin are not uncommon.

The cause of many of these diseases is not known. Most are chronic with no curative treatment despite effective palliative therapy. Cosmetic morbidity is obviously caused by skin diseases of all kinds but psychosocial development in childhood, education, jobs, interpersonal relationships and childrearing can all

Depression and Physical Illness. Edited by M.M. Robertson and C.L.E. Katona
© 1997 John Wiley & Sons Ltd

be affected profoundly by skin disease. The disturbance of sleep by itch is bound to affect psychosocial function, distort perception and alter mood.

Unfortunately, dermatological diagnosis and management is given a low priority by most medical schools. The dermatological competence of graduates is therefore poor; there are few opportunities for postgraduate training and dermatology is not a mandatory part of training rotations for general practice or internal medicine. Lack of knowledge, confidence and sometimes interest is readily perceived by patients.

Skin disease and psychology

Given the psychological importance of skin and the perception of body image, emotional reactions to skin disease are natural, predictable and even appropriate. It is not surprising, therefore, that secondary or reactive (somatopsychic) psychological and psychiatric problems including depression are sometimes encountered; patients with severe chronic dermatoses such as eczema and psoriasis frequently abuse alcohol and tobacco, thus compounding the skin disease (because alcohol is a cutaneous vasodilator and will worsen the erythematous component of all inflammatory dermatoses) and sometimes confounding its management (for example, psoriatics requiring methotrexate are required to forgo *all* alcohol because of enhanced liver toxicity: some severe cases deny themselves this treatment because they cannot or will not stop drinking). A corollary of some syndromic congenital skin disorders (genodermatoses) is learning disability and this may have psychiatric consequences including depression.

Perhaps it is surprising that reactive problems are not even more abundant in general, and that depression in particular is not rife amongst dermatology patients; or perhaps the morbidity is missed and underappreciated. Dermatology outpatients have a higher prevalence of psychiatric disorders than the general population and dermatological inpatients have more than general medical inpatients (Hughes *et al.* 1983). It has been suggested that effective treatment of as many as 30% (Rostenberg, 1960; Koo and Pham, 1992) of dermatology outpatients requires recognition of psychological factors and their management (Sneddon and Sneddon, 1983): dermatologists may not do well in this regard, unless intuitively.

At one time or another psychological factors have been implicated in the causation or exacerbation of several skin diseases. It is widely believed, probably correctly, that some eczematous dermatoses are provoked by psychological factors including depression: palmoplantar vesicular eczema (pompholyx), adult atopic dermatitis and seborrhoeic dermatitis (Maietta *et al.*, 1990) are cases in point. Most dermatologists will acknowledge that stressful situations and significant life events can cause a deterioration in most inflammatory dermatoses (such as eczema and psoriasis) and alter the patient's perception of their symptoms. They will agree that depressive symptoms often accompany the development of some cases of alopecia areata, idiopathic urticaria, aphthous mouth ulceration, rosacea, lichen simplex and idiopathic generalized pruritus.

There is another group of patients whose clinical presentation implies to the physician a primary psychological or psychiatric origin for their illness. Symptomatology seems exaggerated, anxiety is accentuated and the perception of body image is distorted often in the absence of physical signs; or the physical signs cannot be explained by any organic pathophysiological process other than excoriation or self-inflicted injury. Dermatitis artefacta, dermatological non-disease, delusions of parasitosis and dysmorphophobia (especially in acne) are examples where depression may often be present and where there is a risk of suicide.

In this chapter, as well as a historical account of the subject, we have tried to provide for nondermatologists a synopsis of the principal skin diseases that may be associated with depression and those skin complaints that may represent a primary psychiatric disturbance that includes depression, illustrated by clinical vignettes. The differential diagnosis of depression in dermatology patients is discussed (again abetted by sketches of clinical cases). The use of antidepressants and other psychotropic medication in dermatology is considered (and it is to be hoped that this will be of use of dermatologists) and the cutaneous side-effects of antidepressants and other drugs are briefly reviewed. Also discussed is the psychological and psychotherapeutic management of depressed patients (an area in which dermatologists have little formal training).

HISTORICAL

In "On symptoms or signs of melancholy in the body", *Anatomy of Melancholy*, Book 1 by Robert Burton, 1621, there is reference to "a kind of itching ... on the superficies of the skin". The relationship between depression, a common symptom of mental distress and a common psychiatric disorder, and pruritus, a common skin complaint, remains a subject of study in the late 20th century.

The modern history of psychocutaneous medicine was critically reviewed by Whitlock (1976). Nineteenth century ideas of "cutaneous neurosis" (Wilson, 1867) had in mind a disorder of the nervous system rather than a psychological illness. The subsequent speculative psychoanalytic psychodermatology of the early 20th century (Wittkower and Russell, 1953; Obermayer, 1955) was unattractively unscientific to modern dermatologists (Rook, 1976). Of more interest were the ideas of the newer biological psychiatry, while the phenomenological approach to psychopathology seemed more objective. Normal and abnormal brain chemistry became better understood and psychoanalytic psychology was both replaced and complemented by approaches based on experimental psychology and behaviourism: cognitive therapy was introduced (Beck, 1976).

Psychodermatology in recent years has seen many attempts at synthesis, with the work of Panconesi (1984) in Italy, Koblenzer (1987) and Koo and Pham (1992) in the USA, and Cotterill (1983) and Wessely (1990) in the UK. When Bos (1995) addressed the 6th International Congress on Dermatology and Psychiatry, he described his subject as "psychoneuroimmunodermatology", a cumbersome term which nevertheless highlighted the complex interrelationships that exist between mind and skin.

SKIN COMPLAINTS THAT MAY BE ASSOCIATED WITH DEPRESSION

Primary dermatological conditions

Generalized pruritus

Most patients presenting with generalized pruritus will be found to have a primary skin disorder or disease (xerosis (dryness), eczema, psoriasis, urticaria, pediculosis, scabies, lichen planus, dermatitis herpetiformis, etc.) or an underlying metabolic (occult iron deficiency, diabetes, renal, hepatic or thyroid dysfunction) or neoplastic disease (haematopoietic malignancy or solid tissue carcinoma). However, a small proportion of usually elderly patients are identified in whom no discernible cause can be found. Sometimes this is rather uncritically called psychogenic pruritus (Musaph, 1983). Certainly some, but not all, patients can be depressed but separating cause and effect is difficult (Sheehan-Dare *et al.*, 1990).

Psoriasis

Psoriasis is a chronic disease of red scaly patches or plaques affecting greater or lesser areas of the skin surface. Scalp, perianal, genital and nail involvement is characteristic. One per cent of patients may be afflicted by a disabling arthropathy. Treatment is supportive and not curative. It may involve prolonged daily attention to skin care involving messy, smelly treatments and regular attendance at a skin clinic or admissions to hospital. Agents used include topical moisturizers, tar, dithranol, vitamin D analogues and steroids, phototherapy with UVB and UVA or systemic treatment with a retinoid, cyclosporin or methotrexate.

Psoriasis has been associated with depressive disease and suicidal ideation and case reports of completed suicide exist (Fava *et al.*, 1980; Lyketsos *et al.*, 1985; Gupta *et al.*, 1988; Preston, 1969; Sanborn *et al.*, 1972; Gupta *et al.*, 1993: see below).

Atopic dermatitis

Atopic dermatitis is a very common skin disease of variable and unpredictable severity. Classically it starts in the first few months of life and burns itself out in early childhood but in any one case the prognosis is uncertain. There is an inherited subtle immunodysregulatory fault that renders patients hypersensitive to common environmental allergens such as the house dust mite. Treatment is with moisturizers, topical steroids, topical and systemic antibiotics (if infected), oral antihistamines, phototherapy and sometimes systemic immunosuppression with azathiaprine or cyclosporin. Behavioural psychotherapy to eliminate self-damaging behaviour is useful for the chronic syndrome (Bridgett *et al.*, 1996).

Lichen simplex

Lichen simplex is the term given to solitary patches or plaques of eczema in a clinical context where focal itch and reactive scratching predominates. Treatment is with occlusion, topical steroids and oral antihistamines.

The problem is common in the anogenital region and the over-appreciation of itch at these sites in both sexes is often branded by doctors as "psychological". Patients can get depressed, but antidepressant medication may be effective independently—possibly by ill-defined actions on the mediation of the sensation of itch by cutaneous nerves.

Nodular prurigo

Nodular prurigo is a condition characterized by a more generalized perception of intense itch and the development of nodular eczematized and excoriated lesions in response to persistent scratching. There is an association with the atopic diathesis and systemic illness such as bowel disease. Occlusion, topical or intralesional or even systemic steroids and oral antihistamines are the usual lines of treatment but sometimes other modalities such as phototherapy, non-steroidal anti-inflammatory drugs and thalidomide are indicated. A tenuous association with psychological morbidity is often suspected.

Acne

Acne is a common disorder of skin rich in sebaceous glands (face, chest, back) characterized by seborrhoea, comedones, papules, pustules, nodules, cysts, scars and in black people (e.g. Afro-Caribbean), postinflammatory hyperpigmentation. The unsightliness, the chronicity and the permanence of the cosmetic consequences demand that it be treated aggressively. Topical keratolytics, antibiotics and retinoids, and oral antibiotics and hormonal manipulation (in women) can effectively palliate most (90%) cases. A near miraculous innovation in the last 15 years has been the systemic retinoid, isotretinoin (Roaccutane). This agent is profoundly sebostatic and cures most patients with severe disease. The challenge to dermatologists is to identify and treat patients before significant long-term damage is done to the skin.

Poor self-image correlates with the severity of the disease (Shuster *et al.*, 1978). Acne interferes with social activities in adults (Jowett and Ryan, 1985) and in adolescents, for example sport and dating (Motley and Finlay, 1989), and unemployment is higher in patients with acne (Cunliffe, 1986). Both depression and anxiety can be important features of acne (Gupta *et al.*, 1990) Wu *et al.*, 1988; Koo and Smith, 1991). Treatment with isotretinoin usually ameliorates the depression and anxiety associated with acne (Rubinow *et al.*, 1987; MacDonald Hull *et al.*, 1991). Depressed mood can also be a side-effect of isotretinoin.

Rosacea

Rosacea is a very common disorder of the facial cutaneous vasculature that presents with flushing, redness, pustulosis, telangectasia and rhinophyma. It is exacerbated by alcohol, spicy food, coffee and climatic extremes. Treatment is with systemic tetracycline or metronidazole although it is not known why these antibiotics are effective. Depressive symptomatology is not uncommon or surprising given the facial manifestations.

Urticaria

Urticaria defines the appearance of often very symptomatic, itchy, red wheals (hives), whereas angio-oedema refers to deeper cutaneous swelling that may also involve the lips, oral mucosa and pharynx (to the patient's alarm) and which can be life-threatening. The lesions are transient but may last for several hours. They can coalesce and be quite extensive. Empirically, disease persisting for more than 6 weeks is called chronic. Fifty per cent of such patients have lesions lasting 1 year and as many as 20% may be symptomatic for 20 years (Goldstein and Tharp, 1996). Although mast cell histamine release determines the generation of the skin lesions, no specific cause is found in nearly all cases. Most patients can be controlled by oral antihistamines but sometimes oral steroids are necessary; however, they cannot be a chronic therapeutic solution.

Factors potentially involved in the development of depression with urticaria are the intensity of the itch, anxiety about controlling the rash in public or intimate situations and being able to breathe, protracted chronicity, inadequate or absent response to treatment and frustration at the lack of an identifiable cause.

Several studies have implied that significant depression is associated with chronic urticaria (Preston, 1969; Fava *et al.*, 1980; Lyketsos *et al.*, 1985; Hashiro and Okumura, 1994) whereas others have not found it so prevalent (Sheehan-Dare *et al.*, 1990; see below).

Alopecia areata

Alopecia areata is characterized by the abrupt appearance of one or more small or large discs of hair loss usually of the scalp or beard area. The onset of the disease is usually in late adolescence or early adulthood. It is difficult to predict the prognosis but many patients have persistent or recurrent disease. Treatment is with topical or intralesional steroids or by allergic sensitization with diphencyprone but response is uncertain.

Emotional factors are believed to play a role in its precipitation (van der Steen *et al.*, 1992) but it is essentially an autoimmune phenomenon affecting hair follicles (associated with vitiligo and other organ-specific autoimmune diseases like Addison's adrenal deficiency, pernicious anaemia, diabetes mellitus and autoimmune thyroid disease) perhaps triggered by a viral infection.

An increased prevalence of psychiatric disorders has been found in alopecia areata, including depression. Colon *et al.* (1991) reported that 74% of 31 patients had one or more lifetime psychiatric diagnoses: 39% had major depression and 39% had generalized anxiety disorder.

Alopecia due to other causes where the cosmetic effects may be drastic and the prognosis poor can be associated with depressive symptomatology but there is little in the literature to support this assertion. Examples include androgenetic alopecia in men, male pattern hair loss in women, telogen effluvium (postpregnancy hair loss) and scarring alopecia—due to lupus erythematosus, lichen planus or pseudopelade (idiopathic scarring alopecia).

Skin diseases associated with HIV/AIDS

HIV infection and AIDS are associated with a plurality of skin diseases such as dry skin (xerosis), eczema, psoriasis, seborrhoeic dermatitis, warts, mollusca, Kaposi's sarcoma, etc. (Bunker, 1996). The symptomatology and cosmetic insult of these diseases compounds the psychological picture in HIV infection and should not be overlooked, especially when medical attention is often focused on more "serious" pathology in other organ systems.

Genodermatosis

Darier's disease is a *genodermatosis* (genetic skin disorder) of variable cosmetic severity. Patients have greasy clusters of inflamed, often infected papules on the face, trunk and in the axillae, under the breasts and around the genitalia. Treatment is with topical and systemic antibiotics, and topical steroids. Oral retinoids are useful in severe cases. It appears to be the only genetically determined skin disorder that features in the literature pertaining to psychiatric complications of dermatological disease (Denicoff *et al.*, 1990). Not surprisingly, significant suicidal ideation was found and these finding must be pertinent to analogous situations, as reviewed below.

Port-wine stain

Port-wine stain commonly occurs on the face and the reaction in some adolescents and adults may be maladaptive and depressive. The tunable dye laser has revolutionized management of these congenital vascular naevi.

Case 1: Acne, port-wine stain and depression reaction
An 18-year-old schoolgirl was admitted unconscious having taken an overdose of an unspecified number of her mother's benzodiazepine tranquillizers. She had a large facial port-wine stain and severe acne vulgaris. She survived, the psychological impact of her skin problems was realized for the first time by her family and she came to dermatological attention for the first time. A 6 month course of isotretinoin cured the acne and over 1 year the port-wine stain was considerably attenuated by laser treatment. Common conditions that most people cope with can be disastrous for the individual.

Connective tissue disease

Connective tissue diseases such as systemic lupus erythematosus, rheumatoid arthritis and systemic sclerosis affect the skin. In discoid lupus erythematosus only the skin is affected with photosensitivity, red scaly patches, scarring and permanent hair loss. Treatment is with sunscreens, topical steroids and oral antimalarials and can be quite successful. However, dermatologists are used to encountering depression and despair in their chronic, especially female, cases (personal observation).

Keloid scarring

Keloid scarring refers to prominent protuberant firm scars at sites of injury and is commonest in Afro-Caribbeans. The most frequent sites are in the facial, chest and back acne areas, on the ear lobes (from piercing), on the nape of the neck (in young black men) and in caesarean section scars (in black women). Treatments with occlusion, topical and intralesional steroids and by re-excision (even accompanied by radiotherapy) are often disappointing, so depression can be encountered although there is no overt literature on this topic.

Case 2: Mild acne, keloid, depressive neurosis and nondelusional dysmorphophobia
A 24-year-old apprentice carpenter presented with an 8 year history of mild acne vulgaris of the chest and back, with complicating modest keloid scarring. As a result of his skin condition he had developed a depressive neurosis (dysthymia)

with a morbid preoccupation with his scarring (nondelusional dysmorphophobia) which profoundly limited his social life. Over a 12 month period he responded well to a combination of intradermal corticosteroid therapy and cognitive–behavioural psychotherapy.

Skin cancer

Most skin cancer (nonmelanoma skin cancer) is due to basal cell carcinoma (rodent ulcer). This may be recurrent and multifocal and locally invasive but it is not metastatic. Squamous cell carcinoma is rarer and can metastasize. Malignant melanoma is the most feared skin cancer because of the poor prognosis of some lesions (defined histologically by the Breslow thickness).

Primary psychiatric conditions

Trichotillomania

Trichotillomania is self-inflicted alopecia from avulsion of hair. The scalp is most commonly involved but other sites such as the eyebrows may be the focus of the pulling. Sometimes patients eat the hair (trichophagy) and this can be serious if hair balls (trichobezoars) form and cause intestinal obstruction.

Dermatological nondisease

Dermatological nondisease refers to a clinical presentation where subjective symptoms (often extravagantly expressed) predominate over objective physical signs which may be completely absent or explicable as a secondary phenomenon—picking, scratching, etc. Patients are frequently depressed and obsessive about their appearance (see below). The face, the scalp and the perineum are the commonest sites and women are mainly the patients except, probably, for anogenital disorders. Burning or pain (face, mouth, tongue, anus, genitalia) is described rather than itching; redness is imagined or overstated, hair is believed to be falling out and thinning on the scalp, or to be in excess on the face. Some cases of pruritus ani, vulvodynia and scrotal rosacea probably fall into this category.

Acne excoriée

Acne excoriée refers to the situation where minor acne is picked at incessantly, often with needles and tweezers. The resulting acute signs (and chronic scarring) are far in excess of that anticipated by the degree of the cutaneous disease process. Psychological disturbance is commonplace. Disproportionately aggressive dermatological treatment is often indicated (see p. 236).

Dermatitis artefacta

Dermatitis artefacta is part of the constellation of factitious disease. It is suspected when the history is inconsistent with the signs. Malingering may also be suspected. The distribution and the morphology of the lesions varies but bizarre and rectilinear geometric forms of eczema, erosion and ulceration predominate. Self-involvement in generating the dermatosis is denied. Depression is not common but *"la belle indifference"* may be encountered (see below).

Delusions of parasitosis

Delusions of parasitosis (Munro, 1980; Musalek *et al.*, 1990) may be a monosymptomatic delusional state where the patient and sometimes a spouse are unshakeably convinced that they are being bitten by insects. They may have nonspecific excoriations to show on the skin and frequently bring to the clinic a collection of detritus (dirt, crumbs, hair, cloth) that they want to have analysed entomologically. They may have seen several doctors and specialists and been the scourge of the local Environmental Health Office. They may also be depressed, but do not readily accept psychiatric help or treatment.

COMORBIDITY AND CAUSATION

Theoretical possibilities

Various possibilities evidently exist for the relationship between coexisting skin disease and depressive illness. When stressful life events are also considered the aetiological complexity increases (Hughes *et al.*, 1983; Cossidente and Sarti, 1984; Wessely and Lewis, 1989; Koo and Pham, 1992; Cotterill, 1995). Depressive illness may be simply coincidental with skin disease; skin disease may cause depression; depression may lead to, or exacerbate, a skin complaint; or the two conditions may be mutually interactive. Life events may be implicated in causing depressive illness, and in precipitating or exacerbating a skin disease. Finally, systemic disease and medical treatments may produce both skin lesions and psychiatric disturbances including depression.

Skin disease and depression

Research can be made difficult if there is a need to establish temporal relationships between the variables under study. Evidence is then sometimes indirect. Unfortunately, however, many reports imply causation based on assumption, rather than factual evidence, indirect or direct. Wessely and Lewis (1989) found

40% of all attenders ($N=173$) at a dermatology clinic in London had psychiatric disorder, "the majority being minor affective disorder". A minority (5%) had a primary psychiatric disorder. Most commonly, psychological illness seemed secondary to skin disease (75%). In the remainder, comorbidity was considered coincidental. Koo and Pham (1992), in a general review, saw primary agitated depression as often the basis of psychogenic excoriation; other primary psychiatric conditions such as dermatitis artefacta and delusions of parasitosis could also involve depression. As cause of secondary depression, mention was made of leprosy, psoriasis and vitiligo. It was pointed out that the emotional reaction reflects not only personal psychological devastation, but also the stigma imposed by society. Examples of psychophysiological disorders were atopic dermatitis, acne vulgaris and urticaria. In these conditions emotional distress, including depressive illness, could exacerbate the skin disease, and the worsened skin condition could then exacerbate the emotional state. A vicious circle is created.

When Koo and Smith (1991) reviewed the psychological aspects of acne, they found evidence in the literature of acne causing clinical depression, although "anxiety, stress and frustration rather than depression" were identified as emotional factors most likely to exacerbate the skin conditions. A potentially severe reciprocal interaction between emotional illness including depression, and acne was found in acne excoriée.

Case 3: Acne excoriée and depression
A 36-year-old single librarian gave a 23 year history of acne vulgaris on the face, chest, back and shoulders together with a 16 year history of recurrent depressive disorder requiring both antidepressant medications and electroconvulsant therapy. She agreed she was now habitually picking her facial lesions "without realizing it". She was assessed and followed up by a liaison psychiatrist for 18 months. With continuing psychotropic medication together with cognitive–behavioural therapy her habit remitted, allowing a successful course of suppressive isotretinoin to complete her treatment. Physical treatment can thus be complementary to psychological management.

Gupta *et al.* (1994) also found in a small series of male acne patients a positive association between both anxiety and depression, and excoriative behaviour. In women (*acne excoriée des jeunes filles*) personality factors are reported as more relevant (Sneddon and Sneddon, 1983).

In their community survey of alopecia areata and psychiatric disorders, Koo *et al.* (1994) found a significant prevalence of psychiatric comorbidity including major depressive episodes, during the clinical course of the skin disease. No observation was offered on the nature of the link. Using DSM-IIIR criteria, they found that 23.3% of 294 patients with alopecia areata had at least one DSM-III criterion of major depressive episode, generalized anxiety disorder, social phobia or paranoid disorder, compared with 4.7–8.2% in the general population. Evidence of a major depressive episode was uncovered in 8.8% of the total group compared with a prevalence of 1.3–3.5% in the general population. They recommended that dermatologists recognize and treat this cohort of patients.

Case 4: Alopecia areata and depression

A 22-year-old hairdresser presented tearfully with a 3 month history of extensive alopecia areata involving about 40% of her scalp. Her general practitioner had treated her with topical steroids and amitriptyline 75 mg at night, with no effect. Intralesional steroid treatment with triamcinolone was strikingly effective after 2 months and she stopped the antidepressant. The disease relapsed severely 6 weeks later. It was revealed that she was being beaten up regularly by her boyfriend. She left him and went back to live with her mother and was treated anew with intralesional steroids. Two months later hair growth was occurring in all affected areas: she failed to attend for further follow up. Thus specific antidepressant therapy may not always lead to successful management.

When Maietta *et al.* (1990) reported on a positive relationship between depressive syndromes and seborrhoeic dermatitis, the relationship remained unclear despite an initial supposition that seborrhoeic dermatitis was sensitive to emotional states. Sheehan-Dare *et al.* (1990) reported on the association they found between generalized pruritus and chronic urticaria, and psychological symptoms. Using the Beck Depression Inventory, they found depressive symptomatology was significantly associated with pruritus, but not with chronic urticaria: the nature of the relationship was not commented on. Hashiro and Okumura (1994) used the Self-rating Depression Scale to compare a small group of patients with chronic urticaria with normal controls, and found an increased risk of depression with urticaria. There was no comparison with any other skin disease, and no comment was offered on the nature of the comorbidity. Gupta and colleagues (1994) looked at 252 outpatients with pruritus associated with psoriasis, atopic dermatitis and chronic idiopathic urticaria and found a direct correlation between pruritus severity and depressive scores in all three dermatoses. The depressive symptoms may have been primary or secondary to the skin disorder and may have "reduced the threshold for pruritus".

The comorbidity complexities of skin disease and depression were well illustrated by Macdonald Hull *et al.* (1991). In a small series of 16 patients with mild acne, all also showing evidence of dysmorphophobia (including severe depression), they provided evidence in favour of vigorous dermatological treatment. Although psychiatric treatment was offered, it was only taken up by one patient.

Gupta *et al.* (1993), in a study of a heterogeneous group (10–90% of body surface affected; inpatients and outpatients) of 217 patients with psoriasis from Ann Arbor, Michigan, showed that death wish and suicidal ideation were associated with both higher depression scores on a self-related (Carroll Rating) scale and self-related assessments of psoriasis severity. The severity of the psoriasis also correlated directly with overall depression scores. They comment "... the comorbidity between depressive symptoms, suicidal ideation and psoriasis severity is in contrast with reports that severe depression and suicidal ideation are mainly a feature of life-threatening medical disorders such as malignancies...".

In contrast with the last two studies, Brandberg *et al.* (1995) looked for and expected a comorbidity between a life-threatening skin disease, malignant melanoma, and emotional illness. Follow up over 2 years of 144 patients found only a modest incidence of depressive and anxiety complaints, with no relationship to severity of physical illness, and no cases of clinical depressive illness.

Depression and skin complaints

For the less common skin complaints where psychiatric morbidity is primary and a skin condition as such may be absent, it is the diagnosis of the particular mental disorder that is important. Cotterill (1995) equates "dermatological nondisease" to cutaneous dysmorphophobia. The presentation is "rich in symptoms, especially in cutaneous areas important in body image, but poor in signs of organic disease". Depression is the commonest basis, and risk of suicide is important. He reports also delusions of parasitosis sometimes being associated with depressive illness. Cotterill's third primary psychiatric condition, dermatitis artefacta, provides a wide range of behavioural abnormality "from nail biting... to suicide". The depressed mood seems associated with personality factors more than depressive illness.

Case 5: Dermatitis artefacta and suicide
A 44-year-old male freelance writer gave a 10 year history of depressive neurosis complicated by intermittent trichotillomania, and neurotic excoriation of the face and buttocks. Despite continuing individual psychotherapy and a range of psychotropic medication prescribed by a large number of medical practitioners, he subsequently committed suicide.

Sheppard and colleagues (1986) similarly focused on dermatological nondisease, delusions of parasitosis and dermatitis artefacta as important dermatological presentations of psychiatric illness. They described 35 cases seen over 3 years. The majority had dermatological nondisease. Like Cotterill they found depressive illness amongst the varied psychiatric diagnoses made. Fabisch (1980) reported on 50 patients with dermatitis artefacta and his finding that eight showed unipolar depressive illness. He, like Cotterill, saw the inflicted injuries as potentially suicidal. Sneddon and Sneddon (1975) reported on a series of 43 patients with dermatitis artefacta followed up for several years. The chronic psychological illness shown by this series indicated personality factors to be most relevant. In the experience of Lyell (1979) also, dermatitis artefacta was associated most often with an immature personality, and seemed linked to other types of contrived disease as seen in Munchausen's syndrome. Dean *et al.*

(1992) reviewed a related condition, trichotillomania, and reported on three cases. A symptom rather than a diagnosis, hair-pulling was a benign habit in childhood but in adulthood it could either be found as part of an obsessive–compulsive disorder, or as a feature of major depressive illness. Christenson and colleagues (1991) reported on 60 adult hair-pullers; 65% showed mood disorder, while only 15% showed obsessive–compulsive disorder.

Case 6: Trichotillomania and bipolar affective disorder
A 26-year-old female dentist gave a 6 year history of bipolar affective disorder complicated by scalp hair-pulling during depressive episodes. Prophylactic carbemazepine treatment was continued at follow up; her hair-pulling was recognized as an early sign of depressive relapse indicating a need for additional antidepressant therapy.

Koblenzer and Bostrum (1994) gave an account of cutaneous dysaesthesia syndrome, a subvariety of dermatological nondisease: the two other varieties were body dysmorphic disorder and monosymptomatic hypochondriacal psychosis. The cutaneous dysaesthesiae amounted to circumscribed false beliefs and/or perceptions in an otherwise well patient: alternative terms in the literature were olfactory reference syndrome and atypical pain syndrome. Their 14 cases included sensitivity to light, burning scalp, glossodynia, vulvodynia and facial dysaesthesia. They found depressive symptomatology in all their patients, some through depressive illness *per se* and others through borderline personality disorder, or schizoaffective disorder. Successful treatment included use of antidepressant and neuroleptic medication.

Case 7: Chronic cutaneous dysaesthesia, depression and neuroleptic medication
A 32-year-old married charity administrator gave a 2 year history of burning sensations around her eyes, caused by exposure to a variety of light sources including computer visual display units. At assessment she was protecting her eyes with a mask. She was taking a serotonin reuptake inhibitor antidepressant for depressive illness diagnosed by another specialist. She responded well to additional low dosage pimozide combined with cognitive–behaviour therapy, and returned to work symptom free 6 months later.

Systemic factors, skin disease and depression

The links made between depressive illness and skin complaints by both systemic disease and medical treatments are both many and varied. The systemic disorders associated with pruritus reviewed by Koblenzer (1987) could equally be a list from Lishman (1987) of systemic conditions associated with depressive illness. Dermatological adverse drug reactions (Breathnach and Hinter, 1992) can be almost matched by the wide variety of drugs that may be implicated in causing depressed mood as a side-effect (Patten and Love, 1993). More specifically, systemic medication used for skin disease may cause depression as a side-effect (e.g. corticosteroids, retinoids, antiandrogens) while Krahn and Goldberg (1994) review the links between the use of antidepressant medication and a range of skin conditions including acne, psoriasis and alopecia.

DIFFERENTIAL DIAGNOSIS OF DEPRESSION ASSOCIATED WITH SKIN COMPLAINTS

Symptoms, syndromes and diagnosis

Koo and Pham (1992) emphasize that "a dermatological term such as factitious dermatitis does not specify the type of psychopathologic conditions involved". Psychiatric terminology can be equally nondiagnostic. Hay (1970) wrote "dysmorphophobia is nonspecific as a symptom and can occur in different psychiatric syndromes". The same can be said of terms like somatoform disorder (Lipowski, 1988) and monosymptomatic hypochondriasis (Koblenzer and Bostrom, 1994).

Case 8: Acne and dysmorphophobia
A 37-year-old single business woman with a past history of acne gave a 12 month history of fearing she could develop further acne on her face if she touched others suffering with the condition. She agreed her own skin condition was excellent. Assessment revealed an obsessive–compulsive neurosis and a mild reactive depressive episode. She was referred for cognitive–behaviour therapy, with the possibility also of treatment with a serotonin reuptake inhibitor antidepressant. Only careful assessment led to appropriate management.

The process of differential diagnosis in psychodermatology begins with a translation of dermatological terminology into psychiatric: with the common dermatoses this may seem easier than when primary psychiatric disorder underlies a skin complaint. The dermatological terms then, e.g. dermatitis artefacta, dermatological nondisease, and delusions of parasitosis, have a misleading diagnostic flavour to them.

Common dermatological complaints

Depression as a symptom is ubiquitous. With a primary dermatological condition such as acne vulgaris, a depressive complaint is either linked to underlying personality factors, or is part of a depressive episode that is either a reaction to the skin condition itself, or perhaps a reaction to a life event that may also have exacerbated the skin condition (Kenyon, 1966; Koo and Smith, 1991). Although there are no direct links between acneiform eruptions and the depression of manic-depressive illness and schizoaffective psychoses, the dermatological side-effects of lithium carbonate (Table 2) provide an indirect link. The depressive complaints reported as associated with isotretinoin treatment of acne (Hazen, 1983) are uncommon, but as an organic cause of depression they complete the hierarchy of possible diagnostic categories for a depressed state linked to a common skin disease.

Clarification of the nature of a depressive state associated with a particular skin condition is a necessary step towards planning appropriate management. However, authors such as Koo *et al.* (1994) and Colon *et al.* (1991), although reporting a significant relationship between "major depression" and alopecia areata, leave the diagnosis of depression imprecise. Fried (1994) concluded that pruritus and excoriation need careful organic investigation before psychological explanations are sought, but failed to clarify the "depression" and "psychoses" that "frequently underlie or accompany pruritus and self-excoriation". Koblenzer (1987) found psychogenic pruritus "may be a feature of overt neurotic depression" but "may occasionally occur in patients with psychosis". These statements seem tentative compared with the apparently isolated report of Edwards (1954) on pruritus in melancholia: "Six cases of melancholia complicated by pruritus and skin reactions are described. All cases benefited from ECT, although in one case neither the depression nor the skin condition was cured until leucotomy was performed."

Specific medical treatment is not always required.

Case 9: Pruritus and depression
A 45-year-old separated female secretary gave a 22 year history of perineal pruritus that had failed to respond to a wide variety of somatic treatments. Assessment revealed a concomitant history of mild to moderate recurrent depressive disorder directly related to marital discord, including physical and sexual abuse. Exploratory and supportive psychotherapy without antidepressant therapy enabled her to become symptom-free at 3 year follow up, coincidental with her divorce. Thus, social change can be effective in relief of symptoms.

Primary psychiatric disorders

The hierarchy of psychiatric diagnostic categories is particularly relevant to primary psychiatric disorders with depression. Hardy and Cotterill (1982) established that almost one-half of their series of 12 patients with cutaneous dysmorphophobia "were either moderately or severely depressed". In the following case the depressive illness followed successful treatment of a delusional state.

Case 10: Dysmorphophobia and postpsychotic depression
A 64-year-old married and recently retired instrument maker presented initially with a several year history of believing that the skin over his face and legs was diseased and could contaminate others. Physical examination was unremarkable, while his mental state revealed belief abnormalities consistent with the diagnosis of paranoid schizophrenia. He responded well initially to oral neuroleptic

treatment, but subsequently re-presented 6 months later with a recrudescence of his hypochondriasis, now showing features of a moderate depressive episode. This responded well to tricyclic antidepressant medication, and he remained asymptomatic 12 months later at follow up.

Appropriate treatment requires a differentiation between depressed mood of a personality disorder and depression that is a reaction to circumstances and events. Otherwise depression may be part of recurrent depression as in manic-depressive illness, or as seen in schizoaffective schizophrenia. At the top of the hierarchy are the organic causes of depression.

The differential diagnosis of cutaneous monosymptomatic hypochondriacal psychosis (Munro, 1980) from, for example, neurotic states needs therefore to be refined further in clinical practice. Musalek *et al.* (1990) after a prospective study of 34 patients with delusional parasitosis concluded that the term was "neither a nosological entity nor due to a specific psychiatric illness ... all organic, endogenous, psychic and social factors may play a role in (its) pathogenesis". It was a syndrome which could be superimposed on all psychiatric disorders. Koo (1991) put this process differently by presenting a series of cases to illustrate that "many clinical conditions can mimic monosymptomatic hypochondriacal psychosis", including temporal lobe epilepsy, multiple sclerosis, substance abuse, schizophrenia and depressive illness.

Dermatitis artefacta, or factitious dermatitis, and its stablemate pathomimicry (Millard, 1984) provide a similar problem in clinical practice, made even more complex when it is not the patient but the mother (Meadow, 1982) of the patient who may be suffering from a psychiatric disorder. If obsessional habits and conscious malingering are distinguished from dermatitis artefacta (Koblenzer, 1987) the latter syndrome can be further categorized according to psychopathology. Depressive illness in schizoaffective schizophrenia associated with factitious dermatitis is uncommon, and will be associated with a relevant delusional system. When a depressed state is part of an abnormal emotional reaction provoked by an intolerable life situation, the mood disturbance can be concealed behind the mask of "*la belle indifference*". It is, however, at the level of personality disorder that most cases are found, where the psychiatric term "borderline personality disorder" overlaps with the less formal "multiple referral syndrome" (Sneddon, 1983). Van Moffaert (1991) reported on an analysis of 89 dermatitis artefacta patients and found that while borderline personality was associated with self-inflicted dermatological lesions on the limbs, depressive illness was associated with lesions in the genital and breast areas.

Systemic disease

As an example of a possible systemic organic cause of both clinical depression and skin disease, Muller *et al.* (1992) reported a case of systemic sclerosis, where a 10 year history of depressive illness coincided with a history of

Raynaud's syndrome, and skin findings including telangectasia on the nose, forehead and palms.

Of the collagen vascular diseases, systemic lupus erythematosus (SLE) is particularly noteworthy in relation to psychiatric disorder (Feinglass *et al.*, 1976).

Case 11: SLE and depression

A 35-year-old married female administrator with three children presented with a 2 year history of depressed mood and an associated urticarial eruption that had developed into a bullous eruption. Although assessment revealed a past history of recurrent mild depressive episodes associated with life events, her current depressed mood was more variable than previously, and associated with both mild memory disturbance, and brief episodes of inexplicable anger. SLE was diagnosed. All her symptoms remitted on systemic corticosteroid treatment.

PSYCHOTROPIC MEDICATION AND SKIN COMPLAINTS

"Psychopharmacologic agents provide a useful option in the management of psychodermatologic disorders" (Koo and Pham, 1992) as defined as (a) psychophysiological (where the severity of the primary skin disease is influenced by the patient's emotions), (b) primary psychiatric disorders (in which the skin conditions are self-induced), and (c) secondary psychiatric disorders where the psychological symptoms stem from the impact of the skin disease. Psychopharmacological agents can also be used in dermatology for non-psychiatric reasons. As well as treating psychodermatological disorders directly, psychotropic drugs have direct dermatological effects. These can be both unintentional side-effects and also useful intentional effects.

Direct treatment of psychiatric disorder

Possibly the antidepressant most used by British dermatologists is amitriptyline. The dose is usually 25–75 mg (i.e. lower than in psychiatric practice) taken at night. Dothiepin, at similar doses, is an alternative. A third popular and similar tricyclic is doxepin 10–30 mg daily (usually given at night although with total daily doses above 100 mg the administration is advisedly divided). The sedative action of these tricyclic antidepressant drugs may be useful in patients with poor sleep due to pruritus. This seems particularly true in atopic dermatitis where trimipramine may prevent scratching by generally improving the quality of sleep (Savin *et al.*, 1979).

It is reported that dermatology patients are more sensitive to psychotropic medications (Koo and Pham, 1992). Although this seems unsupported by any objective evidence, cautious introduction at a low dosage and gradual increase to achieve control of symptoms followed by reduction titration of dosage, if possible, seems the best practice.

The use of benzodiazepine anxiolytics in managing symptoms in long-standing dermatological disorders is best avoided because of the risk of dependency. Fortunately, tricyclic antidepressants are also useful anxiolytics, with no such attendant risk involved.

Should obsessive–compulsive disorder accompany depression (as in some patients with acne excoriée, neurotic excoriations or trichotillomania) then clomipramine may be indicated (Swedo *et al.*, 1989; McTavish and Benfield, 1990). The dose is 25 mg to as much as 250 mg daily. The selective serotonin reuptake inhibitor (SSRI) antidepressant drug fluoxetine 20–40 mg a day is the subject of considerable literature attesting to its efficacy in treating obsessive–compulsive disorder but no controlled studies have so far been published about its particular role in dermatological disorders. The drug should not be given to suicidal or agitated patients (Koo and Pham, 1991). The possible side-effects of fluoxetine can be avoided by the use of other SSRI antidepressants.

The use of a neuroleptic is worth considering if there is no response to an antidepressant (Koblenzer and Bostrom, 1994). If pimozide is chosen its dose should be modest (1–4 mg daily). Special care is needed in the presence of hepatic or renal insufficiency and its use is contraindicated by hypokalaemia or a history of cardiac dysrhythmia: it is prudent to screen for dysrhythmia and monitor any cardiac effects by ECG.

Direct dermatological effects of psychotropic drugs

Doxepin has been claimed to have a special place in dermatological practice because its antihistamine effects at both H1 and H2 receptors (Koo and Pham, 1991; Bernstein *et al.*, 1981) make it useful in the management of concomitant itch in eczema, urticaria and neurotic excoriations (Krahn and Goldberg, 1994; Koo and Pham, 1992; Figueiredo *et al.*, 1990; Lawlor and Greaves, 1990; Rao *et al.*, 1988; Harris *et al.*, 1987) and idiopathic itch in generalized/senile pruritus. However, the whole class of tricyclics are antihistaminergic. *In vitro* specificity may not correlate with an *in vivo* or clinical effect. Detailed and exhaustive studies are lacking.

If anxiety is an additional feature then the benzodiazepine anxiolytic alprazolam may be the drug of choice because it is short-acting and has antidepressant effects, whereas other benzodiazepines can be depressants (Koo and Pham, 1992). The dose is 0.125–0.5 mg four times daily for 2–3 weeks.

Table 1 gives a summary of the dermatological conditions benefiting from psychotropic medication.

Dermatological side-effects of antidepressant medication

An oft-repeated axiom amongst dermatologists is "any drug, any rash". The cutaneous complications of psychotropic medication are well reviewed by Krahn and Goldberg (1994).

Table 1. Dermatological conditions benefiting from psychotropic medication.

Dermatological condition	Treatment
Postherpetic neuralgia	Amitriptyline, desipramine, pimozide
Chronic urticaria	Doxepin
Idopathic generalized pruritus	Doxepin
Nocturnal scratching (atopic eczema)	Trimipramine
Herpes simplex	Lithium
Aphthous ulcers	Phenelzine
Leishmaniasis	Chlorpromazine

Table 2 gives a summary of the dermatological side-effects caused by drugs used in depressive illness.

MANAGEMENT OF DEPRESSIVE SYNDROMES ASSOCIATED WITH SKIN COMPLAINTS

Dermatologists or psychiatrists?

Sheppard and colleagues (1986) ask, "Who should be the primary agent in the treatment of these patients? The fact that most of the literature concerning (psychogenic skin) disorders is to be found in the dermatological rather than the psychiatric literature emphasizes the reluctance of many of these patients to avail themselves of psychiatric help, and the efforts of dermatologists to offer psychological help." Wessely and Lewis (1989) saw the role of the psychiatrist being with the small percentage of dermatology patients found with primary psychiatric illness, while the majority "with minor affective disorder" should be managed by the dermatologist. There was, however, a need for greater skill amongst dermatologists in detecting psychological illness, as well as training in appropriate treatment. Koo and Pham (1992) observed that the "average dermatologist has neither the time nor the training to conduct psychotherapy or behaviour modification", but the appropriate use of psychopharmacological medication was better than no therapy at all. Attention to the common characteristics of unsuccessful doctor–patient consultations, as amusingly summarized by Cotterill (1989), seems advisable. Cotterill (1986) had earlier observed that the failure to bridge important communication gaps between doctors and patients goes a long way towards explaining the current vogue for alternative medicine.

The relevance of dermatologists managing the more common reactive depressive syndromes becomes clear when it is appreciated that successful dermatological treatment of common conditions such as atopic eczema, acne and psoriasis is often effective in relieving an associated depressive illness.

Table 2. Dermatological side-effects of drugs used in the management of depressive illness.

Drug	Side-effect
Tricyclics (especially desipramine)	Urticaria, angiooedema, purpura, exfoliative dermatitis, erythema multiforme (Stevens–Johnson syndrome), leukocytoclastic vasculitis, photosensitivity, alopecia
MAOIs	Photosensitivity
SSRIs	Urticaria, angioneurotic oedema, miliaria, alopecia
Benzodiazepines	Photosensitivity
Phenothiazines	Urticaria, purpura, toxic erythema, oedema, lupus eythematosus, photosensitivity, blue–grey discoloration
Lithium	Psoriasis, acne, folliculitis, pityriasis versicolor, leg ulcers, pruritus, toxic erythema, urticaria, lichen simplex, exfoliative dermatitis, lupus erythematosus, exacerbation of Darier's disease, warts
Carbamazepine	Pruritus, erythema, purpura, exfoliative dermatitis, lupus erthematosus, alopecia
Sodium valproate	Lupus erythematosus, scleroderma, vasculitis, alopecia

Case 12: Acne and depressive reaction
A 24-year-old single female clerk gave a 10 month history of concern over mild acne vulgaris. Assessment revealed a moderate depressive episode complicated by suicidal thoughts, an inability to continue with work, and failed social relationships. Conventional topical treatment with systemic antibiotics profoundly improved her skin condition, and her depressive disorder remitted without specific treatment.

Case 13: Psoriasis and depressive reaction
A 22-year-old single waiter presented with a 15 year history of widespread psoriasis which had recently failed to respond to a variety of alternative therapies. Mental state examination revealed a mild depressive episode with profound social withdrawal and a family history of both psoriasis and depressive illness. Conventional treatment including ultraviolet light therapy led to remission of his skin condition and his depressive illness remitted without specific treatment.

When such reactive depression is linked to disorders of pigmentation, to scarring and to other benign yet cosmetically distressing conditions, the possible usefulness of cosmetic camouflage (Rayner, 1995) should be considered. Available through most dermatology services, and in the UK through the Red Cross, this approach can complement both dermatological and psychological treatments.

Case 14: Acne, pigmentary change, scarring and cosmetic camouflage
A 32-year-old separated female physical fitness instructor from Zimbabwe with two children gave a 15 year history of acne, particularly troublesome on her face over the last 5 years. Examination revealed deep excoriations with both hypo- and hyperpigmentary scarring, and evidence of a prolonged depressive reaction. Conventional dermatological treatment, supplemented with behaviour modification to eliminate picking behaviour, was arranged. Her depressed state responded positively to supportive psychotherapy and cosmetic camouflage advice.

Medical treatments

The direct dermatological effects of psychotropic medication (Krahn and Goldberg, 1994; Koo and Pham, 1992) may be implicated in the findings of Preston (1969) who reported dramatic improvement in both skin condition and depression when using tricyclic antidepressants for a wide range of primary skin conditions complicated by depression. The various pharmacological possibilities currently available for depression, psychogenic pruritus and excoriation are usefully summarized by Fried (1994). The possibility also exists that antipsychotic agents such as pimozide may be effective (Munro, 1978) not only because of dopamine receptor blockage, but also through their ability to act as opiate antagonists (Krahn and Goldberg, 1994).

Having clarified the psychiatric diagnosis when depressive disorder is associated with a skin disease, *if* antidepressant medication is indicated, the choice can follow the usual clinical guidelines for the identified psychiatric syndrome.

Psychological management

Fabisch (1980) pointed out that the onset of dermatitis is frequently related to significant life events; the visible lesions are an attempt at nonverbal communication. Sneddon and Sneddon (1975) remarked on the unwillingness of such patients to see psychiatrists; long-term follow up revealed that: "recovery seemed to occur when life circumstances changed rather than as a result of treatment". The importance of maintaining a supportive and understanding relationship with patients showing dermatitis artefacta is summarized in what is known as (Sneddon and Sneddon, 1975) the dictum of Lyell (1972): "only indirectly indicate that the nature of their activities is known; sympathize, and give an opportunity to talk; do not confront either the patient or the relatives, else contact with the patient will be lost, and the result can be disastrous" (Lyell, 1976, 1979). Millard (1984) described 13 patients who had simulated their original dermatological disease, and coined the term dermatological pathomimicry: it is distinct from dermatitis artefacta in both lacking "the hollow history", and in presenting physical signs of an original and recognizable skin condition. For such patients support was seen to reinforce their maladaptive behaviour, while appropriate and careful confrontation could lead to recovery.

Despite the availability of effective antidepressant medication and the scarcity of appropriately trained therapists, there remains a place for psychodynamic therapy in the management of depression related to skin disease. Koblenzer (1995) emphasizes that insight-oriented psychotherapy can successfully complement conventional treatment in selected cases of recalcitrant inflammatory dermatoses.

Case 15: Atopic dermatitis and psychodynamic psychotherapy
A 35-year-old marked male credit analyst presented with a life-long history of troublesome atopic skin disease. Over a period of several months conventional treatment of his skin condition, combined with behaviour therapy to reduce his self-damaging scratching and rubbing, brought his eczema into remission. A mild depressive episode then followed, and his skin condition relapsed. Exploratory psychotherapy revealed his depression was related to a life-long experience of continuous physical illness. Continuing insight-oriented psychotherapy was recommended as an adjunct to his dermatological treatment programme.

Van Moffaert (1992) saw the link between psychological stress and bodily symptom as being a "coded message" that needed decoding and understanding by both doctor and patient.

Case 16: Vulvodynia: a somatization disorder
A 35-year-old single female senior secretary and personal assistant gave an 8 month history of intermittent burning sensations in the perineum. Mental state examination revealed a dysthmia of 5 years' duration, associated with vaginismus. Exploratory interviews and homework tasks including a diary of symptoms and emotional experiences established a direct link between her physical symptoms and stressful life experience. She found it difficult to take time off work for psychotherapy, which became impossible when she accepted a post abroad.

Somatization (Lipowski, 1988), the tendency to experience and communicate somatic distress in response to psychosocial stress and to seek medical advice, was the process described by Harrington (1989) in a series of 20 patients with vulvodynia: "this unhappy group of patients transfers a psychological problem to the vulval site". Management involved discovering "the triggering factor" and in "providing an explanation as to why the vulva was the site of the symptoms". Such an approach has now become formalized in cognitive–behaviour therapy (Salkovskis, 1992) and its effectiveness demonstrated in the treatment of medically unexplained physical symptoms (Speckens *et al.*, 1995).

Lyell (1983) in his account of the management of delusions of parasitosis discusses how to approach the issue that "the parasites are imaginary. It may not be necessary to broach this thorny question, if the patient is satisfied that the dermatologist believes in the sensations". This possibility of finding a common ground with the patients' view of their illness is important in achieving compliance with medical treatment of psychotic illness (Kemp, 1996).

Case 17: Ekbom's syndrome

A 45-year-old single cosmetics saleswoman gave a 12 month history of delusions of parasitosis (Ekbom's syndrome). She accepted low dose pimozide therapy on the understanding that, as topical treatment had failed, her skin condition needed treating from "inside out". A subsequent moderate depressive episode was subsequently successfully treated with a tricyclic antidepressant, compliance being encouraged by explaining how depression made her more vulnerable to her "skin complaint". At follow up her condition is significantly improved, although she remained symptomatic.

SUICIDE AND SKIN DISEASE

The number of patients with skin disease who kill themselves seems relatively small, but risk is present and not always obvious. Although perhaps more likely in patients with primary psychiatric disorder, it is sometimes reported as a feature of secondary reactive depressive illness.

There are few reports in the literature of successful suicide associated with dermatitis artefacta. Although Cotterill (1995) and Fabish (1980) saw suicide as a possible outcome, and Sneddon (1983) refers to "direct confrontation" as usually "disastrous", Sneddon and Sneddon (1974) when reviewing the long-term follow up of 41 patients with dermatitis artefacta found "only one patient (had) successfully committed suicide".

Cotterill (1995) gave a brief account of 13 dermatological patients who were known to have committed suicide in the Leeds region over 20 years. The largest group were those with dermatological nondisease and associated depressive illness. Females with facial symptomatology were at particular risk. Otherwise all patients with actual severe skin pathology of important body image areas, such as the face, were "at high risk of reactive depression and suicide". Any chronic, severe and debilitating organic skin disease should be associated with a risk of suicide. Denicoff *et al.* (1990) gave an account of suicidal ideation associated with Darier' disease, and Gupta *et al.* (1993) of suicidal ideation associated with psoriasis. Sandborn *et al.* (1972) provided case reports of psoriasis associated with suicidal ideation and successful suicide. In each case suicide seemed precipitated by further psychosocial stress added to a life already made difficult by chronic physical illness.

Cotterill (1991) reported the case of "a man of 71 with long-standing psoriasis who for 10 years attended a special psoriasis bathroom for treatment 5 days per week. His wife died and his psoriasis got worse. He was put on hydroxyurea, which cured his psoriasis, but 1 year later he killed himself by throwing himself under a train. It was apparent that this man's daily contact with the nurse in the psoriasis bathroom was essential to him, particularly after the death of his wife. By prescribing hydroxyurea the disease was treated successfully, but the patient was not".

CONCLUSIONS

The fascinating interrelationship between skin and mind is richly illustrated by the example of depression and its role in the understanding of many skin complaints.

For common skin conditions such as acne, psoriasis and atopic dermatitis there has in recent years been a change in emphasis from previous psychosomatic theories towards a more pragmatic somatopsychic approach. However, when a skin complaint is based on a primary psychiatric disorder, successful management depends on precise psychiatric diagnosis.

The increasing awareness of the usefulness of psychotropic medication in the management of skin complaints seems often related to direct dermatological effects. Reflecting perhaps the common embryological origins of brain and skin, this aspect of psychodermatology may prove particularly rewarding for future research.

REFERENCES

Beck A (1976) *Cognitive Therapy and the Emotional Disorders*. New York: International Universities Press.

Bernstein JE, Whitney DH and Soltani K (1981) Inhibition of histamine-induced pruritus by topical tricyclic antidepressants. *J Am Acad Dermatol*, **5**, 582–585.

Bos JD (1995) Concepts of psychoneuroimmunology in dermatology. *Proceedings of the 6th International Congress on Dermatology and Psychiatry*, Amsterdam, the Netherlands, 20–22 April.

Brandberg Y, Mansson-Brahme E, Ringborg U and Sjoden PO (1995) Psychological reactions in patients with malignant melanoma. *Eur J Cancer*, **31A**, 157–162.

Breathnach SM and Hinter H (1992) *Adverse Drug Reactions and the Skin*. Oxford: Blackwell.

Bridgett CK, Noren P and Staughton RCD (1996) *Atopic Skin Disease*. Petersfield: Wrightson.

Bunker CB (1996) Dermatological problems in HIV infection and AIDS. In: E Millar (ed) *Medical Management of HIV and AIDS*. Berlin, Heidelberg, New York: Springer-Verlag, 162–189.

Christenson GA, Mackenzie TB and Mitchell JE (1991) Characteristics of 60 adult hairpullers. *Am J Psychiatry*, **148**, 365–370.

Colon EA, Popkin MK, Callies AL *et al.* (1991) Lifetime prevalence of psychiatric disorders in patients with alopecia areata. *Compr Psychiatry*, **32**, 245–251.

Cossidente A and Sarti MG (1984) Psychiatric syndromes with dermatogic expression. *Clin Dermatol*, **2: 4**, 201–236.

Cotterill J (1983) Psychiatry and Skin Disease. *Recent Adv Derm*. 6th Edn. London: Churchill Livingston.

Cotterill J (1986) Alternative medicine and dermatology. *Recent Adv Derm*, 7th Edn, Champion. London: Churchill Livingston. 251–263.

Cotterill JA (1989) The use of games analysis in the dermatological consultation. *Proceedings of the 2nd International Congress on Dermatology and Psychiatry*. Leeds, England, 9–11 July.

Cotterill J (1991) Suicide in dermatological patients. *Proceedings of 3rd International Congress on Dermatology and Psychiatry*. Florence, Italy, 20–21 September.

Cotterill JA (1995) Skin and the psyche. *Proc R Coll Physicians Edinb*, **25**, 29–33.

Cunliffe WJ (1986) Acne and unemployment. *Br J Dermatol*, **115**, 379–383.

Dean JT, Nelson E and Moss L (1992) Pathologic hair-pulling: a review of the literature and case reports. *Compr Psychiatry*, **33**, 84–91.

Denicoff KD, Lehman ZA, Rubinow DR *et al.* (1990) Suicidal ideation in Darier's disease. *J Am Acad Dermatol*, **22**, 196–198.

Edwards KCS (1954) Pruritus in melancholia. *Br Med J*, **2**, 1527–1529.

Fabisch W (1980) Psychiatric aspects of dermatitis artefacta. *Br J Dermatol*, **102**, 29–34.

Fava GA, Perini GI, Santonastaso P and Fornasa CV (1980) Life events and psychological stress in dermatological disorders: Psoriasis, chronic urticaria and fungal infections. *Br J Med Psychiatry*, **53**, 277–282.

Feinglass EJ, Arnett FC, Dorsch CA, Zizik TM and Stevens MB (1976) Neuropsychiatric manifestations of systemic lupus erythematodes: Diagnosis, clinical spectrum and relationship to other features of the disease. *Medicine*, **55**, 323–339.

Figueiredo A, Ribeiro CA, Goncao M, Almeida L, Poiares-Baptista A and Teixera F (1990) Mechanism of action of doxepin in the treatment of chronic urticaria. *Fund Clin Pharmacol*, **4**, 147–158.

Fried RG (1994) Evaluation and treatment of "psychogenic" pruritus and self-excoriation. *J Am Acad Dermatol*, **30(6)**, 993–999.

Goldstein SM and Tharp MD (1996) Urticaria In: EK Arndt, JK Robinson, PE LeBoit and BU Wintroub (eds) *Cutaneous Medicine and Surgery*. Philadelphia: WB Saunders, 392–406.

Gupta MA, Gupta AK, Kirkby S *et al.* (1988). Pruritus in psoriasis, a prospective study of some psychiatric and dermatologic correlates. *Arch Dermatol*, **124**, 1052–1057.

Gupta MA, Gupta AK, Schork NJ *et al.* (1990) Psychiatric aspects of mild to moderate facial acne: some preliminary observations. *Int J Dermatol*, **29**, 719–721.

Gupta MA, Schork NJ, Gupta AK, Kirkby S and Ellis CN (1993) Suicidal ideation in psoriasis. *Int J Dermatol*, **32**, 188–190.

Gupta MA, Gupta AK and Schork NJ (1994) Psychosomatic study of self-excoriative behaviour among male acne patients: preliminary observations. *Int J Dermatol*, **33**, 846–848.

Hardy GE and Cotterill JA (1982) A study of depression and obsessionality in dysmorphophobic and psoriatic patients. *B J Psychiatry*, **140**, 19–22.

Harrington C (1989) Vulvodynia. *Proceedings of the 2nd International Congress on Psychiatry and Dermatology*. Leeds, England, 9–11 July.

Harris BA, Sherertz EF and Flowers FP (1987) Improvement of chronic neurotic excoriation with oral doxepin therapy. *Int J Dermatol*, **26**, 541–543.

Hashiro M and Okumura M (1994) Anxiety, depression, psychosomatic symptoms and autonomic nervous function in patients with chronic urticaria. *J Dermatol Sci*, **8**, 129–135.

Hay GG (1970) Dysmorphophobia. *Br J Psychiatry*, **116**, 399–406.

Hazen PG (1983) Depression: A side-effect of 13 cis-retinoic acid therapy. *J Am Acad Dermatol*, **9**, 278–279.

Hughes J, Barraclough B, Hamblin L *et al.* (1983) Psychiatric symptoms in dermatology patients. *Br J Psychiatry*, **143**, 51–54.

Jowett S and Ryan T (1985) Skin disease and handicap: an analysis of the impact of skin conditions. *Soc Sci Med*, **20**, 425–429.

Kemp R (1996) Compliance therapy in psychotic patients: randomised controlled trial. *Br Med J*, **312**, 345–351.

Kenyon F (1966) The psychosomatic effects of acne. *Br J Dermatol*, **78**, 344–351.

Koblenzer CS (1987) *Psychocutaneous Disease*. Orlando, Florida: Grune and Stratton.

Koblenzer CS (1995) Psychotherapy for intractable inflammatory dermatoses. *J Am Acad Dermatol*, **32(4)**, 609–612.

Koblenzer CS and Bostrom P (1994) Chronic cutaneous dysesthesia syndrome: A psychotic phenomenon or a depressive symptom? *J Am Acad Dermatol*, **30**, 370–374.

Koo JYM (1991) Differential diagnosis of monosymptomatic hypochondriacal psychosis. *Proceedings of the 3rd International Congress on Dermatology and Psychiatry*. Florence, Italy.

Koo JYM and Pham C (1992) Psychodermatology: Practical guidelines on pharmacotherapy. *Arch Dermatol*, **128**, 381–388.

Koo JYM and Smith LL (1991) Psychological aspects of acne. *Pediatr Dermatol*, **8**, 185–188.

Koo JYM, Shellow WVR, Hallman CP and Edwards JE (1994) Alopecia areata and increased prevalence of psychiatric disorders. *Int J Dermatol*, **33(12)**, 849–850.

Krahn LE and Goldberg RL (1994) Psychotropic medications and the skin. In: PA Silver (ed) *Psychotropic Drug Use in the Medically Ill. Adv Psychosom Med*. Basel: Karger, **21**, 90–106.

Lawlor F and Greaves MW (1990) The development of recent strategies in the treatment of urticaria as a result of clinically oriented research. *Z Hautkrankheiten*, **65**, 17–27.

Lipowski ZS (1988) Somatization: The concept and its clinical application. *Am J Psychiatry*, **145**, 1358–1368.

Lishman WA (1987) *Organic Psychiatry: The Psychological Consequences of Cerebral Disorder*. Oxford: Blackwell.

Lyell A (1972) Dermatitis artefacta and self-inflicted disease. *Scottish Med J*, **17**, 187–196.

Lyell A (1976) Dermatitis artefacta in relation to the syndrome of contrived disease. *Clin Exp Dermatol*, **1**, 109–126.

Lyell A (1979) Cutaneous artefactual disease. *J Am Acad Dermatol*, **1**, 391–407.

Lyell A (1983) Delusions of parasitosis. *Br J Dermatol*, **108**, 485–499.

Lyketsos GC, Stratigos J, Tawil G *et al.* (1985) Hostile personality characteristics, dysthymic states and neurotic symptoms in urticaria, psoriasis and alopecia. *Psychother Psychosom*, **44**, 122–131.

MacDonald Hull S, Cunliffe WJ and Hughes BR (1991) Treatment of the depressed and dysmorphophobic acne patient. *Clin Exp Dermatol*, **16**, 210–211.

Maietta G, Fornaro P, Rongioletti F and Rebora A (1990) Patients with mood depression have a high prevalence of seborrhoeic dermatitis. *Acta Dermatol Venereol*, **70**, 432–434.

McTavish D and Benfield P (1990) Clomipramine: an overview of its pharmacological properties and a view of its therapeutic use in obsessive–compulsive disorder and panic disorder. *Drugs*, **39**, 136–153.

Meadow R (1982) Munchausen's syndrome by proxy. *Arch Dis Child*, **57**, 92–98.

Millard L (1984) Dermatological pathomimicry: A form of patient maladjustment. *Lancet*, **ii**, 969–971.

Motley RJ and Finlay AY (1989) How much disability is caused by acne? *Clin Exp Dermatol*, **14**, 194–198.

Muller N, Gizycki-Nienhaus B, Gunther W and Meurer M (1992) Depression as a cerebral manifestation of scleroderma: immunological findings in serum and cerebrospinal fluid. *Biol Psychiatry*, **31**, 1151–1156.

Munro A (1978) Monosymptomatic hypochondriacal psychosis manifesting as delusions of parasitosis. *Arch Dermatol*, **114**, 940–943.

Munro A (1980) Monosymptomatic hypochondriacal psychosis. *Br J Hosp Med*, **24**, 34–38.

Musalek M *et al.* (1990) The position of delusional parasitosis in psychiatric nosology. *Psychopathology*, **23**, 115–124.

Musaph H (1983) Psychogenic pruritus. *Semin Dermatol*, **2**, 217–222.

Obermayer ME (1955) *Psychocutaneous Medicine*. Springfield, Illinois: Charles C Thomas.

Panconesi E (1984) Stress and skin disease: Psychosomatic dermatology. *Clin Dermatol*, **2**, 4.

Patten SB and Love EJ (1993) Can drugs cause depression? A review of the evidence. *J Psychiatr Neurosci*, **18(3)**, 92–99.

Preston K (1969) Depression and skin diseases. *Med J Aust*, **1**, 326–329.

Rao KS, Menon PK, Hilman BC, Sebastian CS and Bairnsfather L (1988) Duration of the suppressive effect of tricyclic antidepressants on histamine-induced wheal-and-flare reactions in human skin. *J Allergy Clin Immunol*, **82i**, 752–757.

Rayner VL (1995) Camouflage therapy. *Dermatol Clin*, **13(2)**, 467–472.

Rook A (1976) Foreword. In: FA Whitlock (ed) *Psychophysiological Aspects of Skin Disease*. London: Saunders, v–vi.

Rostenberg A Jr (1960) The role of psychogenic factors in skin disease. *Arch Dermatol*, **81**, 81–83.

Rubinow DR, Peck GL, Squillace KM and Gantt CG (1987) Reduced anxiety and depression in cystic acne patients after successful treatment with oral isotretinoin. *J Am Acad Dermatol*, **17**, 25–32.

Salkovskis P (1992) The cognitive-behavioural approach. In: F Creed *et al.* (eds) *Medical Symptoms not Explained by Organic Disease*. London: Royal College of Psychiatrists and Royal College of Physicians of London, 70–84.

Sanborn III PE, Sanborn CJ, Cimbolic P and Niswander GP (1972) Suicide and stress-related dermatoses. *Dis Nerv System*, **33**, 391–394.

Savin JA, Parterson WD, Adam K and Oswald I (1979) Effects of trimeprazine and trimipramine on nocturnal scratching with atopic eczema. *Arch Dermatol*, **115**, 313–315.

Sheehan-Dare RA, Henderson MJ and Cotteril JA (1990) Anxiety and depression in patients with chronic urticaria and generalised pruritus. *Br J Dermatol*, **123**, 769–774.

Sheppard N *et al.* (1986) Psychogenic skin disease: A review of 35 cases. *Br J Psychiatry*, **149**, 636–643.

Shuster S, Fisher GH, Harris E and Binnell D (1978) The effect of skin disease on self image. *Br J Dermatol*, **99 (Suppl 16)**, 18–19.

Sneddon IB (1983) Simulated disease: Problems in diagnosis and management. *J R Coll Physicians Lond*, **17**, 199–205.

Sneddon I and Sneddon J (1974) What happens to patients with artefacts? *Br J Dermatol*, **10**, 13.

Sneddon I and Sneddon J (1975) Self-inflicted injury: A follow-up of 43 patients. *Br Med J*, **3**, 527–530.

Sneddon J and Sneddon IB (1983) Acne excoriée: a protective device. *Clin Exp Dermatol*, **8**, 65–68.

Speckens AEM *et al.* (1995) Cognitive behavioural therapy for medically unexplained physical symptoms: A randomised controlled trial. *Br Med J*, **311**, 1328–1332.

Swedo SE, Leonard HL, Rapoport JL, Lenane MC, Goldberger EL and Cheslow DL (1989) A double-blind comparison of clomipramine and despiramine in the treatment of trichotillomania (hair pulling). *N Engl J Med*, **321**, 497–501.

Van der Steen P, Boezeman J, Duller P *et al.* (1992) Can alopecia areata be triggered by emotional stress? An uncontrolled evaluation of 178 patients with extensive hair loss. *Acta Dermatol Venereol*, **72**, 279–280.

Van Moffaert M (1991) Localization of self-inflicted dermatological lesions: What do they tell the dermatologist? *Acta Derm Venereal (Stokh)*, **156**, 23–27.

Van Moffaert M (1992) Psychodermatology: An overview. *Psychother Psychosom,* **58 (3– 4)**, 125–136.

Wessely SC (1990) Dermatological complaints. In CM Bass (ed) *Somatization*. London: Blackwell, 276–300.

Wessely SC and Lewis GH (1989) The classification of psychiatric morbidity in attenders at a dermatology clinic. *Br J Psychiatry*, **155**, 686–691.

Whitlock FA (1976) *Psychophysiological Aspects of Skin Disease*. London: W.B. Saunders, 154–164.

Wilson E (1867) *Diseases of the Skin*. London: Churchill.

Wittkower E and Russell B (1953) *Emotional Factors in Skin Disease*. London: Cassell.

Wu SF, Kinder BN, Trunnell TN and Fulton JE (1988) Role of anxiety and anger in acne patients: a relation with the severity of the disorder. *J Am Acad Dermatol*, **18**, 325– 333.

14

Depression associated with endocrine disorders

Elizabeth B. Boswell, Theodore J. Anfinson and Charles B. Nemeroff

INTRODUCTION

Mood disorders, particularly major depression, have for centuries been observed at unusually high prevalence rates in patients with endocrine diseases. Recognition of psychiatric symptoms associated with endocrine disturbances has in part led investigators to develop the field of psychoneuroendocrinology. Endocrine disorders may be accompanied by various psychiatric symptoms and syndromes. Conversely, many psychiatric illnesses, particularly major depression, are accompanied by highly reproducible neuroendocrine abnormalities. Table 1 illustrates the prevalence of depression in selected endocrine disturbances where prospective data are available.

Psychiatric disorders are most commonly associated with endocrine abnormalities involving the thyroid and adrenal glands, parathyroid glands, diabetes mellitus, and disorders of prolactin secretion. The following review will emphasize the epidemiology and phenomenology of major depression associated with the above-mentioned disorders. The clinical features of each disorder will be presented along with the data from the psychiatric literature to assist the clinician in reviewing the context in which the psychiatric symptoms occur. A brief review of the neuroendocrine abnormalities associated with major depression will be made.

Depression and Physical Illness. Edited by M.M. Robertson and C.L.E. Katona
© 1997 John Wiley & Sons Ltd

Table 1. Prevalence of depression in selected endocrine disorders.

Disorder	Prevalence of depression (%)
Diabetes mellitus	36
Hypothyroidism	50
Hyperthyroidism	28
Cushing's syndrome	63
Hyperparathyroidism	8

The case literature was carefully reviewed and the qualitative nature of the depressive symptoms in a given case are emphasized. This approach is similar to that utilized by Whybrow and Hurwitz (1976) in their classic review of the psychiatric manifestations of endocrine disorders. Studies utilizing a prospective design and structured interview techniques are emphasized. Particular attention is given to the temporal relationship between the onset of psychiatric symptoms and the underlying endocrine disturbance and the response to treatment. In general, the literature suggests that treatment should be initially directed at correcting the underlying endocrine disturbance and following the patient closely for resolution of psychiatric symptoms. If, after normalization of endocrine function, psychiatric symptoms persist, then psychopharmacological intervention may be necessary.

Assessing depression in the medical setting

Frequently, the clinician is faced with the dilemma of diagnosing major depression in a patient with concurrent medical illness. Depression occurring with diabetes mellitus is demonstrative of the various issues a clinician might encounter. Is the fatigue and appetite disturbance a manifestation of the depressive disorder or part of the symptom profile of diabetes mellitus? What is the validity of current diagnostic criteria for major depression in the setting of medical illness?

A variety of epidemiological studies reveal that approximately 30–50% of patients with major depression remain undiagnosed in the medical setting (Cohen-Cole et al., 1993). Many patients do not receive appropriate evaluation and treatment because the clinician fails to identify depressive symptoms or considers the patient to "have a good reason to be depressed".

According to DSM-IV, major depression is diagnosed by the presence of five of nine symptoms every day for a 2 week period of time. Symptoms which are clearly due to physical illness should not be included. Depressed mood or anhedonia must be present as one of the five symptoms. It is important to note that while a depressed mood *may* be present in major depression, other symptoms must be present to fulfil diagnostic criteria for major depression.

The literature does offer some guidelines to aid the clinician in distinguishing whether or not depression is present when some of the depressive symptoms may be due to the physical illness. Lustman and colleagues (1986) evaluated the prevalence of depression in a sample of 114 patients with diabetes mellitus, and compared the prevalence rates with and without inclusion of symptoms which may be attributable to the underlying diabetes. They noted that when the symptoms of weight loss, fatigue, hypersomnia, psychomotor retardation, and decreased libido were excluded, due to their association with diabetes, the rate of depression changed from 36.0% to 32.5%. Lustman concluded that DSM-IIIR criteria are a valid measure of depression in diabetic individuals. The risk of overdiagnosing depression in the medical setting has been estimated at 1.5–8% (Cohen-Cole *et al.*, 1993). It appears that the likelihood of under-diagnosing major depression is far greater than the risk of over-diagnosing major depression in the medical setting. From a clinical point of view it is probably best to maximize sensitivity in diagnosing depression and diagnose depression based on the presence of depressive symptoms using DSM-IV criteria.

Treatment options

In general, treatment of the psychiatric manifestations of endocrine disorders is directed towards correcting the underlying endocrine disturbance. When psychiatric symptoms are extremely disabling or persist after normalization of endocrine function, treatment directed at the psychiatric symptoms may be warranted.

DIABETES MELLITUS

Clinical features of the disorder

Type I or insulin-dependent diabetes mellitus (IDDM) typically presents with hunger, fatigue, weight loss, polyuria and polydipsia. The majority of cases present by age 30. The diagnosis of diabetes mellitus is based upon demonstration of an unequivocally high random glucose (> 200 mg/dl), an elevated fasting glucose (≥ 140 mg/dl) on more than one occasion, or sustained elevation of serum glucose following a 75 g oral glucose challenge. Patients with IDDM are frequently underweight. These patients are insulin deficient and require insulin to prevent weight loss, ketoacidosis, or death.

Patients with type II or non-insulin-dependent diabetes mellitus (NIDDM) frequently present asymptomatically, being detected only through the use of blood screening. NIDDM typically occurs after the age of 40 and patients are usually obese. Common presenting symptoms include polydipsia, polyuria, polyphagia, weight loss or gain, pruritus, dry mouth, visual disturbance, fatigue, and candidal vaginitis or balanitis. Diagnosis is made upon demonstration of hyperglycaemia. The most serious metabolic complication of NIDDM is hyperosmolar hyperglycaemic nonketotic coma.

Depression associated with diabetes mellitus

It is important that the clinician learns to recognize and treat depression in diabetic patients. The literature indicates that depressive symptoms are common in diabetes and careful psychiatric assessment is indicated (Gavard et al., 1993). In addition to the impact of major depression on quality of life, some studies have suggested that depression may be associated with poorer glucose control (Lustman et al., 1986; Mazze et al., 1984). Additionally, depression may negatively impact patients' participation in treatment for diabetes (McGill et al., 1992). Two large community studies have evaluated the overall prevalence of psychiatric disorders in patients with diabetes mellitus. In the first study, a sample of 2554 persons revealed that the presence of psychiatric disorders was not higher among patients with diabetes than in those without medical illness (Wells et al., 1988). Conversely, another community study of 1536 persons utilizing the diagnostic interview schedule (DIS) revealed that the prevalence of psychiatric disorders was higher in patients with diabetes (43.1%) and other chronic medical conditions (50.7%), when compared with controls (26.2%). Depressive disorders accounted for the significant difference noted between diabetics and controls (Weyerer et al., 1989).

Lustman and others (1983) have discussed the various aetiologies of depression associated with medical illness. Depression may occur as a reactive depression associated with the development of a chronic, disabling disease. Major depression may occur coincidently in a person with diabetes mellitus. Certain medications may contribute to the development of depressive symptoms. Additionally, some patients may have a predisposition to becoming depressed in periods of stress due to characterological, temperamental, biological or developmental factors (Lustman et al., 1983). Clinical experience suggests that grief reactions frequently accompany the losses associated with end-organ complications of diabetes mellitus such as loss of vision and renal failure.

As noted above, depressive disorders accounted for the difference in prevalence of psychiatric diagnoses in a community sample comparing diabetics with members of the community without a medical illness (Weyerer et al., 1989). Gavard and colleagues (1993) reviewed 20 studies on the prevalence of depression in diabetes mellitus. In nine controlled studies, they noted prevalence rates of major depression varied from 8.5 to 27.3%. In 11 uncontrolled studies the prevalence rates were 11.0–19.9%. Studies utilizing symptom subscales revealed depressive symptom rates ranging from 21.8 to 60.0% in controlled studies and 10 to 28% in uncontrolled studies. These prevalence rates are at least three times that of the prevalence rate of major depression in the general population.

This review cited numerous methodological problems accounting for the wide variance in prevalence rates (Gavard *et al.*, 1993).

The phenomenology of depression associated with diabetes is very similar to primary major depressive disorder. Lustman and colleagues (1992b) administered the Beck Depression Inventory (BDI) to a sample of 41 depressed diabetic patients (DSM-IIIR criteria), 68 depressed patients without medical illness, and 58 nondepressed diabetic patients. The prevalence and severity of depressive symptoms were similar in depressed diabetic patients and other patients without medical illness who had major depression.

Depression associated with diabetes also resembles primary major depressive disorder in other ways, including a higher occurrence of a positive family history of depression when comparing depressed diabetics with diabetics without depression (Lustman *et al.*, 1987). A female predominance is also seen in diabetic patients with depression (Robinson *et al.*, 1988).

Two contrasting features have been noted in depression associated with IDDM versus that of NIDDM. First, the age of onset of depression in patients with IDDM is 22.1 years and in patients with NIDDM the age of onset is approximately 28.6 years. Second, in patients with NIDDM, the depressive symptoms appear to precede the development of diabetes, while in IDDM the diabetic presentation precedes that of the depressive phenomenology (Lustman *et al.*, 1988).

The occurrence of major depression has been shown to have an adverse impact on treatment in patients with diabetes. Marcus and others (1992) followed attendance of patients with obesity and NIDDM at a weight loss clinic. They found that in patients with coincident depression, attendance was less frequent. Additionally, the extent of hyperglycaemia is correlated with the depression severity in patients with IDDM (Sachs *et al.*, 1991). Finally, patients with diabetic complications had higher BDI scores than diabetics without complications, or nondiabetic controls. (Leedom *et al.*, 1991; Tun *et al.*, 1990).

The use of antidepressants for the treatment of depression in diabetes warrants some discussion. The various classes of antidepressants have different effects on appetite, weight, glucose control, cognition, cholinergic systems, and sexual function. Some antidepressants may exacerbate orthostatic hypotension associated with diabetic autonomic neuropathy (Lustman *et al.*, 1992b; Goodnick *et al.*, 1995).

Monoamine oxidase inhibitors (MAOIs) tend to produce weight gain. In addition, hypoglycaemia may be exacerbated by MAOI treatment. The tricyclics tend to produce carbohydrate craving and are associated with noticeable increases in appetite, weight, and blood glucose. The selective serotonin reuptake inhibitors (SSRIs) are associated with slight reductions in serum glucose and body weight. The SSRIs show little effect on appetite (Goodnick *et al.*, 1995).

Antidepressant medications may also negatively impact cognitive functioning in diabetic patients. The cognitive impairment associated with sedating or anti-

Table 2. Comparison of antidepressant classes used in treatment of diabetes mellitus with depression.

Agent	Blood glucose	Weight	Appetite	Memory
MAOI	↓35 mg%	8% > 15 lb	0	11% impaired
TCA	↑ to 150%	↑2.4 lb	↑86–200%	9.8[a]
SSRI	↓20%	↓2–3 lb	0/↓	6.4[b]

[a]Mean ranking on psychometric testing of patients treated with four TCAs (lofepramine, desipramine, dothiepin, amitriptyline); [b]Mean ranking on psychometric testing of patients treated with four SSRIs (sertraline, paroxetine, fluvoxamine, fluoxetine). Adapted from Goodnick PJ, Henry JH, Buki VMV, Treatment of depression in patients with diabetes. *The Journal of Clinical Psychiatry.* **56**, 128–136, Copyright 1995. Physicians Postgraduate Press. Reprinted by permission.

cholinergic medications may interfere with the daily management of diabetes (Lustman *et al.*, 1992b). Several studies have shown cognitive impairment in some diabetic patients (Ryan *et al.*, 1985; Golden *et al.*, 1989). Therefore, following the strict diet required for treatment with MAOIs is problematic, especially in diabetics who already have stringent dietary restrictions (Goodnick *et al.*, 1995). In addition to their cognitive effects, anticholinergic medications may decrease bowel motility worsening underlying diabetes-related gastroparesis or constipation (Lustman *et al.*, 1992b).

Goodnick and colleagues (1995) recommend the use of SSRIs as the first choice of antidepressant in the diabetic patient because of the combined effects of improved glucose control, slight weight loss, and minimal cognitive and anticholinergic effects.

Table 2 summarizes the relative effects of antidepressants on important clinical features of the diabetic patient.

DISORDERS OF THYROID FUNCTION

Hypothyroidism

Clinical features of the disorder

Common clinical manifestations of hypothyroidism include weight gain, fatigue, cold intolerance, slow and hoarse speech, constipation, cognitive slowing, depressed mood, and diminished energy and libido. On physical examination, patients with hypothyroidism may exhibit weight gain, hypothermia, bradycardia, thickening of the nails and hair, dryness of the skin, thickening of the tongue and facial skin, and a delayed relaxation phase of deep tendon reflexes. The thyroid gland may be enlarged depending upon the aetiology of the

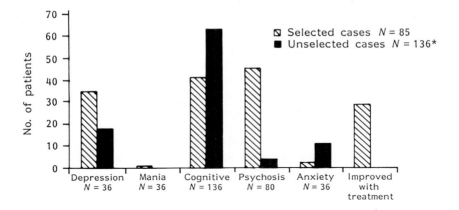

Figure 1. Psychiatric symptoms in hypothyroidism. Number under column reflects number of patients in whom symptom was sought. Adapted from case literature summarized in Table 3.

syndrome. Primary hypothyroidism is the most common cause of hypothyroidism. Laboratory findings include decreased circulating thyroid hormone and elevated thyroid stimulating hormone (TSH) concentrations. Klee (1986) notes that serum TSH is the most useful screening test for primary hypothyroidism.

Hypothyroidism is seen most frequently in women between the ages of 40 and 60. It is a common disorder with an overall incidence of approximately 1.0% in women and 0.1% in men. Autoimmune thyroiditis is the most common cause of hypothyroidism, otherwise known as Hashimoto's disease or chronic lymphocytic thyroiditis. Other common causes of hypothyroidism include the consequences of radioactive iodine therapy or surgery for hyperthyroidism, external neck irradiation, iodine deficiency, and as a side-effect of certain medications (lithium, iodine-containing drugs).

Depression associated with hypothyroidism

Psychiatric complaints may be the initial concern or most prominent sign in patients presenting with hypothyroidism (Hall, 1983). Early studies of psychiatric manifestations of hypothyroidism emphasized psychosis and delirium associated with the condition. In our review of the literature, depression was second only to cognitive dysfunction as the most frequent psychiatric syndrome to occur in unselected hypothyroid patients. Although most psychiatrically ill hypothyroid patients have depressive symptoms, only 50% of unselected hypothyroid patients have a syndromal picture of depression (Figure 1). Mania is exceedingly rare, with only one case report in the literature (Hall *et al.*, 1982).

The literature addressing prevalence of depression in hypothroidism is summarized in Table 3. The Whybrow *et al.* (1969) study is notable in that five or seven hypothyroid patients appeared clinically depressed, one with a psychotic depression. The hypothyroid group scored higher on depressive scales as measured by the Minnesota Multiphasic Personality Inventory (MMPI), Clyde Mood Scale, and the Brief Psychiatric Rating Scale (BPRS), when compared to hyperthyroid patients. Jain (1972) could not demonstrate a relationship between the severity of depression as measured by Hamilton and Beck inventories and the severity of hypothyroidism.

Cognitive disturbance is the most commonly reported psychiatric symptom in hypothyroidism, occurring in 46.3% of unselected cases and 48.2% of psychiatrically ill hypothyroid patients (Figure 1). The severity of the disturbance varies from mild subjective cognitive slowing to severe delirium and encephalopathy.

Anxiety occurs in approximately 30% of unselected hypothyroid patients. Clinical experience suggests it is often accompanied by significant depressive symptoms and is more generalized in nature.

Psychosis is the most common symptom reported in the case literature in hypothyroidism (52.9%), but it represents only 5% of the psychiatric morbidity in unselected samples. This disparity likely reflects a reporting bias due to the dramatic nature of psychotic symptoms. The psychotic symptoms may occur comorbidly with depression or independent of a significant affective disturbance.

Treatment options

Most psychiatric symptoms are alleviated after euthyroidism is achieved. If affective symptoms continue after normal thyroid function is attained, then antidepressant treatment may be indicated. Hypothyroid patients may be sensitive to sedating and anticholinergic side-effects of medications (Kornstein and Gardner, 1993). The use of tricyclic antidepressants may induce rapid cycling in some hypothyroid patients (Cowdry *et al.*, 1983). Less sedating medications such as the SSRIs be the best alternative for the treatment of persistent depressive symptoms.

Hyperthyroidism

Clinical features of the disorder

Symptoms of hyperthyroidism vary among patients, but the most common manifestations include diaphoresis, heat intolerance, fatigue, dyspnoea, palpitations, proximal muscle weakness, anxiety, weight loss despite an increased appetite, hyperdefecation, and visual complaints. Clinicians may observe anxiety, psychomotor agitation, tachycardia (often with atrial fibrillation), bounding peripheral pulses, moist and warm skin, thinning of the individual hair shafts as

Table 3. Psychiatric symptoms in hypothyroidism.

Study	N	Type of psychiatric disturbance				
		Cognitive	Psychosis	Depression	Mania	Anxiety
Selected hypothyroid cases						
Asher, 1949	14	12	9	5		
Miller, 1952	2					
Wiesel, 1952	1		1	1		
Jonas, 1952	1			1		1
Pitts, 1961	3	3	2	3		
Logothetis, 1963	4	4	3	2		
Libow and Durell, 1965	1		1	1		
Tonks, 1964	18	5	7	6		
Pomeranze, 1966	1			1		
Ward, 1967	1	1				
Treadway et al., 1967	1	1	1	1		
Hall et al., 1982	4	1	1	3	1	1
Unselected hypothyroid populations						
Crown, 1949	4	4				
Reitan, 1953	15	15				
Schon, 1962	24	24				
Jellinek, 1962	56	6	noted	noted	noted	noted
Easson, 1966	19	1	11	2		
Whybrow et al., 1969	7	6	1	5		1
Jain, 1972	30	8	3	13		10

Number in column reflects number of patients exhibiting specific symptom/syndrome well as alopecia, tremor and hyperreflexia. Eye findings range from simple retraction of the upper lid with lid lag to overt exophthalmos with impairment of extraocular movement. The thyroid gland is usually enlarged, although in the elderly and in those with substernal thyroid tissue the thyroid will often be normal in size. The most common cause of hyperthyroidism is Graves' disease, a systemic autoimmune disease. Less common causes include toxic nodular goitre, subacute thyroiditis, and excessive thyroid hormone replacement.

Depression associated with hyperthyroidism

Clinical lore has emphasized the universal presence of psychiatric symptoms in patients with hyperthyroidism. However, careful review of the literature suggests that serious psychiatric symptoms occur in only a minority of patients. Most commonly, depression, anxiety, and cognitive changes are seen, with manic and psychotic manifestations encountered less frequently. Table 4 summarizes the case literature and studies involving unselected hyperthyroid patients; Figure 2 compares the prevalence of psychiatric symptoms in these two groups.

The most common psychiatric manifestation of hyperthyroidism according to our review was major depression. Approximately 28% of unselected patients with hyperthroidism had major depression (Figure 2). Symptoms of major depression may precede the development of physical manifestations of hyperthyroidism in some patients. Sonino and others (1993b) reported on the largest sample in the literature and noted that major depression occurred in 23% of 70 patients with Graves' disease. Depression occurred in the prodromal phase in 14% of these patients. Similarly, Wilson and colleagues (1962) reported that 24 of 26 patients with hyperthyroidism noted mood changes and neurovegetative symptoms involving sleep, appetite, libido, and psychomotor activity prior to the occurrence of physical signs and symptoms of hyperthyroidism. No further psychiatric intervention was needed in any of these patients after euthyroidism was achieved.

Kathol and Delahunt (1986) provided the first study to use modern operational criteria for the assessment of psychiatric disorders in hyperthyroid patients. They noted that 10 of 32 patients with untreated hyperthyroidism fulfilled DSM-III criteria for major depression. The likelihood of major depression was not correlated with the severity of hyperthyroidism. Trzepacz and colleagues (1988a) noted that nine of 13 untreated Graves' disease patients fulfilled criteria for major depression using Research Diagnostic Criteria (RDC) and the Schedule For Affective Disorder and Schizophrenia (SADS) index. They found that weight loss in the presence of a voracious appetite represented a striking phenomenological difference when compared to patients with typical major depression.

Apathetic thyrotoxicosis is a condition usually seen in elderly patients with a longer duration of symptoms and more dramatic weight loss. The clinical

Table 4. Psychiatric symptoms in hyperthyroidism

Study	N	Type of psychiatric disturbance				
		Cognitive	Psychosis	Depression	Mania	Anxiety
Selected hyperthyroid cases						
Bursten, 1961	10	3	10	1	1	
Taylor, 1975	1		1	1		
Katerndahl and Vandecreek, 1983	1			1		1
Unselected hyperthyroid populations						
Lidz, 1949	15			9		
Mandelbrote et al., 1955	25			noted		noted
Kleinschmidt et al., 1956	17		2	noted	noted	
Robbins and Vinson, 1960	10	1	1			1
Wilson et al., 1962	26	14		15	2	6
Artunkal and Togrol, 1964	20					
Hermann et al., 1965	24	noted	1			noted
Whybrow et al., 1969	10	4	2	2		2
Thomas et al., 1970	9			6		
MacCrimmon et al., 1979	19					
Rockey and Griep, 1980	14			1		11
Kathol and Delahunt, 1986	33			10		20
Trzepacz et al., 1988a	13			9	3	8

Number in column reflects number of patients exhibiting specific symptom/syndrome

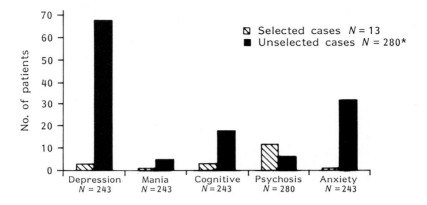

Figure 2. Psychiatric symptoms in hyperthyroidism. Number under column reflects number of unselected patients in whom symptom was sought. Adapted from case literature summarized in Table 4.

appearance is typically that of an elderly patient with depression, apathy, and an increased prevalence of cardiovascular events and decreased prevalence of ocular manifestations of hyperthyroidism. Thomas and colleagues (1970) found that six of nine patients with apathetic thyrotoxicosis had features of mental depression. Specific depression criteria, however, were not described.

Other psychiatric manifestations of hyperthyroidism

The prevalence of cognitive disturbance in thyrotoxicosis is 7.4%, considerably less than that observed in hypothyroidism. The cognitive changes associated with thyrotoxicosis range from subtle defects in attention and concentration to overt delirium.

Although anxiety is frequently believed to be a cardinal feature of hyperthyroidism, it actually occurs in only 23% of unselected patients in whom anxiety symptoms were sought (Figure 2). Anxiety due to hyperthyroidism is generally of insidious onset, often preceding overt physical signs of the disorder (Dietch, 1981). Two recent studies applied operational criteria for anxiety disorders to untreated Graves' disease patients. Trzepacz and colleagues (1988) revealed that eight of 13 patients had generalized anxiety disorder, four of 13 met criteria for panic disorder, and one had agoraphobia using RDC criteria. Kathol and Delahunt (1986) noted that 15 of 32 patients with untreated Graves' disease fulfilled DSM-III criteria for generalized anxiety disorder. Both groups noted that the severity of anxiety correlated with the severity of hyperthyroidism and that most patients with anxiety had concurrent major depression.

Psychosis is an uncommon manifestation of thyrotoxicosis, occurring in 2.1% of unselected patients. Earlier estimates of prevalence ranged from 15 to 25% (Clower *et al.*, 1968). Review of the symptoms reported in these patients, however, would lead many of them to be classified as having affective disorders.

Treatment options

In hyperthyroidism, many of the signs and symptoms can be reversed by the use of beta-adrenergic blocking agents. Benzodiazepines may be the safest medication for short-term use in alleviating anxiety and agitation in hyperthyroidism (Kornstein and Gardner, 1993). The use of tricyclic antidepressants in the setting of hyperthyroidism may exacerbate tachycardia or induce arrhythmias (Loosen, 1988). Tachycardia and arrhythmias may also be exacerbated by the use of neuroleptics (Wilson and Jefferson, 1985). Furthermore, dystonic reactions may be more likely to occur with the use of some neuroleptics in the setting of hyperthyroidism (Witschy and Redmond, 1981).

Subclinical hypothyroidism and the spectrum of thyroid axis abnormalities

A continuum of disturbance in thyroid function has recently been identified given the more sophisticated measures of thyroid function. Grade I (overt) hypothyroidism is manifested by decreased circulating thyroid hormone and an elevated thyroid-stimulating hormone (TSH) concentration and is accompanied by clinical symptoms of hypothyroidism. In Grade II hypothyroidism, TSH is elevated, but thyroid hormone levels are normal. An exaggerated TSH response to exogenously administered thyrotropin-releasing hormone (TRH), the so-called TRH stimulation test, is seen in both Grade I and Grade II hypothyroidism. Grade II hypothyroidism is sometimes referred to as "subclinical hypothyroidism". In Grade III hypothyroidism the TSH response to exogenously administered TRH is exaggerated, but TSH, T_3 and T_4 levels are normal. Grade IV or symptomless thyroiditis is characterized by the presence of antithyroid antibodies in the serum. However, circulating basal TSH and T_4 levels are normal in addition to a normal TRH stimulation test.

Several studies have scrutinized the relationship between affective illness and subclinical hypothyroidism. The clinical significance of such associations, however, remains unclear. Patients with major depression show an increased prevalence of Grade II hypothyroidism (Gold *et al.*, 1981; Haggerty *et al.*, 1987). Subclinical hypothyroidism may also be a risk factor for the development of major depression. Haggerty and colleagues (1993) compared the lifetime occurrence of major depression in 16 patients with Grade II hypothyroidism with 15 patients with normal thyroid function. Patients with Grade II hypothyroidism had a lifetime history of major depression of 56% compared to a rate of 20% in controls. Hamilton Depression Rating Scale scores did not differ between the groups.

Depressed patients with Grade II hypothyroidism may respond poorly to antidepressant treatment (Prange *et al.*, 1988; Targum *et al.*, 1984; Joffe and Levitt, 1992). Some studies have associated rapid cycling bipolar disorder with Grade II hypothyroidism, although discrepant reports have also appeared (Cowdry *et al.*, 1983; Bauer and Whybrow, 1990; Joffe *et al.*, 1986; Wehr *et al.*, 1988).

Whether or not hormone replacement therapy is indicated in subclinical (Grade II) hypothyroidism is an area of current controversy. In a study of 33 patients with Grade II hypothyroidism, eight of 14 patients receiving L-thyroxine reported symptomatic improvement compared to three of 12 patients receiving placebo (Cooper *et al.*, 1984). In a discussion of two patients with psychiatric symptoms and Grade II hypothyroidism, mood and psychotic symptoms improved after treatment with L-thyroxine, antidepressants and antipsychotics, while no improvement in cognitive symptoms was seen (Haggerty *et al.*, 1986).

Hypothalamic–pituitary–thyroid axis and depression

Affective symptoms have long been identified in thyroid disease leading many investigators to search for the role of thyroid axis abnormalities in affective disorders. Use of thyroid hormone supplementation has been found to increase the rapidity of action of tricyclic antidepressants (Prange *et al.*, 1969) and was as effective as lithium in converting depressed TCA nonresponders into responders (Joffe *et al.*, 1993). The precise relationship between the hypothalamic–pituitary–thyroid (HPT) axis and affective disorder remains obscure. The complexities of the HPT axis in depression are illustrated by several contradicting observations. First, symptoms of depression are observed in both hypothyroidism and hyperthyroidism. Secondly, the majority of depressed patients have thyroid function within the normal range (Joffe and Sokolov, 1994). Nonetheless, several intriguing findings have been made.

Elevated levels of TRH in cerebrospinal fluid have been found in drug-free patients with major depression (Kirkegaard *et al.*, 1979; Banki *et al.*, 1988). In 1972, Prange and others found that approximately 25% of depressed patients with major depression exhibited a blunted TSH response to exogenously administered TRH. Conversely, Extein and others (1981) found that 15% of depressed patients showed an exaggerated TSH response to TRH.

Depressed patients have also been found to have a higher than expected incidence of symptomless autoimmune thyroiditis (SAT), defined by the presence of circulating antimicrosomal thyroid and/or antithyroglobulin antibodies (Gold *et al.*, 1982). Further research is needed to clarify the relationship between depression and HPT axis abnormalities.

DISORDERS OF ADRENAL FUNCTION

Cushing's syndrome and disease

Clinical features of the disorder

Common presenting signs and symptoms of Cushing's syndrome include centripetal obesity, moon facies, hirsutism, menstrual irregularities, hypertension, proximal muscle weakness, red to purple striae, acne, and easy bruisability. Patients may also have osteopenia and glucose intolerance. The most common cause of Cushing's syndrome is high dose corticosteroid administration. Other common causes of Cushing's syndrome include excessive production of adrenocorticotropic hormone (ACTH) from a pituitary adenoma, neoplasms of the adrenal cortex, and ectopic production of ACTH by malignancies. Cushing's disease refers to those cases of hypercortisolism due to ACTH production from a pituitary adenoma. Laboratory diagnosis of Cushing's syndrome depends upon the demonstration of cortisol elevation or an abnormal dexamethasone suppression test.

Depression associated with Cushing's syndrome

The occurrence of depression in Cushing's syndrome has been well documented in the literature (Spillane, 1951; Whybrow and Hurwitz, 1976; Zeiger *et al.*, 1993). In 1913, Harvey Cushing noted psychiatric disturbance, particularly depression, in his first description of the illness that bears his name (Cushing, 1932). Mood disorders, especially unipolar depression, are by far the most frequently reported psychiatric manifestations of Cushing's syndrome. Depression was frequently noted in reports prior to 1980, but most studies were retrospective in design and did not use diagnostic criteria. Whybrow and Hurwitz (1976) found depressive symptoms reported in 35% of patients with Cushing's syndrome, compared with a 3.7% prevalence of mania in their classic review. Furthermore, suicide attempts (Starkman *et al.*, 1981a; Haskett, 1985; Gotch, 1994) and completed suicides (Jeffcoate, 1979; Ziegler, 1993) have been reported during the course of Cushing's syndrome. Recently, investigators have further clarified the psychiatric sequelae of Cushing's syndrome by using structured interviews and diagnostic criteria. Haskett (1985) applied Research Diagnostic Criteria (RDC) to 30 patients with Cushing's syndrome and found that 16 (53%) fulfilled criteria for unipolar depression and nine (30%) met criteria for bipolar disorder. Other recent studies suggest that prevalence rates of depressive symptoms in Cushing's syndrome are as high as 77–94% (Starkman *et al.*, 1981a; Mazet *et al.*, 1981).

Mixed anxiety and depressive states are the most common psychiatric manifestation of Cushing's syndrome according to recent investigations (Loosen

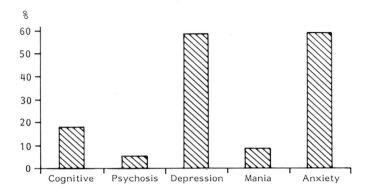

Figure 3. Psychiatric symptoms in Cushing's syndrome. Relative prevalence of major psychiatric symptoms in cases of Cushing's syndrome using broad clinical or structured interview. Adapted from data discussed in text.

et al., 1992; Mazet *et al.*, 1981). Starkman and colleagues (1981a) found anxiety symptoms to be present in 63% of 35 patients with Cushing's syndrome. Loosen and colleagues (1992) used the Structured Clinical Interview for DSM-IIIR (SCID) to study 20 Cushing's disease patients and 20 patients with major depressive disorder. Loosen noted that generalized anxiety disorder was the most common psychiatric diagnosis (79%) in the Cushing's patients. Major depression was present in 68% and panic disorder in 53%. With the exception of one, all patients with major depression had comorbid anxiety diagnoses. Phenomenologically, depressed patients with Cushing's syndrome appear to have more irritability and mood lability (Starkman *et al.*, 1981b; Haskett, 1985). This syndrome of mixed depression and anxiety has been underappreciated, most likely due to reporting and investigator bias. Figure 3 illustrates the prevalence of psychiatric disorders in Cushing's states in studies utilizing prospective methodology. Depressive symptoms occurring in patients with Cushing's disease appear to be intermittent in contrast to the chronicity of symptoms in primary major depression (Haskett, 1985; Starkman *et al.*, 1981b; Loosen *et al.*, 1992).

Depressive symptoms may occur early in the course of Cushing's syndrome. Sonino and colleagues (1993b) noted that prodromal depressive symptoms occurred in 27% of 66 patients with Cushing's syndrome. Jeffcoate (1979) suggested that patients with antecedent psychiatric symptoms have a less favourable psychiatric outcome after treatment of the endocrine disorder.

The mood disorder associated with Cushing's syndrome appears to resolve following treatment of the endocrine disorder. Treatment usually involves metyrapone, adrenalectomy, pituitary irradiation or resection. Sonino found that 70% of depressed Cushing's syndrome patients improved with reduction of serum cortisol (Sonino *et al.*, 1993b). In a series of 34 patients with Cushing's syndrome, bilateral adrenalectomy resulted in improvement of depressive symptoms in eight of nine patients described as depressed (Zieger *et al.*, 1993). A reduction in Hamilton Depression Rating Scale scores in 26 patients with Cushing's syndrome was reported following successful treatment (Kelly *et al.*, 1983). In addition, improvement following treatment may be related to severity of depressive symptoms. Jeffcoate (1979) studied 38 patients with Cushing's syndrome and found that eight of nine moderately to severely depressed patients responded to reduction of plasma cortisol with an improvement in depressive symptoms compared with improvement in only six of 13 mildly depressed patients (Jeffcoate *et al.*, 1979). Starkman and colleagues (1981a) also noted that improvement in depressive symptoms correlated with the reduction in plasma cortisol concentrations.

Bipolar illness and hypomania are relatively infrequent findings in Cushing's syndrome. Starkman and colleagues (1981a) noted hypomania in three and mania in one of 35 patients with Cushing's syndrome. Mazet and colleagues (1981) reported manic symptoms in seven of 50 patients with Cushing's syndrome. However, Haskett (1985) found a higher occurrence of bipolar illness in Cushing's disease. He reported a prevalence rate of 30% for bipolar disorder using the Schedule for Affective Disorders and Schizophrenia—Lifetime Version (SADS-L).

Other psychiatric symptoms associated with Cushing's syndrome

There are only rare reports of psychosis and delirium in the Cushing's disease literature. Psychotic symptoms in Cushing's syndrome are usually noted with a coincident depressive disorder (Cohen, 1980; Haskett *et al.*, 1985). Cognitive impairment in Cushing's syndrome had been relatively infrequently reported, and when documented was mild (Whelan *et al.*, 1980), until the report of Starkman *et al.* (1992).

Treatment options

Psychiatric symptoms usually improve upon normalization of cortisol levels. If psychotic symptoms or extreme agitation are present, low dose neuroleptics or ECT may be helpful (Kornstein and Gardner, 1993). If depressive symptoms persist after normalization of serum cortisol levels, then antidepressant treatment is indicated.

Exogenous corticosteroid administration

Corticosteroids are currently used for a variety of medical conditions. Psychiatric sequelae to steroid use were reported shortly after steroids were introduced

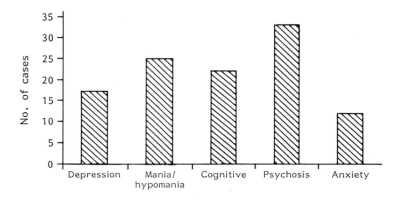

Figure 4. Psychiatric symptoms with corticosteroid administration. Findings from the case literature. Adapted from Hall *et al.*, 1979 and Perry *et al.*, 1984.

into clinical practice (Clark *et al.*, 1952). The phenomenology of psychiatric symptoms in endogenous hypercortisolaemia is quite different to that seen in exogenously administered steroids (Murphy, 1991). Psychiatric sequelae have been reported in most corticosteroid preparations including ACTH (which stimulate cortisol release), cortisone, prednisone, prednisolone, methylprednisolone, and inhaled beclomethasone (Ling *et al.*, 1981; Perry *et al.*, 1984; Rosenberg, 1976; Hayreh and Watson, 1970). Affective symptoms are the most commonly reported psychiatric complication of steroid use, although psychosis, delirium, and anxiety have also been reported (Ling *et al.*, 1981; Perry *et al.*, 1984; Hall *et al.*, 1979; Campbell, 1987; Silva, 1995). Murphy (1991) noted that euphoria and a generally improved mental state is the most common psychiatric manifestation of exogenous corticosteroid use. Irritability, psychomotor agitation, and insomnia are also common. Depression is relatively rare following exogenous steroid use compared to the high incidence of depression with endogenous hypercortisolaemia. Figure 4 illustrates the relative prevalence of depression compared to other psychiatric disturbances following exogenous corticosteroid administration.

There are no controlled studies on the relationship between the corticosteroid dose and the severity of psychiatric symptoms. However, the prevalence of psychiatric disturbances associated with corticosteroid administration does appear to be a dose-related phenomenon. In a prospective study of 718 hospitalized patients receiving prednisone, 1.3% had psychiatric reactions at a dosage less than or equal to 40 mg per day. At a dosage of 41–80 mg per day the rate increased to 4.6%. The rate of psychiatric symptoms increased to 18.4% at 80 mg or more per day of prednisone (Figure 5) (Boston Collaborative Drug Surveillance Program, 1972). Bender *et al.* (1991) prospectively studied 32

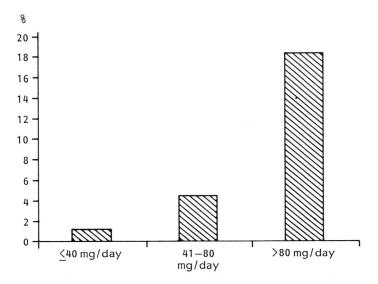

Figure 5. Prevalence of corticosteroid-related psychiatric disturbances: relationship to dose. Adapted from Boston Collaborative Drug Surveillance Program (1972) Acute adverse reactions to prednisone in relation to dosage. *Clin Pharm Ther*, **13**, 694–698.

asthmatic children and found that high dose prednisone (mean 61.4 mg/day) was associated with more depression and anxiety symptoms and decreased verbal memory compared with low dose prednisone (7 mg/day). Newcomer *et al.* (1994) demonstrated that extended treatment (4 days) with dexamethasone, as opposed to a single-dose treatment, resulted in a decrease in declarative memory performance as measured by the paragraph recall test. The memory deficits did not appear to reflect a deficit in arousal or attention.

Treatment options

Hall *et al.* (1979) reported on the use of neuroleptics in corticosteroid-induced psychotic disorders with or without discontinuation of the corticosteroid. Interestingly, the clinical course worsened in patients who received tricyclic antidepressants for treatment of affective symptoms during corticosteroid administration (Hall *et al.*, 1979). Occasionally, a reduction in the dose of corticosteroids may alleviate the psychiatric symptoms (Kornstein and Gardner, 1993). Falk and colleagues (1979) reported on the successful use of prophylactic lithium in therapeutic doses to reduce the psychiatric complications associated with ACTH administration in the setting of multiple sclerosis. Finally, valproic acid may also be helpful in the treatment of mood disorders associated with corticosteroid administration (Abbas and Styras, 1994).

Addison's disease (adrenal insufficiency)

Clinical features of the disorder

Adrenal insufficiency may present acutely or be a chronic condition. Chronic adrenal insufficiency is manifested by fatigue, malaise, weakness, weight loss, anorexia, hyperpigmentation, hypotension, nausea, and vomiting. Metabolic abnormalities include hyponatraemia, hyperkalaemia, metabolic acidosis, anaemia, and eosinophilia. Acute adrenal insufficiency is a more dramatic presentation involving painful gastrointestinal symptoms which may mimic a surgical abdomen. Fever and shock may also be present.

Depression associated with adrenal insufficiency

Psychiatric symptoms are relatively uncommon in adrenal insufficiency. Engel and Margolin (1941) reviewed 25 cases of Addison's disease. Disturbances in cognition were reported in 16 of these patients. Whybrow and Hurwitz (1976) further reviewed these cases and clarified that two patients had delirium, one patient had psychosis, and five had depressive symptoms. Three other cases are present in the literature, characterized by symptoms of anxiety and depression (Thompson, 1973; Varadaraj and Cooper, 1986).

Hypothalamic–pituitary–adrenal axis and depression

Hypercortisolaemia has been widely documented in patients with major depression (Gibbons and McHugh, 1963; Carrol *et al.*, 1976; Rosenbaum *et al.*, 1983). In 1965, Bunnery and Fawcett measured 24-hour 17-OHCSE in 143 depressed patients. Patients who had severe or completed suicide attempts had the highest levels of cortisol. Elevated cortisol levels return to normal following recovery from depression (Sachar *et al.*, 1970).

Hypercortisolaemia appears to represent a state, as opposed to a trait, marker for depression (Nathan *et al.*, 1995). Murphy and colleagues (1991) studied 10 patients with treatment-resistant depression and found that treatment with a steroid suppressive agent resulted in significant improvement in six patients.

There is a growing body of literature relating stressful life events to the activation of the hypothalamic–pituitary–adrenal (HPA) axis. In 1988, Sonino and others investigated the presence of stressful life events in 30 consecutive patients with Cushing's syndrome and 30 controls using Paykel's Interview for Recent Life Events. Patients with Cushing's syndrome had significantly more stressful life events. In a larger study in 1993(a), Sonino and colleagues noted that patients with the pituitary-dependent form of the disease had a higher number of total negative life events prior to the onset of the disease as compared to patients with pituitary-independent Cushing's syndrome.

Carrol (1968) reported nonsuppression of plasma hydroxycorticosteroid levels after administration of the synthetic glucocorticoid dexamethasone in depressed patients. Dexamethasone suppression test (DST) nonsuppression has been highly correlated with more severe forms of depression, such as psychotic depression (Evans and Nemeroff, 1983). Persistent DST nonsuppression may be associated with early relapse or a poorer prognosis (Arana *et al.*, 1985).

Increased levels of corticotropin-releasing factor (CRF) have been found in cerebrospinal fluid in depressed patients (Arato *et al.*, 1986; Nemeroff *et al.*, 1984; Risch *et al.*, 1992). Pituitary gland enlargement (Krishnan *et al.*, 1991) and adrenal gland enlargement have been reported in depressed patients (Amsterdam *et al.*, 1987; Nemeroff *et al.*, 1992).

DISORDERS OF PROLACTIN SECRETION

Hyperprolactinaemia

Clinical features of the disorder

Gonadal dysfunction is the primary feature of hyperprolactinaemia. In females, amenorrhoea, galactorrhoea, and infertility are the primary manifestations of hyperprolactinaemia. In males, impotence is the primary symptom, although gynaecomastia and galactorrhoea can occur. Demonstration of an elevated serum prolactin level ($>25\,\text{ng/ml}$) is required for diagnosis. Prolactin-secreting pituitary adenomas are the most common cause of hyperprolactinaemia. Drug-induced causes of hyperprolactinaemia need to be considered in the differential diagnosis. Drugs associated with hyperprolactinaemia include antipsychotics, other dopamine receptor antagonists, reserpine, methyldopa, amitriptyline, imipramine, amoxapine, verapamil, cimetidine, oestrogens, and opiates (Kornstein and Gardner, 1993). Other endocrinopathies, hepatic, and renal disease may also be associated with hyperprolactinaemia. Magnetic resonance imaging of the sella is the preferred modality for pituitary imaging. Treatment involves the use of dopamine agonists, e.g. bromocriptine, or transsphenoidal pituitary surgery.

Depression associated with hyperprolactinaemia

Major depression has been reported to occur in hyperprolactinaemia. Mastrogiacomo and colleagues (1983a) found that one-third of 18 women with hyperprolactinaemia fulfilled DSM-III criteria for major depression. Hostility and irritability characterized the depression as opposed to dysphoria. Fava and others (1981) found that women with hyperprolactinaemic amenorrhoea reported greater levels of depression, hostility, and anxiety on a self-rating scale than normal healthy women and other women with amenorrhoea and normal prolactin levels. Several studies have revealed the findings of aggression and hostility associated with hyperprolactinaemia. In laboratory animals, high levels of aggression have been observed in lactating mammals in association with high prolactin levels (Erskine *et al.*, 1980). In humans, initial studies suggested a relationship between prolactin levels and hostility among patients with premenstrual syndrome (Steiner *et al.*, 1984). In a later investigation, hyperprolactinaemic patients were compared with family practice patient controls, psychiatric patient controls, and nonpatient employees utilizing the Kellner Symptom Questionnaire (SQ). The SQ is a 92 item self-report scale concerning emotional symptoms and statements of well-being. Four scales are contained within the questionnaire, concerning depression, anxiety, somatization, and anger–hostility. Hyperprolactinaemic patients showed higher scores on the anger–hostility domain of the SQ than the family practice controls and nonpatient employees (Kellner *et al.*, 1984). Another study compared 10 postpartum patients with 10 hyperprolactinaemic patients and 10 employee controls. Hostility scores were higher in the postpartum group than in either the controls or the patients with hyperprolactinaemia. The hyperprolactinaemic patients scored higher on depression scales than either the postpartum patients or the controls (Mastrogiacomo *et al.*, 1983b).

The literature suggests that hyperprolactinaemia may be related to depressive disorders. Bromocriptine is a dopamine agonist used to suppress secretion of prolactin. The use of bromocriptine resulted in a reduction in depression, anxiety, and anger–hostility scales of the SQ. This improvement in symptoms correlated with the reduction in serum prolactin levels (Buckman and Kellner, 1982). In another study, six patients with hyperprolactinaemia were given bromocriptine in a double-blind crossover study and significant reductions in Hamilton depression rating scales were noted (Koppelman, 1987). Furthermore, bromocriptine has been shown to have antidepressant properties in primary depression (Theohar *et al.*, 1981).

DISORDERS OF CALCIUM REGULATION

Hyperparathyroidism

Clinical features of the disorder

Hyperparathyroidism is a disorder characterized by elevated calcium levels due to excessive parathyroid hormone (PTH) production. Most cases are due to a single parathyroid adenoma which secretes excessive PTH. Hyperplasia of multiple glands is the second most common aetiology and usually occurs in the setting of one of the multiple endocrine neoplasia syndromes. Diagnosis depends upon the demonstration of elevated circulating parathyroid hormone. With recent advances in automated screening laboratory panels, the presentation of primary hyperparathyroidism is far less dramatic than in previous decades (Heath, 1991). Most patients at presentation today are either asymptomatic or have vague, nonspecific complaints. Patients may complain of anorexia, fatigue, malaise, weakness, increased thirst, and cognitive changes. Other manifestations include nephrolithiasis, proximal weakness of the lower extremities, chondrocalcinosis, and band keratopathy. Rarely, the clinician may see subperiosteal bone resorption and osteitis fibrosa cystica.

Hypercalcaemia has a vast differential diagnosis, but in the hospital setting an elevated calcium level is often associated with malignancy. Malignancies in which hypercalcaemia frequently occur include those of the lung, breast, prostate, cervix, renal cell, multiple myeloma, and head and neck cancers. A parathyroid hormone-related peptide secreted by the underlying neoplasm has been reported (Insogna, 1989).

Depression associated with hyperparathyroidism

Hyperparathyroidism has been associated with a variety of psychiatric alterations including mood, anxiety, psychotic, and cognitive symptoms. The literature emphasizes that changes in mental status parallel the elevation in calcium concentrations. In general, depressive symptoms occur when serum calcium is mildly to moderately elevated (Brown *et al.*, 1987a). Most of the literature consists of case reports and small case series, with prospective studies occurring more recently. Table 5 summarizes the case literature. In their comprehensive review, Alarcon and Franceschini (1984) noted that affective and cognitive changes were the predominant symptoms in hyperparathyroidism and that most of the patients were elderly females.

Ljunghall and colleagues (1991) studied 32 patients with primary hyperparathyroidism before and after surgery using the Comprehensive Psychopathological Rating Scale. Symptoms most commonly reported included fatiguability, lassitude, decreased memory and concentration, dysphoria, insomnia, anxiety, and irritability. Karpati and Frame (1964) performed a retrospective study of 33 patients with primary hyperparathyroidism and found that 14 patients had psychiatric symptoms. Anxiety was the most commonly noted symptom and four patients had depression and cognitive symptoms. In a prospective study of 54 patients with hyperparathyroidism, Petersen (1968) noted that over 50% had psychiatric symptoms and the severity of the psychiatric symptoms correlated with the magnitude of the serum calcium elevation.

According to our review, the psychiatric symptoms associated with hypercalcaemia improve as the hypercalcaemia is corrected. Solomon and colleagues (1994) prospectively studied 19 patients scheduled for hyperparathy-

Table 5. Psychiatric symptoms in hyperparathyroidism: Case reports.

Reference	Year	Age/Sex	Symptoms	Serum Ca^{2+} (mg%)	Improved with treatment
Fitz and Hallman	1952	55/M	Psychosis	14	yes
		52/M	Delirium	19	yes
Nielsen	1955	47/F	Mood symptoms	13	yes
Bogdanoff	1956	58/F	Depression/Anxiety	15.4	
Thomas	1958	69/F	Delirium	18.3	
Lehrer and Levitt	1960	62/F	Delirium	13.3	no (died)
Reinfrank	1961	38/M	Depression	11.1	yes
Agras and Oliveau	1964	64/F	Psychotic, depression	15	yes
Karpati and Frame	1964	40/F	Depression	12.8	yes
		64/F	Depression/anxiety	11.6	yes
		?/F	Delirium	12.2	yes
		43/F	Anxiety/obsessive–compulsive symptoms	11.6	yes
Jacobs and Merritt	1965	63/F	Delirium	21.2	yes
Reilly and Wilson	1965	34/M	Psychosis	11.6	yes
		62/F	Delirium	12.2	yes
		67/F	Anxiety/Depression symptoms	13.8	yes
Noble	1974	53/F	Depression	14.2	no
Gatewood et al	1975	63/M	Delirium	11.9	yes
Rosenblatt and Faillace	1977	30/M	Psychosis	12.9	yes
Alarcon and Franceschini	1984	53/F	Psychosis	13.0	yes
Kleinfeld et al.	1984	67/F	Psychosis	13.2	yes
Borer and Bhanot	1985	45/F	Depression/delirium	12.3	no; suicide 4 months later
Oztunc et al.	1986	45/M	Delirium	12.4	
Brown et al.	1987a	49/F	Depression/anxiety	11.4	no
		60/F	Depression/anxiety	11.2	no
		73/F	Anxiety	10.9	no
		59/F	Psychosis/cognitive changes	12.5	no
Brown RS et al.	1987b	68/M	Psychosis	12/3	yes
Hayabara et al	1987	68/F	Psychosis	11.0	yes
		60/F	Delirium	15.0	yes
Thurling	1987	52/F	Psychosis	14.8	yes

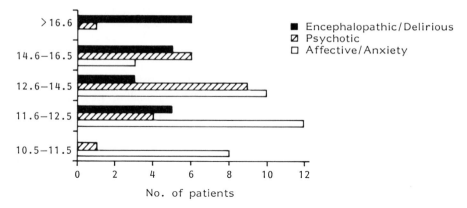

Figure 6. Psychiatric symptoms in hyperparathyroidism. Phenomenological association with changes in serum calcium. Adapted from Peterson *et al.* (1960) updated to include case data from Table 5.

roidectomy. They measured the preoperative symptoms of psychological distress using the Symptom Checklist–90–Revised (SCL-90-R) and found that these symptoms improved within 1 month following corrective surgery for the hyperparathyroidism. Brown *et al.* (1987a) demonstrated the relationship between the psychiatric symptoms and the level of hypercalcaemia. A detailed neurobehavioural assessment and a psychiatric interview was performed on 34 patients with hyperparathyroidism in a prospective study. They found that only 29% of patients were neurobehaviourally asymptomatic. Signs of affective disorder were present in 32% of patients and 39% had evidence of cognitive impairment. Furthermore, the severity of psychiatric symptoms progressed with elevations in serum calcium. At a mean calcium of 10.9 mg%, patients were psychiatrically asymptomatic. Serum calcium levels of approximately 11.3 mg% were associated with affective symptoms and cognitive impairment was observed with calcium concentrations of 12.2 mg% or greater. Surprisingly, no improvement in psychiatric symptoms occurred with correction of the serum calcium in their series. Figure 6 summarizes the case literature and illustrates the relationship between serum calcium levels and the nature of the psychiatric disturbance.

Hypoparathyroidism

Clinical signs and symptoms of the disorder

Hypoparathyroidism is manifested by a decrease in serum calcium concentrations and a corresponding increase in serum phosphorus concentrations. The disorder is most often due to accidental removal of the parathyroid gland during thyroid gland surgery or radical neck dissection. The cardinal symptom of decreased serum calcium is neuromuscular irritability, ranging from paraesthesiae to muscle cramps, carpopedal spasm, laryngospasm, and seizures. Deep tendon reflexes, however, are often decreased to absent. Cataracts and occasionally papilloedema may be found on ocular examination. Dermatological findings include alopecia, transverse nail growth, dry, scaling, pigmented skin, and a propensity to develop candidal infections (Juan, 1979).

Depression associated with hypoparathyroidism

Depressive symptoms have been reported in hypoparathyroidism in addition to irritability, anxiety, psychotic and cognitive alterations. The most common psychiatric symptom associated with hypoparathyroidism is cognitive dysfunction. Anxiety has been recognized by recent authors as a feature of hypoparathyroidism (Carlson, 1986; Lawlor, 1988).

Denko and Kaelbling (1962) conducted the most comprehensive assessment of the psychiatric manifestations of hypoparathyroidism. They reviewed 268 cases of hypoparathyroidism selected for psychiatric symptoms and compared them to 58 cases of pseudohypoparathyroidism and 11 cases of pseudopseudohypoparathyroidism. Among patients with hypoparathyroidism, they noted severe intellectual impairment in 56 cases, organic brain syndromes in 47, psychotic symptoms in 29, and 32 patients with neurotic symptoms. Fifty-seven patients were considered to have undiagnosable psychiatric illness. Further analysis of the data reveals that several of these undiagnosable patients had affective and anxiety symptoms.

In general, hypoparathyroidism due to neck surgery is quickly detected, and therefore presents quite differently when compared with those patients with the idiopathic form. While the overall prevalence of cognitive dysfunction was approximately 50% in both groups, isolated intellectual dysfunction was more uncommon in patients with surgical hypoparathyroidism (3.7% versus 19.0%), and delirium was much more prevalent in the surgical cases (29.2% versus 17.2%). Depressive, psychotic, and anxiety symptoms were more common in the surgical group than in the patients with idiopathic hypoparathyroidism. Depressive symptoms were present in 13.2% of surgical cases, compared to 4.9% of the idiopathic group. Psychotic symptoms were present in 19.8% of surgical cases versus 6.2% of the patients with idiopathic hypoparathyroidism. Anxiety symptoms were noted in 17.9% of surgical cases, and in 11.7% of idiopathic cases. Interestingly, manic symptoms were equally represented in both groups, being present in 4.3% of idiopathic hypoparathyroid patients and 4.7% of surgical cases. These results are summarized in Figure. 7.

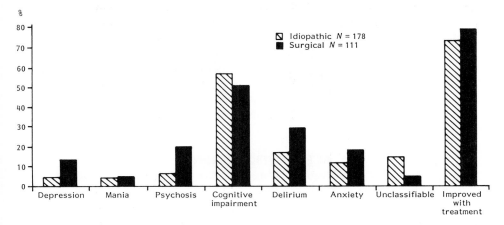

Figure 7. Psychiatric symptoms in hypoparathyroidism. Adapted from Denko and Kaelbling, 1962.

Improvement with treatment

When the underlying hypoparathyroidism was corrected, the vast majority of patients in the Denko and Kaelbling series showed improvement in their psychiatric symptoms. A total of 74% of the idiopathic hypoparathyroidism patients improved, compared with 79% of the surgical cases. Residual symptoms were noted in many patients, however. More recently, other authors have noted an improvement in symptoms with normalization of serum calcium concentrations (Carlson, 1986; Gertner *et al.*, 1976; Hossain, 1970; Lawlor, 1988).

DISCUSSION

We have attempted to provide a clinically relevant discussion of the prevalence and phenomenology of depression and related psychiatric disorders associated with endocrine disease. Further investigation is needed to determine if depression is the direct result of the endocrinopathy or due to other factors. The pathophysiological mechanisms involved in the development of depression in endocrine disturbances undoubtedly vary with the particular endocrine disorder. Therefore, an understanding of these relationships is also crucial to the development of hypotheses concerning the precise mechanisms by which endocrine disorders can produce psychiatric symptoms.

It appears that the severity of the endocrine disturbance is often correlated with the prevalence or severity of depressive symptoms, although this is not always the case. In addition, it is important to note that serious psychiatric syndromes often present in only a minority of patients. Potential risk factors (i.e. genetic predisposition, etc.) for the development of psychiatric symptoms in endocrine disease need to be identified as well. Treatment of patients with comorbid endocrine and depressive disorders remains idiosyncratic because of the absence of controlled treatment trials in this population.

ACKNOWLEDGEMENTS

This research was supported by NIMH MH-51761.

REFERENCES

Abbas A and Styra R (1994) Valproate prophylaxis against steroid induced psychosis. *Can J Psychiatry*, **39**, 188–189.

Agras S and Oliveau DC (1964) Primary hyperparathyroidism and psychosis. *Can Med J*, **91**, 1366–1367.

Akelaitis AJE (1936) Psychiatric aspects of myxedema. *J Nerv Ment Dis*, **83**, 22–36.

Alarcon RD and Franceschini JA (1984) Hyperparathyroidism and paranoid psychosis— case report and review of the literature. *Br J Psychiatry*, **145**, 477–486.

Amsterdam JD, Marinelli DL, Arger P *et al.* (1987) Assessment of adrenal gland volume by computed tomography in depressed patients and healthy volunteers: a pilot study. *Psychiatry Res*, **21**, 189–197.

Arana GW, Baldessarini RJ and Ornsteen M (1985) The dexamethasone suppression test for diagnosis and prognosis in psychiatry. *Arch Gen Psychiatry*, **42**, 1193–1204.

Arato M, Banki CM, Nemeroff CB *et al.* (1986) Hypothalamic–pituitary–adrenal axis and suicide. *Ann N Y Acad Sci*, **487**, 263–270.

Artunkal S and Togrol B (1964) Psychological studies in hyperthyroidism. In: MP Cameron and M O'Connor (eds) *Brain–thyroid relationships*. Ciba Foundation Study Group, No. 18, London: Churchill, 125.

Asher R (1949) Myxoedematous madness. *Br Med J*, **ii**, 555–562.

Banki CM, Bissette G, Arato M *et al.* (1988) Elevation of immunoreactive CSF TRH in depressed patients. *Am J Psychiatry*, **145**, 1526–1531.

Bardgett ME, Taylor GT, Csernansky JG *et al.* (1994) Chronic corticosterone treatment impairs spontaneous alternation behaviour in rats. *Behav Neurol Biol*, **61**, 186–190.

Bauer MS and Whybrow PC (1988) Thyroid hormones and the central nervous system in affective illness: interactions that may have clinical significance. *Integr Psychiatry*, **6**, 75–100.

Bauer MS, Whybrow PC and Winokur A (1990) Rapid-cycling bipolar affective disorder I association with grade I hypothyroidism. *Arch Gen Psychiatry*, **47**, 427.

Bender BG, Lerner JA and Poland JE (1991) Association between corticosteroids and psychologic change in hospitalized asthmatic children. *Ann Allergy*, **66**, 414–419.

Bernstein IC (1965) A case of hypothyroidism presenting as psychiatric illness. *Psychosomatics*, **6**, 215–216.

Bogdanoff MD (1956) Hyperparathyroidism. *Am J Med*, **21**, 583–595.

Borer MS and Bhanot VK (1985) Hyperparathyroidism: neuropsychiatric manifestations. *Psychosomatics*, **26**, 597–601.

Boston Collaborative Drug Surveillance Program (1972) Acute adverse reactions to prednisone in relation to dosage. *Clin Pharmacol Ther*, **13**, 694–698.

Brain L, Jellinek EH and Ball K (1966) Hashimoto's disease and encephalopathy. *Lancet*, **ii**, 512–516.

Brown GG, Preisman RC and Kleerkoper M (1987a) Neurobehavioural symptoms in mild primary hyperparathyroidism: related to hypercalcemia but not improved by parathyroidectomy. *Henry Ford Hosp Med J*, **35**, 211–215.

Brown RS, Fischman A and Showalter CR (1987b) Primary hyperparathyroidism, hypercalcemia, paranoid delusions, homicide and attempted murder. *J Forensic Sci*, **32**, 1460–1463.

Buckman MT and Kellner R (1985) Reduction of distress in hyperprolactinemia with bromocriptine. *Am J Psychiatry*, **142**, 242–244.

Bunney WE and Fawcett SA (1965) Possibility of a biochemical test for suicidal potential. *Arch Gen Psychiatry*, **13**, 232–239.

Bursten B (1961) Psychosis associated with thyrotoxicosis. *Arch Gen Psychiatry*, **4**, 267–273.

Carlson RJ (1986) Longitudinal observations of two cases of organic anxiety syndrome. *Psychosomatics*, **27**, 529–531.

Carroll BJ, Martin FI and Davis B (1968) Pituitary–adrenal function in depression. *Lancet*, **556**, 1373–1374.

Carroll BJ, Curtis GC, Davies BM, Mendels J and Sugerman AA (1976) Urinary-free cortisol excretion in depression. *J Psychol Med*, **6**, 43–47.

Clark LD, Bauer W and Cobb S (1952) Preliminary observations on mental disturbances occurring in patients under therapy with cortisone and ACTH. *N Engl J Med*, **246**, 205–216.

Clark LD, Quarton GC, Cobb S *et al.* (1953) Further observations on mental disturbances associated with cortisone and ACTH therapy. *N Engl J Med*, **249**, 178–183.

Clower CG, Young AJ and Kepas D (1968) Psychotic states resulting from disorders of thyroid function. *Hopkins Med J*, **124**, 305–310.

Cogan MG, Covey CM, Arieff AI *et al.* (1978) Central nervous system manifestations of hyperparathyroidism. *Am J Med*, **65**, 963–970.

Cohen SI (1980) Cushing's syndrome: A psychiatric study of 29 patients. *Br J Psychiatry*, **136**, 120–124.

Cohen-Cole S, Brown FW and McDaniel JS (1993) Assessment of depression and grief reactions in the medically ill. In: A Stoudemire and BS Fogel (eds) *Psychiatric Care of the Medical Patient*. New York: Oxford University Press, 53–69.

Cooper DS, Halpain R, Wood LC, Lever AA and Ridgeway EC (1984) L-thyroxine therapy in subclinical hypothyroidism, a double blind placebo-controlled trial. *Ann Intern Med*, **101**, 18.

Cowdry RW, Wehr TA, Ziz AP *et al.* (1983) Thyroid abnormalities associated with rapid-cycling bipolar illness. *Arch Gen Psychiatry*, **40**, 414–420.

Crowley RM (1940) Psychosis with myxoedema. *Am J Psychiatry*, **96**, 1105–1116.

Crown S (1949) Notes on an experimental study of intellectual deterioration. *Br Med J*, **2**, 684–685.

Cushing H (1932) The basophil adenomas of the pituitary body and their clinical manifestations (pituitary basophilism). *Bull Johns Hopkins Hosp*, **50**, 137–195.

Deary IJ, Hepburn DA, MacLeod KM *et al.* (1993) Partitioning the symptoms of hypoglycemia using multi-sample confirmatory factor analysis. *Diabetologia*, **36**, 771–777.

Denko J and Kaelbling R (1962) The psychiatric aspects of hypoparathyroidism. *Acta Psychiatr Scand*, **164 (Suppl)**, 1–70.

Dietch JT (1981) Diagnosis of organic anxiety disorders. *Psychosomatics*, **22**, 661.

Dunlap HF and Moersch FP (1935) Psychic manifestations associated with hyperthyroidism. *Am J Psychiatry*, **91**, 1215–1236.

Easson WM (1966) Myxedema with psychosis. *Arch Gen Psychiatry*, **14**, 277–283.

Engel GL and Margolin SG (1942) Neuropsychiatric disturbances in Addison's disease and the role of impaired carbohydrate metabolism in production of abnormal cerebral function. *Arch Neurol Psychiatry*, **45**, 881–884.

Erskine MS, Barfield JR and Goldman BD (1978) Intraspecific fighting during late pregnancy and lactation in rats and effects of litter removal. *Behav Neurol Biol*, **23**, 206–213.

Erskine MS, Barfield RJ and Goldman BD (1980) Postpartum aggression in rats. I. Effects of hypophysectomy. *J Comp Physiol Psychol*, **94**, 484–494.

Evans DL and Nemeroff CB (1983) Use of dexamethasone suppression test using DSM III criteria on an inpatient psychiatric unit. *Biol Psychiatry*, **18**, 505–511.

Extein I, Pottash ALC and Gold MS (1981) The thyrotropin-releasing hormone test in the diagnosis of unipolar depression. *Psychiatry Res*, **5**, 311–316.

Falk WE, Mahnke MW and Pozkanzer DC (1979) Lithium prophylaxis of corticotropin-induced psychosis. *JAMA*, **241**, 1011–1012.

Fava G (1994) Affective disorders and endocrine disease: New insights from psychosomatic studies. *Psychosomatics*, **35**, 341–353.

Fava GA, Fava M, Kellner R *et al.* (1981) Depression, hostility and anxiety in hyperprolactinemic amenorrhea. *Psychother Psychosom*, **36**, 122–128.

Fitch TE and Hallman BL (1952) Mental changes associated with hyperparathyroidism. *Arch Intern Med*, **89**, 547–551.

Gatewood JW, Organ CH and Mead BT (1975) Mental changes associated with hyperparathyroidism. *Am J Psychiatry*, **132**, 129–132.

Gavard JA, Lustman PJ and Clouse RE (1993) Prevalence of depression in adults with diabetes—an epidemiological evaluation. *Diabetes Care*, **16**, 1167–1178.

Gertner JM, Hodsman AB and Neuberger JN (1976) 1-Alpha-hydroxycalciferol in the treatment of hypocalcaemic psychosis. *Clin Endocrinol*, **5**, 539–543.

Ghazi AAM, Mofid D, Rahimi F *et al.* Oestrogen and cortisol producing adrenal tumor. *Arch Dis Child*, **71**, 358–359.

Gibson JG (1962) Emotions and the thyroid gland. A critical appraisal. *J Psychosom Res*, **6**, 93–116.

Gibson JL and McHugh PR (1963) Plasma cortisol in depressive illness. *Psychiatric Res*, **1**, 162–171.

Gifford S and Gunderson JG (1970) Cushing's disease as a psychosomatic disorder: A selective review of the clinical and experimental literature and a report of ten cases. *Medicine (Balt)*, **49**, 397–409.

Glynne-Jones R and Vernon CC (1986) Is steroid psychosis preventable by divided doses? *Lancet*, **2**, 1404.

Gold MS, Pottash ALC and Extein I (1981) Hypothyroidism and depression: evidence from complete thyroid function evaluation. *JAMA*, **245**, 1919–1922.

Gold MS, Pottash AC and Extein I (1982) Symptomless auto immune thyroiditis in depression. *Psychiatr Res*, **6**, 261–269.

Golden MP, Ingersoll GM, Brack CJ *et al.* (1989) Longitudinal relationship of asymptomatic hypoglycemia to cognitive function in IDDM. *Diabetes Care*, **12**, 89–93.

Goodnick PJ, Henry JH and Buki VMV (1995) Treatment of depression in patients with diabetes. *J Clin Psychiatry*, **56**, 128–136.

Gotch PM (1994) Cushing's syndrome from the patient's perspective. *Endocrinol Metab Clin North Am*, **23**, 607–617.

Green AI and Austin CP (1993) Psychopathology of pancreatic cancer—A psychobiologic probe. *Psychosomatics*, **34**, 208–221.

Haggerty JJ, Evans DL and Prange AJ (1986) Organic brain syndrome associated with marginal hypothyroidism. *Am J Psychiatry*, **143**, 785–786.

Haggerty JJ, Simon JS, Evans DL *et al.* (1987) Elevated TSH levels and thyroid antibodies in psychiatric inpatients: Relationship to diagnosis and DST response. *Am J Psychiatry*, **144**, 1491–1493.

Haggerty JJ Jr, Stern RA, Mason GA *et al.* (1993) Subclinical hypothyroidism: a modifiable risk factor for depression. *Am J Psychiatry*, **150**, 508–510.

Hall RCW (1983) Psychiatric effects of thyroid hormone disturbance. *Psychosomatics*, **24**, 7.

Hall RCW, Popkin MK, Stickney SK *et al.* (1979) Presentation of the steroid psychosis. *J Nerv Ment Dis*, **167**, 229–236.

Hall RCW, Popkin MK, DeVaul R *et al.* (1982) Psychiatric manifestations of Hashimoto's thyroiditis. *Psychosomatics*, **23**, 337–342.

Halonen H, Hiekkala H, Huupponen T *et al.* (1983) A follow-up EEG study in diabetic children. *Ann Clin Res*, **15**, 167–172.

Harrison G (1983) Hypercalcaemia in a psychogeriatric population. *Br J Psychiatry*, **142**, 384–387.

Haskett RF (1985) Diagnostic categorization of psychiatric disturbance in Cushing's syndrome. *Am J Psychiatry*, **142**, 911–926.

Haumont D, Dorchy H and Pelc S (1979) EEG abnormalities in diabetic children: Influence of hypoglycemia and vascular complications. *Clin Paediatr*, **18**, 750–753.

Hayabara T, Hashimoto K, Izumi H *et al.* (1987) Neuropsychiatric disorders in primary hyperparathyroidism. *Jpn J Psychiatr Neurol*, **41**, 33–40.

Hayreh SS and Watson PG (1970) Prednisolone-21-stearooylglycolate in scleritis. *Br J Ophthalmol*, **54**, 394–398.

Heath H III (1991) Clinical spectrum of primary hyperparathyroidism: Evolution with changes in medical practice and technology. *J Bone Min Res*, **6 (Suppl 2)**, S63–70.

Hehrmann R, Thiele J, Tidow G *et al.* (1980) Acute hyperparathyroidism—Clinical, laboratory, and ultrastructural findings in a variant of primary hyperparathyroidism. *Klin Wochenschr*, **58**, 501–510.

Henderson LM, Behan PO, Aarli J *et al.* (1987) Hashimoto's encephalopathy: A new neuroimmunological syndrome. *Ann Neurol*, **22**, 140–141.

Hermann HT and Quarton GC (1965) Psychological changes and psychogenesis in thyroid hormone disorders. *J Clin Endocrinol*, **25**, 327–338.

Hofeldt FD (1989) Reactive hypoglycemia. *Endocrinol Metab Clin North Am*, **18**, 185–201.

Hossain M (1970) Neurologic and psychiatric manifestations in idiopathic hypoparathyroidism: response to treatment. *J Neurol Neurosurg Psychiatry*, **33**, 153–156.

Hudson JI, Hudson MS, Griffing GT *et al.* (1987) Phenomenology and family history of affective disorder in Cushing's disease. *Am J Psychiatry*, **144**, 951–953.

Hutchison GB, Evans JA and Davidson DC (1958) Pitfalls in the diagnosis of pheochromocytoma. *Ann Intern Med*, **48**, 300–309.

Insogna KL (1989) Humoral hypercalcemia of malignancy: the role of parathyroid hormone-related peptide. *Endocrinol Metab Clin North Am*, **18**, 779–794.

Jacobs JK and Merritt CR (1966) Magnesium deficiency in hyperparathyroidism: case report of toxic psychosis. *Ann Surg*, **162**, 260–262.

Jain VK (1972) A psychiatric study of hypothyroidism. *Psychiatric Clin*, **5**, 121–130.

Jeffcoate WJ, Silverstone JT, Edwards CRW *et al.* (1979) Psychiatric manifestations of Cushing's syndrome: Response to lowering of plasma cortisol. *Q J Med*, **191**, 465–472.

Jellinek EH (1962) Fits, faints, coma, and dementia in myxoedema. *Lancet*, **ii**, 1010–1012.

Joborn C, Hetta J, Johansson H *et al.* (1988) Psychiatric morbidity in primary hyperparathyroidism. *World J Surg*, **12**, 476–481.

Joborn C, Hetta J, Lind L *et al.* (1989) Self-rated psychiatric symptoms in patients operated on because of primary hyperparathyroidism and in patients with lond-standing mild hypercalcemia. *Surgery*, **105**, 72–78.

Joborn C, Hetter J, Rastad J *et al.* (1988) Psychiatric symptoms and cerebrospinal fluid monoamine metabolites in primary hyperparathryoidism. *Biol Psychiatry*, **23**, 149–158.

Joffe RT and Levitt AJ (1992) Major depression and subclinical hypothyroidism. *Psychoneuroendocrinology*, **17**, 215–221.

Joffe RT and Sokolov STH (1994) Thyroid hormones, the brain, and affective disorders. *Crit Rev Neurobiol*, **8**, 45–63.

Joffe RT, Kutcher S and MacDonald C (1986) Thyroid function and bipolar affective disorder. *Psychiatry Res*, **25**, 117–121.

Joffe RT, Singer W, Levitt AJ *et al.* (1993) A placebo-controlled comparison of lithium and triodothyronine augmentation of tricyclic antidepressants in unipolar refractory depression. *Arch Gen Psychiatry*, **50**, 387–394.

Jonas AD (1952) Hypothyroidism and neurotic depression. *Am Practitioner*, **3**, 103–105.

Juan D (1979) Hypocalcemia—differential diagnosis and mechanisms. *Arch Intern Med*, **139**, 1166–1171.

Karnosh LJ and Stout RE (1935) Psychosis of myxoedema. *Am J Psychiatry*, **91**, 1263–1274.

Karpati G and Frame B (1964) Neuropsychiatric disorders in primary hyperapara-thyroidism. *Arch Neurol*, **10**, 387–397.

Katerndahl DA and Vandecreek L (1983) Hyperthyroidism and panic attacks. *Psychosomatics*, **24**, 491–496.

Kathol RG and Delahunt JW (1986) The relationship of anxiety and depression to symptoms of hyperthyroidism using operational criteria. *Gen Hosp Psychiatry*, **8**, 23–28.

Kellner R, Buckman MT, Fava M, Fava GA and Mastrogiacomo I (1984) Prolactin, aggression, and hostility: A discussion of recent studies. *Psychiatric Dev*, **2**, 131–138.

Kelly WF, Checkley SA, Bender DA *et al.* (1983) Cushing's syndrome and depression—a prospective study of 26 patients. *Br Psychiatry*, **142**, 16–19.

Kirkegaard CJ, Faber J, Hummer L *et al.* (1979) Increased levels of TRH in cerebrospinal fluid from patients with endogenous depression. *Psychoneuroendocrinology*, **4**, 227–235.

Klee GC and Hay ID (1986) Assessment of sensitive thyrotropin assays for an expanded role in thyroid function testing: Proposed criteria for analytic performance and clinical utility. *J Clin Endocrinol Metab*, **64**, 461.

Kleinschmidt HJ, Waxenberg SE and Cucker R (1956) Psychophysiology and psychiatric management of thyrotoxicosis: a two-year follow-up study. *J Mt. Sinai Hosp NY*, **23**, 131.

Koppelman MCS, Parry BL, Hamilton JA *et al.* (1987) Effect of bromocriptine on affect and libido in hyperprolactinemia. *Am J Psychiatry*, **144**, 1037–1041.

Kornstein SE and Gardner DF (1993) Endocrine disorders. In: A Stoudemire and BS Fogel (eds) *Psychiatric Care of the Medical Patient*, New York: Oxford University Press.

Krishnan KRR, Doraiswamy PM, Luri SN *et al.* (1991) Pituitary size in depression. *J Clin Endocrinol Metab*, **72**, 256–259.

Lawlor BA (1988) Hypocalcemia, hypoparathyroidism, and organic anxiety syndrome. *J Clin Psychiatry*, **49**, 317–318.

Leedom L, Meehan WJ, Procoi W *et al*. (1991) Symptoms of depression in patients with type II diabetes mellitus. *Psychosomatics*, **32**, 280–286.

Lehrer G and Levitt M (1960) Neuropsychiatric presentation of hypercalcemia. *J Mt Sinai Hosp*, **27**, 10–18.

Libow LS and Durell J (1965) Clinical studies on the relationship between psychosis and the regulation of thyroid gland activity. *Psychosom Med*, **27**, 369–376.

Lidz T and Whitehorn JC (1949) Psychiatric problems in a thyroid clinic. *JAMA*, **139**, 698–701.

Linder J, Brismar K, Granberg PO *et al*. (1988) Characteristic changes in psychiatric symptoms, cortisol and melatonin but not prolactin in primary hyperparathryoidism. *Acta Psychiatr Scand*, **78**, 32–40.

Ling MH, Perry PJ and Tsuang MT (1981) Side-effects of corticosteroid therapy: Psychiatric aspects. *Arch Gen Psychiatry*, **38**, 741–747.

Ljunghall S, Hellman P, Rastad J *et al*. (1991) Primary hyperparathyroidism: Epidemiology, diagnosis, and clinical picture. *World J Surg*, **15**, 681–687.

Logothetis J (1963) Psychotic behaviour as the initial indicator of adult myxedema. *J Nerv Ment Dis*, **136**, 561–568.

Loosen, PT (1988) Thyroid function in affective disorders and alcoholism. *Endocrinol Metab Clin North Am*, **17**, 55–82.

Loosen PT, Chambliss R, DeBold CR *et al*. (1992) Psychiatric phenomenology in Cushing's disease. *Pharmacopsychiatry*, **25**, 192–198.

Lustman, PJ, Amado H and Wetzel RD (1983) Depression in diabetics: a critical appraisal. *Compr Psychiatry*, **24**, 65–74.

Lustman PJ, Clouse RE, Carrey RM and Griffith LS (1987) Characteristics of depression in adults with diabetes. In: *Proc National Institutes of Mental Health Conference on Mental Disorders in General Health Care Setting*. Seattle, WT, **1**: 127–129.

Lustman PJ, Griffith LS and Clouse RE (1988) Depression in adults with diabetes: results of a 5-year-follow-up study. *Diabetes Care*, **11**, 605–610.

Lustman PJ, Freedland KE, Carney RM *et al*. (1992a) Similarity of depression in diabetic and psychiatric patients. *Psychosom Med*, **54**, 602–611.

Lustman PJ, Griffith LS, Gavard JA *et al*. (1992b) Depression in adults with diabetes. *Diabetes Care*, **15**, 1631–1639.

Lustman PJ, Harper GW, Griffith LS *et al*. (1986) Use of the diagnostic interview schedule in patients with diabetes mellitus. *J Nerv Ment Dis*, **174**, 743–746.

MacCrimmon DJ, Wallace JE, Goldberg WM *et al*. (1979) Emotional disturbance and cognitive deficits in hyperthyroidism. *Psychosom Med*, **41 (4)**, 331–340.

Malouf R and Brust JCM (1985) Hypoglycemia: causes, neurological manifestations, and outcome. *Ann Neurol*, **17**, 421–430.

Mandelbrote BM and Wittkower ED (1955) Emotional factors in Grave's disease. *Psychosom Med*, **17**, 109.

Marcus MD, Wing RR, Guare J, Blair EH and Jawad A (1992) Lifetime prevalence of major depression and its effect on treatment outcome in obese type II diabetic patients *Diabetes Care*, **15**, 253–255.

Mastrogiacomo I, Fava M, Fava GA *et al*. (1983a) Correlations between psychological symptoms in hyperprolactinemic amenorrhea. *Neuroendocrinol Lett*, **5**, 117–122.

Mastrogiacomo I, Fava M, Fava G *et al*. (1983b) Postpartum hostility and prolactin. *Int J Psychiatry Med*, **12**, 289–294.

Mazet Ph, Simon D, Luton J-P *et al*. (1981) Syndrome de Cushing: Symptomatologie psychique et personnalite de 50 malades. *Nouv Presse Med*, **10**, 2565–2570.

288   *E.B. Boswell, T.J. Anfinson and C.B. Nemeroff*

Mazze RS, Lucido D and Shanoon H (1984) Psychological and social correlates of glycemic control. *Diabetes Care,* **7**, 360–366.

McGill JB, Lustman PJ, Griffith LS, Freedland RE, Gavarel JA and Clouse RE (1992) Relationship of depression to compliance with self-monitoring of glucose (Abstract). *Diabetes,* **41(suppl. 1)**, 84A.

Miller R (1952) Mental symptoms from myxedema. *J Lab Clin Med,* **40**, 267–270.

Minisola S, Romagnoli E, Scarnecchia M *et al.* (1993) Parathyroid storm: Immediate recognition and pathophysiological considerations. *Bone,* **14**, 703–704.

Modlin IM, Farndon JR, Shepherd A *et al.* (1979) Phaeochromocytomas in 72 patients: Clinical and diagnostic features, treatment and long term results. *Br J Surg,* **66**, 456–465.

Morley JE, Shafer RB, Elson MK *et al.* (1980) Amphetamine-induced hyperthyroxinemia. *Ann Intern Med,* **93**, 707–709.

Murphy BEP (1991a) Steroids and depression. *J Steroid Biochem, Molec Biol,* **38**, 537–559.

Nathan TI, Musselman DL, Schatzberg AF and Nemeroff CB (1995) Biology of mood disorders. In: AF Schatzberg and CB Nemeroff (eds) *Textbook of Psychopharmacology.* Washington, D.C.: American Psychiatric Press.

Nemeroff CB (1989) Clinical significance of psychoneuroendocrinology in psychiatry: Focus on the thyroid and adrenal. *J Clin Psychiatry,* **50 (5 Suppl)**, 13–20.

Nemeroff CB, Widerlov E, Bissette G *et al.* (1984) Elevated concentrations of CSF corticotropin-releasing factor-like immunoreactivity in depressed patients. *Science,* **226**, 1342–1344.

Nemeroff CB, Krishnan KKR, Reed D *et al.* (1992) Adrenal gland enlargement in major depression: a computed tomographic study. *Arch Gen Psychiatry,* **49**, 384–387.

Newcomer JW, Craft S, Hershey T *et al.* (1994) Glucocorticoid-induced impairment in declarative memory performance in adult humans. *J Neurosci,* **14**, 2047–2053.

Nielsen H (1955) Familial occurrence, gastro-intestinal symptoms and mental disturbances in hyperparathyroidism. *Acta Med Scand,* **15**, 359–366.

Noble P (1974) Depressive illness and hyperparathyroidism. *Proc R Soc Med,* **67**, 1066–1067.

Nordenstrom J, Strigard K, Perbeck L *et al.* (1992) Hyperparathyroidism associated with treatment of manic-depressive disorders by lithium. *Eur J Surg,* **158**, 207–211.

Numann PJ, Torppa AJ and Blumetti AE (1984) Neuropsychologic deficits associated with primary hyperparathyroidism. *Surgery,* **96**, 1119–1123.

Oztunç A, Guscott RG, Soni J *et al.* (1986) Psychosis resulting in suicide in a patient with primary hyperparathyroidism. *Can J Psychiatry,* **31**, 342–343.

Packard FH (1909) An analysis of psychoses associated with Graves' disease. *Am J Insanity,* **66 (2)**, 189–201.

Perlmuter LC, Hakami MK, Hodgson-Harrington C *et al.* (1984) Decreased cognitive function in aging non-insulin-dependent patients. *Am J Med,* **77**, 1043–1048.

Perry PJ, Tsuang MT and Hwang MH (1984) Prednisolone psychosis: clinical observations. *Drug Intell Clin Pharm,* **18**, 603–609.

Petersen P (1968) Psychiatric disorders in primary hyperparathyroidism. *J Clin Endocrinol Metab,* **28**, 1491–1495.

Pitts FN and Guze SB (1961) Psychiatric disorders and myxedema. *Am J Psychiatry,* **118**, 142.

Plouin PF, Degoulet P, Tugaye A *et al.* (1981) Le depistage du pheochromocytome: chez quels hypertendus? Etude semiologique chez 2585 hypertendus dont 11 ayant un pheochromocytome. *Nouv Presse Med,* **10**, 869–872.

Pomeranze J and King EF (1966) Psychosis as first sign of thyroid dysfunction. *Geriatrics*, **21**, 211–212.

Pramming S, Thorsteinsson B, Theilgaard A *et al.* (1986) Cognitive function during hypoglycemia in type I diabetes mellitus. *Br Med J*, **292**, 647–650.

Prange AJ, Wilson IC, Rabon AM *et al.* (1969) Enhancement of imipramine antidepressant activity by thyroid hormone. *Am J Psychiatry*, **126**, 457–469.

Prange AJ, Haggerty JJ, Rice J *et al.* (1988) Marginal hypothyroidism in mental illness: preliminary assessments of prevalence and significance. *Proc XVIth CINP Conference, Munich*, 15–19 August.

Reaven GM, Thompson LW, Nahum D *et al.* (1990) Relationship between hyperglycemia and cognitive function in older NIDDM patients. *Diabetes Care*, **13**, 16–21.

Reilly EL and Wilson WP (1965) Mental symptoms in hyperparathyroidism (A report of three cases). *Dis Nerv Syst*, **26**, 361–363.

Reinfrank RF (1961) Primary hyperparathyroidism with depression. *Arch Intern Med*, **108**, 162–166.

Reitan RM (1953) Intellectual functions in myxedema. *Arch Neurol Psychiatry*, **69**, 436–449.

Rennick PM, Wilder RM, Sargent J *et al.* (1968) Retinopathy as an indicator of cognitive-perceptual-motor impairment in diabetic adults (Summary). *Proc 76th Annu Conv Am Psychol Assoc*, 473–474.

Risch SC, Lewine RJ, Kalin NH, *et al.* (1992) Limbic–hypothalamic–pituitary–adrenal axis activity and ventricular-to-brain ratio in affective illness and schizophrenia. *Neuropsychopharmacology*, **6**, 95–100.

Robbins LR and Vinson DB (1960) Objective psychological assessment of the thyrotoxic patient and the response to treatment: preliminary report. *J Clin Endocrinol*, **20**, 120–129.

Robinson N, Fuller JH and Edmeades SP (1988) Depression and diabetes. *Diab Med*, **5**, 268–274.

Rockey PH and Griep RJ (1980) Behavioural dysfunction in hyperthyroidism. *Arch Intern Med*, **140**, 1194–1197.

Rosenbaum AH, Maruta T, Schatzberg AF *et al.* (1983) Toward a biochemical classification of depressive disorders, VII: urinary free cortisol and urinary MHPG in depression. *Am J Psychiatry*, **140**, 314–317.

Rosenberg FR, Sander S and Nelson CT (1976) Pemphigus—A 20-year review of 107 patients treated with corticosteroids. *Arch Dermatol*, **112**, 962–970.

Rosenblatt S and Faillace LA (1977) Psychiatric manifestations of hyperparathyroidism. *Tex Med*, **73**, 59–60.

Rovet JF, Ehrlich RM and Hoppe M (1987) Intellectual deficits associated with early onset of insulin-dependent diabetes mellitus in children. *Diabetes Care*, **10**, 510–515.

Royce PC (1971) Severely impaired consciousness in myxedema—a review. *Am J Med Sci*, **261**, 46–50.

Ryan CM (1988) Neurobehavioural complications of type-I diabetes—examination of possible risk factors. *Diabetes Care*, **11**, 86–93.

Ryan CM, Vega A and Drash A (1985) Cognitive deficits in adolescents who developed diabetes early in life. *Pediatrics*, **75**, 921–927.

Sacher E, Hellman L, Fukuslima D and Gallagher T (1970) Cortisol production in depressive illness. *Arch Gen Psychiatry*, **23**, 289–298.

Sachs G, Spiess R, Moser G *et al.* (1991) Glycosylated hemoglobin and diabetes self-monitoring (compliance) in depressed and non-depressed type I diabetes patients. *Psychother Psychosom Med Psychol*, **41**, 306–312.

Schon M, Sutherland AM and Rawson RW (1962) Hormones and neuroses—The psychological effects of thyroid deficiency. *Proceedings of the 3rd World Congress of Psychiatry, Toronto,* Toronto: University of Toronto Press, 835–839.

Shaw PJ, Walls TJ, Newman PK *et al.* (1991) Hashimoto's encephalopathy: A steroid-responsive disorder associated with high anti-thyroid antibody titers—report of 5 cases. *Neurology,* **41**, 228–233.

Shein M, Apter A, Dickerman Z *et al.* (1986) Encephalopathy in compensated Hashimoto thyroiditis: a clinical expression of autoimmune cerebral vasculitis. *Brain Dev,* **8**, 60–64.

Siegal FP (1978) Lithium for steroid-induced psychosis. *N Engl J Med,* **299**, 155–156.

Silva RG and Tolstunov L (1995) Steroid-induced psychosis: report of a case. *J Oral Maxillofac Surg,* **53**, 183–186.

Skenazy JA and Bigler ED (1984) Neuropsychological findings in diabetes mellitus. *J Clin Psychol,* **40**, 246–258.

Sobrinho LG, Nunes MCP, Calhaz-Jorge C *et al.* (1984) Hyperprolactinemia in women with paternal deprivation during childhood. *Obstet Gynecol,* **64**, 465–468.

Soininen H, Puranen M, Helkala E-L, *et al.* (1992) Diabetes mellitus and brain atrophy: a computerized tomography study in an elderly population. *Neurobiol Aging,* **13**, 717–721.

Solomon BL, Schaaf M and Smallridge RC (1994) Psychologic symptoms before and after parathyroid surgery. *Am J Med,* **96**, 101–106.

Sonino N, Fava GA, Grandi S *et al.* (1991) Stressful life events in the pathogenesis of Cushing's syndrome. *Clin Endocrinol,* **29**, 617–623.

Sonino N, Fava GA and Boscaro M (1993a) A role for life events in the pathogenesis of Cushing's disease. *Clin Endocrinol,* **38**, 261–264.

Sonino N, Fava G, Belluardo P *et al.* (1993b) Course of depression in Cushing's syndrome: response to treatment and comparison with Graves' disease. *Horm Res,* **39**, 202–206.

Spillane JD (1951) Nervous and mental disorders in Cushing's syndrome. *Brain,* **74**, 72–94.

Starkman MN and Schteingart DE (1981) Neuropsychiatric manifestations of patients with Cushing's syndrome. *Arch Intern Med,* **141**, 215–219.

Starkman MN, Schteingart DE and Schork MA (1981) Depressed mood and other psychiatric manifestations of Cushing's syndrome: Relationship to hormone levels. *Psychosom Med,* **43**, 3–18.

Starkman MN, Zelnick TC, Nesse RM *et al.* (1985) Anxiety in patients with pheochromocytomas. *Arch Intern Med,* **145**, 248–252.

Starkman MN, Schteingart DE and Schork MA (1986) Cushing's syndrome after treatment. *Psychiatry Res,* **19**, 177–188.

Starkman MN, Gebarski SS, Berent S *et al.* (1992) Hippocampal formation volume, memory dysfunction, and cortisol levels in patient's with Cushing's syndrome. *Biol Psychiatry,* **32**, 756–765.

Steiner M, Haskett RF, Carroll BJ, Hays S and Rubin RT (1984) Plasma prolactin and severe premenstrual tension. *Psychoneuroendocrinology,* **9**, 29–35.

Targum SD, Greenberg RD, Harmon RL *et al.* (1984) Thyroid hormone and the TRH stimulation test in refractory depression. *J Clin Psychiatry,* **45**, 345.

Taylor JW (1975) Depression in thyrotoxicosis. *Am J Psychiatry,* **132**, 552–553.

Theohar C, Fischer-Cornelssen K, Akesson HO *et al.* (1981) Bromocriptine as antidepressant: Double blind comparative study with imipramine in psychogenic and endogenous depression. *Current Ther Res,* **30**, 830–842.

Thomas WC (1958) Hypercalcemic crisis due to hyperparathyroidism. *Am J Med,* **24**, 229–239.

Thomas FB, Mazzaferri EL and Skillman TG (1970) Apathetic thyrotoxicosis: a distinctive clinical and laboratory entity. *Ann Intern Med*, **72**, 679–685.

Thompson WF (1973) Psychiatric aspects of Addison's disease: report of a case. *Med Ann Dis Columbia*, **42**, 62–64.

Thrush DC and Boddie HG (1974) Episodic encephalopathy associated with thyroid disorders. *J Neurol Neurosurg Psychiatry*, **37**, 696–700.

Thurling ML (1987) Primary hyperparathyroidism in a schizophrenic woman. *Can J Psychiatry*, **32**, 785–787.

Tominaga Y, Grimelius L, Johansson H *et al*. (1992) Histological and clinical features of non-familial primary hyperparathyroid hyperplasia. *Path Res Pract*, **188**, 115–122.

Tonks CM (1964) Mental illness in hypothyroid patients. *Br J Psychiatry*, **110**, 706–710.

Treadway CR, Prange AJ, Doehne EF *et al*. (1967) Myxedema psychosis: Clinical and biochemical changes during recovery. *J Psychiatr Res*, **5**, 289–296.

Trethowan WH and Cobb S (1952) Neuropsychiatric aspects of Cushing's syndrome. *Arch Neurol Psychiatry*, **67**, 283–309.

Trzepacz P, McCue M, Klein I *et al*. (1988a) A psychiatric and neuropsychological study of patients with untreated Graves' disease. *Gen Hosp Psychiatry*, **10**, 49–55.

Trzepacz P, McCue M, Klein I *et al*. (1988b) Psychiatric and neuropsychological response to propranolol in Graves' disease. *Biol Psychiatry*, **23**, 678–688.

Trzepacz P, Roberts M, Greenhouse J *et al*. (1989) Graves' disease: an analysis of thyroid hormone levels and hyperthyroid signs and symptoms. *Am J Med*, **87**, 558–561.

Tun PA, Nathar DM and Pulmater LC (1990) Cognitive and affective disorders in elderly diabetes. *Clin Geriatric Med*, **6**, 731–746.

Varadaraj R and Cooper AJ (1986) Addison's disease presenting with psychiatric symptoms (letter). *Am J Psychiatry*, **143**, 553–554.

Wallfelt C, Ljunghall S, Berstrom R *et al*. (1990) Clinical characteristics and surgical treatment of sporadic primary hyperparathyroidism with emphasis on chief cell hyperplasia. *Surgery*, **107**, 13–19.

Ward DJ and Rastall ML (1967) Prognosis in "myxoedematous madness". *Br J Psychiatry*, **113**, 149–151.

Wehr T, Sack D, Rosenthal N *et al*. (1989) Rapid cycling affective disorder: Contributing factors in treatment response in 51 patients. *Am J Psychiatry*, **145**, 179–184.

Wells KB, Golding JM and Burnam MA (1988) Psychiatric disorder in a sample of the general population with and without chronic medical conditions. *Am J Psychiatry*, **145**, 976–981.

Weyerer S, Hewer W, Pfeifer-Kurda M *et al*. (1989) Psychiatric disorders and diabetes—results from a community study. *J Psychosom Res*, **33**, 633–640.

Whelan TB, Schteingart DE, Starkman MN *et al*. (1980) Neuropsychological deficits in Cushing's syndrome. *J Nerv Ment Dis*, **168**, 753–757.

Whybrow PC and Hurwitz T (1976) Psychological disturbances associated with endocrine disease and hormone therapy. In: EJ Sachar (ed) *Hormones, Behaviour, and Psychopathology*. New York: Raven Press, 125–143.

Whybrow PC, Prange AJ and Treadway CR (1969) Mental changes accompanying thyroid gland dysfunction. *Arch Gen Psychiatry*, **20**, 48–63.

Wiesel C (1952) Psychosis with myxedema. *J Kentucky Med Assoc*, **50**, 395–397.

Wilson WH and Jefferson JW (1985) Thyroid disease, behaviour and psychopathology. *Psychosomatics*, **26**, 481–492.

Wilson WP, Johnson JE and Smith RB (1962) Affective change in thyrotoxicosis and experimental hypermetabolism. *Recent Adv Biol Psychiatry*, **4**, 234–243.

Witschy JK and Redmond FC (1981) Extrapyramidal reactions to fluphenazine potentiated by thyrotoxicosis. *Am J Psychiatry*, **138**, 246–247.

Zeiger MA, Fraker DL, Pass HI *et al.* (1993) Effective reversibility of the signs and symptoms of hypercortisolism by bilateral adrenalectomy. *Surgery*, **114**, 1138–1143.

Zieger MA, Fraker DL, Pass HI, Nienan LK, Cutler GB, Chrousos GP and Norton JA (1993) Effective reversibility of the signs and symptoms of hypercortisolism by the bilateral adrenalectomy. *Surgery*, **114**, 1138–43.

Ziegler LH (1930) Psychosis associated with myxoedema. *J Neurol Psychopathol*, **11**, 20–27.

15

Depression and gastrointestinal and liver disorders

Geoffrey G. Lloyd

Gastroenterologists are referred many patients whose symptoms cannot be explained by organic pathology but who are considered to have a functional disorder. The term "functional" in gastroenterology is used to describe "a variable combination of chronic or recurrent gastrointestinal symptoms which cannot be explained by structural or chemical abnormalities" (Irritable Bowel Syndrome Working Team Report, 1988). These include oesophageal spasm, psychogenic vomiting, nonulcer dyspepsia, irritable bowel syndrome and proctalgia fugax. They are associated with a high prevalence of psychiatric disorder, including depression, but are classified by the International Classification of Disease (ICD-10) in the category of somatoform autonomic dysfunction (Lloyd, 1992).

Harvey *et al.* (1983) in a survey of 2000 patients referred over a 5 year period observed that approximately one-half had no organic disease but had various functional disorders of the gut. MacDonald and Bouchier (1980) interviewed 100 patients newly referred to a gastroenterology clinic and obtained complete data on 87. Nonorganic gastrointestinal disease was diagnosed in 32, of whom 17 were considered to have a psychiatric disorder; six of these had a severe depressive illness. Psychiatric disorder was less common in 35 patients diagnosed as having an organic gastrointestinal illness, only seven being considered to have psychiatric diagnoses, of which two were diagnosed as having severe depression. The other 20 patients had nongastrointestinal conditions.

Depression and Physical Illness. Edited by M.M. Robertson and C.L.E. Katona
© 1997 John Wiley & Sons Ltd

FUNCTIONAL GASTROINTESTINAL DISORDERS

Irritable bowel syndrome

Irritable bowel syndrome (IBS) is the gut syndrome most extensively studied from a psychiatric viewpoint. It is characterized by abdominal pain, which is normally relieved by defecation, variable bowel habit, abdominal distension, excessive flatus and audible borborygmi. Although the presenting symptoms are focused on the lower bowel it has become apparent that there are several noncolonic symptoms including fatigue, nausea, vomiting, dysphagia, frequency of micturition and dyspareunia.

Many studies have demonstrated a high prevalence of psychiatric disorders in patients with IBS attending hospital clinics (Creed and Guthrie, 1987). Some of the earlier studies could be criticized on methodological grounds but more recent studies have overcome these criticisms by using standardized methods of assessment and operational diagnostic criteria. Walker *et al.* (1990) compared 28 patients with IBS with 19 patients with inflammatory bowel disease, the patients being assessed with the Diagnostic Interview Schedule (DIS) and diagnoses made according to DSM-IIIR. Significantly more of the IBS patients had lifetime diagnoses of major depression, panic disorder and phobic disorder. Indeed 26 of the 28 IBS patients had at least one lifetime psychiatric diagnosis most of which had developed before the onset of their irritable bowel symptoms.

Toner *et al.* (1990) compared IBS patients with nonclinical controls, reporting a significantly higher prevalence of psychiatric disorders, particularly anxiety and depression, in the patient group. However, they observed a much lower lifetime prevalence (61%) than in the patients studied by Walker *et al.* (1990). Blanchard *et al.* (1990), using different assessment methods, found higher levels of anxiety and depression among IBS patients than among patients with inflammatory bowel disease who were more depressed than healthy control subjects. Lydiard *et al.* (1993) also reported a high lifetime prevalence of psychiatric disorders, particularly anxiety and mood disorders. Among 35 patients attending a university gastroenterology service 33 met lifetime criteria for one or more DSM-IIIR disorders. Nine met criteria for major depression, two for dysthymic disorder and one for bipolar disorder.

A larger study by Walker *et al.* (1995) confirmed a high prevalence of major depression and current panic disorder in IBS patients who also reported a higher prevalence of childhood sexual abuse, an observation which has previously been described by Drossman *et al.* (1990). Leserman *et al.* (1996) found that female gastroenterology patients with a history of prior sexual abuse reported more pain, more nongastrointestinal somatic symptoms and more previous operations than those without a history of sexual abuse. Sexual abuse may thus explain why women with IBS often suffer from sexual dysfunction (Guthrie *et al.*, 1987).

The high prevalence of psychiatric illness among IBS patients attending hospital clinics has influenced the aetiological hypothesis that IBS is a psycho-physiological disorder of gut motility. But this explanation is not supported by community studies of people with IBS symptoms (Whitehead *et al.*, 1988; Smith *et al.*, 1990). These have shown that people with IBS symptoms who do not consult their doctor have levels of psychological distress similar to asympto-matic control subjects. Whitehead and Crowell (1991) have therefore suggested that psychological symptoms influence the decision to seek medical treatment but have no part in the aetiology of IBS.

Nonulcer dyspepsia

This is the latest in a series of terms used to describe the persistent upper abdominal pain for which no focal or systemic disease can be detected. In a review of the literature Morris (1991) concluded that a significant proportion of patients have a psychiatric disorder, predominantly anxiety or depression, or personality traits which influence their dyspeptic complaints.

Langeluddecke *et al.* (1990) detected significantly higher levels of anxiety, tension and hostility in a group of nonulcer dyspeptic patients compared with a control group who had proven peptic ulcer disease. However, they found no differences in levels of depression or the tendency to suppress anger. In contrast Haug *et al.* (1994) found higher levels of neuroticism, anxiety, depression and DSM-III psychiatric disorders in patients with functional dyspepsia compared with controls. On all these measures patients with duodenal ulcer obtained scores intermediate between the other two groups. Together with dyspeptic symptoms there may be complaints of allergies to certain foods. The true prevalence of food allergy is not known but many who claim to be allergic have no evidence of allergy on objective testing. There is a high prevalence of psychiatric morbidity in patients who present in this manner and Rix *et al.* (1984) have concluded that symptoms supposedly related to food allergy often have a psychogenic basis.

Appendicectomy and abdominal pain

A substantial proportion of patients who undergo appendicectomy for abdominal pain have no histological evidence of acute appendicitis. The appendix is reported as normal or only mildly inflamed. Psychosocial factors have often been implicated as being aetiologically significant in this group, a view which has been given credibility with the application of standardized research methods. Creed (1981) demonstrated that depression was much more common in patients with noninflamed appendices than in those with acute inflammation and was associated with persistent abdominal pain during the years after operation. Patients with noninflamed appendices were also more likely to report exposure to severely threatening life events before surgery, irrespective of whether or not they were depressed. Beaurepaire *et al.* (1992) found that patients with noninflamed appendices and those with acute appendicitis had higher depression scores than healthy control subjects. Of the noninflamed group 38% had depression scores in the clinical range compared with 28% of the acutely inflamed group and 14% of controls.

The important role of life events has been highlighted by Craig and Brown (1984) who compared patients diagnosed as having organic gastrointestinal disorders with those diagnosed as having a functional disorder such as IBS, nonulcer dyspepsia and other nonspecific abdominal pain. Severely threatening life events were significantly more common during the 38 weeks before the onset of symptoms in the functional group than in the organic group and in a community control group. Most of these severely threatening life events involved losses and disappointment and appeared similar to those life events implicated in the onset of depression.

Relationship between depression and abdominal pain

Several facts emerge from the literature on abdominal pain associated with functional bowel disorders. Those patients who are referred to hospital clinics are more likely to report exposure to stressful life events prior to the onset of their symptoms, and they are also likely to have a high lifetime and current prevalence of psychiatric illness, particularly depression and anxiety disorders. A further observation which has emerged recently is that patients with functional abdominal symptoms who do not consult doctors have levels of psychological symptoms no higher than symptom-free controls.

Abdominal pain is a common bodily sensation which for most people does not acquire the status of a medical symptom. It is ignored, tolerated or forgotten. Heaton (1992) has estimated that of every 100 women aged between 20 and 39, 80 experience recurrent abdominal pain but approximately 56 forget about it with time. Of the 24 who can recall their pain, about 14 do not bother to report it to their doctor, leaving only 10 who consult their doctor because of it.

Stressful life events and psychiatric symptoms, particularly depression, may thus be the crucial influences in determining whether or not patients with abdominal pain decide to consult their doctor and request treatment. Life events may influence consulting behaviour directly or indirectly by way of their precipitation of a depressive illness. Once a depressive illness develops there may be changes in bowel motility which give rise to painful sensations. Furthermore, depression is known to amplify the perception of pain and to increase the likelihood of seeking medical treatment for pain which would otherwise be tolerated or dismissed as inconsequential.

It follows that it is an essential aspect of good clinical practice to enquire about life circumstances, interpersonal relationships and psychological symptoms when assessing patients with functional bowel disorders. These factors may have led to the decision to seek medical help for symptoms which had been tolerated for many years, they may have caused an acute exacerbation of symptoms or they may prolong symptoms which would otherwise have subsided spontaneously.

Management

The somatic symptoms of functional bowel disorders usually respond well to straightforward advice and reassurance combined with dietary modification. Many patients with irritable bowel syndrome are worried that they have cancer and a confident exclusion of this diagnosis alleviates the psychological symptoms in most cases. Simple symptomatic treatment with antispasmodic drugs and bulking agents also results in clinical improvement although these drugs are sometimes used indiscriminately. The same caveat applies to antidepressant medication. Many clinicians believe tricyclic antidepressants to be especially beneficial, both by elevating a depressed mood and by reducing abdominal symptoms, the latter perhaps by virtue of their anticholinergic effect on gut motility. Although tricyclics are widely used in gastroenterology practice the evidence for their efficacy is not yet supported by methodologically sound controlled trials.

Various psychological treatments have been used with patients whose symptoms are refractory to physical methods of management. Whorwell (1991) has pioneered the use of hypnotherapy which is directed towards modifying bowel motility. Patients are first provided with a basic explanation of gut physiology which they are expected to modify during subsequent sessions. After induction of the hypnotic state patients are asked to place a hand on their abdomen and to relate the feeling of warmth to the relief of pain, spasm and bloating. They are then asked to visualize a flowing river and imagine it representing their gut. Finally, they are asked to modify the flow to achieve a more acceptable bowel habit. Whorwell acknowledges that conventionally trained doctors may feel uncomfortable with the concepts and terminology used in hypnosis but he emphasizes that the technique is easy to learn and can be modified according to the doctor's own temperament. Some patients may take several weeks to derive benefit but evidence is accumulating to support the benefits of this approach (Whorwell *et al.*, 1984; Harvey *et al.*, 1989).

Behaviour therapy has also been claimed to be effective. Schwarz *et al.* (1990) reported a 4 year follow up of an uncontrolled study, a behavioural approach which included education about IBS, instruction in cognitive coping strategies, progressive muscle relaxation and thermal biofeedback. Twenty seven patients completed the treatment and of the 19 who were contacted 4 years later 17 rated themselves as more than 50% improved. Corney *et al.* (1991) conducted a better-designed study in which 42 patients with IBS were allocated either to conventional medical treatment or to behavioural psychotherapy. The medical treatment involved explanation, dietary advice and the prescription of bulk laxatives, antispasmodics and various other medications. The behavioural treatment comprised advice on pain management and bowel retraining and coping with situations or activities which had previously been avoided. After 9 months both groups had improved on several measures but the behaviour therapy group showed significantly more improvement on two avoidance scores. The authors concluded that in view of the considerable time invested in behaviour therapy it was probably no more effective than medical treatment. Short-term cognitive therapy has been found to improve various somatic symptoms of functional dyspepsia but it did not influence the associated psychological symptoms (Haug *et al.*, 1994).

The best evidence for the effectiveness of psychological treatment is derived from two controlled studies of dynamic psychotherapy (Svedlund *et al.*, 1983; Guthrie *et al.*, 1991) both of which showed psychotherapy to be superior to routine medical treatment. In Guthrie's study patients with overt depression and anxiety did particularly well and improvement in bowel symptoms was considered to be mediated via an improvement in psychological status. Dynamic psychotherapy involves a close, often dependent relationship between the patient and therapist. Analysis of the transference is an important aspect of treatment as is an understanding of the relationship between symptoms and emotional feelings and problems in the patient's life. One of the drawbacks of this type of treatment is the time required to effect change. Patients may need to be seen at least once weekly for several months, occasionally for years. This makes it an impractical therapy for the large number of patients with chronic functional symptoms, but fortunately current trends in psychotherapy are favouring treatment which is brief and focused.

ORGANIC GASTROINTESTINAL DISORDERS

The prevalence of psychiatric disorders is known to be increased in physically ill people, whether the association be assessed in the community, in primary care or in the general hospital. The commonest disorders are depression and anxiety disorders, and often a combination of the two which represents an undifferentiated reaction to illness. Several factors influence the development of psychological symptoms including personality traits, a previous history of depression or anxiety, social problems at the onset of illness and the availability of social support.

Factors pertaining to the illness and its treatment are also important. In the case of gastrointestinal disorders there are often distressing symptoms such as vomiting, diarrhoea and rectal bleeding which impose major restrictions on lifestyle. Fatigue may result from anaemia due to blood loss or from nutritional deficiencies due to malabsorption syndromes. Dietary restrictions may be an essential component of treatment and many find them annoying and socially embarrassing. If surgical treatment is required the prospect of a permanent ileostomy or colostomy can cause considerable distress. Radiotherapy can have a depressing effect on mood although this is usually transient. Drugs used in gastroenterology which can cause or aggravate depressive symptoms include steroids, analgesics, cytotoxics and cyclosporin.

Duodenal ulcer

Duodenal ulcer was at one time considered a psychosomatic disorder but the influence of psychological factors in its development is now believed to be modest (Lewin and Lewis, 1995). The association with depression which has been found in some studies reflects the chronicity of the symptoms and is likely to be a consequence of rather than a causal factor for duodenal ulcer (Tennant *et al.*, 1986).

Malignant disease

Depression is commonly associated with malignant disease, the estimated prevalence varying according to the methods of assessment used and reaching 50% in some series (McDaniel *et al.*, 1995). Carcinoma of the pancreas was previously considered to have a specific link with depression in that it was believed to present frequently with symptoms of a depressive illness. Such an association has not been confirmed however and the apparent relationship probably reflects the difficulty in establishing the diagnosis of pancreatic cancer in the days before intra-abdominal imaging became available. Cancer of the pancreas is notorious for producing few localizing signs in its early development. Symptoms such as anorexia, weight loss, fatigue and diffuse abdominal pain are the usual complaints; their nonspecific nature may well lead to a spurious diagnosis of a depressive illness before other manifestations of the tumour become apparent.

The association between depression and gastrointestinal malignancies is probably no different from that with cancer in other organs. Depression is usually precipitated by the emotional impact of the disease and the prospect of a reduced life-span, together with the distress brought about by persistent pain and other physical complications which affect quality of life. The effects of treatment, particularly chemotherapy and radiotherapy, may temporarily accentuate depressive symptoms. In the case of bowel cancer the construction of a colostomy is another factor which can induce depression by virtue of its effect on body image and self-confidence.

When depression develops in cancer patients it is often not recognized and therefore not treated. A depressed mood may be considered an understandable and inevitable response to a potentially fatal disease; furthermore, the diagnosis may be clouded by the presence of anorexia, weight loss and other somatic symptoms which are conventionally relied upon to establish a diagnosis of depression but which may also be due to the malignancy itself. In the presence of cancer, greater weight has to be given to the psychological manifestations of a depressive illness, particularly loss of interest, loss of enjoyment (anhedonia) and suicidal thinking.

Inflammatory bowel disease

Crohn's disease and ulcerative colitis are chronic, relapsing illnesses with many distressing symptoms including abdominal pain, profuse diarrhoea and bleeding. Complications include anaemia, malabsorption, malnutrition and general debility. The treatment is often unpleasant, a substantial proportion of patients requiring a permanent stoma, so it would not be surprising if many developed psychiatric disorders.

The evidence for this is surprisingly scanty. Helzer *et al.* (1984) observed a higher lifetime prevalence of psychiatric disorder, particularly depression, in patients with Crohn's disease compared with controls who had other chronic medical conditions. There was no association between the severity of the psychiatric disorder and the activity of the inflammatory disease. Andrews *et al.* (1987) have described high levels of anxiety and depression in patients with Crohn's disease and ulcerative colitis but unfortunately did not study a control group. In patients with Crohn's disease, but not ulcerative colitis, there was a clear association between the presence of psychiatric illness and the degree of physical morbidity. North *et al.* (1990) have reviewed the literature on ulcerative colitis and concluded there was no increased prevalence of psychopathology. Ulcerative colitis was one of Alexander's seven classic psychosomatic disorders but North *et al.* concluded that methodological errors had biased the published literature and that the model of ulcerative colitis as a psychosomatic disorder was not supported by studies that were methodologically sound. However, Walker *et al.* (1995) did find higher rates of affective disorder, anxiety and somatization in patients with inflammatory bowel disease compared with general population data, but not as high as in patients with irritable bowel syndrome. The diagnosis of a current psychiatric diagnosis in inflammatory bowel disease patients was associated with a previous history of sexual and physical victimization, increased disability and a higher number of medically unexplained symptoms.

Management

Effective physical treatment is probably the best remedy for depression in physical illness but unfortunately many gastrointestinal disorders are chronic or recurrent, with little prospect of a lasting cure. The support which an experienced physician can provide does much to alleviate depression but doctors often underestimate their capacity to lighten a patient's spirits. Medication is required if the severity of depression fulfils the criteria of a depressive illness. Tricyclic antidepressants have been used for many years with apparent success but are now being replaced by the serotonin reuptake inhibitors which appear to be better tolerated by the physically ill. The evidence suggests that depression in these patients is undertreated, perhaps because doctors ignore the patient's emotional cues or regard depression as understandable and therefore inevitable in the presence of serious physical pathology. Regrettably, there have been few well-designed trials of antidepressant medication in the physically ill. There is certainly a need to compare different antidepressants in these patients with regard to their efficacy, side-effects and acceptability.

Specific psychological treatment has been evaluated for patients with malignant disease, especially breast cancer, but to date no study has specifically assessed its role in gastrointestinal cancer. Cognitive–behaviour therapy is the approach which offers the greatest practical advantage and its place in the management of malignant disease deserves further evaluation.

LIVER DISEASE

There has been renewed interest in the role of the viral infections in causing a prolonged fatigue state whose symptoms show a considerable overlap with those of a depressive illness. Viral hepatitis is one of the syndromes which has been described as predisposing to a chronic fatigue syndrome with prominent depressive symptoms in the convalescent period (Martini and Strohmeyer, 1974). Other authors have disputed this, detecting no specific link between hepatitis and chronic fatigue. At present the case remains unproven and large-scale prospective studies are required to establish whether hepatitis predisposes to depression. Some light has been shed on this topic by a study by McDonald *et al.* (1987) who found an increase in psychiatric symptoms, assessed by standardized methods, in patients with chronic hepatitis B treated with interferon alpha compared with similar patients who did not receive interferon. The commonest psychiatric symptoms were depression, anxiety, fatigue and poor concentration. The authors speculated that if exogenous interferon could increase psychiatric morbidity, similar changes in psychological symptoms might be produced by endogenously produced interferon following viral infections.

Little evidence is available on the relationship between depression and cirrhosis. The evaluation of affective disorders in this patients is difficult because the physical effects of cirrhosis often lead to fatigue, anorexia and weight loss, symptoms which may be mistaken for those of a depressive illness (Collis and Lloyd, 1992). Ewusi-Mensah *et al.* (1983) reported that one-third of a group of nonalcoholic cirrhotics had a psychiatric disorder, most commonly minor depression or anxiety. The prevalence was much higher among alcoholic cirrhotics; a similar finding has been reported by Sarin *et al.* (1988). This observation is what would be expected on commonsense grounds, given the widespread occupational, domestic and social problems which are associated with a long history of heavy drinking. But it does emphasize the importance of a close working relationship between physicians and psychiatrists in the management of patients with alcoholic liver disease.

Transplantation is now an established treatment for end-stage liver disease. Psychological criteria are often considered in the selection of candidates but patients are rarely turned down on the grounds of psychiatric disorder. Levenson and Olbrisch (1993) surveyed all transplant centres in the USA to determine which psychological criteria were used to evaluate transplant candidates. In no centre was a history of affective disorder considered to be an absolute contraindication; a recent suicide attempt was considered a contraindication by 17.4%, a history of multiple suicide attempts by 41.3% and current suicidal ideation by 50.0%. A current affective disorder was regarded as an absolute contraindication in 17.4% of centres. Most transplant centres now undertake to operate on patients with alcoholic cirrhosis provided they have been abstinent for at least 6 months, have a stable psychological background and have no evidence of extrahepatic alcoholic damage (Sherlock, 1995).

Quality of life usually improves following transplantation. Major psychiatric disorders are uncommon with the exception of transient delirium in the immediate postoperative period. Collis *et al.* (1995) found that of 30 patients interviewed posttransplant eight had a psychiatric disorder. Of these, four had mild mixed anxiety and depressive disorders, two adjustment disorders, one a severe depressive disorder and one an organic mood disorder. Drugs use to suppress rejection, particularly steroids, are well known to cause mood disturbances, either depression or mania.

CONCLUSIONS

In gastroenterological practice psychological and organic factors interact in a number of different ways. In the functional disorders the symptoms are, in many cases, the somatic presentation of an underlying psychiatric disorder; in the organic disorders there are significant psychological sequelae to the distress of chronic disability and in alcoholic liver disease the physical pathology is the result of a long-standing behavioural disorder. Whatever the mechanism, there is a high prevalence of psychiatric illness in any representative sample of patients with gastrointestinal disorders. The physician needs to be alert to this problem to be able to treat the minor forms of psychiatric illness and to have easy access to a psychiatric opinion for the more intractable cases. Collaborative treatment will pay dividends for these patients.

REFERENCES

Andrews H, Barczak P and Allan RN (1987) Psychiatric illness in patients with inflammatory bowel disease. *Gut,* **28**, 1600–1604.

Beaurepaire JE, Jones M, Eckstein RP, Smith RC, Piper DW and Tennant C (1992) The acute appendicitis syndrome: Psychological aspects of the inflamed and non-inflamed appendix. *J Psychosom Res,* **36**, 425–437.

Blanchard EB, Scharff L, Schwarz SP, Suls JM and Barlow DH (1990) The role of anxiety and depression in the irritable bowel syndrome. *Behav Res Ther,* **28**, 401–405.

Collis I and Lloyd G (1992) Psychiatric aspects of liver disease. *Br J Psychiatry*, **161**, 12–22.

Collis I, Burroughs A, Rolles K and Lloyd G (1995) Psychiatric and social outcome of liver transplantation. *Br J Psychiatry*, **166**, 521–524.

Corney RH, Stanton R, Newell R, Clare A and Fairclough P (1991) Behavioural psychotherapy in the treatment of irritable bowel syndrome. *J Psychosom Res*, **35**, 461–469.

Craig TKJ and Brown GW (1984) Goal frustration and life-events in the aetiology of painful gastrointestinal disorder. *J Psychosom Res*, **28**, 411–421.

Creed F (1981) Life-events and appendicectomy. *Lancet*, **1**, 381–385.

Creed F and Guthrie E (1987) Psychological factors and the irritable bowel syndrome. *Gut*, **28**, 1307–1318.

Drossman DA, Leserman J, Nachman G, Li ZM, Gluck H, Toomey TC and Mitchell CM (1990) Sexual and physical abuse in women with functional or organic gastrointestinal disorders. *Ann Intern Med*, **113**, 828–833.

Ewusi-Mensah I, Saunders JB, Wodak AD *et al.* (1983) Psychiatric morbidity in patients with alcoholic liver disease. *Brit Med J*, **287**, 1417–1419.

Guthrie E, Creed F and Whorwell PJ (1987) Severe sexual dysfunction in women with the irritable bowel syndrome: comparison with inflammatory bowel disease and duodenal ulceration. *Br Med J*, **295**, 577–578.

Guthrie E, Creed F, Dawson D and Tomensen B (1991) A controlled trial of psychological treatment for the irritable bowel syndrome. *Gastroenterology*, **100**, 450–457.

Harvey RF, Salih SY and Read AE (1983) Organic and functional disorders in 2000 gastroenterology out-patients. *Lancet*, **1**, 632–634.

Harvey RF, Hinton RA, Gunary RM and Barry RE (1989) Individual and group hypnotherapy in treatment of refractory irritable bowel syndrome. *Lancet*, **i**, 424–425.

Haug, TT, Svebak S, Wilhelmsen I, Berstad A and Ursin H (1994) Psychological factors and somatic symptoms in functional dyspepsia: a comparison with duodenal ulcer and healthy controls. *J Psychosom Res*, **38**, 281–291.

Heaton K (1992) What makes people with abdominal pain consult their doctor? In: F Creed, R Mayou and A Hopkins (eds) *Medical Symptoms not Explained by Organic Disease*. London: Royal College of Psychiatrists and Royal College of Physicians, 1–8.

Helzer HE, Chammas S, Norland CC, Stillings WA and Alpers DH (1984) A study of the association between Crohn's disease and psychiatric illness. *Gastroenterology*, **86**, 324–330.

Irritable Bowel Syndrome Working Team Report (1988) *Handbook of International Congress of Gastroenterologists*, Rome.

Langeluddecke P, Goulston K and Tennant C (1990) Psychological factors in dyspepsia of unknown cause: a comparison with peptic ulcer disease. *J Psychosom Res*, **34**, 215–222.

Leserman J, Drossman DA, Li Z, Toomey TC, Nachman G and Glogan L (1996) Sexual and physical abuse history in gastroenterology practice: how types of abuse impact health status. *Psychsom Med*, **58**, 4–15.

Levenson JL and Olbrisch ME (1993) Psychosocial evaluation of organ transplant candidates: a comparative survey of process, criteria and outcomes in heart, liver and kidney transplantation. *Psychosomatics*, **34**, 314–323.

Lewin J and Lewis S (1995) Organic and psychological risk factors for duodenal ulcer. *J Psychosom Res*, **39**, 531–548.

Lloyd GG (1992) Functional gastrointestinal disorders: psychological factors in aetiology and management. In: RE Pounder (ed) *Recent Advances in Gastroenterology*, 9th Edition. Edinburgh: Churchill Livingstone, 63–71.

Lydiard RB, Fossey MD, Marsh W and Ballenger JC (1993) Prevalence of psychiatric disorders in patients with irritable bowel syndrome. *Psychosomatics*, **34**, 229–234.

McDaniel JS, Musselman DL, Porter MR, Reed DA and Nemeroff CB (1995) Depression in patients with cancer: diagnosis, biology and treatment. *Arch Gen Psychiatry*, **52**, 89–99.

MacDonald AJ and Bouchier IAD (1980) Non-organic gastrointestinal illness: a medical and psychiatric study. *Br J Psychiatry*, **136**, 276–283.

McDonald EM, Mann AH and Thomas HC (1987) Interferons as mediators of psychiatric morbidity. *Lancet*, **ii**, 1175–1178.

Martini GA and Strohmeyer G (1974) Posthepatitis syndromes. *Clin Gastroenterol*, **3**, 377–390.

Morris C (1991) Non-ulcer dyspepsia. *J Psychosom Res*, **35**, 129–140.

North CS, Clouse RE, Spitznagel EL and Alpers DH (1990) The relation of ulcerative colitis to psychiatric factors: a review of findings and methods. *Am J Psychiatry*, **147**, 974–981.

Rix KJB, Pearson DJ and Bentley SJ (1984) A psychiatric study of patients with supposed food allergy. *Br J Psychiatry*, **145**, 121–126.

Sarin SK, Sachder G, Jildha RC *et al.* (1988) Patterns of psychiatric morbidity and alcohol dependence in patients with alcoholic liver disease. *Digestive Dis Sci*, **33**, 443–448.

Schwarz SP, Taylor AE, Scharf L and Blanchard EB (1990) Behaviourally treated irritable bowel syndrome patients: A four year follow-up. *Behav Res Ther*, **28**, 331–335.

Sherlock S (1995) Alcoholic liver disease. *Lancet*, **345**, 227–229.

Smith RC, Greenbaum DS, Vancouver JB *et al.* (1990) Psychosocial factors are associated with health care seeking rather than diagnosis in irritable bowel syndrome. *Gastroenterology*, **98**, 293–301.

Svedlund J, Sjodin I, Ottoson JO and Dotevall G (1983) Controlled study of psychotherapy in irritable bowel syndrome. *Lancet*, **i**, 589–592.

Tennant C, Goulston K and Langeluddecke P (1986) Psychological correlates of gastric and duodenal ulcer disease. *Psychol Med*, **16**, 365–371.

Toner BB, Garfinkel PE and Jeejeebhoy KN (1990) Psychological factors in irritable bowel syndrome. *Can J Psychiatry*, **35**, 158–161.

Walker EA, Roy-Byrne PP, Katon WJ, Li L, Amos D and Tirenek G (1990) Psychiatric illness and irritable bowel syndrome: a comparison with inflammatory bowel disease. *Am J Psychiatry*, **147**, 1656–1661.

Walker EA, Gelfand AN, Gelfand MD and Katon WJ (1995) Psychiatric diagnoses, sexual and physical victimisation and disability in patients with irritable bowel syndrome or inflammatory bowel disease. *Psychol Med*, **25**, 1259–1267.

Whitehead WE and Crowell MD (1991) Psychologic considerations in the irritable bowel syndrome. *Gastroenterol Clin N Am*, **20**, 249–267.

Whitehead WE, Bosmajian L, Zonderman AB, Costa PT and Schuster MM (1988) Symptoms of psychologic distress associated with irritable bowel syndrome: comparison of community and medical clinic samples. *Gastroenterology*, **95**, 709–714.

Whorwell PJ (1991) Use of hypnotherapy in gastrointestinal disease. *Br J Hosp Med*, **45**, 27–29.

Whorwell PJ, Prior A and Faragher EB (1984) Controlled trial of hypnotherapy in the treatment of severe refractory irritable bowel syndrome. *Lancet*, **ii**, 1232–1234.

16

Depression in neurological disorders

Mary M. Robertson

INTRODUCTION

Depression is common in neurological illness. However, the relationship between the depression and the specific neurological disorders is complex. General problems in the area will be addressed in the introduction, while the problems relating to specific disorders will be discussed individually.

Ron (1995) divides neurological disorders into three types (a) generalized disorders (e.g. Alzheimer's disease, multiple sclerosis), (b) localized disorders (Parkinson's disease, Huntington's disease) and (c) discrete disorders (stroke, tumours). This typology will be adhered to in this chapter, but Alzheimer's disease and tumours will not be discussed as they are included in other chapters.

PREVALENCE OF PSYCHIATRIC ILLNESS IN NEUROLOGICAL PATIENTS

Several studies have attempted to examine the prevalence of depression across the range of neurological disorders, and the results and conclusions of these will be presented in chronological order.

Kirk and Saunders (1977) conducted a retrospective case note study of 2716 patients attending a neurological outpatients clinic, and documented that 13.2%

Depression and Physical Illness. Edited by M.M. Robertson and C.L.E. Katona
© 1997 John Wiley & Sons Ltd

had a primary psychiatric illness, as assessed by clinical interview. Eighty-two per cent of psychiatric disorders included neurosis and personality disorders, 17% had affective disorders, while only 1% had schizophrenia. The same authors (Kirk and Saunders, 1979) then studied 342 neurological outpatients prospectively, using a clinical interview by a neurologist and the General Health Questionnaire (GHQ). Clinical assessment revealed 27% with psychiatric disorders, whilst the GHQ showed a probable psychiatric morbidity of 48% with a cut-off score of 11/12, and 21% using a cut-off score of 26/27.

DePaulo and Folstein (1978) used the Mini-Mental State (MMS) and GHQ to detect cognitive defects and emotional disturbances in 126 consecutively admitted neurological patients. Of the patients tested 67% had cognitive defects, emotional disturbance or both; 50% demonstrated emotional disturbance as indicated by a score of five or more on the GHQ. In 30% of patients psychiatric disturbance was not recognized by the treating physician; psychiatric consultation was only requested for 9% of patients during the study period. The most common neurological diagnosis in this study was cerebrovascular disease (22%). Continuing their work in the area, DePaulo *et al.* (1980) administered the MMS and GHQ to a total of 197 neurological inpatients; 126 of these were those included in the DePaulo and Folstein (1978) investigation. Once again, 50% showed emotional disturbance. The highest rates of emotional disturbance indicated by GHQ scores were found in patients with myaesthenia gravis (73% abnormal) and multiple sclerosis (68%), followed by Parkinson's disease (50%), stroke (50%) and amyotrophic lateral sclerosis (15%).

Schiffer (1983) systematically interviewed 241 consecutive inpatients ($N=57$) and outpatients ($N=184$) of a neurology service for emotional disorders. The 16 symptom areas of the Brief Psychiatric Rating Scale (BPRS) were assessed. Of these, 101 (41.9%) were sufficiently symptomatic to justify a DSM-111 diagnosis. Overall, 17.5% of both inpatient and outpatient groups had a primary psychiatric difficulty. In this group the most common primary psychiatric diagnoses were conversion disorder and somatoform disorders, while depression ($N=2$) and anxiety ($N=4$) together accounted for 2.5%. Secondary psychiatric diagnoses occurred in 59 (24%) patients; alcohol abuse and depressive disorder were the most common psychiatric diagnoses to accompany a primary neurological illness. The most commonly associated diagnoses were alcohol abuse, epilepsy, depression, pain syndromes, and anxiety and pain syndromes ($N=5$). In the group of simultaneous diagnoses (i.e. secondary psychiatric diagnoses), the neurological disorders antedated the psychiatric disorders in 38 (65%) of the patients.

Bridges and Goldberg (1984) estimated the prevalence of psychiatric morbidity in 100 neurological inpatients using the GHQ and the Clinical Interview Schedule (CIS). Psychiatric morbidity was judged to be 39%, of which 72% was unrecognized by the neurologists. In this study, the satisfactory GHQ threshold score was 11/12. The psychiatric diagnoses encountered among the patients assessed by the CIS were mostly minor affective disorders: depression (24%), mixed depression and anxiety (6%) and anxiety states (4%).

Schofield and Duane (1987) examined 199 neurological inpatients and found reactive depression to be the most common psychiatric diagnosis, encountered in 36% of patients; 2% had a diagnosis of manic depressive illness. The most common neurological illness in their cohort was epilepsy (21% of admissions).

Metcalfe *et al.* (1988) assessed 93 female neurological inpatients using the GHQ, the Illness Behaviour Questionnaire (IBQ) and the CIS. They reported an overall prevalence of definite psychiatric disorder, diagnosed by the CIS (and thus satisfying DSM criteria), in 34%, with depression being the most common diagnosis. The most common neurological disorders were spondylosis and cerebrovascular disease (14% each), multiple sclerosis, epilepsy and headache (13% each). In an elegant subsequent investigation, the same group (Creed *et al.*, 1990) studied 133 patients admitted to a neurological ward, assessing them for the presence of both organic neurological disease, psychiatric disorder, and abnormal illness behaviour using the CIS and IBQ. Many patients either had clear organic disease or somatic presentation of psychiatric disorder ("somatization"), but one-third fell between these two extremes and either had a complex mixture of the two types of illness or could not be accurately diagnosed. Not only does this study highlight the difficulties when trying to diagnose psychiatric illness (and thus also depression) in patients with neurological illness, but the authors also discuss the problems of "primary" and "secondary" psychiatric disorders in neurological patients. Of the 78 patients whose complaints were not regarded as wholly explicable in terms of organic disease, 45 had an affective disorder, with 31 (40%) being depressed, 13 (17%) anxious and 1 (1%) hypomanic (Creed *et al.*, 1990).

In a survey of patient encounters in neurological practice in the UK, Hopkins *et al.* (1989) documented that only 6% of 411 new patients seen received primary diagnoses of anxiety, depression and personality disorders.

It is also worth noting that many patients presenting to neurologists may not have a disorder with an "organic" basis. Mace and Trimble (1991) surveyed 168 neurologists, and replies suggested that between them they were seeing over 36 000 new patients a year whose symptoms lacked a neurological basis; moreover, very low proportions of these patients were referred by the participating neurologists to other specialists (including psychiatrists) for further diagnosis and treatment. Many neurological patients who are referred to psychiatrists end up with diagnoses of somatization and conversion disorders. In a large chart survey study, Tomasson *et al.* (1991) identified 51 patients with conversion disorder and 65 with somatization disorder. Of these, 41% of the conversion disorder patients and 18% of the somatization disorder patients presented to neurology or neurosurgery clinics. The most common specific main complaints for conversion disorder patients were fits (24%), paralysis (10) and a lump in the throat (8%). For the somatization disorder patients the most frequent chief complaint was depressed or dysphoric mood (15%), followed by abdominal pain (11%) and chest pain (8%). Of importance is that of the 51 conversion disorder patients, 18% had a history of major depression and 16% had attempted suicide; significantly more patients in the somatization group had a history of major depression (48%) and attempted suicide (51%). This illustrates further the difficulties of detecting and treating depression in patients who present themselves to neurologists.

It is worth noting that in a least three studies (De Paulo and Folstein, 1978; Bridges and Goldberg, 1984; Mace and Trimble, 1991) there was clinical under-recognition of psychiatric illness amongst neurological patients, compared to detection when instruments were used during investigation situations. This should be borne in mind by the neurological liaison psychiatrist, and suggests that more work in the area needs to be carried out. If similar underdetection results, the work of such liaison psychiatrists may well have to change, and include detection of psychiatric disorder, rather than solely management of those patients referred; this would of course have personnel, and thus financial, implications.

In summary, many patients who attend neurological clinics have emotional or psychiatric disorders, the most common of which appear to be depression and anxiety. The prevalence figures range from 27% to 50% (average figure about 38%), with only two studies yielding much lower rates (Kirk and Saunders, 1977; Hopkins *et al.*, 1989 6%). The low values in the former may well have been accounted for because the figure of 13.2% was for primary psychiatric illness. The low figures of the latter may well have been because the study was a survey of neurologists and their responses, rather than the neurological patients being assessed; and, as mentioned earlier, there seems to be clinical under-recognition of psychiatric disorder in neurological patients. The neurological illness may well antedate the psychiatric illness and due to under-recognition may well be untreated. The psychiatric and neurological disorders may be related in several ways. Thus, there may be a primary psychiatric illness or there may be comorbidity; that is the two disorders (psychiatric and neurological) co-occurring. Some of these neurological patients with psychiatric disorder may well also attempt suicide.

Notwithstanding the inherent difficulties noted above, an attempt will be made to review the literature on depression in specific neurological disorders, acknowledging that the review is not exhaustive, but hopefully covering classic texts and giving practical guidelines to recognition and treatment.

GENERALIZED DISORDERS

Multiple sclerosis

Multiple sclerosis (MS), the most common of the demyelinating disorders, is a chronic disorder in which the irregular demyelination of both the central and peripheral portions of the nervous system results in varying degrees of motor, sensory and cognitive dysfunction (Joffe *et al.*, 1987), with progressive deterioration, remissions and exacerbations (Schubert and Foliart, 1993).

Affective disturbances are common in patients with MS and can be of varying types. Until fairly recently, euphoria was thought to be a cardinal symptom of MS. Thus, Brown and Davis (1922) reported that 90% of MS patients had "mental alterations", with euphoria being present in 71%. Cottrell and Wilson (1926) reported that of 100 MS patients 63% had euphoria, 10% had depression, and 23% had labile mood. Wechsler (1921) reported that 9% of 1773 MS patients had euphoria, while 12% had depression. It has been suggested that what was once considered the psychological symptom of euphoria, would now probably be reclassified as the neurological symptom of frontal lobe disinhibition (McNamara, 1991).

Several case reports (e.g. Kellner *et al.*, 1984; Peselow *et al.*, 1981; Kept *et al.*, 1977) and one epidemiological study (Schiffer *et al.*, 1986) have suggested that people with MS have a specific vulnerability to bipolar disorder.

It is now, however, recognized that depression is the most common psychiatric disorder encountered in MS. One of the first physicians to note the association was the French neurologist Charcot (1881). Subsequently, early studies reported that depression occurred in 18% (Kahana *et al.*, 1971) to 20% (Braceland and Giffin, 1950) of patients with MS. Surridge (1969) undertook the first controlled study of psychiatric changes in MS and found no significant differences in the incidence of depressive symptoms in 108 MS patients (27% compared with 13% depression rate among 39 controls with muscular dystrophy), thus concluding that the majority of the MS patients were suffering from a "reactive" illness, rather than from a disorder specific to MS. Subsequent studies also supported this "reactive" hypothesis (Baretz and Stephenson, 1981; Melvor *et al.*, 1984).

Others, however, such as Whitlock and Siskind (1980), compared 30 MS patients with 30 patients with other neurological illnesses and found that those with MS were significantly more depressed at interview than patients with equal disability from other disorders; in addition, eight of the MS patients (but none of the controls) were depressed before the onset of the neurological illness, arguing against a "reactive" hypothesis.

At least two other investigations (Dalos *et al.*, 1983; Feinstein *et al.*, 1993) have demonstrated that clinical exacerbations in MS have been associated with increased psychiatric morbidity, suggesting a primarily biological nature to the depression.

Schiffer (1987) studied 20 patients with MS and major depressive episodes and suggested that because he found the depression to be heterogeneous, there is probably not a single pathophysiological explanation, whether neurological (organic) or psychological ("reactive"). Devins and Sedland (1987) suggest other psychological responses to MS as important in the aetiology of the depression, including loss of control, general illness-related factors and a response to the personal intrusiveness of MS.

There have been several studies investigating psychopathology and magnetic resonance imaging (MRI) in patients with MS. One of the first was that of Honer *et al.* (1987) who studied eight MS cases with psychiatric disorders (six with affective disorders) and compared them to eight MS controls without psychiatric disorders. Family history was available for seven patients and none had a relative with a defined psychiatric disorder. In all cases the onset of the psychiatric disorder was coincident with or subsequent to the diagnosis of MS. Episodes of psychiatric disturbance did not consistently correlate with neurological exacerbations of MS. Cases had a larger number of clinical neurological sites involved and the psychiatric group had significantly more temporal lobe involvement on MRI (Honer *et al.*, 1987). In another investigation, those patients in whom increasing MRI abnormalities and relapses occurred during the study, showed an increase in their anxiety and depression; the authors commented that whether the worsening depression was due to an increasing lesion load or a subjective response to deterioration in physical well-being, or a combination of the two is difficult to discern (Feinstein *et al.*, 1993). In a careful MRI study, six out of 25 (24%) moderately disabled MS patients were diagnosed as suffering from depressive mood disorder. In correlational analysis, depression was unrelated to age, gender, duration of illness, status of disability, or the results of cognitive assessment; no relationship between the depression scores and the different MRI measures was identified (Moller *et al.*, 1994).

It is also worth noting that several cases have been documented where MS presented initially as a depressive illness (Young *et al.*, 1976; Goodstein and Ferrel, 1977; Salloway *et al.*, 1988) rather than with neurological signs, while in a study it has been shown that 16% of MS patients were referred for psychiatric treatment during the time between the onset of illness and their final diagnosis of MS (Skegg *et al.*, 1988).

A large study by Joffe and colleagues (1987), using many standardized psychiatric interview schedules and diagnostic criteria (e.g. Kurtzke Functional and Disability Scales for MS), reported a 72% incidence of psychiatric problems in 100 consecutive MS patients, the most common being depression (42%). Thirteen per cent fulfilled criteria for manic-depressive illness; this is significantly higher than the reported prevalence of 1% in the general population. There was no direct relationship between the degree of functional disability and clinical disorders of mood.

Finally, Schubert and Foliart (1993) undertook a meta-analysis of six controlled studies comparing depression in MS patients and in comparison groups. Overall, MS patients scored significantly higher on measures of depression than the comparison groups, which were primarily other chronic illness groups.

Treatment of depression in MS has not been widely studied. However, Larcombe and Wilson (1984) randomly allocated 20 depressed MS patients either to cognitive–behaviour therapy (CBT) or to a waiting list control condition. Results showed that CBT resulted in clinically and statistically significant improvement in the depression in these patients. Crawford and McIvor (1985) found that group psychotherapy was of value in treating patients with depression and MS. Finally, Schieffer and Wineman (1990) undertook the only double-blind antidepressant trial in 28 depressed patients with MS who were not receiving concurrent corticosteroid therapy. Fourteen were randomly assigned to a 5 week trial of desipramine and individual psychotherapy, and 14 to placebo plus psychotherapy. Patients treated with desipramine improved significantly more than the placebo group. Side-effects (e.g. postural hypotension, constipation, jitteriness, oedema, dizziness, rash) were a limiting factor in the treatment.

Patients with MS often complain of fatigue (which should be differentiated from depression), and the fatigue responds well to amantadine (Rosenberg and Appenzeller, 1988). It should also be noted that patients with MS may be taking tricyclic antidepressants (TCAs) for their bladder problems, and it may therefore be preferable to increase the dose of the TCA rather than introduce another antidepressant.

In summary, depression certainly appears to be more common in patients with MS when compared to control groups. The aetiology of the depression may well be multifactorial, with both organic and psychological factors being important. MRI studies are useful in the group, although whether or not depressed mood is associated with specific MRI changes is as yet uncertain; at least one study has hinted at temporal lobe involvement. Treatment of the depression should ideally include both psychotherapy and antidepressants, although side-effects with the TCAs may be a problem. It is therefore suggested that the newer specific serotonin reuptake inhibitors (SSRIs) may be more appropriately used in this group.

Epilepsy

A relationship between depression and epilepsy has been described since antiquity, when both Hippocrates (Lewis, 1934) and Areteus (Temkin, 1971) discussed a relationship between the two disorders. More recently, several authors from Griesinger in the 1850s to White, Barham, Baugh and Jones in the early 1900s have discussed melancholia interlinked with epilepsy (Robertson, 1988a,b).

Peri-ictal depression is not very common and, although only a few reports of this condition are available, lowered mood around seizures has been documented throughout the ages and can have serious sequelae such as attempted suicide. Prolonged depressive moods have been observed during status epilepticus, "petit mal" status, temporal lobe epilepsy (TLE) status, nonconvulsive status and partial seizure status (Robertson, 1992). The depression in these cases is secondary to organic brain disease (an ictal episode), and the management therefore should be directed at the treatment of the cause, namely ictal activity, with antiepileptic drugs (AEDs) being used.

Interictal depression is the most common and clinically important affective disorder in people with epilepsy (PWE). It has been demonstrated that 20% of TLE patients become moderately or severely depressed (Currie *et al.*, 1971), and that 62% of patients with medically intractable complex partial seizures (CPS) have had a history of depression, of whom 38% met criteria for major depressive illness (Victoroff *et al.*, 1990). Indaco *et al.* (1992) reported that no less than 50% of outpatients with epilepsy were depressed according to DSM criteria. Mendez *et al.* (1986) reported that the frequency of interictal depression in community-based PWE was greater than in a control population with similar socioeconomic and disability levels, suggesting that depression in PWE is more than a nonspecific reaction to a chronic disability.

Interictal depression prevalence can also be deduced from clinical observations as well as investigations into psychopathology in PWE using a variety of standardized psychiatric scales, all of which have demonstrated that depression is increased in PWE and is higher than in control populations, and several of which have found higher depression scores for patients with psychomotor or TLE compared to those with generalized seizures (see Robertson, 1988a,b, 1992). Dodrill and Batzell (1986) suggested that the number of seizure types was far more relevant to emotional or psychiatric problems in epilepsy than was the particular seizure type. Patients with TLE often have more than one seizure type and therefore as a consequence appear to be more maladjusted.

Many studies have explored specific aspects of interictal depression in PWE. Those using standardized rating scales have documented that the majority of individuals were rated as nonendogenous, the severity of the depression seems to be moderate to severe, and features of depression are high anxiety, neuroticism, hostility, sadness, obsessionalism, dependence, altered sexual interest, paranoia, irritability, humourlessness, an abnormal affect and hallucinations (Roy, 1979; Mendez *et al.*, 1986; Palia and Harper, 1986; Robertson *et al.*, 1987), while, in one series, 13 out of 66 were psychotic (Robertson *et al.*, 1987).

Depressed PWE have often also been reported to have had a significant past history of depression, deliberate drug overdosage, and self-harm (Roy, 1979; Palia and Harper, 1986; Robertson *et al.*, 1987) but not more so than a depressed group without epilepsy (Mendez *et al.*, 1986).

Several reports have indicated that a family history of depression or suicide is important in depressed PWE (Hancock and Bevilacqua, 1971; Brent *et al.*, 1987; Robertson *et al.*, 1987), while Mendez *et al.* (1986) failed to confirm this.

Gender may be important in the aetiology of depression in PWE. Depression in the general population is more common in women than men (Bird and Harrison, 1987) and in depressed PWE populations this has also been reported to be the case in some (Palia and Harper, 1986; Robertson *et al.*, 1987;

Hermann and Whitman, 1989) but not other investigations (Fenton, 1986; Mendez *et al.*, 1986), in which males predominated. Altschuler *et al.* (1990) found that a left temporal lobe depressed epileptic group (see below) had an insignificantly larger number of males and left-handed subjects. No sex differences for the occurrence of depression in PWE were reported by Victoroff *et al.* (1990).

Several psychosocial models of depression have been suggested (see Robertson, 1988b) and some of these may apply to PWE. Many have reported on the stigma and social prejudice to which PWE are subject, while others suggest they do not feel stigmatized (Robertson, 1988a,b). Several investigations have found that PWE have a substantial number of psychosocial problems at school, in emotional, interpersonal, vocational, and financial matters; they show an increase in stressful life events and family discord and also have problems coping with epileptic attacks; they have a poor adjustment to seizures, at least some of which stemmed from poor seizure control, caused by poor compliance with AED medication, lack of self-esteem, inability to accept a diagnosis of epilepsy or not being willing to disclose the fact of having epilepsy to others (Beran and Read, 1981; Danesi, 1984; Danesi *et al.*, 1981; Dodrill *et al.*, 1984a,b; Arntson *et al.*, 1986; Fenton, 1986; Hoare and Kerley, 1991). Many of these have been found specifically to relate to depression in PWE (Palia and Harper, 1986; Brent *et al.*, 1987; Hermann and Whitman, 1989). The case for epilepsy being a human analogue of the learned helplessness theory of depression (Seligman, 1975; Abramson *et al.*, 1978) has been argued eloquently by Hermann (1979). In a careful study, Hermann and Whitman (1989) showed that increased stressful life events, poor adjustment to seizures and financial stress were predictive of increased depression.

While several have noted a decrease in seizure frequency prior to the onset of the lowered mood (Dongier, 1959/60; Flor-Henry, 1969; Betts, 1974; Standage and Fenton, 1975), others found that depression was associated with an increase in seizures (Dodrill and Batzel, 1986; Fenton, 1986). The majority of investigations have, however, found that depressive symptomatology is not intimately related to epilepsy variables such as age of onset of epilepsy, the presence of an intracranial lesion, or seizure frequency (Mendez *et al.*, 1986; Robertson *et al.*, 1987, 1994; Roy, 1979; Hermann and Wyler, 1989; Trimble and Perez, 1982; Fralin *et al.*, 1987; Kramer *et al.*, 1987). However, complex partial seizures (CPS) and TLE (Mendez *et al.*, 1986; Robertson *et al.*, 1987) and, in particular, left-sided lesions (Nielsen and Kristensen, 1981; Perini *et al.*, 1983; Perini and Mendius, 1984; Palia and Harper, 1986; Mendez *et al.*, 1986; Robertson *et al.*, 1987; Altshuler *et al.*, 1990; Victoroff *et al.*, 1990; Strauss *et al.*, 1992; Seidenberg *et al.*, 1995) have been recently implicated in depression in PWE. In addition, the severity of the depression has been shown to correlate significantly with the duration of the epilepsy, and an association was found between CPS and a past history of depression (Robertson *et al.*, 1987).

The left side appears to be more implicated, but whether this is specific as suggested by some (Mendez *et al.*, 1986; Altshuler *et al.*, 1990; Victoroff *et al.*, 1990), or because the left hemisphere and frontotemporal areas seem particularly vulnerable as far as psychopathology is concerned, as evidenced by studies on head injury (Lishman, 1968) and stroke patients (Robinson *et al.*, 1984), or because, when focal abnormalities are found, foci on the left side appear to be more common (Scott, 1985), is, as yet, not certain.

Some investigators have found no associations between mood and AED medication (Mendez *et al.*, 1986; Altshuler *et al.*, 1990), but they are the exception, and many studies have found that AEDs affect the mental state of PWE. Several AEDs have been shown to be positively psychotropic. Thus, as early as 1971, carbamazepine (CBZ) was noted to have a psychotropic effect in PWE (Dalby, 1971). Since then, there have been many studies showing the psychotropic action of CBZ (Trimble *et al.*, 1980; Rodin and Schmaltz, 1984; Andrewes *et al.*, 1986; Robertson *et al.*, 1987; Post *et al.*, 1983a,b). Valproate (VPA) has been shown to be a useful adjunct in manic-depressive illness, depression and mania (Emrich *et al.*, 1984). A recent investigation has indicated that the new AED, lamotrigine, may well, in addition to alleviating seizures, have a positive psychotropic action as, when compared to placebo, scores on a Health-related Quality of Life model were higher for lamotrigine on the happiness and mastery scales (Smith *et al.*, 1993a,b). Phenobarbitone (PB), on the other hand, has been shown to affect mood adversely, being associated with depression, suicidal ideation and suicidal behaviour (Brent, 1986; Brent *et al.*, 1987, 1990; Robertson *et al.*, 1987; Smith and Collins, 1987; Barabas and Matthews, 1988; Victoroff *et al.*, 1990). Vigabatrin has also been noted to alter mood adversely (Ring and Reynolds, 1990, 1992; Ring *et al.*, 1990).

The treatment of interictal depressive phenomena should initially be directed towards the identification and possible cause. Thus, if a patient is undergoing a depressive reaction on acquiring the label of epilepsy, the support and help of a social worker who has knowledge of epilepsy and experience in its management can help the person "work through" his or her grief (Betts, 1981). Several studies have indicated that a high seizure frequency interferes with psychosocial functioning and may masquerade as depression. Behavioural methods of decreasing seizure frequency ought to be considered, using biofeedback techniques, operant conditioning, and relaxation (see Robertson, 1988a). Psychotherapy is important in the treatment of PWE with depression, especially when one considers the psychosocial causes of mood changes and the literature on stigma and epilepsy. One may opt for supportive therapy alone or a combination of formal psychotherapy (such as cognitive, interpersonal, or behavioural approaches) and antidepressants, which, as recently shown, is more effective than either treatment alone (see Robertson, 1988a). Assessment and rationalization of the patient's AED medication is also important, and improvement in the mental state of patients with a reduction of polypharmacy, and discontinuation with PB has been reported (Shorvon and Reynolds, 1979; Thompson and Trimble, 1982, 1983). If monotherapy is possible and all other factors, such as type of epilepsy, are taken into account, CBZ would seem the most appropriate AED.

What is the role of antidepressants in depressed PWE? Only two studies have looked at this. Ojemann *et al.*, (1983) conducted a retrospective case note study on 19 depressed PWE. The TCA doxepin given at a mean dose of 161 mg daily improved the depression; in addition, seizure frequency was reduced in the majority of patients, and increased in two. Robertson and Trimble (1985) conducted a double-blind placebo-controlled study on 42 depressed PWE assessing the efficacy and safety of the TCA, amitriptyline, and nomifensine. At 6 weeks the majority of patients responded significantly and there were no significant differences between the two drugs and placebo; at 12 weeks nomifensine was superior to amitriptyline. Of note is that there were no clinically significant differences in seizures between the drugs.

It is well known that virtually all non-monoamine oxidase inhibitor (MAOI) antidepressants lower the seizure threshold (Trimble, 1978). Medications most likely to be implicated with seizures are amoxapine, bupropion, chlomipramine, maprotiline, mianserin and trazodone, while the drugs which are less likely to be associated, and are therefore safer, are the MAOIs, doxepin, viloxazine, protriptyline, butriptyline, and the SSRIs fluoxetine, fluvoxamine, paroxetine and sertraline (Edwards, 1985; Edwards and Wheal, 1992; Rosenstein *et al.*, 1993). To the best of the author's knowledge, no seizures have been reported in association with the new MAOI (RIMA), moclobemide, which is safer than the "old" MAOIs, and this may well be the antidepressant of choice in depressed PWE. Moreover, it has been demonstrated that moclobemide is relatively free of psychomotor and cognitive impairment (Hindmarch and Kerr, 1992) which are characteristic of TCAs, and this is a further reason for prescribing moclobemide in these patients. Other nonsedating or less sedative antidepressants (e.g. the SSRIs) may also be of use, because most AEDs which the patient will be taking have sedative side-effects. Many clinicians, however, prefer to use antidepressants they know well, and commence with small doses, increasing the dose gradually (see Robertson, 1988a,b). One should discontinue the antidepressant if there is an increase in seizures, and the patient should be admitted to hospital if there is a resultant poor seizure control or a risk of status. One should also regularly monitor AED levels, as they are usually affected by antidepressants. For example, the effect of phenytoin may by increased by imipramine, nortryptiline and viloxazine (Perucca and Richens, 1977), while CBZ toxicity has been caused by viloxazine (Pisani *et al.*, 1984, 1986).

As suicide and parasuicide are common in PWE (Mackay, 1979; Barraclough, 1981; Matthews and Barabas, 1981), safer antidepressants in overdosage (e.g. SSRIs) should probably be used. Finally, ECT is particularly important to consider when suicide is a real danger or in cases of severe paranoid agitation, in which the patient's seizure frequency appears to have diminished prior to the onset of the depression. Paradoxically, some of these patients appear to have a particularly high seizure threshold during the administration of ECT (see Robertson, 1988a,b). Finally, as the relationship between depression and epilepsy is complex, the treatment, which can also be complex, is best handled by someone well versed in both disorders.

Headache

Not only is headache very common, but also there are many types of headaches including chronic tension-type headache (CTTH), episodic tension-type headache, chronic daily headache (CDH), migraine, drug-induced headache, cluster headache (chronic or episodic), idiopathic stabbing headache, headache associated with structural lesions, headache associated with metabolic disorder, trigeminal neuralgia and temporal arteritis, the latter two of which may present as facial pain (Solomon *et al.*, 1992; Feinmann and Peatfield, 1993; Sanin *et al.*, 1994), and chronic post-traumatic headache (Duckro *et al.*, 1995). In one large study embracing 400 patients attending a headache clinic, patients were classified according to the International Headache Society (IHS) headache classification (Headache Classification Committee of the IHS, 1988). Results showed that the majority had more than two types of headache; even though migraine was the most common diagnosis, only 25% of those with a migraine diagnosis had it as the only diagnosis. Thirty-seven per cent of patients suffered from CDH (Sanin *et al.*, 1994).

The relationship between headache and depression is undisputed, but there has been controversy as to whether this relationship reflects pathology which pre-existed the headache disorder, the consequences of living with chronic pain, or the contribution to both pain and depression resulting from deficient levels of brain serotonin (5-hydroxytryptamine (5-HT)) and/or other neurotransmitters (Kaiser, 1992).

Although there is much written about depression and headache, and depression has been included as a criterion for the diagnosis or definition of, for example, tension-type headache (Pfaffenrath *et al.*, 1994), the clearest evidence appears to be for an association between migraine and depression, based on clinical, epidemiological and familial association studies (Glover *et al.*, 1993; Breslau *et al.*, 1994; Devlen, 1994; Merikangas, 1994). Indeed, the low 5-HT levels in migraine and depression have attracted much attention (Glover *et al.*, 1993), but differences between migraine and depression have also been noted, especially the brief and self-limiting nature of migraine attacks, and, as part of the migraine cascade occurs outside the blood–brain barrier, migraine attacks can be ameliorated by drugs which only act peripherally (Glover *et al.*, 1993). Although most of the literature on headache and depression concerns adult patients, it is important to know that headache and depression have also been associated in both children (Ling *et al.*, 1970) and adolescents (Kaiser, 1992).

The treatment of headache can be with analgesics (Feinmann and Peatfield, 1993), and indeed, some people with headaches overuse analgesics (Solomon *et al.*, 1992). Cluster headaches respond to verapamil, corticosteroids, or lithium; trigeminal neuralgia usually responds to carbamazepine; temporal arteritis responds to corticosteroids (Feinmann and Peatfield, 1993). Migraine can be treated with anti-inflammatory analgesics, dihydroergotamine, metoclopramide, sumatriptan, propanolol, butorphanol, domperidone, pizotifen or VPA (Feinmann and Peatfield, 1993; Silberstein, 1994).

However, partly because of the association between depression and headache, antidepressants have often been used in patients with headache. For example, the TCA amitriptyline was, for many years, considered the drug of first choice in the therapy of CTTH (Lance and Curran, 1964; Diamond and Baltes, 1971), and the efficacy of antidepressants in CTTH (even without depressive symptoms) has been thought to be due to their analgesic properties, which are based on an inhibition of the 5-HT reuptake centrally, presynaptically, as well as peripherally in platelets. Other antidepressants used successfully in headache include amitriptylinoxide (Pfaffenrath *et al.*, 1994) and phenelzine (Turkewitz *et al.*, 1992), while sulpiride, a neuroleptic, has also been used with good effect (Langemark and Olesen, 1994). Bearing in mind that the new SSRIs are more 5-HT specific than the older TCAs, and that 5-HT has been involved in both headache and migraine, it is perhaps not surprising that the SSRIs fluoxetine (Adly *et al.*, 1992; Saper *et al.*, 1994) and fluvoxamine (Bank, 1994; Manna *et al.*, 1994) have both been used successfully in both migraine and CTTH, while paroxetine (Foster and Bafaloukos, 1994) has been successful in chronic daily headache.

LOCALIZED DISORDERS

Parkinson's disease

Parkinson's disease (PD) is one of the most common neurological disorders of later life with an estimated prevalence of around 1%. The classic neurological manifestations are a pill-rolling tremor, rigidity and hypokinesia resulting in poverty of movement (akinesis/bradykinesis) leading to slowness in initiating movement; numerous other symptoms may also occur and include ocular–motor abnormalities, postural changes, flexed posture, festinant gait, excessive salivation, seborrhoea, constipation, subjective sensory disturbance and marked fatigue (Lishman, 1987). Cummings (1992) notes that despite dramatic advances being made in the field (e.g. transplantation of foetal tissue into the basal ganglia which may permanently ameliorate the motor disability (Lindvall and

Bjorklund, 1989; Lindvall *et al.*, 1989), many aspects of PD, including the psychobehavioural manifestations, remain ill-understood.

Psychiatric sequelae are common in PD and fall into four main groups:

1. Cognitive decline (global dementia, focal cognitive deficits, drug-induced confusional states, depression-related cognitive difficulties).
2. Affective disorders (depressive symptoms, depressive illness meeting diagnostic criteria).
3. Psychotic (depressive psychosis, drug-induced psychosis) (Ring, 1993).
4. Changes in personality or personality traits (Todes and Lees, 1985).

Depression was first noted by Parkinson himself in his initial description of the disease, when he described a particular patient; "a previously sanguine man ... now dejected and melancholic" (Mayeux, 1990). Today, an association between PD and depression is well established, but it is unclear to what extent the depression is reactive to a serious disabling illness, or whether it is an integral part of the disease process. This has been comprehensively reviewed by Brown and Marsden (1984), Mayeux (1990), Ring and Trimble (1991) and, more recently, by both Cummings (1992) and Ring (1993); the descriptions of depression will be collated from these, unless otherwise individually referenced.

Reviewing 26 previous studies, Cummings (1992) reported a mean rate of depression of 40% (range 4–70%). Some of these utilized the Beck Depression Inventory (BDI) to measure depression, but this method has been criticized because the scale contains somatic items such as "motor slowing" which may also be part of the motor disorder itself. A more recent study by Dooneief *et al.* (1992) found an inception rate for depression of 1.86% per year in PD subjects.

It has been suggested that there are three types of depression encountered in PD. Around one-half of those with depression satisfy criteria for major depression, while slightly less than one-half qualify for dysthymia (minor depression). A third, atypical depression, has been described (e.g. Schiffer *et al.*, 1988), characterized by anxiety and panic disorder. There are two aetiological models regarding the depression of PD: firstly, that it is "reactive" to the physical disability, and, secondly, that it is "endogenous", i.e. independent of the physical handicap. It is of interest that minor depression and dysthymia are more closely related to the motor state of PD and also more likely to remit. A study by Robins (1976) compared a group of age- and sex-matched patients who also had severe disabling disease (hemiplegia, paraplegia, arthritis) and found higher rates of depression among the PD patients than among controls, suggesting that the depression might be a more integral part of the PD disease process (endogenous) rather than simply being reactive to the disability. Mayeux and colleagues (1981) found that about one-quarter of depressed PD patients were depressed before the onset of motor manifestations.

The depression in PD patients shows some phenomenological differences from primary major depression. In PD there are high levels of dysphoria, anxiety and pessimism concerning the future, as well as irritability, sadness and suicidal ideation. However, guilt, self-reproach, delusions or hallucinations are less common. Despite a high rate of suicidal ideation, completed suicide appears to be rare. Risk factors for depression include female gender, a past personal history of depression (but not a family history of depression), bradykinesis, gait instability (rather than tremor-dominant syndromes), a greater degree of left brain involvement and an earlier age of onset of the PD (but not current age). The course of the depression has received little attention, but suffice it to say that patients with PD can be broadly divided into two groups, one with and one without mood changes, and the groups are relatively stable over time.

The aetiology of the depression of PD is unknown, but it is tempting to speculate on the role of brain monoamines, as both disorders are thought to result from a functional deficiency of central monoamines particularly dopamine (DA) and serotonin (5-HT). The depression seen in PD may be a predictor of future dementia (Stern *et al.*, 1993), and patients with PD and depression show a greater intellectual decline (Starkstein *et al.*, 1989), with particular problems in frontal lobe tasks (Cooper *et al.*, 1991; Ring, 1993).

Mayeux (1990) suggests that the aetiology of depression in PD is multi-factorial. The same degenerative process which affects the DA system and causes the motor manifestations may affect the 5-HT system in PD; added risk factors of advanced age, poor health and disability may also precipitate the depressed mood. He suggests that the most likely explanation is an interaction between the two factors (i.e. the degenerative process added to the risk factors).

It is worth noting that several antiparkinsonian medications (e.g. amantadine, bromocriptine, carbidopa, levodopa) may also precipitate depression (Wise and Taylor, 1990). When managing the depression, therefore, manipulation of these agents may be an initial step. Thereafter, standard antidepressive remedies such as the TCAs and ECT appear to be effective in treating the depression (see Cummings, 1992). Anderson *et al.* (1980) reported the successful use of nortriptyline in treating depression in 19 PD patients in a double-blind placebo-controlled trial, all of whom were also receiving L-dopa; the PD symptoms, however, did not respond. Mayeux *et al.*, (1988) documented the successful use of the 5-HT precursor 5-hydroxytryptophan (5-HTP) in treating depression in PD patients. The SSRIs have also been shown to be useful in depression in PD patients (Mayeux, 1990). Paroxetine may be particularly useful in those patients who have depression associated with panic disorder (Oehrberg *et al.*, 1995). ECT may alleviate not only the depression, but sometimes also the motor symptoms of the PD (Lebensohn and Jenkins, 1975; Abrams, 1989). It should be noted that MAOIs are absolutely contraindicated during treatment with levodopa or carbidopa–levodopa (Silver *et al.*, 1990).

In summary, it would appear that depression in PD is common, but that the true incidence and prevalence are not known. The relationship between the two disorders is complex, with many factors being suggested as aetiologically significant. There appear to be phenomenological differences between the depression seen in PD and major depression. The treatment of the depression may first involve manipulation of the anti-PD drugs, followed by, in most cases, the prescribing of traditional antidepressants, with possibly the SSRIs being particularly useful.

Depressive psychosis, usually as a side-effect of medication, is relatively common in PD. Its management involves manipulation of anti-PD drugs, and may eventually require either ECT, or a combination of antidepressants and antipsychotics. If the latter is necessary, clozapine, an antipsychotic without extrapyramidal adverse effects, may prove useful.

Huntington's disease

Huntington's disease (HD) is characterized by abnormal choreiform involuntary movements, psychiatric disturbances such as changes in behaviour and personality, cognitive impairment, or frank dementia (Hayden, 1981). it is inherited as an autosomal dominant condition, linked to a polymorphic DNA marker that maps to human chromosome 4 (Gusella *et al.*, 1983), although a new mutation has been suggested (Wolff *et al.*, 1989).

Psychiatric syndromes are widely recognized in HD, and even Huntington (1872) included in his original description a "tendency to that insanity that leads to suicide". A classic study of the psychosocial sequelae of HD is that of Dewhurst *et al.* (1970), documenting a nonspecific psychiatric prodromal illness which usually precedes the movement disorder; the psychiatric symptoms are often the presenting features and attempted suicide also occurs in HD. Di-Maio *et al.* (1993a) studied 2793 subjects with HD to evaluate the risk of suicide in them and family members; suicide was the reported cause of death in 205 subjects (7.3%) which included those affected and those at risk; this rate is considerably higher than in the USA general population. The authors suggested that this increased suicide risk must be carefully considered in planning genetic counselling for predictive testing in HD (see below).

Affective disorder, especially depressive psychoses, schizophreniform psychoses, and changes of personality occur in HD and can lead to misdiagnosis. It has been suggested that depression associated with HD may differ neurochemically from that seen in major depression and that this has a specific relationship to HD, rather than being a nonspecific prodromal feature of dementia (for review see Robertson, 1990). Peyser and Folstein (1990) report that depression occurs in 38%, while mania only occurs in 10% of patients with HD. In addition, affective disorders can occur 20 years before neurological signs, are not randomly distributed, but occur in a subset of HD families

(Peyser and Folstein, 1990). A study conducted on 510 HD patients demonstrated that the most frequent psychiatric onset symptom was depression, with stressful life events reported in 43% of patients (Di-Maio *et al.*, 1993b).

Folstein (1991) notes that HD can cause psychiatric disorder in two ways: first by the direct action of the gene on striatal neurones, and secondly by the indirect effects of the disordered family environment on the children, regardless of whether or not they have inherited the HD gene (see below).

The dementia of HD coined "subcortical dementia" by McHugh and Folstein (1975) is characterized by poor cognitive function, slowing of mental operations, and decline in memory function, but with no dysfunction of language (aphasia) or focal deficits of perception (agnosia and apraxia). It has also been noted that many patients with HD have insight into their intellectual impairment. Initially, the dementia may therefore masquerade as depression, but later on when the patient is more demented (and has insight) he or she may become "reactively" depressed.

There is no treatment for HD itself, and therefore treatment is symptomatic. Traditional antidepressants (TCAs and SSRIs) and neuroleptics (with less side-effects and safe in overdose) should be considered if necessary; clozapine, an atypical neuroleptic with less extrapyramidal side-effects, may be useful in the associated psychoses (Sajatovic *et al.*, 1991).

In summary, a variety of psychiatric manifestations may occur in HD, but depression seems to be particularly common. The depression may, moreover, be neurochemically different from primary major depressive illness. Suicide and attempted suicide are also common in patients with HD, and this should be borne in mind both when considering genetic testing and prescribing antidepressants.

Gilles de la Tourette syndrome

Gilles de la Tourette syndrome (GTS) is a movement disorder characterized by both multiple motor tics and one or more vocal tics (noises) (ICD-10, WHO, 1992; DSM-IV, APA, 1994). GTS, once thought to be a rarity, is found in all cultures, presenting with similar clinical characteristics. The exact prevalence of GTS is unknown, but the generally accepted figure is 0.5/1000 (approximately 110 000 patients in the USA and 25 000 in the UK). The majority of studies agree that it occurs 1.5–3 times more commonly in males and it is found in all social classes (Robertson, 1989, 1994; APA, 1994). The age of onset of symptoms ranges from 2 to 15 years, with a mean of 7 years being most common.

Associated behaviours and psychopathology of GTS include obsessive–compulsive behaviours (OCB) (Robertson, 1995) and attention deficit hyperactivity disorder (Robertson and Eapen, 1992) as well as affective disorders (depression and anxiety).

Controlled studies have shown increased rates of depression when compared to controls (Robertson *et al.*, 1993). Depression is more severe among those with a longer history of GTS (Robertson *et al.*, 1988), suggesting that it may possibly be reactive to having a chronic disabling and stigmatizing disorder (Robertson, 1994).

The treatment of the depression in GTS is by the use of standard anti-depressants, but, as suicide has been reported in this population (Robertson *et al.*, 1995), and GTS patients may be impulsive (Comings, 1990), it is suggested that antidepressants safer in overdose are preferred. In addition, the SSRIs can be used to treat the OCB aspects of the syndrome. Thus, as the depression and OCB can co-occur in many patients, it may be wise to prescribe an SSRI as the antidepressant of choice.

Hepatolenticular degeneration (Wilson's disease)

Hepatolenticular degeneration (also known as Wilson's disease (WD)) is an uncommon (estimated incidence about 30 per million) inborn error of metabolism, transmitted by an autosomal recessive gene, and characterized by an accumulation of copper in liver, brain, kidney, cornea and bone. It was originally described by Wilson (1912) who recognized both hepatic and neuro-logical involvement, as well as the familial nature of the disorder. Martin (1968) suggested that WD could be divided into two types; a juvenile form with an onset between 7 and 15 years, and a late form, which usually begins around the age of 30. Psychiatric manifestations can occur in both types, but the psychoses usually occur with the latter type. Kayser–Fleischer rings (characteristic, visible deposits of copper in the eye) are usually, but not always, associated with neurological damage (Willeit and Kiechl, 1991).

Psychiatric symptoms usually appear late in the disease, but can precede neurological and hepatic signs and symptoms in about 20%. Psychiatric aspects of 649 WD patients were reviewed by Dening (1985), who identified four symptom clusters in 170 individuals who displayed psychiatric symptoms (26%). The two most common were affective symptomatology (e.g. emotional lability and incongruity, and clinical pictures resembling a depressive neurosis or bipolar manic depressive disorder), and behavioural/personality changes (e.g. aggression, childish self-destructive or antisocial activities, along with schizoid, hysterical and psychopathic personality traits) (Dening, 1985).

Akil *et al.* (1991) reviewed the case records of 42 WD patients and inter-viewed 17. Five patients were asymptomatic, 65% reported psychiatric symptoms at the time of initial presentation, severe enough to warrant psychia-tric intervention in almost half, before the diagnosis of WD was made (Akil *et al.*, 1991). Personality changes, particularly irritability and aggression, were most common (45.9%), followed by depression (27%). Cognitive changes, anxiety, psychoses and catatonia, while less frequent, also occurred (Akil *et al.*, 1991).

Oder *et al.* (1991) studied WD patients ($N=45$) and found that psychiatric symptoms and behavioural disorders were common, varying from mild personality and psychological disturbances to severe psychiatric illness (major affective syndromes and schizophreniform psychoses). Disturbances of mood were observed in 27%, all of whom had neurological abnormalities. There was a history of attempted suicide in 16% of patients, and a history of organic delusional syndrome in 7%.

Dening and Berrios (1989) assessed psychiatric symptoms in 195 WD cases retrospectively and found that 99 patients (51%) had some psychopathology, and 39 (20%) had seen a psychiatrist before the diagnosis of WD. The most common psychiatric features were abnormal behaviour and personality change, although depression and cognitive impairment were also rated frequently (Dening and Berrios, 1989).

Treatment of WD itself is essential and there are several "anti-copper" drugs such as dimercaprol (Peters *et al.*, 1945) and penicillamine (Walshe, 1956), which probably remains the treatment of choice. Once WD is being treated with, say, penicillamine, the treatment of the affective disorder is with traditional antidepressants, using medications with less side-effects.

Spasmodic torticollis

Spasmodic torticollis (ST) is the most common focal dystonia (Fahn *et al.*, 1987), caused by involuntary contractions of the neck muscles resulting in abnormal postures and/or involuntary movements of the head, leading to a "wry neck" (neck and head rotated and twisted laterally). Although patients with ST find it very distressing, it was previously thought that these patients suffered no increase of formal psychiatric illness (Sheehy and Marsden, 1982). More recently, several groups have found that obsessive–compulsive symptoms (OCS) and depression are more common in ST patients (Jahanshahi, 1991; Bihari *et al.*, 1992). Moreover, Jahanshahi and Marsden (1988, 1992) reported that symptomatic improvement of ST with botulinum toxin injection was associated with a significant reduction of depression, suggesting that the depression is a consequence of the postural abnormality. Thus, if a patient with ST is depressed, treatment of the ST itself may ameliorate the depression. Alternatively, traditional antidepressants may be prescribed, avoiding those with side-effects, particularly of the dystonic variety.

Myaesthenia gravis

There have been several case reports in the literature of an association between myaesthenia gravis (MG) and depression (Bernstein *et al.*, 1973; Hescheles and Kavanagh, 1976; Sternbach, 1991; Pande and Grunhaus, 1990; Junger and Wright, 1990) and bipolar illness (Stewart and Naylor, 1990).

However, the few studies in the area have not consistently shown increased depression.

Iwasaki *et al.* (1993) compared five female MG patients with controls on a variety of standardized measures and found that the MG patients were significantly more depressed than the controls.

In a controlled study, however, Tennant *et al.* (1986) suggested that trait anxiety and supression of anger may predispose to MG, but there was no association with depression. They assessed 31 MG patients and 31 matched normal controls on a range of psychological indices and found that there was no increased depression in the MG patients (Tennant *et al.*, 1986). Rohr (1992) reported that retrospectively, 20% of more than 200 MG patients (mean duration 10 years) reported being initially diagnosed as having a psychiatric disorder. Younger women were significantly most at risk of a psychiatric misdiagnosis, whereas men were more often subject to somatic misdiagnoses. In addition, the misdiagnoses coincided with higher depression scores. Depression was also related to the dosage of anticholinesterase medication as well as to the self-reported muscular weakness (Rohr, 1992). Rohr (1993) subsequently examined 240 MG patients and found that those with facial muscular symptoms had high scores on measures of social phobia, but not depression.

Treatment of the depressed MG patient might prove problematic, especially with the TCA antidepressants, which could theoretically worsen MG by aggravating the cholinergic deficiency. Nevertheless, successful treatment of depression in MG patients has been reported with TCAs (Sternbach, 1991), as well as with ECT (Pande and Grunhaus, 1990) and plasma exchange (Iwasaki *et al.*, 1993). There have been no documentations of the treatment of depression in MG with the newer antidepressants (e.g. SSRIs) and these may well prove useful.

DISCRETE DISORDERS

Cerebrovascular accident (stroke)

Stroke has an annual incidence in Britain of approximately 200 cases for every 100 000 population, and a prevalence of about 500 for every 100 000 (Wade *et al.*, 1985). Kraepelin (1921) was one of the first clinicians to note an association between depression and stroke. Thereafter, it was acknowledged not only that mood disorder may be a specific complication of stroke (Folstein *et al.*, 1977), but also that depression is recognized to be the most commonly reported poststroke psychiatric condition (Burvill *et al.*, 1995). Despite agreement on an increased risk of mood disorder following stroke, there remains some uncertainty on its aetiology and management (Eastwood *et al.*, 1989). Review of the literature suggests, moreover, that the relationship between stroke and depression is complex.

There are several classic reviews (House, 1987; Starkstein and Robinson, 1989; 1993) and investigations (Robinson and Coyle, 1980; Robinson and Szetela, 1981; Robinson and Price, 1982; Robinson *et al.*, 1984; House *et al.*, 1989; Sharpe *et al.*, 1990) on mood disorders after stroke, and especially poststroke depression (PSD). An attempt will be made to examine the conclusions of these, as well as to review more recent studies, and to offer some suggestions as to the mechanisms and management of depression in this population.

Many investigations have indicated that depression is common after stroke, and quoted rates of PSD have ranged from 18% to 61% (House, 1987), with up to as many as 50% of stroke patients developing depression during the acute poststroke period; among outpatient stroke populations, the prevalence of depression is around 30% (Starkstein and Robinson, 1989). The discrepant and varying figures quoted have arisen for a variety of reasons, including the different settings from which the patients have been derived (with selection bias towards inpatients and long-term outpatients), small numbers of subjects, the use of different and at times ill-defined selection criteria, different assessment instruments, uncertainty of the methods used to measure psychiatric symptoms and the failure to use control groups (Burvill *et al.*, 1995).

Astrom *et al.* (1993) undertook a 3 year longitudinal study of poststroke patients, and demonstrated that the prevalence of major depression was 25% at the acute stage, and approximately the same (31%) at 3 months, decreasing to 16% at 12 months, plateauing at 19% at 2 years, and increasing to 29% at 3 years. The most important predictors of immediate major depression were left anterior brain lesion, dysphasia and living alone. Dependence in activities of daily living was the most important predictor at 3 months. From 12 months on few social contacts outside the immediate family contributed most to depression, and at 3 years, cerebral atrophy also contributed. At 1 year, 60% of the patients with early depression (0–3 months) had recovered, and those who had not recovered at that follow up ran a high risk of development of chronic depression (Astrom *et al.*, 1993). This suggests that contributions from biological, psychological and social factors interact in the development and maintenance of PSD. Other risk factors for PSD include a history of previous psychiatric and cerebrovascular disorder (Eastwood *et al.*, 1989).

A carefully performed population-based study (Burvill *et al.*, 1995), employing recognized standardized psychiatric measures and encompassing 294 patients, reported that 9% of male and 13% of female patients examined had evidence of depression at the time of the stroke. The prevalence of depression 4 months after stroke was 23% (18–28%), with 15% (11–19%) major depression and 8% (5–11%) minor depression. There were no significant differences between the sexes or between patients with first-ever or recurrent strokes. Twelve months after stroke 56% of men continued to be depressed (40% major and 16% minor depression), as were 30% of women (12% major and 18% minor depression).

The early seminal investigations by Robinson and his coworkers (Robinson and Coyle, 1980; Robinson and Szetela, 1980; Robinson and Price, 1982; Robinson *et al.*, 1980, 1982, 1984) documented an association between depression and *left* frontal lesions, as demonstrated by computerized topography (CT). The Robinson group has, moreover, latterly consistently reported a significant association between major depression and left hemisphere anterior lesions involving cortical (mostly frontal) and subcortical (mainly basal ganglia) areas (see Starkstein and Robinson, 1993). These findings have been replicated/ supported by some (Eastwood *et al.*, 1989; Astrom *et al.*, 1993; Hermann *et al.*, 1995) but not all authors (House *et al.*, 1991; Sharpe *et al.*, 1990; Folstein *et al.*, 1977). Folstein *et al.* (1977) have, on the other hand, reported a relationship between depression and *right* hemisphere lesions. The Robinson group (Starkstein *et al.*, 1987) furthermore reported that the severity of the depression was significantly correlated with the proximity of the lesion to the frontal pole. On the other hand, the same authors (Paradiso *et al.* in Starkstein and Robinson, 1996) recently reported that dysthymia in the acute poststroke period was significantly correlated with proximity of the lesion to the occipital pole in the left hemisphere. One study demonstrated that psychiatric symptom scores were greater with larger volume brain lesions (Sharpe *et al.*, 1990). These findings show that although there is some evidence that PSD (major) is associated with left hemisphere anterior lesions, not all studies have shown this. There are many reasons for this including, for example, neuroimaging methods employed, differing definitions of depression (major versus minor), depressive symptomatology rather than depression, time after stroke, duration of the depression and factors considered above (e.g. Burvill *et al.*, 1995).

Several studies have also examined associated psychiatric features of patients with PSD. In a community study, with a non-hierarchic approach to diagnosis of those with depression, 26% of men and 39% of women had an anxiety disorder, mainly agoraphobia (Burvill *et al.*, 1995). Another community-based study reported that anxiety disorders, especially agoraphobia, were relatively common (20% if diagnosed in the presence of depression) but were not related to lesion location or volume (Sharpe *et al.*, 1990).

Although both social and physical disability after stroke have also been implicated in the aetiology of the PSD (Robinson *et al.*, 1984; Ebrahim *et al.*, 1987; Wade *et al.*, 1987), the majority of studies have consistently found that the severity of depression is not closely related to the severity of physical impairment (see Starkstein and Robinson, 1989).

In conclusion, it would appear that the aetiology of PSD is multifactorial, including the actual cerebral insult, psychological and social factors (e.g. living alone, social network) and a history of both previous psychiatric disorder and previous stroke.

A wide variety of treatment strategies have been reported as useful in PSD including nortriptyline (Lipsey *et al.*, 1984; Lazarus *et al.*, 1994), trazodone

(Reding *et al.*, 1986), methylphenidate (Lingam *et al.*, 1988; Lazarus *et al.*, 1994), ECT (Murray *et al.*, 1986) and both group (Oradei *et al.*, 1974) and family (Watziawick and Coyne, 1980) psychotherapy. Finkelstein *et al.* (1987) conducted a retrospective case note review of PSD patients and showed that those patients who responded well to antidepressants were those who were prescribed significantly larger doses of medication for a longer period of time than those who failed to respond. It has also been noted, however, that care needs to be taken in prescribing antidepressants because blood concentrations may be unpredictable in the elderly (Carr and Hobson, 1977). Lazarus *et al.* (1994) compared nortriptyline and methylphenidate in a retrospective case note study and found that response rate and side-effects were similar. Patients, however, responded to methylphenidate much more rapidly (2.4 days) than to nortriptyline (27 days) and the authors therefore suggested that methylphenidate may be particularly useful in this group (Lazarus *et al.*, 1994). The present author, however, notes that potential problems which may arise with long-term methylphenidate ingestion include addiction, psychosis and weight loss. While discussing treatment in this group, it may be wise to note that MAOIs may be particularly dangerous in poststroke patients because of the dangers of a tyramine-induced hypertensive crisis and further strokes (Silver *et al.*, 1990). There has been one study to date investigating the treatment of PSD. Andersen *et al.* (1994) treated 66 consecutive patients with PSD using citalopram and placebo, under double-blind conditions: citalopram was significantly superior to placebo and was well-tolerated. This suggests that the SSRIs with their relative lack of serious side-effects (particularly sedation) may well be the agents of choice.

While discussing the management of PSD, it would be prudent to note that rehabilitation has been recommended as the most effective treatment of the depression in at least four studies (see Eastwood *et al.*, 1989). Such rehabilitation needs to be combined with reassurance, advice and education for both patient and family (House, 1987).

GENERAL CONCLUSIONS AND GUIDELINES FOR TREATMENT

There is no doubt that depression is common in neurological disorders although the exact prevalence is unknown in the majority of disorders. In general, it would appear that depression is more common in patients with neurological disorders than in the general population, although to the best of the author's knowledge there are no studies comparing the relative prevalence/ incidence in the various disorders. Of importance is that the depression may be missed, undiagnosed, and thus, not treated. In many of the neurological disorders suicide and attempted suicide are also more common than in the general population. It appears that, in general, the aetiology of the depression is complex with both "organic" and "reactive" or psychological mechanisms being involved. Iatrogenic factors include the depression encountered in people with epilepsy, being particularly associated with antiepileptic drugs such as phenobarbitone.

The treatment of depression can be complex and it is generally advisable for someone with a specialist interest to manage depressed neurological patients. However, there are general guidelines which may be adhered to.

Silver *et al.* (1990) have reviewed the relevant literature. In general, they suggest that neurological patients who exhibit or complain of depressed mood, have somatic symptoms of depression and those who have problems with motivation or difficulties in rehabilitation, should receive a therapeutic trial of antidepressants. In addition, they suggest that, by and large, the choice of anti-depressant should depend primarily on the side-effect profile. Thus, those antidepressants with the fewest sedative, hypotensive and anticholinergic side-effects are preferable. For example, nortriptyline (with few anticholinergic effects and a low liability to cause orthostatic hypotension) may be started at a dose of 10 mg per day and increased by 10 mg every 3 days. Ideally, they recommend that antidepressant plasma levels should be monitored. Should the patient become severely hypotensive, confused or sedated, the dose of anti-depressant should be reduced. Finally, antidepressant medication should be continued for at least 6 months after clinical improvement is observed (Silver *et al.*, 1990). In the same study, the authors also note that the SSRI fluoxetine does not have any anticholinergic properties and therefore it may not produce the cognitive problems which may occur with the TCAs.

It is suggested by the present author that SSRIs in general (fluoxetine, fluvox-amine, paroxetine, sertraline, citalopram) may well be useful in treating depres-sion in neurological patients because of their side-effect profile (Montgomery *et al.*, 1994; Hindmarch, 1995) and safety in overdose, although no trials are known indicating superiority of any particular agent. Other new agents with side-effect profiles different to those of the traditional TCAs may also be useful in depressed neurological patients, and these include the TCA, lofepramine, and the serotonin and noradrenaline reuptake inhibitor (SNRI) venlafaxine. In addition, the RIMA, moclobemide, has been shown to be free of adverse behavioural effects (Hindmarch and Kerr, 1992) and may be useful in this group, especially in depressed people with epilepsy.

Stimulants such as methylphenidate or dextroamphetamine can be used in neurological patients who require a rapid antidepressant effect or when they are unable to tolerate traditional heterocyclic antidepressants (Silver *et al.*, 1990). The present author is more cautious, however, noting the potential problems of long-term methylphenidate ingestion such as addiction, psychosis and severe weight loss.

ECT is a highly effective and underutilized modality in the treatment of depression in neurological patients. Silver *et al.* (1990) report that the nondominant unilateral ECT, with 2–3 days in between each treatment and fewer treatments in the course (4–6), results in improvement of depressive symptoms without major memory side-effects.

Finally, psychotherapy for both the patient and carers may well be of added help. Specific psychotherapies have proved useful in some disorders (e.g. cognitive–behaviour therapy in people with epilepsy and multiple sclerosis), while support and reassurance are often useful as adjuncts to pharmacological measures in many depressed neurological patients.

REFERENCES

Abrams R (1989) ECT for Parkinson's disease. *Am J Psychiatry*, **146**, 1391–1393.

Abramson LY, Seligman MEP and Teasdale JD (1978) Learned helplessness in humans: critique and reformulation. *J Abnorm Psychol*, **87**, 49–74.

Adly C, Staumanis J and Chesson A (1992) Fluoxetine prophylaxis of migraine. *Headache*, **32(2)**, 101–104.

Akil M, Schwatz JA, Dutchak D, Yuzbasiyan Gurkan B and Brewer GJ (1991) The psychiatric presentations of Wilson's disease. *J Neuropsychiatry Clin Neurosci*, **3(4)**, 377–382.

Altshuler LL, Devinsky O, Post RM and Theodore W (1990) Depression, anxiety, and temporal lobe epilepsy. Laterality of focus and symptoms. *Arch Neurol*, **47**, 284–288.

American Psychiatric Association (1994) *Diagnostic and Statistical Manual of Mental Disorders* (4th edition) (DSM IV). Washington DC: American Psychiatric Association.

Andersen G, Vestergaard K and Lauritzen L (1994) Effective treatment of poststroke depression with the selective serotonin reuptake inhibitor citalopram. *Stroke*, **25(6)**, 1099–1104.

Anderson J, Aabro E, Gulmann N *et al.* (1980) Anti-depressive treatment in Parkinson's disease: a controlled trial of the effect of nortriptyline in patients with Parkinson's disease treated with L-dopa. *Acta Neurol Scand*, **62**, 210–219.

Andrewes DG, Bullen JD, Tomlinson L, Elwes RDC and Reynolds EH (1986) A comparative study of the cognitive effects of phenytoin and carbamazepine in new referrals with epilepsy. *Epilepsia*, **27**, 128–134.

Arntson P, Droge D, Norton R and Murray E (1986) The perceived psychosocial consequences of epilepsy. In: S Whitman and BP Hermann (eds) *Psychopathology in Epilepsy: Social Dimensions*. New York: Oxford University Press, 143–161.

Astrom M, Adolfsson R and Apslund K (1993) Major depression in stroke patients. *Stroke*, **24**, 976–982.

Bank J (1994) A comparative study of amitriptyline and fluvoxamine in migraine prophylaxis. *Headache*, **34**, 476–478.

Barabas G and Matthews WS (1988) Barbiturate anticonvulsants as a cause of severe depression. *Pediatrics*, **82**, 284–285.

Baretz RM and Stephenson GR (1981) Emotional responses to multiple sclerosis. *Psychosomatics*, **22**, 117–127.

Barraclough B (1981) Suicide and epilepsy. In: EH Reynolds and MR Trimble (eds) *Epilepsy and Psychiatry*. Edinburgh: Churchill Livingstone, 72–76.

Beran RG and Read T (1981) Patient perspectives of epilepsy. *Clin Exp Neurol*, **17**, 56–69.

Bernstein AE, Flegenheimer W and Roose LJ (1973) Transference and counter-transference problems in a critically ill patient. *Psychiatry Med*, **4(2)**, 191–199.

Betts TA (1974) A follow-up study of a cohort of patients with epilepsy admitted to psychiatric care in an English city. In: P Harris and C Mawdsley (eds) *Epilepsy: Proceedings of the Hans Berger Centenary Symposium*. Edinburgh: Churchill Livingstone, 326–338.

Betts TA (1981) Depression, anxiety and epilepsy. In: EH Reynolds and MR Trimble (eds) *Epilepsy and Psychiatry*. Edinburgh: Churchill Livingstone, 60–71.

Bihari K, Hill JL and Murphy DL (1992) Obsessive–compulsive characteristics in patients with idiopathic spasmodic torticollis. *Psychiatry Res*, **42(3)**, 267–272.

Bird JM and Harrison G (1987) *Examination Notes in Psychiatry*. Bristol: Wright.

Braceland FJ and Giffen ME (1950) The mental changes associated with multiple sclerosis (an interim report). *Res Publ Assoc Res Nerv Ment Dis*, **28**, 450–455.

Brent DA (1986) Overrepresentation of epileptics in a consecutive series of suicide attempters seen at a children's hospital. *J Am Acad Child Psychiatry*, **25**, 242–246.

Brent DA, Crumrine PK, Varma RR, Allan M and Allman C (1987) Phenobarbital treatment and major depressive disorder in children with epilepsy. *Pediatrics*, **80**, 909–917.

Brent DA, Crumrine PK, Varma K, Brown RV and Allan MJ (1990) Phenobarbital treatment and major depressive disorder in children with epilepsy: A naturalistic follow-up. *Pediatrics*, **85(6)**, 1086–1091.

Breslau N, Davis GC, Schultz LR and Peterson EL (1994) Migraine and major depression: a longitudinal study. *Headache*, **34**, 387–393.

Bridges KW and Goldberg DP (1984) Psychiatric illness in inpatients with neurological disorders: patients' views on discussion of emotional problems with neurologists. *Br Med J*, **289**, 656–658.

Brown S and Davis TK (1922) The mental symptoms of multiple sclerosis. *Arch Neurol Psychiatry*, **7**, 629–634.

Brown RG and Marsden CD (1984) How common is dementia in Parkinson's disease? *Lancet*, **ii**, 1262–1265.

Burvill GA, Johnson GA, Jamrozik KD, Anderson CS, Stewart-Wynne EG and Chakera TMH (1995) Prevalence of depression after stroke: the Perth community stroke study. *Br J Psychiatry*, **166**, 320–327.

Carr AC and Hobson RP (1977) High serum concentrations of antidepressants in elderly patients. *Br Med J*, **ii**, 1151.

Charcot JM (1881) Disseminated sclerosis: its symptomatology. G Sigerson (transl). London: New Sydenham Society, 2.

Comings DE (1990) *Tourette Syndrome and Human Behavior*. Duarte California: Hope Press.

Cooper JA, Sagar HJ, Jordan N, Harvey NS and Sullivan EV (1991) Cognitive impairment in early, untreated Parkinson's disease and its relationship to motor disability. *Brain*, **114(5)**, 2095–2122.

Cottrell SS and Wilson SA (1926) The affective symptomatology of disseminated sclerosis. *J Neurol Psychopathol*, **7**, 1–20.

Crawford JD and McIvor GP (1985) Group psychotherapy: Benefits in multiple sclerosis. *Arch Phys Med Rehab*, **66**, 810–813.

Creed F, Firth D, Timol M, Metcalfe R and Pollock S (1990) Somatization and illness behaviour in a neurology ward. *J Psychsom Res*, **34(4)**, 427–437.

Cummings JL (1992) Depression and Parkinson's disease: A review. *Am J Psychiatry*, **149(4)**, 443–454.

Currie S, Heathfiled KWG, Henson RA and Scott DF (1971) Clinical course and prognosis of temporal lobe epilepsy. A survey of 666 patients. *Brain*, **94**, 173–190.

Dalby MA (1971) Antiepileptic and psychotropic effect of carbamazepine (Tegretol) in the treatment of psychomotor epilepsy. *Epilepsia*, **12**, 325–334.

Dalos NP, Rabins PV, Brooks BR and O'Donnell P (1983) Disease activity and emotional state in multiple sclerosis. *Ann Neurol*, **13**, 573–577.

Danesi MA (1984) Patient perspectives on epilepsy in a developing country. *Epilepsia*, **25**, 184–190.

Danesi MA, Odusote KA, Roberts OO and Adu EO (1981) Social problems of adolescent and adult epileptics in a developing country, as seen in Lagos, Nigeria. *Epilepsia*, **22(6)**, 689–696.

Dening TR (1985) Psychiatric aspects of Wilson's disease. *Br J Psychiatry*, **147**, 677–682.

Dening TR and Berrios GE (1989) Wilson's disease. Psychiatric symptoms in 195 cases. *Arch Gen Psychiatry*, **46(12)**, 1126–1134.

DePaulo JR and Folstein MF (1978) Psychiatric disturbances in neurological patients: Detection, recognition and hospital course. *Ann Neurol*, **4**, 225–228.

DePaulo JR, Folstein MF and Gordon B (1980) Psychiatric screening on a neurological ward. *Psychol Med*, **10**, 125–132.

Devins GM and Sedland TP (1987) Emotional impact of MS: recent findings and suggestions for future research. *Psychol Bull*, **101**, 363–375.

Devlen J (1994) Anxiety and depression in migraine. *J Soc Med*, **87**, 338–341.

Dewhurst K, Oliver JE and McKnight LA (1970) Socio-psychiatric consequences of Huntington's disease. *Br J Psychiatry*, **116**, 255–258.

Di Maio L, Squitieri F, Napolitano G, Campanella G, Trofatter JA and Conneally PM (1993a) Suicide risk in Huntington's disease. *J Med Genet*, **30(4)**, 293–295.

Di Maio L, Squitieri F, Napolitano G, Campanella G, Trofatter JA and Conneally PM (1993b) Onset symptoms in 510 patients with Huntington's disease. *J Med Genet*, **30(4)**, 289–292.

Diamond S and Baltes BJ (1971) Chronic tension headache treated with amitriptyline—a double blind study. *Headache*, **11**, 110–116.

Dodrill CB and Batzel LW (1986) Inter-ictal behavioural features of patients with epilepsy. *Epilepsia*, **27: Suppl 2**, S64–S76.

Dodrill CB, Breyer DN, Diamond MB, Dubinsky BL and Geary BB (1984a) Psychosocial problems among adults with epilepsy. *Epilepsia*, **25**, 168–175.

Dodrill CB, Beier R, Kasparick M, Tacke I, Tacke U and Tan S Y (1984b) Psychosocial problems in adults with epilepsy: Comparison of findings from four countries. *Epilepsia*, **25**, 176–183.

Dongier S (1959/60) Statistical study of clinical and electroencephalographic manifestations of 536 psychotic episodes occurring in 516 epileptics between clinical seizures. *Epilepsia*, **1**, 117–142.

Dooneief G, Mirabello E, Bell K, Marder K, Stern Y and Mayeux R (1992) An estimate of the incidence of depression in idiopathic Parkinson's disease. *Arch Neurol*, **49(3)**, 305–307.

Duckro PN, Chibnall JT and Tomaxic TJ (1995) Anger, depression and disability: a pathway analysis of relationships in a sample of chronic posttraumatic headache patients. *Headache*, **35**, 7–9.

Eastwood MR, Rifat SL, Nobbs H and Ruderman J (1989) Mood disorder following cerebrovascular accident. *Br J Psychiatry*, **154**, 195–200.

Ebrahim S, Barer D and Nouri F (1987) Affective illness after surgery. *Br J Psychiatry*, **151**, 52–56.

Edwards JG (1985) Antidepressants and seizures: Epidemiological and clinical aspects. In: MR Trimble (ed) *The Psychopharmacology of Epilepsy*. Chichester: Wiley, 119–139.

Edwards JG and Wheal HV (1992) Assessment of epileptogenic potential: experimental, clinical and epidemiological approaches. *J Psychopharmacol*, **6(2)**, 204–213.

Emrich HM, Dose M and von Zerssen D (1984). Action of sodium valproate and of oxcarbazepine in patients with affective disorders. In: HM Emrich, T Okuma and AA Muller (eds) *Anticonvulsants in Affective Disorders*. Amsterdam: Excerpta Medica, 45–55.

Fahn S, Marsden CD and Calne DB (1987) Classification and investigation of dystonia. In: CD Marsden and S Fahn (eds) *Movement Disorders 2*. London: Butterworths, 332–358.

Feinmann C and Peatfield R (1993) Orofacial neuralgia: diagnosis and treatment guidelines. *Drugs*, **49(2)**, 263–268.

Feinstein A, Ron M and Thompson A (1993) A serial study of psychometric and magnetic resonance imaging changes in multiple sclerosis. *Brain*, **116**, 569–602.

Fenton GW (1986) Minor psychiatric morbidity in people with epilepsy: evidence for a gender difference. Presented at the Annual Meeting of the Royal College of Psychiatrists, Southampton, United Kingdom, 8–10 July, 1986.

Finkelstein S, Weintraub RJ, Karmouz N *et al.* (1987) Antidepressant drug treatment for poststroke depression: retrospective study. *Arch Phys Med Rehabil*, **68**, 772–776.

Flor-Henry P (1969) Psychosis and temporal lobe epilepsy: a controlled investigation. *Epilepsia*, **10**, 363–395.

Folstein MF, Maiberger R and McHugh PR (1977) Mood disorder as a specific complication of stroke. *J Neurol Neurosurg Psychiatry*, **40**, 1018–1022.

Folstein SE (1991) The psychopathology of Huntington's disease. *Res Publ Assoc Res Nerv Ment Dis*, **69**, 181–191.

Foster CA and Bafaloukos J (1994) Paroxetine in the treatment of chronic daily headache. *Headache*, **34(10)**, 587–589.

Fralin C, Kramer LD, Berman NG and Locke GE (1987) Interictal depression in urban minority epileptics. *Epilepsia*, **28**, 598.

Glover V, Jarman J and Sandler M (1993) Migraine and depression: biological aspects. *J Psychiatry Res*, **27**, 223–231.

Goodstein RK and Ferrel RB (1977) Multiple sclerosis presenting as depressive illness. *Dis Nerv System*, **38**, 127–131.

Gusella JF, Wexler NS, Conneally PM, Naylor SL, Anderson MA, Tanzi RE, Watkins PL, Ottina K, Wallace MR, Sakuguchi AY, Young AB, Shoulson I, Bonilla E and Martin JB (1983) A polymorphic DNA marker genetically linked to Huntington's disease. *Nature*, **306**, 234–283.

Hancock JC and Bevilacqua AR (1971) Temporal lobe dysrhythmia and impulsive or suicidal behavior: preliminary report. *South Med J*, **64(10)**, 1189–1193.

Hayden MR (1981) *Huntington's Chorea*. New York: Springer.

Headache Classification Committee of the International Headache Society (1988) Classification and diagnostic criteria for headache disorders, cranial neuralgias and facial pain. *Cephalalgia*, **7(Suppl 8)**, 1–96.

Hermann BP (1979) Psychopathology in epilepsy and learned helplessness. *Med Hypotheses*, **5**, 723–729.

Hermann BP and Whitman S (1989) Psychosocial predictors of interictal depression. *J Epilepsy*, **2**, 231–237.

Hermann BP and Wyler AR (1989) Depression, locus of control, and the effects of epilepsy surgery. *Epilepsia*, **30**, 332–338.

Hermann M, Bartels C, Schumacher M and Wallesch CW (1995) Poststroke depression: Is there a pathoanatomic correlate for depression in the postacute stage of stroke? *Stroke*, **26**, 850–856.

Hescheles D and Kavanagh T (1976) Technical eclecticism and open-case consultation: a psychotherapeutic training model. *Psychol Rep*, **39(3:2)**, 1043–1046.

Hindmarch I (1995) The behavioural toxicity of the selective serotonin reuptake inhibitors. *Int Clin Psychopharmacol*, **9(Suppl)**, 13–17.

Hindmarch I and Kerr J (1992) Behavioural toxicity of antidepressants with particular reference to moclobemine. *Psychopharmacology (Berlin)*, **106(Suppl)**, 49–55.

Hoare P and Kerley S (1991) Psychosocial adjustment of children with chronic epilepsy and their families. *Dev Med Child Neurol*, **33**, 201–215.

Honer WG, Hurwitz T, Li DKB, Palmer M and Paty DW (1987) Temporal lobe involvement in multiple sclerosis patients with psychiatric disorders. *Arch Neurol*, **44**, 187–190.

Hopkins A, Menken M and DeFriese (1989) A record of patient encounters in neurological practice in the United Kingdom. *J Neurol Neurosurg Psychiatry*, **52**, 436–438.

House A (1987) Depressed after stroke. *Br Med J*, **294**, 76–78.

House A, Dennis M, Molyneux A, Warlow C and Hawton K (1989) Emotionalism after stroke. *Br Med J*, **298**, 991–994.

House A, Dennis M, Mogridge L, Warlow C, Hawton K and Jones L (1991) Mood disorders in the year after first stroke. *Br J Psychiatry*, **158**, 83–92.

Huntington G (1872) On chorea. *Medical and Surgical Reporter*, **26**, 317–321.

Indaco A, Carrieri PB, Nappi C, Gentile S and Striano S (1992) Interictal depression in epilepsy. *Epilepsy Res*, **12**, 45–50.

Iwasaki Y, Kinoshita M, Ikeda K, Shiojima T and Kurihara T (1993) Neuropsychological function before and after plasma exchange in myasthenia gravis. *J Neurol Sci*, **114(2)**, 223–226.

Jahanashahi M (1991) Psychosocial factors and depression in torticollis. *J Psychosom Res*, **35(4–5)**, 493–507.

Jahanshahi M and Marsden CD (1988) Depression in torticollis: a controlled study. *Psychol Med*, **18**, 925–933.

Jahanashahi M and Marsden CD (1992) Psychological functioning before and after treatment of torticollis with botulinum toxin. *J Neurol Neurosurg Psychiatry*, **55(3)**, 229–231.

Joffe RT, Lippert GP, Gray TA, Sawa G and Horvath Z (1987) Mood disorder and multiple sclerosis. *Arch Neurol*, **44**, 376–378.

Junger SS and Wright RB (1990) Dysphagia due to a pharyngeal mucocoele mimicking myasthenia. *J Neurol Neurosurg Psychiatry*, **53(3)**, 268.

Kahana E, Leibowitz U and Alter M (1971) Cerebral multiple sclerosis. *Neurology*, **21**, 1179–1185.

Kaiser RS (1992) Depression in adolescent headache patients. *Headache*, **32**, 340–344.

Kellner CH, Davenport Y and Post RM (1984) Rapidly cycling bipolar disorder and multiple sclerosis. *Am J Psychiatry*, **141**, 112–113.

Kemp K, Lion JR and Magram G (1977) Lithium in the treatment of a manic patient with multiple sclerosis: A case report. *Dis Nerv System*, **38**, 210–211.

Kirk C and Saunders M (1977) Primary psychiatric illness in a neurological outpatient department in north-east England. *J Psychosom Res*, **21**, 1–5.

Kirk CA and Saunders M (1979) Psychiatric illness in a neurological out-patient department in north-east England. *Acta Psychiatr Scand*, **60**, 427–437.

Kraepelin E (1921) *Manic-Depressive Insanity and Paranoia*. Edinburgh: E and S Livingstone.

Kramer LD, Fralin C, Berman NG and Locke GE (1987) Relationship of seizure frequency and interictal depression. *Epilepsia*, **28**, 629.

Lance JW and Curran DA (1964) Treatment of chronic tension headache. *Lancet*, **1**, 1236–1239.

Langemark M and Olesen J (1994) Sulpiride and paroxetine in the treatment of chronic tension-type headache. An explanatory double-blind trial. *Headache*, **34**, 20–24.

Larcombe NA and Wilson PH (1984) An evaluation of cognitive-behaviour therapy for depression in patients with multiple sclerosis. *Br J Psychiatry*, **145**, 366–371.

Lazarus LW, Moberg PJ, Langsley PR and Lingam VR (1994) Methylphenidate and nortriptyline in the treatment of poststroke depression: a retrospective comparison. *Arch Phys Med Rehabil*, **75**, 403–406.

Lebensohn ZM and Jenkins RB (1975) Improvement of parkinsonism in depressed patients treated with ECT. *Am J Psychiatry*, **132**, 283–285.

Lewis AJ (1934) Melancholia: a historical review. *J Ment Sci*, **80**, 1–42.

Lindvall O and Bjorklund A (1989) Transplantation strategies in the treatment of Parkinson's disease: experimental basis and clinical trials. *Acta Neurol Scand*, **126(Suppl)**, 197–210.

Lindvall O, Rehncroma S, Brundin P *et al.* (1989) Human fetal dopamine neurons grafted into the striatum in two patients with severe Parkinson's disease. A detailed methodology and a 6-month follow-up. *Arch Neurol*, **46(6)**, 615–631.

Ling W, Oftedal G and Weinberg W (1970) Depressive illness in childhood presenting as severe headache. *Am J Dis Child*, **120**, 122–124.

Lingam VR, Lazarus LW, Groves L and Oh SH (1988) Methylphenidate in treating poststroke depression. *J Clin Psychiatry*, **49**, 151–153.

Lipsey JR, Robinson RG, Pearlson GD *et al.* (1984) Nortriptyline treatment of poststroke depression: a double blind study. *Lancet*, **1**, 297–300.

Lishman WA (1968) Brain damage in relation to psychiatric disability after head injury. *Br J Psychiatry*, **114**, 373–410.

Lishman WA (1987) *Organic Psychiatry. The Psychological Consequences of Cerebral Disorder*. Oxford: Blackwell Scientific.

Mace CJ and Trimble MR (1991) "Hysteria", "functional" or "psychogenic"? A survey of British neurologists' preferences. *J R Soc Med*, **84**, 471–475.

Mackay A (1979) Self-poisoning—a complication of epilepsy. *Br J Psychiatry*, **134**, 277–282.

Manna V, Bolino F and Di Cicco L (1994) Chronic tension-type headache, mood depression and serotonin: therapeutic effects of fluvoxamine and mianserine. *Headache*, **34**, 44–49.

Matthews WS and Barabas G (1981) Suicide and epilepsy. A review of the literature. *Psychosomatics*, **22**, 515–524.

Mayeux R (1990) Depression in the patient with Parkinson's disease. *J Clin Psychiatry*, **51(7 suppl)**, 20–23.

Mayeux RM, Stern Y, Rosen J *et al.* (1981) Intellectual impairment and Parkinson's disease. *Neurology*, **31**, 645–650.

Mayeux R, Stern Y, Sano M *et al.* (1988) The relationship of serotonin to depression in Parkinson's disease. *Mov Disord*, **3**, 237–244.

McHugh PR and Folstein MF (1975) Psychiatric syndromes of Huntington's chorea. In DF Benson and D Blumer (eds) *Psychiatric Aspects of Neurologic Disease*. New York: Grune and Stratton, 267–285.

McNamara ME (1991) Psychological factors affecting neurological conditions: Depression and stroke, multiple sclerosis, Parkinson's disease and epilepsy. *Psychosomatics*, **32**, 255–267.

Melvor GP, Riklan M and Reznikoff M (1984) Depression in multiple sclerosis as a function of length and severity of illness, age, remissions, and perceived social support. *J Clin Psychol*, **40**, 1028–1033.

Mendez MF, Cummings JL and Benson DF (1986) Depression in epilepsy. *Arch Neurol*, **43**, 766–770.

Merikangas KR (1994) Psychopathology and headache syndromes in the community. *Headache*, **34**, S17–S26.

Metcalfe R, Firth D, Pollock S and Creed F (1988) Psychiatric morbidity and illness behaviour in female neurological inpatients. *J Neurol Neurosurg Psychiatry*, **51**, 1387–1390.

Moller A, Wiedemann G, Rohde U, Backmund H and Sonntag A (1994) Correlates of cognitive impairment and depressive mood disorder in multiple sclerosis. *Acta Psychiatr Scand*, **89**, 117–121.

Montgomery SA, Henry J, McDonald G, Dinan T, Lader M, Hindmarch I, Clare A and Nutt D (1994) Selective serotonin reuptake inhibitors: meta-analysis of discontinuation rates. *Int Clin Psychopharmacol*, **9(1)**, 47–53.

Murray GB, Shea V and Conn DK (1986) Electroconvulsive therapy for poststroke depression. *J Clin Psychiatry*, **47**, 258–260.

Nielsen H and Kristensen O (1981) Personality correlates of sphenoidal EEG-foci in temporal lobe epilepsy. *Acta Neurol Scand*, **64**, 289–300.

Oder W, Grimm G, Kollegger H, Ferenci P, Schnedier B and Deecke L (1991) Neurological and neuropsychiatric spectrum of Wilson's disease: a prospective study of 45 cases. *J Neurol*, **238(5)**, 281–287.

Oehrberg S, Christiansen PE, Behnke K, Borup AL, Severin B, Soegarrd J, Calberg H, Judge R, Ohrstrom JK and Manniche PM (1995) Paroxetine in the treatment of panic disorder: a randomised, double-blind, placebo-controlled study. *Br J Psychiatry*, **167**, 374–379.

Ojemann LM, Friel PN, Trejo WJ and Dudley DL (1983) Effect of doxepin on seizure frequency in depressed epileptic patients. *Neurology*, **33**, 646–648.

Oradei DM and Wahe NS (1974) Group psychotherapy with stroke patients during the immediate recovery phase. *Am J Orthopsychiatry*, **44**, 386–390.

Palisa SS and Harper MA (1986) Mood disorders in epilepsy: A survey of psychiatric patients. Presented at the Annual Meeting of the Royal College of Psychiatrists. The University of Southampton, UK, 8–10 July 1986.

Pande AC and Grunhaus LJ (1990) ECT for depression in the presence of myasthenia gravis. *Convulsive Ther*, **6(2)**, 172–175.

Perini G and Mendius R (1984) Depression and anxiety in complex partial seizures. *J Nerv Ment Dis*, **172**, 287–290.

Perini G, Suny MD and Mendius R (1983) Interictal emotions and behavioural profiles in left and right temporal lobe epileptics. *Psychosom Med*, **45**, 1, 83.

Perucca E and Richens A (1977) Interaction between phenytoin and imipramine. *Br J Clin Pharmacol*, **4**, 485–486.

Peselow ED, Deutsch SI and Fieve RR (1981) Coexistent manic symptoms and multiple sclerosis. *Psychomatics*, **22**, 824–825.

Peters RA, Stocken LA and Thompson RHS (1945) British antilewisite (BAL). *Nature (London)*, **15**, 656.

Peyser CE and Folstein SE (1990) Huntington's disease as a model for mood disorders. Clues from neuropathology and neurochemistry. *Mol Chem Neuropathol*, **12(2)**, 99–119.

Pfaffenrath V, Diener H-C, Isler H, Meyer C, Scholz E, Taneri Z, Wessely P and Zaiser-Kaschel H (1994) Efficacy and tolerability of amitriptylinoxide in the treatment of chronic tension-type headache: a multi-centre controlled study. *Cephalalgia*, **14**, 149–155.

Pisani F, Narbone MC, Fazio A *et al.* (1984) Effect of viloxazine on serum carbamazepine levels in epileptic patients. *Epilepsia*, **25**, 482–485.

Pisani F, Fazio A, Oteri G *et al.* (1986) Carbamazepine–viloxazine interaction in patients with epilepsy. *J Neurol Neurosurg Psychiatry*, **49**, 1142–1145.

Post RM, Uhde TW, Ballenger JC, Chatterji DC, Greene RF and Bunney WE Jr (1983a) Carbamazepine and its 10,11-epoxide metabolite in plasma and CSF. *Arch Gen Psychiatry*, **40**, 673–676.

Post RM, Uhde TW, Ballenger JC and Squillace KM (1983b) Prophylactic efficacy of carbamazepine in manic-depressive illness. *Am J Psychiatry*, **140**, 1602–1604.

Purdon Martin J (1968) Wilson's disease In: PJ Vinken and GW Bruyn (eds) *Diseases of the Basal Ganglia. Handbook of Clinical Neurology*. Vol 6. Amsterdam: North-Holland. 267–277.

Reding MJ, Orto LA, Winter SW *et al.* (1986) Antidepressant therapy after stroke: a double blind trial. *Arch Neurol*, **43**, 763–765.

Ring H (1993) Psychological and social problems of Parkinson's disease. *Br J Hosp Med*, **49(2)**, 111–116.

Ring HA and Reynolds EH (1990) Vigabatrin and behaviour disturbance. *Lancet*, **335**, 970.

Ring HA and Reynolds EH (1992) Vigabatrin. In TA Pedley and BS Meldrum (eds) *Recent Advances in Epilepsy* (5th edn). Edinburgh: Churchill Livingstone, 177–195.

Ring HA and Trimble MR (1991) Affective disturbance in Parkinson's disease. *Int J Geriatric Psychiatry*, **6**, 385–393.

Ring HA, Heller AJ, Farr IN and Reynolds EH (1990) Vigabatrin: rational treatment for chronic epilepsy. *J Neurol Neurosurg Psychiatry*, **53**, 1051–1055.

Robertson MM (1988a) Depression in patients with epilepsy reconsidered. In: TA Pedley and BS Meldrum (eds) *Recent Advances in Epilepsy*, Vol 4. Edinburgh: Churchill Livingstone, 205–240.

Robertson MM (1988b) Epilepsy and mood. In: MR Trimble and EH Reynolds (eds) *Epilepsy, Behaviour and Cognitive Function*. Chichester: Wiley, 145–157.

Robertson MM (1989) The Gilles de la Tourette syndrome: The current status. *Br J Psychiatry*, **154**, 147–169.

Robertson MM (1990) The psychiatric aspects of movement disorders. *Curr Opin Psychiatry*, **3**, 83–89.

Robertson MM (1992) Affect and mood in epilepsy: an overview with a focus on depression. *Acta Neurol Scand*, **86 (Suppl)**, 127–132.

Robertson MM (1994) Gilles de la Tourette syndrome: an update. *J Child Psychol Psychiatry*, **35**, 597–611.

Robertson MM (1995) The relationship between Gilles de la Tourette syndrome and obsessive–compulsive disorder. *J Serotonin Res*, **Suppl 1**, 49–62.

Robertson MM and Eapen V (1992) Pharmacologic controversy of CNS stimulants in Gilles de la Tourette's syndrome. *Clin Neuropharmacol*, **15**, 408–425.

Robertson MM and Trimble MR (1985) The treatment of depression in patients with epilepsy: a double-blind trial. *J Affect Disord*, **9**, 127–136.

Robertson MM, Trimble MR and Townsend HRA (1987) The phenomenology of depression in epilepsy. *Epilepsia*, **28**, 364–372.

Robertson MM, Trimble MR and Lees AJ (1988) The psychopathology of the Gilles de la Tourette syndrome: A phenomenological analysis. *Br J Psychiatry*, **152**, 383–390.

Robertson MM, Channon S, Baker JE and Flynn D (1993) The psychopathology of Gilles de la Tourette syndrome: A controlled study. *Br J Psychiatry*, **162**, 114–117.

Robertson MM, Channon S and Baker J (1994) Depressive symptomatology in a general hospital sample of outpatients with temporal lobe epilepsy: A controlled study. *Epilepsia*, **35(4)**, 771–777.

Robertson MM, Eapen V and van de Wetering BJM (1995) Suicide in Gilles de la Tourette's syndrome: Report of two cases. *J Clin Psychiatry*, **56(8)**, 378.

Robins AH (1976) Depression in patients with parkinsonism. *Br J Psychiatry*, **128**, 141–145.

Robinson RG and Coyle JT (1980) The differential effect of right versus left hemispheric cerebral infarction on catecholamines and behaviour in the rat. *Brain Res*, **188**, 63–78.

Robinson RG and Price TR (1982) Post-stroke depressive disorders: A follow-up study of 103 patients. *Stroke*, **13(5)**, 635–641.

Robinson RG and Szetala B (1981) Mood change following left hemisphere brain injury. *Ann Neurol*, **9**, 447–453.

Robinson R, Coyle JT and Szetela B (1980) Mood change following left hemisphere brain injury. *Ann Neurol*, **9**, 447–454.

Robinson RG, Coyle JT and Price TR (1982) Post-stroke depressive disorders: a follow-up study of 103 patients. *Stroke*, **13**, 635–641.

Robinson RG, Coyle JT, Starr LB and Price TR (1984) A two-year longitudinal study of mood disorders following stroke: prevalence and duration at 6 months follow-up. *Br J Psychiatry*, **144**, 256–262.

Rodin E and Schmaltz S (1984) The Bear–Fedio personality inventory and temporal lobe epilepsy. *Neurology*, **34**, 591–596.

Rohr W (1992) Myasthenia gravis in the frontier of psychiatric diagnosis. *Psychiatr Praxis*, **19(5)**, 157–163.

Rohr W (1993) Situational anxiety in myasthenia gravis. *Psychother Psychosom Med Psychol*, **43 (3–4)**, 93–99.

Ron MA (1995) Affective disorders in neurological practice. Glaxo Wellcome Lecture Series, 22nd November 1995. The National Hospital For Neurology and Neurosurgery, Queen Square.

Rosenberg GA and Appenzeller O (1988) Amantadine, fatigue, and multiple sclerosis. *Arch Neurol*, **45**, 1104–1106.

Rosenstein DL, Nelson JC and Jacobs SC (1993) Seizures associated with antidepressants: a review. *J Clin Psychiatry*, **54**, 289–299.

Roy A (1979) Some determinants of affective symptoms in epileptics. *Can J Psychiatry*, **24**, 554–556.

Sajatovic M, Verbanac P, Ramirez LF and Meltzer HY (1991) Clozapine treatment of psychiatric symptoms resistant to neuroleptic treatment in patients with Huntington's chorea. *Neurology*, **41(1)**, 156.

Salloway S, Price LH, Charney DS and Shapiro M (1988) Multiple sclerosis presenting as major depression: A diagnosis suggested by MRI scan but not CT scan. *J Clin Psychiatry*, **49**, 364–366.

Sanin LC, Mathew NT, Bellmeyer LR and Ali S (1994) The International Headache Society (IHS) headache classification as applied to a headache clinic population. *Cephalalgia*, **14**, 443–446.

Saper JR, Silberstein SD, Lake AE and Winters ME (1994) Double-blind trial of fluoxetine: chronic daily headache and migraine. *Headache*, **34(9)**, 497–502.

Schiffer RB, Wineman NM and Weitkamp LR (1986) Association between bipolar affective disorder and multiple sclerosis. *Am J Psychiatry*, **143**, 94–95.

Schiffer RB (1983) Psychiatric aspects of clinical neurology. *Am J Psychiatry*, **140**, 205–207.

Schiffer RB (1987) The spectrum of depression in multiple sclerosis. *Arch Neurol*, **44**, 596–599.

Schiffer RB and Wineman NM (1990) Antidepressant pharmacotherapy of depression associated with multiple sclerosis. *Am J Psychiatry*, **147**, 1493–1497.

Schiffer RB, Kurlan R, Rubin A and Boer S (1988) Evidence for atypical depression in Parkinson's disease. *Am J Psychiatry*, **145**, 1020–1022.

Schofield A and Duane MMA (1987) Neurologic referrals to a psychiatric consultation liaison service. *Gen Hosp Psychiatry*, **9**, 280–286.

Schubert DSP and Foliart RH (1993) Increased depression in multiple sclerosis patients. *Psychosomatics*, **34, no 2**, 124–129.

Scott DF (1985) Left and right cerebral hemisphere differences in the occurrence of epilepsy. *Br J Med Psychol*, **58**, 189–192.

Seidenberg M, Hermann B, Noe A and Wyler AR (1995) Depression in temporal lobe epilepsy: interaction between laterality of lesion and Wisconsin Card Sort Performance. *Neuropsychiatry, Neuropsychol Behav Neurol*, **8(2)**, 81–87.

Seligman MEP (1975) *Helplessness: On Depression, Development and Death*. San Francisco: WH Freeman.

Sharpe M, Hawton K, House A, Molyneux A, Sandercock P, Bamford J and Warlow C (1990) Mood disorders in long-term survivors of stroke: associations with brain lesion and volume. *Psychol Med*, **20**, 815–828.

Sheehy MP and Marsden CD (1982) Writers' cramp—a focal dystonia. *Brain*, **105(Pt 3)**, 461–480.

Shorvon SD and Reynolds EH (1977) Unnecessary polypharmacy for epilepsy. *Br Med J*, **i**, 1635–1637.

Shorvon S and Reynolds EH (1979) Reduction in polypharmacy for epilepsy. *Br Med J*, **2**, 1023–1025.

Silberstein SD (1994) Treatment of the migraine attack. *Curr Opin Neurol*, **7(3)**, 258–263.

Silver JM, Hales RE and Yudofsku SC (1990) Psychopharmacology of depression in neurologic disorders. *J Clin Psychiatry*, **51**, 33–39.

Skegg K, Corwin PA and Skegg DC (1988) How often is multiple sclerosis mistaken for a psychiatric disorder? *Psychol Med*, **18**, 733–736.

Smith DB and Collins JB (1987) Behavioral effects of carbamezepine, phenobarbital, phenytoin and primidone. *Epilepsia*, **28**, 598.

Smith D, Chadwick D, Baker G, Davis G and Dewey M (1993a) Seizure severity and the quality of life. *Epilepsia*, **34 (Suppl 5)**, S31–S35.

Smith DB, Baker G, Davies G, Dewey M and Chadwick DW (1993b) Outcomes of add-on treatment with Lamotrigine in partial epilepsy. *Epilepsia*, **34 (2)**, 312–322.

Solomon S, Lipton RB and Newman LC (1992) Clinical features of chronic daily headache. *Headache*, **32**, 325–329.

Standage KF and Fenton GW (1975) Psychiatric symptom profiles of patients with epilepsy: a controlled investigation. *Psychol Med*, **5**, 152–160.

Starkstein SE and Robinson RG (1989) Affective disorders and cerebral vascular disease. *Br J Psychiatry*, **154**, 170–182.

Starkstein SE and Robinson RG (1993) *Depression in Neurologic Disease*. Baltimore: The Johns Hopkins University Press.

Starkstein SE and Robinson RG (1996) Co-morbidity of dysthymia and neurological disorders. *World Health Organisation Neuroscience Series* (in press).

Starkstein SE, Preziosi RJ, Berthier ML, Bolduc PL, Mayberg HS and Robinson RG (1989) Depression and cognitive impairment in Parkinson's disease. *Brain*, **112**, 114–115.

Stern Y, Richards M, Sano M and Mayeux R (1993) Comparison of cognitive changes in patients with Alzheimer's and Parkinson's disease. *Arch Neurol*, **50(10)**, 1040–1045.

Sternbach H (1991) Depression misdiagnosed as neuromuscular disease: Case reports and review. *Ann Clin Psychiatry*, **3(1)**, 37–41.

Stewart JB and Naylor GJ (1990) Manic-depressive psychosis in a patient with mitochondrial myopathy: A case report. *Med Sci Res*, **18(7)**, 265–266.

Strauss E, Wada J and Moll A (1992) Depression in male and female subjects with complete partial seizures. *Arch Neurol*, **49(4)**, 391–392.

Surridge D (1969) An investigation into some psychiatric aspects of multiple sclerosis. *Br J Psychiatry*, **115**, 749–764.

Temkin O (1971) *The Falling Sickness* (2nd edn revised). Baltimore: Johns Hopkins Press.

Tennant CC, Wilby J and Nicholson GA (1986) Psychological correlates of myasthenia gravis: a brief report. *J Psychosom Res*, **30(5)**, 575–580.

Thompson PJ and Trimble MR (1982) Comparative effects of anticonvulsant drugs on cognitive functioning. *Br J Clin Pract*, **18**, 154–156.

Thomson PJ and Trimble MR (1983) Anticonvulsant drugs and cognitive functions. *Epilepsia*, **33**, 531–544.

Todes CJ and Lees AJ (1985) The pre-morbid personality of patients with Parkinson's disease. *J Neurol Neurosurg Psychiatry*, **48**, 97–100.

Tommason K, Kent D and Coryell W (1991) Somatization and conversion disorders: Comorbidity and demographics at presentation. *Acta Psychiatr Scand*, **84**, 288–293.

Trimble MR (1978) Non-monoamine oxidase inhibitor antidepressant and epilepsy: A review. *Epilepsia*, **19**, 241–250.

Trimble MR and Perez MM (1982) Quantification of psychopathology in adult patients with epilepsy. In: BM Kulig, H Meinardi and G Stores (eds) *Epilepsy and Behaviour '79* and *Proceedings of WOPSASSEPY I 1980*. Lisse: Swets and Zeitlinger, 118–126.

Trimble MR, Corbett JA and Donaldson D (1980) Folic acid and mental symptoms in children with epilepsy. *J Neurol Neurosurg Psychiatry*, **43**, 1030–1034.

Turkewitz LJ, Casaly JS, Dawson GA and Wirth O (1992) Phenelzine therapy for headache patients with concomitant depression and anxiety. *Headache*, **32**, 203–207.

Victoroff JI, Benson DF, Engel J Jr, Grafton S and Mazziotta JC (1990) Interictal depression in patients with medically intractable complex partial seizures: Electroencephalography and cerebral metabolic correlates. *Ann Neurol*, **28**, 221.

Wade DT, Hewer LJ, Skilbeck CE and David RM (1985) *Stroke: A Critical Approach to Diagnosis, Treatment and Management:* London: Chapman and Hall.

Wade DT, Legh-Smith J and Hewer RA (1987) Depressed mood after stroke: A community study of its frequency. *Br J Psychiatry*, **151**, 200–205.

Walshe JM (1956) Penicillamine. A new oral therapy for Wilson's disease *Am J Med*, **21**, 487–495.

Watziawick P and Coyne JC (1980) Depression following stroke: brief, problem focused family treatment. *Fam Treatment*, **19**, 13–18.

Wechsler IS (1921) Statistics of multiple sclerosis including a study of the infantile, congenital, familial and hereditary forms and the mental and psychic symptoms. *Arch Neurol Psychiatry*, **8**, 59–75.

Whitlock FA and Siskind MM (1980) Depression as a major symptom of multiple sclerosis. *J Neurol Neurosurg Psychiatry*, **43**, 861–865.

Willeit J and Kiechl SJ (1991) Wilson's disease with neurological impairment but no Kayser–Fleischer rings. *Lancet*, **337**, 1426.

Wilson SAK (1912) Progressive lenticular degeneration: A familial nervous disease associated with cirrhosis of the liver. *Brain*, **34**, 296–509.

Wise MG and Taylor SE (1990) Anxiety and mood disorders in medically ill patients. *J Clin Psychiatry*, **51 (suppl 1)**, 27–32.

Wolff G, Deuschl G, Wienker TF, Hummel K, Lucking CH, Schumacher M, Hammer J and Oepen G (1989) New mutations to Huntington's disease. *J Med Genet*, **26(1)**, 18–27.

World Health Organisation (1992) *International Classification of Diseases and Health Related Problems* (10th Revision). Geneva : WHO.

Young AC, Saunders J and Ponsford JR (1976) Mental changes as an early feature of multiple sclerosis. *J Neurol Neurosurg Psychiatry*, **39**, 1008–1013.

17

Depression in traumatic brain injury patients

George P. Prigatano and Jay D. Summers

INTRODUCTION

Depression, in its mild to severe forms, is readily apparent in many brain dysfunctional patients (as well as in their family members). The exact role that disturbed brain function plays in directly producing depression is an area of considerable discussion, speculation, and investigation. Informative reviews have been published by Crews and Harrison (1995), Kinsbourne (1988) and Brumback (1993). The latter discusses the neurophysiological and neurochemical bases of depression.

Although psychiatrists have long been interested in the diagnosis and treatment of depression (e.g. Feighner and Boyer, 1991; Beck *et al.*, 1979), evaluating and rehabilitating brain dysfunctional patients who demonstrate significant depression remains a formidable clinical task. In reviewing suicidal behaviour in brain dysfunctional patients who had undergone an intensive neuropsychologically orientated rehabilitation programme (as described by Prigatano and Others, 1986), Klonoff and Lage (1995) noted that 24 of 111 traumatically brain-injured (TBI) patients (i.e. 21.8%) showed significant depression. Furthermore, 14 (12.6%) reported "suicidal ideation". In this population, two patients (1.8%) eventually took their life.

This chapter reapproaches the problem of depression in TBI patients with a model of personality disorders that emanated from neuropsychological rehabili-

Depression and Physical Illness. Edited by M.M. Robertson and C.L.E. Katona
© 1997 John Wiley & Sons Ltd

tation. The focus of such rehabilitation is to return brain dysfunctional individuals to a productive lifestyle. Because this approach and its effectiveness have been described elsewhere (Prigatano et al., 1994, 1986), this chapter concentrates on TBI as a diagnostic condition and on the model of personality disorders that has been useful in working with this patient group. Data related to the model are then presented. The chapter concludes with a discussion of practical issues involved in the clinical neuropsychological assessment and management of depression after TBI.

PERSONALITY DISORDERS ASSOCIATED WITH TBI

A wide variety of emotional and motivational disturbances have been reported to follow TBI (Prigatano, 1987, 1992): irritability, impulsiveness, restlessness, loss of interest in the environment, easy fatiguability, and occasional paranoia and depression. There is no well-accepted estimate of the incidence or prevalence of depression associated with TBI.

Although the definition of TBI is specific, the condition is associated with different degrees of brain pathology. As discussed elsewhere (Prigatano, 1992), TBI refers to a situation in which external forces are applied to the skull and its contents with such force that damage to the brain itself is either confirmed or strongly suspected. Macroscopic or microscopic changes may occur, and lesions may be present throughout the cerebrum, cerebellum and brain stem (Adams, 1975; Becker and Povlishock, 1985; Jennett and Teasdale, 1981). As noted earlier, "commonly there is evidence of bilateral (but not symmetrical) frontal-temporal injuries in the context of diffuse deep white matter injury" (Prigatano, 1992, pp. 360–361).

Clinically, patients with mild to moderate injuries (defined as admitting Glasgow Coma Scale (GCS) scores between 13 and 15 and between 9 and 12, respectively, the absence of a space-occupying lesion, and no deterioration in the patient's condition in the first 24 h) verbalize feelings of depression *more* often than patients with severe injuries (i.e. GCS scores between 3 and 8 with or without space-occupying lesions). Patients with blunted affect who have lost interest in their environment and whose appetites have decreased may be described as depressed by family members or inexperienced rehabilitation therapists. Such patients often present with behavioural characteristics that indicate a bilateral frontal lobe injury, which is associated with cognitive and affective disturbances that mimic depression. These patients, however, are not considered to be clinically depressed (Prigatano and Others, 1986; Stuss and Benson, 1986).

When any personality disturbance after brain injury is evaluated, it is important to state the presumed relationship between the nature of the personality disorder and its relationship to brain damage. The underlying model can then be tested empirically. Historically, personality disturbances associated with brain injury acquired from various aetiologies have been studied from two different perspectives: that of traditional psychiatry and that of neurology and neuropsychiatry.

In the psychiatric tradition, the individual's personality characteristics after brain injury are thought to represent a rich mixture of premorbid personality characteristics and the generalized effects of brain damage. For example, a patient's loss of the abstract attitude after brain injury may result in less efficient ego defences or coping mechanisms. The individual may struggle to cope with the effects of brain injury with fewer cognitive resources. Consequently, premorbid personality features may manifest themselves in "primitive" forms. Schilder (1934), Goldstein (1952), and Weinstein and Kahn (1955) have articulated this perspective.

From the perspective of neuropsychiatry and neurology, personality disturbances may reflect the direct effects of a specific brain lesion or dysfunction. Premorbid states of psychological coping may contribute little to the patient's symptom picture. The work of Cummings (e.g. Petry *et al.*, 1988) and Robinson (e.g. Robinson and Chait, 1985) represents contemporary examples of this tradition.

Work with brain dysfunctional patients within the context of postacute rehabilitation has emphasized that both approaches have merit and must be synthesized to create a practical working model for understanding personality disorders associated with brain injury. Clearly, brain damage does not occur in a psychological vacuum. It can occur at various times in the life cycle and can affect people at different stages of their psychosocial development (see Erikson, 1978). Yet, specific areas of brain dysfunction can affect differentially various symptoms that are summarized under the term depression. The question has always been how to separate the factors or symptoms directly caused by the brain injury from those that are indirectly related to the injury.

In the context of this approach, personality disorders after brain injury have been classified into three broad categories (Prigatano and Others, 1986; Prigatano, 1987, 1992). Behavioural disturbances (including disturbances of mood or affect) classified as neuropsychologically mediated are a direct effect of brain damage. Some behavioural disturbances are in response to disordered cognition as well as to common sensory, motor, and psychosocial changes after brain injury. In this case, the patients struggle to adapt given their impaired function; consequently, they may show a variety of symptoms that are only indirectly related to brain injury (Goldstein, 1952). These disturbances have been labelled reactionary problems. Finally, some personality or behavioural disturbances (including major depressive disorders) may have long predated the onset of a brain injury. These disturbances are referred to as characterological problems if they are independent of the direct or indirect effects of brain damage. If this model is useful, research should support it.

DEPRESSION INDEPENDENT OF BRAIN DAMAGE

Typically, most people treated for depression have no history that suggests acquired brain damage. Patients can be classified according to the DSM-IV (American Psychiatric Association, 1994) as demonstrating a major depressive episode, a major depressive disorder, a dysthymic disorder, an unspecified depressive disorder, or several other diagnostic conditions. None of these diagnostic categories includes the criterion of brain damage even though many depressed patients complain of difficulties with memory and concentration that suggest subtle brain dysfunction.

Feighner and Boyer (1991) note that "depression is an extremely common, debilitating, but treatable psychiatric illness ... It is a multifaceted symptom, syndrome and disease which reveals important parts of itself to those who approach it from different perspectives" (p. xi). When taken from the perspective of traditional psychiatry and clinical psychology, depression seems to have many potential aetiologies: neurotransmitter disturbances (Kupfer, 1991), faulty beliefs about the self that seem to develop over several years (Beck et al., 1979), or an abrupt and tragic personal loss. Other factors can also precipitate the onset of a dysphoric mood and the associated cognitive and vegetative symptoms (see Freedman et al, 1985).

A major problem confronting the field is to provide a clear and concise definition of depression. Unfortunately no such definition is readily available. In fact, DSM-IV fails to provide a single definition for depression under its Glossary of Technical Terms. DSM-IV, however, offers many "descriptive features" that are associated with a major depressive episode: tearfulness, brooding, obsessive rumination, excessive worry, complaints of somatic discomfort, loss of appetite, subjective reports of sadness, and empty feelings. Sleep and eating disturbances are often present and associated with a loss of energy, fatigue, and a decreased ability to concentrate, remember, and think.

Typically, depression can be separated from normal sadness in one important way. Sadness is a normal reaction to a significant loss in life. Yet sadness frequently responds to good news; depression does not. In practical terms, depressed patients seem to take little if any pleasure in good things that happen to them. They persist in a dysphoric state that has disastrous consequences for their adaptation. Patients who exhibit depressive symptomatology after a brain injury are often classified as showing a major depressive episode or as demonstrating a dysthymic personality disturbance.

Common symptoms exhibited by depressed brain dysfunctional patients are a dysphoric mood; negative thought patterns that do not respond to logic; failure to experience pleasure or satisfaction in appetite or sexual drive; sleep disturbances; a progressive lack of interest in the environment (versus aspontaneity); flattened affect which, in part, reflects a failure to show spontaneity in facial expressions or tone of voice as well as failing to perceive affect in others. Depressed patients tend to cry often and report mental fatigue.

The diagnosis of depression in brain dysfunctional patients can be a difficult task (Ross and Rush, 1981). Lesions of the left hemisphere can affect patients' ability to verbalize about their emotional state. Right hemisphere lesions can affect patients' ability to express emotion (including facial expressions, and body postures). Damage to brain stem or limbic regions can induce vegetative symptoms, altering behaviours such as appetite, sexual drive, or sleep. Such brain lesions can also influence internal feeling states and produce dysphoria. Except for sleep disturbances (Prigatano *et al.*, 1982; Manseau and Broghton, submitted for publication), however, it is difficult to find studies that show a relationship between any of these disturbances and specific brain lesions. Therefore, for any given patient, these symptoms must be evaluated on an individual basis to identify the most likely causes.

DIRECT EFFECTS OF BRAIN DYSFUNCTION AND DEPRESSION

Some studies, however, do suggest that a direct relationship exists between brain injury and depression. The work of Robinson *et al.* (Robinson *et al.*, 1983, 1984a,b, 1987; Robinson and Szetela, 1981; Robinson and Price, 1982; Starkstein *et al.*, 1987, 1988) has most clearly documented a potential relationship between brain lesion location and the existence of a major depressive episode. For example, they found that a major depressive episode soon after a stroke was frequently associated with left hemisphere injury (Robinson and Price, 1982; Robinson *et al.*, 1983, 1984a,b; Starkstein *et al.*, 1987). In particular, left frontal lesions tended to correlate with a major depressive episode in this patient group.

As stroke patients recovered or as time passed, however, depression was less easily correlated with a left anterior cerebral dysfunction. After the first 2 years poststroke, the prevalence of depression remained stable, but the composition of the group changed (Robinson *et al.*, 1987). All patients who were initially depressed improved, in terms of depression, after 2 years. The mood of patients who were not initially depressed, however, deteriorated 2 years after stroke. These findings suggest that with time, depression is correlated with factors other than lesion location.

Depression also can exist when multiple areas of the brain are damaged. Studying acute TBI patients, Fedoroff *et al.* (1992) reported that "the presence of left dorsolateral frontal lesions and/or left basal ganglia lesions and, to a lesser extent, parietal–occipital and right hemisphere lesions were associated with an increased probability of developing major depression" (p. 918). As is often the case in TBI patients who suffer brain damage attributable to acceleration or deceleration forces applied to the skull, lesions are often bilateral and asymmetrical. This pattern precludes an easy correlation between lesion location and specific personality disturbances (Prigatano, 1992), including depression.

The model of Robinson and his colleagues (Fedoroff *et al.*, 1992) suggests that multiple brain sites may be involved in the genesis of depression, including left and right hemisphere lesions. Electrophysiological studies provide some interesting clues about the relative roles of the two hemispheres in the genesis of depression. Davidson (1992) has suggested that the right and left anterior cerebral structures play fundamentally different roles in the genesis of emotion. The left frontal and anterior temporal regions purportedly play a dominant role in approach behaviours while the right frontal–anterior temporal regions play a major role in withdrawal behaviour. Therefore, damage to the left hemisphere can produce disturbances of approach while damage to the right hemisphere can produce disturbances of withdrawal. This innovative theory has been tested from several different perspectives and offers some promising insights in the study of depression. The reader is referred to Davidson's (1992) excellent review of this topic and its implications.

For the purpose of the present discussion, Davidson (1992) points out that "a patient with left anterior damage" may develop "depressive symptomatology" only if "exposed to the requisite environmental stresses"(p. 129). He also reviews evidence that indicates that "remitted depressives, like the acutely depressed subjects, had significantly less left frontal activation than the healthy controls in the frontal region" (p. 140). Collectively, the findings that he reviewed suggest that even if patients have decreased left frontal activation, they may not develop depression unless subjected to other precipitating factors. For example, if such an individual sustained a right hemisphere injury, it might precipitate the onset of depressive symptoms. Theoretically, this possibility is interesting because it suggests a dynamic relationship between the right and left hemispheres. It also suggests that premorbid characteristics (including biological characteristics) may contribute to the complexity of depressive symptomatology seen after TBI. These notions are compatible with recent (Fedoroff *et al.*, 1992) as well as earlier literature (Lishman, 1968). These studies suggest that sometimes damage to the brain directly produces depressive symptomatology.

DEPRESSION AS AN INDIRECT EFFECT OF BRAIN INJURY

Observing the behaviour of brain-injured soldiers, Goldstein (1942) noted that some symptoms appear to be in response to the struggles imposed by the brain injury, some reflected a tendency to avoid the struggle, and other symptoms reflected the struggle itself. Goldstein also reported the phenomenon of the "catastrophic reaction", in which anxiety and depression play predominant roles.

If depression is an indirect effect of brain damage, it should *not* correlate readily with the measures of severity of brain injury or location. Moreover, its frequency and severity should change over time depending mostly on environmental conditions. Finally, it should be related to premorbid factors. What data support this perspective?

Levin and Grossman (1978) developed a profile of behavioural disturbances in relation to the severity of closed head injury (CHI). They reported that depression, as judged by the Brief Psychiatric Rating Scale (BPRS), was not significantly related to severity of brain injury (Figure 1). Using a cross-sectional design, Godfrey *et al.* (1993) studied self-reports of depression in TBI patients 6 months, 1 year and 2–3 years after injury. Their reports of depression were compared to those of an orthopaedic control group. Six months after injury, the level of depression reported by TBI patients was comparable to that reported by the orthopaedic controls. One year after injury, however, TBI patients reported higher levels of depression. This trend was also evident 2–3 years after injury. Finally, Fedoroff *et al.* (1992) noted that of TBI patients who showed evidence of a major depression, 70.6% had a history of premorbid psychiatric disturbance compared to 37% of the TBI patients who did not demonstrate a major depressive disorder. The difference was statistically significant. Collectively, these findings argue that depression can be an indirect effect of brain injury. Problems of adjustment (including depression) may also have existed premorbidly and be independent of the TBI.

It has been our clinical impression that as TBI patients become more cognitively alert to their environment and begin to experience problems related to social isolation (Kozloff, 1987) and a wide variety of behavioural limitations (Godfrey *et al.*, 1993) their self-reports of depression increase. An interesting question remains, however. What specific symptoms might be related to the brain injury and what specific symptoms seem to be in reaction to the brain injury?

SYMPTOMS OF DEPRESSION AFTER TBI

Ross and Rush (1981) state that pathological crying, in the absence of bilateral lesions causing pseudobulbar palsy, is likely to be indicative of depression. Jorge *et al.* (1993a,b) studied specific vegetative and psychological symptoms of depression in 66 TBI patients over 1 year. Initially, 20% of the patients reported the presence of depressed mood. At 1 year follow up the percentage was comparable (26%), but some patients had been lost to follow up. Vegetative signs of depression varied over time. For example, at the time of initial evaluation, 42% of the depressed patients had sleep disturbances that had disappeared 1 year after injury. In contrast, reports of loss of libido had increased to 60% by the 1 year follow up examination compared to 32% at the initial evalua-

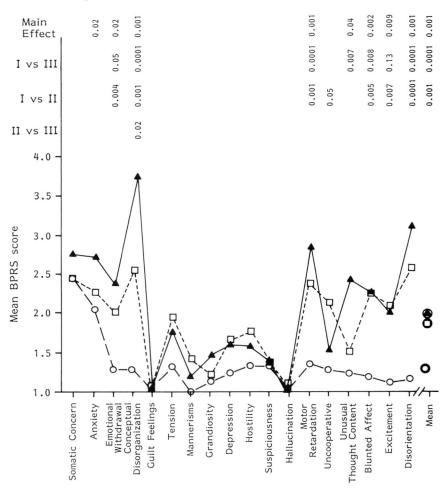

Figure 1. Mean score by each grade of injury on individual scales of Brief Psychiatric Rating Scale (BPRS), with grand mean and results of analysis of covariance. Scale scores were adjusted for effects of variation in the injury-rating interval. Order of scales corresponds to that of published BPRS. Open circles connected by solid line indicate grade I; open circles connected by dashed line, grade II; solid triangles connected by solid line, grade III. Reprinted from Levin and Grossman with permission of *Arch Neurol*, November, 1978, Vol. 35. Copyright 1978, American Medical Association.

tion. These findings are reminiscent of an earlier report (Thomsen, 1984) in which TBI patients often were judged to show increased tiredness and sensitivity to stress 10–15 years after injury compared to 2.5 years after injury. More information is needed on the relationship between specific symptoms associ-

Table 1. A comparison made by a person who suffered from depression before and after brain injury

Characteristic	Depression before TBI	Depression after TBI
Environmental stress	Generally absent	May be present
Worry loop	Present	Absent
Nervous pulsing pain	Present	Not present
Daily mood cycle	Chronic on waking; at my best in evening	Unpredictable, generally at best in morning
Weight loss	Severe	Overweight
Sleep disturbance	Quick to sleep late evening; wake within 1–3 hours	Sleep 10–12 hours starting any time, difficult to wake
Follow and understand discussion	Difficult, tend to ignore and act on own	Equally difficult but lack clear vision on what to do
Ability to perform	Enhanced	Reduced
Headaches	Plagued by depression	Nonexistent
Memory	Diary not required	Require comprehensive diary
Concentration	Could read a book	Cannot read a book
Mood	Unhappy and sad, prefer to retreat	Frustrated and childish, likely to lose temper and be violent
Smell and taste	Sensitive	Do not exist
Balance	Satisfactory	Poor
Wife on appearance	Patient has become expert at hiding his feelings, you never know what he is thinking	Paitent loses his temper without any warning, says hurtful things

ated with depression and neurophysiological and neuropsychological changes caused by brain injury.

In this regard, a table constructed by a patient in which he compares his symptoms of depression before and after brain injury is informative. Table 1 lists many of the symptoms of depression as well as symptoms of brain injury. For example, prior to brain injury the individual reports having a "worry loop". By this he meant that he often would have "deep and profound concentration on any problem". After the brain injury, this was absent. Before the brain injury he would frequently wake after only 1–3 hours sleep. After the brain injury he required anywhere from 10–12 hours sleep and noted it was extremely difficult to wake.

The patient also notes a change in his smell and taste, as well as balance, something that did not exist prior to his brain injury. Also, while his mood was initially described as unhappy and sad and he tended to retreat prior to his brain injury, after the brain injury he used the words frustrated and childish to describe himself, as well as a tendency for him to lose his temper.

This table nicely describes how varying symptoms can change as a result of brain injury. By detailed interviewing of such patients clinicians will get further insights as to what symptoms may be specifically caused by brain injury and what symptoms are independent of it.

CLINICAL ASSESSMENT AND MANAGEMENT OF DEPRESSION IN TBI PATIENTS

Three brief case examples highlight the realities of assessing and managing depression in TBI patients. A 32-year-old carpenter fell from a ladder and was rendered unconscious. His admitting GCS score was 14, but a computed tomography (CT) scan revealed small punctate areas of hypodensity in the left parietal region. The patient reported being quick to anger and noted problems with "short-term memory". Upon further questioning, he indicated that he would often cry easily—something he did not do before the injury. His wife was vocal about her concerns that he was now "depressed". In the initial interview he was almost "euphoric". However, his profile on the Minnesota Multiphasic Personality Inventory—2 (MMPI-2) obtained at that time showed substantial elevations on scales 2 and 7, suggesting a long-standing depressive disorder. Later, his wife reported a history of depression in her husband's family. A parent and sibling committed suicide in their 30s.

Symptoms of crying could be attributed to depression but in this case appeared to be attributed to emotional lability—a common problem after TBI (Prigatano, 1992).

Thus, in this case, depression did not appear to be "caused" by the patient's brain injury—it most likely existed independent of it. Yet, his brain injury created certain cognitive deficits that may have increased his risk for depression and suicide, and he was treated psychiatrically—rather than within the context of a neuropsychologically orientated rehabilitation programme.

A second patient, a young adult married female, suffered a TBI in a car accident in which she was a passenger. Her admitting GCS score was 7. Computed tomography (CT) of the brain revealed a "thin-rimmed subdural haematoma in the left frontal region and along the posterior parietal and inferotemporal lobe". Her attending neurologist noted that she had "cognitive deficits" and described her as "depressed" about 1 month after her injury. The patient complained of headaches and was given an antidepressant medication that had little impact on her headaches. She cried frequently but reported no vegetative signs of depression. He appetite was good, she slept reasonably well, and her libido had declined only slightly. Neuropsychological examination revealed mild-to-moderate cognitive deficits 4 months after TBI even though her GCS score had been 7 upon her admission to the hospital. She also had problems with memory and speed-of-information processing (Prigatano, 1996;

Dikmen *et al.*, 1995). While discussing her reaction to neuropsychological testing, she commented that testing "gave her a severe headache". When asked to do sustained cognitive tasks, she experienced slowness of thought—a phenomenon she found quite distressing. Because physically she appeared fine, her husband had the impression that she was now simply "lazy". To avoid continued marital tension, she felt a strong need to return to work even though she did not feel ready to do so. Her headaches and dysphoric mood come closest to what Goldstein described as the "indirect effects" of brain injury. They represent a form of catastrophic reaction. By helping her to understand her symptoms and guiding her and her husband to a realistic perspective of the aftermath of her brain injury, her headaches, anxiety, and depression declined. Prohibiting work for 6 months until she had experienced further cognitive recovery was a major step in managing her dysphoric mood. No medication was necessary to reduce her headaches and nor was a neuropsychologically orientated rehabilitation programme warranted. With an adequate under-standing of the effects of her brain injury, she and her husband were able to manage their problems much more effectively.

In contrast, an 18-year-old male who also suffered a severe TBI from an automobile accident did need a neuropsychologically orientated rehabilitation programme. His admitting GCS score was 3. CT revealed a right frontal epidural haematoma as well as an interparenchymal haematoma in the right frontal and left temporal regions (Figure 2). Five months after his injury, the patient stated that he was depressed and had been for several months. He had recurring suicidal ideation and was immediately placed on antidepressant medications. Thoughts of suicide stopped abruptly. Like many patients with such TBIs, he perceived no difficulties with his cognitive functioning. He was eager to return to school and to his athletic-orientated life-style. He showed clear indications of neuropsychological impairment. His speed of finger movement was slow, his memory had decreased, and his abstract reasoning and problem-solving skills were impaired. Because the patient's abilities before his injury were above average, his level of performance on neuropsychological tests suggested that his cognitive deficits were mild. In reality, however, the patient's status had changed dramatically compared to his premorbid state. He has resisted neuropsycho-logically orientated rehabilitation and yet remains in need of it. Without it, his psychiatric status has begun to decline and he has started to use nonprescribed drugs. This patient needs a combination of neuropsychologically orientated rehabilitation and psychiatric treatment because his problems reflect major brain dysfunction in the context of pre-existing behavioural problems. Certainly, his difficulties with depression and poor insight seem to be directly related to his brain injury.

These case studies document the need for individual evaluation of a patient's symptom profile. Because different factors can contribute to the symptoms of TBI patients, proper evaluation is needed to ensure that appropriate forms of

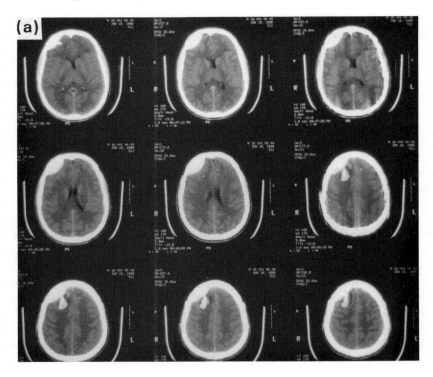

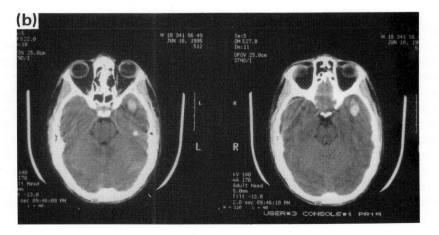

Figure 2. Computed tomography scans of a patient who became severely depressed within 1 month of his brain injury show (a) right frontal and (b) left anterior temporal lesions (see text for details)

Table 2. Factors to consider in evaluating depression in TBI patients

Is a diagnostic disorder present?
    Major depressive disorder
    Major depressive episode
    Dysthymic personality disorder
Are there specific symptoms that need to be further evaluated and treated?
    Dysphoric mood—feeling "bad," "blue," no joy, sense of hopelessness, helplessness,
    no value or meaning to one's life or behaviour
    Negative thought patterns that do not respond to logic:
        • "The situation is hopeless"
        • "I am worthless; a fraud"
    Failure to experience pleasure or satisfaction in appetitive drives:
        • Loss of appetite
        • Loss of libido or sexual drive
    Sleep disturbances, presence or absence of dreaming (absence of dreaming may be
    indicative of acquired brain injury)
    Loss of interest in the environment (vs. aspontaneity)
    "Flat affect" or mood:
        • Failure to show spontaneous facial features
        • Monotone voice
        • Failure to perceive affect in others
    (Pathological) crying
    Mental fatigue
    Suicidal ideation:
        • "I want to die"
        • "Sometimes I wonder if I should have survived the accident"

management or intervention are instituted. For example, the first patient
described above was treated psychiatrically. The second patient and her spouse
needed education and help to manage environmental stressors. Despite his
resistance, the third patient needs a neuropsychologically orientated rehabilitation programme.

No simple checklist exists for the evaluation of TBI patients. Table 2,
however, lists several factors that should be reviewed when TBI patients present
with symptoms that suggest depression. By reviewing these symptoms and by
considering their potential aetiologies, clinicians can better evaluate what form
of intervention would be most helpful for an individual patient.

THE RELATIONSHIP OF DEPRESSION TO IMPAIRED SELF-AWARENESS AFTER TBI

There has been a growing appreciation that many TBI patients show a lack
of insight into their behavioural and neuropsychological disturbances several

weeks or months after injury (Prigatano and Others, 1986). For some patients, this lack of insight appears to be permanent. As patients report more disabilities and have higher levels of neuropsychological impairment, they also report more depression (Godfrey *et al.*, 1993). Is there a relationship between impaired self-awareness after TBI and depression?

Starkstein *et al.* (1992) studied depression in patients with cerebral vascular lesions who showed various degrees of anosognosia. They found no relationship between anosognosia and depression and suggested that "anosognosia does not protect stroke patients from depressive feelings" (p. 1446). Godfrey *et al.* (1993), however, suggested that "the return of insight (following TBI) is associated with increased risk of emotional dysfunction" (p. 503), which includes feelings of depression. While definitive studies are lacking, TBI patients may experience greater social isolation and job failures as time passes (Kozloff, 1987). They may also experience increased behavioural problems and depression. Clinically, however, many of these patients do not seem to recognize (i.e. be aware) that their brain injury is directly responsible for their failures.

When impaired self-awareness is a direct consequence of brain damage (i.e. a negative symptom), there seems to be little if any connection between depression and the patient's state of knowledge. If the patients, however, are partially aware of their impairment, they may use premorbid coping mechanisms to deal with their problems (Prigatano and Weinstein, 1996) even if these mechanisms are no longer adaptive. In this case, patients are exhibiting a denial of disability that can be interpreted as a "positive symptom" after brain injury (Prigatano and Weinstein, 1996). In fact, depression may ensue in TBI patients who have partial knowledge of their disability. A correlation, but not necessarily a causal relationship, may exist between partial knowledge or insight and depressive symptomatology after TBI. This area, however, requires considerably more investigation before our understanding of how impaired self-awareness and depression are related is definitive.

ANTIDEPRESSANT MEDICATIONS AFTER TBI

Many TBI patients are put on antidepressant medications. To our knowledge, there have been no double crossover studies which have systematically assessed the efficacy of such pharmacological interventions for this heterogeneous group of subjects. In general, the pharmacological methods for treating TBI patients have been similar to those used for other neurological subgroups (see Chapter 16). Given, however, that the incidence of pre-existing psychiatric disorders may be higher in TBI patients than in other neurological groups of patients (e.g. those with Parkinson's disease), determining what medications are most helpful in relieving depression in TBI patients is a complicated task.

It has been our clinical impression that if a patient has had a history of premorbid depression which meets DSM-IV criteria for a major depressive disorder, they may respond differentially to antidepressant medications after TBI, but this has not been systematically tested. What is clear, however, is that antidepressant medications are frequently given to TBI patients and these drugs may affect many functions besides their mood state. For example, in one study using antidepressant medications with TBI patients, it was demonstrated that improved arousal and initiation occurred for certain patients, thereby apparently helping them with their overall adaptation and outcome even when depression was not present (Reinhard *et al.*, 1995). Definition of the roles of various neurotransmitter agents in dealing with the complex array of symptoms associated with brain injury is badly needed.

For the further discussion of the role of various psychotropic medications used to treat depression after TBI, the reader is referred to two articles which detail this topic (Silver, 1991a,b).

SUMMARY

TBI produces a wide variety of neuropathological disturbances with associated personality changes. Some of these patients manifest signs and symptoms of depression over time. Certain symptoms may reflect the direct effects of brain injury while others appear to be indirect effects. The clinician must observe patients closely for possible major depressive episodes, particularly immediately after brain injury. In such cases, pharmacological intervention may be necessary. The specific symptoms of depression, which include dysphoric mood, negative thought patterns, loss of interest in the environment, and other vegetative signs, must be treated on an individual basis and can respond to a variety of techniques. Neuropsychological rehabilitation attempts to help postacute patients with severe TBI return to a productive life-style and to reduce their social isolation. If successful, the patient's level of irritability and depressive symptomatology often decreases. Many of these TBI patients will still experience some dysphoria, but their emotional state seems to resemble typical human sadness rather than a true depressive disorder. In such cases, at least a portion of the initial depressive symptoms were likely a reflection of indirect effects of brain injury. As patients can cope more effectively with the consequences of their brain injury, their depressive symptomatology tends to improve substantially and their clinical management is thus enhanced.

ACKNOWLEDGEMENTS

The authors thank the staff of the Neuroscience Publications Office of the Barrow Neurological Institute for their help in preparing this manuscript and Shelley A. Kick, PhD, for editorial assistance.

REFERENCES

American Psychiatric Association (1994) *Diagnostic and Statistical Manual of Mental Disorders*, Washington, DC: American Psychiatric Association.

Adams JH (1975) The neuropathology of head injuries. In: PJ Vinken and GW Bruyn (eds) *Handbook of Clinical Neurology*, Vol. 23. New York: Elsevier-North Holland, 35–65.

Beck AT, Rush JA, Shaw BF and Emery G (1979) *Cognitive Therapy of Depression*. New York: Guilford.

Becker DP and Povlishock JT (1985) *Central Nervous System Trauma Status Report: 1985*. (Prepared for the National Institute of Neurological and Communicative Disorders and Stroke. Grant NS19591), Bethesda, MD: National Institutes of Health.

Brumback RA (1993) Is depression a neurologic disease? *Neurol Clin*, **11(1)**, 79–104.

Crews WD and Harrison DW (1995), The neuropsychology of depression and its implications for cognitive therapy. *Neuropsychol Rev*, **5(2)**, 81–123.

Davidson R (1992) Anterior cerebral asymmetry and the nature of emotion. *Brain Cogn*, **20**, 125–151.

Dikmen S, Machamer JE, Winn HR and Temkin NR (1995) Neuropsychological outcome at 1-year post head injury. *Neuropsychology*, **9(1)**, 80–90.

Erikson (1978) Stages of psychological development. In: CS Hall and G Lindzey (eds). *Theories of Personality*, 3rd edn. New York: Wiley, 87–108.

Fedoroff JP, Starkstein SE, Forrester AW, Geisler FH, Jorge RE, Arndt SV and Robinson RG (1992) Depression in patients with acute traumatic brain injury. *Am J Psychiatry*, **149**, 918–923.

Feighner JP and Boyer WM (1991) *Perspectives in Psychiatry*, Volume 2: *Diagnosis of Depression*. Chichester: Wiley.

Freedman AM, Kaplan HI and Sadock BJ (1985) *Modern Synopsis of Comprehensive Textbook of Psychiatry/II*, Baltimore, MD: Williams and Wilkins.

Godfrey HP, Partridge FM, Knight RG and Bishara S (1993) Course of insight disorder and emotional dysfunction following closed head injury: a controlled cross-sectional follow-up study. *J Clin Exp Neuropsychol*, **15**, 503–515.

Goldstein K (1942) *Aftereffects of Brain Injury in War*. New York: Grune and Stratton.

Goldstein K (1952) The effect of brain damage on the personality. *Psychiatry*, **15**, 245–260.

Hall CS and Lindzey G (1978) *Theories of Personality* (3rd edn). New York: Wiley.

Jennett B and Teasdale G (1981) *Management of Head Injuries*. Philadelphia, PA: F.A. Davis.

Jorge RE, Robinson RG, Arndt S, Forrester AW, Geisler F and Starkstein SE (1993a) Comparison between acute- and delayed-onset depression following traumatic brain injury. *J Neuropsychiatry*, **5**, 43–49.

Jorge RE, Robinson RG, Arndt SV, Starkstein SE, Forrester AW and Geisler F (1993b)

Depression following traumatic brain injury: a 1 year longitudinal study. *J Affect Disord*, **27**, 233–243.

Kinsbourne M (1988) *Cerebral Hemisphere Function in Depression*, Washington, DC: American Psychiatric Press.

Klonoff PS and Lage GA (1995) Suicide in patients with traumatic brain injury: Risk and prevention. *J Head Trauma Rehabil*, **10(6)**, 16–24.

Kozloff R (1987) Network of social support and the outcome from severe head injury. *J Head Trauma Rehabil*, **2(3)**, 14–23.

Kupfer DJ (1991) Biological markers of depression. In: JP Feighner and WF Boyer (eds) *The Diagnosis of Depression*. Chichester: Wiley, 79–98.

Levin HS and Grossman RG (1978) Behavioural sequelae of closed head injury. A quantitative study. *Arch Neurol*, **35**, 720–727.

Lishman WA (1968) Brain damage in relation to psychiatric disability after head injury. *Br J Psychiatry*, **114**, 373–410.

Manseau C and Broughton R (submitted for publication). Organic insomnia as a consequence of closed head injury.

Petry S, Cummings JL, Hill MA and Shapira J (1988) Personality alterations in dementia of the Alzheimer's type. *Arch Neurol*, **45**, 1187–1190.

Prigatano GP (1987) Psychiatric aspects of head injury: Problem areas and suggested guidelines for research. In: H Levin, J Graftman and HM Eisenberg (eds) *Neurobehavioural Recovery from Head Injury*. New York: Oxford University Press, 215–231.

Prigatano GP (1992) Personality disturbances associated with traumatic brain injury. *J Consult Clin Psychol*, **60**, 360–368.

Prigatano GP (1996). Neuropsychological testing after traumatic brain injury. In RW Evans (ed) *Neurology and Trauma*. Philadelphia: W.B. Saunders, 222–230.

Prigatano GP and Others (1986) *Neuropsychological Rehabilitation After Brain Injury*. Baltimore, MD: Johns Hopkins University.

Prigatano GP and Weinstein EA (1996). Edwin A. Weinstein's contributions to neuropsychological rehabilitation. *Neuropsychol Rehabil*, **6(4)**, 305–326.

Prigatano GP, Stahl M, Orr W and Zeiner H (1982) Sleep and dreaming disturbances in closed head injury patients. *J Neurol Neurosurg Psychiatry*, **45**, 78–80.

Prigatano GP, Klonoff PS, O'Brien KP, Altman I, Amin K, Chiapello DA, Shepherd J, Cunningham M and Mora M (1994) Productivity after neuropsychologically oriented, milieu rehabilitation. *J Head Trauma Rehabil*, **9(1)**, 91–102.

Reinhard DL, Whyte J and Sandel ME (1995) Improved arousal and initiation following tricyclic antidepressant use in severe brain injury. *Arch Phys Med Rehabil*, **77**, 80–83.

Robinson RG and Chait RM (1985) Emotional correlates of structural brain injury with particular emphasis on post-stroke mood disorders. *Crit Rev Clin Neurobiol*, **1(4)**, 285–317.

Robinson RG and Price TR (1982) Post-stroke depressive disorders: A follow-up study of 103 patients. *Stroke*, **13**, 635–641.

Robinson RG and Szetela B (1981) Mood change following left hemispheric brain injury. *Ann Neurol*, **9**, 447–453.

Robinson RG, Kubos KL, Starr LB, Rao K and Price TR (1983) Mood changes in stroke patients: Relationship to lesion location. *Compr Psychiatry*, **24**, 555–556.

Robinson RG, Starr LB, Lipsey JR, Rao K and Price TR (1984a) A two-year longitudinal study of post-stroke mood disorders: Dynamic changes in associated variables over the first six months of follow-up. *Stroke*, **15**, 510–517.

Robinson RG, Starr LB, Kubos KL, Rao K and Price TR (1984b) Mood disorders in stroke patients: Importance of location of lesion. *Brain*, **197**, 91–93.

Robinson RG, Bloduc PL and Price TR (1987) Two-year longitudinal study of poststroke mood disorders: diagnosis and outcome at one and two years. *Stroke*, **18**, 837–843.

Ross ED and Rush AJ (1981) Diagnosis and neuroanatomical correlates of depression in brain-damaged patients: Implications for a neurology of depression. *Arch Gen Psychiatry*, **38**, 1344–1354.

Schilder P (1934) Psychic disturbances after head injuries. *Am J Psychiatry*, **91**, 155–188.

Silver JM, Yodufsky SC and Hales RE (1991a) Depression in traumatic brain injury. *Neuropsychiatry Neuropsychol Behav Neurol*, **4**, 12–23.

Silver JM, Hales RE and Yudofsky SC (1991b) Psychopharmacology of depression in neurologic disorders. *J Clin Psychiatry*, **51(1, Suppl)**, 33–39.

Starkstein SE, Robinson RG and Price TR (1987) Comparison of cortical and subcortical lesions in the production of poststroke mood disorders. *Brain*, **110**, 1045–1059.

Starkstein SE, Robinson RG and Price TR (1988) Comparison of patients with and without poststroke major depression matched for size and location of lesion. *Arch Gen Psychiatry*, **45**, 247–252.

Starkstein SE, Fedoroff JP, Price TR, Leiguarda R and Robinson RG (1992) Anosognosia in patients with cerebrovascular lesions: A study of causative factors. *Stroke*, **23**, 1446–1453.

Stuss DT and Benson DF (1986) *The Frontal Lobes*. New York: Raven Press.

Thomsen IV (1984) Late outcome of very severe blunt head trauma: A 10–15 year second follow-up. *J Neurol Neurosurg Psychiatry*, **47**, 260–268.

Weinstein EA and Kahn RL (1955) *Denial of Illness: Symbolic and Physiological Aspects*. Springfield IL: Charles C Thomas.

18

Depression in renal failure and its treatment

Tom Sensky

INTRODUCTION

Chronic renal failure is the irreversible and substantial loss of renal function, causing ill health. In its early stages, it may produce few if any symptoms. As it becomes more severe, it may present with a variety of symptoms, including those of hypertension, anaemia and hyperparathyroidism. In end-stage renal failure, some form of replacement therapy becomes essential to sustain life.

The prevalence of treated end-stage renal disease (measured as the population receiving renal replacement therapies) varies considerably, from 17 per million in Egypt to 660 and 840 per million in the USA and Japan, respectively (United States Renal Data System, 1993). In European Community countries, the prevalence is in the range 300–430 per million. Each year, between 50 and 180 new patients per million population are accepted into renal replacement treatment programmes (D'Amico, 1995). In European countries, the most common cause of end-stage renal failure is glomerulonephritis, accounting for 23% of all cases. In the USA, diabetes is the most common cause (30% of cases) (D'Amico, 1995). Other common causes include hypertension, polycystic kidney disease, pyelonephritis, and analgesic nephropathy.

Renal replacement therapies include haemodialysis, continuous ambulatory peritoneal dialysis, and transplantation. Haemodialysis involves extracorporeal circulation of blood through a dialysis machine for periods of several hours two

Depression and Physical Illness. Edited by M.M. Robertson and C.L.E. Katona
© 1997 John Wiley & Sons Ltd

or three times weekly. Solute and fluid transfer takes place across a semiperme-able membrane in the dialysis machine. Between dialyses, the patient needs to adhere to a diet, restricted in salts and protein, and must also restrict fluid intake. Some people who are on maintenance dialysis still have some residual urine output, and for such individuals, the fluid restrictions can be less severe. Good vascular access is essential for haemodialysis, and commonly involves surgical preparation of an arteriovenous fistula, usually at the wrist. Maintaining adequate vascular access over time is a major problem in some cases, and further vascular grafts may be needed to replace the initial access site when this becomes unusable. The process of dialysis itself can be uncomfortable for some patients, who experience muscle cramps, nausea and hypotension. Patients can dialyse either in a hospital or satellite dialysis unit, or at home. Home dialysis requires a room to be set aside for dialysis and its equipment, and assistance from family and professionals with the dialyses themselves and with maintenance of the equipment.

In peritoneal dialysis, the peritoneum substitutes for the semipermeable membrane of the dialysis machine. Dialysis fluid is placed into the peritoneum via a catheter, and removed and replaced with fresh fluid at regular intervals. Continuous ambulatory peritoneal dialysis involves making several such fluid exchanges daily. This technique is much simpler than haemodialysis, and can therefore readily be undertaken at home. It does not require the same degree of dietary and fluid restriction as haemodialysis. However, peritonitis is a common complication, and is the most frequent reason for hospital admission.

In the longer term, all forms of dialysis can lead to complications including renal bone disease, hypertension, atherosclerosis, and cerebrovascular disease. Anaemia was previously common, but is now treated with erythropoetin, which can have dramatic benefits for patients' quality of life (Evans et al., 1990).

For many people with end-stage renal disease, transplantation is the preferred treatment. A successful kidney graft allows the individual to return to a relatively normal life-style, not dependent on diets or technologies. While overall quality of life is better after transplantation than on dialysis, transplantation also has burdens and complications. Although short-term survival of the transplanted kidney has increased in recent years, with four in five grafted kidneys remaining viable after 1 year (Mallick et al., 1995), long-term morbidity and mortality remain problems. In the second decade after transplantation, approximately 3–4% of transplant recipients die, mainly from atherosclerotic vascular disease, sepsis, liver failure and malignancies. Other long-term complications include post-transplant diabetes, avascular necrosis and other musculoskeletal problems, cataracts, and recurrence of the original renal disease in the trans-planted kidney. In addition, each year after the first decade, approximately one in 50 kidney grafts is lost (First, 1993). After a failed transplant, another can be undertaken but finding a suitable donor kidney is more difficult, due to the patient's HLA sensitization as a result of the previous graft.

The transplanted kidney may be obtained from a cadaveric or a live donor. Given the difficulties of meeting the demands for kidney grafts from cadaveric donors, there has been increased use of live related donors and, more recently, also of live unrelated donors such as spouses and friends. The decision to donate a kidney involves complex ethical issues (Kasiske and Bia, 1995), not least because the benefits to the donor of giving the "gift of life" (Simmons *et al.*, 1977) to the recipient are tempered by a small but significant mortality rate (approximately 0.03%) and a 5 year morbidity rate of 0.2%.

End-stage renal failure can occur at all ages. This chapter will focus on its impact for adults, and will concentrate on the effects of renal failure itself, and its management. Although the disease which gave rise to the renal failure (such as diabetes) will in many cases make a substantial contribution to psychological morbidity, consideration of these other physical factors is beyond the scope of this chapter.

PSYCHOLOGICAL IMPACT OF RENAL REPLACEMENT THERAPIES

The experience of haemodialysis is arguably unique. Twice or three times weekly, the person becomes a patient, with life depending on the dialysis machine and on those who maintain it and assist in the procedure. Off dialysis, the same individual might show no signs to casual observers or even friends of being unwell. During these times off dialysis, families can put considerable pressure on the individual to lead a "normal" life. This may be exacerbated by the patient's feelings of indebtedness towards the family for tolerating the dialysis, which usually becomes part of the family ritual, especially if the patient dialyses at home. This process has been described as a form of double bind (Alexander, 1976).

There are two important differences between transplanting kidneys and other organs. First, transplantation is one of several options for replacement therapy for people with end-stage renal failure. A person in terminal heart or liver failure would die without a transplant. A person in renal failure can continue on dialysis. Despite the advantages of transplantation, some individuals elect to remain on dialysis (Callender *et al.*, 1989). Some individuals, because they are able to exercise this choice, consider themselves responsible for the consequences, even when the choice is illusory, and medical advice points to only one viable option. Renal transplantation is unusual also in that kidneys can and are transplanted from live donors. Live donors are also used in bone marrow transplantation, but here, the organ tends to be perceived as less tangible than the kidney. Renal transplant recipients may form a special relationship with their new kidney. Thus one woman in her 50s commented that "it's a funny old kidney this—it always wakes up at night ..." (referring to her nocturia). Live donors continue to be sought because the demand for transplants far exceeds the cadaveric kidneys available. However, others have argued that live kidney donation is often a "gift of love", which not only offers the recipient the prospect of much improved quality of life, but also in many instances has a very positive emotional and psychological impact on the donor (Simmons *et al.*, 1987). Often, the relationship between recipient and donor becomes much closer, which may have complex repercussions for the families involved. Nevertheless, live kidney donation has very complex effects on everyone concerned. If such a transplant fails, both donor and recipient sometimes feel overwhelming guilt and responsibility, which may be shared by others in the family who encouraged the transplant. Until recently, live donors have been close relatives of the recipients. Even the process of finding a suitable related donor within the family is complex (Sensky and Mee, 1989). The increasing success rate of transplants from nonrelated live donors has opened up new possibilities of kidney donation by spouses and others, but this also brings with it even more complex relationship changes. One illustration of the complexity of these relationships is the unexpected finding that people on dialysis have a worse outcome if their families appear cohesive (Reiss *et al.*, 1986).

DEPRESSION—PRESENTATION AND DIFFERENTIAL DIAGNOSIS

As with other types of physical illness, the diagnosis of depression in people on chronic dialysis is complicated by the fact that the biological symptoms of depression are common, even in the absence of a depressive disorder. Symptoms which are generally unhelpful in diagnosing depression in this patient group include fatigue, loss of energy, apathy, insomnia, and decreased sexual interest (Smith *et al.*, 1985; Craven *et al.*, 1987; Hinrichsen *et al.*, 1989). Most of these symptoms are associated with uraemia. Restless legs syndrome is commonly associated with sleep disturbance among those on dialysis (Walker *et al.*, 1995), and this may prove helpful in distinguishing insomnia due to uraemia from that associated with depression. Other symptoms reported to be more specifically associated with depressive disorder in renal failure include depressed mood, loss of interest, slowed or confused thinking, and anorexia and weight loss (Craven *et al.*, 1987). Cognitive features, such as feelings of worthlessness or excessive guilt, may also point to depression (Craven *et al.*, 1987; Williams and Scott, 1988; Kimmel *et al.*, 1993). However, even these symptoms must be interpreted with caution. For example, anorexia and nausea are associated with uraemia. Depressive ruminations and suicidal ideation associated with uraemia may improve after dialysis (Wise, 1974).

Among those on renal replacement therapies, suicidal ideation or behaviour constitutes a particular diagnostic problem. Noncompliance with medications or diet can rapidly put the patient at serious risk. For example, the combination of dietary abuse and missing a dialysis rapidly leads to elevated serum potassium levels which can be lethal. When such noncompliance occurs, it is in some instances motivated by suicidal thoughts. However, such behaviour may be motivated by factors other than depression or the wish to die (Rodin, 1980). For example, Leon, an Afro-Caribbean in his late teens, had been on dialysis for over a year. He was very critical of renal unit staff, blaming them for his ill-health and for his failure to get an early transplant. Unit staff tried to be as supportive as possible, but considered that whatever they did for him, he judged inadequate. He commonly abused his diet, and sometimes missed dialyses. This behaviour caused much concern to staff. Far from being suicidal, Leon's view was that life had treated him unfairly, he was not going to give in to his difficulties but try to brush them aside, and if he wanted to direct his anger at renal unit staff, he was entitled to. James, a married man in his 40s who had been on haemodialysis for over 20 years, offers an even more complex example. Three previous transplants had eventually been rejected, and he was on haemodialysis. Having become progressively more disabled by arthropathy, he now needed to use a wheelchair. Despite this, he had shown no evidence of clinical depression throughout. He and his wife (a nurse) had made a pact that, if his pain and disability became intolerable, she would help him to die by administering an injection of insulin. He had talked about this openly for some years. During a particularly difficult time, they resolved to carry out the plan. However, they were interrupted in their preparations by their two young sons, whose arrival on the scene made James and his wife realize that they could not go through with their plan. Subsequently, James experienced his first episode of depression, which required specialist intervention. His talk of suicide reflected his belief that there was one way in which he could again take control over his illness if it became intolerable, and he had continued to tolerate his illness until he realized that this belief of taking control was not sustainable.

Depression among people on chronic dialysis has a substantial list of different diagnoses in addition to uraemia. Anaemia, common in this patient group, can present with fatigue and loss of energy. Erythropoetin, used to treat the anaemia, commonly leads to improved subjective well-being (Nissenson, 1989). Electrolyte disturbances associated with poor dietary compliance can give rise to dysphoria, anxiety and confusion (Brown and Brown, 1995). Dialysis disequilibrium syndrome, associated with rapid reduction in blood nitrogen levels, commonly presents with fatigue, headaches and restlessness. Dialysis dementia may also present with a depression-like picture. Thankfully, this has become more uncommon since the recognition that aluminium contributes to its aetiology and that in renal failure, even small doses of aluminium may accumulate in the body (Sherrard, 1991).

The difficulties in diagnosing depression in dialysis do not apply to the same extent to people with a renal transplant. Transplantation corrects some of the factors giving rise to symptoms which masquerade as depression. However, cyclosporin, used for immunosuppression, can give rise to symptoms of fatigue and anorexia. Similarly, steroids and other drugs used for immunosuppression can produce a variety of symptoms.

PREVALENCE OF DEPRESSION

Reported prevalence rates of depression vary between zero and 100% (Smith *et al.*, 1985). Some studies have relied on instruments such as the General Health Questionnaire (GHQ) or the Beck Depression Inventory (BDI) (Sensky, 1993). These will tend to overestimate depression, since ratings will be inflated by the somatic symptoms commonly found in renal failure even in the absence of depression (see above). In one study of 60 patients on different forms of renal replacement therapy, for example, 47% of the sample scored as depressed on the BDI, but only 5% warranted a DSM-III diagnosis of depression (Smith *et al.*, 1985). This applies not only among those on renal replacement therapy, but also in medical inpatients generally (Clark *et al.*, 1983). In an attempt to circumvent this problem, some researchers have used a modified version of the BDI, including only the cognitive variables (Sacks *et al.*, 1990).

Where ascertainment has been rigorous, reported point prevalence rates have been within a narrower range, similar to those reported in other chronic illnesses. Smith *et al.* (1985) reported a prevalence of 5%, based on the use of the Schedule for Affective Disorders and Schizophrenia. Using the Present State Examination, House found a prevalence of 13% (House, 1987). Craven *et al.* (1987) found a prevalence of 8%, using the Diagnostic Interview Schedule. Hinrichsen and colleagues found that 7% of their haemodialysis sample met Research Diagnostic Criteria for major depression (Hinrichsen *et al.*, 1989).

Some studies have attempted to compare rates of depression in different types of dialysis—haemodialysis (either hospital-based or at home) and continuous ambulatory peritoneal dialysis. Unfortunately, it is hard to draw firm conclusions from such studies, because few researchers have paid sufficient attention to potentially confounding variables (Sensky, 1993). Many researchers have approached this question as though patients are randomly assigned to treatment methods, which is not so. Those who dialyse at home are less likely to be very ill or unemployed, and are more likely to have adequate social supports. It is, therefore, hardly surprising if those on home dialysis have lower rates of depression. This probably has no *direct* relationship with the type of treatment.

After transplantation, overall psychiatric morbidity is reduced. One study reported a prevalence rate of psychiatric morbidity of 46% after transplantation and 48% on dialysis (Kalman *et al.*, 1983). However, this relied on the use of the General Health Questionnaire to measure "caseness". Others who have used more rigorous methods to compare people on dialysis with those who have a viable transplant have found lower rates of psychiatric morbidity among the latter (House, 1987; Sensky, 1989). The prevalence rate of depression is of the order of 5% (Blazer *et al.*, 1976).

AETIOLOGY OF DEPRESSION IN END-STAGE RENAL DISEASE

Individuals who develop end-stage renal failure experience multiple loss events, often of their good health, their freedom, and sometimes of employment and close relationships. In addition, they live with the continuing threat to their health and even their lives. Those who develop psychiatric disorders tend to show evidence of family problems (House, 1987). Spouses of people on haemodialysis report elevated levels of depression and anxiety (Speidel *et al.*, 1979). However, this surfeit of negative life events, chronic difficulties and ambivalent social support cannot alone account for depression in this patient group, for two main reasons. First, the prevalence of psychiatric disorder in general, and depression in particular, is much the same in end-stage renal failure as in other chronic physical illnesses in which adverse life events are possibly less frequent. Secondly, one of the key predictors of psychiatric disorder in the patient group is a past history of psychiatric disorder, predating the onset of the renal failure (Sensky, 1989). As in other physical illnesses, depression is often more closely associated with patients' perceptions of their disease than with (objective) disease severity (Sacks *et al.*, 1990).

Other specific organic aetiological factors may be important in individual cases. For example, depression is the most common psychiatric presentation of hyperparathyroidism, common in this patient group. Parathyroidectomy can improve mood disturbance (Brown and Brown, 1995). Chronic renal failure gives rise to disturbances in noradrenaline and serotonin metabolism. It has been suggested that the combination in renal failure of reduced intraneuronal noradrenaline and decreased noradrenaline release can cause dysphoria (Brown and Brown, 1995). Currently available data on the changes in serotonin are inconsistent, with some reports suggesting marked elevation in plasma levels (Kerr *et al.*, 1992), and others finding the opposite (Steyn *et al.*, 1992). To what extent such peripheral changes in serotonin metabolism reflect brain changes is unknown. In some instances, iatrogenic factors may also play a part. For example, hypertension is common in chronic renal failure, and the use of some beta-blocking drugs may predispose to depression.

Numerous psychological factors have also been cited as potentially important in the onset and maintenance of depression in renal failure. In a study based on the learned helplessness concept, depression was found to correlate with the patient's experience of his circumstances as uncontrollable, his illness as intrusive, and with an external locus of control (Devins *et al.*, 1981, 1983). In another study, depression scores correlated with external locus of control, and inversely with beliefs in control by professionals and family (Sensky, 1989). This suggests that depression is less frequent among those who either have confidence in their own ability to control their illness and symptoms, or who can place their trust and confidence in professionals and family. However, while such beliefs may be adaptive when they reflect the patient's actual circumstances, they can lead to increased depression when the patient has evidence that this illness is difficult to control, for example after experiencing a failed transplant (Christensen *et al.*, 1991) (see also the case of James, above). Possibly related to this is the finding that lower rates of mood disturbance are associated with the use of denial (Fricchione *et al.*, 1992). Psychodynamic models of dialysis have tended to emphasize the difficulties of loss of health, and adjustment to illness (Israel, 1986), as well as concerns about control (Viederman, 1978; Levy, 1981). Low tolerance of frustration and aggression have been reported to be common among people on renal dialysis (Kaplan De Nour and Czaczkes, 1972) (also illustrated by the case of Leon, above), and depression has been seen by some as the introjection of this aggression (Israel, 1986).

One factor common to many of these psychological models is the concept of gradual adjustment and adaptation to chronic renal failure. Consistent with this is the finding by some researchers that the prevalence of psychiatric morbidity is inversely related to the duration of treatment (Maher *et al.*, 1983; House, 1987).

After transplantation, affective disorders have in the past been commonly associated with organic factors which are less likely to occur now, such as use of high dose steroids for immunosuppression (Blazer *et al.*, 1976; McCabe and Corry, 1978). Because a successful transplant can make such a great difference to the individual and the family, depression has been described as "paradoxical" (Greene, 1984). However, psychological factors can be important in aetiology, as illustrated by the case of Elsie, a woman in her 50s who had her first transplant after several years on dialysis. In earlier years, she was the matriarch of a close and very caring family, who ran a greengrocer's shop. As she became increasingly disabled through her renal failure, others in the family gradually took over her roles. One key role remained—she cared for her granddaughter for some years, while the child's mother was herself going through difficulties. Her successful transplant came shortly after her daughter's life settled to the extent that the child returned to live with her mother. Although physically well following her transplant, Elsie was left without any of the roles in life which had previously served to define her as a person. She became increasingly depressed and anxious, particularly about harm coming to the family. She expected her daughters to telephone her several times daily, to confirm that they were safe and well. On one occasion, she commented that "worrying is all I am good at now". Graham, a 29-year-old single unemployed computer programmer, had been on dialysis for some years before having a successful transplant. He was referred for psychiatric assessment because his rehabilitation was progressing extremely slowly, and because he developed headaches and chest pains whenever he tried to work at the computer for more than a few minutes. It eventually emerged that his life had been focused on the dialysis unit. He had no social life outside the unit, and had excused his lack of social contacts and work by saying that he was not well enough to pursue these while on dialysis. When he was able to acknowledge this, he became depressed for the first time.

These two cases illustrate the complexities of adjustment to transplantation, which has proved difficult to assess systematically, particularly quantitatively. However successful the transplant from the medical viewpoint, the new organ, often initially viewed as "alien", must be incorporated into the recipient's body image (Stewart, 1983). Sometimes, the recipient fears that, through the transplant, he will acquire characteristics of the donor (Belk, 1990). When the transplanted kidney has come from a live donor, this can sometimes cause problems. Thus, for example, a brother can worry that his sexuality will change as a result of his sister donating a kidney to him. This particular fear is made more troublesome by the fact that many people on dialysis suffer sexual problems and look to transplantation to correct these.

Psychiatric morbidity 12 months after transplantation is predicted by depression before transplantation, but not to the same extent by social supports, or social adjustment (Sensky, 1989). Depression 12 months after transplantation correlated with the degree of change of "powerful others" locus of control. One might have expected that adaptation would be more successful if the patient was able to modify his locus of control beliefs with his changing circumstances. However, this finding suggests that being able to preserve some of one's beliefs about control may be adaptive.

IMPACT OF DEPRESSION

A key feature of depression is its effect on the individual's perceptions of his life and appraisal of his circumstances (Sensky, 1990). This applies equally in those with renal failure as in others. Depression alters appraisal of the illness and of treatment (Sacks *et al.*, 1990; Sensky and Catalan, 1992), and influences the individual's assessment of quality of life (Sensky, 1988).

The relationship in chronic renal failure between depression and reduced survival rates has been well documented (Zairnik *et al.*, 1977; Wai *et al.*, 1981; Richmond *et al.*, 1982; Burton *et al.*, 1986; Kimmel *et al.*, 1993). However, others have failed to find such an association (Devins *et al.*, 1990). High rates of suicide have been described among people on renal replacement therapy. Even among those with transplants, a suicide rate of 15% has been reported (Washer *et al.*, 1983). In this study, suicides were most commonly associated with previous psychiatric morbidity and with failed transplants. One problem with such data is the difficulty in reliably ascertaining the cause of death. In haemodialysis, failure to adhere to fluid and dietary restrictions can rapidly become life-threatening (Plough and Salem, 1982; Friend *et al.*, 1986). People on haemodialysis therefore possess a readily available means to kill themselves. Depression may be one reason why a person decides not to adhere to the medical regime (see below), but there are undoubtedly other reasons (see again the case of Leon, above). It is quite likely that suicide is overreported as a cause of death among those on dialysis. After transplantation, failure to follow the immunosuppression regime can be life-threatening, but again, there are a multitude of reasons why an individual may choose to do this.

Evidence that depression can influence adherence to dietary or fluid restrictions in haemodialysis has been equivocal. Many published studies have methodological shortcomings, notably that they have assumed that the same psychological factors are likely to influence adherence to both dietary and fluid restrictions. There is no *a priori* reason to make this assumption, and nor is it supported by research evidence (Sensky, 1993). In a recent study examining the possible impact on adherence of a range of psychological factors, depression was associated with more erratic adherence to diet, but not with adherence to fluid restrictions (Sensky *et al.*, 1996). However, the relationship between depression and adherence was complex, and is probably mediated by other factors. Thus among younger patients, erratic dietary adherence was associated with a combination of depression, poor social adjustment and strong beliefs in the control of one's health by others. By contrast, among older patients, strong beliefs in control of illness by others plus depression were associated with the least erratic compliance. Superficially, this finding may appear counterintuitive. However, there is no reason why similar beliefs, about locus of control for example, should lead to similar behaviour across all age groups. In this instance, older people, with greater experience of renal failure and its management, might be more inclined than young patients to show flexibility in their treatment regime—"reasoned" rather than "ritual" adherence (O'Brien, 1990).

MANAGEMENT OF DEPRESSION

From what has been said above, the first consideration must be careful attention to assessment and diagnosis. Once a diagnosis of depression has been reached, it is essential to review the overall management to date, and to identify possible organic and/or iatrogenic aetiological factors which can be reversed or brought under better control. Beyond this, clinical depression requires treatment in those with renal failure just as in others. As in other physical illnesses, depression in chronic renal failure should never be assumed to be an understandable or inevitable consequence of the illness and therefore an integral part of the illness, not requiring specific treatment.

There have been few clinical trials of antidepressant drugs in people with chronic renal failure, and these have been confined to open studies involving only a few patients (Rosser, 1976; Kennedy *et al.*, 1989). Nevertheless, such studies demonstrate that antidepressant therapy can be as effective in those with renal failure as in people who are physically healthy. Prescribing in renal failure requires caution and attention to each individual's physical state (Bennett *et al.*, 1987; Bennett, 1988). Uraemia (or its management) can have profound effects on the bioavailability of a drug, as well as distribution and metabolism (Bennett *et al.*, 1987). Long-term haemodialysis leads to increased plasma levels of the conjugated metabolites of some tricyclic antidepressants, and also plasma levels of the parent drug may be reduced (Sandoz *et al.*, 1984; Lieberman *et al.*, 1985). One reason for this latter finding is that volume of distribution of the drug may be altered through reduction in protein binding, which affects some drugs (such as diazepam) but not others (such as imipramine and maprotiline) (Lynn *et al.*, 1981; Vanholder *et al.*, 1988). Protein binding is also important in influencing the removal of a drug during dialysis. A further complication is that reduced levels of serum albumin are not uncommon in patients with chronic renal failure.

The choice of a particular antidepressant drug must depend on careful evaluation in each case, considered individually. Table 1 summarizes some information relevant to this decision. Drugs which are excreted by the kidney, either unchanged or in the form of pharmacologically active metabolites, should be avoided in those on haemodialysis. These include nomifensine, which has a much prolonged half-life in chronic renal failure, as well as citalopram, amoxapine, viloxazine and venlafaxine. Theoretically, if drugs are removed by dialysis, they could be used in treating someone on continuous peritoneal dialysis. However, very little research has been published on the pharmacokinetics of antidepressant drugs in peritoneal dialysis. It has been implied that, because serotonin levels are raised in chronic renal failure, use of selective serotonin reuptake inhibiting drugs might be more hazardous in this group of patients than in others (Brown and Brown, 1995). While it is always important to be vigilant for signs of the serotonin syndrome, there appear to have been no published reports of this in chronic renal failure to date. Also, as noted above, the evidence of raised serotonin levels in chronic renal failure is equivocal. Furthermore, a similar argument could be applied to the use of other antidepressant drugs, since chronic renal failure also leads to changes in the metabolism of other neurotransmitters besides serotonin (Brown and Brown, 1995).

Other physical treatments may also be used in chronic renal failure. What appears to be the largest published clinical trial of the treatment of depression in people on haemodialysis reported significant benefits of S-adenosyl-L-methionine, compared with placebo (Ancarani *et al.*, 1993). When clinically indicated,

Table 1. Properties of selected antidepressant drugs and their evaluation in end-stage renal failure

Drug	Half-life (hours)[a]	% Protein binding	Renal excretion[a]	Evaluation of pharmaco-kinetics[b]	Clinical trial in ESRF[c]
Amitriptyline	8–80	96	0	Y	Y
Amoxapine	8–30	90	+	N	N
Citalopram	36	<80	+ +	N	N
Clomipramine	21	98	0	N	N
Dothiepin	56	82–98	0	N	N
Fluoxetine	220	95	0	Y	N
Fluvoxamine	17–22	77	0	Y	Y
Imipramine	4–54	86	0	Y	Y
Lofepramine	17–28	99	0	N	N
Maprotiline	27–58	89	0	Y	Y
Mianserin	10–20	96	0	N	N
Moclobemide	1–2	50	0	Y	N
Nefazodone	2–4	>99	0	Y	N
Nomifensine	3	–	+ + +	N	N
Paroxetine	17	95	0	Y	N
Phenelzine	1	–	0	N	N
Sertraline	22–36	98	0	Y	Y
Trazodone	10–12	95	+	N	N
Venlafaxine	5–11	27–30	+	Y	N
Viloxazine	2–5	85–90	+	N	N

[a]including active metabolites where applicable, [b]Y = publications or reports available on pharmacokinetics in end-stage renal failure, [c]Y = publications or reports available of clinical use with patients in end-stage renal failure

electroconvulsive therapy can be effective, although anaesthetic risks are increased (Pearlman et al., 1988).

Particularly given the potential hazards of prescribing drugs in those on dialysis, cognitive–behavioural therapy warrants consideration in treating depression in this patient group. Cognitive therapy has been shown to be effective in treating depression, and there is no reason why it should be less effective in this patient group than in others (Sensky, 1993; Sensky and Wright, 1993). Often, people with chronic physical illness have beliefs or attitudes which do not serve them well. Such dysfunctional beliefs are commonly erroneous, and are a very appropriate focus for a cognitive intervention. Cognitive and biological treatments are not incompatible, and can be combined very effectively (Wright et al., 1993). Graham, mentioned above, who became depressed following a successful transplant, was treated with a combination of an antidepressant and cognitive therapy. He worked to review some of his skills and strengths which were, ironically, demonstrated by his experiences since he had to go onto dialysis. Even though his circle of acquaintances was confined to staff on the renal unit and other dialysis patients, he was able to recognize that these contacts demonstrated that he still had social and personal skills, which gave him more confidence to contemplate new relationships. His fiancée had ended their relationship when he first started dialysis, and he believed that he would never be able to form another close relationship. The therapy allowed him to challenge this belief. By breaking down the tasks and skills he needed to return to a "normal" life, he was able to set himself a step-by-step plan for this, which made the task more manageable and reduced his anxiety and hopelessness. Jane, a married mother of two in her late 30s, felt very guilty about her illness and her need to dialyse. She did everything possible to reduce the impact of her illness on the family. When she started cognitive therapy for depression, it became apparent that, in her attempt to "compensate" the family for her illness, she had completely neglected her own needs and wishes. The only independent time which she permitted herself was while she was on dialysis. Despite her pleasure in her family, her life had become increasingly burdensome. The therapy allowed her to recognize this, and then to negotiate with the family to have more opportunity to pursue the artistic interests which had previously given her pleasure and satisfaction, but which she had increasingly denied herself.

Cognitive therapy can also be useful in managing some of the problems possibly associated with depression, such as inadequate adherence to dietary or fluid restrictions (even though the associations between depression and adherence remain equivocal, they are undoubtedly important in individual cases). Tony, who had diabetes as well as chronic renal failure, usually took great interest and pride in his cooking. When he became depressed, his eating habits became more careless, and this was reflected in his blood tests. Initially, he was angry with renal clinic staff for drawing his attention to his poor adherence, accusing them of adding yet another burden to cope with. However, this belief and others were successfully challenged and modified in therapy.

CONCLUSIONS

There are several theoretical reasons, psychological as well as biological, why people on renal replacement therapies might be particularly prone to episodes of depression. However, no convincing evidence is currently available to support the importance of such special aetiological factors, and the best available data indicate that the prevalence of depression among those on long-term dialysis is no different from that reported in other chronic physical illnesses. Successful transplantation may lead to a reduced prevalence of depression, but the aetiology of depression under such circumstances is even less clear.

The management of depression in chronic renal failure, as in other physical illnesses, depends on careful assessment and diagnosis, with the management plan taking into careful consideration the individual's illness as well as his depression and circumstances. In principle, depression in this patient group should otherwise be managed in the same way as in other physical illnesses. There is relatively little published information on the pharmacokinetics and/or clinical efficacy of antidepressant drugs in chronic renal failure. Most of the data available have been gathered from samples of people on haemodialysis, and are unlikely to apply to those on continuous ambulatory peritoneal dialysis. As in other chronic physical illnesses, depression and problems associated with it are amenable to treatment using cognitive–behavioural therapy.

REFERENCES

Alexander L (1976) The double-bind theory and haemodialysis. *Arch Gen Psychiatry*, **33**, 1353–1356.

Ancarani E, Biondi B, Bolleta A and Cestra D (1993) Major depression complicating haemodialysis in patients with chronic renal failure: A multicenter, double-blind, controlled clinical trial of S-adenosyl-L-methionine versus placebo. *Curr Ther Res*, **54**, 680–686.

Belk RW (1990) Me and thee versus mine and thine: how perceptions of the body influence organ donation and transplantation. In: J Shanteau and RJ Harris (eds) *Organ Donation and Transplantation: Psychological and Behavioural Factors*. Washington DC: American Psychological Press, 139–149.

Bennett WM (1988) Guide to drug dosage in renal failure. *Clin Pharmacokinet*, **15**, 326–354.

Bennett WM, Aronoff GR, Golper TA, Morrison G, Singer I and Brater DC (1987) *Drug Prescribing in Renal Failure: Dosing Guidelines for Adults*. Philadelphia: American College of Physicians.

Blazer DG, Petrie WM and Wilson WP (1976) Affective psychoses following renal transplant. *Dis Nerv System*, **37**, 663–667.

Brown TM and Brown RLS (1995) Neuropsychiatric consequences of renal failure. *Psychosomatics*, **36**, 244–253.

Burton HJ, Kline SA, Lindsay RM and Heidenheim AP (1986) The relationship of depression to survival in chronic renal failure. *Psychosom Med*, **48**, 261–268.

Callender CO, Jennings PS, Bayton JA, Flores JC, Tagunicar H, Yeager C and Bond O (1989) Psychologic factors related to dialysis in kidney transplant decisions. *Transplant Proc*, **21**, 1976–1978.

Christensen AJ, Turner CW, Smith TW, Holman JM and Gregory MC (1991) Health locus of control and depression in end-stage renal disease. *J Consult Clin Psychol*, **59**, 419–424.

Clark DC, Cavanaugh SV and Gibbons RD (1983) The core symptoms of depression in medical and psychiatric patients. *J Nerv Ment Dis*, **171**, 705–713.

Craven JL, Rodin GM, Johnson L *et al.* (1987) The diagnosis of major depression in renal dialysis patients. *Psychosom Med*, **49**, 482–492.

D'Amico G (1995) Comparability of the different registries on renal replacement therapy. *Am J Kidney Dis*, **25**, 113–118.

Devins GM, Binik YM, Hollomby DJ, Barre PR and Guttman RD (1981) Helplessness and depression in end-stage renal disease. *J Abnorm Psychol*, **90**, 531–545.

Devins GM, Binik YM, Hutchinson TA, Hollomby DJ, Barre PE and Guttman RD (1983) The emotional impact of end-stage renal disease: importance of patients' perceptions of intrusiveness and control. *Int J Psychiatry Med*, **13**, 327–343.

Devins GM, Mann J, Mandin H, Paul LC, Hons RB, Burgess ED, Taub K, Schorr S, Letourneau PK and Buckle S (1990) Psychosocial predictors of survival in end-stage renal disease. *J Nerv Ment Dis*, **178**, 127–133.

Evans RW, Rader B and Manninen DL (1990) The quality of life of hemodialysis recipients treated with recombinant human erythropoietin. Cooperative Multicenter EPO Clinical Trial Group. *JAMA*, **263**, 825–830.

First MR (1993) Long-term complications after transplantation. *Am J Kidney Dis*, **22**, 477–486.

Fricchione GL, Howanitz E, Jandorf L, Kroessler D, Zervas I and Woznicki RM (1992) Psychological adjustment to end-stage renal disease and the implications of denial. *Psychosomatics*, **33**, 85–91.

Friend R, Singletary Y, Mendell NR and Nurse H (1986) Group participation and survival among patients with end-stage renal disease. *Am J Public Health*, **76**, 670–672.

Greene WA (1984) Paradoxical depression in successfully transplanted patients. *Dialysis Transplant*, **12**, 149–151.

Hinrichsen GA, Lieberman JA, Pollack S and Steinberg H (1989) Depression in haemodialysis patients. *Psychosomatics*, **30**, 284–289.

House A (1987) Psychosocial problems of patients on the renal unit and their relation to treatment outcome. *J Psychosom Res*, **31**, 441–452.

Israel M (1986) Depression in dialysis patients: a review of psychological factors. *Can J Psychiatry*, **31**, 445–451.

Kalman TP, Wilson PG and Kalman CM (1983) Psychiatric morbidity in long-term transplant recipients and in patients undergoing haemodialysis. *JAMA*, **250**, 55–58.

Kaplan De Nour A and Czaczkes JW (1972) Personality factors in chronic haemodialysis causing non-compliance with medical regimen. *Psychosom Med*, **34**, 333–344.

Kasiske BL and Bia MJ (1995) The evaluation and selection of living kidney donors. *American J Kidney Dis*, **26**, 387–398.

Kennedy SH, Craven JL, Rodin GM and Roin GMR (1989) Major depression in renal dialysis patients: an open trial of antidepressant therapy. *J Clin Psychiatry*, **50**, 60–63.

Kerr PG, Argiles A and Mion C (1992) Whole blood serotonin levels are markedly elevated in patients on dialytic therapy. *Am J Nephrol*, **12**, 14–18.

Kimmel PL, Weihs K and Peterson RA (1993) Survival in hemodialysis patients: the role of depression. *J Am Soc Nephrol*, **4**, 12–27.

Levy NB (1981) Psychological reactions to machine dependency: haemodialysis. *Psychiatr Clin North Am*, **4**, 351–363.

Lieberman JA, Cooper TB, Suckow RF, Steinberg H, Borenstein M, Brenner R and Kane JM (1985) Tricyclic antidepressant and metabolite levels in chronic renal failure. *Clin Pharmacol Ther*, **37**, 301–307.

Lynn K, Braithwaite R, Dawling S and Rosser R (1981) Comparison of the serum binding of maprotiline and phenytoin in uraemic patients on haemodialysis. *Eur J Clin Pharmacol*, **19**, 73–77.

Maher BA, Lamping DL, Dickinson CA, Murawski BJ, Oliver DC and Santiago GC (1983) Psychosocial aspects of chronic haemodialysis: The National Cooperative Dialysis study. *Kidney International*, **23(Suppl 13)**, S50–S57.

Mallick NP, Jones E and Selwood N (1995) The European (European Dialysis and Transplantation Association—European Renal Association) Registry. *Am J Kidney Dis,* **25**, 176–187.

McCabe MS and Corry RJ (1978) Psychiatric illness and human renal transplantation. *J Clin Psychiatry,* **39**, 393–400.

Nissenson AR (1989) Recombinant human erythropoietin: Impact on brain and cognitive function, exercise tolerance, sexual potency and quality of life. *Semin Nephrol,* **9(1 Suppl 2)**, 25–31.

O'Brien ME (1990) Compliance behaviour and long-term maintenance dialysis. *Am J Kidney Dis,* **15**, 209–214.

Pearlman C, Carson W and Metz A (1988) Hemodialysis, chronic renal failure, and ECT. *Convulsive Ther,* **4**, 332–333.

Plough AL and Salem A (1982) Social and contextual factors in the analyses of mortality in end-stage renal disease: Implications for health policy. *Am J Public Health,* **72**, 1293–1295.

Reiss D, Gonzalez S and Kramer N (1986) Family process, chronic illness, and death: On the weakness of strong bonds. *Arch Gen Psychiatry,* **43**, 795–804.

Richmond JM, Lindsay RM, Burton HJ, Conley J and Wai L (1982) Psychological and physiological factors predicting outcome on home haemodialysis. *Clin Nephrol,* **17**, 109–113.

Rodin GM (1980) Renal dialysis and the liaison psychiatrist. *Can J Psychiatry,* **25**, 473–477.

Rosser R (1976) Depression during renal dialysis and following transplantation. *Proc R Soc Med,* **69**, 832–834.

Sacks CR, Peterson RA and Kimmel PL (1990) Perception of illness and depression in chronic renal disease. *Am J Kidney Dis,* **15**, 31–39.

Sandoz M, Vandel S, Vandel B, Bonin B, Hory B, St Hillier Y and Volmat R (1984) Metabolism of amitriptyline in patients with chronic renal failure. *Eur J Clin Pharmacol,* **26**, 227–232.

Sensky T (1988) Measurement of quality of life in end-stage renal failure. *N Engl J Med,* **319**, 3153.

Sensky T (1989) Psychiatric morbidity in renal transplantation. *Psychother Psychosom,* **52**, 41–46.

Sensky T (1990) Patients' reactions to illness: Cognitive factors determine responses and are amenable to treatment. *Br Med J,* **300**, 622–623.

Sensky T (1993) Cognitive therapy in physical illness. In: M Hodes and S Moorey (eds) *Psychological Treatment in Human Disease and Illness.* London: Gaskell Press.

Sensky T (1993) Psychosomatic aspects of end-stage renal failure. *Psychother Psychosom,* **59**, 56–68.

Sensky T and Catalan J (1992) Asking patients about their treatment: Why their answers should not always be taken at face value. *Br Med J,* **305**, 1109–1110.

Sensky T and Mee AD (1989) Dilemmas faced by dialysis patients in search of a living related kidney donor. *Dialysis Transplantation,* **18**, 243–249.

Sensky T and Wright J (1993) Cognitive therapy with medical patients. In: JH Wright, ME Thase, AT Beck and JW Ludgate (eds) *Cognitive Therapy with Inpatients: Developing a Cognitive Milieu,* New York: Guilford Press, 219–246.

Sensky T, Leger C and Gilmour S (1996) Psychosocial and cognitive factors associated with adherence to dietary and fluid restriction regimens by people on chronic haemodialysis. *Psychother Psychosom,* **65**, 36–42.

Sherrard DJ (1991) Aluminium—much ado about something. *N Engl J Med,* **324**, 558–559.

Simmons RG, Klein SD and Simmons RL (1977) *The Gift of Life: The Social and Psychological Impact of Organ Transplant.* New York: Wiley.

Simmons RG, Marine SK and Simmons RL (1987) *Gift of Life: The Effect of Organ Transplantation on Individual, Family and Societal Dynamics.* New Brunswick NJ: Transaction.

Smith MD, Hong BA and Robson AM (1985) Diagnosis of depression in patients with end-stage renal disease. *Am J Med,* **79**, 160–166.

Speidel H, Koch V, Balck F and Kneiss J (1979) Problems in interaction between patients undergoing long-term haemodialysis and their partners. *Psychother Psychosom,* **31**, 235–242.

Stewart RS (1983) Psychiatric issues in renal dialysis and transplantation. *Hosp Community Psychiatry,* **34**, 623–628.

Steyn ME, Viljoen M, Ubbink JB, van Rensburg BW and Reinach SG (1992) Whole blood serotonin levels in chronic renal failure. *Life Sciences,* **51**, 359–366.

United States Renal Data System (1993) Excerpts from the 1993 USRDS Annual Data Report. *Am J Kidney Dis,* **22.**

Vanholder R, Van Landschoot N, De Smet R, Shoots A and Ringoir S (1988) Drug protein binding in chronic renal failure: Evaluation of nine drugs. *Kidney Int,* **33**, 996–1004.

Viederman M (1978) On the vicissitudes of the need for control in patients confronted with haemodialysis. *Compr Psychiatry,* **19**, 455–467.

Wai L, Richmond J, Burton H and Lindsay RM (1981) Influence of psychosocial factors on survival of home-dialysis patients. *Lancet,* **ii**, 1155–1156.

Walker S, Fine A and Kryger MH (1995) Sleep complaints are common in a dialysis unit. *Am J Kidney Dis,* **26**, 751–756.

Washer GF, Schroter GPJ, Starzl TE and Weil R (1983) Causes of death after kidney transplantation. *JAMA,* **250**, 49–54.

Williams JMG and Scott J (1988) Autobiographical memory in depression. *Psychol Med,* **18**, 689–695.

Wise TN (1974) The pitfalls of diagnosing depression in chronic renal disease. *Psychosomatics,* **15**, 83–84.

Wright JH, Thase ME and Sensky T (1993) Cognitive and biological therapies: A combined approach. In: JH Wright, ME Thase, AT Beck and JW Ludgate (eds), *Cognitive Therapy with Inpatients: Developing a Cognitive Milieu.* New York: Guilford Press, 193–218.

Zairnik JP, Freeman CW, Sherrard DJ and Calsyn DA (1977) Psychological correlates of survival on renal dialysis. *J Nerv Ment Dis,* **164**, 210–213.

19

Depression in arthritis and musculoskeletal disorders

Jerry C. Parker and Gail E. Wright

The term "arthritis" refers to inflammation of one or more joints and is, therefore, highly nonspecific. In fact, there are over 127 forms of arthritis ranging from relatively minor conditions, such as bursitis, to major disabling diseases, such as rheumatoid arthritis (Fries, 1986). Taken as a whole, the arthritides have a major socioeconomic impact. In the USA the combined direct and indirect costs of arthritis are estimated to be $17 billion per year (Burkhauser *et al.*, 1986). In the case of a disabling condition such as rheumatoid arthritis (RA), 37% of those afflicted experience a reduction in work capacity (Yelin *et al.*, 1987). As a group, people with RA earn only 50% of their expected income in comparison to age- and education-matched controls (Meenan *et al.*, 1981).

Arthritis is particularly costly and disabling for the elderly (Yelin, 1992). For persons over 70 years of age, 55% report some form of arthritis, and 78% of the afflicted elderly report physical limitations (Yelin, 1992). Thirty-six per cent of elderly people with arthritis report limitations in their activities of daily living. The data are unequivocal that arthritis is a major contributor to both economic hardship and physical disability in all age groups, but particularly in the elderly (Yelin, 1992).

Beyond these socioeconomic aspects, arthritis also exacts a heavy psychological and emotional toll on many people who have one or more of the

Depression and Physical Illness. Edited by M.M. Robertson and C.L.E. Katona
© 1997 John Wiley & Sons Ltd

diseases. Again, using RA as an example, 40% of people with RA experience limitations in their social roles (Liang *et al.*, 1984). Sixty-one per cent report family-related problems (Liang *et al.*, 1984), and over 50% report sexual difficulties (Blake *et al.*, 1987; Yoshino and Uchida, 1981). Lastly, 89% of people with RA report interference with their leisure/recreational pursuits (Yelin *et al.*, 1987).

Information on the full extent of the psychological and/or psychiatric aspects of arthritis is limited. The prevalence of psychological sequelae from arthritis appears to vary widely on the basis of such factors as demographic characteristics, disease type, disease severity, disease duration, and presence or absence of comorbidities. The manifestation of psychological and/or psychiatric conditions in a given individual also is mediated to some extent by the effectiveness of the coping process (Parker *et al.*, 1989). A sizable percentage of people with arthritis experience emotional distress secondary to multiple stressors such as pain, loss of income, disruption of social roles, and restriction of daily activities. However, the manifestation of psychological and/or psychiatric problems in the arthritides is far from universal; some people with arthritis cope extremely well and are able to avoid emotional and/or psychological problems (DeVellis, 1993).

When people with a chronic medical illness, such as arthritis, develop a concomitant depressive disorder, there are implications for physical functioning. Patients with arthritis who are depressed have been shown to exhibit deteriorated clinical status and higher levels of pain (Wells *et al.*, 1989; Katz and Yelin, 1993). So, from a clinical perspective, the diagnosis and management of depression assumes great importance in the context of chronic medical disease.

PREVALENCE OF DEPRESSION IN SELECTED MUSCULOSKELETAL DISORDERS

The literature on the prevalence of depression in musculoskeletal disorders is confusing for several reasons. First, the term depression is used in multiple ways by different authors. When a stringent definition of depression is used, the prevalence estimates, not surprisingly, are much lower. Second, most studies use convenience samples which vary widely on potentially confounding demographic characteristics, so a consensus across studies is difficult to achieve. Third, some symptoms of depression (e.g. fatigue) are also symptoms of rheumatic disease. Therefore, the inclusion (or exclusion) of these potential overlap symptoms affects the estimates of the prevalence of depression. Until well-controlled studies are conducted on representative samples, data on the prevalence of depression in arthritis must be viewed with caution.

Rheumatoid arthritis

With regard to the prevalence of depression in RA, the data have ranged from a low of 3% (Fifield *et al.*, 1995) to a high of 80% (Rimón and Laakso, 1984). The high figure of Rimón and Laakso is based on self-reports of depressive symptomatology, and in fact, depressive symptoms are known to be widespread in persons with chronic medical illnesses (Rodin *et al.*, 1991). The more conservative estimates of Fifield *et al.* are based on structured diagnostic interviews for major depression, and overlap symptoms are generally excluded. Following a comprehensive literature review, Creed and Ash (1992) concluded that the prevalence of major depression in RA ranges from 17% to 27%; these estimates were based on studies using structured diagnostic interviews and carefully devised research methods. However, the work of Fifield *et al.* suggests that the prevalence of major depression (as a distinct diagnostic entity) may be somewhat lower in RA than has previously been suggested, even though depressive symptomatology in RA is quite common. Further studies are needed to establish more accurately the prevalence of depression in RA.

Osteoarthritis (OA)

Data on the prevalence of depression in OA are particularly lacking. Although not specially addressing depression, Yelin *et al.* (1987) found that 49% of people with OA report losses in social relationships, 42% report losses in work activities, and 57% encounter problems with transportation. Notably, 82% of people with OA experience losses in leisure or recreational activities (Yelin *et al.*, 1987). Given such profound functional losses, a relatively high prevalence of depression for people with OA would be expected. In fact, Hawley and Wolfe (1991) found that depression in OA was approximately as high as the level of depression found in RA. Similarly, Zautra *et al.* (1994) found similar levels of depression in OA and RA patients. Although the literature is limited, the available studies suggest that depression in OA is a substantial clinical problem.

Systemic lupus erythematosus (SLE)

With regard to SLE, Omdal *et al.* (1995) found that patients with SLE have higher levels of depression than controls, although a specific prevalence figure for depression was not reported. Overall, however, Omdal *et al.* found that 47% of people with SLE present with some form of psychological distress. Liang *et al.* (1984), using the Minnesota Multiphasic Personality Inventory (MMPI), found that 41% of a sample of SLE patients had elevated depression scales. Hay *et al.* (1992), using a structured diagnostic interview, found that 20.5% of SLE patients met the criteria for some form of psychiatric diagnosis (11% met the diagnostic criteria for depression). Wekking (1993) reported that 17–21% of persons with SLE exhibit psychiatric symptomatology. Once again, the available literature suggests that depression is considerably more prevalent in persons with SLE than in the general population.

Fibromyalgia

The question of the prevalence of depression in fibromyalgia (including the possibility of an aetiological role) has been extensively debated. At one extreme, Clark *et al.* (1985) found no difference between fibromyalgia patients and a general medical comparison group on measures of depression. Burckhardt *et al.* (1994), however, examined the rates of depression in a fibromyalgia sample and, not surprisingly, found that the prevalence estimates for depression varied depending upon the specific clinical instrument. For example, based on the Beck Depression Inventory, the prevalence of depression in fibromyalgia was 55%; based on the MMPI, 44%; based on the "adjusted" Beck Depression Inventory, 29%; and based on the Computerized-Diagnostic Interview Schedule, 22%. Hudson *et al.* (1985), using a structured diagnostic interview, estimated the prevalence of depression in fibromyalgia to be 71%. Ahles *et al.* (1991) reported that the life-time prevalence of depression in fibromyalgia was 34%. Lastly, Wolfe *et al.* (1984) found that depression scores were higher for patients with fibromyalgia than for an RA comparison group. Therefore, the evidence is strong that the prevalence of depression, and other types of psychological distress, is higher in fibromyalgia than in the general population.

RISK FACTORS FOR DEPRESSION

Risk factors for depression vary according to the specific depression subtype, but the risk factors associated with major depression are useful as a general introduction to the topic. In the general population, a key risk factor for major depression is a history of prior episodes of depression (Depression Guideline Panel, 1993a). If a person has a history of one previous episode of major depression, the probability of a second episode is 50%. Following two previous episodes, the probability of recurrence is 70%. After three previous episodes, the probability of recurrence is 90%. In addition, a history of prior suicide attempts also increases the probability for developing a subsequent depression (Depression Guideline Panel, 1993b). So, in general, prior depression and/or suicide attempts are key risk factors for subsequent depressive episodes.

Similarly, a family history of depressive disorder is a risk factor for major depression (Depression Guideline Panel, 1993b), although the specific mechanism is not entirely clear. First-degree biological relatives have rates of major depression which are 1.5–3.0 times higher than that of the general population (American Psychiatric Association, 1994), but there remains the possibility that childrearing practices, nutrition, or socioeconomic conditions may be responsible for the increased risk of depression in biological relatives.

Another risk factor for major depression is female gender. In the general population, the life-time prevalence of major depression is 10–25% for women as compared to 5–12% for men (American Psychiatric Association, 1994). Once again, the reason for the higher prevalence of depression in women is not entirely clear. There may be a biological vulnerability to depression in women, or conversely, women may simply be more willing to disclose depressive symptoms. Evidence also exists that women bear an inordinate social, psychological, and economic burden in modern, industrialized societies (American Psyciatric Association, 1990), so the higher prevalence of depression in women may be a direct effect of stressful life experiences. Female gender as a risk factor for depression has important implications for persons with arthritis because many rheumatological diseases are significantly more prevalent in women. Therefore, one of the key risk factors for depression (i.e. female gender) is over-represented in the arthritis population.

Medical comorbidity is an additional risk factor for major depression (Rodin *et al.*, 1991). Comorbid medical conditions are particularly relevant for people with arthritis because many of the arthritides involve pain, loss of physical function, and disability. A related risk factor for depression is lack of social support (Revenson *et al.*, 1991), which is also commonly experienced by persons with arthritis. Advancing age, decreased mobility, reduced work capacity, and low self-esteem can all conspire to reduce social contacts for people with arthritis. Finally, stressful life events pose a risk factor for major depression (Turner and Beiser, 1990). For people with arthritis, stressful life events such as social and economic difficulties are common (Parker and Westra, 1989; Yelin *et al.*, 1987). So, in general, several of the risk factors for major depression are over-represented in people with musculoskeletal diseases.

Beyond the general risk factors for depression, there are also unique risk factors for people with arthritis. Newman *et al.* (1989) found that depressed mood in RA was affected by numerous demographic variables, not just disease activity *per se*. For example, Newman *et al.* (1989) found that higher depression was correlated with high levels of physical disability, longer disease duration, greater social isolation, and greater economic distress. In addition, Katz and Yelin (1995) have shown that the loss of valued activities is strongly associated with the development of depression in RA. Therefore, helping arthritis patients find ways to continue to engage in pleasurable activities appears to be a particularly important strategy for minimizing the development of depression.

DIAGNOSIS OF DEPRESSION IN MUSCULOSKELETAL DISORDERS

Impressive evidence exists that depression is severely underdiagnosed in general medical settings (Rodin *et al.*, 1991). According to these authors, over 50% of people with depression may be misdiagnosed by general medical practitioners. There are several possible reasons for the high degree of underdiagnosis. First, general practitioners are often not trained in psychiatric diagnosis. Second, depressive symptoms are easily dismissed as secondary to medical problems; the assumption is that treatment of the medical problem will alleviate the depression. Although medical illness is a risk factor for depression, symptoms do not necessarily dissipate when the medical problems are resolved. In some patients, depressive symptoms may even predate the medical disorder. For others, medical illness causes major disruptions in areas such as work, finances, and family relationships which do not quickly remit after treatment. Therefore, optimal care for people who have both a musculoskeletal disease and depression begins with accurate diagnosis.

Even for experienced practitioners, major pitfalls exist. A pervasive problem is the difficulty in disentangling the symptoms of depression from the symptoms of musculoskeletal disease. As previously noted, overlap symptoms can be confusing. For example, symptoms such as fatigue, loss of energy, and concern about health status might be attributable to *either* depression *or* musculoskeletal disease. Therefore, practitioners must take care to assign symptoms to the appropriate aetiology (or to both aetiologies). The Agency for Health Care Policy and Research guidelines (Depression Guideline Panel, 1993a) for the management of depression suggest that when both depression and a medical condition coexist, the medical condition should be treated first. If the depressive symptoms resolve following medical treatment, no further management of depression is required. However, if the depressive symptoms do not resolve, then depression needs to become a focus of treatment in its own right. This sequential approach requires that practitioners adopt a long-term view of depression and that they monitor depressive symptoms over time.

Another challenge for practitioners who care for patients who have both musculoskeletal disease and depression is the utilization of an appropriate diagnostic framework for psychiatric disorders. Simply categorizing patients as depressed versus nondepressed is insufficient; the many subtypes of depression vary widely in terms of severity and indicated treatment strategies. The distinguishing features of the various subtypes of depression must be recognized so that proper diagnosis can be accomplished. Therefore, a diagnostic framework such as the *Diagnostic and Statistical Manual of Mental Disorder—IV* (DSM-IV) (American Psychiatric Association, 1994) must be used. In the DSM-IV system, there are numerous subcategories of depression which range from major depression at one extreme to conditions such as adjustment disorder with depressed mood at the other extreme. In order to implement proper treatment, an accurate psychiatric diagnosis must first be made.

Several technical aids are available to assist with the diagnosis of depression. One type is the "structured diagnostic interview", which typically is administered on an individual basis by a trained examiner. Diagnostic interviews guide examiners through a sequence of diagnostically relevant questions, and a decision-tree yields a specific diagnosis. Studies of the utility of structured diagnostic interviews have generally found them to be both reliable and valid (Weissman *et al.*, 1995). Examples of structured diagnostic interviews are as follows: (a) Structured Clinical Interview for DSM-IIIR (Spitzer *et al.*, 1990), (b) Inventory to Diagnose Depression (Zimmerman and Coryell, 1987), (c) Diagnostic Interview Schedule (Robins *et al.*, 1985) and (d) Composite International Diagnostic Interview (World Health Organization, 1993).

A second aid in the diagnosis of depression is the self-report questionnaire. Depression questionnaires typically encompass a range of depressive symptoms which patients can either endorse or not endorse as they see fit. Most of the commonly used depression questionnaires have good reliability and validity, but they do not generally yield a specific diagnosis. Therefore, depression questionnaires are best used for screening purposes and/or for the assessment of depression severity. Depression questionnaires also have the disadvantage that the examiner cannot easily pose follow up questions on an item-by-item basis. Nevertheless, self-report questionnaires play an important screening role in the diagnosis of depression. See Chapter 1 for examples of screening questionnaires.

MANAGEMENT OF DEPRESSION IN MUSCULOSKELETAL DISORDERS

Volumes have been written on the treatment of depression (Rodin *et al.*, 1991; Depression Guideline Panel, 1993a; Manning and Frances, 1990), so only a conceptual overview is practicable for this chapter. In general, management of depression begins with the determination of a specific diagnosis. Next, there must be consideration of all comorbidities, some of which may have an aetiological role in depression. For example, if substance abuse is a comorbidity, treatment of the drug- or alcohol-related problem is indicated. Similarly, concurrent medications must be carefully reviewed because numerous pharmacological agents are known to be associated with depression (e.g. cardiovascular drugs, glucocorticoids, psychotropics, anticancer agents, antiinflammatory drugs, and antiinfective agents) (Rodin *et al.*, 1991). When indicated, medication adjustments (or changes) should be made to mitigate depressive symptoms.

When a concomitant medical condition (such as arthritis) exists, effective management of the comorbidity should be pursued. In essence, optimal rheumatological care is the foundation for the subsequent treatment of depression. Likewise, if a concomitant psychiatric disturbance exists, such as an eating disorder, the potentially causative psychiatric condition should first be treated. In addition, if a grief reaction exists, this situational reaction to a problematic life event should be the primary focus of treatment.

After comorbidities have been treated and/or ruled out, direct treatment of depression can proceed. With regard to major depression, there are three essential phases of treatment which are as follows: (a) acute phase, (b) continuation phase, and (c) maintenance phase (Depression Guideline Panel, 1993a). In the acute phase, which typically lasts for 6–12 weeks, the goal is to effect a remission. In the continuation phase, which typically lasts for 4–9 months, the goal is to avoid relapse and to sustain recovery. In the maintenance phase, which typically lasts for one or more years, the goal is to sustain recovery and to prevent recurrence. For less severe forms of depression, the treatment phases may be shorter, or they may have a different character. However, the successful management of depression is typically a long-term process which goes far beyond the treatment of the acute symptoms.

There are four major options for the treatment of depression which are as follows: (a) medication, (b) psychotherapy, (c) combined medication and psychotherapy, and (d) electroconvulsive therapy (ECT). Medication is typically indicated for the more profound forms of depression, especially moderate to severe major depression. Studies have found medication to be effective in approximately 65–70% of cases of major depression (Depression Guideline Panel, 1993a). Interestingly, the major antidepressive medication categories (i.e. tricyclics, heterocyclics, selective serotonin reuptake inhibitors, and monoamine oxidase inhibitors) do not vary substantially in their effectiveness as first-line drugs, so the selection of a medication should be based primarily on the side-effect profile which is most acceptable to the patient.

With regard to psychotherapy, there is again a variety of treatment options which range from dynamic approaches to cognitive–behavioural interventions. Meta-analysis of psychotherapy trials for major depression have revealed that approximately 50% of cases responded effectively to psychotherapy alone (Dobson, 1989). However, psychotherapy as a first-line treatment for depression is only indicated when the depression is of mild to moderate severity and when there is an absence of psychotic symptomatology.

The literature on the combination of medication and psychotherapy does not equivocally reveal that combination treatments are superior to either medication or psychotherapy alone (Manning and Frances, 1990). Therefore, treatment of depression with combined medication and psychotherapy is best reserved for cases in which there is an incomplete response to a single treatment or when there is evidence of a significant psychiatric comorbidity.

ECT is not a first-line treatment for depression. Nevertheless, ECT has been shown to be effective for severely symptomatic patients and for those who present with medication-resistant depression. Therefore, ECT has an important role in the treatment of major depression in selected cases. Typically, ECT is used only in severe depression when patients are acutely suicidal and/or dangerously delusional. ECT also has the disadvantage of having significant side-effects such as short-term retrograde and anterograde amnesia; ECT also carries the risks inherent with general anaesthesia. See Chapter 5 for a detailed discussion of treatment issues.

Another major issue in the treatment of depression is the assessment and management of suicide risk. Death by suicide occurs in approximately 15% of people with major depression (American Psychiatric Association, 1994). In cohorts with concomitant medical illnesses, the rate of suicide can be even higher. In fact, increased disability, itself, can be a risk factor for suicide. Even passive suicidal ideation can reduce medical compliance and self-care and, thereby, result in premature death (Rodin *et al.*, 1991). So, for many reasons, people with depression must be monitored carefully from the standpoint of suicide risk.

There is a somewhat limited literature on the treatment of depression in people with arthritis. Rimón (1974) used a combination of antidepressant medication (chlorimipramine) and supportive psychotherapy to treat 37 depressed RA patients. The combination treatment proved beneficial for 57% of the depressed people with RA. In contrast, Kaplan and Kozin (1981) compared people with RA who received psychotherapy with an age-matched control group; they found no significant difference in level of depression.

Three studies have addressed the success of antidepressive therapy in the context of RA patients. Fowler *et al.* (1977) used low-dose imipramine (75 mg) to treat depressed RA patients and found that depression improved following antidepressant medications, but the study was limited in that the imipramine group had higher initial depression scores. Grant-McFarlane *et al.* (1986) used a randomized double-blind study to assess the effect of low dose trimipramine (25–75 mg) in a sample of RA patients; joint pain and tenderness were reduced, but depression did not improve. Frank *et al.* (1988) treated 47 RA patients in a double-blind, crossover trial comparing amitriptyline, desipramine, trazodone, and a placebo. All three antidepressants had beneficial effects on mood, but only amitriptyline was found to be superior as an analgesic agent.

These preliminary studies suggest that both antidepressants and supportive psychotherapy may be beneficial for patients with RA, but more rigorous studies are needed. In addition, cognitive–behavioural interventions for people with RA need to be carefully studied. Further research will be required to elucidate the optimal treatments for specific depressive disorders in the context of musculoskeletal diseases.

DEPRESSION AND HEALTH CARE COSTS

Depression is a costly problem ($29 billion per year in the USA alone) (Abraham *et al.*, 1991), and depression contributes to substantial disability in its own right (Wells *et al.*, 1989). In fact, Wells *et al.* (1989) have shown that depression is more disabling than several chronic medical diseases, including arthritis. As previously noted, people with musculoskeletal diseases demonstrate a higher prevalence of both depression and other psychological disorders than does the general population. In short, the higher level of psychological distress (e.g. depression) associated with chronic illness often translates into greater disability and higher health care costs.

For example, Clarke *et al.* (1994) found that patients with systemic lupus erythematosus (SLE) who had concomitant psychological and/or physical dysfunction incurred significantly higher health care costs than those patients without the psychological and/or physical comorbidities. Similarly, Cronan *et al.* (1995) found psychological factors to be strong predictors of health care utilization, even stronger than demographic characteristics such as age. The clear implication of the literature is that depression and other psychological problems are both prevalent, and costly, in the population of people with musculoskeletal diseases.

There is also evidence that medical utilization and health care costs are significantly higher for people with arthritis as compared to healthy individuals. Clarke *et al.* (1993) found that people with SLE have four times as many hospitalizations as the general public. OA patients had 142 million office visits in 1980 alone (Weinberger *et al.*, 1990), and RA patients average more than two times the medical costs of the general population (Lubeck *et al.*, 1986). Therefore, strategies to reduce health care costs for people with arthritis are extremely important.

A potential strategy for reducing the health care costs associated with arthritis is the efficient delivery of psychoeducational programmes. Lorig *et al.* (1993) found a 40% reduction in outpatient visits for people with arthritis; the reduction translated into a 4 year saving of $648 per RA patient. In the Hawaii Medicaid Study, Pallak *et al.* (1994) found that patients with chronic diseases, including RA, had lower health care costs following brief psychological interventions. In general, the literature on the medical cost-offset phenomenon shows that psychological interventions are typically cost-effective in medical settings and have the capacity to reduce overall health care costs (Cummings and Follette, 1968; Mumford *et al.*, 1984). Therefore, there is strong evidence, both clinical and economic, that the aggressive treatment of psychological distress, including depression, is an important management strategy for people with musculoskeletal diseases.

CONCLUSION

Several conclusions can be drawn from the literature on depression in arthritis and musculoskeletal diseases. First, the problem of depression is common in the arthritides, but by no means universal. The majority of studies show that a sizable percentage of people with arthritis experience depressive symptoms—far more so than in the healthy population. In addition, the over-representation of factors such as female gender, medical comorbidities, and major life stress appear to contribute to the higher prevalence of depression in the arthritides.

Second, accurate diagnosis of depression is essential, but somewhat difficult, in musculoskeletal conditions. Overlap symptoms such as fatigue and loss of energy must be carefully evaluated; depression should not automatically be dismissed as secondary to a medical condition. Practitioners caring for patients with arthritis must be alert to the various depressive subtypes and vigilant with regard to the prevalence of depression in their patients.

Third, many people with musculoskeletal diseases need to have access to effective treatments for depression. Therefore, practitioners must be willing, when necessary, to consult with mental health professionals who can evaluate for depression and formulate appropriate therapies. For most depressed patients, either a medication regimen or a psychotherapeutic intervention (and sometimes both) will be indicated. Practitioners must be conversant with the available treatments and committed to following their depressed patients over extended timeframes in order to minimize relapse.

Lastly, practitioners should recognize that depression in the context of musculoskeletal conditions is extremely costly, in terms of both exacerbated disability and high levels of health care utilization. In particular, from the stand-point of disability, practitioners must recognize that depression has the potential to be *more* disabling than the musculoskeletal condition itself. Therefore, the overall care of patients with arthritis needs to include the management of potentially disabling psychological conditions, such as depression.

REFERENCES

Abraham IL, Neese JB and Westerman PS (1991) Depression: Nursing implications of a clinical and social problem. *Nurs Clin North Am,* **26(3)**, 527–536.

Ahles TA, Khan SA, Yunus MB, Spiegel DA and Masi AT (1991) Psychiatric status of patients with primary fibromyalgia, patients with rheumatoid arthritis, and subjects without pain: A blind comparison of DSM-III diagnoses. *Am J Psychiatry,* **148**, 1721–1726.

American Psychological Association (1990) *Women and Depression: Risk Factors and Treatment Issues.* Final Report of the American Psychological Association's National

Task Force on Women and Depression. Washington, DC: American Psychological Association.

American Psychiatric Association (1994) *Diagnostic and Statistical Manual of Mental Disorder*. 4th edition, Washington, DC: American Psychiatric Association.

Blake DJ, Maisiak R, Alarcon GS, Holley HL and Brown S (1987) Sexual quality-of-life of patients with arthritis compared to arthritis-free controls. *J Rheumatol*, **14(3)**, 570–576.

Burckhardt CS, O'Reilly CA, Wiens AN, Clark SR, Campbell SM and Bennett RM (1994) Assessing depression in fibromyalgia patients. *Arthritis Care Res*, **7(1)**, 35–39.

Burkhauser RV, Butler JS, Mitchell JM and Pincus T (1986) Effects of arthritis on wage earnings. *J Gerontol*, **41(2)**, 277–281.

Clark S, Campbell SM, Forehand ME, Tindall EA and Bennett RM (1985) Clinical characteristics of fibrositis: II. A "blinded" controlled study using standard psychological tests. *Arthritis Rheum*, **28(2)**, 132–137.

Clarke AE, Esdaile JM, Bloch DA, LaCaille D, Danoff DS and Fries JF (1993) A Canadian study of the total medical costs for patients with systemic lupus erythematosus and the predictors of costs. *Arthritis Rheum*, **36(11)**, 1548–1559.

Clarke AE, Bloch DA, Danoff DS and Esdaile JMK (1994) Decreasing costs and improving outcomes in systemic lupus erythematosus: Using regression trees to develop health policy. *J Rheumatol*, **21**, 2246–2253.

Creed F and Ash G (1992) Depression in rheumatoid arthritis: Aetiology and treatment. *Int Rev Psychiatry*, **4**, 23–34.

Cronan TA, Shaw WS, Gallagher RA and Weisman M (1995) Predicting health care use among older osteoarthritis patients in an HMO. *Arthritis Care Res*, **8(2)**, 66–72.

Cummings NA and Follette WT (1968) Psychiatric services and medical utilization in a prepaid health plan setting; Part II. *Med Care*, **6**, 31–41.

Depression Guideline Panel (1993a) *Depression in Primary Care:* Volume 2. *Treatment of Major Depression. Clinical Practice Guideline, Number 5*. Rockville, Md: U.S. Department of Health and Human Services, Public Health Service.

Depression Guideline Panel (1993b) *Depression in Primary Care:* Volume 1. *Detection and Diagnosis. Clinical Practice Guideline, Number 5*. Rockville, MD: U.S. Department of Health and Human Services, Public Health Service.

DeVellis BM (1993) Depression in rheumatological diseases: Review. *Balliere's Clin Rheumatol*, **7(2)**, 241–257.

Dobson KS (1989) A meta-analysis of the efficacy of cognitive therapy for depression. *J Consult Clin Psychol*, **57(3)**, 414–419.

Fifield J, Reisine S, Tennen H and Sheehan TJ (1995) Depressive symptom reports and depression diagnoses among patients with RA. *Arthritis Care Res*, **8(4)**, S15.

Fowler PD, MacNeill A, Spencer D, Robinson ET and Dick WC (1977) Imipramine, rheumatoid arthritis and rheumatoid factor. *Curr Med Res Opin*, **5(3)**, 241–246.

Frank RG, Beck NC, Parker JC, Kashani JH, Elliott TR, Haut AE, Smith, E, Atwood C, Brownlee-Duffect M and Kay DR (1988) Depression in rheumatoid arthritis. *J Rheumatol*, **15(6)**, 920–925.

Fries JF (1986) *Arthritis: A Comprehensive Guide to Understanding Your Arthritis*. Reading, MA: Addison-Wesley.

Grant-Macfarlane J, Jalali S and Grace EM (1986) Trimipramine in rheumatoid arthritis: A randomized double-blind trial in relieving pain and joint tenderness. *Curr Med Res Opin*, **10(2)**, 89–93.

Hawley DJ and Wolfe F (1991) Pain, disability, and pain/disability relationships in seven rheumatic disorders: A study of 1,522 patients. *J Rheumatol*, **18(10)**, 1552–1557.

Hay EM, Black D, Huddy A Creed F, Tomenson B, Bernstein RM and Lennox Holt PJ

(1992) Psychiatric disorder and cognitive impairment in systemic lupus erythematosus. *Arthritis Rheum*, **35(4)**, 411–416.

Hudson JI, Hudson MS, Pliner LF, Goldenberg DL and Pope HG Jr (1985) Fibromyalgia and major affective disorder: A controlled phenomenology and family history study. *Am J Psychiatry*, **142(4)**, 441–446.

Kaplan S and Kozin F (1981) A controlled study of group counselling in rheumatoid arthritis. *J Rheumatol*, **8(1)**, 91–99.

Katz PP and Yelin EH (1993) Prevalence and correlates of depressive symptoms among persons with rheumatoid arthritis. *J Rheumatol*, **20(5)**, 790–796.

Katz PP and Yelin EH (1995) The development of depressive symptoms among women with rheumatoid arthritis: The role of function. *Arthritis Rheum*, **38(1)**, 49–56.

Liang MH, Larson M, Thompson M, Eaton H, McNamara E, Katz R and Taylor J (1984) Costs and outcomes in rheumatoid arthritis and osteoarthritis. *Arthritis Rheum*, **27(5)**, 522–529.

Liang MH, Rogers M, Larson M, Eaton HM, Murawski BJ, Taylor JE, Swafford J and Schur PH (1984) The psychosocial impact of systemic lupus erythematosus and rheumatoid arthritis. *Arthritis Rheum*, **27(1)**, 13–19.

Lorig KR, Mazonson PD and Holman HR (1993) Evidence suggesting that health education for self-management in patients with chronic arthritis has sustained health benefits while reducing health care costs. *Arthritis Rheum*, **36(4)**, 439–446.

Lubeck DP, Spitz PW, Fries JF, Wolfe F, Mitchell DM and Roth SH (1986) A multicenter study of annual health service utilization and costs in rheumatoid arthritis. *Arthritis Rheum*, **29(4)**, 488–493.

Manning DW and Frances AJ (1990) Combined therapy for depression: Critical review of the literature. In: DW Manning and AJ Frances (eds) *Combined Pharmachotherapy and Psychotherapy for Depression*. Washington, DC: American Psychiatric Press.

Meenan RF, Yelin EH, Nevitt M and Epstein WV (1981) The impact of chronic disease: A sociomedical profile of rheumatoid arthritis. *Arthritis Rheum*, **24(3)**, 544–548.

Mumford E, Schlesinger HJ, Glass GV, Patrick C and Cuerdon T (1984) A new look at evidence about reduced cost of medical utilization following mental health treatment. *Am J Psychiatry*, **141**, 1145–1158.

Newman SP, Fitzpatrick R, Lamb R and Shipley M (1989) The origins of depressed mood in rheumatoid arthritis. *J Rheumatol*, **16(6)**, 740–744.

Omdal R, Husby G and Mellgren SI (1995) Mental health status in systemic lupus erythematosus. *Scand J Rheumatol*, **24**, 142–145.

Pallak MS, Cumming NA, Dörken H and Henke CJ (1994) Medical costs, Medicaid, and managed mental health treatment: The Hawaii study. *Managed Care Q*, **2(2)**, 64–70.

Parker JC and Westra BD (1989) Stress, psychological factors and rheumatoid arthritis. *Curr Opin Rheumatol*, **1**, 39–43.

Parker JC, Smarr KL, Buescher KL, Phillips LR, Frank RG, Beck NC, Anderson SK and Walker SE (1989) Pain control and rational thinking: Implications for rheumatoid arthritis. *Arthritis Rheum*, **32(8)**, 984–990.

Revenson TA, Schiaffino KM, Majerovitz SD and Gibofsky A (1991) Social support as a double-edged sword: The relation of positive and problematic support to depression among rheumatoid arthritis patients. *Soc Sci Med*, **33(7)**, 807–813.

Rimón R (1974) Depression in rheumatoid arthritis. *Ann Clin Res*, **6**, 171–175.

Rimón R and Laakso RL (1984) Overt psychopathology in rheumatoid arthritis: A fifteen-year follow-up study. *Scand J Rheumatol*, **13**, 324–328.

Robins LN, Helzer JE, Orvaschel H, Anthony JC, Blazer DG, Burnam A and Burke JD Jr (1985) The Diagnostic Interview Schedule. In: WW Eaton and LG Kessler (eds) *Epide-*

miologic Field Methods in Psychiatry: the NIMH Epidemiologic Catchment Area Program. New York: Academic Press.

Rodin G, Craven J and Littlefield C (1991) *Depression in the Medically Ill: An Integrated Approach.* New York: Brunner/Mazel.

Spitzer RL, Williams JBW, Gibbon M and First MB (1990) *User's Guide for the Structured Clinical Interview for DSM-IIIR:SCID.* Washington, DC: American Psychiatric Press.

Turner RJ and Beiser M (1990) Major depression and depressive symptomatology among the physically disabled: Assessing the role of chronic stress. *J Nerv Ment Dis,* **178(6)**, 343–350.

Weinberger M, Tierney WM, Booher P and Hiner SL (1990) Social support, stress and functional status in patients with osteoarthritis. *Soc Sci Med,* **30(4)**, 503–508.

Weissman MM, Olfson M, Leon AC, Broadhead WE, Glibert TT, Higgins ES, Barrett JE, Blacklow RS, Keller MB and Hoven C (1995) Brief diagnostic interviews (SDDS-PC) for multiple mental disorders in primary care: A pilot study. *Arch Family Med,* **4**, 220–227.

Wekking EM (1993) Psychiatric symptoms in systemic lupus erythematosus: An update. *Psychosom Med,* **55**, 219–228.

Wells KB, Stewart A, Hays RD, Burnam MA, Rogers W, Daniels M, Berry S, Greenfield S and Ware J (1989) The functioning and well-being of depressed patients: Results from the medical outcomes study. *JAMA,* **262(7)**, 914–919.

Wolfe F, Cathey MA, Kleinheksel SM, Amos SP, Hoffman RG, Young DY and Hawley DJ (1984) Psychological status in primary fibrositis and fibrositis associated with rheumatoid arthritis. *J Rheumatol,* **11(4)**, 500–506.

World Health Organization (1993) *Composite International Diagnostic Interview (CIDI): Version 1.1.* Geneva, Switzerland: World Health Organization.

Yelin E (1992) Arthritis: The cumulative impact of a common chronic condition. *Arthritis Rheum,* **35(5)**, 489–497.

Yelin E, Lubeck D, Holman H and Epstein W (1987) The impact of rheumatoid arthritis and osteoarthritis: The activities of patients with rheumatoid arthritis and osteoarthritis compared to controls. *J Rheumatol,* **14**, 710–717.

Yoshino S and Uchida S (1981) Sexual problems of women with rheumatoid arthritis. *Arch Phys Med Rehabil,* **62**, 122–123.

Zautra AJ, Burleson MH, Matt KS, Roth S and Burrows L (1994) Interpersonal stress, depression, and disease activity in rheumatoid arthritis and osteoarthritis patients. *Health Psychol,* **13(2)**, 139–148.

Zimmerman M and Coryell W (1987) The Inventory to Diagnose Depression (IDD): A self-report scale to diagnose major depressive disorder. *J Consult Clin Psychol,* **55(1)**, 55–59.

20

Depression and respiratory disorders

Ian Collis

Breathing is the physiological function most associated with life itself, and breathlessness one of the most frightening physical symptoms that we can experience, linked as it is with fears of suffocation and death. Respiratory diseases are very common and cause a great deal of sickness and death. Despite this, the psychological aspects of respiratory disorders have not received the same degree of interest and research as other groups of disorders, such as malignancies or HIV (human immunodeficiency virus) disease. The research that has been undertaken in this area has concentrated on the chronic disorders, particularly chronic obstructive airways disease and asthma, which are responsible for most of the disability associated with respiratory disease, and this chapter will be focused in the same way. The first section will discuss the features of the assessment of depression which are common to all patients with respiratory disease; then, the clinical, epidemiological and aetiological aspects of depression in specific respiratory disorders, and in patients who receive assisted ventilation, will be considered; the last section will deal with the relationship between depression and rehabilitation, the management of depression and the problems associated with the use of medications in these patients.

Depression and Physical Illness. Edited by M.M. Robertson and C.L.E. Katona
© 1997 John Wiley & Sons Ltd

ASSESSMENT OF DEPRESSIVE SYMPTOMS

Patients with respiratory disease frequently avoid expressing their emotions because of the fear that this will worsen their breathlessness. This can result in problems in psychiatric assessment: patients often minimize psychological symptoms and psychosocial problems and concentrate on physical symptoms, with the result that depressive disorders may be masked and left untreated. Somatic depressive symptoms, such as sleep disturbance and lack of energy, may be difficult to differentiate from symptoms caused by respiratory disease. Anxiety symptoms may be easier to elicit and often indicate an underlying depressive disorder. Excess alcohol consumption and breathlessness disproportionate to objective pulmonary function tests may also be indicators of depressive illness.

Depressive symptoms in people with respiratory disease occur in a spectrum of psychiatric disorders, from mild adjustment disorders to severe depressive illness. They are often related to losses, such as the development of a negative self-image as a result of the illness, a reduction in self-esteem, or an impairment in relationships or in work or educational performance. Patients with severe pulmonary disease, especially asthmatics, may have experienced being mechanically ventilated and may be afraid of experiencing this again, or dying suddenly or unpredictably, and their depressive thoughts are sometimes strongly focused on these fears. Changes in medications, particularly corticosteroids, can herald depressive episodes, as can deterioration in the patient's physical health. Patients with feelings of pessimism and hopelessness, a lack of drive and motivation, or even ideas of suicide, as a result of depression may not comply with medication and, for example, may not deal with impending asthma attacks efficiently; an unexpected deterioration in health may be an indication of an underlying depressive disorder. In patients with more severe physical illness, symptoms of depression, especially if accompanied by anxiety or agitation, may be secondary to hypoxia or other organic factors; the possibility of an organic mood disorder or delirium should always be considered.

Close links between psychiatric services and general medical services, including primary care, will aid the identification of patients with depressive disorders. The use of instruments such as the Hospital Anxiety and Depression Scale (Zigmond and Snaith, 1983) may help staff to screen for significant depressive symptoms.

FEATURES OF SPECIFIC RESPIRATORY DISORDERS

Chronic obstructive pulmonary disease

Chronic obstructive pulmonary disease consists of a spectrum of lung disorders characterized by chronic airways obstruction: chronic bronchitis; emphysema;

and chronic asthma, where there is a significant irreversible obstructive component. Common symptoms of these disorders are breathlessness, cough, wheezing, and sputum production. The three conditions, especially bronchitis and emphysema, frequently coexist.

Chronic bronchitis is defined clinically as sputum production on most days for 3 months of 2 successive years; symptoms are produced as thickening of the mucosa of the airway lumen and excess mucus cause airways obstruction. Emphysema is defined histologically as dilatation of lung air spaces by destruction of their walls; reduction in the lungs' elasticity results in obstruction of the airways. In asthma, there is mucosal swelling, increased mucus production and constriction of bronchial muscles, leading to generalized airways obstruction; the obstruction is initially paroxysmal and reversible, and in some cases caused by exposure to allergens, but in chronic disease may become at least partly irreversible.

The psychological aspects of chronic pulmonary disorders have been the subject of investigation, using a variety of interviews, psychological tests and self-report inventories, since the early years of this century (Greenburg *et al.*, 1985). Differences in the instruments used in research and between the populations of patients studied have resulted in discrepancies in the results of these studies, particularly in the estimation of the prevalence of psychiatric disorders, as will be discussed later.

Being unable to breathe is a very frightening experience, and the fear of becoming breathless has been regarded as central to the onset of psychological disorders, mainly anxiety and depression, in chronic obstructive pulmonary disease; it has been suggested that this fear is more important than the severity of physical symptoms in causing psychiatric morbidity (Agle and Baum, 1977; Kinsman *et al.*, 1983). Associations have been noted between psychological symptoms and disabling changes in behaviour, such as avoiding activities which result in breathlessness (Agle and Baum, 1977; Fletcher and Martin, 1982). Patients describe situations which are particularly feared, such as taking a shower, shaving, going to the lavatory, going in lifts, and being alone outside home without an inhaler; phobic avoidance of these situations can develop, with a vicious circle of fear, hyperventilation and breathlessness, panic and increasing avoidance, which in turn can lead to depression (Yellowlees *et al.*, 1987). Furthermore, patients with chronic obstructive pulmonary disease attempt to avoid feelings of depression, anxiety, agitation or anger which may lead to worsening breathlessness, and have been described as living in "emotional straitjackets" as a result of this (Dudley *et al.*, 1980). It has even been suggested that the autonomic arousal associated with depression can be a cause of sudden death in patients with chronic asthma (Miller, 1987). This avoidance of situations and emotions may lead to increasing social withdrawal and to worsening depression.

In the context of such distressing physical symptoms and psychosocial disability, it is not surprising that some authors have found a high prevalence of depressive symptoms in patients with chronic obstructive pulmonary disease; however, this has not been a consistent finding.

Agle and Baum (1977), interviewing 23 men with chronic pulmonary disorder who were candidates for a rehabilitation programme, found significant depression in 17 of them (74%). A previous study (Burns and Howell, 1969) indicated that 16 out of 31 patients who had been found to be more breathless than would be predicted by objective measures of their pulmonary function were clinically depressed. McSweeney *et al.* (1980) found the incidence of depression to be 42%, compared with 9% in controls. Karajgi *et al.* (1990) studied, using the Structured Clinical Interview for DSM-IIIR, 31 men and 19 women with a significant chronic irreversible airflow disorder attending an outpatients clinic: five people (10%) had past and three people (6%) current episodes of major depression; one (2%) subject had a current episode of dysthymia; twice as many women as men had mood disorders. The prevalence of mood disorders in this study was consistent with the prevalence found in studies of the general population (Robins *et al.*, 1984). The prevalence of panic disorder, however, at 15%, was 10 times that of the general population. Yellowlees *et al.* (1987), in their study of 32 men and 18 women admitted to a respiratory unit with chronic obstructive airflow disorders, found a prevalence of 12% for major depression and 4% for dysthymic disorder, using DSM-III diagnostic criteria. The prevalence of panic disorder was 24%. It was noted that patients with psychiatric disorders had a higher alcohol intake than other patients.

Bronchial asthma

Asthma is usually a chronic illness which can vary greatly in severity of symptoms. There is intermittent generalized airways obstruction which, at least in the early stages of the condition, is reversible. The airways obstruction is caused by mucosal swelling, constriction of bronchial muscles, and increased production of mucus. The symptoms are wheezing, breathlessness and cough; they may be so mild in some individuals that treatment will not be sought, or so severe that mechanical ventilation may become necessary. Asthma symptoms can be precipitated by allergens, cold, infections, exercise, or anxiety, or may occur without precipitants. The prevalence is some populations is 8% and the disease can occur at any age.

Asthma has traditionally been regarded as a psychosomatic disorder and psychoanalytical theories have related its onset to psychic conflicts and disturbances in the mother–child relationship (Goodman and Turpin, 1986; Thompson and Thompson, 1985a). Evidence has been produced by some studies that bronchoconstriction may be produced by suggestion in some asthmatic patients (McFadden *et al.*, 1969) and that psychological factors may increase use of as-needed medication and medical care in general (Bengtsson,

1984; Dahlem *et al.*, 1977). However, Spittle and Sears' study (1984) of 66 adult patients attending an asthma clinic in New Zealand found no relationship between illness severity, allergy indicated by serum total IgE, and psychological and social factors (including the Brief Psychiatric Ratting Scale); and the study of Janson *et al.* (1994) found that there was a significant correlation between respiratory symptoms and anxiety and depression in their community survey of 715 people, but no association between the diagnosis of asthma on objective criteria and anxiety and depression. It therefore seems that psychological factors may affect symptom severity and use of medical care in individual patients, as it does in people with respiratory symptoms without a diagnosis of asthma, but there is no evidence that asthma is a psychogenic disorder. Similarly, although depressive and anxiety disorders are more common in people with more severe asthma, as will be discussed below, there is no evidence that psychological factors will worsen the overall severity of the disorder.

Anxiety symptoms are common in asthmatic patients (Karajgi *et al.*, 1990) and may be an indication of an underlying depressive disorder. Asthmatics often experience rapid deteriorations in their health, which may herald depressive episodes, and fears of dying or needing mechanical ventilation are common. Changes in corticosteroid medication may be linked with depressive symptoms, and noncompliance with treatment should alert staff to the possibility of a depressive disorder.

Janson *et al.* (1994), in their community survey, found that of 129 subjects who had ever had asthma 2% were definite and 9% possible cases of depression (defined by the Hospital Anxiety and Depression Scale); of the 63 subjects on medication for asthma, 4% were definite cases for depression and 14% possible cases for depression. Yellowlees *et al.* (1988), using the Diagnostic Interview Schedule to form DSM-III diagnoses, found one (3%) case of depressive disorder out of 36 outpatients with asthma and one case (8%) out of 13 patients who had a history of very severe episodes of asthma. The overall picture, therefore, is of a prevalence of depressive disorder amongst people with a diagnosis of asthma comparable to the general population, but with higher rates amongst patients with more severe disease.

Cystic fibrosis

This is one of the commonest inherited diseases, affecting one in 2000 live births. Inheritance is by an autosomal recessive gene. In affected people, symptoms are caused by viscid mucus which blocks and causes damage in glands. In children and young adults there are recurrent chest infections and bronchiectasis, as well as pancreatic disorders, diabetes mellitus, infertility and intestinal obstruction. Treatment has improved the prognosis and most people affected by this condition now survive into early adulthood.

Evidence from most (but not all) studies using matched normal controls (Blair *et al.*, 1994; Kashani *et al.*, 1988; Shepherd *et al.*, 1991; Steinhausen and Schindler, 1981) and from uncontrolled studies (Brown *et al.*, 1994; Walters *et al.*, 1993) suggests that children and adults with cystic fibrosis do not have greater levels of psychopathology than the general population, cope well with their disease and have excellent psychosocial functioning (although with lower educational attainment and levels of employment than the general population). Depressive and anxiety symptoms may be more common in patients with cystic fibrosis over the age of 16 than in younger patients (Pearson *et al.*, 1991). The use of denial with regard to the course and ultimate outcome of the disease may be important in maintaining psychological health (Brown *et al.*, 1994; Bywater, 1981), something which needs to be considered during psychiatric intervention with this group of patients. Where depressive symptoms do occur, they may be related to worries about the future, a deterioration in health (especially pulmonary function), self-image, or problems within the family. Often families, especially mothers, carry the burden of the illness and may need special help.

Tuberculosis

In tuberculosis there is initial infection with *Mycobacterium tuberculosis*, usually through the lungs; this stage of the disease is mostly asymptomatic, but there may be fever, lassitude, cough and sputum. Infection spreads throughout the body, but immunity develops and the disease becomes quiescent until reactivated later in life, when there will be systemic symptoms such as lassitude, weight loss and fever, and often organ-specific (including respiratory) symptoms. Treatment of pulmonary tuberculosis involves taking antituberculous drugs for several months. There has been relatively little research into the prevalence and nature of psychiatric morbidity in people with tuberculosis and into their need for psychiatric intervention. The lack of studies in this area may be related to the decline, until recently, of the prevalence of the disease. Depressive symptoms in patients with tuberculosis may be related to loss of job, loss of role in family, long hospitalization, or a perception of being infected or dirty (Moran, 1985). There may be difficulties in identifying depression in people with tuberculosis, who are often poor, with literacy or language problems (Westaway and Wolmarans, 1994). Isoniazid, a drug used to treat tuberculosis, may be the cause of depression in some patients.

Occupationally acquired pulmonary disease

Once again, there is little research in this area. Mesotheliomas are pleural tumours which cause chest pain, breathlessness and pleural effusions; if malignant there is usually a history of exposure to asbestos. The prognosis is very poor. One study (Lebovits, 1985) suggested that nearly one-half of patients with industrially acquired mesotheliomas has major depression, compared with 6% of controls. Patients with occupational asthma may have a lower quality of life and more emotional dysfunction than other asthma patients (Malo *et al.*, 1993). There is little research into the psychiatric consequences of occupationally acquired asbestosis, extrinsic allergic alveolitis or pneumoconiosis.

Obstructive sleep apnoea

In this condition there is occlusion of the oropharynx during sleep, preventing inspiration, and causing the patient to wake, usually with loud snorting and snoring sounds. The main symptoms are: disturbed sleep, daytime sleepiness, poor concentration and memory, morning headaches, personality change and sexual dysfunction. The upper airways obstruction may be due to enlarged tonsils, nasal obstruction, mandibular deformity, enlargement of the tongue, or systemic conditions such as obesity or hypothyroidism. The disorder is found in about 12% of men aged 40–75 years (Young *et al.*, 1993). The typical patient is a middle-aged man who leads a sedentary life-style, is obese, smokes and drinks alcohol.

Several studies have found a high prevalence of depressive disorders in patients with obstructive sleep apnoea. Reynolds *et al.* (1984) found, using Research Diagnostic Criteria, that of 25 consecutive male patients attending a clinic, three had a history of major depression, two of chronic intermittent depression, and one of cyclothymia. Another study of 25 subjects (Guilleminault and Dement, 1977) reported elevated depression scores on the Minnesota Multiphasic Personality Inventory in 28%. Millman *et al.* (1989) found 45% of their 55 patients had significant depressive symptoms. However, there is an overlap between the symptoms of obstructive sleep apnoea and depression; common features include fatigue, decreased energy and libido, impaired concentration: this may lead to the overdiagnosis of depression, especially when using self-report questionnaires. This conclusion is reached by Lee *et al.* (1993), who report finding only two cases of DSM-IIIR major depression in 128 patients with obstructive sleep apnoea.

The first line of treatment of depressive symptoms in obstructive sleep apnoea is to treat the apnoeic episodes by weight loss, nocturnal nasal continuous positive airways pressure (CPAP), or uvulopalatopharyngoplasty (Millman *et al.*, 1989; Kaplan, 1992). Antidepressant or psychological therapy may be necessary in some cases; interestingly, tricyclic antidepressants seem to improve the symptoms of obstructive sleep apnoea, perhaps through reducing REM (random eye movement) sleep (Lee *et al.*, 1993; Kaplan, 1992).

Finally, as well as depressive symptoms being frequently reported in patients with obstructive sleep apnoea, mild sleep apnoea may be common in depressed patients; Reynolds *et al.* (1982) reported that 15% of subjects with depression defined by the Research Diagnostic Criteria had mild sleep apnoea.

However, it is not clear that this is higher than the prevalence in the general population or that treating the apnoeic episodes will improve the depressive symptoms in this group of patients.

Lung cancer

Lung cancer is common in developed countries, constituting about one-fifth of cases of cancer. Its major risk factor is smoking cigarettes and it is therefore largely a self-induced disorder. Symptoms include cough, breathlessness, haemoptysis, chest pain, severe and persistent fatigue, malaise, and weight loss. Insomnia is found in about one-half of patients with diagnosed lung cancer (Bernhard and Ganz, 1991). There may also be unpleasant symptoms produced as adverse effects of treatment, including nausea and vomiting, sedation, hair loss and sexual dysfunction. There is often some difficulty in diagnosing depressive disorders in lung cancer patients: many of the somatic symptoms of depression overlap with the systemic symptoms of the tumour or with the consequences of treatment, and some of the psychological features of depression are commonly found as part of the adjustment of the patient to the diagnosis or as aspects of organic psychiatric disorders.

Ginsburg *et al.* (1995) interviewed 52 Canadian patients with recently diagnosed lung cancer who were receiving radiotherapy or chemotherapy; the time between diagnosis and psychiatric evaluation ranged from 6 to 150 days. They found two patients (4%) who had depressive disorders on the criteria of the Diagnostic Interview Schedule; one had major depression, the other dysthymia. Five (10%) other patients had adjustment disorders with depressed mood, and one patient had an adjustment disorder with anxious mood. No other current psychiatric diagnoses were made; two patients (4%) had experienced adjustment disorders following the diagnosis of lung cancer which had resolved by the time of the interview; 44% had experienced significant symptoms of low mood after learning they had cancer; 13% had thought of suicide. Hughes (1985) found a prevalence of 16% of major depression in 50 patients with inoperable lung cancer. Goldberg *et al.* (1984), in a small study, found that depressive symptoms were closely related to the patients' physical state.

Upper respiratory tract disorders

A number of small studies have linked the onset of the common cold to stressful life events, although there is no evidence that it is linked to affective disorders. There has been some discussion of the relationship between chronic rhinitis and psychological disorders. Bell *et al.* (1991) in a survey of 379 college students found that self-reported depressive symptoms were no more common in subjects with hay fever than in other subjects, although one-half of the 17 subjects with a history of a diagnosis of depression suffered from hay fever compared to a quarter of the rest of the sample.

ASSISTED VENTILATION AND DEPRESSION

Assisted ventilation may become necessary as respiratory failure worsens. It may range from continuous positive airways pressure, where an oxygen–air mixture is breathed through a mask, to controlled ventilation through an endotracheal tube with sedation and neuromuscular blocking drugs. Psychiatric symptoms appearing in patients with respiratory disease of this severity are often secondary to cerebral dysfunction, and appropriate investigations, including arterial blood gas measurements, should be made. Psychopathology may be caused by cerebral anoxia or hypercapnia, but other metabolic disturbances, infections, and medications may also be important.

The environment in intensive care units, with constant noise from the respirator, interruption of sleep, sensory deprivation or overload, extreme dependence and vulnerability, and uncomfortable or painful procedures, is an important cause of emotional distress and depression in these patients; there is also the patient's fear of death and disability and uncertainty about the future. However, it is difficulty in communicating that is probably the greatest stress (Gale and O'Shanick, 1985). These problems can be ameliorated by training staff in overcoming communication problems, by keeping patients informed and involving them as much as possible in decisions about their treatment, maintaining continuity of care by staff, and taking measures to reduce sensory distortions. The prevalence of depression resulting from the above problems has not been established, and practical difficulties make research in this area difficult.

DEPRESSIVE DISORDERS AND REHABILITATION

Emotional factors, such as depression, may cause breathlessness disproportionate to lung dysfunction in some individuals and psychiatric intervention may reduce breathlessness (Burns and Howell, 1969). Negative cognitions associated with depression, such as low self-esteem and pessimism about the future, are associated with increased time off work and reduced exercise tolerance in chronic obstructive pulmonary disease (Rutter, 1970; Morgan *et al.*, 1983). Psychological assessment may help to identify those patients who will benefit from rehabilitation and to identify those who require specific psychiatric or psychological interventions. Treatment of depression and psychological interventions aimed at negative cognitions may be expected to improve disability from respiratory symptoms.

MANAGEMENT OF DEPRESSION IN PATIENTS WITH RESPIRATORY DISORDERS

Psychological, social, and physical treatments for depression all have their place in the treatment of depressive disorders in patients with respiratory disease. Where depressive disorders are suspected, a full psychiatric assessment is necessary to establish the diagnosis, and to evaluate the nature and severity of the symptoms, including the risk of suicide. It is important to assess the psychological and social factors contributing to the depression, including systems of social support, functioning within the family and at work, self-image, and the meaning and significance of the physical illness to the patient. Physical factors often play an important role in precipitating depression: these include a recent worsening of respiratory symptoms, underlying metabolic disturbances, infections, a deterioration in respiratory function, or the onset of nonrespiratory diseases. Treatment of the physical disorder will often produce a significant improvement in mood symptoms.

Research provides little evidence about the efficacy of the various forms of psychotherapeutic and pharmacotherapeutic treatments in this group of patients. The use of antidepressants should be considered in patients with depressive disorders who have not responded to treatment of their underlying physical illness or to brief psychological interventions. The use of medications in these patients is discussed below. Various psychotherapeutic approaches have been used, and clinical experience has often shown a combination of drug therapy and psychotherapy to be effective, especially in containing the patient's despair and in maintaining some hope for the future while treatment continues. Psychological interventions often aim to boost the patient's coping mechanisms and personality resources, which may help to prevent recurrences of depression. Social and family interventions can also reduce factors which maintain the depression.

DEPRESSION AND MEDICATION USE IN PATIENTS WITH PULMONARY DISEASE

Psychotropic drugs

Psychotropic medications are centrally acting drugs, and the main concern of clinicians using them in patients with lung disease is the risk of depression of the respiratory drive and excessive sedation. Doses of medication need to be carefully adjusted and effects closely monitored because of this and because, although the pharmacokinetics of psychotropic drugs in respiratory disease have not been extensively studied, it is likely that in severe lung disease both uptake of drugs from the gastrointestinal tract and clearance from the body are reduced. Caution needs to be used in assessing whether psychological symptoms, especially agitation and anxiety, are due to hypoxia; sedating medication may worsen these symptoms and it is therefore very important to assess and treat hypoxia before using it. Furthermore, patients with pulmonary disease are often elderly and often suffer from other diseases; they may be susceptible to the adverse effects of medication because of this.

Antidepressants

Tricyclic antidepressants appear to be safe to use in therapeutic doses in patients with stable pulmonary disease, and nonsedating tricyclics may improve respiratory function, especially in asthma; in overdose, they can rapidly cause respiratory arrest (Rubey and Lydiard, 1994; Thompson and Thompson, 1985b). In obstructive sleep apnoea, as discussed above, tricyclic antidepressants can improve symptoms of the disorder. It is prudent to choose a less-sedating tricyclic antidepressant, such as protriptyline, to start with a low dose, and to increase the dose slowly. There is little evidence about the use of monoamine oxidase inhibitors (MAOIs) and newer antidepressants in chronic pulmonary disease; there seem to be no case reports of their causing a deterioration in respiratory function when used in patients with pulmonary disorders. The lack of sedation associated with the use of specific serotonin reuptake inhibitors suggests some theoretical advantages in using this group of antidepressant drugs in patients with respiratory impairment. Patients are frequently taking other medications and the possibility of interactions with antidepressants should always be considered. MAOIs and tricyclics increase the adverse effects of antimuscarinic drugs and hypertension (a hypertensive crisis with MAOIs) can result if they are used with sympathomimetic drugs. Both groups of drugs can increase the side-effects of antihistamines: tricyclics should not be used with terfenadine because of the risk of cardiac arrhythmias; the manufacturers of promethazine recommend that it should not be used within 14 days of taking an MAOI.

Lithium and anticonvulsants

Carbamazepine, sodium valproate and lithium do not cause respiratory depression in therapeutic doses but seriously ill patients will need to have careful monitoring of blood levels of medication.

Antipsychotics

Antipsychotic medications, which may be used as part of the treatment of depression complicated by agitation or psychotic symptoms, can compromise respiratory function by causing sedation, laryngopharyngeal dystonias, or tardive dyskinesias affecting respiration. Benzodiazepines are probably preferable in agitated patients; in psychotic patients, a high potency antipsychotic such as haloperidol is the drug of choice, in combination with an anticholinergic drug such as benztropine to reduce the risk of extrapyramidal side-effects (Rubey and Lydiard, 1994).

Benzodiazepines

Although the use of benzodiazepines in chronic pulmonary disease has been more widely studied than that of other psychotropic drugs, results have been contradictory, probably as a result of differences in severity of disease in groups of patients studied, duration of administration of the drug and duration of the illness, and route of administration of the drug (Block *et al.*, 1984; Clark *et al.*, 1971; Kronenberg *et al.*, 1975; Model and Berry, 1974; Woodcock *et al.*, 1981). Particular care is necessary if there are coexisting medical diseases or if the patient is elderly, and benzodiazepines should be avoided in unstable pulmonary disease or if there is hypercapnia (Rubey and Lydiard, 1994). Use of benzodiazepines may be hazardous if the patient is receiving other central nervous system depressants, such as opioid analgesics. There is no evidence that any benzodiazepine is superior to another in this group of patients; there would appear to be a theoretical advantage in using drugs with a shorter half-life. Of course, treatment with these drugs should be as brief as possible.

Depressive symptoms caused by medical drugs

Medications used to treat respiratory diseases may cause depressive symptoms which are often worsened by treatment with antidepressant drugs and which are most effectively treated by reducing the dose of the drug concerned or choosing an alternative therapy. Drugs which may cause depressive symptoms include corticosteroids, isoniazid, ethionamide, cycloserine, theophylline, and phenylephrine.

REFERENCES

Agle DP and Baum GL (1977) Psychological aspects of chronic obstructive pulmonary disease. *Med Clin North Am*, **61**, 749–758.
Bell IR, Jasnoski ML, Kagan J *et al.* (1991) Depression and allergies: a study of non-clinical population. *Psychother Psychosom*, **55**, 24–31.
Bengtsson U (1984) Emotions and asthma. *Eur J Resp Dis*, **65 (Suppl 136)**, 123–129.
Blair C, Cull A and Freeman CP (1994) Psychosocial functioning in young adults with cystic fibrosis and their families. *Thorax*, **49**, 798–802.
Block AJ, Dolly R and Slayton PC (1984) Does flurazepam ingestion affect breathing and oxygenation during sleep in patients with chronic obstructive lung disease? *Am Rev Respir Dis*, **129**, 230–233.

Brown C, Rowley S and Helms P (1994) Symptoms, health and illness behaviour in cystic fibrosis. *Soc Sci Med*, **39**, 375–379.

Burns BH and Howell JBL (1969) Disproportionately severe breathlessness in chronic bronchitis and emphysema. *Q J Med*, **38**, 277–294.

Bywater EM (1981) Adolescents with cystic fibrosis: psychosocial adjustment. *Arch Dis Child*, **56**, 538–543.

Clark TJH, Collins JV and Tong D (1971) Respiratory depression caused by nitrazepam in patients with respiratory failure. *Lancet*, **ii**, 737–738.

Dahlem NW, Kinsman RA and Horton DJ (1977) Panic-fear in asthma: requests for as-needed medications in relation to pulmonary function measurements. *J Allergy Clin Immunol*, **60**, 295–300.

Dudley DL, Glaser EM, Jorgenson BN *et al.* (1980) Psychosocial concomitants to rehabilitation in chronic obstructive pulmonary disease: Part 1. Psychosocial and psychological considerations. *Chest*, **77**, 413–420.

Fletcher EC and Martin RJ (1982) Sexual dysfunction and erectile impotence in chronic obstructive pulmonary disease. *Chest*, **81**, 413–421.

Gale J and O'Shanick GJ (1985) Psychiatric aspects of respirator treatment and pulmonary intensive care. *Adv Psychosom Med*, **14**, 93–108.

Ginsberg ML, Quirt C, Ginsburg AD *et al.* (1995) Psychiatric illness and psychosocial concerns of patients with newly diagnosed lung cancer. *Can Med Assoc J*, **152**, 701–708.

Goldberg RJ, Wool MS, Glicksman A *et al.* (1984) Relationship of the social environment and patients' physical status to depression in lung cancer patients and their spouses. *J Psychosoc Oncol*, **2**, 73–80.

Goodman TA and Turpin JP (1986) The psychology of asthma: implications for treatment. In: ME Gershwin (ed) *Bronchial Asthma*. Orlando, Florida: Grune and Stratton, 541–560.

Greenburg GD, Ryan JJ and Bourlier PF (1985) Psychological and neuropsychological aspects of COPD. *Psychosomatics*, **26**, 29–33.

Guilleminault C and Dement WC (1977) Sleep apnea syndrome due to upper airway obstruction *Arch Intern Med*, **137**, 296–300.

Hughes JE (1985) Depressive illness and lung cancer, II: Follow up of inoperable patients. *Eur J Surg Oncol*, **11**, 21–24.

Janson C, Björnsson E, Hetta J *et al.* (1994) Anxiety and depression in relation to respiratory symptoms and asthma. *Am J Respir Crit Care Med*, **149**, 930–934.

Kaplan R (1992) Obstructive sleep apnoea and depression: Diagnostic and treatment implications. *Aus NZ J Psychiatry*, **26**, 586–591.

Karajgi B, Rifkin A, Doddi S *et al.* (1990) The prevalence of anxiety disorders in patients with chronic obstructive pulmonary disease. *Am J Psychiatry*, **147**, 200–201.

Kashani JH, Barbero GJ, Wilfley DE *et al.* (1988) Psychological concomitants of cystic fibrosis in children and adolescents. *Adolescence*, **23**, 873–880.

Kinsman RA, Yaroush RA, Fernandez E *et al.* (1983) Symptoms and experiences in chronic bronchitis and emphysema. *Chest*, **83**, 755–761.

Kronenberg RS, Cosio MG and Stevenson JE (1975) The use of oral diazepam in patients with obstructive lung disease and hypercapnia. *Ann Intern Med*, **83**, 83–84.

Lebovits AH (1985) Industrially acquired pulmonary disease. *Adv Psychosom Med*, **14**, 68–92.

Lee S, Wing YK and Chen CN (1993) Obstructive sleep apnoea and depression *Aus NZ J Psychiatry*, **27**, 162–166.

McFadden ER, Luparello T, Lyons HA *et al.* (1969) The mechanism of action of suggestion in the induction of acute asthma attacks. *Psychosom Med*, **31**, 134–143.

McSweeney AJ, Heaton RK, Grant I *et al.* (1980) Chronic obstructive pulmonary disease: Socioemotional adjustment and life quality. *Chest*, **77**, 309–311.

Malo JL, Boulet LP, Dewitte JD, *et al.* (1993) Quality of life of subjects with occupational asthma. *J Allergy Clin Immunol*, **91**, 1121–1127.

Miller BD (1987) Depression and asthma: a potentially lethal mixture. *J Allergy Clin Immunol*, **80**, 481–486.

Millman RP, Fogel BF and McNamara ME (1989) Depression as a manifestation of obstructive sleep apnea: reversal with positive airway pressure. *J Clin Psychiatry*, **50**, 348–351.

Model DG and Berry DJ (1974) Effects of chlordiazepoxide in respiratory failure due to chronic bronchitis. *Lancet*, **ii**, 869.

Moran M (1985) Psychiatric aspects of tuberculosis. *Adv Psychosom Med*, **14**, 109–118.

Morgan AD, Peck DF, Buchanan DR *et al.* (1983) Effect of attitudes and belief on exercise tolerance in chronic bronchitis. *Br Med J*, **286**, 171–173.

Pearson DA, Pumariega AJ and Seilheimer DK (1991) The development of psychiatric symptomatology in patients with cystic fibrosis. *J Am Acad Child Adolesc Psychiatry*, **30**, 290–297.

Reynolds CF, Coble PA, Spiket DG *et al.* (1982) Prevalence of sleep apnoea and nocturnal myoclonus in major affective disorders: Clinical and polysomnographic findings. *J Nerv Ment Dis*, **170**, 565–567.

Reynolds CF, Kupfer DJ, McEachran AB *et al.* (1984) Depressive psychopathology in male sleep apnoeics. *J Clin Psychiatry*, **45**, 287–290.

Robins LN, Helzer JE, Weissman MM *et al.* (1984) Lifetime prevalence of specific psychiatric disorders in three sites. *Arch Gen Psychiatry*, **41**, 949–958.

Rubey RN and Lydiard RB (1994) Psychopharmacology in the medically ill. *Adv Psychosom Med*, **21**, 1–27.

Rutter BM (1970) The prognostic significance of psychological factors in the management of chronic bronchitis. *Psychol Med*, **9**, 63–70.

Shepherd SL, Hovell MF, Harwood IR *et al.* (1991) A comparative study of the psychosocial assets of adults with cystic fibrosis and their healthy peers. *Chest*, **97**, 1310–1316.

Spittle BJ and Sears MR (1984) Bronchial asthma: lack of relationship between allergic factors, illness severity and psychosocial variables in adult patients attending an asthma clinic. *Psychol Med*, **14**, 847–852.

Steinhausen HC and Schindler HP (1981) Psychosocial adaptation in children and adolescents with cystic fibrosis. *J Dev Behav Ped*, **2**, 74–77.

Thompson WL and Thompson TL (1985a) Psychiatric aspects of asthma in adults. *Adv Psychosom Med*, **14**, 33–47.

Thompson WL and Thompson TL (1985b) Use of medications in patients with chronic pulmonary disease. *Adv Psychosom Med*, **14**, 136–148.

Walters S, Britton J and Hodson ME (1993) Demographic and social characteristics of adults with cystic fibrosis in the United Kingdom. *Br Med J*, **306**, 549–552.

Westaway MS and Wolmarans L (1994) Depression and self-esteem: rapid screening for depression in black, low literacy, hospitalized tuberculosis patients. *Soc Sci Med*, **35**, 1311–1315.

Woodcock AA, Gross ER and Geddes DM (1981) Drug treatment of pink puffers: contrasting effects of diazepam and promethazine in pink puffers. *Br Med J*, **283**, 343–346.

Yellowlees PM, Alpers JH, Bowden JJ *et al.* (1987) Psychiatric morbidity in patients with chronic airflow obstruction. *Med J Aust*, **146**, 305–307.

Yellowlees PM, Haynes S, Potts N *et al.* (1988) Psychiatric morbidity in patients with life-threatening asthma: initial report of a controlled study. *Med J Aust*, **149**, 246–249.

Young T, Palta M, Dempsey J *et al.* (1993) Occurrence of sleep disordered breathing among middle-aged adults. *N Eng J Med,* **328**, 1230–1235.

Zigmond AS and Snaith RP (1983) The Hospital Anxiety and Depression Scale. *Acta Psychiatr Scand,* **B67**, 361–370.

21

Depression and substance misuse

Stuart Cox and Emily Finch

INTRODUCTION

The fact that symptoms of depression and substance misuse commonly occur together has been recognized for many years, but received little focused attention from psychiatrists until the advent of multiaxial classifications such as the DSM-IIIR (American Psychiatric Association, 1987). The term *comorbidity* (Feinstein, 1970) is used to describe the simultaneous occurrence of signs or symptoms from more than one psychiatric diagnosis, although the literature also refers to *dual-diagnosis* and less formally to "*double-trouble*". In this chapter we will be using "depression" in any of the senses in which it occurs in the DSM-IV (American Psychiatric Association, 1994) or ICD-10 (World Health Organisation, 1992), but to avoid ambiguity we shall try to specify whether depressed mood, depressive symptoms, or full depressive illness is being referred to. Similarly, the term substance abuse (*misuse* in the UK) has its meaning defined within DSM-IV, but in some places we will refer specifically to substance *dependence*. Before examining the separate relationships between depression and alcohol or drug misuse, it is useful to consider some general points.

The first general point is the importance of this type of comorbidity. The rate of deliberate self-harm and completed suicide in substance misusing patients is alarmingly high, and assessment of depression and suicidal intent is mandatory. Miller *et al.* (1991) report that 25% of drug and alcohol misusers eventually kill themselves.

Depression and Physical Illness. Edited by M.M. Robertson and C.L.E. Katona
© 1997 John Wiley & Sons Ltd

The second general point is that a number of different relationships might explain the coexistence of depression and substance misuse. In this chapter we shall examine which of these models best fits the observed comorbidity associated with each substance. In the classification below, *primary* refers to the causative condition, which might be expected to appear *first* in a complete case history.

1. *Depression as the primary disorder.* In this relationship, depression is the trigger that causes substance misuse. Depression may make the patient more likely to yield to the temptation of substance misuse. Conversely, substance misuse may be an attempt to self-medicate for deficiencies in processing negative affective states (Khantzian, 1985, 1990), or restore some neurochemical deficiency (Tollefson, 1991). Interestingly, substance misusers themselves very often report that the motivation for drug misuse is to relieve depression (Weiss *et al.*, 1992a) .

2. *Substance misuse as the primary disorder.* In this case, the substance misuse triggers depression either in response to a chaotic life-style, or because the substance *itself* is capable of causing an organic mood disorder, either during intoxication or withdrawal.

3. *Depression and substance misuse are both manifestations of another underlying disorder.* Substance misuse (particularly alcohol misuse) and depression are both common in psychotic illnesses and in patients with neurotic anxiety disorders. Both depression and substance misuse are also common in men with antisocial personality disorder. Borderline personality disorder is characterized by affective instability, and the substance misuse frequently shown by these patients is one manifestation of poor impulse control. Lastly, although not amounting to a formal psychiatric diagnosis, the psychopathology of substance misusers may make them more vulnerable to depressive episodes of all kinds.

4. *Depression and substance misuse are different manifestations of the same disorder.* A relationship of this type has been proposed (Winokur *et al.*, 1971) to explain the increased rates of alcohol misuse and depression seen in family studies. The suggestion is that depression and alcohol misuse are both part of "depressive spectrum disorder" which manifests as alcohol misuse and personality disorder in men, but as depression in women.

The third general point is the caution that needs to be exercised in making a diagnosis of depression in the presence of substance misuse. The difficulties of making a diagnosis of depression in the presence of physical illness have been extensively reported—see, for example, Snaith (1987), and also Chapter 2. Moreover, self-rating instruments, such as the Beck Depression Inventory (BDI), show less correlation with DSM-III diagnosis than clinician-administered rating scales (Hesselbrock *et al.*, 1983). The difficulty of accurately measuring prevalence, especially if depressed mood is not clearly distinguished from depressive illness, is highlighted by a study of 59 alcohol misusing patients whose rate of depression varied from 20% using the Diagnostic Interview Schedule (DIS) to 42% using the symptom checklist–90 (SCL-90) questionnaire (Choquette, 1994). In methadone users, Batson *et al.* (1993) also found that the more stringent definition of depression used by the DIS lead to much lower rates than the BDI.

A related difficulty is that many of the signs and symptoms of depression may be mimicked by the somatic effects of misused substances. Acute withdrawal, especially from CNS depressant drugs such as opiates and alcohol, may produce agitation, restlessness, tearfulness, somatic complaints, loss of libido, sleep disturbance and poor appetite; without invoking any effect of the drug on mood itself. When these "biological" symptoms are added to the psychological effects of more prolonged withdrawal, such as low mood, anergia, anhedonia, poor concentration, and irritability, it can readily be seen that accurate diagnosis of a *separate* depressive syndrome is compromised. No unique clinical features help to identify the depression caused by substance misuse (Patten and Lamarre, 1992). Depressed mood, without any other defining symptoms, may occur during the repeated intoxication and hangover associated with active substance misuse. Lastly, although the full picture of depressive illness may be present early in withdrawal, these symptoms may melt away as detoxification proceeds.

In contrast to the difficulty in deciding whether particular *signs and symptoms* have been caused by substance misuse or by a coexistent depressive disorder, McKenna and Ross (1994) have identified features from the *case history* that may usefully predict a separate depressive disorder. Their finding that seven factors, including a history of sexual abuse, the patient's own rationale for misusing substances, an age of onset over 20 years, and the use or misuse of at least four separate substances, predict the likelihood of an underlying depressive disorder, needs replication and confirmation by longitudinal studies.

The remainder of this chapter will focus on the relationship between individual drugs and depression. In each case we will, whenever possible, refer to the epidemiology, the aetiology and the assessment, management and treatment of these patients, together with some indication of prognosis.

ALCOHOL MISUSE

The frequent comorbidity of alcohol misuse and depression exemplifies all the problems of classification and diagnosis described in the introduction. Nevertheless, symptoms of depression are extremely common in alcohol misusing patients; in particular the symptom of depressed mood can occur at every stage of alcohol misuse. The "maudlin drunk", intoxicated and consumed with his or her woes, is an archetype; "boozer's gloom" (Madden, 1993) manifests as sadness and remorse during the recovery from a hangover. The experience of depressed mood may cause a drinker to seek help for the first time. Depressed mood is encountered in the context of chronic alcohol misuse, or during detoxification, and is sometimes unmasked after abstinence is achieved.

Despite the protean manifestations of depression in the context of alcohol misuse, clinicians need to be aware of the greatly increased risk of deliberate self-harm and completed suicide that occurs in alcohol misuse and dependence. Merril *et al.* (1992) report that in the UK, 34% of men and 15% of women attempting suicide have alcohol problems, without meriting a diagnosis of alcohol dependence. Compared with the rest of the population, the relative risk of completed suicide in alcohol dependence may be as high as 25 times, and 15% of people with alcohol dependence eventually commit suicide (Miles, 1979) although a recent study gave a relative risk of only 7.5 (Rorsow and Amundsen, 1995).

The epidemiology of comorbidity between alcohol and depression

The co-occurrence of depression and alcohol misuse frequency seen by clinicians does not preclude the possibility of a spurious correlation. Indeed, Schuckit (1994) observes that a majority of the Western population consumes alcohol, and possibly one-third of people who drink have, at some time, experienced a temporary alcohol-related problem. Moreover, most people have experienced the intense distress that accompanies loss or grief. Thus, lifetime histories of the symptoms of both alcohol misuse and major depression must occur together quite frequently.

How frequent is depression in the context of alcohol misuse? Factors influencing reported rates are the type of sample, the diagnostic criteria used and the methodology employed. Table 1 gives rates of depression from inpatient studies.

As indicated in the comments in Table 1, rates are higher when considering symptoms rather than depressive disorder, lower the more restrictive the diagnostic criteria, and lifetime rates of depression were higher than rates for the current episode of alcohol misuse. The matter is further complicated by differing rates in men and women (Hesselbrock *et al.*, 1985) with men having substantially higher incidence.

Inpatient samples are subject to bias because individuals with the combination of depression and alcohol misuse are more likely to present for treatment than individuals with alcohol problems alone (Berkson's bias). Moreover, at presentation, alcohol misusers with depression seem to have worse alcohol symptoms and histories than their nondepressed colleagues (McMahon and

Table 1. Prevalence of comorbidity of depression and alcohol misuse in treatment samples.

Author(s)	Percentage	Comments
Nakamura *et al.*, 1983	71	Depressive symptoms
Tyndel, 1974	30	Depressive symptoms
Woodruff *et al.*, 1973	53	Feighner criteria, major depression, lifetime rate
Hasin *et al.*, 1988	46	RDC criteria, major depression, lifetime rate
Yates *et al.*, 1988	10	DSM-III criteria, major depression, current rate at time of assessment, males only
Davidson, 1995	67	RDC criteria, major depression, current rate

Table 2. The prevalence of depression and alcohol misuse in community samples.

Author(s)	Prevalence (%)	Relative risk	Comments
Weissman and Myers, 1980	71	–	Lifetime comorbidity
	15.4	1.8	Current alcohol abuse and current depression
Helzer *et al.*, 1988	–	1.3–2.1	Lifetime relative risk
Helzer and Pryzbeck, 1988b	78 (males),	–	Lifetime risk of depression in
	44 (females)	–	primary alcohol misusers
Regier *et al.*, 1990	13.4	1.9	Lifetime prevalence of depression in alcohol misuse/dependence

Davidson, 1986). Rates from community epidemiological studies are given in Table 2.

The converse relationship, that of alcohol misuse occurring in depressed populations, also holds: The massive Epidemiological Catchment Area (ECA) study showed that nearly 22% of patients with depression also have a lifetime diagnosis of alcohol misuse (Regier *et al.*, 1990). It should be remembered, however, that the presence of alcohol misuse in people with a lifetime diagnosis of depression does not imply anything about causation; it is merely a measure of coincidence. Preliminary results from another large community epidemiological study, the National Comorbidity Survey (Kessler, 1994), have shown that psychiatric morbidity in the population is highly clustered in individuals who are highly comorbid, and presumably highly vulnerable. Disaggregation of these results, to show which conditions cluster together, is awaited.

A much higher relative risk of comorbid alcohol misuse is seen when bipolar disorder is considered, with a relative risk of over 6 for men, and 10 for women. The ECA study mentioned above gives rates of over 43% for comorbidity of alcohol misuse and bipolar disorder. However, the nature of the increased risk is unclear although the alcohol misuse seems to occur in the manic rather than the depressed phases of the illness. Alcohol misuse may be a symptom of the manic phase of the disorder, but it has also been suggested that manic patients may attempt to self-medicate symptoms such as agitation and sleeplessness, as in the first relationship in the introduction where depression is the primary disorder.

It thus seems that the increased rates of depression seen in treatment samples is confirmed by community studies, albeit to a smaller degree, and that the two conditions *do* more commonly occur together than by chance alone.

The aetiology of comorbid depression and alcohol misuse

Which of the possible relationships in the introduction best explains the observed comorbidity? Relatively little evidence points to depression causing alcohol abuse (Petty and Nasrallah, 1981) and most depressed people do not increase their alcohol intake. Lipton (1994) reports that light to moderate drinkers may be less likely to develop depression secondary to chronic stress. Woodruff *et al.* (1973) studied three patient groups: patients with alcohol misuse alone, patients with depression alone, and patients with both. On a number of measures of demographic and case history variables, the comorbid group closely resembled patients with alcohol misuse alone, rather than patients with depression alone. Moreover, their comorbid patients reported the onset of alcohol misuse prior to the onset of depression. Whilst the use of case histories that have been supplied by the patients themselves is open to criticism because of poor or biased recall, most of the evidence seems to point to the onset of alcohol problems before the first appearance of depression.

Family, twin and adoption studies

Despite their success in determining the extent of heritability in other areas of psychiatry, such studies have yielded equivocal results when considering comorbidity for alcohol misuse and depression. Some studies indicate the presence of a possible depressive spectrum disorder (Winokur *et al.*, 1971), but other studies quotes by Merikangas and Gelernter (1990) indicate independent transmission. The interested reader is referred to the extensive reviews of the subject by Schuckit (1986) and Cloninger *et al.* (1979). Schuckit (1994) suggests that the observed excess comorbidity may be because both mood disturbance and alcohol abuse are common in people with antisocial personality disorder (the third relationship in the introduction) or because of assortative mating—people with either depression or substance misuse problems are more likely to have children together.

Clinical studies

Useful aetiological data have been obtained from clinical studies. A study of 577 male "alcoholics" revealed the presence of intense feelings of sadness in up to 80%, although the rate of depression varied according to the criteria employed (Schuckit, 1985). However, when stringent history taking was employed, only 5% of this population reported episodes of depression in the absence of drinking. Similarly, Brown and Schuckit (1988) have said that 40% of primarily "alcoholic" men reported significant levels of depression after 9 days of abstinence, but the rate dropped to 4% 4 weeks later, without any specific therapy for their depression. Similarly, Davidson (1995) reported that 67% of alcohol misusing inpatients had symptoms which met research diagnostic criteria (RDC) for major depression, shortly after admission, but only 13% of these patients remained depressed after detoxification. Roggala and Uhl (1995) showed that a relapse into renewed alcohol misuse was accompanied by an immediate relapse into depression.

Longitudinal studies

One longitudinal study of potential comorbidity (Schuckit, 1991) failed to reveal any increase in the incidence of major depressive episodes in 200 sons of probands with alcohol misuse at 10 year follow up. In another follow up study of 239 alcohol misusing men, Schuckit *et al.* (1994) found that only 2% of patients who remained abstinent developed a major depressive episode, compared with 4% in those who relapsed. Harrington *et al.* (1990) reported no excess of alcohol dependency developing by age 30 in patients who had manifested major affective illness in adolescence although other work comes to the opposite conclusion (Burke *et al.*, 1994). Lastly, laboratory studies of susceptible individuals showed that alcohol administration can directly cause symptoms of depression and anxiety (van der Spruy, 1972; Gibson and Becker, 1973).

Thus, despite conflicting evidence concerning coheritability, it does seem as if the majority of the excess depression seen in alcohol misusing patients resolves with abstinence, and that alcohol is the primary problem, causing an organic mood disorder, as in the second relationship in the introduction. A smaller group show residual depression or develop new depressive episodes when abstinent, and need to be considered from both clinical and theoretical perspectives as different.

Neuropathology of alcohol

Early theories about the neurotropic effects of alcohol (ethanol) focused upon its ability to fluidize biological membranes. Such theories, at least in simple form, have been abandoned because the fluidizing effect only occurs at tissue concentrations of ethanol that would be supralethal in man and animals. However, recent developments have shown that ethanol may differentially partition into membranes around certain membrane-bound proteins (Bloom, 1991), but the clinical relevance of such studies is, as yet, unclear.

Recent work on alcohol has focused on its effect on receptors such as the GABA, NMDA (glutamate), serotonergic (5-hydroxytryptamine, 5-HT) and dopaminergic systems. Alcohol potentiates transmission at the GABA channel, and thus has an anxiolytic effect similar to the benzodiazepines (Tabakoff and Hoffman, 1993). Moreover, alcohol antagonizes transmission at the NMDA subclass of glutamate receptors, and so has an anti-anxiogenic effect. Thus withdrawal of alcohol can produce anxiety symptoms, which, of course, are a part of the syndrome of depressive disorder. Alcohol withdrawal can produce other symptoms of noradrenergic overactivity, leading to agitation, restlessness and insomnia (Mueller et al., 1993). These symptoms lead to further effects, such as irritability and poor concentration thus building towards a picture of depressive disorder.

But what of the "core" symptoms of depressive illness—depressed mood and anhedonia? Tollefson (1991), among others, has produced an elegant model which proposes that individuals with a tendency towards alcohol misuse may have a pre-existing serotonergic deficit. This deficit is relieved by acute alcohol administration, which causes the presynaptic terminals to release their stored serotonin, but leaving them further depleted. That serotonin is intimately involved in the genesis of depression and impulse disorders is now generally accepted, and would suggest that serotonin reuptake inhibitors (SSRI) might be of particular benefit in treating the depression associated with alcohol misuse.

Lastly, alcohol may directly or indirectly stimulate (Koob, 1992) the dopaminergic pathways from the ventral tegmental region of the brain stem to the nucleus accumbens. It is this pathway that is widely supposed to form the anatomical substrate for the mediation of pleasurable reward. Withdrawal of alcohol might be expected to produce a state of lack of pleasure—just the anhedonia that is found in clinical practice. This is almost certainly an oversimplification, but future work will elucidate the relationship between alcohol misuse, withdrawal, elation and anhedonia.

Assessment, treatment and prognosis

Assessment and treatment

In earlier sections it was shown that there is a profound overlap between symptoms of depression and alcohol misuse; that alcohol can certainly cause an organic mood disorder in susceptible people; and that the majority of patients presenting with both alcohol misuse and depression do not remain depressed after abstinence is achieved. Conversely, a return to alcohol misuse is frequently accompanied by a return of depressive symptoms. Therefore, it is not surprising that clinicians have found that attempting to treat depression while patients continue to misuse alcohol is unrewarding. Indeed, treatment of such patients has been succinctly described as "like painting over rust" (D. Kelly, personal communication). Treatment of depression in active drinkers may lead both patient and physician to wrongly attribute the primary problem as depression and not alcohol, but confronting patients before they are engaged in treatment is unhelpful; clinicians should also remember that a minority of patients *do* manifest depression after detoxification.

In contrast to the uncertain aetiological relationship between these two disorders there is a consensus appearing in the literature regarding treatment (see, for example, Davidson, 1995; Mueller *et al.*, 1993; Madden, 1993). Assessment and treatment of depressive symptoms should be delayed at least 3–4 weeks after abstinence is achieved, by which time the majority of patients will no longer need specific treatment for depression. Secondary depression in the context of alcohol misuse remits more quickly than primary depressive symptoms (Brown *et al.*, 1995). Moreover, the minority of studies which demonstrate a marked improvement in mood when antidepressant therapy is started early in the treatment regime, are confounded by the natural remission of symptoms which occur as abstinence is achieved. Probably the only exception to this general rule is in patients who either have a strongly positive family history for depressive illness or who have a demonstrated history of depression occurring in the absence of alcohol misuse. However, Nunes *et al.* (1993) report that imipramine may help primary depressed alcoholic misusers who continue to drink.

After the appropriate delay, is there any guidance about the most appropriate antidepressant to use? Merikangas and Gelernter (1990) quote five studies of tricyclic antidepressants, four of which showed that they were superior to placebo. The same authors summarize the results of studies using lithium without definite conclusions. Trials of SSRIs in comorbid and alcohol abusing populations are beginning to appear in the literature: Cornelius *et al.* (1993) noted a reduction of both depressive symptoms and alcohol consumption with fluoxetine. The serotonergic hypothesis that links depression and alcohol misuse would also suggest that SSRIs should have a beneficial effect upon the tendency of alcohol misusers to relapse after successful treatment. Unfortunately, a recent placebo-controlled trial of fluoxetine failed to demonstrate such an effect (Kranzler *et al.*, 1995). Despite this negative result, the well-documented reduction of alcohol consumption in both human and animal experiments produced by the SSRIs (see, for example, Naranjo and Bremner, 1993) must make this a fertile area for future research.

There are other good clinical reasons for making the SSRIs a first choice in these patients. The SSRIs have reduced toxicity in overdosage and they are much less potent central nervous system (CNS) depressants. They have well-documented effects in suppressing "appetitive" (consuming) behaviours of many kinds, including alcohol consumption. They have a more benign side-effect profile than the tricyclic antidepressants. Lastly, there is preliminary evidence that SSRIs may improve functioning in patients with Korsakov's-type brain damage (Martin *et al.*, 1995).

There are few studies in the literature about psychotherapeutic approaches to comorbidity. However, Silvers (1993), using a method of cognitive restructuring, abolished all symptoms of craving and withdrawal in 79% of patients in a small study. Less familiar to Western psychiatrists is the technique of transcranial electrical treatment (TEF) which produces changes in brain monoamines and GABA, with useful effects upon mood and anxiety in alcohol misuse (Krupitsky *et al.*, 1991).

Prognosis and outcome

Depression has a relatively benign outcome in the majority of alcohol misusers, provided that they continue to exert appropriate control over their alcohol use. Do patients with comorbidity have a worse prognosis than those patients who present with only one of the two disorders? Mueller *et al.* (1993) propose a worse prognosis for patients with "double trouble" and the same author (Mueller *et al.*, 1994) has shown that in a 10 year follow up, patients who continue to drink have a worse prognosis for their current depression; somewhat surprisingly, however, patient's drinking status did not predict the development of new depressive illness. Lastly, Davidson and Ritson (1993) state that although the presence of depression may hasten the development of alcohol dependence, the outcome of alcohol misuse in patients who remain depressed is unclear, and Petty (1992) has suggested that a poorer outcome for future alcohol misuse may be present when depression persists after detoxification.

ILLICIT DRUG MISUSE

The relationship between depression and substance misuse is complex and drug users with comorbid depression are common. The presence of depressive symptoms or depressive illness in a substance misuser may have important prognostic significance. For instance, either a diagnosis of a depressive syndrome or elevated scores on rating scales to measure depression have been found to be powerful predictors of substance abuse-related outcome in opiate users (Rounsaville *et al.*, 1982). There is other evidence that this group is more difficult to manage than alcohol misusers. Users of heroin and cocaine with high scores on the Beck Depression Inventory, the Symptom Checklist—90 (SCL-90) and the General Health Questionnaire (GHQ) have higher levels of injecting and needle sharing than the general injecting population, putting them at greater risk of HIV (human immunodeficiency virus) and hepatitis (Metzger *et al.*, 1991; Latkin and Mandell, 1993). Like alcohol misusers, substance misusers have higher suicide rates than the general population (Rossow, 1994). Drug users with depression therefore require more intensive psychiatric and addiction management.

Illicit drug misusers differ from alcoholics in many ways despite many attempts to group them together. Their drug use is illegal, so they tend to be a more deviant group who are under substantial legal and social stress. However, opiate drugs are less likely to cause an organic mood disorder than alcohol. Illicit drug misusers are a substantially younger group which of course affects any chance associations between their illicit drug misuse and depressive illness. Follow up studies are difficult because they are a mobile group who are difficult to trace. Also, it must be remembered, that a variety of substances may be misused together, and each may have a very different affect on mood. Assessment of depressive symptoms and syndromes may be difficult in the presence of drug effects. The behaviour associated with an addicted life-style itself may make assessment even more difficult. The amount of drug abused or the amount of time spent in using it will affect its relationship with depression and will certainly affect the strength of any aetiological relationship. Drug misusers also often misuse alcohol.

The epidemiology of comorbidity between drug abuse and depression

Unfortunately, identifying coexisting psychiatric disorders in a substance misusing population presents several specific methodological problems that can complicate the diagnostic process (Weiss *et al.*, 1996b). The timing of an interview may affect the reliability and validity of a patient's response. Repeating the same diagnostic interview can produce poor long-term and short-term diagnostic agreement (Rounsaville *et al.*, 1991b). Different interview techniques and diagnostic criteria can also affect the prevalence of depressive syndromes. In addition, researchers tend to use different abstinence criteria (the length of time a subject must be drug free) before a depression diagnosis is made. In the USA many opiate misusers are managed in methadone mainte-

Table 3. The prevalence of current depression in illicit drug misusers.

Author	Population	Diagnostic criteria	Prevalence (%)
Rounsaville et al., 1980	62 narcotic addicts	SADS-L, RDC	42
Rounsaville et al., 1982	157 narcotic addicts	RDC	17 major depression, 44 any depression
Woody et al., 1983	110 opiate addicts	SADS-L	43 any depression
Khantzian and Treece, 1985	133 methadone maintenance.	DSM-III	48 any depression
Mirin et al., 1988	160 opiate using inpatients	DSM-III	17.6 major of atypical depression
Regier et al., 1990 (ECA study)	Community sample of opiate misusers	DIS/DSM-III	26.4 any depression
El-Guebaly, 1990	Review	DIS/DSM-III	15–30
Mirin et al., 1988	Inpatient cocaine misusers	DSM-III	30.6 major or atypical depression
Rounsaville et al., 1991a	Inpatient and outpatient primary cocaine users	RDC	4.7 major depression 44 any depression

nance programmes and stable clients may be on methadone although classed as "drug free" in research. Depressive symptoms decline significantly in patients after entry to methadone maintenance programmes, making valid assessment of depression in these clients difficult (Strain et al., 1992).

The prevalence of depression in illicit drug users varies from 15% to almost 50% depending on the study (see Table 3). Most of the studies have been conducted on opiate users. The differences in prevalence between opiate and stimulant users may be an effect of the drug itself; but an alternative explanation may be that cocaine users tend to be a more heterogeneous group whose levels of dependence vary substantially. Opiate users who come to treatment tend to be heavily dependent and function badly. The cocaine users may be a less deviant and dysfunctional group initially resulting in lower levels of depressive disorder.

Another study of opiate users in Sydney, Australia has looked at minor psychopathology and symptoms rather than syndromes. This found that using the GHQ, 61% of the subjects achieved "caseness" compared with a rate of approximately 20% in Australian community samples (Swift et al., 1990). In a study that also suggests a high level of depressive symptoms, Dinwiddie et al. (1992) looked at a history of suicide attempts in intravenous drug users and found a ratio of 8.27 for a suicide attempt compared with non-drug users.

Effects of different substances

Opiates

Opiates are CNS depressants, with the desired effect of euphoria. They induce a profound dependence, and drug-seeking behaviour becomes the overriding activity in an addicted life-style. Opioid withdrawal is associated with substantial levels of dysphoria, and in view of its half-life of about 6 hours, the dependent heroin user will be experiencing withdrawal several times a day (Handelsman *et al.*, 1992). Indeed this dysphoria may be one factor driving continued heroin use as a mechanism to avoid the aversive symptoms of withdrawal. Depressive symptoms in heroin addicts decrease significantly after a period of stabilization on methadone, which may be a consequence of its much longer half-life, resulting in an individual not experiencing withdrawal symptoms (Strain *et al.*, 1992; Finch *et al.*, 1994). These findings do suggest that the diagnosis of syndromal depression such as a major depressive disorder should be made only after a prolonged period of abstinence or at least prolonged periods of stabilization on opioid replacement drugs.

Stimulants

Depressive symptoms are a well-established part of the cocaine withdrawal syndrome which follows three phases: crash, withdrawal and extinction (Gawin and Ellinwood, 1988), although this concept is not universally accepted (Lago and Kosten, 1994). During the withdrawal phase patients experience fluctuating depression which is usually not severe enough to cause clinical concern but may well cue further craving and precipitate relapse (Strang *et al.*, 1993). Cocaine acts by blocking the reuptake of all monoamine neurotransmitters and has a central action on 5-HT receptors. The most abuse-specific action, however, seems to be its action as a potent blocker of the dopamine reuptake system (Stamford *et al.*, 1988). These actions have created substantial interest in the use of antidepressants to treat the symptoms of the withdrawal crash experienced by cocaine users since, theoretically, the increased availability of monoamines after use of antidepressants may mitigate their rebound depletion following cocaine administration. There are some reports of permanent depletion of dopaminergic neurones after the administration of cocaine, possibly associated with long-term symptoms of depression (Wyatt *et al.*, 1987). The vast majority of cocaine abstainers do not show prolonged mood changes however.

Amphetamines are also associated with depressive symptoms during withdrawal but again patients rarely show long-term effects following prolonged abstinence. Amphetamine withdrawal has been less extensively studied but seems similar to cocaine withdrawal (Lago and Kosten, 1994).

Cannabis

Transient depression is a typical cannabis effect. Andreasson and Allebeck (1990) reported an increased proportion of deaths by suicide among heavy cannabis users in 15 year follow up of Swedish conscripts. Anecdotally, there are reports that cannabis may precipitate relapse in patients with pre-existing mood disorder and that serious or prolonged mood disorder can occur. However, the dysphoric reactions commonly occurring with cannabis use are brief and self-limiting.

Other drugs

MDMA (Ecstasy) has been associated with a range of different psychiatric disturbances. The evidence is primarily in case reports, and several report the presence of depression and suicidal behaviour (Schifano and Magni, 1994). Lysergic acid diethylamide (LSD) has mainly been associated with flashbacks but not with depression. Steroid abuse is also known to be associated with dysphoric mood states (Williamson and Young, 1992).

The aetiology of comorbid depression and drug misuse

The understanding of the aetiology of depression in substance misusers requires an understanding of the possible relationship between the conditions. These relationships are set out in the introduction. Organic mood disorders, which fit with the second aetiological relationship outlined in the introduction, have been discussed above; other aetiological theories are discussed below.

The self-medication hypothesis

There has been substantial interest in the "self-medication hypothesis". This conforms consistently with the first relationship outlined in the introduction. Khantzian (1985) states that drug-dependent individuals are predisposed to addition because they suffer from depression and other psychiatric disorders. He goes on to say that the choice of drug is not random. Opiate addicts prefer opiates because of their effects on rage and aggression; cocaine is chosen because of its ability to relieve distress associated with depression and other dysphoric mood states. However, in a study of 32 patients who met DSM-IIIR criteria for an Axis I disorder of depression it was found that only opiate users reported that drugs improved their psychiatric symptoms, while cocaine users did not (Castaneda *et al.*, 1989). Another study reported that drug use to relieve depressive symptoms was more common in men with major depression although these authors did find that most patients reported using drugs in response to depressive symptoms (Weiss *et al.*, 1992a).

In summary, it does seem that some drug users do use drugs to relieve symptoms of depression but specific relationships between the drug and particular symptoms have not been established.

Family studies

There has been very little work looking at the genetics of drug misuse and even less in patients with a comorbid depressive illness. Rounsaville *et al.* (1991b) have investigated the relationship between comorbid drug users and psychiatric disorder and substance misuse disorders in their families. They found that relatives of opiate addicts with major depression had substantially higher rates of major depression, indicating that these opiate addicts were a subtype with a genetic predisposition to depression. A study of the siblings of cocaine users with comorbid major depression found that they had a wide range of psychiatric disorders, suggesting that those cocaine users may be predisposed to a wide range of psychiatric disorders not just depression (Luthar and Rounsaville, 1993). These studies do suggest that there may be some kind of common genetic predisposition to substance misuse and other Axis I psychiatric disorders, corresponding with the fourth relationship discussed in the introduction.

Assessment, treatment and prognosis

Assessment

The assessment of psychiatric symptoms in drug users may be problematic. As discussed above, drug users do seem to have a high prevalence of both depressive syndromes and minor transient dysphoric states. The diagnosis of a true depressive syndrome may be difficult.

The problem of instability of symptoms over time may be overcome by carrying out repeated mental state examinations over a few weeks. Persistent depressive symptoms may indicate serious pathology. Histories need to be taken carefully to establish whether or not depression occurred before the substance misuse became a problem. In practice, however, this can be difficult as many drug users who are using drugs heavily may have been using them since adolescence. It may be useful to ask about family history of major depression and about life events or major trauma which may have triggered a depressive illness. In trying to establish a causative role for the drug in provoking depressive symptoms, it may be possible to identify recent changes in patterns of drug use. A new phase of heavy cocaine use in combination with opiates, or a recent escalation in the amount of drug used, for example, when injecting replaces smoking in heroin users, can often precipitate the onset of depression.

To establish confidently the role of a particular drug in a depressive illness a period of abstinence (usually about 1 month) is required. However, in clinical practice this may not be possible as a patient may find it impossible to stay drug-free for that long. This may differ from alcohol misusers who as a less deviant group are able, at least temporarily, to conform to treatment programmes. Nevertheless, a period of stable drug use, for instance by maintenance on an adequate dose of methadone, can distinguish between minor states of dysphoria, and the presence of major depressive disorder.

Treatment

There is some evidence that tricyclic antidepressants are effective in the treatment of drug misusers with depression. In a study of 17 stable patients receiving methadone maintenance who met DSM-IIIR criteria for depression there was substantial improvement in both mood and illicit drug use after treatment with imipramine (Nunes *et al.*, 1991). However, this contrasted with an earlier randomized controlled trial which failed to show a difference in response to amitriptyline in a group of methadone maintenance patients with DSM-III depression (Kleber *et al.*, 1983). This study and another demonstrated the positive effect of drug treatment itself on the symptoms of depression (Magruder-Habib, 1992). In a study of interpersonal psychotherapy for methadone-maintained opiate users, Woody *et al.* (1983) found that the treatment was most successful in those who were depressed.

The practical management of depressive symptoms in drug users requires the following stages. Firstly, an adequate assessment and in order to do this a period of stabilization of drug use, if not detoxification, may be required. This may be achievable in an outpatient prescribing programme but more chaotic patients may require a period of inpatient treatment. Only if the symptoms persist beyond stabilization or detoxification should a course of antidepressant be used.

In cocaine users the procedure may differ. The cocaine withdrawal syndrome has depressive symptoms as one of its central features and there has been substantial interest in the use of antidepressants to treat depression-induced cocaine craving during the withdrawal period. The results of randomized controlled trials have been conflicting (Kosten *et al.*, 1992; Arndt *et al.*, 1992). However, many clinicians find a course of a tricyclic or an SSRI useful in managing cocaine-induced craving in inpatients despite unpromising early research effort for their efficacy (Grabowski *et al.*, 1995). Of course, persistent depressive symptoms in a cocaine user require assessment in the same way as in an opiate user.

Prognosis and outcome

As stated above, depressive symptoms in substance misusers often remit substantially when they receive adequate treatment for their substance misuse.

In a study mentioned earlier of 157 opiate addicts there was a substantial drop in the prevalence of major depression when they were followed up after 6 months (Rounsaville *et al.*, 1986). However, this was only related to retention in treatment. The prognosis for patients with depression and substance misuse is less good than for those with substance misuse alone. There is a problem with finding adequate treatment services as patients may find it difficult to comply with substance misuse programmes, and may not be accepted for treatment by general psychiatrists because of their drug use. In general, there, is a need for more treatment services designed to met the needs of the substance misuser with a psychiatric problem.

CONCLUSIONS

Theoretical studies which have examined the comorbidity of depression and substance misuse have given differing results. Attempts to clarify their aetiology have given interesting data; but, as yet, no definite consensus has emerged about the causal relationship that may exist between either alcohol or drug misuse and depression. Historically, there has also been confusion between depressed mood, depressive symptoms and the full depressive syndrome.

There are few longitudinal studies in alcohol misuse, and even fewer in illicit drug misuse, that help to elucidate the aetiology of the observed comorbidity. A potential approach for the future is to start considering a greater constellation of variables rather than just depression and/or substance misuse: the presence or absence of antisocial personality disorder, and personality traits such as anxiety, sensation seeking and low versus high arousal personality types may all interact, together with gender, in the genesis of substance misusing behaviour.

In contrast to the difficulty of establishing how, when and why alcohol and depression interact, consensus is now appearing in considering treatment options for patients with "double trouble". The majority of these patients are best treated by detoxification. When abstinence is achieved, most will no longer be experiencing depressive symptoms. For the minority who do have both autonomous depression and alcohol misuse, use of antidepressant medication is not only useful, but may be lifesaving, given the elevated rate of completed suicide.

In illicit drug misuse, the picture is more complicated. Detoxification is less successful in illicit drug misusers, and consideration must be given to assessment of mood following a period of stable drug use. Indeed, antidepressants may be useful in patients with stable opiate use. Provision of services which address the problems of alcohol and drug misuse with comorbid depressive illness is one of the challenges for the future.

REFERENCES

American Psychiatric Association (1987) *Diagnostic and Statistical Manual of Mental Disorder* (3rd edn, revised). Washington, DC: APA.

American Psychiatric Association (1994) *Diagnostic and Statistical Manual of Mental Disorders* (4th edn). Washington, DC: APA.

Andreasson S and Allebeck P (1990) Cannabis and mortality among young men: a longitudinal study of Swedish conscripts. *Scand J Soc Med*, **18**, 9–15.

Arndt IO, Dorozynsky L, Woody GE *et al*. (1992) Desipramine treatment of cocaine dependence in methadone maintained patients. *Arch Gen Psychiatry*, **49**, 888–893.

Batson HW, Brown LS, Zaballero AR, Chu A and Alterman AI (1993) Conflicting measurements of depression in a substance abuse population. *J Subst Abuse*, **5**, 93–100.

Bloom FE (1991) Alcohol and anaesthetic actions: are they mediated by lipid or protein? In: RE Meyer, GF Koob, MJ Lewis and SM Paul (eds). *Neuropharmacology of Ethanol, New Approaches*. Boston: Birkhauser, 1–19.

Brown SA and Schuckit MA (1988) Changes in depression in abstinent alcoholics. *J Stud Alcohol*, **49**, 412–417.

Brown, SA, Inaba, RK, Gillin JC *et al*. (1995) Alcoholism, and affective disorder: Clinical course of depressive symptoms. *Am J Psychiatry*, **152**, 45–52.

Burke JD, Burke KC and Rae DS (1994) Increased rates of drug abuse and dependence after onset of mood or anxiety disorders in adolescence. *Hosp Commun Psychiatry*, **45**, 451–455.

Castaneda R, Galanter M and France H (1989) Self-medication among addicts with primary psychiatic disorders. *Compr Psychiatry*, **30**, 80–83.

Choquetta KA (1994) Assessing depression in alcoholics with the BDI, SCL-90, and DIS criteria. *J Subst Abuse*, **6**, 295–304.

Cloninger CR, Reich T and Wetzel R (1979) Alcoholism and affective disorders: Familial association and genetic models. In: DW Goodwin and CK Erickson (eds). *Alcoholism and Affective Disorders: Clinical, Genetic, and Biochemical Studies*. New York: SP Medical and Scientific Books.

Cornelius JR, Salloum IM, Cornelius MD *et al*. (1993) Fluoxetine trial in depressed alcoholics. *Pscyhopharmacol Bull*, **29**, 195–199.

Davidson KM (1995) Diagnosis of depression in alcohol dependence: Changes in prevalence with drinking status. *Br J Psychiatry*, **166**, 199–204.

Davidson KM and Ritson, EB (1993) The relationship between alcohol dependence and depression. *Alcohol Alcohol*, **28**, 147–155.

Dinwiddie SH, Reich T and Cloninger CR (1992) Psychiatric comorbidity and suicidality among intravenous drug users. *J Clin Psychiatry*, **53**, 364–369.

El-Guebaly N (1990) Substance abuse and mental disorders: The dual diagnosis concept. *Can J Psychiatry*, **35**, 261–267.

Feinstein AR (1970) The pre-therapeutic classification of co-morbidity in chronic disease. *J Chronic Disord*, **23**, 455–468.

Finch EJL, Groves I, Feinamnn C *et al*. (1994) A low threshold methadone stabilisation programme—description and first stage evaluation. *Addiction Res*, **3:1**, 63–71.

Gawin FH and Ellinwood EH (1988) Cocaine and other stimulants. *New Engl J Med*, **318**, 1173.

Gershon ES, Hamvovit J and Guroff JJ (1982) A family study of schizoaffective, bipolar I, bipolar II, unipolar, and normal control probands. *Arch Gen Psychiatry*, **39**, 1157–1167.

Gibson S and Becker J (1973) Changes in alcoholics' self-reported depression. *J Stud Alcohol*, **34**, 829–836.

Grabowski J, Rhoades H, Elk R *et al.* (1995) Fluoxetine is ineffective for treatment of cocaine dependence or concurrent opiate and cocaine dependence: two placebo-controlled double-blind trials. *J Clin Psychopharmacol*, **15(3)**, 163–174.

Handelsman L, Aronson MJ, Hess R *et al.* (1992) The dysphoria of heroin addiction. *Am J Drug Alcohol Abuse*, **18(3)**, 275–287.

Harrington R, Fudge H, Rutter M, Pickles A and Hill J (1990) Adult outcomes of childhood and adolescent depression. *Arch Gen Psychiatry*, **47**, 465–473.

Hasin DS, Grant BF and Endicott J (1988) Lifetime psychiatric co-morbidity in hospitalized alcoholics. *Int J Addict*, **23**, 827–850.

Helzer JE and Pryzbeck TR (1988) The co-occurence of alcoholism with other psychiatric disorders in the general population and its impact on treatment. *J Stud Alcohol*, **49**, 219–224.

Helzer JE, Canino GJ, Hwu HG *et al.* (1988) Alcoholism: a cross-national comparison of population surveys with the diagnostic interview schedule. In RM Rose and JE Barret (eds). *Alcoholism: Origins and Outcome*. New York: Raven Press, 31–48.

Hesselbrock MN, Hesselbrock VM, Tennen H, Meyer RE and Workman KL (1983) Methodological considerations in the assessment of depression of alcoholics. *J Consult Clin Psychol*, **51**, 399–405.

Hesselbrock MN, Meyer RE and Keener JJ (1985) Psychopathology in hospitalised alcoholics. *Arch Gen Psychiatry*, **42**, 1050–1055.

Ingraham IF and Wender PH (1992) Risk for affective disorder and alcohol and other drug abuse in the relatives of affectively ill adoptees. *J Affect Dis*, **26**, 45–51.

Kessler RC (1994) The National Comorbidity Survey of the USA. *Int Rev Psychiatry*, **6**, 365–376.

Khantzian EJ and Treece C (1985) DSM-III psychiatric diagnosis of narcotic addicts. *Arch Gen Psychiatry*, **42**, 1067–1071.

Khantzian EJ (1985) The self medication hypothesis of addictive disorders: focus on heroin and cocaine dependence. *Am J Psychiatry*, **142**, 1259–1264.

Khantzian EJ (1990) Self-regulation and self-medication factors in alcoholism and the addictions. *Recent Dev Alcohol*, **8**, 255–271.

Kleber HD, Weissman MM, Rounsaville BJ *et al.* (1983) Imipramine as a treatment for depression in addicts. *Arch Gen Psychiatry*, **40**, 649–653.

Koob GF (1992) Drugs of abuse: anatomy, pharmacology and function of reward pathways. *Trends Pharmacol Sci*, **13**, 177–184.

Kosten TR, Morgan CM, Falcione J *et al.* (1992) Pharmacotherapy for cocaine-abusing methadone maintained patients using amantadine or desipramine. *Am J Psychiatry*, **49**, 894–898.

Kranzler HR, Burleson JA, Korner P *et al.* (1995) Placebo-controlled trial of fluoxetine as an adjunct to relapse prevention in alcoholics. *Am J Psychiatry*, **152**, 391–397.

Krupitsky EM, Burakov AM, Karandashova GF, Katsnelson JS and Lebedev, VP (1991) The administration of transcranial electrical treatment for affective disturbances in alcoholic patients. *Drug Alcohol Depend*, **27**, 1–6.

Lago JA and Kosten TR (1994) Stimulant withdrawal. *Addiction*, **89**, 1477–1481.

Latkin CA and Mandell W (1993) Depression as an antecedent of frequency of intravenous drug use in an urban, nontreatment sample. *Int J Addict*, **28(14)**, 1601–1612.

Lipton RI (1994) The effect of moderate alcohol use on the relationship between stress and depression. *Am J Public Health*, **84**, 1913–1917.

Luthar S and Rounsaville BJ (1993) Substance misuse and comorbid psychopathology in a high risk group: A study of siblings of cocaine misusers. *Int J Addict*, **28(5)**, 415–434.

Madden JS (1993) Alcohol and depression. *Br J Hosp Med*, **50**, 261–264.

Magruder-Habib K, Hubbard R and Ginzburg HM (1992) Effects of drug misuse treatment on symptoms of depression and suicide. *Int J Addict*, **27(9)**, 1035–1065.

Martin PR, Adinoff B, Lane E *et al.* (1995) Fluvoxamine treatment of alcoholic amnestic disorder. *Eur Neuropsychopharmacol*, **5**, 27–33.

McKenna C and Ross C (1994) Diagnostic conundrums in substance misusers with psychiatric symptoms. *Am J Drug Alc Abuse*, **20**, 397–412.

McMahon RC and Davidson RS (1986) An examination of depressed vs non-depressed alcoholics in inpatient treatment. *J Clin Psychol*, **42**, 177–184.

Merikanas KR and Gelernter CS (1990) Comorbidity for alcoholism and depression. *Psychiatric Clin North Am*, **13**, 613–632.

Merril J, Milner G, Owens J and Vale A (1992) Alcohol and attempted suicide. *Br J Addict*, **87**, 83–90.

Metzger D, Woody G, De Philippis D *et al.* (1991) Risk factors for needle sharing among methadone treated patients. *Am J Psychiatry*, **148**, 636–640.

Miles CP (1979) Conditions predisposing to suicide: A review. *J Nerv Ment Dis*, **164**, 231–246.

Miller NS, Mahler JC and Gold MS (1991) Suicide risk associated with drug and alcohol dependence. *J Addict Disord*, **10**, 49–61.

Mirin SM, Weiss RD and Michael J (1988) Psychopathology in substance abusers: diagnosis and treatment. *Am J Drug Alcohol Abuse*, **14(2)**, 139–157.

Mueller TI, Brown RA and Recupero PR (1993) Depression and substance misuse. *Rhode Island Med*, **76**, 409–413.

Mueller TI, Lavori PW, Keller MB *et al.* (1994) Prognostic effect of the variable course of alcoholism on the 10-year course of depression. *Am J Psychiatry*, **151**, 701–706.

Nakamura MM, Overall JE, Hollister RE and Radcliffe E (1983) Factors affecting outcome of depressive symptoms in alcoholics. *Alcohol Clin Exp Res*, **7**, 188–193.

Naranjo CA and Bremner KE (1993) Clinical pharmacology of serotonin-altering medications for decreasing alcohol consumption. *Alcohol Alcohol*, **Suppl 2**, 221–229.

Nunes EV, Quitkin FM, Bradu R and Stewart JW (1991) Imipramine treatment of methadone maintenance patients with affective disorder and illicit drug use. *Am J Psychiatry*, **148**, 667–669.

Nunes EV, McGrath PJ, Quitkin FM and Stewart JP (1993) Imipramine treatment of alcoholism, with co-morbid depression. *Am J Psychiatry*, **150**, 963–965.

Patten SB and Lamarre CJ (1992) Can drug induced depressions be identified by their clinical features? *Can J Psychiatry*, **37**, 213–215.

Petty F (1992) The depressed alcoholic. Clinical features and medical management. *Gen Hosp Psychiatry*, **14**, 258–264.

Petty F and Nasrallah HA (1981) Secondary depression in alcoholism: implications for future research. *Compr Psychiatry*, **22**, 587–595.

Reigier DA, Farmer ME and Rae DS (1990) Comorbidity of mental disorders with alcohol and other drug abuse: Results from the Epidemiologic Catchment Area (ECA) study. *JAMA*, **264**, 2511–2518.

Roggale H and Uhl A (1995) Depression and relapse in treated chronic alcoholics. *Int J Addict*, **30**, 337–349.

Rossow I and Amundsen A (1995) Alcohol abuse and suicide: A 40-year prospective study of Norwegian conscripts. *Addiction*, **90**, 685–691.

Rossow I (1994) Suicide in drug addicts in Norway. *Addiction*, **89**, 1667–1673.

Rounsaville BJ, Weissman MM, Cris-Christopher K *et al.* (1982) Diagnosis and symptoms of depression in opiate addicts. *Arch Gen Psychiatry*, **39**, 151–156.

Rounsaville BJ, Kosten TR and Kleber HD (1986) Long-term changes in current psychiatric diagnosis of treated opiate addicts. *Compr Psychiatry*, **27(5)**, 480–498.

Rounsaville BJ, Rosenberger P, Wilber CH *et al.* (1980) A comparison of the SADS/RDC and DSM III: Diagnosing drug abusers. *J Nerv Ment Dis*, **168**, 90–97.

Rounsaville B, Foley Anton S, Carroll K, *et al.* (1991a) Psychiatric diagnosis of treatment seeking cocaine abusers. *Arch Gen Psychiatry*, **48**, 43–51.

Rounsaville BJ, Kosten TR, Weissman MM *et al.* (1991b) Psychiatric disorders in relatives of probands with opiate addictions. *Arch Gen Psychiatry*, **48**, 33–42.

Schifano F and Magni G (1994) MDMA ('Ecstasy') abuse: Psychopathological features and craving for chocolate: A case series. *Biol Psychiatry*, **46**, 763–767.

Schuckit MA (1985) The clinical implications of primary diagnostic groups among alcoholics. *Arch Gen Psychiatry*, **42**, 1043–1049.

Schuckit MA (1986) Genetic and clinical implications of alcoholism and affective disorder. *Am J Psychiatry*, **143**, 140–147.

Schuckit MA (1991) A 10-year follow-up of sons of alcoholics. *Alcohol*, **51**, 147–149.

Schuckit MA (1994) Alcohol and depression: A clinical perspective. *Acta Psychiatr Scand*, **Suppl 377**, 28–32.

Schuckit MA, Irwin M and Smith TL (1994) One-year incidence rate of major depression and other psychiatric disorders in 239 alcoholic men. *Addiction*, **89**, 441–445.

Silvers EP (1993) A psychotherapeutic approach to substance misuse. *Am J Drug Alc Abuse*, **19**, 51–54.

Snaith RP (1987) The concepts of mild depression. *Br J Psychiatry*, **150**, 387–393.

Stamford JA, Kruk ZL and Millar J (1988) Effects of uptake inhibitors on stimulated dopamine release and uptake in the nucleus accumbens studied by fast cyclic voltammetry. *Br J Pharmacol*, **94**, 348.

Strain E, Stitzer M and Bigelow GE (1992) Early treatment time course of depressive symptoms in opiate addicts. *J Nerv Mental Dis*, **179(4)**, 215–221.

Strang J, Johns A and Caan W (1993) Cocaine in the UK—1991. *Br J Psychiatry*, **162**, 1–13.

Swift W, Williams G, Neill O and Grenyer B (1990) The prevalence of minor psychopathology in opioid users seeking treatment. *Br J Addict*, **85**, 629–634.

Tabakoff B and Hoffman PL (1993) The neurochemistry of alcohol. *Curr Opin Psychiatry*, **6**, 388–394.

Tollefson GD (1991) Anxiety and alcoholism: a serotonin link. *Br J Psychiatry*, **159 (suppl. 12)**, 34–39.

Tyndel M (1974) Psychiatric study of one thousand alcoholic patients. *Can Psychiatr Assoc*, **19**, 21–24.

Van der Spruy HIJ (1972) The influence of alcohol on the mood of the alcoholic. *Br J Addict*, **67**, 255–265.

Weiss RD, Griffin ML and Mirin SM (1992a) Drug abuse as self medication for depression, an empirical study. *Am J Drug Alcohol Abuse*, **18**, 121–129.

Weiss RS, Mirin S and Griffin M (1992b) Methodological considerations in the diagnosis of coexisting psychiatric disorders in substance abusers. *Br J Addict*, **87**, 179–187.

Weissman MM and Myers JK (1980) Clinical depression in alcoholism. *Am J Psychiatry*, **137**, 372–373.

Williamson DJ and Young AH (1992) Psychiatric effects of androgenic and anabolic androgenic steroid abuse in men: A brief review of the literature. *J Psychopharmacol*, **6(1)**, 20–26.

Winokur G, Rimmer J and Reich T (1971) Alcoholism. Is there more than one type of alcoholism? *Br J Psychiatry*, **118**, 525–531.

Woodruff RA, Guze SB, Clayton PJ and Carr D (1973) Alcoholism and depression. *Arch Gen Psychiatry*, **28**, 97–100.

World Health Organisation (1992) *The Tenth Revision of the International Classification of Diseases and Related Health Problems*. Geneva: WHO.

Woody GE, Luborsky L, McLellan AT *et al.* (1983) Psychotherapy for opiate addicts: Does it help? *Arch Gen Psychiatry*, **40**, 639–645.

Wyatt RJ, Fawcett R and Karoum F (1987) A persistent decrease in frontal cortex dopamine from cocaine. Presentation at the 26th Annual Meeting of the American College of Neuropsychopharmacology (Abstracts), San Juan, Puerto Rico, 7–11 December 1987.

Yates WR, Petty F and Brown K (1988) Factors associated with depression in primary alcoholics. *Compr Psychiatry*, **29**, 28–33.

22

Depression and cancer

Peter Maguire

INTRODUCTION

The diagnosis of cancer carries with it the threat of loss of life. The treatments used often cause loss of important bodily parts or functions, and loss of role. So, it is not surprising that depression is common. The factors leading to depression will be discussed, and problems in ensuring adequate recognition and treatment highlighted before ways of managing it are described.

PREVALENCE OF AFFECTIVE DISORDERS

Derogatis *et al.* (1983) used standardized psychiatric interviews and a self-rating symptom checklist, the SCL-90, to determine the psychiatric morbidity in 215 cancer patients. They included patients who had been admitted to an outpatient clinic or ward in three major cancer hospitals. Of the patients 44% were judged to be suffering from a psychiatric illness, and affective disorders predominated (85%).

Since this information has been available for over a decade, ways should have been found of reducing the prevalence of these affective disorders in cancer patients. However, recent studies have confirmed that it remains high in cancer patients and their partners. For example, a longitudinal study of 673 patients found that depressive disorders occurred in up to one-fifth of newly diagnosed

Depression and Physical Illness. Edited by M.M. Robertson and C.L.E. Katona
© 1997 John Wiley & Sons Ltd

patients within the first year after diagnosis (Parle *et al.*, 1996a). This chapter considers why there has been no change in the prevalence of these disorders and discusses how they might be reduced or prevented.

AETIOLOGY

Prevention ought to be possible if strong and easily identifiable predictive factors could be found. Failure to deal with key hurdles associated with a cancer diagnosis renders patients more vulnerable to affective disorders.

Hurdles associated with diagnosis

Uncertainty about the future

The diagnosis of cancer is associated with uncertainty about whether or not the disease will recur and cause premature death. Regular hospital follow up can exacerbate patients' uncertainties, particularly if different doctors give inconsistent information. The frequent mention of cancer in magazine articles and television programmes can further intensify patients' fears. Worries are likely to be especially strong if patients have had adverse experience of cancer in close friends and relatives, particularly if a friend or relative was reassured that they would survive but later died. Patients may, therefore, continue to be plagued by worry about their future.

Search for meaning

Patients find it easier to cope with a life-threatening illness if they can find an adequate explanation for why they have developed the illness. Common questions include "Why me?" "Why now?", "What have I done to bring this on myself?" The problem with having cancer is that few risk factors have been identified. Patients and relatives, therefore, tend to project lay theories into the resulting vacuum. Popular theories include the notion that their cancer is caused by a flaw in their personality or inability to cope, especially an inability to express feelings of anger. Alternatively, they may blame others for their predicament.

Loss of control

Patients also cope better if they believe they can contribute towards their recovery. For example, patients with coronary heart disease can try to lose weight, adopt a healthier diet, give up smoking and do more physical exercise. Given the absence of known risk factors there is little cancer patients can do to contribute to their survival. Those patients who feel helpless after their diagnosis are likely to become clinically depressed. Those cancer patients who seek to fight their illness by utilizing techniques such as diet, relaxation, visualization, yoga or meditation or who become involved in volunteer organizations and self-help groups usually cope much better unless their method of dealing with their illness becomes an overriding obsession.

Stigma

Some cancer patients feel that they are no longer "clean". They use words such as "dirty", or "contagious" to describe how they feel about themselves. Such feelings of stigma are common in patients with cancers, like those of the cervix, which have been linked to promiscuity. Patients who feel stigmatized are less likely to be open about their predicament with other people and will receive less practical and emotional support.

Openness about the diagnosis

Those patients who have been able to be open about their predicament to close friends, relatives and employers cope much better than those who keep it a secret. Secretiveness is associated with a poor psychological adaptation.

Sense of isolation

Some cancer patients become increasingly isolated because family and friends find it embarrassing to meet them and talk about their predicament. Moreover, regular contact may remind friends and relatives of their own mortality. It can be deeply distressing to see somebody you love deteriorate physically or mentally, especially if they are suffering from unpleasant symptoms such as pain, weight loss or vomiting.

Medical support

It should be expected that doctors and nurses will ensure that cancer patients are followed up regularly and given practical and emotional support. Unfortunately, this may not be the case. Some doctors and nurses find it very hard to communicate effectively with cancer patients (see later). They may, therefore, avoid seeing patients unless it is absolutely necessary. This leads to patients perceiving that the emotional and practical support is inadequate.

Overall, it has been found that if any patient experiences major problems with one or more of these hurdles they are at high risk of developing major depression.

It is, therefore, important to explore how cancer patients are coping with these hurdles. This can be done by asking, "How do you see your illness working out?" (uncertainty), "Have you come up with any explanation as to why you have become ill this time?" (search for meaning), "Have you found anything you can do to contribute to your recovery?" (contributing to survival), "Has being ill changed how you feel about yourself as a person?" (stigma), "Have you been able to be open with people about your illness and treatment?" (openness), "Have you been seeing as many people as you did before your illness? (isolation), and "How much support to do you feel you have been getting from the doctors and nurses?" (perception of medical and nursing support).

Contribution of surgery

Those who develop persisting body image problems associated with avoidance of looking at the affected part following surgery which has removed an important body part (for example, mastectomy) are also at high risk of mood disturbance (Maguire *et al.*, 1983). Three types of body image problem may develop singly or in combination. First, the patient cannot accept that she is no longer physically whole. This loss of physical integrity causes her to feel vulnerable psychologically. She finds it harder to adapt to other stressful life events even when these are unrelated to cancer. Second, patients may experience a heightened self-consciousness. They worry that people have only to look at them to realize they have lost a breast even when they have tried to conceal their shape by wearing baggy clothes. Third, some women feel less attractive and feminine. They are not reassured by their partners' claims that they love them as much as they did before surgery. The visible evidence provided by the absence of the body part can also trigger worries about disease recurrence. The loss of key bodily functions is also linked with increased body image problems and depression. Up to 32% of patients who have a stoma formed after a cancer of the large bowel is removed become clinically depressed (Williams and Johnston, 1983; Thomas *et al.*, 1987). They cannot accept the stoma (because it represents an obscene part of themselves) and/or the bag. They fear the bag will bulge, leak, smell, burst or make a noise. They also worry that it could have profound effects on their personal relationships and employment. Should they mention their stoma to a potential partner and if so at what point can they risk doing so? Loss of bodily functions such as the loss of voice after laryngectomy cause similar problems in adaptation and depression.

Impact of other cancer treatments

Radiotherapy is usually explained to patients on the basis that it destroys any residual cancer cells. This information can have a paradoxical effect when patients were told they had a good prognosis. Fallowfield *et al.* (1986) found that as many patients undergoing breast conservation followed by radiotherapy developed a depressive disorder as those who had a mastectomy alone. They were worried that some cancer had been left behind. Women with cancer of the cervix who receive radiotherapy from a radiation source placed in the vagina can suffer anatomical damage including stenosis, fibrosis and fistulae. This can lead to serious sexual problems. Being diagnosed with cervical cancer also heightens feelings of stigma. The development of sexual problems and feeling stigmatized have been strongly linked with the later development of depression (Bos-Branolte, 1988). A strong relationship has also been found between adverse effects of radiotherapy and later depression (Devlen *et al.*, 1987).

The adverse effects of chemotherapy have also been linked to later depression (Devlen *et al.*, 1987; Hughson *et al.*, 1986). Conditioned nausea and vomiting is an especially potent factor (Hughson *et al.*, 1986). Characteristically, patients experience nausea and vomiting during the first two courses of treatment. They then find that any sound, sight or smell which reminds them of treatment provokes the same adverse effects. This can lead to phobic avoidance of treatment.

In other patients on chemotherapy, the development of acute depression may be better understood as due to a direct and rapid effect on the brain. Some patients become acutely depressed within a few hours of a chemotherapy infusion and may develop a depressive stupor.

Chemotherapy can affect sexual functioning adversely through impairing hormone production. Oestrogen production may be suppressed and the levels of follicular stimulating and luteinizing hormones elevated. This leads to infertility and a premature menopause in premenopausal women. In men, there may be a relative or complete lack of the ability to produce sperm and infertility. Alkylating agents are most likely to produce these sexual problems. When sexual problems persist once patients are disease free and off treatment there is an increased risk of depression (Maguire, 1985).

Other drugs used to treat cancer, such as steroids, also contribute to the development of depression.

Disease status

The prevalence of depression is higher when patients are aware that they have a poor prognosis (Hughes, 1985). Metabolic factors such as hypercalcaemia should also be considered. The onset of depression may also herald a recurrence of cancer or metastatic spread.

Influence of the coping process

Recent research has found that how patients appraise their predicament at the time of diagnosis predicts the later development of depression. Patients who react by having a greater number of more severe concerns and who feel unable to resolve these are most likely to develop depression (Parle *et al.*, 1996a). The onset of depression has also been linked to patients perceiving that the information they have been given about their disease was inadequate to their needs (Fallowfield *et al.*, 1990). Thus, patients who are given too much or too little information are more at risk of depression than those who feel the information they were given was appropriate to their needs.

The development of depression has also been linked to being younger, being female, having concerns about the illness itself, treatment, feeling different, feeling upset, the future, finances, relationship with partner and sexuality (Harrison and Maguire, 1995).

Other factors which increase the risk of depression include a past psychiatric history, low self-esteem, high levels of emotional distress at the time of diagnosis and lack of perceived emotional support.

PROBLEMS IN RECOGNITION

Objective studies in the 1980s found that only a small proportion of patients who developed depressive disorders were recognized as needing help and referred appropriately (Maguire, 1992). Even on a medical oncology unit where a liaison psychiatry service was established the recognition rate was only 40% (Hardman *et al.*, 1989). So, research has been conducted to determine the reasons for this.

There are three main reasons. Doctors and nurses involved in cancer care fear asking the kinds of questions that would elicit patients' concerns and mood disturbance because they believe this will harm patients psychologically. They feel they lack the relevant interviewing and counselling skills and worry that they will not be able to deal with any problems that emerge. They also fear they will be unsupported if they work in this way (Parle *et al.*, 1996b). Three approaches have, therefore, been pursued in a bid to improve the recognition and treatment of those with depressive disorders.

The role of specialist nurses

Specialist cancer nurses were employed and trained in those skills found to promote patient disclosure of their concerns. They were also encouraged to relinquish strategies that inhibit patient disclosure. It was hypothesized that the provision of information, advice, and practical and emotional support by a specialist nurse would prevent psychiatric morbidity including depression. If depression still developed, the nurses would detect this and refer the patient for psychiatric help. In a randomized controlled trial it was found that this counselling and monitoring approach led to a six-fold improvement in the ability of specialist nurses (90%) to recognize patients who developed depression compared with nurses without this training in key interviewing skills (15%). Consequently, there was a difference in the psychiatric referral rate: 75% of patients who developed depression in the counselling and monitoring group were referred for psychiatric help compared with only 15% of the control group. Because psychiatric intervention was effective there was a three- to four-fold reduction in the incidence of depression in the counselled and monitored group compared with controls (Maguire *et al.*, 1980). However, it was found that some patients preferred not to be visited by a nurse, particularly those who were coping well. Visits by the specialist nurses reactivated latent worries in some patients and led to an increase in their anxiety. Regular follow up also fostered dependency. Patients looked more to the nurse for help rather than to their own family. The specialist nurses were faced with an accumulating load since they were expected to see every mastectomy patient in the counselling group every 2 months after discharge.

It was decided, therefore, to develop a more economic approach which put more responsibility on patients to seek help if they needed it. In the limited intervention approach patients were seen once by a specialist nurse who assessed them thoroughly. Patients were then informed that if there were no problems it would be up to them to contact the nurse at a future date if any problems developed. This approach was then compared to the original 2 monthly follow up and an intervention condition involving only ward and community nurses in assessing patients' problems before and after mastectomy.

In a randomized controlled trial (Wilkinson *et al.*, 1988) it was found that the limited intervention approach was as good as the full intervention. However, the ward and community approach was of limited value. Few nurses achieved the necessary level of competence in their assessments of patients' mood (Faulkner and Maguire, 1984).

Other disadvantages of the specialist nurses' role in psychological care became evident. All psychological care tended to be delegated to them by other members of the health care team. They also seemed eager to monopolize it. It would be much healthier if all those involved in cancer care could acquire the necessary assessment skills so that the chances of a patient who becomes depressed being recognized and treated appropriately are optimized. Both psychiatrists and clinical psychologists could contribute to this training (Burton and Watson, 1994).

TRAINING HEALTH PROFESSIONALS IN ASSESSMENT SKILLS

Residential multidisciplinary workshops were developed to help health professionals improve their communication and counselling skills (Maguire and

Faulkner, 1988). A study was then conducted to check if hypotheses about which interviewing behaviours facilitated an inhibited disclosure were correct.

The use of open directive questions, asking questions with a psychological focus, clarifying psychological aspects, the use of empathy and educated guesses and the summarizing of what the patient has said all promoted disclosure of key concerns and mood disturbance. Without such training the majority of health professionals in cancer care use as many if not more behaviours that inhibit patient disclosure of key concerns than behaviours which promote disclosure.

While this training was beneficial in participants helping patients disclose their concerns and feelings nurses reacted to this greater disclosure by blocking. They were still afraid of harming the patient (Maguire, 1985). Other factors causing blocking included a perceived lack of support from professional colleagues (Booth, 1993; Wilkinson, 1991) and fears about death and dying (Wilkinson, 1991).

Razavi *et al.* (1993) explored the impact of workshops in communication skills on cancer nurses. While they were able to change nurses' attitudes to death and dying in a more positive direction, their workshops had little impact on key skills. A key issue, therefore, is how much attention should be paid in training to the attitudes and fears of health professionals about the consequences of establishing the true nature of patients' predicaments compared with time spent on skills.

We restructured our workshops to focus more on attitudes and feelings while maintaining an emphasis on skills and the need to integrate physical and psychological enquiry when taking a history. Evaluation found that our workshops proved even more effective. They equipped health professionals with the skills and confidence necessary to elicit depression as well as patients' other concerns. However, we have not demonstrated yet that skills acquired in this way improve the ability of health care professionals other than specialist nurses to recognize and refer patients who are depressed within their day-to-day practice.

SCREENING FOR AFFECTIVE DISORDERS

An alternative to training health professionals in the necessary assessment skills is to rely on self-rating questionnaires to diagnose depression. Razavi (1990) found that the Hospital Anxiety and Depression Scale (HADS) performed well in a screening role in a research setting. Similarly, Ibbotson *et al.* (1994) found that the Rotterdam Symptom Checklist and HADS performed well but their thresholds for identifying probable cases of depression were affected by disease and treatment status. These had to be adjusted to achieve an optimal positive predictive value. Practically, the results meant that for every five patients who scored above threshold, only 2 would be found to be true cases of depression.

Further work was conducted to test the feasibility of using these scales in clinical practice. A total of 357 outpatients attending a cancer hospital were screened for probable caseness using the HADS and the Rotterdam Symptoms Checklist. Of 139 high scorers, 69 were randomized to specialist nurse intervention and 70 to routine care. Only 26 (23%) of those referred to the specialist nurses were seen by them: the nurses were too busy to catch up with some patients, while other patients refused to be seen. Practical problems included having to catch buses, or go for investigations or treatments at the time when a specialist nurse was available to assess them.

An alternative approach is to use these screening questionnaires to notify the treating clinician or ward nurses of those patients judged to be probable cases. This is only likely to be effective if doctors and nurses can be helped to improve their ability to assess when mood disorders are present. Currently, they tend to be poor at detecting which patients are highly distressed (Ford *et al.*, 1994).

PREVENTING AFFECTIVE DISORDERS

The provision of information about diagnosis and treatment, practical advice about how to cope with the illness and any treatment complications coupled with the opportunity to talk about problems and feelings has not been found to prevent the development of clinical depression (Wilkinson *et al.*, 1988).

Thus while Fawzi *et al.* (1993) achieved a reduction in depression and fatigue scores as measured by the Profile of Moods States when they placed patients in psychoeducational groups (health education, problem solving, stress management, and psychological support) a reduction in depression and fatigue scores did not seem of clinical importance. Similarly, cognitive–behavioural interventions (Greer *et al.*, 1992) and nondirective counselling (Burton and Parker, 1995) did not reduce the prevalence of probable cases of depression as measured on self-rating scales. So, it remains to be shown that psychological interventions reduce the development of affective disorders. Interventions are more likely to be effective if they focus on those at high risk.

FOCUSING ON THOSE AT HIGH RISK

Worden and Weisman (1984) carried out a pioneering study to screen out patients within 10 days of diagnosis who were at risk of high emotional distress. Patients were then randomized to a psychotherapeutic or cognitive–behavioural intervention. Patients offered help reported less fatigue and confusion, increased vigour and less frustration, anxiety and apathy. However, there were no changes in the number and nature of their concerns or in levels of depression.

Greer *et al.* (1992) studied the impact of six sessions of a cognitive–behavioural approach (adjuvant psychological therapy). While there was a significant reduction in probable cases of anxiety there was no impact on depression. So, ways still need to be found of intervening effectively with patients at risk of affective disorder in respect of the development of depression. Recent work by Parle *et al.* (1996a) suggests this might be achieved by identifying patients with four or more concerns and high scores on the HADS and then intervening to change patients' appraisal towards a more adaptive one. The effectiveness of their immediate debriefing approach is currently being compared to delayed intervention and routine care within a randomized controlled trial.

The prevalence of affective disorders including depression also ought to be reduced if it were possible to train doctors to determine and respond to patients' information needs, elicit their concerns and help resolve them.

MANAGEMENT OF DEPRESSION

The management of depression must begin with careful exploration of possible causal and maintaining factors. It is important to give the patient a chance to disclose any key concerns and the feelings associated with them. This will result in the patient feeling understood and make it much more likely that the patient will comply with the offered antidepressant medication.

Indications for antidepressant medication include: persistent low mood for 2–4 weeks where the mood disturbance has been significantly greater (both quantitatively and qualitatively) compared with periods when the patient has been experiencing normal mood variation; patients are unable to distract themselves out of this depressed mood; and patients who are complaining of at least four other symptoms including repeated or early morning waking, irritability, impairment of attention and concentration, restlessness or retardation, loss of energy, social withdrawal, negative ideation, suicidal ideation, diurnal variation of mood, loss of appetite or weight, and constipation.

The assessment needs to allow for the possibility that some of those symptoms (like loss of weight and loss of energy) may be due to the presence of disease. However, if in doubt, it is worth treating the depression since many of the symptoms attributed to disease may lessen because they were due to depression.

When prescribing antidepressant medication it is important to explain to the patient that they do not cause physical dependence. The patient should also be given an explanatory model. This should include the fact that depression is due to a change in brain chemistry caused by the stress of the cancer and/or its treatment. The drug will need to be taken for at least 4–6 months to prevent any relapse of depression, and the giving of antidepressant medication is only the first step in helping patients with their predicament. The antidepressant medication should be taken as prescribed and not just when the patient is feeling low. The patient should be warned of common side-effects and offered a life-line to the clinician if they experience any untoward side-effects. Finally, they should be informed that any improvement in their mood disturbance and associated symptoms may take 2–4 weeks.

Drugs such as dothiepin in a dose of 75–150 mg are usually helpful in patients who are both depressed and agitated. Those who are more retarded or suffering from panic disorder benefit from selective serotonin reuptake inhibitors such as fluoxetine or paroxetine.

When there are obvious maintaining factors such as inappropriately negative views of the cancer prognosis or body image problems it is often necessary to offer the patient cognitive behavioural therapy once their mood has begun to improve. Other patients may have interpersonal difficulties and a more psychodynamic approach may be more helpful.

Only a minority of cancer patients who suffer from depression become suicidal but some patients can be at high risk, particularly when they experience pain, have major body image problems (particularly with stomas) or wrongly believe that their cancer has spread to their brain or is causing other parts of their body to rot. Patients who suffer severe complications from treatment (like major neuropathies secondary to chemotherapy) are also at risk. So the risk of suicide needs to be established.

Over 80% (Chaturvedi *et al.*, 1994) of cancer patients treated in this way for depression recover completely. If they fail to do so they need to be reassessed, for it is likely that other causes and maintaining factors exist which have not been detected. Alternatively, it may mean that there has been some progression of disease or metabolic problems.

CONCLUSION

Depression remains an important clinical problem in cancer patients and their relatives. Effort should continue, therefore, to find ways of improving the recognition, treatment and prevention of these disorders.

REFERENCES

Booth K (1993) Helping patients with cancer. *PhD Thesis*, University of Manchester.
Bos-Branolte G, Rijshouwer YM, Zeielsstra EM and Duivenvoorden HJ (1988) Psychological morbidity in survivors of gynaecological cancers. *Int J Gynaecol Oncol*, **9**, 61–76.

Burton MV and Parker RW (1995) A randomised controlled trial of preoperative psychological preparation for mastectomy. *Psycho-Oncol,* **4,** 1–20.

Burton M and Watson M (1994) Clinical psychology services for patients with cancer and their families. *Clin Psychol Forum,* **21,** 26–29.

Chaturvedi SK, Maguire P and Hopwood P (1994) Antidepressant medications in cancer patients. *Psycho-Oncol,* **4,** 57–60.

Derogatis LR, Morrow GR, Fetting J, Penman D, Piasetsky S and Schmale AM (1983) The prevalence of psychiatric disorders among cancer patients. *JAMA,* **249(6),** 751–757.

Devlen J, Maguire P, Phillips P, Crowther D and Chambers H (1987) Psychological problems associated with diagnosis and treatment of lymphomas. I. Retrospective study. *Br Med J,* **295,** 953–954.

Fallowfield LJ, Baum M and Maguire GP (1986) Effects of breast conservation on psychological morbidity associated with diagnosis and treatment of early breast cancer. *Br Med J,* **293,** 1331–1334.

Fallowfield LJ, Hall A, Maguire GP and Baum M (1990) Psychological outcomes of different treatment policies in women with early breast cancer outside a clinical trial. *Br Med J,* **301,** 275–280.

Faulkner A and Maguire P (1984) Training ward nurses to monitor cancer patients. *Clin Oncol,* **9,** 319–324.

Fawzy IF, Fawzy NW, Hyun CS, Eloshoff R, Guthrie D, Fahey JL and Morton DL (1993) Effects of an early structured psychiatric intervention, coping and affective state on recurrence and survival 6 years later. *Arch Gen Psychiatry,* **50,** 681–689.

Ford S, Fallowfield L and Lewis S (1994) Can oncologists detect distress in their outpatients? *Br J Cancer,* **70,** 767–770.

Greer S, Moorey S, Baruch JD, Watson M, Robertson BM, Bason A, Rowden L, Law M and Bliss J (1992) Adjuvant psychological therapy for patients with cancer: A prospective randomised trial. *Br Med J,* **304,** 675–680.

Hardman A, Maguire P and Crowther D (1989) The recognition of psychiatric morbidity on a medical oncology ward. *J Psychosom Res,* **33,** 235–237.

Harrison J and Maguire P (1995) Influence of age on psychological adjustment to cancer. *Psycho-Oncol,* **4,** 33–38.

Hughes JE (1985) Depressive illness in lung cancer. I. Depression before diagnosis. II, Follow up of inoperable patients. *Eur J Cancer,* **11,** 15–20.

Hughson AVM, Cooper AF, McArdle CS and Smith DC (1986) Psychological impact of adjuvant chemotherapy in the first two years after mastectomy. *Br Med J,* (Clin. Res.), **293,** 1268–1271.

Ibbotson T, Maguire P, Selby P, Priestman T and Wallace L (1994) Screening for anxiety and depression in cancer patients. Effects of disease and treatment. *Eur J Cancer,* **30a,** 37–40.

Maguire GP, Tait A, Brooke M, Thomas C and Sellwood R (1980) Effects of counselling on the psychiatric morbidity associated with mastectomy. *Br Med J,* **281,** 1454–1456.

Maguire P, Brooke M, Tait A, Thomas C and Sellwood R (1983) Effect of counselling on physical disability and social recovery after mastectomy. *Clin Oncol,* **9,** 319–324.

Maguire P (1985) Barriers to psychological care of the dying. *Br Med J,* **291,** 1711–1713.

Maguire P (1992) Improving the recognition and treatment of affective disorders in cancer patients. In: K Granville-Grossman (ed) *Recent Advances in Clinical Psychology.* Edinburgh: Churchill Livingstone.

Maguire P and Faulkner A (1988) How to improve the counselling skills of doctors and nurses involved in cancer care. *Brit Med J,* **297,** 847–849.

Maguire P, Booth K, Elliott C and Hillier V (1996) Helping cancer patients disclose their concerns. *Eur J Cancer,* **32A,** 78–81.

Parle M, Jones B and Maguire P (1996a) Maladaptive coping and affective disorders among cancer patients. *Psychol Med*, **26**, 735–744.

Parle M, Maguire P and Heaven C (1996b) Improving communication with cancer patients. *Soc Sci Med*, (In press).

Razavi D, Delvaux N, Farvacques C and Robaye E (1990) Screening for adjustment disorder and major depressive disorders in cancer patients. *Br J Psychiatry*, **156**, 79–83.

Razavi D, Delvaux N, Marchal S, Bredart A, Farvacques C and Paesmans M (1993) Effects of a 24 hour psychological training programme on attitudes, communication skills and occupational stress in oncology: a randomised study. *Eur J Cancer*, **29A**, 1858–1863.

Thomas C, Medden F and Jehu D (1987) Psychological effects of stomas: II. Factors influencing outcome. *J Psychosom Res*, **31**, 317–323.

Wilkinson S (1991) Factors which influence how nurses communicate with cancer patients. *J Adv Nursing*, **16**, 677–688.

Wilkinson S, Maguire P and Tait A (1988) Life after breast cancer. *Nursing Times*, **54**, 34–37.

Williams NS and Johnson D (1983) The quality of life after rectal excision for low rectal cancer. *Br J Surgery*, **70**, 460–462.

Worden JW and Weisman AD (1984) Preventative psychological intervention with newly diagnosed cancer patients. *Gen Hosp Psychiatry*, **6 (4)**, 243–249.

23

Depression in palliative care

N. Swire and R.J.D. George

The neuropsychiatric symptoms and syndromes of mood disorders, such as depression, have an important place in any agenda that focuses on symptom control in the terminal patient. Depression produces considerable unnecessary suffering, increased physical distress (Craig, 1989), poorer physical and psychosocial functioning, poor judgement (Conwell *et al.*, 1990; Fogel and Mor, 1993), decreased ability to adhere to medical recommendations (Goldberg, 1983) and suicide (Holland, 1987). It therefore matters that we recognize and treat this condition. However, several factors combine to create a barrier to that recognition.

SADNESS OR CLINICAL DEPRESSION?

Firstly, are the symptoms of sadness, tearfulness and depression of mood indicative of an underlying major depression, due to the "syndrome" adjustment disorder with depressed mood, or part of normal grieving in the face of a life-threatening illness (Clayton, 1974; Cohen-Cole and Stoudemire, 1987)? Some state that because sadness and grief are expected emotional responses to serious illness it cannot be given a pathological label (Rosen *et al.*, 1987). Rather it should be considered part of the normal grieving process (Kraft, 1990). Moreover, if the symptoms worsen and the patient is even suicidal this can still be viewed as understandable and not appropriate for or amenable to

Depression and Physical Illness. Edited by M.M. Robertson and C.L.E. Katona
© 1997 John Wiley & Sons Ltd

treatment. However, most palliative physicians consider that a growing body of evidence challenges these assumptions, the symptoms and syndromes of depression cause unacceptable reduction in quality of life and they merit appropriate measures.

Whilst diagnosis is the first step towards treatment and prevention of life-threatening consequences, it is difficult in the physically ill, and especially so in the dying patient. Three areas of controversy affect the diagnosis of depression in the terminally ill: diagnostic criteria, symptom severity thresholds, and the problem of somatic symptoms.

DIAGNOSTIC CRITERIA

The standard diagnostic classification systems were not originally intended for use in medically ill populations. Although superficially similar, using different systems can produce very different prevalence rates of depression. For instance, (Kathol *et al.*, 1990) found that the diagnosis of depression in 152 cancer patients differed by as much as 13% depending on the diagnostic system used.

Stressful life events such as serious medical illness (Maguire *et al.*, 1978) produce the normal reactions of shock, denial, fear, anger, unhappiness and sorrow. Such psychological distress predictably increases at the time of medical diagnosis (Fawzy *et al.*, 1990) and at relapse or recurrence (Cella *et al.*, 1990), or with loss of function and with signs of progression of the disease (Bolund, 1985). These realities are unpleasant and often intensely distressing for the patient but the emotional response is not usually persistent or incapacitating (Massie and Holland, 1984) as an individual's psychological strategies allow personal effective adjustment. The diagnosis of depression should be entertained if the reactions seem to be prolonged and pervasive.

Depression may be subdivided into "major depressive disorder" and "adjustment disorder". A third alternative, in the medically ill population, is the diagnosis of organic affective disorder.

Major depressive disorder

The key factor to make a diagnosis of a major depressive episode is the pervasiveness of the symptoms. The DSM-IV criteria are summarized below.

For at least 2 weeks nearly every day, depression of mood or loss of interest or pleasure (Wing *et al.*, 1990), plus at least four of the following:

1. Weight loss or gain, e.g. more than 5% body weight in a month; decreased or increased appetite.
2. Insomnia, hypersomnia.
3. Psychomotor agitation or retardation.

4. Fatigue or loss of energy.
5. Feelings of worthlessness or guilt.
6. Decreased concentration, indecisiveness.
7. Recurrent thoughts of death, suicidal ideation.

In severe cases gross mental and physical slowness occurs. The differential diagnosis (Gulledge and Calabrese, 1988) is an anxiety-based stupor where thought is disrupted by concentration problems and the patient is literally "frozen with fear". In these cases the signs of hyperarousal should be apparent (Brittlebank and Regnaud, 1990). In some cases features of the two disorders may coexist (Fawcett and Kravity, 1983).

Adjustment disorder with depressed mood

Symptoms of an adjustment disorder often fluctuate in severity from day to day and patients can be distracted from their distress, albeit temporarily. Some will seem withdrawn (Maguire *et al.*, 1993), but practically, patients may not present with classic depressive symptoms. Instead the psychological coping stategies may be more apparent with, for instance, excessive and persistent anger or bitterness. They may be labelled as a "difficult patient" and be noncompliant or refuse treatment (Goldberg, 1983a).

Organic affective disorder

An alternative diagnosis to consider, especially if there is evidence of cognitive impairment, is organic affective disorder. In terminal illnesses organic brain syndromes with an associated depressive component are common (MacKenzie and Popkin, 1987; Yarnell and Battin, 1988) and often have multiple causes (Levine *et al.*, 1978). Although the aetiology of these organic states is notoriously difficult to unravel, the cause irreversible or not remedial to medical intervention, some are easily treated by correcting the underlying cause.

Drugs (Med Lett Drugs Therapeutics, 1993; McCabe, 1991) and metabolic disturbances (Goldberg, 1983b) are the most common precipitants of organic brain syndromes followed by neurological, endocrine and nutritional disorders, and distressing symptoms (Dworkin and Gitlin, 1991). Psychiatric manifestations vary. For example, cancer-related hypercalcaemia, although more commonly causing confusion, can induce severe depression (Weizman *et al.*, 1979). Likewise corticosteroids, which are used widely in palliative care, can cause almost any mood state to occur including anxiety, paranoia and mania, in addition to depressions (Murphy, 1991).

Patients with any advanced disease, especially when complicated by renal and hepatic failure, are at particular risk of psychopathology. Altered pharmacokinetics of a suspect drug may simply need dose reduction or occasionally a change in the timing of doses to improve mental state. When it is not possible to stop treatment, as may be the case with chemotherapy, antidepressant medication should be used. Chemotherapeutic agents at highest risk of associated depression include vincristine and vinblastine, used in the treatment of leukaemias, L-asparaginase used in the treatment of lymphomas, and procarbazine when used in high doses (Peterson and Popkin, 1980).

Psychiatric disturbance may be the presenting feature of a variety of medical illnesses, including pancreatic cancer (where it may preclude diagnosis) (Holland *et al.*, 1986; Shakin and Holland, 1988), hypothyroidism, adrenal insufficiency, and primary or metastatic brain tumours. Frontal lobe tumours in particular may present as apathy, social withdrawal and depression and otherwise be clinically silent. Lastly, psychological morbidity and depression (Massie and Holland, 1987) is often a confounding factor complicating severe and intractable pain (Hopwood *et al.*, 1991), or other untreated symptoms, from whatever cause. An aggressive approach is essential, as adequate analgesia and good symptom control can quickly resolve depressive symptoms.

SYMPTOM-SEVERITY THRESHOLDS

The second issue that may influence the diagnosis of depression is the severity with which symptoms must be expressed before they are considered clinically significant. Whether evaluated in a clinical interview or indicated by patients on self-report questionnaires, measurement of the level of severity of depressive symptoms does not directly reflect the rates of diagnosis of a specific clinical syndrome, although they may be highly correlated. Certainly, small differences between investigators in the application of symptom-severity thresholds can result in large differences in the prevalence rates for depression (Zimmerman *et al.*, 1990). For instance, Chochinov *et al.* (1994) found that a variation of 1-point per item of the Schedule for Affective Disorders and Schizophrenia (Endicott and Spitzer, 1978) (a structured diagnostic interview used as a research assessment method for depression in the medically ill patient (Spitzer *et al.*, 1978)) resulted in a doubling of the prevalence figure produced.

THE PROBLEM OF SOMATIC SYMPTOMS

The third issue is the lack of specificity of the physical symptoms used in the criteria. Since the symptoms of poor concentration, anorexia, weight loss, low energy and fatigue are common in all terminally ill patients, how best should they be interpreted in the light of a potential diagnosis of depression? Four possible approaches to this problem have been described (Breitbart *et al.*, 1995).

The first solution is to avoid inclusion of all items which, although symptoms of depression, are also likely to occur in a population of very ill patients. For instance, Buckberg *et al.* (1984) eliminated anorexia and fatigue from the diagnostic criteria in diagnosing depression in these patients. Similarly, on comparing the diagnosis of depression in the medically ill and in psychiatric populations, Cavanaugh (1984) suggests that major depression in a patient with cancer is most accurately diagnosed from cognitive or mood symptoms. He emphasizes the loss of self-esteem and the sense of worthlessness and of feeling a burden to others. He makes the point that these patients tend to feel "bad about themselves" as compared with patients who are suffering from adjustment disorders who feel "bad about their situation".

This is also the approach of all self-report screening instruments; the Hospital Anxiety and Depression Scale (HADS) (Zigmond and Snaith, 1983) which concentrates on psychological measures, and the Beck Depression Inventory (BDI) (Beck and Beck, 1972; Beck *et al.*, 1961), the Carroll Rating System (CRS) (Golden *et al.*, 1991) and the General Health Questionnaire-30 (GHQ) which have a strong emphasis on cognitive affective symptoms. The concern over these rating scales is that the deletion of all somatic items risks under-diagnosis. In practice, the rate of diagnosis is more affected by the cut-off score rather than the tool itself. To avoid false-negative results, most instruments are used with relatively low symptom-severity thresholds so that, instead of under-diagnosis, over-diagnosis becomes a problem. Because of their low specificity, these scales should be complemented with a psychiatric interview.

A second approach is to ignore the dilemma and include all symptoms whether or not they may be secondary to the illness or its treatment rather than due to neuropsychiatric disturbance (Cassem, 1990; Rifkin *et al.*, 1985); in other words, to follow the set criteria to the letter ignoring their possible aetiology. This approach is likely to lead to a high false-positive rate (Noyes and Kathol, 1986) and the DSM-IV includes a directive not to include symptoms which are clearly due to a physical disorder.

There are two compromise solutions. The first approach is to substitute physical symptoms of uncertain aetiology with psychological one (Hughes, 1985). This approach is best exemplified by the Endicott Substitution Criteria (Endicott, 1984) (see Table 1). However several investigators have found that there is no particular advantage to this approach (Rapp and Vrana, 1989). Chochinov *et al.* (1994) in studying the results produced by the different systems found that identical prevalence rates of 9.2% for major depression and 3.8% for minor depression (total 13%) were found utilizing Research Diagnostic Criteria (RDC) high-threshold criteria and high-threshold Endicott criteria. In other words the symptom-severity thresholds had greater impact on the final rate rather than the approach to somatic symptoms.

The final approach is to consider the likely aetiology of any somatic symptoms and if probably due to the disease process to exclude them, but to

Table 1. Endicott substitution criteria.

Physical/somatic symptom	Psychological symptom substitute
Change in appetite, weight	Tearfulness, depressed appearance
Sleep disturbance	Social withdrawal, decreased talkativeness
Fatigue, loss of energy	Brooding, self-pity, pessimism
Diminished ability to think or concentrate, indecisiveness	Lack of reactivity

include them if a depressive disorder is the likely cause. Consequently, if the physical symptoms seem temporally related to the psychic or out of proportion to the physical illness they may be helpful diagnostically. The Diagnostic Interview Schedule (DIS) (Rodin *et al.*, 1981) for use with DSM-IV includes a decision-tree to assist in determining which symptoms are a result of physical illness and suggests that these not be included as diagnostic criteria. This may produce the best balance between potential under-diagnosis resulting from the elimination of all somatic criteria and potential over-diagnosis when all are included (Rodin *et al.*, 1991).

This approach relies on intimate knowledge of the patient and his disease by the doctor and becomes more problematic as the disease progresses, as near death all physical criteria have a high probability of disease aetiology. In these circumstances, an alternative diagnosis is organic affective disorder. However, the general consensus to this distinction is that it appears entirely arbitrary as to which factors are seen as contributory and those that are causally related. Fogel (1990) argues that the diagnosis of organic affective disorder is discarded and that instead the diagnosis of a major depressive episode should be based on the standard criteria with any contributory biological factors being mentioned separately.

VALIDATED DIAGNOSTIC SYSTEMS

In summary, to accomplish the very challenging task of assessing depression in patients with a terminal illness, it is essential to use a validated diagnostic system such as DSM-IV. The various systems produce divergent rates of prevalence but using the higher thresholds appears to reduce these differences. Similarly, including potentially confounding symptoms related to physical illness does not seem to change the overall prevalence rate as much as the stringency of the applied criteria themselves. Several types of study tools based on these standardized criteria have been validated for the medically ill population, although there is no currently recognized method for assessing depression that is validated and standardized and designed to accommodate terminally ill patients (Cody, 1990).

CLINICAL ASSESSMENT

Clinically, the self-reporting tools are gaining more favour (Razavi *et al.*, 1992). Firstly, they are brief and easily completed by even a severely ill patient. Secondly, although they tend to concentrate on psychological symptoms such as the severity of dysphoric mood, the degree of hopelessness, guilt or worthlessness, and the presence of suicidal thoughts, the contents are generally acceptable to the patient, as well as a possible prompt for further discussion, although, because of the sensitivity of such issues as suicidal ideation in terminal patients, some palliative care physicians feel they may be better used within the safety of an interview. Thirdly, they have a high sensitivity (in other words one can say with a high degree of confidence that patients with a negative test do not have depression).

One disadvantage is their low specificity with relatively high false-positive rates. Thus any patient identified by one of the screens as having depression ideally requires further evaluation and follow up with a clinical interview using the standardized diagnostic criteria. Despite this problem these self-reporting instruments are easy for both patient and doctor to use. They are helpful screening tools and can also be used as an ongoing method of assessing response to treatment (Lloyd-Williams, 1993).

On interviewing a patient with mood disturbance, apart from standard assessment, the practitioner needs to explore the patient's understanding of his disease and its implications and the impact of the illness on the patient and the people around him. It is invaluable to know of the support systems available to the patient and whether use is being made of them. Current psychosocial stresses, which may not be specifically related to the illness, also need to be taken into account. Past losses and how the patient coped with them, past psychosocial functioning and psychiatric history help complete the picture.

Finally, in the medically ill patient, cognitive assessment is essential to help rule out an organic confusional state (Folstein *et al.*, 1984). In this population one of the shortened screening instruments, such as the 10-question abbreviated mental test score (Jitapunkul *et al.*, 1991) or the mini mental state examination, are suitable tools, being short, clear, not requiring self-administration and well tolerated by patients and their families. Similarly, special consideration must be given to the physical state of the patient, especially the presence and severity of pain, the use of mood altering drugs and the likelihood of any cerebral pathology.

PREVALENCE

Considering the degree of controversy surrounding the question of diagnosis it will come as no surprise that the reported prevalence rates, in the studies done (almost every clinical series described consisted of patients with malignancies), range from as low as 3.7% to as high as 58% (Buckberg and Holland, 1980; Dean, 1987; Derogatis *et al.*, 1983; Evans *et al.*, 1986; Morton *et al.*, 1984; Plumb and Holland, 1981; Weddington *et al.*, 1986). This apparent lack of consistency is significant for clinical practice. Is depression a very common disorder that is under-recognized in the medically ill or have clinicians tended to be over-inclusive in their approach to diagnosis (Lansky *et al.*, 1985)?

The large variation in prevalence rates may relate to a number of factors including the type or stage of the illness and the subsequent level of physical impairment, demographic characteristics of the population, and variations in diagnostic systems as well as in the application of diagnostic criteria. Moreover, the highest frequencies are reported in studies that depend on clinician reports with an absence of defined criteria, with advanced stages of illness and thus more severe levels of impairment (Hinton, 1972); while the lowest rates reported have used defined criteria in patients with good physical functioning, including some patients who were ambulatory.

Recent research suggests that mood disturbance is significantly associated with severity of the disease (Coyle *et al.*, 1990) and physical disability (Cassileth *et al.*, 1985), symptom distress (McCorkle and Quint-Benoliel, 1983), poor social support and a previous psychiatric history. There is also a significant correlation between depression and cognitive impairment (Massie *et al.*, 1979; Power *et al.*, 1993). Adjustment disorders are common at 25–35% with a small, but significant, minority of patients becoming seriously depressed (approximately 5–15% of the total population of cancer patients). Among hospitalized cancer patients, with significant levels of physical impairment, at least 25% suffer from a clinically important depression (Lynch, 1995). This is similar to the rates of depression seen in patients with non-psychiatric general medical conditions at between 12% to 36%.

UNDER-DIAGNOSIS OF THE PROBLEM

However, just as in general medical settings depression in the terminally ill appears to be significantly under-diagnosed (Maguire, 1985a) and subsequently under-treated (Jaeger *et al.*, 1985; Steifel *et al.*, 1990). The data on antidepressant medication usage in hospices suggest that few patients are treated for depression and even fewer receive the appropriate medication (Curtis and Walsh, 1993) (Goldberg and Mor (1985) found 3% of hospice patients were prescribed antidepressant medication). Similarly, Derogatis *et al.* (1979) found that of 1579 patients with cancer, 51% were prescribed psychotropic drugs, but antidepressants only totalled 1%. Several factors may contribute to this under-recognition.

Firstly, the medical approach, which focuses primarily on physiological treatment and symptom management, may overlook or discount emotional or psychological needs (Derogatis *et al.*, 1976) and subsequently misinterpret the presenting symptoms. For instance a patient's lack of co-operation may be seen as evidence of laziness, manipulation, attention-seeking or noncompliance rather than a possible manifestation of mood disturbance.

Secondly, in ignoring psychiatric symptoms clinicians may unwittingly collude with patients in agreeing that psychosocial issues are not important enough to warrant mentioning (Saunders and Valente, 1988), or even that they are something to be faced by that individual alone and that there is little that can be done to relieve their distress (a common assumption held by depressed people). Subsequently patients may be reluctant to bother the team for fear of being stigmatized as a noncoper. They may be embarrassed to report depressive symptoms but may instead report somatic symptoms (Gerber *et al.*, 1992). Not surprisingly, fewer than one in four patients volunteer psychological problems spontaneously to the treatment team (Comaroff and Maguire, 1981).

Lastly, clinicians may hesitate to ask about the emotional impact of a physical illness. Maguire (1985a) found that oncology nurses and doctors were reluctant to talk in depth to patients with cancer due to the fear that discussions may lead to such subjects as death. The professionals identified lack of confidence about their ability to handle such difficult subjects and the emotional sequelae (Buckman, 1984), or that in opening up "the can of worms" their lack of psychosocial skills may cause more harm than good (Maguire, 1984).

It would seem that relying on clinical acumen alone does not pick up the majority of patients with depression (Pascretta and Massie, 1990). Hardman *et al.* (1989) found that physicians and nurses recognized only 49% of depressed patients on a medical oncology unit. He suggests that training in interview skills could substantially improve the identification and referral rates of patients with psychiatric morbidity. An alternative approach is to use some form of screening tool and then concentrate on in-depth interviews with those patients who register as possibly depressed (Razavi *et al.*, 1990). Finally, if the diagnosis of depression is still in doubt a psychiatric referral should be made.

TREATMENT OPTIONS

For reviews of treatment options see Hughes (1986) and Mermelstein and Lesko (1992). In those patients with a terminal diagnosis yet relatively good physical function, the diagnosis between adjustment disorder and depression can often be easily made. For those cases in which the clinician harbours doubt a trial of antidepressant or a trial of time (e.g. waiting to see if the mood changes or is constant over a set period of time such as 2 weeks) are both possible.

Most clinicians favour open discussion and a good listening ear for the management of adjustment reactions. However, clinical depression may not respond positively to this technique, or may even be worsened, so the distinction is important. In this group, especially those with serious suicidal ideation, psychiatric referral (Breitbart, 1987) and more active treatment including pharmacological approaches should be considered.

Treatment decisions are much more difficult when dealing with the terminal stages of an illness. Firstly, aetiology is likely to be multifactorial with the physical effects of illness and treatments, the psychological reaction to progressive disablement and the grief at the impending loss of life and loved ones, all contributing variously to the mood state. Secondly, there is often not enough time to just "wait and see" if the mood might improve on its own or to even wait for the benefits of conventional antidepressant medication.

Because of the diversity of possible contributory factors to the state of depression a wide spectrum of measures, including the physical, psychosocial and existential aspects of an individual, as well as therapeutics, needs to be considered in its management (Massie and Holland, 1990). These are complementary and only rarely will one intervention relieve the patient's depression.

PHYSICAL ASPECTS

Adequate symptom control is the cornerstone in the treatment of depression in the dying. Pain and other disagreeable symptoms are a major source of distress for terminally ill patients and must be relieved as a priority. The speed of resolution of depressive symptoms can be impressive simply with good palliative medicine. In addition, fear of possible distressing symptoms looms large in the minds of people facing death (Levin et al., 1985; Wanzer et al., 1989). Patients and families often obtain remarkable psychological benefit from simple reassurance of a physician's availability and commitment to addressing the patient's discomfort.

Similarly, organic causes should be treated where possible. For those cases which do not respond, or are not accessible to medical intervention, some relief may be produced with appropriate practical support as well as the use of psychotropic agents.

PSYCHOSOCIAL ASPECTS

For some patients the psychological demands of a life-threatening illness can be more daunting than the physical ones (Jones et al., 1989). Whether the diagnosis is seen as a threat or challenge (Lipowski, 1983) its psychological impact will tend to rise in proportion to the uncertainty, helplessness and loss of control that physical deterioration brings (Kurtz et al., 1994). All patients encounter a series of additional losses: social roles and daily activities that contribute to a sense of self-worth, well-being and meaning. Some personality types may find these psychological burdens overwhelming, particularly if complicated by other significant losses, current life stresses, or a lack of social support (Alloway and Bebbington, 1987). A previous history of major depression or other psychiatric disorders is important.

Usually social supports (Barrera and Ainlay, 1983) facilitate these normal bereavements and anxieties but terminal illness regularly stresses key interpersonal relationships—occasionally eliciting enhanced coping behaviours—but also producing dysfunctional patterns. The patient may find the family (biological or social) unable to meet his overt needs of physical and emotional care, let alone deeply felt longings and fears, because of their own psychological burdens and grieving processes (Givèn *et al.*, 1993). This in turn may compound the fear and guilt common among the terminally ill of being a burden and hinder the completion of tasks such as "goodbyes", "thank-yous" and "sorries" between the patient and significant others.

In adjustment disorders formal psychotherapy, both cognitive and behavioural is helpful in the less unwell population of terminally ill patients (Meyer and Mark, 1995; Weisman *et al.*, 1980). When this is not available or the patient is too debilitated, a palliative care team can provide important support through informal (Valente *et al.*, 1994) or formal counselling; showing interest and concern, facilitating the expression of fears and feelings and offering encouragement, and the assurance of continuity in practical and emotional care, to both the patient and significant others. When faced with a patient who has a major depressive disorder, however, it is important to delay formal techniques until antidepressant medication is being effective. The reason for this is that such patients are unable to think positively at that stage and their symptoms may be made worse rather than improved by counselling (Beck *et al.*, 1979).

EXISTENTIAL ASPECTS (Saunders, 1988)

The understanding of self, of life, suffering (Patterson, 1984) and death all impact on an individual's view of and emotional response to their illness and their life in general (Conrad, 1985). Spiritual issues around meaning can significantly impact on a patient's mood (Austin and Jennings, 1993). They are often unexpressed without permission and it is important at the very least to offer a sympathetic listening ear (Morrison, 1992), and more concrete pastoral help if necessary.

For some patients it will be sufficient simply to have shared their deepest fears with another human being. In other cases the sheer enormity of the problem articulated may only be matched by the clinician's ignorance. Spiritual advice acceptable to that individual is then called for. Counselling on spiritual issues requires a degree of skill but even an inexperienced professional can be a fellow "traveller" and offer sympathy and companionship (Speck, 1988). In most cases assurance to the patient that they are not the only ones to feel that way, that they are normal and experiencing something common to man, familiar to us all, and that in the uniqueness of their dying they are not unique in their suffering, may provide all the support that is needed (Doyle, 1992).

PHARMACOLOGICAL ASPECTS (Goldberg and Cullen, 1986)

Tricyclic antidepressants, coupled with supportive psychotherapy, have traditionally been the mainstay of treatment in the medically ill, monoamine oxidase inhibitors (MAOIs), lithium, and electroconvulsive therapy (ECT) being reserved for refractory cases and special circumstances. Excepting ECT, these traditional antidepressants, together with the newer selective serotonin reuptake inhibitors (SSRIs) (DeVane, 1992), take 2–3 weeks to exert their antidepressant effect. Although patients may benefit from the anxiolytic or sedative effect much earlier, they are only suitable for patients with a reasonable prognosis.

There are few controlled studies on antidepressant drug treatment for depressive disorders in patients with cancer, even fewer that focus on the terminally ill oncology patient and none that cover other fatal diagnostic categories. General principles therefore have to be followed (Potter *et al.*, 1991).

CONVENTIONAL THERAPIES

The traditional slow onset mood elevators have roughly equivalent clinical efficacy (Popkin *et al.*, 1985) and the choice of agent should be based on the clinical state of the patient and on whether or not the anticipated side-effects or additional actions, such as sedation or activation, are likely to be particularly troublesome or beneficial (Small, 1989). For instance the MAOIs, used in the treatment of atypical depressions, are generally considered unsuitable for depressed cancer patients because of dietary restrictions and dangerous interactions with the opiates. Similarly the tricyclic antidepressants need to be taken with care when patients have a history of cardiac disease, prostatism, glaucoma or intestinal obstruction.

Because of the high risk of noxious side-effects and multiple drug interactions in this population, initial dosages, especially of tricyclics, should be low and increased only cautiously, especially in the elderly and debilitated. Experience suggests that patients with medical illnesses seem to respond to lower doses than a healthy population, although this remains to be validated scientifically, and it is best to tailor the final dosage according to response and the severity of side-effects (Billings and Block, 1995). The newer SSRIs avoid most of these problems (Edwards, 1992). They have few side-effects, the most common problem being some initial nausea. As optimum doses can be used from the outset, one avoids the risk that therapeutic dosages are never reached (Shuster *et al.*, 1992).

RAPID ONSET MOOD ELEVATORS

For those patients who are severely ill and have a brief life expectancy or cannot wait up to 4 weeks for a response to an antidepressant, the more quick-acting therapies should be considered. Psychostimulants (for example methyl-phenidate, dextroamphetamine, premoline (Breitbart and Mermelstein, 1992) and mazindol) have been shown to be effective antidepressants in medically ill patients (Katon and Raskind, 1980; Kaufman and Murray, 1982; Masand *et al.*, 1991; Woods *et al.*, 1986) including the terminally ill with cancer (Burns and Eisendrath, 1994) and those with acquired immune deficiency syndrome (Fernandez *et al.*, 1988; Holmes *et al.*, 1989). Fernandez *et al.* (1987), using methylphenidate, showed a marked improvement in 33% (10/30) of his depressed cancer patients with moderate improvement experienced by a further 43% (13/30).

Few data exist on their long-term use (Steibel and Kemp, 1990) but a thera-peutic response to a psychostimulant can be seen in hours to days. As well as relieving depressive symptoms they may also counter physical symptoms, such as fatigue, occurring independently of the depression. Unexpectedly, although known to cause anorexia, in the medically ill patient they often increase appetite. Psychostimulants have no anticholinergic or cardiac conductive side-effects like the tricyclic antidepressants and interact with opiates favourably, unlike the MAOIs, with enhanced analgesic effect and reduced opioid-related sedation (Bruera *et al.*, 1987, 1989). Common troublesome side-effects are agitation, confusion, insomnia, paranoia and anxiety. Consequently they are contraindicated in the patient with delirium, although they may offer a quick way of discriminating between dementia and depression.

Flupenthixol dihydrochloride (Lloyd-Williams, 1994), although acting more slowly than the psychostimulants, should produce a response within a week at therapeutic dosages. Reported side-effects include insomnia and restlessness and rarely anticholinergic effects.

Phototherapy may be a useful option. As the mobility of patients in the terminal phase of illness is severely reduced they are often exposed to little direct sunlight which may exacerbate mood changes. Cohen *et al.* (1994) report the successful use of phototherapy in three terminally ill patients to alleviate the symptoms of depression. This treatment has few clinical side-effects and the onset of action is seen within 3–4 days of starting treatment. Finally, in the healthier patient ECT needs to be remembered. The indications for ECT are no different in this group of patients than for any other patient although the fitness of the individual for a general anaesthetic will need careful consideration (Valente, 1990).

OUTCOME AND THE RISK OF SUICIDE (Breitbart, 1989)

Major depression in the terminally ill can be successfully treated in the majority of cases where survival allows enough time for antidepressant medication to be effective (Katon and Sullivan, 1990; Ramsay, 1992). Subsequent improvement in mood and function can dramatically improve an individual's quality of life (Brugha, 1993) and reduce the stress on both informal and formal carers (Oberst *et al.*, 1989). With improvement in self-esteem and reduction in feelings of worthlessness, usefulness and hopelessness (Bursztain *et al.*, 1986) this in turn can lead to a reduction in the "desire for death" often expressed by terminally ill patients (Chochinov, 1992) and the real risk of suicide (Breitbart, 1987; Cote *et al.*, 1992; Storm *et al.*, 1992) or requests of assisted suicide.

Transient thoughts of death or suicide are not unusual in patients with life-threatening diagnoses (Chochinov *et al.*, 1995) but a pervasive desire for death should not be regarded as normal in this population (Leibenluft and Goldberg, 1988). As with the general population the wish for death is significantly associated with the diagnosis of major depression (Brown *et al.*, 1986; Salzburg *et al.*, 1989). Depression is a factor in 50% of all suicides and depressed patients have a 25-fold risk of suicide (Bulik *et al.*, 1990). As the prevalence of depression increases with advancing illness so does the risk of suicide. A survey among cancer patients by Farberow *et al.* (1963) showed that 86% of suicides occurred in the terminal phase.

EUTHANASIA

The confounding factor of depression impacts directly on the issue of euthanasia. The concern is that the desire for death may be indicative of this potentially treatable psychiatric disorder (Cain and Conwell, 1993). Similar worries have been expressed over the role of uncontrolled symptoms (Helig, 1988), especially pain (Foley, 1991; Van der Maas *et al.*, 1991), and the various social factors that may undermine the capacity to cope (Chernyl *et al.*, 1994). Many of these known precipitants for depression and "wish for death" are found in terminally ill patients. All are remedial to good palliative care (Hendin and Klerman, 1993) and psychosocial support (American Medical Association Council on Ethical and Judicial Affairs, 1992; Richman, 1992). It therefore seems reasonable not to take the request for assisted suicide at face value in a terminal patient (Baile *et al.*, 1993; Block and Billings, 1994).

SUMMARY

In conclusion, depression is not an inevitable accompaniment of terminal illness. Its diagnosis is complicated by the issues surrounding diagnostic criteria, symptom severity thresholds and the controversy of somatic symptoms. In the clinical setting the screening instruments can aid the detection of significant mood changes. Adjustment disorders are common but only a minority of patients will suffer from a major depressive disorder.

Mood disturbance is significantly associated with the presence of pain, physical and cognitive impairment, social isolation and previous psychiatric illness. These and other precipitants need to be tackled appropriately. In addition to psychological support the relief of major depression requires medication at therapeutic levels. As well as traditional remedies, rapid onset antidepressant therapies are available. Finally, the appropriate treatment of depression does not change a patient's circumstances but can make them more bearable and may temper the wish for early death.

REFERENCE

Alloway R and Bebbington P (1987) The buffer theory of social support—a review of the literature. *Psychol Med*, **17**, 91–108.

American Medical Association Council of Ethical and Judicial Affairs (1992) Decisions near the end of life. *JAMA*, **267**, 2229–2233.

Austin D and Jennings CJ (1993) Grief and religious belief: Does belief moderate depression? *Death Studies*, **17**, 487–496.

Baile WF, DiMaggio JR Schapira DV and Janofsky JS (1993) The request for assistance in dying: the need for psychiatric consultation. *Cancer* **72(9)**, 2786–2791.

Barrera M Jr and Ainlay SL (1983) The structure of social support: A conceptual and empirical analysis. *J Community Psychol*, **9**, 435–447.

Beck AT and Beck RW (1972) Screening depressed patients in family practice: A rapid technique. *Postgrad Med*, **52**, 81–85.

Beck AT, Rush AJ, Shaw BF and Emery G (1979) *Cognitive Therapy of Depression*. New York: Guilford Press.

Beck AT, Ward CH, Mendelson M, Mock JE and Erbaugh J (1961) An inventory measuring depression. *Arch Gen Psychiatry*, **4**,,461–571.

Billings JA and Block S (1995) Palliative medicine update: Depression. *J Palliat Care*, **11** **(1)**, 48–54.

Block SD and Billings JA (1994) Patient requests to hasten death: Evaluation and management in terminal care. *Arch Intern Med*, **154**, 2039–2047.

Bolund C (1985) Suicide and cancer, II. Medical and care factors in suicides by cancer patients in Sweden, 1973–76. *J Psychosoc Oncol*, **3(1)**, 31–52.

Breitbart W (1987) suicide in cancer patients. *Oncology*, **1(2)**, 49–55.

Breitbart W (1989) Suicide. In: JC Holland and JH Rowland (eds) *Handbook of Psycho-oncology: Psychological Care of the Patient with Cancer*. New York: Oxford University Press.

Breitbart W and Mermelstein H (1992) Pemoline. An alternative psychostimulant for the management of depressive disorders in cancer patients. *Psychosomatics*, **33(3)**, 352–356.

Breitbart, W, Bruera E, Chochinov H and Lynch M (1995) Neuropsychiatric syndromes and psychological symptoms in patients with advanced cancer. *J Pain Symptom Manag*, **10(2)**, 131–141.

Brittlebank A and Regnaud C (1990) Terror or depression? A case report. *Palliat Med*, **4**, 317–319.

Brown JH, Henteleff P, Barakat S and Rowe CJ (1986) Is it normal for terminally ill patients to desire death? *Am J Psychiatry*, **143(2)**, 208–211.

Bruera E, Chadwick S, Brennies C, Hanson J and MacDonald RN (1987) Methylphenidate associated with narcotics for the treatment of cancer pain. *Cancer Treat Rep*, **71**, 67–70.

Bruera E, Brennies C, Paterson AH and MacDonald RN (1989) Use of methylphenidate as an adjuvant to narcotic analgesics in patients with advanced cancer. *J Pain Symptom Manag*, **4**, 3–6.

Brugha TS (1993) Depression in the terminally ill. *Br J Hosp Med*, **50 (4)**, 175–181.

Buckberg JB and Holland JC (1980) A prevalence study of depression in a cancer hospital population. *Proc Am Assoc Cancer Res*, **21**, 382.

Buckberg JB, Penman D and Holland JC (1984) Depression in hospitalised cancer patients. *Psychosom Med*, **46**, 199–212.

Buckman R (1984) Breaking bad news: why is it still so difficult? *Br Med J*, **i**, 1597–1599

Bulik CM, Carpenter LL, Kupfer DJ and Frank E (1990) Features associated with suicide attempts in recurrent major depression. *J Affect Disord*, **18**, 29–37.

Burns MM and Eisendrath SJ (1994) Dextroamphetamine treatment for depression in terminally ill patients. *Psychosomatics*, **35**, 80–83.

Bursztain H, Gutheil TG, Warren MJ and Brodsky A (1986) Depression, self-love, time and the "right" to suicide. *Gen Hosp Psychiatry*, **8**, 91–95.

Cain ED and Conwell YC (1993) Self-determined death, the physician, and medical priorities: Is there time to talk? *JAMA*, **270**, 875–876.

Cassem EH (1990) Depression and anxiety secondary to medical illness. *Psychiatr Clin North Am*, **13**, 597–612.

Cassileth BR, Lusk EJ, Strouse TB, Miller DS, Brown LL and Cross PA (1985) A psychological analysis of cancer patients and their next of kin. *Cancer*, **55**, 72–76.

Cavanaugh S (1984) Diagnosing depression in the hospitalised patient with chronic medical illness. *J Clin Psychiatry*, **45**, 13–16.

Cella DF, Mahon SM and Donovan MI (1990) Cancer recurrence as a traumatic event. *Behav Med*, **16(1)**, 15–22.

Chernyl NI, Coyle N and Foley KN (1994) The treatment of suffering when patients request elective death. *J Palliat Care*, **10**, 71–79.

Chochinov HM, Wilson KG, Enns M and Lander S (1994) The prevalence of depression in the terminally ill: Effects of diagnostic criteria and symptom threshold judgements. *Am J Psychiat*, **151**, 537–540.

Chochinov HM, Wilson KG, Enns M, Mowchun N, Lander S, Levitt M and Clinch JJ (1995) Desire for death in the terminally ill. *Am J Psychiatry*, **152**, 1185–1191.

Clayton P (1974) Mourning and depression: Their similarities and differences. *Can J Psychiatry*, **1**, 309–312.

Cody M (1990) Depression and the use of antidepressants in patients with cancer. *Palliat Med*, **4**, 271–278.

Cohen SR, Steiner W and Mount BM (1994) Phototherapy in the treatment of depression in the terminally ill. *J Pain Symptom Manag*, **9(8)**, 534–536.

Cohen-Cole SA and Stoudemire A (1987) Major depression and physical illness: Special considerations in diagnosis and biologic treatment. *Psychiatr Clin North Am*, **10(1)**, 1–17.

Comaroff J and Maguire P (1981) Ambiguity and the search for meaning, childhood leukaemia in the modern clinical context. *Soc Sci Med*, **1513**, 115–123.

Conrad NL (1985) Spiritual support for the dying. *Nurs Clin North Am*, **20(2)**, 415–426.

Conwell Y, Caine ED and Oslen K (1990) Suicide and cancer in late life. *Hosp Community Psychiatry*, **41(2)**, 1334–1338.

Cote TR, Biggar RJ and Dannenberg AL (1992) Risk of suicide among patients with AIDS. *JAMA*, **268**, 2066–2068.

Coyle N, Adelhardt J, Foley K and Portenoy R (1990) Character of terminal illness in advanced cancer patients: pain and other symptoms during the last 4 weeks of life. *J Pain Symptom Manag*, **5(2)**, 83–93.

Craig KD (1989) Emotional aspects of pain. In: D Wall and R Melzack (eds) *Textbook of Pain*. 2nd Edn. London: Churchill Livingstone, 220–230.

Curtis EB and Walsh TD (1993) Prescribing practices of a palliative care service. *J Pain Symptom Manag*, **8**, 312–316.

Dean C (1987) Psychiatric morbidity following mastectomy: Preoperative predictors and types of illness. *J Psychosom Res*, **31**, 385–392.

Derogatis LR, Abeloff MD and McBeth CD (1976) Cancer patients and their physicians in the perception of psychological symptoms. *Psychosomatics*, **17**, 197–201.

Derogatis LT, Feldstein M, Morrow G, Schmale A, Schmitt M, Gates C, Murawski B, Holland J, Penman D, Melisaratos N, Enelow AJ and Adler LM (1979) A survey of psychotropic drug prescriptions in an oncology population. *Cancer*, **44**, 1919–1929.

Derogatis LT, Morrow GR *et al.* (1983) The prevalence of psychiatric disorders among cancer patients. *JAMA*, **249**, 751–757.

DeVane CL (1992) Pharmacokinetics of the selective serotonin reuptake inhibitors. *J Clin Psychiatry*, **42 (2 suppl)**, 13–20.

Doyle D (1992) Have we looked beyond the physical and psychosocial? *J Pain Symptom Manag*, **7(5)**, 302–311.

Dworkin RH and Gitlin MJ (1991) Clinical aspects of depression in chronic pain patients. *Clin J Pain*, **7**, 79–94.

Edwards JG (1992) Selective serotonin reuptake inhibitors. A modest though welcome advance in the treatment of depression. *Br Med J*, **304**, 1644–1646.

Endicott J (1984) Measurement of depression in patients with cancer. *Cancer*, **53**, 2243–2249.

Endicott J and Spitzer RL (1978) A diagnostic interview: The Schedule for Affective Disorders and Schizophrenia. *Arch Gen Psychiatry*, **35**, 837–844.

Evans DL, McCartney CF *et al.* (1986) Depression in women treated for gynaecological cancer: Clinical and neuroendocrine assessment. *Am J Psychiatry*, **143**, 447–452.

Farberow NL, Schneidman ES and Leonard CV (1963) Suicide among general medical and surgical hospital patients with malignant neoplasms. *Med Bull*, **9**, US Veterans Administration, Washington DC.

Fawcett J and Kravity HM (1983) Anxiety syndromes and their relationship to depressive illness. *J Clin Psychiatry*, **44**, 8–11.

Fawzy FI, Cousins N, Fawzy NW, Kemeny ME, Elashoff R and Morton D (1990) A structured psychiatric intervention for cancer patients. *Arch Gen Psychiatry*, **47**, 720–735.

Fernandez F, Adams F, Holmes V *et al.* (1987) Methylphenidate for depressive disorders in cancer patients: An alternative to standard antidepressants. *Psychostimulants Psychosomatics*, **29**, 455–462.

Fernandez F, Adams F, Levy JK, Holmes VF, Neidhart M and Mansell PW (1988) Cognitive impairment due to AIDS-related complex and its response to psycho-stimulants. *Psychosomatics*, **29**, 38–46.

Fogel BS (1990) Major depression versus organic mood disorder: A questionable distinction. *J Clin Psychiatry*, **51**, 53–56.

Fogel BS and Mor V (1993) Depressed mood and care preferences in patients with AIDS. *Gen Hosp Psychiatry*, **15**, 203–207.

Foley KM (1991) The relationship of pain and symptom management to patients requests for physician-assisted suicide. *J Pain Symptom Manag*, **6**, 289–297.

Folstein MF, Fetting JH, Lobo A, Niaz U and Capozzoli K (1984) Cognitive assessment of cancer patients. *Cancer*, **53**, 2250–2255.

Gerber PD, Barrett JE, Barrett JA, Oxman TE, Manheimer E, Smith R and Whiting RD (1992) The relationship of presenting physical complaints to depressive symptoms in primary care patients. *J Gen Intern Med*, **7**, 170–173.

Given CW, Stommel M, Given B, Osuch J, Kurtz M and Kurtz JC (1993) The influence of cancer patients' symptoms, functional states on patient depression and family reaction and depression. *Health Psychol*, **12(4)**, 277–285.

Goldberg RJ (1983a) Systematic understanding of cancer patients who refuse treatment. *Psychother Psychosom*, **39**, 1507–1512.

Goldberg RJ (1983b) Psychiatric symptoms in cancer patients: Is the cause organic or psychologic? *Cancer*, **74**, 263–273.

Goldberg RJ and Cullen LO (1986) Use of psychotropics in cancer patients. *Psychosomatics*, **27**, 687–700.

Goldberg RJ and Mor V (1985) A survey of psychotropic use in terminal cancer patients. *Psychosomatics*, **26**, 745–751.

Golden RN, McCartney CF, *et al.* (1991) The detection of depression by self-report in women with gynecological cancer. *Int J Psychiatry Med*, **21**, 17–27.

Gulledge AD and Calabrese JR (1988) Diagnosis of anxiety and depression. *Med Clin North Am*, **72**, 753–763.

Hardman A, Maguire P and Crowther D (1989) The recognition of psychiatric morbidity on a medical oncology ward. *J Psychosom Res*, **33(2)**, 235–239.

Helig S (1988) The San Francisco medical society euthanasia survey: Results and analysis. *San Francisco Medicine*, **61(8)**, 24–34.

Hendin H and Klerman G (1993) Physician-assisted suicide: The dangers of legalization *Am J Psychiatry*, **150**, 143–145.

Hinton J (1972) Psychiatric consultation in fatal illness. *Proc R Soc Med*, **65**, 29–32.

Holland JC (1987) Managing depression in the patient with cancer. *Cancer*, **37(6)**, 366–371.

Holland JC, Hughes AH, Tross S, *et al.* (1986) Comparative psychological disturbance in patients with pancreatic and gastric cancer. *Am J Psychiatry*, **143**, 982–986.

Holmes VF, Fernandez F and Levy JK (1989) Psychostimulant response in AIDS-related complex patients. *J Clin Psychiatry*, **52(6)**, 263–267.

Hopwood P, Howell A and Maguire P (1991) Psychiatric morbidity in patients with advanced cancer of the breast: Prevalence measured by two self-rating questionnaires. *Br J Cancer*, **64**, 349–352.

Hughes J (1985) Depressive illness and lung cancer. Follow up of inoperable patients. *Eur J Surg Oncol*, **11**, 21–24.

Hughes J (1986) Depression in cancer patients. In: BA Stoll and AD Weisman (eds) *Coping with Cancer Stress*, Dordrecht: Martinus Nijhoff.

Jaeger H, Morrow GR and Brescia F (1985) A survey of psychotropic drug utilization by patients with advanced neoplastic disease. *Gen Hosp Psychiatry*, **7**, 353–360.

Jitapunkul S, Pillay L and Ebrahim S (1991) The abbreviated Mental Test: Its use and validity. *Age Ageing*, **20**, 332–336.

Jones K, Johnston M and Speck P (1989) Despair felt by the patient and the professional carer: A case study of the use of cognitive behavioural methods. *Palliat Med*, **3**, 39–46.

Kathol RG, Mutgi A, Williams J, Clamon G and Noyes R (1990) Diagnosis of major depression in cancer patients according to four sets of criteria. *Am J Psychiatry*, **147 (8)**, 1021–1024.

Katon W and Raskind M (1980) Treatment of depression in the medically ill elderly with methylphenidate. *Am J Psychiatry*, **137**, 963–965.

Katon W and Sullivan MD (1990) Depression and chronic medical illness. *J Clin Psychiatry*, **51 (Suppl)**, 3–11.

Kaufmann MW and Murray GB (1982) The use of d-amphetamine in medically ill depressed patients. *J Clin Psychiatry*, **43**, 463–464.

Kraft T (1990) Use of hypnotherapy in anxiety management in the terminally ill: A preliminary study. *Br J Exp Clin Hypn*, **7**, 27–33.

Kurtz ME, Given B, Kurtz JC and Given CW (1994) The interaction of age, symptoms and survival status on physical and mental health of patients with cancer and their families. *Cancer Suppl*, **74(7)**, 2071–2078.

Lansky SB, List MA, Hermann CA, Ets-Hokin EG, DasGupta TA, Wilbanks GD and Hendrickson FR (1985) Absense of major depressive disorder in female cancer patients. *J Clin Oncol*, **3**, 1553–1560.

Leibenluft E and Goldberg RL (1988) The suicidal, terminally ill patient with depression. *Psychosomatics*, **29**, 379–386.

Levin DN, Cleeland CS and Dar R (1985) Public attitudes toward cancer pain. *Cancer*, **86**, 2334–2339.

Levine P, Silverfarb PM and Lipowski ZJ (1978) Mental disorders in cancer patients—a study of 100 psychiatric referrals. *Cancer*, **42**, 1385–1391.

Lipowski ZJ (1983) Psychosocial reactions to physical illness. *Can Med Assoc J*, **128**, 1069–1072.

Lloyd-Williams M (1993) The use of the HAD scale in research. *Palliat Care Today*, **11 (111)**, 39.

Lloyd-Williams M (1994) Treatment of depression with flupenthixol in terminally ill patients. *Eur J Cancer Care*, **3**, 133–134.

Lynch ME (1995) The assessment and prevalence of affective disorders in advanced cancer. *J Palliat Care*, **11(1)**, 10–18.

Mackenzie TB and Popkin MK (1987) Suicide in the medical patient. *Int J Psychiatry Med*, **17**, 3–22.

MaGuire P (1984) The recognition and treatment of affective disorders in cancer patients. *Int Rev Appl Psychol*, **33**, 479–491.

Maguire P (1985a) Improving the detection of psychiatric problems in cancer patients. *Soc Sci Med*, **20**, 819–823.

Maguire P (1985b) Barriers to psychological care of the dying. *Br Med J*, **291**, 1711–1713.

Maguire P, Lee EG, Bevington DJ, Kuchemann CS, Crabtree RJ and Cornell CE (1978) Psychiatric problems in the first year after mastectomy. *Med Pract*, **1**, 963–965.

Maguire P, Faulkner A and Regnaud C (1993) Handling the withdrawn patient–a flow diagram. *Palliat Med*, **7**, 333–338.

Masand P, Pickett P and Murray GB (1991) Psychostimulants for secondary depression in medical illness. *Psychosomatics*, **32**, 203–208.

Massie MJ and Holland JC (1984) Diagnosis and treatment of depression in the cancer patient. *J Clin Psychiatry*, **45**, 25–28.

Massie MJ and Holland JC (1987) The cancer patient with pain: Psychiatric complications and their management. *Med Clin North Am*, **71**, 243–248.

Massie MJ and Holland JC (1990) Depression and the cancer patient. *J Clin Psychiatry*, **51 (July suppl)**, 12–15.

Massie MJ, Holland J and Glass E (1979) The diagnosis of depression in hospitalised patients with cancer. *Proc Am Assoc Cancer Res Am Soc Clin Oncol*, **20**, 432–444.

McCabe MS (1991) Psychological support for the patient on chemotherapy. *Oncology*, **5(7)**, 91–103.

McCorkle R and Quint-Benoliel J (1983) Symptom distress, current concerns and mood disturbance after diagnosis of life-threatening illness. *Soc Sci Med*, **17**, 431–438.

Med Lett Drugs Therapeutics (1993) Drugs that cause psychiatric symptoms. *Med Lett Drugs Ther*, **35(901)**, 65–70.

Mermelstein HT and Lesko L (1992) Depression in patients with cancer. *Psychooncology*, **1**, 199–215.

Meyer TJ and Mark MM (1995) Effects of psychosocial interventions with adult cancer patients: A meta-analysis of randomized experiments. *Health psychol*, **14(2)**, 101–108.

Morrison R (1992) Diagnosing spiritual pain in patients. *Nursing Standard*, **6(25)**, 36–38.

Morton RP, Davies ADM *et al.* (1984) Quality of life in treated head and neck cancer patients: A preliminary report. *Clin Otolaryngol*, **9**, 181–185.

Murphy BEP (1991) Steroids and depression. *J Steroid Biochem Molec Biol*, **38**, 537–559.

Noyes R and Kathol RG (1986) Depression and cancer. *Psychiatr Dev*, **2**, 77–100.

Oberst MT, Thomas SE, Gass KA and Ward SE (1989) Caregiving demands and appraisal of stress among family caregivers. *Cancer Nurs*, **12**, 209–215.

Pasacretta JV and Massie MJ (1990) Nurses' reports of psychiatric complications in patients with cancel. *Oncol Nurs Forum*, **17(3)**, 347–353.

Patterson RA (1984) The search for meaning: A pastoral response to suffering. *Hosp Prog*, **65**, 46–49.

Peterson LG and Popkin MK (1980) Neuropsychiatric effects of chemotherapeutic agents for cancer. *Psychosomatics*, **21**, 141–153.

Plumb MM and Holland J (1981) Comparative studies of psychological function in patients with advanced cancer: II. Interviewer-rated current and past psychological symptoms. *Psychosom Med*, **43**, 243–254.

Popkin MK, Callies AL and MacKenzie TB (1985) The outcome of antidepressant use in the medically ill. *Arch Gen Psychiatry*, **42**, 1160–1163.

Potter WZ, Rudorfer MV and Manji H (1991) The pharmacologic treatment of depression. *N Engl J Med*, **325**, 633–642.

Power D, Kelly S, Gilsenan J, Kearney M, O'Mahony D, Walsh JB and Coakley D (1993) Suitable screening tests for cognitive impairment and depression in the terminally ill—a prospective prevalence study. *Palliat Med*, **7**, 213–218.

Ramsay N (1992) Referral to a laison psychiatrist from a palliative care unit. *Palliat Med*, **6**, 54–60.

Rapp SR and Vrana S (1989) Substituting nonsomatic for somatic symptoms in the diagnosis of depression in elderly male medical patients. *Am J Psychiatry*, **146**, 1197–1200.

Razavi D, Delvaux N, Farvacques C and Robaye E (1990) Screening for adjustment disorders and major depressive disorders in cancer inpatients. *Br J Psychiat*, **156**, 79–83.

Razavi D, Delvaux N, Bredart A, Paesmans N, Debusscher L, Bron D and Stryckmans P (1992) Screening for psychiatric disorders in a lymphoma outpatient population. *Eur J Cancer*, **28A**, 1869–1872.

Richman J (1992) A rational approach to a rational suicide. *Suicide Life Threat Behav*, **22**, 130–141.

Rifkin A, Reardon G, Siris S *et al.* (1985) Trimipramine in physical illness with depression. *J Clin Psychiatry*, **46**, 4–8.

Robins LN, Helzer JE, Croughan J and Ratcliff KF (1981) National institute of Mental Health diagnostic interview schedule: Its history, characteristics, and validity. *Arch Gen Psychiatry*, **38**, 381–397.

Rodin G, Craven J and Littlefield C (1991) *Depression in the Medically Ill*, New York: Brunner/Mazel, Chapter 1 and 2.

Rosen DH, Gregory RJ, Pollock D and Schiffmann A (1987) Depression in patients referred for psychiatric consultation; a need for a new diagnosis. *Gen Hosp Psychiatry*, **9**, 391–397.

Salzburg D, Breitbart W, Fishman B, Stiefel F, Holland J and Foley K (1989) The relationship of pain and depression to suicidal ideation in cancer patients. (abstract). *Am Soc Clin Oncol*, **8**, A1215.

Saunders C (1988) Spiritual pain. *Hosp Chap*, **102**, 30.

Saunders JM and Valente SM (1988) Cancer and suicide. *Oncol Nurs Forum*, **15(5)**, 575–581.

Shakin EJ and Holland J (1988) Depression and pancreatic cancer. *J Pain Symptom Manag*, **3**, 194–198.

Shuster JL, Stern TA and Greenberg DB (1992) Pros and cons of fluoxetine for the depressed cancer patient. *Oncology*, **6(11)**, 45–55.

Small GW (1989) Tricyclic antidepressants for medically ill geriatric patients. *J Clin Psychiatry*, **50 (7 suppl)**, 27–31.

Song F, Freemantle N, Sehldon TA *et al.* (1993) Selective serotonin reuptake inhibitors: Meta-analysis of efficacy and acceptability. *Br Med J*, **306**, 683–687.

Speck P (1988) *Being There—Pastoral Care in Times of Illness*. London: SPCK.

Spitzer RL, Endicott J and Robins E (1978) Research diagnostic criteria, rationale and reliability. *Arch Gen Psychiatry*, **35**, 773–782.

Steibel V and Kemp J (1990) Long-term methylphenidate use in the medically ill patient with organic mood syndrome. *Psychosomatics*, **31**, 454–456.

Stiefel FR, Kornblith A and Holland JC (1990) Changes in prescription patterns of psychotropic drugs for cancer patients during a 10-year period. *Cancer*, **65**, 1048–1053.

Storm HH, Christensen N and Jensen OM (1992) Suicides among Danish patients with cancer. *Cancer*, **69**, 1507–1512.

Valente SM (1990) Electroconvulsive therapy. *Arch Psychiatr Nurs*, **V(4)**, 223–228.

Valente SM, Saunders JM and Cohen MZ (1994) Evaluating depression among patients with cancer. *Cancer Pract*, **2(1)**, 65–71.

van der Mass PJ, van Delden JJM, Pijnenborg L and Looman CWN (1991) Euthanasia and other medical decisions concerning the end of life. *Lancet*, **338**, 669–674.

Wanzer, SH, Federman DD, Adelstein J *et al.* (1989) The physician's responsibility toward hopelessly ill patients: A second look. *N Engl J Med*, **320**, 844–849.

Weddington WW, Segraves KB and Simon MA (1986) Current and life-time incidence of psychiatric disorders among a group of extremity sarcoma survivors. *J Psychosomatic Res*, **30**, 121–125.

Weisman AD, Worden JW and Sobel HJ (1980) *Psychosocial Screening and Intervention with Cancer Patients: Research Report*. Mass: Shea Bros.

Weizman A, Eldar M, Shoenfeld M *et al.* (1979) Hypercalcaemia-induced psychopathology in malignant diseases. *Br J Psychiatry*, **135**, 363–366.

Wing JK, Babor T, Brugha T *et al.* (1990) Schedules for clinical assessment in neuropsychiatry. *Arch Gen Psychiatry*, **47**, 589–593.

Woods SW, Tesar GE, Murray GB and Cassem EH (1986) Psychostimulant treatment of depressive disorders secondary to medical illness *J Clin Psychiatry*, **47**, 12–15.

Yarnell SK and Battin MP (1988) AIDS, psychiatry and euthanasia. *Psychiatr Ann*, **818**, 598–603.

Zigmond A S and Snaith R P (1983) The hospital anxiety and depression scale. *Acta Psychiatr Scand*, **67**, 361–370.

Zimmerman M, Coryell W H and Black D W (1990) Variability in the application of contemporary diagnostic criteria: Endogenous depression as an example. *Am J Psychiatry*, **147**, 1173–1179.

24

Pain and depression

Boudewijn Van Houdenhove and Patrick Onghena

INTRODUCTION

Pain and depression can both be considered as perhaps the most serious forms of human suffering. Clinical experience shows that physical pain and the emotional suffering of depression are often strongly interwoven and interactions in both directions may occur. During the last decade, research endeavours have mainly focused on further clarifying the prevalence, nature and treatment implications of the association between *chronic pain* and depression. The purpose of this chapter is to review the present state of knowledge, including controversies and unresolved questions, and the practical consequences of this complex relationship for the clinician.

DEFINITIONS

Pain

According to the International Association for the Study of Pain (IASP) pain is "an unpleasant sensory and emotional experience associated with actual or potential tissue damage, or described in terms of such damage" (IASP, 1986). This definition implies that pain is much more than a merely sensory phenomenon, and explicitly calls attention to the psychological aspects of pain experience.

Depression and Physical Illness. Edited by M.M. Robertson and C.L.E. Katona
© 1997 John Wiley & Sons Ltd

A further understanding of the role of psychological factors in pain is provided by the "gate control theory", which includes a neurologically based framework of psychological pain modulation, and a differentiation of sensori-perceptual, affective–motivational and cognitive–evaluative pain aspects (Melzack and Wall, 1965). Another well-known and influential schema that includes essential psychological components is Loeser's (1982) differentiation of the pain phenomenon in four dimensions, namely: "nociception", "pain perception", "suffering" and "pain behaviour".

Psychological factors may sometimes be judged to have a major role in the onset, severity, exacerbation, or maintenance of the pain. In these cases, the pain may be coded according to the *Diagnostic and Statistical Manual of Mental Disorders* (DSM-IV) as one of the "somatoform disorders", either as "pain disorder associated with psychological factors" (307.80), or as "pain disorder associated with both psychological factors and a general medical condition" (307.89).

Chronic pain

Most authors define chronic pain pragmatically as pain that persists beyond 6 months (Sternbach, 1974). Continued nociception or nociception-induced changes within the nervous system can significantly contribute to pain persistence. Moreover, most pain clinicians and researchers agree that psychosocial or psychiatric factors may play a crucial role in the development, continuation or amplification of chronic pain (Egle and Hoffmann, 1993; Wall and Melzack, 1994; Novy et al., 1995a).

Depression is considered to be an important psychological variable in chronic pain, and the complex relationship between the two is beyond doubt of great theoretical as well as practical concern (Romano and Turner, 1985).

THE COMORBIDITY BETWEEN CHRONIC PAIN AND DEPRESSION

Chronic pain and depression have been found to co-occur in patients with "psychogenic" pain (e.g. Merskey, 1965; Valdes et al., 1989), as well as in patients who manifest organically based pain (e.g. King, 1993), including cancer pain (Heim and Oei, 1993). Depressive symptoms tend to be more evident in females with pain than in males (Magni et al., 1993). Elderly chronic pain patients may be particularly at risk for depression (Roy, 1986; Herr and Mobily, 1992; Williamson and Schulz, 1992; Turk et al., 1995). Other risk factors seem to be the single state, low education and income (Magni et al., 1990, 1993), and litigation problems (Solomon and Tunks, 1991) (Table 1).

Several reviewers (e.g. Romano and Turner, 1985; Gupta, 1986; Craig, 1994; Merskey, 1994) point to the great inconsistencies in the literature on the preva-

Table 1. Risk factors for depression in chronic
pain patients.

Female sex
Older age
Single state
Low education
Low income
Litigation problems

lence of depressive symptoms or diagnosable depression in chronic pain
patients, varying from 0 to 87%. For example, the frequent finding of a concomitant depression in chronic pain patients led certain authors (Lindsay and
Wycoff, 1981) to identify a "depression–pain syndrome", whereas a recent study
reported both pain clinic patients and nonclinical pain patients to score on the
Beck Depression Inventory (BDI) in the nondepressed range (Roy *et al.*, 1990).
The majority of studies in various groups of chronic pain patients, however,
report a frequency of clinically diagnosed depression ranging from 30 to 60%
(Magni, 1987). When only major depressive episodes are considered, this is
reduced from 8 to 50% (Smith, 1992). In any case, depression seems to be
more common in chronic pain than in other chronic medical populations, and
this may be explained by the unique psychological experience of living with
chronic pain (Banks and Kerns, 1996).

The marked variation in prevalence rates clearly depends on differences
between studies, with regard to types and locations of pain, diagnostic criteria
used to define both depression and chronic pain, characteristics of the sample
recruited, and assessment of depression. In particular the latter two issues have
been addressed in recent research.

The problem of selection bias

The majority of data on the chronic pain/depression comorbidity have been
gathered in highly selected groups ("convenience samples"). These are
generally made up of patients referred to hospitals or specialist centres such as
pain clinics, which evidently attract pain sufferers who are more prone to
present psychological problems (Magni *et al.*, 1992; Gamsa, 1994). Consequently, it is not surprising that, when Crook *et al.* (1989) compared pain clinic
patients with chronic pain patients in a family practice, the former were more
likely to be depressed.

Recently, several investigations have been carried in the general population to
avoid the problem of selection bias (Table 2). In one of the first population-
based studies, Dworkin *et al.* (1990), using the Depression scale of the
Symptom Checklist—90 Revised, found depression to be associated with

Table 2. Population-based prevalence studies on depression in chronic pain patients.

Author	Type of pain	N	Measure	% depressed
Magni *et al.* (1990)	Musculoskeletal	416 (Non-institutionalized civilian population of the USA)	CES-D ⩾ 20	18.3
	No chronic pain	2388 (id.)	id.	8.8
Magni *et al.* (1992)	Abdominal	205 (Mexican/ Cuban Americans)	id.	18.7
	No chronic pain	3970 (id.)	id.	8.0
	Abdominal	113 (Puerto Ricans)	id.	40.8
	No chronic pain	1210 (id.)	id.	19.1

multiple pains and pain-related disability. Magni *et al.* (1990) using the Depression Scale of the Centre for Epidemiological Studies (CES-D) in a large-scale population-based survey found that 18.3% of subjects with chronic musculoskeletal pain suffered from depression, in contrast to 8.8% of the population who did not have chronic pain. In a second population survey, Magni *et al.* (1992) reported data on abdominal pain and depression; interestingly (but without manifest explanation), marked differences in depression rates were observed between Mexican and Cuban Americans (18.7%) and Puerto Ricans (40.8%). Finally, in a recent Finnish population study (Rajala *et al.*, 1995) it was found that musculoskeletal pains were more common among depressed people than in the nondepressed population, and many of the depressed people suffered from multiple pains.

One may conclude that population-based investigations, although providing varying data dependent on measurement and pain location, do confirm the close link between chronic pain and depression found in more select groups.

Assessment problems

There is a substantial symptomatology overlap in depression and chronic pain: e.g. sleep disturbances, fatigue, weight loss, motor retardation, and social withdrawal are common symptoms in both. This may cause a tendency to *overestimate* depression in pain patients and is likely to have contributed to inconsistencies in reported prevalence rates (Romano and Turner, 1985; Brown, 1990; Sullivan *et al.*, 1992).

Several investigators have documented this overestimation in standardized assessment (particularly with the BDI), a phenomenon that is known as criterion contamination (Pincus and Callahan, 1993). Williams and Richardson (1993) conclude that the use of the total BDI score in chronic pain patients may give a misleading impression of the nature and degree of affective disturbance in this group of patients, and Volk *et al.* (1993) specify that this may cause an approximately 20% false-positive rate in the identification of clinically significant depression. Chibnall and Tait (1994) caution that particularly the "work inhibition" and "fatigue" items of the BDI may not be relevant. Recently it has been put forward that further investigations of the constituents of depression as measured by the BDI may contribute to the understanding of the interrelations of chronic pain and depression (Novy *et al.*, 1995b).

On the other hand, Turk and Okifuji (1994) found that the CES-D did have predictive validity for depression in chronic pain patients, using a cut-off score of 19; they mentioned, moreover, that the removal of somatic items did not enhance the effectiveness of the CES-D.

It should further be noted that patients' response bias may also distort prevalence figures of depression: since many chronic pain patients have a tendency to deny emotional problems, this may led to an *underestimation* of coexistent depression as well (Craig, 1994).

THE NATURE AND DIRECTION OF THE PAIN/DEPRESSION RELATIONSHIP

Correlational studies (Table 3)

Depression has often been found to be correlated with higher pain intensity (Haythornthwaite *et al.*, 1991; Affleck *et al.*, 1991; Herr *et al.*, 1993; Johnson *et al.*, 1993; Casten *et al.*, 1995). However, this positive correlation has recently

Table 3. Correlation between depression and some pain-related aspects.

Pain aspect	Correlation with depression
Pain intensity	+/−
Pain tolerance	?
Pain extent	+
Pain behaviour	+/−
Conflict about pain	+
Social support	−

been observed in older, but not in younger patients (Turk *et al.*, 1995). Moreover, a close relationship between depression and reported pain severity has been shown to be more manifest in women than in men (Haley *et al.*, 1985).

Some laboratory studies have demonstrated a correlation between lower mood and lower pain tolerance (Zelman *et al.*, 1991), but in the clinical setting the exact relationship between depressed mood, pain perception and pain tolerance remains unclear (Geisser *et al.*, 1993). Furthermore, depression also appears to be positively correlated with higher pain extent (Tait *et al.*, 1990).

Studies investigating the relationship between depression and pain behaviour have generated inconsistent results. While some authors have found a positive correlation between the two in patients with various chronic pain problems (Keefe *et al.*, 1986; Haythornthwaite *et al.*, 1991), this has not been confirmed in patients with rheumatoid arthritis (Anderson *et al.*, 1987), and in fibromyalgia patients (Buckelew *et al.*, 1994).

Watt-Watson *et al.* (1988) demonstrated the interrelationships between depression and pain intensity, coping responses and family functioning. From a social perspective, in arthritis sufferers both pain and depression have been found to be associated with an inability to participate in the workplace (Fifield *et al.*, 1991), whereas in patients with myofascial pain more severe depression was correlated with more pain, more conflict about pain and less network social support (Faucett, 1994).

Studies on temporal relationships

In their review of the literature, Romano and Turner (1985) conclude that relatively few patients seem to develop pain after the onset of depression, a clearly greater number become depressed subsequent to the onset of pain, and most patients develop pain and depression simultaneously. They state, however, that these conclusions may be biased by problems inherent to the collection of retrospective self-report data.

Some prospective studies have recently been carried out to avoid this methodological problem. Two such studies in chronic musculoskeletal pain patients led the authors (Leino and Magni, 1993; Magni *et al.*, 1994) to conclude that "evidence was found for both the views that depression promotes pain, and pain promotes depression" (although in both cases the predictive power was relatively weak, particularly for depression predicting pain). Von Korff *et al.* (1993) examined first onset rates of five common pain symptoms and assessed, on a prospective basis, whether depressive symptoms at baseline were associated with onset risks; they found that, relative to the nondepressed, individuals with moderate-to-severe depressive symptoms were more likely to develop headache and chest pain (however, presence of a pain condition was a more consistent predictor of subsequent risks of developing a new pain condition). In another prospective study, Potter and Jones (1992) found that the presence of depression, high pain intensity scores and the increasing use of passive coping strategies were associated with the development of chronic musculoskeletal pain. Similarly, depression—among other psychosocial and biological variables—has been found to be an important predictor of pain to become chronic in herpes zoster patients (Dworkin *et al.*, 1992), and lumbar disc patients (Hasenbring *et al.*, 1994). Thus, prospective investigations confirm that at least in a significant proportion of chronic pain patients depression precedes chronic pain or coincides with its development.

Depression: consequence or cause of chronic pain?

It is often overlooked that, given the high point prevalence of both chronic pain and depression, there may in some cases be no causal relationship at all, but a purely chance association (Gupta, 1986). The pain patient's depression may originate in other forms of life stress, and thus be unrelated (or only partly related) to the pain problem.

The aetiological aspects of the chronic pain/depression relationship still remain largely unresolved, because most studies on this topic are cross-sectional, limiting by definition causal inferences (the above-mentioned prospective studies are notable exceptions). Nevertheless, some authors interpret their correlational findings as an indication that emotional disturbance is more likely to be a consequence than a cause of chronic pain (e.g. Gamsa, 1990; Gaskin *et al.*, 1992). It should be emphasized, however, that the causal direction between the two syndromes could ultimately only be validated within the context of a true longitudinal or causal design (Geisser *et al.*, 1994a).

Despite the lack of definite empirical data, there are several aetiological hypotheses concerning the relationship between chronic pain and depression. They may be summarized as shown in Figure 1 and in the following list.

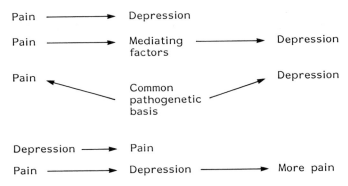

Figure 1. Pain/depression relationship: aetiological hypotheses.

1. Depression is a direct consequence (or an inherent part) of the chronic pain experience.
2. Chronic pain causes depression through mediating (psychological or somatic) factors.
3. Depression and pain have a common pathogenetic basis.
4. Depression causes (and may be masked by) pain.
5. Depression perpetuates or exacerbates pain once it develops.

Depression as a direct consequence (or inherent part) of chronic pain

Depression among chronic pain patients has often been explained as an understandable and even expected consequence of the long-term suffering from pain and the limitations it imposes on the patient's life (Sternbach, 1974). More specifically, Hendler (1984) has described the psychological reactions to chronic pain in terms of a multi-staged grief process, that may result in a final adaptation, but may also often be blocked in a prolonged depressive state.

There is some empirical evidence for the direct link between chronic pain and depression. Brown's (1990) study of depression in rheumatoid arthritis patients, for example, provides support for a causal model in which pain predicts depression, but only after an extended period of time (1 year in the study). Other authors suggest that chronic pain and depression are associated by recursive, vicious cycles in which pain increases unpleasant affect, promoting access to memories of unpleasant events, which, in turn, intensifies the unpleasant affect and helps perpetuate pain (Eich et al., 1990). However, hypotheses concerning a direct (or inherent) relationship between chronic pain and depression leave the question unanswered why only a proportion of pain patients develop depression.

Mediating factors between chronic pain and depression (Table 4)

Cognition, behaviour and coping style

Lefebvre (1981) and more recently Ingram et al. (1990), Skevington (1993), Krause et al. (1994), and Smith et al. (1994a,b) observed marked cognitive distortion and helplessness in some chronic pain patients, which was in turn associated with increased levels of self-reported or clinically diagnosed depression.

In line with these findings, Turk, Kerns and their colleagues (Kerns and Turk, 1984; Kerns and Haythornthwaite, 1988; Rudy et al., 1988; Turk et al., 1995) have proposed a cognitive–behavioural mediation model to explain the variation of emotional distress in chronic pain patients. According to this

Table 4. Mediating factors between chronic pain and depression.

Cognition, behaviour and coping style (e.g. low activity; catastrophizing)
Familial and social factors (e.g. low marital satisfaction)
Inhibited anger (or other negative affect)
Vulnerability (e.g. genetic or developmental-psychological)
Iatrogenic factors (e.g. some medications; negative attitudes)

---

model, pain alone is not a sufficient condition for the development of depression; specific cognitive appraisal variables such as the patients' perceptions of the impact of pain on their lives, decline in activities associated with the resultant loss of social rewards, and decline in perceptions of self-control and personal mastery are necessary to mediate this relationship. (For a recent, comprehensive discussion of the model see also Banks and Kerns, 1996.)

Rudy *et al.* (1988) directly tested the model and found that, although pain and depression were modestly correlated, this relationship was virtually zero when perceptions of impact (i.e. disability) and life control were controlled for. Other studies have subsequently supported the validity of the cognitive–behavioural mediation model of pain and depression (e.g. Cheatle *et al.*, 1990; Haythornthwaite *et al.*, 1991; Kleinke, 1991; Devins *et al.*, 1993; Holzberg *et al.*, 1993).

Some specific pain-coping reactions are considered to be significantly related to depression. One of those is *catastrophizing*, which means judgements of an inability to persist in coping efforts, excessive worry about the future, and the tendency to view pain and the individual's life situation as overwhelming (Keefe *et al.*, 1989; Jensen *et al.*, 1991). Recent research evidence indicates that catastrophizing seems not to be merely a symptom of depression (as suggested by some authors, e.g. Sullivan and D'Eon, 1990) but to represent a related but separate construct (Geisser *et al.*, 1994 a,b).

In addition, idiosyncratic personal beliefs about pain (such as self-blame) have also been demonstrated to mediate depressive symptoms in chronic pain patients (Williams *et al.*, 1994).

Family and social factors

Kerns and Turk (1984) and Kerns and Haythornthwaite (1988) suggest a positive role for marital satisfaction and support as a buffer from depressive symptoms in chronic pain patients. In a later study, Kerns *et al.* (1990) found that pain patients who experience a generally low level of marital satisfaction as well as a high frequency of punishing responses contingent on demonstrations of pain are more likely to experience depressive symptoms. Perceived pain-related spousal support may moderate the potentially depressive effect of a low level of activity in chronic pain patients (Goldberg *et al.*, 1993). However, the exact effect of spousal support on pain (and particularly on pain behaviour), and its potentially mediating influence on the relationship between pain and depression remains unclear and deserves further study (Revenson *et al.*, 1991; Turk *et al.*, 1995).

Inhibited anger

There has been a long-standing notion in psychodynamic theory that individuals who do not express anger outwards but instead turn it upon themselves with self-blame run the risk of depression. This mechanism could play a mediating role in depression among chronic pain sufferers because they are often said to inhibit anger ("anger-in") (Kerns *et al.*, 1994; Fernandez and Turk, 1995).

However, systematic empirical support for this mechanism is scarce. Achterberg-Lawlis (1982) reported that anger was associated with depressive symptoms in arthritis sufferers, and Wade *et al.* (1990) showed that anger in chronic pain patients significantly predicted scores on the Beck Depression Inventory (BDI) and the depression score of the Minnesota Multiphasic Personality Inventory (MMPI). Beutler *et al.* (1986, 1988) and Corbishley *et al.* (1990) also found evidence for inhibited expression of anger in depressed chronic pain patients; they moreover added a biological viewpoint arguing that the inability to express intense negative affect coinciding with chronic pain could deactivate the production of endogenous opioids and natural killer cells which in turn could reduce the body's defence against disease, pain and depression.

Vulnerability factors

France and his colleagues carried out a series of biological and family studies in which they tried to differentiate depressed from nondepressed chronic pain patients (for a review see Krishnan *et al.*, 1988). Their results compelled them to speculate that a subset of chronic pain patients may have a genetic vulnerability to depression with an associated underlying neurochemical substrate.

From a developmental–psychological perspective, Goldberg (1994) found a significant positive relationship between depression in chronic pain patients and a history of childhood sexual and physical abuse, while there was no significant relationship between abuse and chronic pain as such. Likewise, Taylor *et al.* (1995) reported that the differences they found between abused and nonabused fibromyalgia patients could almost all be seen as symptoms of depression.

Iatrogenic factors

Some authors (Aronoff *et al.*, 1986; Craig, 1994) draw attention to the fact that commonplace treatment recommendations for patients with persistent pain, such as withdrawal from work and other activities, prolonged bed-rest, and the use of narcotic analgesics and benzodiazepines may provoke or exacerbate depression. Negative attitudes and behaviours on the part of the health care provider (e.g. nonchalance, impatience, or suggestions that the patient's pain is psychological) may have similar effects (Banks and Kerns, 1996).

A common pathogenetic basis between depression and pain?

Neurobiological models

There is broad empirical evidence for the hypothesis that chronic pain syndromes unexplainable by manifest organic lesions ("idiopathic" or "indeterminate" pain) and depressive disorders may share certain common pathogenetic mechanisms (Table 5). First, biological similarities between these pain syndromes and depression include low serum and urine melatonin levels, low cerebrospinal fluid (CSF) 5-HIAA levels, low platelet monoamine oxidase (MAO) levels, low (^{3}H) imipramine receptor binding, cortisol hypersecretion, pathological dexamethasone suppression tests, shortened rapid eye movements latency in sleep electroencephalograph (EEG), and normal or high Fraction I CSF endorphin levels (for a recent review, see von Knorring and Ekselius, 1994). Secondly, several studies have reported marked therapeutic effects of antidepressants in chronic pain, but the exact mechanisms of action of these

Table 5. Evidence of neurobiological links between chronic idiopathic pain and depression

Condition	Neurobiological effect
In both syndromes	Low melatonin in serum/urine
	Low CSF 5-HIAA
	Low platelet MAO
	Low (^{3}H) imipramine binding
	Cortisol hypersecretion
	Pathological DST
	Shortened REM latency
	Normal/high fraction I CSF endorphin
	Therapeutic effects of antidepressants
In chronic idiopathic pain patients	High prevalence of depression and "depressive spectrum disorders"

medications remain unclear (Onghena and Van Houdenhove, 1992) (see further). Thirdly, a relatively high percentage of subjects with chronic indeterminate pain appears to have a family history of depression and "depressive spectrum disorders" such as migraine and irritable bowel syndrome (Magni, 1987).

Von Knorring and Ekselius (1994) conclude that one important common pathogenetic mechanism in both depressive disorder and chronic idiopathic pain seems to be disturbances in the serotoninergic system. From a clinical perspective, Merskey (1994) similarly assumes that "there are sometimes pain patients whose cerebral pathophysiology is such that they will respond to antidepressants in the same way as patients with depression, but who lack the evidence of a depressed mood".

Psychodynamic models

In psychoanalytical theory it has long been assumed that both pain and depression may be psychodynamically related to the "emotional pain" of affective loss, feelings of guilt and narcissistic injury (Van Houdenhove, 1991; Egle, 1993).

Unresolved affective loss and guilt are the core characteristics of Engel's (1959) "pain-prone patient" concept. Blumer and Heilbronn (1982) later extended this concept by linking it more explicitly to the psychodynamic and biological features of depression, and defining it as a distinct nosological entity within the spectrum of depressive disorder ("pain-prone disorder"). According to this model, pain is neither primary nor secondary to depression, but rather is a "synchronous expression" of the disorder.

The link between pain, depression and narcissistic injury has been illustrated in interview-based psychoanalytically orientated studies by Blazer (1980) and Van Houdenhove (1987). These authors identify a subgroup of chronic pain patients with marked narcissistic personality traits, and more specifically, an exaggerated premorbid investment of their physical strength and endurance. When confronted with a physical illness or trauma, these people's self-esteem may become seriously threatened, and focusing on physical pain may be the best solution to preserve their psychic equilibrium and ward off an impending depression.

Several other psychoanalytically orientated studies have provided data that are compatible with a possible "psychodynamic bridge" between pain and depression. For example, Violon (1980) found the histories of atypical facial pain patients and cluster headache patients to be characterized by early affective deprivation and pre-existent depression. The above-mentioned studies of Beutler et al. (1986, 1988) about the role of inhibited expression of negative affect in depressed pain patients can also be interpreted within the hypothesis of common psychodynamic features in the two syndromes. Also supportive are the findings of Schors (1990) that psychogenic pain patients without depression showed more chronicity than depressed pain patients, suggesting that in the former pain could be understood as a substitution. However, attempts to validate empirically a common psychodynamic basis between pain and depression appear to be inherently problematic, since the results of psychoanalytically orientated studies are very hard to test by controlled psychometric research (Gamsa, 1994).

Trait models

Pain and depression may be related through common psychological traits that modulate symptom perception. For example, Costa and McCrae (1985) believe that some individuals have more tendency than others to experience negative, distressing emotions, and are also more likely to report dysphoric physical symptoms. Similarly, Watson and Pennebaker (1989) have described a general trait of somatopsychic distress which they call "negative affectivity". From this perspective, depression and pain may both be indicative of an underlying sensitivity to dysphoric symptoms, physical as well as psychological. Support for this hypothesis was provided by Affleck *et al.* (1992) who found in a prospective study that rheumatoid arthritis patients higher in neuroticism reported more intense pain and more negative mood, and by Wade *et al.* (1992) who concluded from a canonical correlation analysis that "personality traits influence the ways in which people cognitively process the meanings that chronic pain holds for their life, and hence the extent to which they suffer".

Depression as a cause of pain

It is well established that depressed individuals often complain of diffuse and, more rarely, localized pain (von Knorring *et al.*, 1983). Particularly in the elderly, depression often manifests as hypochondriacal complaints about pain and other somatic symptoms (Katona, 1994). Pain as a symptom of depression may be mediated by a number of psychological and/or physiological mechanisms, including anxiety, tension, somatic preoccupation, and biochemical changes. However, in many of these patients, pain appears not to be a major presenting complaint and treatment for it is not sought (Romano and Turner, 1985).

Although the "masked depression" concept has gained some acceptance in the depression literature (see e.g. Lopez-Ibor, 1991), the idea that chronic pain could be explained by an underlying depression has encountered much resistance among chronic pain researchers (with some exceptions; see for example Chaturvedi, 1989). Notably Blumer and Heilbronn (1982), who characterize their "pain-prone disorder" concept as a "masked depression *par excellence*", have been blamed by authoritative investigators for giving rise to diagnostic and conceptual confusion (Turk and Salovey, 1984; Gamsa, 1994). According to

Dworkin and Gitlin (1991), instead of diagnosing a "masked depression" in chronic pain patients, the latter could better be given a dual diagnosis of both a depressive and a pain disorder.

In an attempt to elucidate the problem, Van Houdenhove (1991) suggests that the "masked depression" concept as related to pain should be considered neither as a diagnostic nor a nosological entity, nor as a psychodynamic concept (as implicated by Blumer and Heilbronn, 1982). The term primarily refers to a *communication problem* between the pain patient and his doctor: there may indeed be multiple (more or less conscious) reasons why depressive patients tend to hide their mood problem behind a pain problem, such as the wish to avoid psychiatric stigma, the traits of alexithymia and the idiosyncratic influences of social and cultural norms (Katon *et al.*, 1982). On the other hand (as outlined above), psychodynamic theory hypothesizes that some people may *somatize* the affective distress associated with unconscious needs or conflicts in order to *avoid* depression, a process that must be distinguished from masked depression and would be comparable to a conversion process (see also Van Houdenhove *et al.*, 1992). In any case, the interrelationships between depression, pain and somatization are complex and still not well understood (Lipowski, 1990).

Depression as a perpetuating or exacerbating factor in pain

Once pain develops, a concomitant depression may profoundly influence its subsequent evolution. In this respect, Fields (1991) proposes a neurobiological model which implies that different factors mediate the relationship between depression and the sensory experience of pain compared to the affective and the evaluative aspects. More specifically, the author contends that depression directly impacts the sensory transmission of pain through an increased somatic focus which activates pain-facilitating neurones, whereas negative appraisals about pain such as catastrophizing mediate the impact of depression on the evaluative and affective aspects. Partial empirical support for this model has been provided by Geisser *et al.* (1993, 1994a).

CLINICAL ASPECTS

Many faces of depression in chronic pain patients

Roy (1982) and more recently Dworkin and Gitlin (1991) extensively discuss the different ways in which chronic pain patients may manifest depression. First, the severity of depressive symptoms may substantially vary among patients, and some only show variable or temporary emotional instability, irritability, helplessness or demoralization, without reaching diagnostic criteria of depressive disorder. Secondly, in those with a diagnosable depression, several DSM-IV subtypes may be differentiated (e.g. "substance-induced mood disorder" in case of the depressive effects of certain analgesic medications). Thirdly, persistent pain is often associated with both depression and anxiety states (Varma *et al.*, 1991; Kuch *et al.*, 1993; Casten *et al.*, 1995), and there is also a frequent coexistence between chronic pain, depression and chronic fatigue (Covington, 1991). In any case, when a pain patient has a concomitant depressive disorder—whatever its origin or diagnostic features—this has to be considered as an integral part of the chronic pain experience and is of paramount importance in developing an optimal treatment plan (Dworkin and Gitlin, 1991).

Clinical-diagnostic difficulties

As already mentioned, common symptoms may make the diagnosis of depression in chronic pain patients difficult, and this may be particularly the case in elderly people (Herr and Mobily, 1992). Careful questioning of the patient's mood, and examination of the cognitive aspects of depression such as anhedonia, lowered self-esteem, pessimism about the future, feelings of guilt and indecisiveness may provide useful diagnostic cues to the clinician. Not infrequently, however, diagnosis is additionally hampered by the patient's tendency to describe these symptoms as part of his pain experience, thereby denying the reality of an associated depressive disorder. From a biological point of view, the dexamethasone suppression test (DST) appears not to be useful for the detection of depression in chronic pain patients, because it may be significantly affected by other clinical variables (Ward *et al.*, 1992).

Impact of depression on the chronic pain patient and his family

Clinical experience shows that a concomitant depression may profoundly worsen the quality of life of chronic pain patients, by adding emotional suffering to physical suffering and (often in a vicious cycle) reinforcing sleep problems, apathy, and a general loss of interest and pleasure. The "emotional pain" of depression may even be experienced as more distressing than the physical pain (Osmond *et al.*, 1984). In a recent survey of patients with chronic nonmalignant pain who were members of a self-help organization, respondents identified depression as one of the worst problems caused by their chronic pain, and 50% admitted being hopeless and having considered suicide (Hitchcock *et al.*, 1994). As a matter of fact, suicide in chronic pain patients does not appear to be exceptional, and has been found to be associated with complex psychiatric, social, vocational and litigation problems (Fishbain *et al.*, 1989, 1991; Fishbain, 1995).

Although (as discussed above) correlational studies strictly do not allow causal inferences, several clinical investigations suggest that affective distress may have a considerable impact on the total pain experience. For example, in rheumatoid arthritis patients it has been shown that depression explained more variance in pain than did variables related to physical health (Hagglund *et al.*, 1989; Parker *et al.*, 1992).

Furthermore, the presence of depression has been found to be an important predictor of disability in chronic pain patients (Haley *et al.*, 1985; Dworkin *et al.*, 1986; Doan and Wadden, 1989), and it may also predict lack of motivation for psychological pain treatment (Kerns and Haythornthwaite, 1988). In the same vein, treatment failures in chronic pain rehabilitation programmes may reflect inadequate attention to concomitant depression (Dworkin and Gitlin, 1991).

Finally, it may be assumed that when a chronic pain patient suffers from depression, this involves an additional burden for the whole family (Snelling, 1994). In some cases, the spouse may become depressed as well (Schwartz *et al.*, 1991).

DEPRESSION IN SPECIFIC PAIN SYNDROMES

Depression and chronic low back pain (CLBP)

In an extensive review of the literature, Sullivan *et al.* (1992) conclude that 62% of CLBP patients, seen in a clinical setting, may show significant depressive symptoms. The prevalence of major depression, however, has been found to be much less (21%), although this percentage is still approximately three to four times higher than that reported in the general population. Dysphoric mood is frequent in both the elderly and the nonelderly with chronic back pain (Herr *et al.*, 1993). A few studies have provided data suggesting that the probability of being depressed is highest in the first 2–3 years following the onset of CLBP (Turner and Romano, 1984; Love, 1987).

In general, studies on depression in specific samples of CLBP patients have provided data similar to those in other chronic pain groups. For example, Wesley *et al.* (1991) found that commonly used measurements of depression (such as the BDI and the Hamilton Psychiatric Rating Scale for Depression) are confounded with pain symptomatology in CLBP patients. Furthermore, depression in CLBP patients appears to be strongly related to catastrophizing (Main and Waddell, 1991), passive–avoidant coping strategies (Weickgenant *et al.*, 1993), helplessness (Keefe *et al.*, 1992), and higher disability (Strong *et al.*, 1994a,b).

Atkinson *et al.* (1988) showed that CLBP patients with depressed mood reported significantly more untoward life events and ongoing life difficulties related to the back pain, than pain patients without depressed mood, and control subjects. In a later study the authors (Atkinson *et al.*, 1991) concluded that alcohol use disorders rather than depression may increase risk of developing CLBP, but the risk of new onset and recurrent major depression remains high for men throughout their CLBP career. The same research group recently also found a significant correlation between major depression, alcohol dependence and an increased severity of somatization among CLBP patients (Bacon *et al.*, 1994).

Depression and fibromyalgia (FM)

The role of depression in fibromyalgia (FM) (a medically unexplained condition mainly consisting of widespread musculoskeletal pains and fatigue) is controversial (Baumstark and Buckelew, 1992), although clinical experience shows that FM patients often display symptoms of depression (Goldenberg, 1989; Martinez *et al.*, 1995). Studies using psychological assessment instruments have consistently found that clinical samples of FM patients report more affective distress than rheumatoid arthritis patients (Payne *et al.*, 1982; Ahles *et al.*, 1987; Scudds *et al.*, 1987). In contrast Clark *et al.* (1985) found no significant difference on the BDI between a community sample of FM patients and a control sample of general medical patients.

Some studies have demonstrated a higher incidence of current and lifetime major depression in FM patients and their first-degree relatives as compared to control groups (Hudson *et al.*, 1985; Hudson and Pope, 1989), which led the authors to speculate that the syndrome may be part of the "depressive spectrum diseases". In the same vein, the validity of Blumer and Heibronn's depression-related "pain-prone disorder" concept was supported in a psychodynamically orientated investigation of a group of 40 fibromyalgia patients seen in a rheumatological practice (Alfici *et al.*, 1989). Other investigators, however, have not found any evidence for a specific pathogenetic relationship between FM and depression (Kirmayer *et al.*, 1988; Ahles *et al.*, 1991).

Tender points (a primary diagnostic sign of FM) have been shown to be associated with depression, sleep problems and fatigue (Croft *et al.*, 1994). Other studies suggest that depression in FM patients may be related to the same cognitive mediating mechanisms as described in other types of chronic pain patients. For example, Kuch *et al.* (1993) reported that mood in FM patients was more closely tied to patients' ability to cope with pain than to the pain itself.

Depression and pain in the head/face region

There are multiple clinical reports that underscore the close link between depression and various types of headache (Adler *et al.*, 1987; Merikangas *et al.*, 1988; Smith, 1990). A high comorbidity between syndromes has, for example, been reported by Srikiathkachorn (1991) in a group of elderly patients in

Thailand. Referring to the masked depression concept, some authors even consider headache to be "an important marker of depression in the primary care setting" (Chung and Kraybill, 1990).

The interrelationships between headache, depression, and anger seem to be of particular interest. Tschannen et al. (1992) found both male and female chronic headache patients to report higher levels of anger-in than anger-out; a path analysis indicated that anger-in was significantly related to depression, which in turn was directly related to perceived disability. Very similar findings have recently been reported by Duckro et al. (1995) in a sample of post-traumatic headache patients. Biological evidence in accordance with the above data suggests that central serotoninergic transmission can play a role in the pathophysiology of the chronic depressed as well as nondepressed tension-type headache sufferers (Manna et al., 1994).

Much attention has also been given to the association between depression and orofacial disorders, particularly temporomandibular joint pain and dysfunction syndrome (TMJPDS) (for reviews in odontological literature, see Tversky et al., 1991 and Kinney et al., 1992). More concretely, Gallagher et al. (1991) found by means of a structured clinical interview a minimum lifetime prevalence rate for major depression of 41% in women with TMJPDS. Moreover, the high comorbidity between depression and TMJPDS has recently been confirmed in a Finnish population study (Vimpari et al., 1995). Demoralization in myofascial face pain patients may demonstrate a seasonal pattern (being significantly greater in the peak dark months) (Gallagher et al., 1995), and has been found to be associated with changes in the immune system (Marbach et al., 1990). The potential role of depression and precipitating life events in another idiopathic orofacial condition, namely the burning mouth syndrome (glossodynia), has recently been discussed by Van Houdenhove and Joostens (1995).

TREATMENT

The importance of treating depression in chronic pain patients

Several investigators have called for more attention to the treatment of depression in chronic pain patients (e.g. Dworkin and Gitlin, 1991; Sullivan et al., 1992; Smith, 1992). As a matter of fact, treating depression in these patients may improve their general well-being and quality of life, by reducing additional affective distress and incapacitating symptoms such as lack of energy, sleep disturbances, anxiety, tension, and restlessness. Moreover, this may also have a beneficial influence on different aspects of the pain experience itself (pain intensity and quality, pain behaviour, disability, activity level, functional status, coping, etc.). Finally, treatment of a concomitant depressive disorder is likely to increase a patient's responsiveness to pain management techniques and diminish the risk of withdrawal from treatment.

Antidepressants

Clinical experience has shown that when an antidepressant is prescribed to a depressive chronic pain patient, usually the depression as well as the pain are reduced. This pain reduction can be conceptualized according to any of the aetiological models for the association between chronic pain and depression. The antidepressant may indeed alleviate a concomitant or "underlying" ("masked") depression, produce more general sedative or anxiolytic effects (which may enhance pain tolerance, coping, etc.), or exert an independent biochemical influence on central pain-controlling mechanisms (Feinmann, 1985; France *et al.*, 1984; Magni, 1991) (Figure 2).

A meta-analysis of all pre-1990 double-blind placebo-controlled clinical trials concerning the antidepressant-induced analgesic effect provided most evidence for an *independent* mode of action of antidepressants in chronic pain (Onghena and Van Houdenhove, 1992). In a convincing number of studies, pain reduction was indeed accomplished apart from depression reduction or at doses smaller than those usually effective in depression. Moreover, pain reduction was also observed in nondepressed chronic pain patients and in pain with a clear organic basis (Table 6). This has led many authors to further speculate about hitherto unsuspected intrinsic analgesic properties of the antidepressant's molecules (for recent reviews, see Eschalier *et al.*, 1994; Monks, 1994; Max, 1995). Additional evidence for this "biochemical" hypothesis is as follows.

1. The analgesic response seems to come into action much faster (within the first week) than the antidepressant response (usually after the first 2 weeks).
2. Analgesic effects are also observed in animal studies, in experimental models for both acute pain and chronic pain.

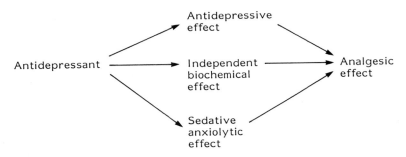

Figure 2. Possible mechanisms of antidepressant-induced analgesia in chronic pain.

Table 6. Descriptive statistics on the effect sizes of the studies involved in the meta-analysis of Onghena and Van Houdenhove (1992), subdivided according to presence of an antidepressant effect, dose of the antidepressant drug, presence of depressive patients, and assumed pain aetiology

	Mean effect size	Standard error of the mean effect size	Number of comparisons
Antidepressant effect			
Absent	0.56	0.15	16
Not reported	0.74	0.18	15
Present	0.55	0.17	9
Dose of the antidepressant drug			
Doses below "antidepressant" range	0.75	0.13	22
Usual "antidepressant" doses	0.51	0.13	18
Inclusion/exclusion of depressive patients			
Mixed	0.52	0.12	26
Depressive patients excluded	0.85	0.21	9
Only depressive patients included	0.94	0.16	4
Assumed aetiology of the pain			
Organic	0.53	0.13	22
Mixed organic/psychogenic	0.80	0.15	10
Psychogenic	0.75	0.21	8

3. Analgesic effects are also observed in people with acute pain, both in laboratory-induced pain and in clinical acute pain.
4. There are remarkable pharmacological similarities between the opiates and some antidepressants (Onghena and Van Houdenhove, 1992; for a methodological discussion see Onghena and Van Houdenhove, 1993; Richardson and Williams, 1993; Turner and Denny, 1993).

Following this meta-analysis, several trials were conducted to further delineate the conditions under which an antidepressant-induced analgesic effect can be expected. In our own study (Onghena et al., 1993), we were unable to replicate a mianserin-induced analgesic effect in depressive patients with chronic organic pain, patients with somatoform pain disorder and vital signs of depression, and patients with chronic organic pain without depression. Although there was a clear mianserin-induced antidepressant effect in depressive patients without pain complaints, there was no evidence for an antidepressive effect in depressive patients with pain complaints. This led us to the conclusion that, if the antidepressant has no analgesic effect (apparently like mianserin), chronic pain can be an obstacle for the adequate pharmacological treatment of depression because the pain acts as a continuous stressor. On the other hand, there are also indications that antidepressive response rates in depressed chronic low back pain patients (approximately 55–75%) are similar to those reported for depressed patients without chronic pain (Sullivan *et al.*, 1992). Furthermore, in a recent pilot study with large doses of mianserin an analgesic effect was observed in patients with abdominal pain (Tanum, 1993).

More recent double-blind placebo-controlled studies confirmed some of the more specific results of our meta-analysis of past research. Carette *et al.* (1994) found an effect of amitriptyline on fibromyalgia symptoms, while Nørregaard *et al.* (1995) did not with the selective serotonin reuptake inhibitor (SSRI) citalopram. Furthermore, no analgesic effects were observed with trazodone in chronic low back pain (Goodkin *et al.*, 1990).

In trials on pain due to diabetic neuropathy, analgesic effects of amitriptyline, imipramine, clomipramine, desipramine, and the SSRIs paroxetine and citalopram were found, whereas no effect of the SSRI fluoxetine or of the nontricyclic mianserin was observed (Sindrup *et al.*, 1990a,b, 1992a,b; Max *et al.*, 1991, 1992). In postherpetic neuralgia, central pain and chronic facial pain the evidence also remains positive (Kishore-Kumar *et al.*, 1990; Panerai *et al.*, 1990; Sharav *et al.*, 1991), but Menkes *et al.* (1995) failed to confirm the analgesic effect of the reversible monoamine inhibitor (MAOI-A) moclobemide in an open small N design with chronic neuropathic pain patients. In two studies without placebo control, positive results with paroxetine in the treatment of chronic headache were reported (Foster and Bafaloukos, 1994; Langemark and Olesen, 1994).

The more specific results of our meta-analysis, complemented with the results of more recent work, can be summarized as follows.

1. There is cumulating evidence that amitriptyline is the most potent "analgesic". It can be effective in low dose, although there are also indications of a positive dose–response relationship (unfortunately associated with a dose–response for the incidence of adverse effects too) (McQuay *et al.*, 1992, 1993; Zitman *et al.*, 1990). Interestingly, the analgesic effect of amitriptyline was confirmed in an animal model of neuropathic pain, and was reversible with naloxone (Ardid and Guilbaud, 1992).

2. By extension, there is also growing evidence that tricyclics in general are most effective in relieving pain, and that less selective (and possibly mildly sedating) antidepressants are more effective than the newer selective compounds (Table 7). More recent work suggests that paroxetine is an exception, and this might be an indication that, with respect to analgesic affects, SSRIs should not be lumped together indistinctly. In any case, this is an indication that more placebo-controlled double-blind studies are warranted to examine the differential effectiveness of SSRIs in chronic pain. Futhermore, it should be stressed that SSRIs may be valuable for elderly or medically unstable patients even if they are only modestly effective, because these drugs have a more favourable safety profile in comparison to

Table 7. Descriptive statistics on the effect sizes of the studies involved in the meta-analysis of Onghena and Van Houdenhove (1992), subdivided according to chemical, biochemical, and activity profiles.

	Mean effect size	Standard error of the mean effect size	Number of comparisons
Chemical profiles			
Tricyclic	0.69	0.10	34
Nontricyclic	0.36	0.17	11
MAOI	1.30	–	1
Biochemical profiles			
Mixed	0.73	0.12	30
Serotonergic	0.32	0.21	8
Noradrenergic	0.40	0.16	7
MAOI	1.30	–	1
Activity profiles			
Sedating	0.67	0.11	30
Neutral	0.55	0.17	13
Activating	0.46	0.42	3

tricyclics (Max, 1995). Likewise, in pain patients with a concomitant or supposed "underlying" depressive disorder, SSRIs or other newer compounds may be a better choice since they are better tolerated than tricyclics at therapeutic doses (see for example Van Houdenhove and Joostens, 1995).

3. Neuropathic pain seems to respond better than other forms of chronic pain. Moreover, pain in the head region (tension and migraine headache, atypical facial pain, etc.) seems to be more responsive than pain in the locomotor system, like for example chronic low back pain (Turner and Denny, 1993) (however, fibromyalgia also seems to respond rather well). Finally—and this is a more methodological remark—it seems to be easier to replicate the antidepressant-induced analgesic effect in a homogeneous group of patients with specific symptoms (e.g. diabetic neuropathy or postherpetic neuralgia) than in a heterogeneous group of patients with unspecified "chronic pain" (Table 8).

Psychotherapeutic strategies

Kramlinger et al. (1983) were among the first to indicate that cognitive–behavioural modalities can effectively alleviate depressive symptoms in chronic pain patients. These findings have been replicated in several other pain management studies (e.g. Maruta et al., 1989) and predictors for individual differences in treatment response have been investigated (e.g. Tota-Faucette et

Table 8. Descriptive statistics on the effect sizes of the studies involved in the meta-analysis of Onghena and Van Houdenhove (1992), subdivided according to pain diagnosis.

	Mean effect size	Standard error of the mean effect size	Number of comparisons
Rheumatological pain	0.37	0.19	10
Not specified or mixed	0.23	0.10	7
Tension headache	1.11	0.15	6
Chronic back pain	0.64	0.13	5
Migraine	0.82	0.26	4
Atypical facial pain	0.81	0.25	3
Postherpetic neuralgia	1.44	0.50	2
Diabetic neuropathy	1.71	–	1
Central poststroke pain	0.70	–	1
Dysaesthetic pain	–0.60	–	1

al., 1993). Further studies have suggested that psychological treatments for chronic pain are often associated with improvements in mood, even if other dimensions of functioning such as level of pain or work status remain unchanged (Linton, 1986; Turner and Clancy, 1986; Stevens *et al.*, 1988; Malone and Strube, 1988). Besides cognitive–behavioural interventions, conjoint therapy that promotes positive marital communication and targets other deficits in marital functioning may be helpful in minimizing depressive symptoms in chronic pain patients (Kerns *et al.*, 1990).

Combined psychopharmacological/psychotherapeutic treatment

Treating chronic pain with antidepressants should always take place within a trustful therapeutic relationship, and include adequate motivation of the patient as well as detailed instructions about expected therapeutic effects, side-effects, etc. to enhance the acceptability of this "psychiatric" medication. Furthermore, many patients may benefit from a combination of pharmacotherapy with some form of psychotherapy (e.g. cognitive–behavioural treatment or relaxation training), preferably within a multidisciplinary setting (Flor *et al.*, 1992).

The effects of separate versus combined treatment have been investigated by Pilowsky and colleagues. In a first study (Pilowsky and Barrow, 1990) they reported that amitriptyline reduced pain intensity and increased the patient's activity level, while psychodynamically orientated psychotherapy improved productivity and increased pain intensity. In a second study (Pilowsky *et al.*, 1995) no significant differences could be demonstrated between the outcome of cognitive–behavioural therapy combined with a low dose of amitriptyline, and supportive therapy with a low dose of amitriptyline. The latter results call attention to the importance of a supporting relationship with a caring and empathic physician, which will undoubtedly also exert a powerful "antidepressive" effect in many chronic pain sufferers.

REFERENCES

Achterberg-Lawlis J (1982) The psychological dimensions of arthritis. *J Consult Clin Psychol,* **50**, 984–992.

Adler CS, Adler SM and Packard RC (eds) (1987) *Psychiatric Aspects of Headache.* Baltimore: Williams & Wilkins.

Affleck G, Tennen H, Urrows E and Higgins P (1991) Individual differences in the day-to-day experience of chronic pain: a prospective daily study of rheumatoid arthritis patients. *Health Psychol,* **10**, 419–426.

Affleck G, Tennen H, Urrows E and Higgins P (1992) Neuroticism and the pain–mood relation in rheumatoid arthritis: Insights from a prospective study. *J Consult Clin Psychol,* **60**, 119–126.

Ahles TA, Yunus MB and Masi AT (1987) Is chronic pain a variant of depressive disease? *Pain,* **29**, 105–112.

Ahles TA, Khan SA, Yunus MB, Spregel DA and Masi AT (1991) Psychiatric status of patients with primary fibromyalgia, patients with rheumatoid arthritis, and subjects without pain: A blind comparison of DSM-III diagnoses. *Am J Psychiatry,* **148**, 1721–1726.

Alfici S, Sigal M and Landau M (1989) Primary fibromyalgia syndrome: A variant of depressive disorder? *Psychother Psychosom,* **51**, 156–161.

Anderson KO, Bradley LA, MacDaniel LK, Young LD, Turner RA, Agudelo LA, Gaby NS, Keefe FJ, Pisko EJ, Snyder RM and Semle EL (1987) The assessment of pain in rheumatoid arthritis: Disease differentiation and temporal stability of a behavioural observation method. *J Rheumatol,* **14**, 700–704.

Ardid D and Guilbaud G (1992) Antinociceptive effects of acute and "chronic" injections of tricyclic antidepressant drugs in a new model of mononeuropathy in rats. *Pain,* **49**, 279–287.

Aronoff GM, Wagner JM and Spangler AS (1986) Chemical interventions for pain. *J Consult Clin Psychol,* **54**, 769–775.

Atkinson JH, Slater MA, Grant I, Patterson TL and Garfin SR (1988) Depressed mood in chronic low back pain: relationship with stressful life events. *Pain,* **35**, 47–55.

Atkinson JH, Slater MA, Patterson TL, Grant I and Garfin SR (1991) Prevalence, onset, and risk of psychiatric disorders in men with chronic low back pain. *Pain,* **45**, 111–121.

Bacon NM, Bacon SF, Atkinson JH, Slater MA, Patterson TL, Grant I and Garfin SR (1994) Somatization symptoms in chronic low back pain patients. *Psychosom Med,* **56**, 118–127.

Banks SM and Kerns RD (1996) Explaining high rates of depression in chronic pain: A diathesis-stress framework. *Psychol Bull,* **119**, 95–110.

Baumstark KF and Buckelew SP (1992) Fibromyalgia: clinical signs, research findings, treatment implications, and future directions. *Ann Behav Med,* **14**, 282–291.

Beutler LE, Engle D, Oro-Beutler ME, Daldrup R and Meredith KE (1986) Inability to express intense affect: A common link between depression and pain. *J Consult Clin Psychol,* **54**, 752–759.

Beutler LE, Daldrup R, Engle D, Guest P, Corbishley A and Meredith KE (1988) Family dynamics and emotional expression among patients with chronic pain and depression. *Pain*, **32**, 65–72.

Blazer D (1980) Narcissism and the development of chronic pain. *Int J Psychiatr Med*, **10**, 69–77.

Blumer D and Heilbronn M (1982) Chronic pain as a variant of depressive disease. *J Nerv Ment Dis*, **170**, 381–414.

Brown GKA (1990) Causal analysis of chronic pain and depression. *Abnorm Psychol*, **99**, 127–137.

Buckelew SP, Parker JC, Keefe PJ, Deuser WE, Crews TM, Conway R, Kay DR and Hewett JE (1994) Self-efficacy and pain behaviour among subjects with fibromyalgia. *Pain*, **59**, 377–384.

Carette S, Bell MJ, Reynolds WJ, Haraoui B, McCain GA, Bykerk VP, Edworthy SM, Baron M, Koehler BE, Fam AG, Bellamy N and Guimont C (1994) Comparison of amitriptyline, cyclobenzaprine, and placebo in the treatment of fibromyalgia: A randomized, double-blind clinical trial. *Arthritis Rheum*, **37**, 32–40.

Casten R, Parmelee P, Kleban MH, Lawton MP and Katz IR (1995) The relationship among anxiety, depression, and pain in a geriatric institutionalized sample. *Pain*, **61**, 271–276.

Chaturvedi SK (1989) Psychalgic depressive disorder: A descriptive and comparative study. *Acta Psychiatr Scand*, **79**, 98–102.

Cheatle MD, Brady JP and Ruland T (1990) Chronic low back pain, depression, and attributional style. *Clin J Pain*, **6**, 114–117.

Chibnall JT and Tait RC (1994) The short form of the Beck Depression Inventory: Validity issues with chronic pain patients. *Clin J Pain*, **10**, 261–266.

Chung MK and Kraybill DE (1990) Headache: A marker of depression. *J Fam Pract*, **31**, 360–364.

Clark S, Campbell SM, Forehand ME, Tindall EA and Benett RM (1985) Clinical characteristics of fibrositis. II. A "blinded" controlled study using standard psychological tests. *Arthritis Rheum*, **28**, 132–137.

Corbishley MA, Hendrickson R, Beutler LE and Engle D (1990) Behavior, affect, and cognition among psychogenic pain patients in group expressive psychotherapy. *J Pain Symptom Manag*, **5**, 241–248.

Costa PT and McCrae RR (1985) Hypochondriasis, neuroticism and aging: When are somatic complaints unfounded? *Am Psychol*, **40**, 19–28.

Covington EC (1991) Depression and chronic fatigue in the patient with chronic pain. *Prim Care*, **18**, 341–358.

Craig KD (1994) Emotional aspect of pain. In: PD Wall and R Melzack (eds) *Textbook of Pain* (3rd edn), Edinburgh: Churchill Livingstone, 261–274.

Croft P, Schollum J and Silman A (1994) Population study of tender points counts and pain as evidence for fibromyalgia. *Br Med J*, **309**, 696–699.

Crook J, Weir R and Tunks E (1989) An epidemiological follow-up survey of persistent pain sufferers in a group family practice and specialty pain clinic. *Pain*, **36**, 49–61.

Devins GM, Seland TP, Klein GM, Edworthy SM and Soary MT (1993) Stability and determinants of psychosocial well-being in multiple sclerosis. *Rehabil Psychol*, **38**, 11–26.

Doan B and Wadden N (1989) Relationship between depressive symptoms and descriptions of chronic pain. *Pain*, **36**, 75–84.

Duckro PN, Chibnall JT and Tomazic TJ (1995) Anger, depression, and disability: A path analysis of relationships in a sample of chronic posttraumatic headache patients. *Headache*, **35**, 7–9.

Dworkin RH and Gitlin JM (1991) Clinical aspects of depression in chronic pain patients. *Clin J Pain,* **7**, 79–94.

Dworkin RH, Richlin D, Handlin D and Brand C (1986) Predicting treatment response in depressed and non-depressed chronic pain patients. *Pain,* **24**, 342–353.

Dworkin SF, Von Korff M and Le Resche L (1990) Multiple pains and psychiatric disturbance: An epidemiological investigation. *Arch Gen Psychiatry,* **47**, 239–244.

Dworkin RH, Hartstein G, Rosner HL, Walther RR, Sweeney EW and Brand C (1992) A high-risk method for studying psychosocial antecedents of chronic pain, the prospective investigation of herpes zoster. *J Abnorm Psychol,* **101**, 200–205.

Egle UT (1993) Psycho-analytische Auffassungen von Schmerz. Historische Entwicklung, gegenwartiger Stand und empirische Belege. *Nevenarzt,* **65**, 289–302.

Egle UT and Hoffmann SO (eds) (1993) *Der Schmerzkranke.* Stuttgart/New York: Schattauer.

Eich E, Rachman S and Lopatka L (1990) Affect, pain, and autobiographical memory. *J Abnorm Psychol,* **99**, 174–178.

Engel GL (1959) Psychogenic pain and the pain-prone patient. *Am J Med,* **26**, 899–918.

Eschalier A, Mestre C, Dubray C and Ardid D (1994) Why are antidepressants effective as pain relief? *CNS Drugs,* **2**, 261–267.

Faucet JA (1994) Depression in painful chronic disorders: The role of pain and conflict about pain. *J Pain Symptom Manag,* **9**, 520–526.

Feinmann C (1985) Pain relief by antidepressants: Possible modes of action. *Pain,* **23**, 1–8.

Fernandez E and Turk DC (1995) The scope and significance of anger in the experience of chronic pain. *Pain,* **61**, 165–175.

Fields H (1991) Depression and pain: A neurobiological model. *Neuropsychiatr Neuropsychol Behav Neurol,* **4**, 83–92.

Fifield J, Reisine ST and Grady K (1991) Work disability and the experience of pain and depression in rheumatoid arthritis. *Soc Sci Med,* **33**, 579–585.

Fishbain DA (1995) Chronic pain and suicide. *Psychother Psychosom,* **63**, 54.

Fishbain DA, Goldberg M, Rosomoff RS and Rosomoff HL (1989) Suicide-homicide and chronic pain. *Clin J Pain,* **5**, 275–277.

Fishbain DA, Goldberg M, Rosomoff RS and Rosomoff HL (1991) Completed suicide in chronic pain. *Clin J Pain,* **7**, 29–36.

Flor H, Fydrich T and Turk DC (1992) Efficacy of multidisciplinary pain treatment centers: A meta-analytic review. *Pain,* **49**, 221–230.

Foster CA and Bafaloukos J (1994) Paroxetine in the treatment of chronic daily headache. *Headache,* **34**, 587–589.

France RD, Houpt JL and Ellinwood EH (1984) Therapeutic effects of antidepressants in chronic pain. *Gen Hosp Psychiatry,* **6**, 55–63.

Gallagher RM, Marbach JJ, Raphael KG, Dohrenwend BP and Cloitre M (1991) Is major depression comorbid with temporomandibular pain and dysfunction syndrome? A pilot study. *Clin J Pain,* **7**, 219–225.

Gallagher RM, Marbach JJ, Raphael KG, Handte J and Dohrenwend BP (1995) Myofascial pain: Seasonal variability in pain intensity and demoralisation. *Pain,* **61**, 113–120.

Gamsa A (1990) Is emotional disturbance a precipitator or a consequence of chronic pain? *Pain,* **42**, 183–195.

Gamsa A (1994) The role of psychological factors in chronic pain. I. A half-century of study. II. A critical appraisal. *Pain,* **57**, 5–29.

Gaskin ME, Greene AF, Robinson ME and Geisser ME (1992) Negative affect and the experience of chronic pain. *J Psychosom Res,* **36**, 707–713.

Geisser ME, Gaskin ME, Robinson ME and Greene AF (1993) The relationship of depression and somatic focus to experimental and clinical pain in chronic pain patients. *Psychol Health*, **8**, 405–415.

Geisser ME, Robinson ME, Keefe FJ and Weiner Ml (1994a) Catastrophizing, depression and the sensory, affective and evaluative aspects of pain. *Pain*, **59**, 79–83.

Geisser ME, Robinson ME and Henson CD (1994b) The Coping Strategies Questionnaire and chronic pain adjustment: a conceptual analysis. *Clin J Pain*, **10**, 98–106.

Goldberg GM, Kerns RD and Rosenberg R (1993) Pain-relevant support as a buffer from depression among chronic pain patients low in instrumental activity. *Clin J Pain*, **9**, 34–40.

Goldberg RT (1994) Childhood abuse, depression, and chronic pain. *Clin J Pain*, **10**, 277–281.

Goldenberg DL (1989) Psychiatric and psychologic aspects of fibromyalgia syndrome. *Rheum Dis Clin North Am*, **15**, 105–114.

Goodkin K, Gullion CM and Agras WS (1990) A randomized, double-blind, placebo-controlled trial of trazodone hydrochloride in chronic low back pain syndrome. *J Clin Psychopharmacol*, **10**, 269–278.

Gupta MA (1986) Is chronic pain a variant of depressive illness? A critical review. *Can J Psychiatry*, **31**, 241–248.

Hagglund K, Haley W, Reveille J and Alarcon G (1989) Predicting individual differences in pain and functional impairment among patients with rheumatoid arthritis. *Arthritis Rheum*, **32**, 851–858.

Haley WE, Turner JA and Romano JM (1985) Depression in chronic pain patients: Relation to pain, activity, and sex differences. *Pain*, **23**, 337–343.

Hasenbring M, Marienfeld G, Kuhlendahl D and Soyka D (1994) Risk factors of chronicity in lumbar disc patients. A prospective investigation of biologic, psychologic, and social predictors of outcome. *Spine*, **19**, 2759–2765.

Haythornthwaite JA, Sieber WJ and Kerns RD (1991) Depression and the chronic pain experience. *Pain*, **46**, 177–184.

Heim HM and Oei TP (1993) Comparison of prostate cancer patients with and without pain. *Pain*, **53**, 159–162.

Hendler N (1984) Depression caused by chronic pain. *J Clin Psychiatry*, **45**, 30–36.

Herr KJ and Mobily PR (1992) Chronic pain and depression. *J Psychosoc Nurs*, **30**, 7–12.

Herr KJ, Mobily PR and Smith C (1993) Depression and the experience of chronic back pain: A study of related variables and age differences. *Clin J Pain*, **9**, 104–114.

Hitchcock LS, Ferrell BR and McCaffery M (1994) The experience of chronic nonmalignant pain. *J Pain Symptom Manag*, **9**, 312–318.

Holzberg AD, Robinson ME and Geisser ME (1993) The relationship of cognitive distortion to depression in chronic pain: The role of ambiguity and desirability in self-ratings. *Clin J Pain*, **9**, 202–206.

Hudson JL and Pope HG (1989) Fibromyalgia and psychopathology: Is fibromyalgia a form of "affective spectrum disorder"? *J Rheumatol*, **16 (suppl 19)**, 15–22.

Hudson JL, Hudson MS, Pliner LF, Goldenberg DL and Pope HG Jr (1985) Fibromyalgia and major affective disorder: A controlled phenomenology and family history study. *Am J Psychiatry*, **142**, 441–446.

Ingram RE, Atkinson JH, Slater MA, Saccuzzo DP and Garfin SR (1990) Negative and positive cognition in depressed and non-depressed chronic pain patients. *Health Psychol*, **9**, 300–311.

Jensen MP, Turner JA, Romano JM and Karoly P (1991) Coping with chronic pain: A review of the literature. *Pain*, **47**, 249–283.

Johnson R, Spence SH, Champion GD and Ziegler JB (1993) Pain, affect and cognition in children: I. The influence of affective state on pain in children. In: GF Gebhart, DL

Hammond and TS Jensen (eds). *Progress in Pain Research and Management* (Proceedings of the 7th World Congress on Pain, Vol 2) Seattle: IASP Press, 870–873.

Katon W, Kleinman A and Rosen G (1982) Depression and somatization: A review (parts 1 and 2). *Am J Med*, **72**, 127.

Katona CLE (1994) *Depression in Old Age*. Chichester: Wiley.

Keefe FJ, Wilkins RH, Cook Jr WA, Crisson JE and Muhlbaier LH (1986) Depression, pain and pain behavior. *J Consult Clin Psychol*, **54**, 665–669.

Keefe F, Brown GK, Wallston KA and Caldwell DS (1989) Coping with rheumatoid arthritis pain: Catastrophizing as a maladaptive strategy. *Pain*, **37**, 51–56.

Keefe FJ, Dunsmore J and Burnett R (1992) Behavioral and cognitive–behavioral approaches to chronic pain: Recent advances and future directions. *J Consult Clin Psychol*, **60**, 528–536.

Kerns RD and Haythornthwaite JA (1988) Depression among chronic pain patients: Cognitive–behavioral analysis and effect on rehabilitation outcome. *J Consult Clin Psychol*, **56**, 870–876.

Kerns RD and Turk DC (1984) Depression and chronic pain: The mediating role of the spouse. *J Marr Fam*, **46**, 845–852.

Kerns RD, Haythornthwaite J, Southwick S and Giller EL Jr (1990) The role of marital interaction in chronic pain and depressive symptoms. *J Psychosom Res*, **34**, 401–408.

Kerns RD, Rosenberg R and Jacob MC (1994) Anger expression and chronic pain. *J Behav Med*, **17**, 57–67.

King SA (1993) Pain in depression and Parkinson's disease. *Am J Psychiatry*, **150**, 353–354.

Kinney RK, Gatchel RJ, Ellis E and Holt C (1992) Major psychological disorders in chronic TMD patients: Implications for successful management. *JAMA*, **123**, 49–54.

Kirmayer LJ, Robins JR and Kapusta MA (1988) Somatization and depression in fibromyalgia syndrome. *Am J Psychiatry*, **145**, 950–954.

Kishore-Kumar R, Max MB, Schafer SC, Gaughan AM, Smoller B, Gracely RH and Dubner R (1990) Desipramine relieves postherpetic neuralgia. *Clin Pharmacol Ther*, **47**, 305–312.

Kleinke CL (1991) How chronic pain patients cope with depression: Relation to treatment outcome in a multidisciplinary clinic. *Rehabil Psychol*, **36**, 207–218.

Kramlinger KG, Swanson DW and Maruta T (1983) Are patients with chronic pain depressed? *Am J Psychiatry*, **140**, 747–749.

Krause SJ, Wiener RL and Tait RC (1994) Depression and pain behavior in patients with chronic pain. *Clin J Pain*, **10**, 122–127.

Krishnan KRR, France RD and Davidson RJ (1988) Depression as a psychopathological disorder in chronic pain. In: RD France and KRR Krishnan (eds). *Chronic Pain*, Washington DC: American Psychiatric Press, 194–218.

Kuch K, Cox B, Evans RJ, Watson PC and Bubela C (1993) To what extent do anxiety and depression interact with chronic pain? *Can J Psychiatry*, **38**, 36–38.

Langemark M and Olesen J (1994) Sulpiride and paroxetine in the treatment of chronic tension-type headache: An explanatory double-blind trial. *Headache*, **34**, 20–24.

Lefebvre MF (1981) Cognitive distortion and cognitive factors in depressed psychiatric and low back pain patients. *J Consult Clin Psychol*, **49**, 517–525.

Leino P and Magni G (1993) Depressive and distress symptoms as predictors in low back pain, neck shoulder pain, and other musculoskeletal morbidity. *Pain*, **53**, 84–94.

Lindsay P and Wycoff M (1981) The depression–pain syndrome and response to antidepressants. *Psychosomatics*, **22**, 511–517.

Linton SJ (1986) Behavioral remediation of chronic pain: A status report. *Pain*, **24**, 125–141.

Lipowski ZJ (1990) Somatization and depression. *Psychosomatics*, **31**, 13–21.

Loeser JD (1982) Concepts of pain. In: M Stanton-Hicks and R Boas (eds). *Chronic Low Back Pain*, New York: Raven Press, 145–148.

Lopez-Ibor JJ Jr (1991) The masking and unmasking of depression. In: JP Feighner and WF Boyer (eds) *Diagnosis of Depression*, Chichester: Wiley, 92–118.

Love AW (1987) Depression in chronic low back pain patients: Diagnostic efficiency of three self-report questionnaires. *J Clin Psychol*, **43**, 84–89.

Magni G (1987) On the relationship between chronic pain and depression when there is no organic lesion. *Pain*, **31**, 1–21.

Magni G (1991) The use of antidepressants in the treatment of chronic pain: A review of the current evidence. *Drugs*, **42**, 730–748.

Magni G, Caldieron C, Rigatti-Luchini S and Merskey H (1990) Chronic musculoskeletal pain and depressive symptoms in the general population. An analysis of the 1st National Health and Nutrition Examination survey data. *Pain*, **43**, 299–307.

Magni G, Rossi M, Rigatti-Luchini S and Merskey H (1992) Chronic abdominal pain and depression. Epidemiologic findings in the United States. Hispanic Health and Nutrition Examination Survey. *Pain*, **49**, 77–85.

Magni G, Marchetti M, Moreschi C, Merskey H and Rigatti-Luchini S (1993) Chronic musculoskeletal pain and depressive symptoms in the National Health and Nutrition Examination. I. Epidemiological follow-up study. *Pain*, **53**, 163–168.

Magni G, Moreschi C, Rigatti-Luchini S and Merskey H (1994) Prospective study on the relationship between depressive symptoms and chronic musculoskeletal pain. *Pain*, **56**, 389–397.

Main CJ and Waddell G (1991) A comparison of cognitive measures in low back pain: Statistical validity at initial assessment. *Pain*, **46**, 287–298.

Malone MD and Strube MJ (1988) Meta-analysis of non-medical treatments for chronic pain. *Pain*, **34**, 231–244.

Manna V, Bolino F and Di Cicco L (1994) Chronic ternsion-type headache, mood depression and serotonin. Therapeutic effects of fluvoxamine and mianserin. *Headache*, **34**, 44–49.

Marback JJ, Schleifer SJ and Keller SE (1990) Facial pain, distress, and immune function. *Brain Behav Immun*, **4**, 243–254.

Martinez JE, Ferraz MB, Fontana AM and Atra E (1995) Psychological aspects of Brazilean women with fibromyalgia. *J Psychosom Res*, **39**, 167–174.

Maruta T, Vatterot MK and McHardy MJ (1989) Pain management as an antidepressant: Long-term resolution of pain-associated depression. *Pain*, **36**, 335–337.

Max MB (1995) Antidepressant drugs as treatments for chronic pain: Efficacy and mechanisms. In: B Bromm and J Desmedt (eds). *Advances in Pain Research and Therapy*, (vol. 22), New York: Raven Press, 501–515.

Max MB, Kishore-Kumar R, Schafer SC, Meister B, Gracely RH, Smoller B and Dubner R (1991) Efficacy of desipramine in painful diabetic neuropathy: A placebo-controlled trial. *Pain*, **45**, 3–9.

Max MB, Lynch SA, Muir J, Shoaf SE, Smoller B and Dubner R (1992) Effects of desipramine, amitriptyline, and fluoxetine on pain in diabetic neuropathy. *N Engl J Med*, **326**, 1250–1256.

McQuay HJ, Carroll D and Glynn CJ (1992) Low dose amitriptyline in the treatment of chronic pain. *Anaesthesia*, **47**, 646–652.

McQuay HJ, Carroll D and Glynn CJ (1993) Dose-response for analgesic effect of amitriptyline in chronic pain. *Anaesthesia*, **48**, 281–285.

Melzack R and Wall PD (1965) Pain mechanisms: A new theory. *Science*, **150**, 971–979.

Menkes DB, Fawcett JP, Busch AF and Jones D (1995) Moclobemide in chronic neuropathic pain: Preliminary case report. _Clin J Pain_, **11**, 134–138.

Merikangas KR, Risch NJ, Merikangas JR, Weissman MM and Kidd KK (1988) Migraine and depression: Association and familial transmission. _J Psychiatr Res_, **22**, 119–129.

Merskey H (1965) The characteristics of persistent pain in psychological illness. _J Psychosom Res_, **9**, 291–298.

Merskey H (1986) Classification of chronic pain: Description of chronic pain syndromes and definitions of chronic pain terms. _Pain_, **suppl 3**, S1–S225.

Merskey H (1994) Pain and psychological medicine. In: PD Wall and R Melzack (eds). _Textbook of Pain_ (3rd edn), Edinburgh: Churchill Livingstone, 903–922.

Monks R (1994) Psychotropic drugs. In: PD Wall and R Melzack (eds). _Textbook of Pain_ (3rd edn), Edinburgh: Churchill Livingstone, 963–989.

Nøregaard J, Volkmann H and Danneskiold-Samsøe B (1995) A randomized controlled trial of citalopram in the treatment of fibromyalgia. _Pain_, **61**, 445–449.

Novy DM, Nelson DV, Francis DT and Turk DC (1995a) Perspectives of chronic pain: An evaluative comparison of restrictive and comprehensive models. _Psychol Bull_, **118**, 238–247.

Novy DM, Nelson DV, Berry LA and Averill PM (1995b) What does the Beck Inventory measure in chronic pain? A reappraisal. _Pain_, **61**, 261–270.

Onghena P and Van Houdenhove B (1992) Antidepressant-induced analgesia: A meta-analysis of 39 placebo-controlled studies. _Pain_, **49**, 205–219.

Onghena P and Van Houdenhove B (1993) Meta-analysis of placebo-controlled double-blind trials on antidepressant-induced analgesia in chronic pain: A reply to Richardson and Williams. _Pain_, **52**, 248–249.

Onghena P, De Cuyper H, Van Houdenhove B and Verstraeten D (1993) Mianserin and chronic pain: A double-blind placebo-controlled process and outcome study. _Acta Psychiatr Scand_, **88**, 198–204.

Osmond H, Mullaly R and Bisbee C (1984) The pain of depression compared with physical pain. _Practitioner_, **228**, 849–853.

Panerai AE, Monza G, Movilia P, Bianchi M, Francucci BM and Tiengo M (1990) A randomized, within-patient, cross-over, placebo-controlled trial on the efficacy and tolerability of the tricyclic antidepressants chlorimipramine and nortriptyline in central pain. _Acta Neurol Scand_, **82**, 34–38.

Parker J, Smarr K, Angelone E, Mothersead P, Lee B, Walter S, Bridges A and Caldwell C (1992) Psychological factors, immunological activation and disease activity in rheumatoid arthritis. _Arthritis Care Res_, **5**, 196–201.

Payne TC, Leavitt F, Garron DC, Katz RS, Golden HE, Glickman PB and Vanderplate C (1982) Fibrositis and psychologic disturbance. _Arthritis Rheum_, **25**, 213–217.

Pilowsky I and Barrow CG (1990) A controlled study of psychotherapy and amitriptyline used individually and in combination in the treatment of chronic intractable, "psychogenic" pain. _Pain_, **40**, 3–19.

Pilowsky I, Spence N, Rounsefell B, Forsten C and Soda J (1995) Out-patient cognitive–behavioural therapy with amitriptyline for chronic non-malignant pain: A comparative study with 6-month follow-up, _Pain_, **60**, 49–54.

Pincus T and Callahan LF (1993) Depression scales in rheumatoid arthritis: Criterion contamination in interpretation of patient responses. _Patient Educ Couns_, **20**, 133–143.

Potter RG and Jones JM (1992) The evolution of chronic pain among patients with musculoskeletal problems: A pilot study in primary care. _Br J Gen Pract_, **42**, 462–464.

Rajalla U, Keinönen-Kiukaaniemi S, Uusimöki A and Kivelö SL (1995) Musculoskeletal pains and depression in a middle-aged Finnish population. _Pain_, **61**, 451–457.

Revenson TA, Schiaffino KM, Majerovitz SD and Gibofsky A (1991) Social support as a double-edged sword: The relation of positive and problematic support to depression among rheumatoid arthritis patients. *Soc Sci Med*, **33**, 807–813.

Richardson PH and Williams AC (1993) Meta-analysis of antidepressant-induced analgesia in chronic pain: Comment. *Pain*, **52**, 247.

Romano JM and Turner JA (1985) Chronic pain and depression: Does the evidence support a relationship? *Psychol Bull*, **97**, 18–34.

Roy R (1982) Many faces of depression in patients with chronic pain. *Int J Psychiatr Med*, **12**, 109–119.

Roy R (1986) A psychosocial perspective on chronic pain and depression in the elderly. *Soc Work Health Care*, **12**, 27–36.

Roy R, Thomas M and Berger S (1990) A comparative study of Canadian nonclinical and British pain clinic subjects. *Clin J Pain*, **6**, 276–283.

Rudy TE, Kerns RD and Turk DC (1988) Chronic pain and depression: Toward a cognitive–behavioural mediation model. *Pain*, **35**, 129–140.

Schors R (1990) Die depressive Symptomatik bei psychosomatischem Schmerzsyndrom. *Fortschr Med*, **108**, 613–615.

Schwartz L, Slater MA, Birchler GR and Atkinson JH (1991) Depression in spouses of chronic pain patients: The role of patient pain and anger, and marital satisfaction. *Pain*, **44**, 61–67.

Scudds RA, Rollman GB, Harth M and McCain GA (1987) Pain perception and personality measures as discriminators in the classification of fibrositis. *J Rheumatol*, **14**, 563–569.

Sharav Y, Singer E, Schmidt E, Dionne RA and Dubner R (1991) The analgesic effect of amitriptyline in chronic facial pain. *Pain*, **31**, 199–209.

Sindrup SH, Gram LF, Brøsen K, Eshøj O and Mogensen EF (1990a) The selective serotonin reuptake inhibitor paroxetine is effective in the treatment of diabetic neuropathy symptoms. *Pain*, **42**, 134–144.

Sindrup SH, Gram LF, Skjold T, Grodum E, Brøsen K and Beck-Nielsen H (1990b) Clomipramine vs. desipramine vs. placebo in the treatment of diabetic neuropathy symptoms: A double-blind cross-over study. *Br J Clin Pharmacol*, **30**, 683–691.

Sindrup SH, Bjerre U, Dejgaard A, Brøsen K, Aaes-Jørgensen T and Gram LF (1992a) The selective serotonin reuptake inhibitor citalopram relieves the symptoms of diabetic neuropathy. *Clin Pharmacol Ther*, **52**, 547–552.

Sindrup SH, Tuxen C, Gram LF, Grodum E, Skjold T, Brøsen K and Beck-Nielsen H (1992b) Lack of effect of mianserin on the symptoms of diabetic neuropathy. *Eur J Clin Pharmacol*, **43**, 251–255.

Skevington SM (1993) The relationship between pain and depression: A longitudinal study of early synovitis. In: GF Gebhart, DL Hammond and TS Jensen (eds). *Progress in Pain Research and Management* (Proceedings of the 7th World Congress on Pain, vol 2) Seattle: IASP Press, 201–210.

Smith R (1990) Headache and depression. *J Fam Pract*, **31**, 357–358.

Smith GR (1992) The epidemiology and treatment of depression when it coexists with somatoform disorders, somatization, or pain. *Gen Hosp Psychiatry*, **14**, 265–272.

Smith TW, Christensen AJ, Peck JR and Ward JR (1994a) Cognitive distortion, helplessness, and depressed mood in rheumatoid arthritis. *Health Psychol*, **13**, 213–217.

Smith TW, O'Keeffe JL and Christensen AJ (1994b) Cognitive distortion and depression in chronic pain: Association with diagnosed disorders. *J Consult Clin Psychol*, **62**, 195–198.

Snelling J (1994) The effect of chronic pain on the family unit. *J Adv Nurs*, **19**, 543–551.

Solomon P and Tunks E (1991) The role of litigation in predicting disability outcomes in chronic pain patients. *Clin J Pain*, **7**, 300–304.

Srikiathkachorn A (1991) Epidemiology of headache in the Thai elderly: A study in the Bangkae Home for the Aged. *Headache*, **31**, 677–681.

Sternbach RA (1974) *Pain Patients: Traits and Treatment*. New York: Academic Press.

Stevens VM, Peterson RA and Maruta T (1988) Changes in perception of illness and psychological adjustment: Findings of a pain management program. *Clin J Pain*, **4**, 249–256.

Strong J, Ashton R and Large RG (1994a) Function and the patient with chronic low back pain. *Clin J Pain*, **10**, 191–196.

Strong J, Ashton R and Stewart A (1994b) Chronic low back pain: Toward an integrated psychosocial assessment model. *J Consult Clin Psychol*, **62**, 1058–1063.

Sullivan MJL and D'Eon JL (1990) Relation between catastrophizing and depression in chronic pain patients. *J Abnorm Psychol*, **99**, 260–263.

Sullivan MJL, Reesor K, Mikail S and Fisher R (1992) The treatment of depression in chronic low back pain: Review and recommendations. *Pain*, **50**, 5–13.

Tait RC, Chibnall JT and Margolis RB (1990) Pain extent: Relations with psychological state, pain severity, pain history, and disability. *Pain*, **41**, 295–301.

Tanum L (1993) The effect of mianserin in chronic idiopathic abdominal pain: A pilot study. *Nord J Psychiatry*, **47**, 351–354.

Taylor ML, Throtter DR and Csuka ME (1995) The prevalence of sexual abuse in women with fibromyalgia. *Arthritis Rheum*, **38**, 229–234.

Tota-Faucette ME, Gil KM, Williams DA, Keefe FJ and Goli V (1993) Predictors of response to pain management treatment. The role of the family. *Clin J Pain*, **9**, 115–123.

Tschannen TA, Duckro PN, Margolis RB and Tamazic TJ (1992) The relationship of anger, depression and perceived disability among headache patients. *Headache*, **32**, 501–503.

Turk DC and Okifuji A (1994) Detecting depression in chronic pain patients: The adequacy of self-reports. *Behav Ther*, **32**, 9–16.

Turk DC and Salovey P (1984) Chronic pain as a variant of depressive disease: A critical reappraisal. *J Nerv Ment Dis*, **172**, 398–404.

Turk DC, Okifuji A and Scharff L (1995) Chronic pain and depression: Role of perceived impact and perceived control in different age cohorts. *Pain*, **61**, 93–101.

Turner JA and Clancy S (1986) Strategies for coping with low-back pain: Relationship to pain and disability. *Pain*, **24**, 355–363.

Turner JA and Denny MC (1993) Do antidepressant medications relieve chronic low back pain? *J Fam Pract*, **37**, 545–553.

Turner JA and Romano JM (1984) Self-report screening measures for depression in chronic pain patients. *J Clin Psychol*, **40**, 909–913.

Tversky J, Reade PC, Gerschman IA, Holwill BJ and Wright J (1991) Role of depressive illness in the outcome of treatment of temporomandibular joint pain-dysfunction syndrome. *Oral Surg Oral Med Oral Pathol*, **71**, 696–699.

Valdes M, Garcia L, Tressera J, de Pablo J and de Flores T (1989) Psychogenic pain and depression disorders: An empirical study. *J Affect Dis*, **16**, 21–25.

Van Houdenhove B (1987) Prevalence and psychodynamic interpretation of premorbid hyperactivity in patients with chronic pain. *Psychother Psychosom*, **45**, 195–200.

Van Houdenhove B (1991) Interpersonal and psychodynamic links between pain and depression. *Eur J Psychiatry*, **5**, 177–185.

Van Houdenhove B and Joostens P (1995) Burning mouth syndrome: Successful treatment with sertraline and psychotherapy. *Gen Hosp Psychiatry*, **17**, 385–388.

Van Houdenhove B, Verstraeten D, Onghena P and De Cuyper H (1992) Chronic idiopathic pain, mianserin and "masked" depression. *Psychother Psychosom*, **58**, 46–53.

Varma VK, Chaturvedi SK, Malhotra A and Chari P (1991) Psychiatric symptoms in patients with non-organic intractable pain. *Indian J Med Res,* **94**, 60–63.

Vimpari SS, Knuuttila MLE, Sakki TK and Kivelä SL (1995) Depressive symptoms associated with symptoms of the temporomandibular joint pain and dysfunction syndrome. *Psychosom Med,* **57**, 439–444.

Violon A (1980) The onset of facial pain. A psychological study. *Psychother Psychosom,* **35**, 11–16.

Volk RJ, Pace TM and Parchman ML (1993) Screening for depression in primary care patients: Dimensionality of the short form of the Beck Depression Inventory. *Psychol Assess,* **5**, 173–181.

von Knorring L (1975) The experience of pain in depressed patients: A clinical and experimental study. *Neuropsychobiology,* **1**, 155–165.

von Knorring L and Ekselius L (1994) Idiopathic pain and depression. *Qual Life Res,* **3**, 57–68.

Von Korff M, Le Resche L and Dworkin SF (1993) First onset of common pain symptoms: A prospective study of depression as a risk factor. *Pain,* **55**, 251–258.

Wade JB, Price DD, Hamer RM, Schwartz SM and Hart RP (1990) An emotional component analysis of chronic pain. *Pain,* **40**, 303–310.

Wade JB, Dougherty LM, Hart RP, Rafini A and Pride DD (1992) A canonical correlation analysis of the influence of neuroticism and extraversion on chronic pain, suffering, and pain behavior. *Pain,* **51**, 67–73.

Wall PD and Melzack R (eds) (1994) *Textbook of Pain* (3rd edn). Edinburgh: Churchill Livingstone.

Ward NG, Turner JA, Ready B and Bigos S (1992) Chronic pain, depression, and the dexamethasone suppression test. *Pain,* **48**, 331–338.

Watson D and Pennebaker JW (1989) Health complaints, stress and distress: Exploring the role of negative affectivity. *Psychol Rev,* **96**, 233–254.

Watt-Watson JH, Evans RJ and Watson CPN (1988) Relationships among responses and perceptions of pain intensity, depression and family functioning. *Clin J Pain,* **4**, 101–106.

Weickgenant AL, Slater MA, Patterson TL, Atkinson JH, Grant I and Garfin SR (1993) Coping activities in chronic low back pain: Relationship with depression. *Pain,* **53**, 95–103.

Wesley AL, Gatche RJ, Polatin PB, Kinney RK and Mayer TG (1991) Differentiation between somatic and cognitive/affective components in commonly used measurements of depression in patients with chronic low-back pain. Let's not mix apples and oranges. *Spine,* **16**, 213–215.

Williams AC and Richardson PH (1993) What does the BDI measure in chronic pain? *Pain,* **55**, 259–266.

Williams DA, Robinson ME and Geisser ME (1994) Pain beliefs: Assessment and utility. *Pain,* **59**, 71–78.

Williamson GM and Schultz R (1992) Physical illness and symptoms of depression among elderly outpatients. *Psychol Aging,* **7**, 343–351.

Zelman DC, Howland EW, Nichols SN and Cleeland CS (1991) The effects of induced mood on laboratory pain. *Pain,* **46**, 105–111.

Zitman FG, Linssen ACG, Edelbroek PM and Stijnen T (1990) Low dose amitriptyline in chronic pain: The gain is modest. *Pain,* **42**, 35–42.

25

Depression and chronic fatigue syndrome

Matthew Hotopf and Simon Wessely

INTRODUCTION

Whilst unitary biomedical explanations for chronic fatigue syndrome (CFS) remain elusive, the evidence for a significance relationship between fatigue, CFS, and psychiatric disorder is remarkably consistent. The relationship appears worth investigating in more depth for several reasons: firstly, a keener understanding of the relationship between CFS and depression may give insight into causal and perpetuating factors in the illness. Secondly, there is growing evidence that comorbid psychiatric disorder is a poor prognostic indicator in many physical illnesses. If CFS is associated with high levels of psychiatric morbidity for any reason it may be possible to improve quality of life and prognosis in sufferers by treating the psychiatric disorder. Thirdly, although new treatments for CFS are being assessed, and some seem promising, they are not widely available, in contrast to treatments for depression. Finally, suicide is the only known fatal complication of CFS.

The history of CFS has been dominated by the often acrimonious debate on the contribution of physical versus psychological factors in aetiology (Wessely, 1990, 1991) This problem is not specific to CFS but is frequently faced by doctors dealing with patients who present with medically unexplained symptoms (Goldberg and Bridges, 1988). Although the association between

Depression and Physical Illness. Edited by M.M. Robertson and C.L.E. Katona
© 1997 John Wiley & Sons Ltd

such presentations and psychiatric morbidity is strong, patients may resist such explanations. Psychiatry is often misunderstood in this setting. Sufferers (and occasionally doctors) may think psychological explanations trivialize their symptoms or imply they are malingering. Some of the unease shown by sufferers towards psychological explanations reflects the general stigma of psychiatric disorders. This stigma is partly due to the widely held view that those suffering from psychiatric disorders are personally culpable in a way which separates them from sufferers of most physical diseases.

In the clinical setting it is necessary to be aware of these prejudices since they may deny patients effective treatment for depression (Royal Colleges of Physicians, Psychiatrists and General Practitioners, 1996).

In this chapter we review the epidemiology of fatigue and CFS before discussing evidence for an association between CFS and depression and other psychiatric disorders. We then discuss clinical assessment and treatment of sufferers from CFS who have depression. This review is based on a literature search using Medline and Index Medicus, and extensive cross-referencing.

EPIDEMIOLOGY AND DEFINITIONS

Fatigue, as well as being the principal symptom of CFS, is a universal experience. In order to gain an understanding of the epidemiology of CFS it is necessary to describe the epidemiology of fatigue (Lewis and Wessely, 1992). Fatigue is a subjective experience. Previous attempts to quantify fatigue using "objective" measures have proved unsuccessful (Muscio, 1921). The study of fatigue must rely upon the self-report of patients.

Community and primary care surveys (Pawlikowska et al., 1994; David et al., 1990) have demonstrated that severity of fatigue follows a normal distribution within the population (Figure 1). Relatively few individuals report no fatigue in the preceding week and there is no "point of rarity" in the distribution, which might indicate that a subgroup of distinct, severely affected sufferers existed. When asked about the cause of fatigue, most individuals suggest it is due to commonplace stressors such as caring for young children or poor sleep (David et al., 1990; Pawlikowska et al., 1994; Lawrie and Pelosi, 1995).

The definition of fatigue may be tightened to include only those individuals in whom it becomes a problem: either due to its severity, persistence, or interference in everyday life. In a community survey which used the Revised Clinical Interview Schedule (Lewis et al., 1992) on nearly 10 000 individuals, fatigue was the most common of 12 psychological symptoms to be experienced (Meltzer et al., 1995). Similarly, in the American Epidemiologic Catchment Area (ECA) study the lifetime prevalence for fatigue diagnosed on the Diagnostic Interview Schedule (DIS) (Robin et al., 1981) was 23.6% making it one of the top 10 most common physical symptoms (Walker et al., 1993). These high levels of

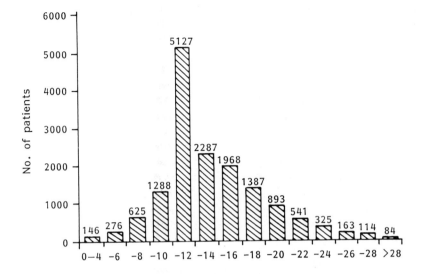

Figure 1. Frequency distribution of fatigue scores (from Pawlikowska *et al.*, 1994). Reproduced with permission from BMJ Publishing Group.

fatigue are witnessed across cultures: it is one of the commonest symptoms in British, French, Algerian, Swedish and Taiwanese populations (Lewis and Wessely, 1992).

If the definition of fatigue is narrowed to cases who present to doctors it remains common. In one study of fatigue in primary care 6.7% of patients presented with this as the main complaint leading to consultation (Cathebras *et al.*, 1992). Patients who consult their general practitioner (GP) for other reasons report high levels of troublesome fatigue when asked directly. Approximately one-quarter to one-third of all GP attenders (Bates *et al.*, 1993; Kroenke *et al.*, 1988) report fatigue when directly asked. In the community and primary care samples, an association has been noted between female gender (David *et al.*, 1990; Kroenke *et al.*, 1988), lower socioeconomic status (Lawrie and Pelosi, 1995) and fatigue.

Chronic fatigue is often defined as fatigue above a certain level of severity which is present for a period of 6 months or more and which is not explained by physical disease. Rates in most epidemiological studies are consistent at 10–19% of the adult population suffering (David *et al.*, 1990; Lawrie and Pelosi, 1995; Pawlikowska *et al.*, 1994; Buchwald *et al.*, 1995).

CFS is defined as chronic fatigue after minimal exertion which becomes disabling by interfering in the sufferer's life. There are now three main definitions, summarized in Table 1 (Sharpe *et al.*, 1991; Fukuda *et al.*, 1994; Lloyd *et*

Table 1. Case definitions for chronic fatigue syndrome.

	Minimum duration (months)	Functional impairment	Cognitive/ neuropsychiatric symptoms	Other symptoms	New onset	Medical exclusions	Psychiatric exclusions
CDC-1988	6	50% decrease in activity	May be present	6 of 8 required	Required	Extensive list of known physical causes	Psychosis, bipolar disorder, substance abuse
CDC-1994	6	Substantial	May be present	4 of 8 required	Required	Clinically important	Melancholic depression, substance abuse, bipolar disorder, psychosis, eating disorders
Australian	6	Substantial	Required	Not specified	Not required	Known physical causes	Psychosis, bipolar disorder, substance abuse, eating disorders
UK	6	Disabling	Mental fatigue required	Not specified	Required	Known physical causes	Psychosis, bipolar disorder, eating disorders, organic brain disease

al., 1990). In this chapter we shall use the British consensus definition (Sharpe *et al.,* 1991) unless otherwise specified. These criteria require debilitating fatigue with a clear onset to have been present for 6 months at least 50% of the time. The British definition does not require the presence of additional physical symptoms, such as myalgia, but suggests that such symptoms are typical. Some psychiatric disorders may preclude the diagnosis, including psychosis, eating disorders and substance abuse; however, depression is no longer excluded. The principal difference between the current American definition and the British one is that the former requires the presence of additional physical symptoms. Clinical descriptions of CFS include an exhaustive range of somatic symptoms affecting practically every bodily system.

Early prevalence studies in CFS were based on recognized cases. An Australian survey indicated a prevalence of 0.37% and a Scottish report showed an overall prevalence of 0.115%. The doctors surveyed in the Scottish report had disparate rates of CFS ranging from 1/60 to 1/10 000 (or even lower, since some doctors reported no cases). This variation almost certainly indicated the enthusiasm (or lack of it) with which doctors applied this relatively novel diagnosis. Subsequent studies which have directly surveyed subjects in epidemiological samples have estimated rates of CFS varying between 0.07 and 1.8% depending on the criteria used (Bates *et al.,* 1993; Lawrie and Pelosi, 1995; Wessely *et al.,* 1997; Buchwald *et al.,* 1995). These rates are an order of magnitude higher than those estimated using physicians as key informants. It is likely that this difference is due to many true cases going unrecognized by doctors and sufferers alike: indeed, in a community-based study of chronic fatigue, only 1% of sufferers from chronic fatigue thought they had CFS (Pawlikowska *et al.,* 1994), and only 12% of those with CFS apply the term to describe their illness (Euba *et al.,* 1996).

DISABILITY AND FATIGUE

Patients presenting to their doctor with complaints of fatigue attend more frequently than those without fatigue (Risdale *et al.,* 1994) despite the fact that the vast majority have normal investigations (Lane *et al.,* 1990; Valdini *et al.,* 1989). Patients who present to their doctors with complaints of fatigue are more likely to attribute their symptoms to physical causes than psychosocial ones when they are compared to patients with similar levels of fatigue who have not consulted (Nelson *et al.,* 1987). Because fatigue is a common and nonspecific symptom, it is not recognized as worrying by most doctors, whereas patients see it as troublesome (Dohrenwend and Crandell, 1970). There are grounds to suggest that fatigue is a particularly disabling symptom. For example, the symptom of fatigue can be as disabling as many severe physical illnesses (Kroenke *et al.,* 1988; Fisk *et al.,* 1994; Wessely *et al.,* 1995b).

Indeed, functional incapacity in CFS may be even worse than that caused by many physical diseases with clear biomedical aetiologies (Wessely *et al.*, 1997).

Fatigue appears to be an especially disabling symptom for individuals with physical illnesses. For example, most individuals suffering from Parkinson's disease rate fatigue as one of the three most troublesome symptoms (Friedman and Friedman, 1993). This study found that fatigue was more strongly predicted by depressive symptoms than Parkinson's symptom severity. Similar results have been reported in patients with systemic lupus erythematosus who seem prone to fatigue when they become depressed (McKinley *et al.*, 1995).

PSYCHIATRIC DISORDER AND FATIGUE

The previous sections have emphasized a dimensional view of fatigue. In ascertaining the relationship between CFS and psychiatric disorder it is necessary to recognize that only a small proportion of people who suffer from fatigue as a symptom meet diagnostic criteria for CFS, and only a minority of patients with CFS are seen in specialist settings. Studies which assess levels of psychiatric morbidity in secondary or tertiary care patients with CFS may be subject to selection bias, It is therefore necessary to assess evidence for a relationship between fatigue and psychiatric disorder in the community.

A recent survey (Pawlikowska *et al.*, 1994) of 15 283 subjects treated both fatigue and psychological distress as dimensions and found a correlation of 0.6 between scores on a fatigue questionnaire (Chalder *et al.*, 1993) and the General Health Questionnaire (GHQ (Goldberg, 1972)) (see Figure 2). This

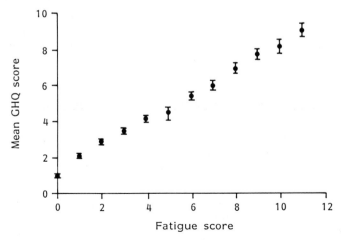

Figure 2. Mean and 95% confidence interval score for GHQ according to fatigue score (from Pawlikowska *et al.*, 1994). Reproduced with permission from BMJ Publishing Group.

correlation has been replicated in another study which used a different fatigue questionnaire (Lawrie and Pelosi, 1995). This relationship appears to span all severities of fatigue.

If fatigue and psychiatric disorder are treated as categories the relationship remains. In the ECA study (Walker *et al.*, 1993), individuals who met criteria for symptomatic fatigue on the DIS had increased rates of depression (odds ratio 14.7 for men and 6.3 for women), dysthymia (odds ratio 10.2 for men and 5.9 for women) and somatization disorder (odds ratio 24.9 for men and 13.4 for women (NB very wide confidence intervals since only very few cases of somatization disorder were identified)). Subjects who reported fatigue were more likely to report other medical symptoms and the female fatigue sufferers were higher users of medical services.

What is the rate of psychiatric disorder among fatigued patients in primary care settings? It has been demonstrated (Gerber *et al.*, 1992) that the complaint of fatigue and sleep disturbance are the two strongest indicators of underlying depression in primary care. Similarly, patients presenting with complaints of fatigue are more likely to have current or lifetime diagnoses of depression than their nonfatigued counterparts (Cathebras *et al.*, 1992). If patients in primary care are screened for fatigue the relationship holds. One primary care study (Kroenke *et al.*, 1988) found that 80% of those with significant fatigue scored above threshold on a depression questionnaire. A similar British study found that 72% of 65 cases met ICD-9 criteria for psychiatric disorder (McDonald *et al.*, 1993). Finally a recent study (Euba *et al.*, 1995) has compared patients with CFS drawn from a community sample and those seen in tertiary care. Rates of psychological distress were similar in both groups, but in the hospital group people from higher socioeconomic class and those who believed their illness had physical origins were over-represented. The studies indicate a strong relationship between symptomatic fatigue and psychological distress and suggest that the high rates of depression seen in CFS are not due to selection bias.

FATIGUE AS A SYMPTOM OF DEPRESSION

Psychiatrists have long recognized fatigue as an important symptom of depression (Stoeckle and Davidson, 1962). In both DSM-IV (American Psychiatric Association, 1994) and ICD-10 (World Health Organization, 1992) fatigue is one of the constituent symptoms of major depressive disorder. It is therefore not surprising to find that "weakness", fatigue, daytime drowsiness, and impaired concentration are some of the commonest symptoms of depressed patients (Matthew *et al.*, 1981; Coulehan *et al.*, 1988). We have traced over 25 studies of the somatic symptoms of depression and found that fatigue is invariably in the top five most common symptoms. A variety of physical symptoms of uncertain origin, such as headaches and dizziness, are very common in depression, and these symptoms also occur frequently in CFS.

The symptom of fatigue appears to predict the onset of depression. The ECA study (Dryman and Eaton, 1991) followed individuals suffering from various symptoms over 1 year, and demonstrated that the complaint of fatigue was associated with onset of depression (odds ratio 2.6 for women and 6.8 for men). A community-based study (Dew *et al.*, 1988) compared patients with depression who had sought help and those who had not. It was found that fatigue, physical symptoms, and sleep disorder were commoner in those who had consulted.

DEPRESSION AND CFS

The relationship between CFS and depression has been reviewed elsewhere (David, 1991). Uncontrolled studies or those which used normal controls (Kruesi *et al.*, 1989; Hickie *et al.*, 1990; Manu *et al.*, 1988, 1989; Gold *et al.*, 1990; Taerk *et al.*, 1987) found high rates of depression and other psychiatric disorders and CFS. These studies could not rule out the possibility that depression was a consequence of experiencing disabling physical symptoms. Subsequent case-control studies (Wessely and Powell, 1989; Katon *et al.*, 1991; Wood *et al.*, 1991, 1994; Pepper *et al.*, 1993) have compared CFS sufferers with patients suffering chronic physical ailments such as rheumatoid arthritis or neuromuscular disorders. These studies are remarkably consistent. Rates of psychiatric disorder are considerably higher in CFS than in physical diseases with about two-thirds of sufferers from CFS having psychiatric disorder and the majority of these suffering from affective disorders. The remainder have a mixture of anxiety and somatoform disorders.

In attempting to investigate possible overlap between the experience of fatigue in those patients with neuromuscular disorders and those with CFS, Wessely and Powell (1989) discriminated between central and peripheral fatigue. Central fatigue relates to difficulties with mental functioning such as attention and concentration, whereas peripheral fatigue relates to post-exertional fatigue and difficulties with locomotor function. Wessely and Powell found that patients with CFS had high levels of peripheral and central fatigue, whereas those with neuromuscular disorder suffered from peripheral fatigue but only complained of central fatigue if they had depression as well. Finally, when compared to patients with depression, those with CFS have similar levels of peripheral and central fatigue. These findings suggest that the experience of central and peripheral fatigue may involve different mechanisms, and that individuals with CFS may have the same mechanism as those with depression. Hence the symptom of effortful cognition, common to both CFS and depression, may reflect common neurobiological processes.

Despite these high levels of depression many patients with CFS who are seen in secondary care are reluctant to accept psychological factors as a possible cause of their fatigue. Powell *et al.* (1990) compared patients with depression and CFS with psychiatric inpatients who had depression alone. They found that despite similar levels of depression the patients with CFS very rarely made psychological attributions or acknowledged their depression. This seemed to protect the depressed CFS patients from feelings of guilt or worthlessness. Thus, in this tertiary care setting, attributing symptoms of CFS to physical problems (in particular viral infections) might protect patients from some of the most unpleasant cognitive symptoms of depression.

DEPRESSION AS A RISK FACTOR

Aetiology

Further evidence for the link between depression and CFS comes from cohort studies which have followed patients after viral illnesses. Although the relationship between viral illness and CFS remains controversial (Hotopf and Wessely, 1994) several studies have demonstrated that previous emotional disorder or high scores on the GHQ are significant predictors of CFS at follow up (Wessely *et al.*, 1995; Hotopf *et al.*, 1996). The studies indicate that some viral illnesses in individuals with previous psychiatric disorder increase their risk of CFS, replicating and extending an early classic study (Imboden *et al.*, 1961).

Prognosis

There have been four studies of prognosis of CFS (Sharpe *et al.*, 1992; Wilson *et al.*, 1994; Clark *et al.*, 1995; Vercoulen *et al.*, 1995). The studies are consistent in demonstrating that psychological factors are of primary importance in determining outcome. Hence three found that life time or current psychiatric disorders predicted poor outcome (Sharpe *et al.*, 1992; Wilson *et al.*, 1994; Clark *et al.*, 1995) and the fourth found a relationship between high self-efficacy and recovery (Vercoulen *et al.*, 1995). It is striking that attributing the illness to viral infection or other physical causes was associated with a poor outcome in three studies (Sharpe *et al.*, 1992; Wilson *et al.*, 1994; Vercoulen *et al.*, 1995). This attribution may be associated with many other beliefs and lead to alterations in life-style: behavioural changes which have also been demonstrated to indicate poor outcome. The finding that depression indicates a poor outcome is not especially surprising. In many physical illnesses, including myocardial infarction (Silverstone, 1990; Frasure-Smith *et al.*, 1993; Ladwig *et al.*, 1994) and back pain (Burton *et al.*, 1995), poor outcome is associated with depression and certain attributional styles. In CFS there is also evidence to suggest that a tendency to "catastrophize" is associated with more disability (Petrie *et al.*, 1994), so the way in which symptoms are interpreted may have a powerful role in the disruption they cause.

EXPLANATIONS FOR THE RELATIONSHIP BETWEEN DEPRESSION AND CFS

Possible explanations for the relationship between CFS and depression have been explored elsewhere (Abbey and Garfinkel, 1991; Ray, 1991; David, 1991; Kendell, 1991). The first and simplest is that they are two categories which consist of similar but not identical overlapping dimensions such as sleep disturbance, poor concentration and fatigue itself. It is perhaps not surprising that the observed overlap exists. In research it has been necessary to adjust definitions of depression so that fatigue is not a main criterion.

Similar points have been made by critics of the concept of CFS who suggest it may be distinguished from "myalgic encephalomyelitis" by the severity of symptoms. It has, for example, been suggested that there is a "true" but rare disease entity which is not associated with depression but has more severe symptoms (Anon, 1993). There is no evidence for this contention: rather the reverse—the more severe the symptoms of CFS, the stronger the association with depression. Thus one epidemiological study (Pawlikowska *et al.*, 1994) showed that the prevalence of psychiatric disorder increased with increasingly restrictive definitions of chronic fatigue. Similarly, an American study (Katon and Russo, 1992) showed that by including multiple physical symptoms in the diagnostic criteria the rate of psychiatric disorder *increases* rather than decreases among sufferers.

The second possibility is that depression is a natural consequence of such a debilitating illness. Although the experience of many CFS sufferers is distressing this is not a sufficient explanation. Studies which have compared rates of depression in CFS and physical illnesses find considerably lower rates in the latter.

Thirdly, the explanation could be that CFS is an atypical "somatized" presentation of depression. Somatization is the process by which psychological distress is translated into physical complaints and is one of the commonest presentations of psychiatric disorder to primary care (Goldberg and Bridges, 1988). The evidence that depressed CFS patients and those with overt depression use different attributions implies that the label of CFS or myalgic encephalomyelitis protects the patient from some of the worst aspects of their underlying depressive illness. The difficulty with this as an explanation is that depression is not invariably present in CFS and there are a large minority of sufferers who have no overt psychiatric disorder.

Finally, some underlying process could be responsible for both depression and CFS. There is evidence for an underactive hypothalamic–pituitary–adrenal (HPA) axis with reduced urinary cortisol, but retained adrenal reactivity to adrenocorticotrophic hormone (ACTH) and raised ACTH levels (Demitrack *et al.*, 1991). These findings suggest a subgroup of sufferers may have alterations of HPA functioning at the level of the hypothalamus. There is also evidence that central serotonergic function is increased in CFS (Bakheit *et al.*, 1992), supported by the finding of increased prolactin responses to d-fenfluramine challenge (Cleare *et al.*, 1995). These findings suggest that the condition may involve alteration of some of the systems classically affected in depression, albeit in the opposite direction, which would be consistent with the hyper-somnia and preserved appetites seen in this group.

Another strand of evidence comes from neuroimaging studies in CFS. The number of studies is small, and it is too soon to reach definite conclusions. MRI studies have found areas of high signal intensity; however, the results of three studies available are inconclusive (Cope *et al.*, 1995; Buchwald *et al.*, 1992; Natelson *et al.*, 1994). One functional neuroimaging study found a substantial increase in defects compared to normal controls. However, there were no striking differences between the pattern of defects in depression and CFS (Schwartz *et al.*, 1994) with changes in both illnesses being confined to the frontal and temporal lobes.

These neurobiological studies are intriguing and might go some way to explain the possible link between depression and CFS. There could be some unknown common factor which causes both. On the other hand, it is feasible that these changes are epiphenomena of some behavioural correlates of both illnesses. For example they could be the neurobiological equivalent of the cardiopulmonary effects of deconditioning or due to the sometimes profound changes in sleep patterns seen in patients with CFS (Buchwald *et al.*, 1994; Morriss *et al.*, 1993).

Whatever the relationship between depression and CFS it is important to avoid making dualistic assumptions about the cause of CFS in individual patients. There are no grounds to suspect, for example, that patients with CFS and no depression have an "organic" form of CFS whereas those with CFS and depression have a "psychogenic" form. Biological factors may play as much a part in the aetiology of CFS with depression as behavioural, social and cultural factors play in the aetiology of CFS without depression.

A MODEL FOR DEPRESSION AND CFS

Whatever mechanisms exist it is clear that depression worsens the prognosis of CFS and may be responsible for maladaptive cognitions, behavioural changes and reduced quality of life. All these factors make depression worth treating in patients with CFS.

Current psychiatric understanding of CFS (Wessely *et al.*, 1989; Surawy *et al.*, 1995) has drawn on cognitive–behavioural models of depression (Beck, 1989) and other psychiatric disorders as well as empirical evidence from longitudinal studies. Models have been devised which describe the onset of the syndrome following some acute event (Surawy *et al.*, 1995; Wessely and Sharpe, 1995). Many patients will describe an acute infection at the onset of their symptoms (Behan and Behan, 1988; Petersen *et al.*, 1991; Wessely and Powell, 1989). Although there is limited evidence from cohort studies that viral infections are responsible, it may be that some patients with a particular attributional style (Cope *et al.*, 1994) or previous psychiatric disorder (Hotopf *et al.*, 1996; Wessely *et al.*, 1995) are most at risk. An initial illness may then lead to the patient entering a vicious circle of inactivity, frustration, resumed activity and relapse, described below.

Inactivity

There is no doubt that rest is helpful for acute fatigue; however, there is no evidence to suggest it plays a helpful part in the management of chronic fatigue, despite the advice commonly given to sufferers. On the contrary, there are physiological grounds to suggest that the extreme inactivity common in CFS has a profound effect on cardiovascular and muscular function (Kottke, 1966; Sharpe and Bass, 1992). Over time, greater levels of inactivity lead to lower exercise tolerance, thereby worsening symptoms.

Not all sufferers are inactive all the time. Another harmful pattern is of inconsistent activity; attempting to do too much too soon. Many clinicians in the field have commented on the somewhat driven perfectionist personality of many sufferers which may lead to extreme bursts of activity following profound inactivity. Again there are sound physiological reasons to suggest that this pattern may lead to worsening of symptoms by causing microtrauma in muscles (Newham, 1988). Thus many patients with CFS may have their worst fears confirmed when attempting exercise.

Cognitions

Some cognitions are associated with a poor prognosis, and are therefore worth challenging during rehabilitation. In particular, the patient with CFS may believe that further exercise will invariably be followed by worsening symptoms, and this is confirmation of the hopelessness of their predicament. In therapy it is necessary to provide a middle ground between the strident perfectionist view that total health involves no symptoms and complete tolerance of activities, and the hopeless view that illness in the form of CFS requires total avoidance of activity.

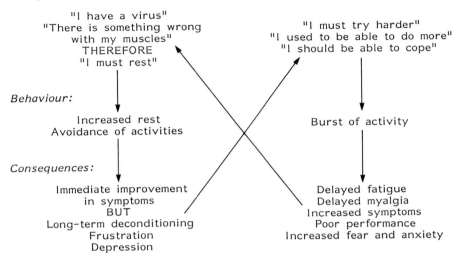

Thoughts:

"I have a virus"
"There is something wrong
with my muscles"
THEREFORE
"I must rest"

"I must try harder"
"I used to be able to do more"
"I should be able to cope"

Behaviour:

Increased rest
Avoidance of activities

Burst of activity

Consequences:

Immediate improvement
in symptoms
BUT
Long-term deconditioning
Frustration
Depression

Delayed fatigue
Delayed myalgia
Increased symptoms
Poor performance
Increased fear and anxiety

Figure 3. A model for the perpetuation of CFS symptoms (adapted from Butler *et al.*, 1991 and Suraway *et al.*, 1995).

Symptom focusing

Once individuals are caught in the vicious circle of inactivity and relapse, it is not surprising that they become more aware of innocent bodily symptoms which others might ignore, seeing them as "warning signals". As concern for these symptoms mounts, they are perceived more readily and tend to confirm maladaptive illness beliefs.

Emotional factors

The model described has some similarities with the influential notion of "learned helplessness" (Seligman, 1974). It is perhaps not surprising that the cycle of inactivity, frustration, resumed activity and relapse leads to such a large proportion suffering from depression (see Figure 3).

ASSESSMENT OF CFS AND DEPRESSION IN CFS SUFFERERS

Referral

Many patients resist referral to a psychiatrist, seeing it as an indication that their symptoms are being trivialized. It is worthwhile establishing close links with colleagues in primary care and medical departments. The ideal solution is a joint clinic where new referrals may be introduced to a psychiatrist in person. Failing this, the physician or GP might explain that the psychiatrist has a special interest in the role of emotional factors and stress in worsening the effects of physical disease.

Engagement

Patients with CFS often have complex histories. It is necessary to arrange a long first appointment (up to 2 hours) to ensure there is time to engage them in therapy. Although some patients with CFS are hostile from the outset when referred to a psychiatrist, it is more common that they are somewhat fearful, but ready to be advised and helped. The best opening gambit is to explain the psychiatrist's role in helping people with CFS and the way in which chronic physical illnesses and physical symptoms are worsened by emotional factors. The next stage is to elicit a careful history of physical symptoms. This serves three purposes; firstly, it reassures the patient that the psychiatrist is capable of listening and taking their symptoms seriously; secondly, it gives the psychiatrist the opportunity to gain insight into the patient's understanding of the cause of the symptoms; and thirdly, it allows the psychiatrist to make links between physical symptoms and life events or emotional distress.

History

Several areas require careful consideration:

Does the patient have a psychiatric diagnosis?

As discussed, depression is common. It may be missed because the patient denies it when asked direct questions regarding mood. Patients may not have negative attributions such as feelings of guilt and worthlessness seen in depression. Anhedonia is a useful clue that patients with CFS may have depression. The biological symptoms of depression are important, but there is commonly an atypical pattern with problems of hypersomnia, weight gain and a reversal of the usual diurnal mood variation with evening worsening of mood. As well as depression, it is important to detect phobic disorders and panic disorder because these are common and may cause special difficulties in rehabilitation. Once again, distinguishing phobic anxiety from lack of energy may not be easy.

What does the patient think are the main causes of his or her symptoms?

Attributions in CFS may predict poor prognosis. If a patient believes that his symptoms are due to a virus which will be reactivated if he exercises, graded exposure to exercise alone is unlikely to be successful, and it will be necessary to challenge some of these cognitions.

In what way have the symptoms affected the patient's life?

Many patients with CFS are seriously restricted by their illness. In its most extreme form they may be bed-bound or unable to perform the simple activities of daily living. In milder cases the patient may have restricted their social life or changed diets. Many patients stop work because of CFS and it is important to gain a full occupational history in order to assess whether there are any factors which seem to reduce their chances of returning to work, for example conflict at work or outstanding compensation issues.

Are there any factors in their personal history which may have contributed to their current illness?

There has been relatively little research into the developmental antecedents of CFS; however, there is increasing evidence to suggest that somatization is more likely in those who have experienced childhood adversity and in particular illness within the family in childhood (Craig *et al.*, 1993). Illness in the individual or his/her relatives may have a special meaning to the patient with CFS.

Who else is the patient seeing for CFS?

Many patients will have seen a wide range of different doctors, which often adds to confusion. It is common for patients to have consulted alternative or "complementary" practitioners, many of whom raise hopes unrealistically high or prescribe countertherapeutic measures. Finally, patients may be involved with one of the self-help charities which may provide emotional support but discourage psychological interventions.

Are there any other obvious perpetuating factors?

Many physiological and psychological processes are likely to be involved in perpetuating the symptoms of CFS. For example, a history of hyperventilation disorder or panic may be responsible for symptoms of fatigue and avoidance. Prolonged inactivity, sleep disorders, and avoidance may all play a part in perpetuating symptoms.

PHYSICAL EXAMINATION AND INVESTIGATIONS

Most physical illnesses may cause fatigue and the differential diagnosis of chronic fatigue includes malignancy, neurological disorders, thyroid disease, electrolyte imbalances (e.g. Addison's disease, hypercalcaemia), chronic infections (tuberculosis, Lyme disease, human immunodeficiency virus (HIV), autoimmune disease (rheumatoid or systemic lupus erythematosus) and sleep apnoea. Whilst the clinician should be aware of these possibilities, they are rarely seen in those suffering from chronic fatigue.

We recommend a routine battery of investigations consisting of full blood count, erythrocyte sedimentation rate, liver function tests, urea and electrolytes, thyroid function tests, and urine protein and sugar. Additional tests, which might be considered if indicated by clinical history or examination, might include: chest X-ray, rheumatoid and antinuclear factors, acetylcholine antibody and serology for the following infectious diseases: Epstein–Barr virus, Lyme disease, brucellosis, Q fever, cytomegalovirus, toxoplasmosis and HIV.

There are some investigations which have enjoyed brief vogues as being "diagnostic", but which have no clinical value: these include enterovirus tests (IgG, IgM, VP-1), lymphocyte subsets, natural killer cell assays and computed tomography, SPECT and MRI scans.

TREATMENT OF CFS AND DEPRESSION

Just as the treatment of depression involves psychological and pharmacological approaches, so too does the treatment of CFS with depression.

Pharmacotherapy

Given the powerful relationship between depression and CFS, it is astonishing that there have been no randomized controlled trials of antidepressants until very recently. What is striking is the burgeoning number of studies on the effects of immunotherapy, antiviral agents, and nutrition. An open study gave encouraging results suggesting that the selective serotonin reuptake inhibitor, sertraline, is effective in the treatment of CFS even in the absence of depression (Behan *et al.*, 1994). This was not replicated in the one controlled antidepressant trial to date (Vercoulen *et al.*, 1995), which showed no advantage of fluoxetine over placebo in treating CFS, despite adequate statistical power. Given this disappointing result, it is not possible to recommend prescribing antidepressants in the absence of depression. Nonetheless, it seems reasonable to give a trial of antidepressants if depression is present.

The choice of antidepressant poses some difficulties as many patients with CFS are especially sensitive to side-effects. Many patients have considerable daytime drowsiness and hypersomnia so sedating antidepressants may not be appropriate. Choice of antidepressant should also be determined by perceived suicide risk.

Tricyclic antidepressants are cheap and effective in depression. Some of the older tricyclics have marked muscarinic side-effects and they are cardiotoxic in overdose. They remain the first choice for patients who are thought to be at low risk of suicide and those with marked sleep disturbance. Doses in CFS should start low (25–50 mg) and be increased gradually to a full dose of 150 mg.

The newer selective serotonin reuptake inhibitors (SSRIs) have the welcome advantage of fewer side-effects and improved safety in overdose. In the treatment of uncomplicated depression, there is no sound evidence to suggest that the considerable excess cost of SSRIs translates into clinical benefits (Hotopf *et al.*, 1996). They are however recommended in the following circumstances:

1. Patients who have a medical contraindication to tricyclic antidepressants.
2. Patients who are thought to be at high risk of suicide (although an alternative is lofepramine).
3. Those who are unable to tolerate a tricyclic antidepressant.

There is some evidence to suggest that the monoamine oxidase inhibitors are especially useful in patients with "atypical" presentations of depression (Bass and Kerwin, 1989) and this presentation is common in CFS.

Psychological treatments

There has been growing interest in psychological treatments for CFS in recent years. This interest has been partly fuelled by the success of cognitive–behavioural therapy (CBT) and behavioural therapies such as problem solving (Wilkinson and Mynors-Wallis, 1994; Mynors-Wallis, 1995) in the treatment of depression and somatoform disorders. Psychological treatments have some specific advantages which make them especially attractive. Theoretically they may have longer lasting benefits and the relapse rate may be less than with antidepressants. Psychological treatments may be preferred by patients in whom there has been growing mistrust of pharmacological treatments.

As in CBT for depression the emphasis of early sessions is educative. If any progress is to be made the patient needs to understand the model given above for CFS and usually the first two or three sessions are given over to explanation and questions. Many patients will have had years of illness and have very set views on CFS.

The next step is to plan activities: this is similar to the notion of graded exposure in the treatment of phobias. A clear account of which activities the patient can and cannot do is necessary. A list of behavioural targets is then set. The aim is to set modest and achievable goals at first and to prohibit sudden increases in activity. As with other behavioural treatments the patient should keep a diary of activities. Activities should be planned and an initial increase in symptoms should be anticipated and explained to the patient. In addition to planned activities, planned rest is important. The aim is to encourage efficient rest which is predetermined and not simply a reaction to symptoms—occasionally it is necessary to reduce some "surges" of activity to ensure consistency at the start of treatment.

These behavioural techniques may be augmented with cognitive strategies aimed at challenging some of the negative automatic thoughts seen in CFS. In particular it may be necessary to challenge the belief that health is a symptomless state and anything less than this is evidence of disease. This idealized notion of health is often allied to a view that the sufferer's health before the onset of symptoms was perfect and that anything short of a complete recovery is useless. If the patient suffers from depression this may be treated along conventional lines.

Additional behavioural techniques for specific difficulties are worth mentioning. Sleep disorder is often a prominent problem and there are several effective nonpharmacological techniques available (Morin *et al.*, 1994). The patient is encouraged to use their bed only for sleep, to get out of bed if sleep does not come within 20 minutes, to go to bed at the same time each night and to avoid stimulants such as caffeine before bedtime. Problem solving is a structured behavioural technique aimed at identifying and overcoming difficulties, by setting achievable goals. CFS affects all aspects of an individual's functioning, and during recovery it is necessary to tackle these: for example, return to social or occupational roles may require specific help.

ASSESSING PSYCHOLOGICAL TREATMENTS

The first published report described an open trial of cognitive–behaviour therapy (CBT) for CFS and showed encouraging results in those who completed the active treatment (Butler *et al.*, 1991). The first true randomized controlled trial (Lloyd *et al.*, 1993) was less encouraging, showing no sustained benefit in the treated group. This study has been criticized because the treatment was brief. A subsequent study (Friedberg and Krupp, 1994) also showed only modest benefits. Two subsequent randomized controlled trials have been completed in London (Deale *et al.*, 1997) and Oxford (Sharpe *et al.*, 1996) which used cognitive and behavioural approaches. The results of these studies are more encouraging: in Sharpe *et al.*, 22/30 patients on active treatment had a good outcome (i.e. return to normal functioning at 1 year) compared with only 7/30 on the inactive ("routine care") treatment (P < 0.001). Deale *et al.* were able to demonstrate similar improvement in functional capacity and fatigue scores over 1 year follow up and a distinct advantage over the placebo treatment, relaxation. It is likely that the differences in results of the early studies and later ones may be due to longer treatment, longer duration of follow up and more stringently applied therapy; however, there is little to say what the "active ingredient" of therapies may be. Fortunately, compliance is good and side-effects are very rare.

SUMMARY

In this chapter we have attempted to review current understanding on the relationship between CFS and depression. There is overwhelming evidence from research that rates of psychiatric disorder in general and depression in particular are high in CFS, although the exact mechanism underlying this relationship remains elusive. There have been exciting advances in the treatment of CFS which owe much to established treatments in depression. It is hoped that future research into the epidemiology, neurobiology and treatment of CFS will further improve the outlook for frequently misunderstood and disabled patients.

ACKNOWLEDGEMENT

Dr Hotopf is supported by a Medical Research Council Clinical Training Fellowship.

REFERENCES

Abbey SE and Garfinkel PE (1991) Chronic fatigue syndrome and depression: Cause effect or covariate? *Rev Infect Dis*, **13 (suppl 1)**, S73–S83.

American Psychiatric Association (1994) *Diagnostic and Statistical Manual of Mental Disorders: DSM IV* (IV edn) Washington DC: APA.

Anon (1993) Report from the National Task Force on Chronic Fatigue Syndrome (CFS), Postviral Fatigue syndrome (PVFS) and Myalgic Encephalomyelitis (ME). Bristol: Westcare.

Bakheit A, Behan P, Dinan T, Gray C and O'Keane V (1992) Possible upregulation of hypothalamic 5-hydroxytryptamine receptors in patients with post viral fatigue syndrome. *Br Med J*, **304**, 1010–1012.

Bass C and Kerwin R (1989) Rediscovering monoamine oxidase inhibitors. *Br Med J*, **298**, 345–346.

Bates DW, Schmitt W, Buchwald D, Ware NC, Lee J, Thoyer E and Komaroff AL (1993) Prevalence of fatigue and chronic fatigue syndrome in a primary care practice. *Arch Intern Med*, **153**, 2759–2765.

Beck AT (1989) *Cognitive Therapy and the Emotional Disorders*. London: Penguin.

Behan P and Behan W (1988) The postviral fatigue syndrome. *Crit Rev Neurobiol*, **42**, 157–178.

Behan P, Haniffah BAG, Doogan DP and Loudon M (1994) A pilot study of sertraline for the treatment of chronic fatigue syndrome. *Clin Infect Dis*, **18 (suppl 1)**, S111.

Buchwald D, Cheney P, Peterson D, Henry B, Wormsley S, Geiger A, Ablashi D, Salahuddin Z, Saxinger C, Biddle R, Kikinis R, Jolesz T, Folks T, Balchandran N, Peter J,

Gallo R and Komaroff A (1992) A chronic illness characterised by fatigue, neurologic and immunologic disorders, and active human herpes type 6 infection. *Ann Intern Med*, **116**, 103–116.

Buchwald D, Pascauly R, Bombardier C and Kith P (1994) Sleep disorders in patients with chronic fatigue. *Clin Infect Dis*, **18 (suppl 1)**, S68–S72.

Buchwald D, Umali P, Umali J, Kith P, Pearlman T and Komaroff AL (1995) Chronic fatigue and the chronic fatigue syndrome: Prevalence in a Pacific Northwest Health Care System. *Ann Intern Med*, **123**, 81–88.

Burton K, Tillotson M, Main C and Hollis S (1995) Psychosocial predictors of outcome in acute and sub-chronic low back trouble. *Spine*, **20**, 722–728.

Butler S, Chalder T, Ron M and Wessely S (1991) Cognitive behaviour therapy in chronic fatigue syndrome. *J Neurol Neurosurg Psychiatry*, **54**, 153–158.

Cathebras PJ, Robbins JM, Kirmayer LJ and Hayton BC (1992) Fatigue in primary care: Prevalence, psychiatric comorbidity, illness behaviour and outcome. *J Gen Intern Med*, **7**, 276–286.

Chalder T, Berelowitz G, Pawlikowska T *et al.* (1993) Development of a fatigue scale. *J Psychosom Res*, **37**, 147–154.

Clark RR, Katon W, Russo J, Kith P, Sintay M and Buchwald D (1995) Chronic fatigue: Risk factors for symptom persistence in a 2½ year follow up study. *Am J Med*, **98**, 187–195.

Cleare A, Bearn J, McGregor A, Allain T, Wessely S and O'Keane V (1995) Contrasting neuroendocrine responses in depression and chronic fatigue syndrome. *J Affect Disord*, **34**, 283–294.

Cope H, David A, Pelosi A and Mann A (1994) Predictors of chronic "postviral" fatigue. *Lancet*, **344**, 864–868.

Cope H, Pernet A, Kendall B and David A (1995) Cognitive functioning and magnetic resonance imaging in chronic fatigue. *Br J Psychiatry*, **187**, 86–94.

Coulehan JL, Schulberg HC, Block MR and Zettler-Segal M (1988) Symptoms patterns of depression in ambulatory medical and psychiatric patients. *J Nerv Ment Dis*, **176**, 284–288.

Craig TKJ, Boardman AP, Mills K, Daly-Jones O and Drake H (1993) The South London somatisation study: Longitudinal course and the influence of early life experiences. *Br J Psychiatry*, **579**, 5888.

David AS (1991) Postviral fatigue syndrome and psychiatry. *Br Med Bull*, **47**, 966–988.

David A, Pelosi A, McDonald E, Stephens D, Ledger D, Rathbone R and Mann A (1990) Tired, weak or in need of rest: Fatigue among general practice attenders. *Br Med J*, **301**, 1199–1202.

Deale A, Chalder T, Marks I and Wessely S (1997) A randomised controlled trial of cognitive behaviour versus relaxation therapy for chronic fatigue syndrome. *Am J Psychiatry*, in press.

Demitrack M, Dale J, Straus S, Laue L, Listwak S, Kruesi M, Chrousos G and Gold P (1991) Evidence for impaired activation of the hypothalamic–pituitary adrenal axis in patients with chronic fatigue syndrome. *J Clin Endocrinol Metab*, **73**, 1224–1234.

Dew MA, Dunn LO, Bromet EJ and Schulberg HC (1988) Factors affecting help-seeking during depression in a community sample. *J Affect Disord*, **14**, 223–234.

Dohrenwend BP and Crandell DL (1970) Psychiatric symptoms in community, clinic and mental hospital groups. *Am J Psychiatry*, **126**, 87–94.

Dryman A and Eaton WW (1991) Affective symptoms associated with the onset of major depression in the community: Findings form the US National Institute of Mental Health Epidemiologic Catchment Area Program. *Acta Psychiatr Scand*, **84**, 1–5.

Euba R, Chalder T, Deale A and Wessely S (1996) A comparison of the characteristics of chronic fatigue syndrome in primary and tertiary care. *Br J Psychiatry*, **168**, 121–126.

Fisk JD, Ritvo PG, Ross L, Haase DA, Marrie TJ and Schlech WF (1994) Measuring the functional impact of fatigue: Initial validation of the fatigue impact scale. *Clin Infect Dis*, **18 (suppl 1)**, S79–S83.

Frasure-Smith N, Lesperance F and Talajic M (1993) Depression following myocardial infarction: Impact on 6-month survival. *JAMA*, **270**, 1819–1825.

Friedberg F and Krupp LB (1994) A comparison of cognitive behavioural treatment for chronic fatigue syndrome and primary depression. *Clin Infect Dis*, **18 (suppl 1)**, S105–S110.

Friedman J and Friedman H (1993) Fatigue in Parkinson's disease. *Neurology*, **43**, 2016–2019.

Fukuda K, Straus S, Hickie I, Sharpe M, Dobbins J and Komaroff A (1994) The chronic fatigue syndrome: A comprehensive approach to its definition and study. *Ann Intern Med*, **121**, 953–959.

Gerber PD, Barrett JE, Barrett JA, Oxman TE, Manheimer E, Smith R and Whiting RD (1992) The relationship of presenting physical complaints to depressive symptoms in primary care patients. *J Gen Intern Med*, **7**, 170–173.

Gold D, Bowden R, Sixbey J, Riggs R, Katon W, Ashley R, Obrigewitch R and Corey L (1990) Chronic fatigue: A prospective clinical and virologic study. *JAMA*, **264**, 48–53.

Goldberg D (1972) *The Detection of Psychiatric Illness by Questionnaire*, London: Oxford University Press.

Goldberg DP and Bridges K (1988) Somatic presentation of psychiatric illness in primary care setting. *J Psychosom Res*, **32**, 137–144.

Hickie I, Lloyd A, Wakefield D and Parker G (1990) The psychiatric status of patients with the chronic fatigue syndrome. *Br J Psychiatry*, **156**, 534–540.

Holmes G, Kaplan J, Gantz N, Kormaroff A, Shonberger L and Straus S (1988) Chronic fatigue syndrome: A working case definition. *Ann Intern Med*, **108**, 387–389.

Hotopf MH and Wessely SC (1994) Viruses, neurosis and fatigue. *J Psychosom Res*, **38**, 499–514.

Hotopf MH, Lewis G and Normand C (1996) Are SSRIs a cost effective alternative to tricyclics? *Br J Psychiatry*, **168**, 404–409.

Hotopf MH, Noah N and Wessely S (1996) Chronic fatigue and psychiatric morbidity following viral meningitis: A controlled study. *J Neurol Neurosurg Psychiatry*, **60**, 504–509.

Imboden JB, Canter A and Cluff LE (1961) Convalescence from influenza: A study of the psychological and clinical determinants. *Arch Intern Med*, **108**, 393–399.

Katon W and Russo J (1992) Chronic fatigue syndrome: A critique of the requirement for multiple physical complaints. *Arch Intern Med*, **152**, 1604–1609.

Katon W, Buchwald D, Simon G, Russo J and Mease P (1991) Psychiatric illness in patients with chronic fatigue and rheumatoid arthritis. *J Gen Intern Med*, **6**, 277–285.

Kendell RE (1991) Chronic fatigue viruses and depression. *Lancet*, **337**, 160–162.

Kottke FJ (1966) The effects of limitation of activity upon the human body. *JAMA*, **196**, 117–122.

Kroenke K, Wood D, Mangelsdorff D, Meier N and Powell J (1988) Chronic fatigue in primary care: Prevalence, patient characteristics and outcome. *JAMA*, **260**, 929–934.

Kruesi MJP, Dale J and Straus SE (1989) Psychiatric diagnoses in patients who have chronic fatigue syndrome. *J Clin Psychiatry*, **50**, 53–56.

Ladwig KH, Roll G, Breithardt G, Budde T and Borggrefe M (1994) Post-infarction depression and incomplete recovery 6 months after acute myocardial infarction. *Lancet*, **343**, 20–23.

Lane TJ, Matthews DA and Manu P (1990) The low yield of physical examinations and laboratory investigations of patients with chronic fatigue. *Am J Med*, **299**, 313–318.

Lawrie SM and Pelosi AJ (1995) Chronic fatigue syndrome in the community: Prevalence and associations. *Br J Psychiatry*, **166**, 793–797.

Lewis G and Wessely S (1992) The epidemiology of chronic fatigue syndrome: More questions than answers. *J Epidemiol Community Health*, **46**, 92–97.

Lewis G, Pelosi AJ, Araya R and Dunn G (1992) Measuring psychiatric disorder in the community: A standardised assessment for lay interviewers. *Psychol Med*, **22**, 465–486.

Lloyd A, Hickie I, Boughton CR, Spencer O and Wakefield D (1990) Prevalence of chronic fatigue syndrome in an Australian population. *Med J Aust*, **153**, 522–528.

Lloyd A, Hickie I, Boughton R, Hickie C, Wilson A, Dwyer J and Wakefield D (1993) Immunologic and psychological therapy for patients with chronic fatigue syndrome. *Am J Med*, **94**, 197–203.

Manu P, Matthews D and Lane T (1988) The mental health of patients with a chief complaint of chronic fatigue: A prospective evaluation and follow up. *Arch Intern Med*, **148**, 2212–2217.

Manu P, Matthews DA, Lane TJ, Tennen H, Hesselbrock V, Mendola R and Affleck G (1989) Depression among patients with a chief complaint of chronic fatigue. *J Affect Disord*, **17**, 165–172.

Matthew RJ, Weinman ML and Mirabi M (1981) Physical symptoms of depression. *Br J Psychiatry*, **139**, 293–296.

McDonald E, David AS, Pelosi AJ and Mann AH (1993) Chronic fatigue in primary care attenders. *Psychol Med*, **23**, 987–998.

McKinley PS, Ouellette SC and Winkel GH (1995) The contributions of disease activity, sleep patterns, and depression to fatigue in systemic lupus erythematosus. *Arthritis Rheum*, **38**, 826–834.

Meltzer H, Gill B and Petticrew M (1995) The prevalence of psychiatric morbidity among adults aged 16–64, living in private households, in Great Britain. *OPCS Surveys of Psychiatric Morbidity in Great Britain*, Report I, London: HMSO, 1–174.

Morin CM, Culbert JP and Schwartz SM (1994) Nonpharmacological interventions for insomnia: A meta-analysis of treatment. *Am J Psychiatry*, **151**, 1172–1180.

Morriss R, Sharpe M, Sharpley AL, Cowen PJ, Hawton K and Morris J (1993) Abnormalities of sleep in patients with the chronic fatigue syndrome. *Br Med J*, **306**, 1161–1164.

Muscio B (1921) Is a fatigue test possible? *Br J Psychol*, **12**, 31–46.

Mynors-Wallis LM (1995) Randomised controlled trial comparing problem solving treatment with amitriptyline and placebo for major depression in primary care. *Br Med J*, **310**, 441–445.

Natelson B, Cohen J, Brassloff I and Lee H-J (1994) A controlled study of brain magnetic resonance imaging in patients with the chronic fatigue syndrome. *J Neurol Sci*, **120**, 213–217.

Nelson E, Kirk H, McHugo G, Douglass R, Ohler J, Wasson J and Zubkoff M (1987) Chief complaint fatigue: A longitudinal study from the patient's perspective. *Fam Pract Res J*, **6**, 175–188.

Newham D (1988) The consequences of eccentric contractions and their relationship to delayed onset of muscle pain. *Eur J Appl Physiol*, **57**, 353–359.

Pawlikowska T, Chalder T, Hirsch SR, Wallace P, Wright DJM and Wessely SC (1994) Population based study of fatigue and psychosocial distress. *Br Med J*, **308**, 763–766.

Pepper CM, Krupp LB, Friedberg F, Doscher C and Coyle PK (1993) A comparison of neuropsychiatric characteristics in chronic fatigue syndrome, multiple sclerosis, and major depression. *J Neuropsychiatry*, **5**, 200–205.

Petersen P, Schenk C and Sterman P (1991) Chronic fatigue syndrome in Minnesota. *Minn Med*, **74**, 21–26.

Petrie K, Moss-Morris R and Weinman J (1994) The impact of catastrophic beliefs on functioning in chronic fatigue syndrome. *J Psychosom Res*, **39**, 31–37.

Powell R, Dolan R and Wessely S (1990) Attributions and self-esteem in depression and chronic fatigue syndromes. *J Psychosom Res*, **34**, 665–673.

Ray C (1991) Chronic fatigue syndrome and depression: Conceptual and methodological ambiguities. *Psychol Med*, **21**, 1–9.

Risdale L, Evans A, Jerrett W, Mandalia S, Osler K and Vora H (1994) Patients who consult with tiredness: Frequency of consultation, perceived cause of tiredness and its association with psychological distress. *Br J Gen Pract*, **44**, 413–416.

Robin LN, Helzer JE, Croughan J and Ratcliff KS (1981) National Institute of Mental Health Diagnostic Interview Schedule; its history, characteristics and validity. *Arch Gen Psychiatry*, **38**, 381–389.

Royal Colleges of Physicians, Psychiatrists and General Practitioners (1996) *Chronic Fatigue Syndrome*: Report of a Joint Working Group of the Royal Colleges of Physicians, Psychiatrists and General Practitioners, 1–58.

Schwartz R, Kormaroff A and Garada B (1994) SPECT imaging of the brain: Comparison of findings in patients with chronic fatigue syndrome, AIDS dementia complex and major unipolar depression. *Am J Roentgenology*, **162**, 943–951.

Seligman, MEP (1974) Depression and learned helplessness. In: RJ Freidman and MM Katz (eds) *The Psychology of Depression: Contemporary Theory and Research*. Washington: Winston-Wiley, 83–113.

Shahar E and Lederer J (1990) Asthenic symptoms in a rural family practice. *J Fam Pract*, **31**, 257–262.

Sharpe M and Bass C (1992) Pathophysiological mechanisms in somatization. *Int Rev Psychiatry*, **4**, 81–97.

Sharpe M, Archard LC, Banatvala JE *et al.* (1991) A report—chronic fatigue syndrome: Guidelines for research. *J R Soc Med*, **84**, 118–121.

Sharpe M, Hawton K, Seagroatt V and Pasvol G (1992) Follow up of patients presenting with fatigue to an infectious diseases clinic. *Br Med J*, **305**, 147–152.

Sharpe M, Hawton K, Simkin S, Surawy C, Hackmann A, Klimes I, Peto T, Warrell D and Seagroatt V (1996) Cognitive therapy for chronic fatigue syndrome: a randomized controlled trial. *Br Med J*, **312**, 22–26.

Silverstone PH (1990) Depression increases mortality and morbidity in acute life-threatening medical illness. *J Psychosom Res*, **34**, 651–657.

Stoeckle JD and Davidson GE (1962) Bodily complaints and other symptoms of depressive reaction. *JAMA*, **180**, 134–139.

Surawy C, Hackmann A, Hawton K and Sharpe M (1995) Chronic fatigue syndrome: A cognitive approach. *Behav Res Ther*, **33**, 535–544.

Taerk GS, Toner BB, Salit IE, Garfinkel PE and Ozersky S (1987) Depression in patients with neuromyasthenia (benign myalgic encephalomyelitis). *Int J Psychiatry Med*, **17**, 49–56.

Valdini A, Steinhardt S and Feldman E (1989) Usefulness of a standard battery of laboratory tests in investigating chronic fatigue in adults. *Fam Pract*, **6**, 286–291.

Vercoulen J, Swanink C and Zitman F (1995) Fluoxetine in chronic fatigue syndrome: A randomized, double-blind, placebo-controlled trial. Submitted.

Vercoulen JHMM, Swanink CMA, Fennis JFM, Galama JMD, van der Meer JWM and Bleijendberg G (1995) Prognosis in chronic fatigue syndrome (CFS): A prospective study on the natural course. *J Neurol Neurosurg Psychiatry* (In Press)

Walker EA, Katon WJ and Jemelka RP (1993) Psychiatric disorders and medical care utilization among people in the general population who report fatigue. *J Gen Intern Med*, **8**, 436–440.

Wessely S (1990) Old wine in new bottles: Neurasthenia and "ME". *Psychol Med*, **20**, 35–53.

Wessely S (1991) History of postviral fatigue syndrome. *Br Med Bull*, **47**, 919–941.

Wessely S and Powell R (1989) Fatigue syndromes: A comparison of chronic "postviral" fatigue with neuromuscular and affective disorders. *J Neurol Neurosurg Psychiatry*, **52**, 940–948.

Wessely S and Sharpe M (1995) Chronic fatigue and chronic fatigue syndrome. In: R Mayou, C Bass and M Sharpe (eds). *The Nature and Treatment of Somatic Symptoms*, Oxford: Oxford University Press, 285–312.

Wessely S, David A, Butler S and Chalder T (1989) Management of chronic (post-viral) fatigue syndrome. *J R Coll Gen Pract*, **39**, 26–29.

Wessely S, Chalder T, Hirsch S, Palikowska T, Wallace P and Wright DJM (1995) Post-infectious fatigue: Prospective cohort study in primary care. *Lancet*, **345**, 1333–1338.

Wessely S, Chalder T, Hirsch S, Wallace P and Wright D (1997) The prevalence and morbidity of chronic fatigue syndrome: a prospective primary care study. *Am J Public Health*, (In Press)

Wilkinson P and Mynors-Wallis L (1994) Problem solving therapy in the treatment of unexplained physical symptoms in primary care: a preliminary study. *J Psychosom Res*, **38**, 591–598.

Wilson A, Hickie I, Lloyd A, Hadzi-Pavlovic D, Boughton C, Dwyer J and Wakefield D (1994) Longitudinal study of outcome of chronic fatigue syndrome. *Br Med J*, **308**, 756–759.

Wood GC, Bentall RP, Gopfert M and Edwards RHT (1991) A comparative psychiatric assessment of patients with chronic fatigue syndrome and muscle disease. *Psychol Med*, **21**, 619–628.

Wood GC, Bentall RP, Gopfert M, Dewey ME and Edwards RHT (1994) The differential response of chronic fatigue, neurotic and muscular dystrophy patients to experimental psychological stress. *Psychol Med*, **24**, 357–364.

World Health Organization (1992) *The Tenth Revision of the International Classification of Diseases and Related Health Problems (ICD-10)*, Geneva: World Health Organization.

26

Depression and hypochondriasis

Gary Jackson

DEFINITIONS

Hypochondriasis

Hypochondriasis is defined in ICD-10 (F45.2) (World Health Organization, 1993) as follows.

A. Either of the following must be present:
1. A persistent belief, of at least 6 months' duration, of the presence of a maximum of two serious physical diseases (of which at least one must be specifically named by the patient).
2. A persistent preoccupation with a presumed deformity or disfigurement (body dysmorphic disorder).
B. Preoccupation with the belief and the symptoms causes persistent distress or interference with personal functioning in daily living, and leads the patient to seek medical treatment or investigations (or equivalent help from local healers).
C. There is persistent refusal to accept medical reassurance that there is no physical cause for the symptoms or physical abnormality. (Short-term acceptance of such reassurance, i.e. for a few weeks during or immediately after investigations, does not exclude this diagnosis.)
D. Most commonly used exclusion clause. The symptoms do not occur only

Depression and Physical Illness. Edited by M.M. Robertson and C.L.E. Katona
© 1997 John Wiley & Sons Ltd

during any of the schizophrenic or related disorders or any of the mood disorders.

The definition according to DSM-IV (F45.2) (American Psychiatric Association, 1995) is as follows.

A. Preoccupation with fears of having, or the idea that one has, a serious disease based on the person's misinterpretation of bodily symptoms.
B. The preoccupation persists despite appropriate medical evaluation and reassurance.
C. The belief in Criterion A. is not of delusional intensity and is not restricted to a circumscribed concern about appearance.
D. The preoccupation causes clinically significant distress or impairment in social, occupational, or other important areas of functioning.
E. The duration of the disturbance is at least 6 months.
F. The preoccupation is not better accounted for by generalized anxiety disorder, obsessive–compulsive disorder, panic disorder, a major depressive episode, separation anxiety, or another somatoform disorder.
Specify if with poor insight (i.e. if, for most of the time during the current episode, the person does not recognize that the concern about having a serious illness is excessive or unreasonable).
(Note : Body dysmorphic disorder is classified separately in DSM-IV whereas in ICD-10 it is not differentiated from hypochondriasis)

Depression

ICD-10 criteria for a major depressive episode (F32.2) (World Health Organization, 1993) are as follows.

A. Five (or more) of the following symptoms have been present during the same 2 week period and represent a change from previous functioning; at least one of the symptoms is either (1) depressed mood or (2) loss of interest or pleasure.
   1. Depressed mood most of the day, nearly every day, as indicated by either subjective report or observation made by others.
   2. Markedly diminished interest or pleasure in all, or almost all, activities most of the day, nearly every day (as indicated by either subjective account or observation made by others).
   3. Significant weight loss when not dieting or weight gain, or decrease or increase in appetite nearly every day.
   4. Insomnia or hypersomnia nearly every day.
   5. Psychomotor retardation or agitation nearly every day.
   6. Fatigue or loss of energy nearly every day.
   7. Feelings of worthlessness or excessive or inappropriate guilt nearly every day.

8. Diminished ability to think or concentrate or indecisiveness nearly every day.
9. Recurrent thoughts of death, recurrent suicidal ideation without a specific plan, or a suicide attempt or a specific plan for committing suicide.
B. The symptoms do not meet criteria for a mixed episode (of depression)
C. The symptoms cause clinically significant distress or impairment in social, occupational or other important areas of functioning.
D. The symptoms are not due to the direct physiological effects of a substance or a general medical condition.
E. The symptoms are not better accounted for by bereavement, the symptoms persist for longer than 2 months or are characterized by marked functional impairment, morbid preoccupation with worthlessness, suicidal ideation, psychotic symptoms, or psychomotor retardation.

HYPOCHONDRIASIS: A BRIEF REVIEW

Essentially, hypochondriasis features a persistent preoccupation with the possibility of having one or more serious and progressive physical disorders. Patients manifest persistent somatic complaints or persistent preoccupation with their physical appearance. Normal or commonplace sensations and appearances are often interpreted by a patient as abnormal and distressing, and attention is usually focused on only one or two organs or systems of the body. The feared physical disorder or disfigurement may be named by the patient, but even so the degree of conviction about its presence and the emphasis upon one disorder rather than another may be vague. The patient usually entertains the possibility that one or another additional physical disorder may exist in addition to the one given pre-eminence. The belief about physical disease is not, however, of delusional quality (i.e. the person can acknowledge the possibility that he or she may be exaggerating the extent of the feared disease, or that there might be no disease at all).

A thorough medical examination and special investigations fail to identify a general medical condition that fully accounts for the person's concerns about disease or for the physical signs or symptoms (although a coexisting medical condition may be present). Such "negative" findings on physical examination and special investigation fail to reassure the patient that the feared condition is not present.

Many individuals, especially those with milder forms of the disorder, remain within the primary care or nonpsychiatric medical specialties. Patients may "doctor shop", with resultant frustration and anger on both sides. Patients are at risk of poor treatment in a number of respects, including overinvestigation (and perhaps even iatrogenic disease) or cursory underassessment such that somatic illness is missed.

Psychiatric referral is often resented, unless accomplished early in the development of the disorder and with tactful collaboration between physician and psychiatrist.

The degree of associated disability is variable; some individuals dominate or manipulate family and social networks as a result of their symptoms, or occupational functioning is impaired often due to much time off for "illness". In contrast, a minority function almost normally.

Serious illnesses, particularly in childhood, and past experience with disease in a family member are associated with the occurrence of hypochondriasis. Psychosocial stressors, in particular the death of someone close to the individual, are thought to precipitate hypochondriasis in some cases.

The individual's cultural background and explanatory model for their symptoms needs to be taken into account in evaluating their inability to be reassured about their symptoms or their continuing preoccupation with them.

Some data suggest that hypochondriasis is associated with "soft" physiological changes, either "primary" or "secondary" as demonstrated for example by electromyogram (EMG) studies (Kellner, 1990).

The prevalence of hypochondriasis in the general population is unknown but the prevalence in general medical practice has been reported to be between 4% and 9%. The disorder is equally common in males and females. The disorder rarely presents for the first time after the age of 50 years (American Psychiatric Association, 1995).

Hypochondriasis as currently defined does not enjoy firm nosological status. Its phenomenology, epidemiological features, prevalence and relationship to other Axis 1 and Axis 2 diagnoses is still under investigation (Bass, 1990; Kellner, 1985; Murphy, 1990; Warwick and Salkovskis, 1990). Some authors have focused on "hypochondriacal personality" or personality involving an "overprotective view of health" either as an additional possible diagnosis or in place of hypochondriasis as an Axis 1 disorder, on the basis of the tendency for hypochondriacal symptoms to be chronic (Tyrer et al., 1990; Schmidt and Lousberg, 1992).

THE RELATIONSHIP BETWEEN DEPRESSION AND HYPOCHONDRIASIS: RESEARCH DATA

The nature of the relationship between hypochondriasis and depression has been debated frequently and over many years. Early references to their relationship can be found in historical medical texts, dating back to the 7th century AD (Dorfman, 1975).

Concerns about physical health or complaints about physical symptoms have long been recognized as not uncommon in depression. This means to say that somatic complaints not uncommonly accompany general depressive symptoms such as, for example, disturbance of mood, appetite, sleep, or anhedonia and psychomotor retardation/agitation. Somatic symptoms or hypochondriacal concerns as part of depression range between a vague feeling that something is wrong (physically) to overvalued ideas about physical symptoms and somatic delusions).

In patients from non-Western cultures, depression may be expressed principally in somatic terms, for example complaints of "nerves" and headaches in Latin and Mediterranean cultures, or of problems with the "heart" in Middle Eastern cultures (American Psychiatric Association, 1995).

Thus at a descriptive, phenomenological level, the coexistence of somatic symptoms and more "classical" depressive symptoms is common. For the purposes of this chapter, in keeping with current diagnostic theory and practice, such depressive-congruent and culture-congruent somatic/hypochondriacal symptoms will be differentiated from hypochondriasis (as defined above) and this chapter will not thus review the substantial research evidence of a high prevalence of somatic complaints in depression.

What is a decidedly more vexed question, is the nature of the coexistence of depression and the full syndrome of hypochondriasis. As hypochondriasis has come to achieve a more robust identity as a syndrome in its own right, particularly following its redefinitions in DSM-IIIR and later DSM-IV and ICD-10, so the need to research the relationship between depression and hypochondriasis (clearly and operationally defined), has returned to prominence. It may be argued that the validity of this endeavour depends on the validity of hypochondriasis as a distinct syndrome/disease which is as yet, as stated above, uncertain. The validity of depressive disorder (as defined by DSM-IV and ICD-10) is more established. There may of course be other syndromes as yet not defined, involving hypochondriacal symptoms and depressive symptoms.

DSM-IV boldly draws a clear line between hypochondriasis and depression with criterion F in the diagnostic rubric: "The preoccupation is not better accounted for by . . . a major depressive episode . . .". ICD-10 stipulates that hypochondriasis should not be diagnosed if the syndrome occurs only during another psychiatric disorder, including a mood disorder, once again distinguishing hypochondriasis from hypochondriacal symptoms accompanying a depression.

A definitive study on the comorbidity of ICD-10 or DSM-IIIR/IV depression and hypochondriasis is still awaited. A number of methodological difficulties have to be overcome in undertaking such research. For example, studies conducted in medical tertiary care settings may involve a different patient population from studies conducted in psychiatric hospitals or primary care settings. In order to clarify the relationship between the two diagnoses in one patient, it would be preferable that no other Axis 1 or any Axis 2 diagnosis was present. Furthermore, a longitudinal design would be desirable, if not fully prospective, then at least with long follow up so that one might observe the relative course of the two disorders. Whether these conditions can be met remains to be seen.

Research work so far has, unsurprisingly, failed to meet most of these criteria and indeed, as the literature available is almost all based on pre-DSM-IV/ICD-10 definitions (and indeed all too often using hypochondriacal symptoms rather than syndrome), its relevance to the conditions as currently defined is limited. Nevertheless, it makes interesting reading.

Before considering some of this literature, comment needs to be made on a confusion which recurs in this body of work, concerning the terms "primary" and "secondary" hypochondriasis. Although the term "primary" is mostly used to denote hypochondriasis without other coexisting Axis 1 disorders, in places it is used to refer to hypochondriasis which occurs with, but predates, other Axis 1 disorders. The term "secondary" hypochondriasis is found referring to hypochondriasis occurring with other Axis 1 diagnoses, following other Axis 1 diagnoses, following major life stress (bereavements, traumatic life events) or following illness (directly or in a close/loved one). These varied uses are confusing. Astute reading includes identifying how the term is used in any one piece of work.

Depressed medical and surgical inpatients have been shown to be more hypochondriacal than nondepressed inpatients (Fava *et al.*, 1982). These authors also found a positive correlation between depression scores and disease conviction and general hypochondriasis. In a retrospective review of medical records of hypochondriacal inpatients, Kenyon (1964) found that 82% of those with another Axis 1 diagnosis concurrent with hypochondriasis had depression. Jacobs *et al.* (1968) found that two-thirds of hypochondriacal outpatients scored in the depressed range on the Zung self-rating depression scale. Barsky *et al.* (1986) studied general medical outpatients and found that depressive symptoms predicted 33% of the variance in hypochondriasis and the two had a zero order correlation of 0.58 ($P = 0.0001$). Other work too has found evidence for significant comorbidity of depression and hypochondriasis (Fava *et al.*, 1982; Jacobs *et al.*, 1968; Kellner *et al.*, 1989; Kreitman *et al.*, 1965; Stenback and Jalava, 1961; Wise *et al.*, 1982).

The concurrence of hypochondriasis and bipolar affective disorder is less certain. Pilowski (1970) reported no increased prevalence of hypochondriasis in bipolar patients, a finding that has yet to be robustly vindicated or challenged.

Tennant *et al.* (1994) produced an interesting "negative" finding in a very specific patient population. They divided a large sample (N = 532) of patients with complaints of myocardial-type chest pain into those with demonstrable myocardial ischaemia, those with normal coronary artery flow, and postmyocardial infarction patients (with no current ischaemia). They found no differences between the groups on depression and hypochondriasis ratings (amongst other variables including anxiety and personality). The groups did differ significantly however on ways of coping and (ways of) anger management.

A more recent, cross-sectional study by El Islam *et al.* (1988) on 100 Kuwaiti depressed psychiatric inpatients found that 69 had hypochondriasis in addition. In 53 of these, the hypochondriasis set in after the depression, whereas in 16 patients the depressed mood appeared after the hypochondriasis. The hypochondriacal depressed patients could not be distinguished from the nonhypochondriacal depressed patients on demographic variables.

More recently still, Barsky *et al.* (1992), studied comorbidity in an adult population with DSM-IIIR hypochondriasis. Patients with hypochondriasis had twice the lifetime prevalence of other Axis 1 disorders than controls, twice as many Diagnostic Interview Schedule (DIS) symptoms and three times the level of personality disorders. Thirty three per cent of hypochondriacal patients had a current Axis 1 diagnosis of major depression and 45.2% a current Axis 1 diagnosis of dysthymic disorder. Looked at in a different way, these data showed that the hypochondriacal patients were 8.1 times as likely to have major depression and 7.1 times as likely to have dysthymia than nonhypochondriacal controls. There were no significant differences on other variables (including demographics) between patients with hypochondriasis alone and patients with hypochondriasis and another Axis 1 disorder. The authors concluded that hypochondriasis alone was relatively rare; the diagnosis in their sample was more usually accompanied by another Axis 1 or Axis 2 (less common) diagnosis.

Ball and Clare (1990) considered a cultural influence in their study—the point prevalence of depression together with hypochondriasis in a Jewish depressed population. Eighty per cent of the Jews as against 30% ($N = 25$ in each group) of the non-Jews had hypochondriasis at assessment. Ebert *et al.* (1994) recently compared matched Turkish and German samples with major depression (DSM-IIIR) on the prevalence of hypochondriacal and somatic preoccupation (as measured with the DIS). They found that the Turkish sample was more preoccupied with somatic complaints than the German group and concluded that their findings confirmed the established perception that in some cultures there is a higher tendency to use referents other than internal psychological referents for emotional expression.

Kramer-Ginsberg *et al.* (1989) assessed 70 old psychiatry inpatients with major depression. On admission, 60% were found to have hypochondriacal symptoms too. At discharge, 40% were still hypochondriacal. It is not made clear whether the depression was treated in all cases by discharge, or whether any specific intervention was made to affect the hypochondriacal symptoms. There was no relationship between the severity of the patients' depression and their hypochondriacal concerns. An additional finding of interest was the lack of association between the state of the patients' physical health and their hypochondriacal concerns. Brown *et al.* (1984) compared patients with onset of depression in the involutional period (age over 50) with patients with onset of depression before age 50. They found that those with onset after 50 years of age had more hypochondriacal symptoms than their younger counterparts. Gouvia *et al.* (1980) emphasized the need to take into account the real somatic illness rates in older people when interpreting hypochondriacal concerns in this population. Having studied 60 later life patients they concluded that hypochondriasis in old age reflects both real health problems and psychopathology, particularly depression and anxiety. Numerous other authors have written on depression and hypochondriasis in the elderly (e.g. Blazer, 1982; Brink, 1982; Hyer *et al.*, 1987; Post, 1962). No work appears, however, to have been published concerning the prevalence of depression in elderly people admitted or presenting with hypochondriasis. This may reflect a historical prejudice to focus on depression.

Having reviewed many of the data to hand, Schmidt (1994) concluded that the correlation between depression (unipolar) and hypochondriasis (unfortunately not uniformly defined) ranged between 0.4 and 0.6.

THE RELATIONSHIP BETWEEN DEPRESSION AND HYPOCHONDRIASIS: EXPLANATORY MODELS

Numerous explanatory models have been proposed for the coexistence of depression and hypochondriasis. Most simplistically, hypochondriasis has been considered to be no more than a "depressive equivalent"; a somatic presentation of depression with no accompanying mood disorder (Lesse, 1983). This approach suggests that hypochondriasis is no more than a different kind of depression. No work to date, however, has convincingly shown that hypochondriasis presents with no depressive affect and responds to antidepressant treatment (to the extent expected from a depressive disorder).

Psychoanalytical theorists considered that hypochondriasis, among other things, may be a defence mechanism, most often employed after loss. Psychoanalytical theory also considered depression as related to loss, thus linking the two syndromes in terms of their origins (Kenyon, 1976). Starcevic (1988) reviews the psychodynamic understandings of hypochondriasis as a component of depression, focusing on issues such as the need for reassurance.

Fava and Kellner (1991) propose in their model of the development of hypochondriasis that it develops following an anxiety-provoking life event. The normal resultant somatic anxiety symptoms are perceived by some people with a particular cognitive style to be threatening, a perception which likely increases the level of anxiety, thus setting off a "snowball" effect, much like the cognitive explanatory model of panic. If this theory were at least in part valid, the coexistence of hypochondriasis and depression may be somewhat explained— depression has been robustly demonstrated often to follow challenging life events.

Concerning the apparent higher rate of hypochondriasis in old age, Costa and McCrae (1985) suggest that individuals have a characteristic level of somatic concerns which are stable over time and which are influenced by personality type (e.g. level of neuroticism). Age then is associated with increasing physical illness which, in individuals with a higher propensity to somatic concern, sets off hypochondriacal concern.

Hypochondriasis has been linked to genetics, learned behaviour in families, the experience of physical illness (directly or indirectly), social class, culture, the individual's cognitive style and personality, reinforcement and secondary gain, hostility, and other factors. Depression too has been linked to a number of these (Kellner, 1985).

Dysfunction of the second somatosensory cortical area, involved with somatic sensation perception, has also been proposed as important in the causation of hypochondriasis (Miller, 1985).

In general terms, it is hardly surprising that depressive symptoms might develop in a patient with much anxiety and somatic symptom preoccupation (as in established hypochondriasis), just as an increased incidence of depression in those with chronic physical illness is recognized. Similarly, as somatic symptom concern is frequent in "regular" depression, the development of these concerns into hypochondriasis in some patients (perhaps because of their cognitive style or personality) might be expected. If hypochondriasis and depression occur simultaneously, having developed seemingly independently (i.e. cannot be explained with psychological rationales), another explanatory model is required.

TREATMENT

Research information on the treatment of hypochondriasis coexisting with depression is limited. Naturally, when it is only hypochondriacal symptoms or concerns which are present as part of the depression, one might expect them to abate as the depression responds to treatment, with reassurance until then.

No publications in the literature argue against this apparently sensible approach. Kellner *et al.* (1986) demonstrated that this expectation is valid in a sample of 20 patients with DSM-III depressive disorder and hypochondriacal fears and beliefs ("melancholia"). They treated the patients with amitriptyline and the hypochondriacal symptoms disappeared as the depression responded.

When the patient appears to be suffering from a full hypochondriacal disorder, and a depression has set in subsequently, it is likely that the depression will need specific treatment and the hypochondriasis separate, specific treatment. Likewise, it is likely when these two conditions coexist without clarity on which came first, that specific treatment will be required for each, more or less in parallel.

The treatment of depression is well rehearsed and will not be reviewed here.

The treatment of hypochondriasis is complex. There is no single agreed best approach, and most treatment trials have been beset with methodological difficulties.

Amongst psychological treatments, analytic psychotherapy has not enjoyed much success (Kellner, 1992). In recent years, the emphasis appears to have shifted to helping the patient address the fears and false beliefs and thus cognitive and behavioural treatment elements have come to be most commonly employed. Desensitization to disturbing hypochondriacal imagery or thoughts has been employed (O'Donnell, 1978) with some success. Informing the patient about plausible reasons for his symptoms (including possible selective perception tendencies), explaining how somatic anxiety symptoms and worry can fuel one another, conducting appropriate investigations and reassuring convincingly, giving advice, engendering the trust of the patient and more specifically dealing with preoccupations (cognitively) are treatment components which have variously been considered important (Barsky et al., 1988; House, 1989; Kellner, 1982; Kukleta, 1991).

An interesting debate has arisen about the role of reassurance. Kellner (1985) has advocated reassurance provided it is constructive (i.e. not repetition of shallow statements, but rather giving helpful information, educating and providing new information as it becomes available, for example after investigations). Salkovskis and Warwick (1986) however argue that reassurance encourages reassurance-seeking behaviour, and illness behaviour more generally, and should thus not be provided.

It is likely that as there is variation in personalities, attitudes and clinical features in hypochondriacal patients, no single psychological treatment approach will be adequate for all patients, and individual "tailoring" will be necessary.

One report of patients with hypochondriasis without depression responding to electroconvulsive therapy has been published (Kenyon, 1964). This work needs replication.

Only two substantial, recent trials of drug treatment for hypochondriasis (without major depression) appear in the literature (Fallon et al., 1993; Wesner and Noyes, 1991). Wesner and Noyes treated 10 patients with hypochondriasis (with "good insight") without major depression on imipramine (150 mg per day). Eight patients improved moderately after 8 weeks of treatment.

Fallon et al. treated 14 patients, seven with hypochondriasis alone and seven with hypochondriasis and another disorder, with fluoxetine at doses up to 80 mg per day for 12 weeks. Six of the patients with hypochondriasis alone responded (much/very much improved), but the response was late in treatment (mostly after 6 weeks). Four of the patients with comorbidity responded comparably.

These studies need to be repeated with larger sample sizes. The mechanism of action of antidepressants in hypochondriasis, if indeed effective, is difficult to explain; for example, might they act directly on the hypochondriacal symptoms mediation mechanism or just reduce anxiety and thus undermine a propagating factor of the hypochondriasis?

NATURAL HISTORY/PROGNOSIS

The prognosis of depressive disorder, treated or untreated, is well documented. As the current diagnostic criteria for hypochondriasis are so new, no long-term follow-up studies have been conducted on hypochondriasis as currently defined. The accumulated literature agrees that the course of both symptoms and disability is usually chronic and fluctuating. Acute onset, shorter duration of illness, medical comorbidity, coexisting anxiety or depression, the absence of a personality disorder and secondary gain appear to afford a better prognosis (American Psychiatric Association, 1995; House, 1989; Pilowski, 1968).

Noyes *et al.* (1994) recently followed up 50 untreated patients with DSM-IIIR hypochondriasis, and 50 controls, for 1 year. At follow up, two-thirds of the hypochondriacal patients still met the diagnostic criteria for the disorder, and the balance still had hypochondriacal symptoms (although in most patients there had been a moderate reduction in hypochondriacal symptom severity). In patients who had coexisting depression at initial assessment, the depression was still present at follow up. Predictors of worse outcome were presence of other psychiatric illness (including depression), longer duration of illness, and severe symptoms. The authors concluded that although symptoms in hypochondriasis wax and wane, a feature of the condition appears to be stability of the diagnosis over time, in a majority of patients.

Thus there is conflicting evidence as to the role played by coexisting depression in hypochondriasis; does it improve or worsen the prognosis? This question too awaits resolution.

REFERENCES

American Psychiatric Association (1995) *DSM IV. Diagnostic and Statistical Manual of Mental Disorders* (4th edn) (International Version). Washington, DC: American Psychiatric Association.

Ball RA and Clare A (1990) Symptoms and social adjustment in Jewish Depressives. *Br J Psychiatry*, **156**, 379–383.

Barsky AJ, Wyshak G and Klerman GL (1986) Hypochondriasis: An evaluation of the DSM-III criteria in medical outpatients. *Arch Gen Psychiatry*, **43**, 493–500.

Barsky AJ, Geringer E and Wool CA (1988) A cognitive-educational treatment for hypochondriasis. *Gen Hosp Psychiatry*, **10**, 322–327.

Barsky AJ, Wyshak G and Klerman GL (1992) Psychiatric comorbidity in DSM-IIIR hypochondriasis. *Am J Psychiatry*, **49**, 101–108.

Bass CM (1990) Assessment and management of patients with functional somatic symptoms. In: CM Bass (ed) *Somatisation: Physical Symptoms and Psychological Illness.* London: Blackwell Scientific.

Blazer D (1982) *Depression in Later Life.* St. Louis: Mosby.

Brink TL (1982) Geriatric depression and hypochondriasis: Incidence, interaction, assessment and treatment. *Psychother Theory, Res Pract,* **19(4)**, 506–511.

Brown RP, Kocsis JH, Glick ID, Dhar AK (1984) Efficacy and feasibility of high dose tricyclic antidepressant treatment in elderly delusional depressives. *J Clin Psychopharmacol,* **4(6)**, 311–315.

Costa P and McCrae R (1985) Hypochondriasis, neuroticism and aging: When are somatic complaints unfounded? *Am Psychol,* **40(1)**, 19–28.

Dorfman W (1975) Hypochondriasis Revisited: A dilemma and challenge to medicine and psychiatry. *Int J Psychiatry Med,* **XVI**, 14–16.

Ebert D and Martus P (1994) Somatization as a core symptom of melancholic type depression. Evidence from a cross-cultural study. *J Affect Disord,* **32**, 253–256.

El Islam M, Malasi T, Suleiman M and Mirza I (1988) The correlates of hypochondriasis in depressed patients. *Int J Psychiatry Med,* **18(3)**, 253–261.

Fallon B, Liebowitz M, Salman E, Schneier F, Jusino C, Hollander E and Klein D (1993) Fluoxetine for hypochondriasis without major depression. *J Clin Psychopharmacol,* **13(6)**, 438–442.

Fava GA and Kellner R (1991) Prodromal symptoms in affective disorders. *Am J Psychiatry,* **148(7)**, 823–830.

Fava GA, Pilowski I, Pierfederici A, Bernardi M and Pathak D (1982) Depression and illness behaviour in a general hospital: A prevalence study. *Psychother Psychosom,* **38**, 141–153.

Gouveia I, Hyer L, Harrison W, Warsaw J and Coutsouridis D (1980) Hypochondriasis in later life: Health or psychopathology. *Clin Gerontol,* **6(1)**, 45–51.

House A (1989) Hypochondriasis and related disorders. *Gen Hosp Psychiatry,* **11**, 156–165.

Hyer L, Gouveia I, Harrison W, Warsaw J, Coutsouridis D (1987) Depression, anxiety, paranoid reactions, hypochondriasis, and cognitive decline of later life inpatients. *J Gerontol,* **42(1)**, 92–94.

Jacobs MA, Anderson LS, Eisman HD, *et al.* (1968) Interaction of psychologic and biologic predisposing factors in allergic disorders. *Psychosom Med,* **29**, 572–585.

Kellner R (1982) Psychotherapeutic strategies in hypochondriasis: A clinical study. *Am J Psychother,* **36**, 146–157.

Kellner R (1985) Functional somatic symptoms and hypochondriasis; a survey of empirical studies. *Arch Gen Psychiatry,* **42**, 821–833.

Kellner R (1990) Somatization. Theories and research. *J Nerv Ment Dis,* **178(3)**, 150–160.

Kellner R (1992) Diagnosis and treatment of hypochondriacal syndromes. *Psychosomatics* **33(3)**, 278–289.

Kellner R, Fava G, Lisansky J, Perini G and Zielezny M (1986) Hypochondriacal fears and beliefs in DSM-III melancholia. *J Affect Disord,* **10**, 21–26.

Kellner R, Abbott P, Winslow WW and Pathak D (1989) Anxiety, depression and somatization in DSM-III hypochondriasis. *Psychosomatics,* **30**, 57–64.

Kenyon FE (1964) Hypochondriasis: A clinical study. *Br J Psychiatry,* **110**, 478–488.

Kenyon FE (1976) Hypochondriacal states. *Br J Psychiatry,* **129**, 1–14.

Kramer-Ginsberg E, Greenwald BS, Aisen PS and Brod-Miller C (1989) Hypochondriasis in the elderly depressed. *J Am Geriatr Soc,* **37**, 507–510.

Kreitman N, Sainsbury P, Pearce K, *et al.* (1965) Hypochondriasis and depression in outpatients at a general hospital. *Brit J Psychiatry,* **111**, 607–615.

Kukleta M (1991) Psychophysiological mechanisms in hypochondriasis. *Homeostasis* (Prague), **33**, 7–12.

Lesse S (1983) The masked depression syndrome—Results of a seventeen-year clinical study. *Am J Psychother*, **XXXVII(4)**, 456–475.

Miller NE (1985) Effects of emotional stress on the immune system. *Pavlov J Biol Sci*, **20(2)**, 47–52.

Murphy MR (1990) Classification of the somatoform disorders. In: CM Bass (ed) *Somatization: Physical Symptoms and Psychological Illness*. London: Blackwell Scientific.

Noyes R, Kathol R, Fisher M, Phillips B, Suelzer M and Woodman C (1994) One-year follow-up of medical outpatients with hypochondriasis. *Psychosomatics*, **35**, 533–545.

O'Donnell JM (1978) Implosive therapy with hypnosis in the treatment of cancer phobia: a case report. *Psychother Theory Res Pract*, **15**, 8–12.

Pilowski I (1968) Response to treatment in hypochondriacal disorders. *Aust NZ J Psychiatry*, **2**, 88–94.

Pilowski I (1970) Primary and secondary hypochondriasis. *Acta Psychiatr Scand*, **46**, 273–285.

Post F (1962) *The Significance of Affective Symptoms in Old Age*. London: Oxford University Press.

Salkovskis P and Warwick HMC (1986) Morbid preoccupations, health anxiety and reassurance: A cognitive–behavioural approach to hypochondriasis. *Behav Res Ther*, **24**, 597–602.

Schmidt AJM (1994) Bottlenecks in the diagnosis of hypochondriasis. *Compr Psychiatry*, **35(4)**, 306–315.

Schmidt AJM and Lousberg R (1992) *De Maastrichter Eigen Gezondheidsattitude en Hypochondrieschaal*: de MEGAH-schaal. Handleiding, Lisse: Swets en Zeitlinger.

Starcevic V (1988) Diagnosis of hypochondriasis: A promenade through the psychiatric nosology. *Am J Psychother*, **XLII(2)**, 197–211.

Stenback A and Jalava V (1961) Hypochondria and depression. *Acta Psychiatr Scand*, **37 (Suppl 62)**, 240–246.

Tennant C, Mihailidou A, Scott A, Smith R, Kellow J, Jones M, Hunyor S, Lorang M and Hoschi R (1994) Psychological symptom profiles in patients with chest pain. *J Pyschosom Res*, **38(4)**, 365–371.

Tyrer P, Fowler-Dixon R, Ferguson B and Keleman A (1990) A plea for the diagnosis of hypochondriacal personality disorder. *J Psychosom Res*, **34**, 637–642.

Warwick HMC and Salkovskis PM (1990) Hypochondriasis. *Behav Ther Res*, **28**, 105–117.

Wesner RB and Noyes R (1991) Imipramine: An effective treatment for illness phobia. *J Affect Disord*, **22**, 43–48.

Wise TN and Rosenthal JB (1982) Depression, illness beliefs and severity of illness. *J Psychosom Res*, **26(2)**, 247–253.

World Health Organization (1993) *International Classification of Mental and Behavioural Disorders*. Geneva: WHO.

27

Iatrogenic depression

Matcheri S. Keshavan

INTRODUCTION

Psychiatrists and other physicians in daily practice face the question of how to use their powerful therapeutic armamentarium without inadvertently causing treatment-induced (or iatrogenic) dysfunction. Depressive symptoms are among the iatrogenic psychiatric syndromes seen in practice and have both clinical and scientific importance. Depressive symptoms cause considerable morbidity and may impair recovery from concomitant medical illnesses, and might often lead to suicidal behaviour. Early detection of such symptoms is critical for effective treatment and prevention of such morbidity. The scientific importance of iatrogenic depression derives from the fact that a clear understanding of the mechanisms underlying these depressions could generate hypotheses regarding the aetiology of primary depressive illness. A case in point is the theory regarding possible impairment in the aminergic neurotransmission in depressive disorders; this hypothesis was stimulated by the observed association between reserpine and depression (Schildkraut and Kety, 1967).

While virtually every class of medications has been implicated in causing depression, evidence supporting such implications varies widely. Studies range from controlled prospective studies to single case reports; however, the published literature does not always provide descriptions of the criteria used to diagnose depressive symptoms. Three caveats should be considered when reviewing literature reporting medications associated with depression. First,

Depression and Physical Illness. Edited by M.M. Robertson and C.L.E. Katona
© 1997 John Wiley & Sons Ltd

descriptions of iatrogenic depression reported in the literature often seem to be a mixture of lethargy, apathy, tiredness, drowsiness, and feeling "sluggish" or slowed-down, and not typical of the clinical depressive syndrome (Edwards, 1989). Thus, one needs to distinguish depression-like symptoms (or "pseudo-depression") from an iatrogenic major depressive illness. Second, it should be borne in mind that depression is a very common problem and leads to a high likelihood of a chance co-occurrence with the institution of a treatment; spontaneous recovery is also common, and could occur by chance together with discontinuation of a treatment. Both these situations can lead to an erroneous assumption of a cause–effect relationship between a treatment and depression (Zelnik, 1987). Third, depressive symptoms in medically ill patients on pharmacological treatment are likely to have a multifactorial aetiology. These factors include the substantial psychological and social stressors that frequently accompany medical illness; the direct neuropsychiatric effects of the medical illnesses themselves, as well as the pharmacological effects of treatment. Patients with a family history of depression, and those with a prior history of mood disorders, may be at a higher risk for drug-induced depression (Pascualy and Veith, 1989). Each of these factors might act interactively to cause iatrogenic depression.

According to DSM-IV (American Psychiatric Association, 1994), a drug-induced depression, if it meets the severity criteria of a major depressive episode, should be categorized as a depressive episode in relation to a general medical condition. In this chapter, the adverse mood disturbances induced by the administration or withdrawal of drugs used in medical and psychiatric practice are described. This review is organized by medication type and is based on reviews of this topic available in the literature (Metzger and Friedman, 1994; Patten and Love, 1993; Dhondt and Hooijer, 1995).

DRUGS CAUSING DEPRESSIVE SYMPTOMS

Antihypertensives

Antihypertensive drugs are among the drugs most commonly reported to be associated with depression. Depression is commonly associated with the use of reserpine, a centrally acting rauwolfia alkaloid, one of the earliest drugs used in the treatment of hypertension; however, reserpine is rather infrequently used currently as an antihypertensive. The depressive effect of reserpine is probably related to its effects on depletion of catecholamine stores at synaptic endings (Schildkraut and Kety, 1967; Goodwin and Bunney, 1971). Goodwin and Bunney (1971) reviewed 16 studies of depression associated with reserpine, and found an average incidence of 20%; however, the definition of depression used in many of these early studies was far from clear. When limited to severe,

Table 1. Drugs associated with depressive symptoms.

Anthypertensive agents	Antibiotics
Reserpine*	Amphotericin
Propranolol	Cycloserine
Clonidine	Dapsone
Methyldopa	Ethionamide
Antiarrhythmic drugs	H$_2$ blockers
Digitalis	Cimetidine
Procainamide	Ranitidine
Anticholesterol drugs	Antipsychotic drugs
Cholestyramine	Psychotropic drug withdrawal
Pravastatine	Stimulants*
Hormonal agents	Benzodiazepines*
Corticosteroids*	Methaqualone
Anabolic steroids	Barbiturates
Oral contraceptives	Anticonvulsants
Cancer chemotherapy agents	Dilantin
Methotrexate	Felbamate
Vinblastine	Phenobarbitone*
Asparaginase	
Procarbazine	
Interferon	

*The literature is relatively more convincing in regard to the cause–effect relationship between these drugs and depressive symptoms. ±cause–effect relationship questionable.

"endogenous" depression, the incidence was closer to 5% (Goodwin *et al.*, 1972). Most cases occurred at doses over 0.5 mg per day; a past history of depression was frequent in these patients. Other features commonly seen in association with reserpine use include visual hallucinations, nightmares, decreased slow-wave sleep, and increased rapid eye movement (REM) sleep.

Beta-adrenergic blocking agents are among the most commonly prescribed antihypertensive drugs. Over the last two decades, an extensive body of literature has accumulated regarding the possible association between the use of beta-blockers and depression. The presence of beta-adrenergic receptors in the brain as well as observations that these agents may reduce brain levels of catecholamines and indoleamines provide biological plausibility to the view that these drugs may cause depression. Two large scale studies using prescription plan databases have found an association between exposure to beta-blockers and the prescription of antidepressants (Avorn *et al.*, 1986; Thiessen *et al.*, 1990). The causal association between depression and beta-blockers, however, remains controversial. In a case control study based on a Medicaid database, it was found that the association between beta-blocker administration and depression was no longer significant when the confounding influence of health-seeking patterns and other illness-associated psychological variables were taken into account (Bright and Everitt, 1992). Some negative studies have also been published (for review see Patten and Love, 1993). Thus, while a causal relationship may exist between beta-blockers and depression, it cannot, at this time, be considered to be established. It has been suggested that hydrophilic beta-blocking agents such as atenolol and nadolol may be superior to lipophilic agents such as propranolol because the former are less likely to cross the blood–brain barrier (Yudofsky, 1992). However, this has been debated (Levenson, 1993). If a depressive syndrome develops after beginning treatment with beta-blockers, one should consider an antihypertensive agent of a different pharmacological class such as a calcium channel blocker or an angiotensin converting enzyme inhibitor. If this is not practical, an antidepressant should be considered for concomitant administration. This approach is generally effective and safe. It should, however, be kept in mind that beta-blockers are likely to have a reduced antihypertensive effect when combined with tricyclic antidepressants because of displacement at the adrenergic receptor.

Clonidine and α-methyldopa are α_2 adrenergic agonists used as antihypertensive agents. The metabolite of methyldopa is an agonist of α_2 adrenergic receptors; clonidine is a direct α_2 adrenergic agonist. Interest in the possible association between these drugs and depression was stimulated both by early observations of depression during treatment with these agents as well as abnormalities of noradrenergic receptor function in patients with depression. While an association between depression and clonidine and α-methyldopa has been widely assumed, few systematic studies have supported a cause–effect relationship. Demuth and Ackerman (1983) reviewed several studies of depression associated with α-methyldopa and concluded that DSM-III criteria of major depression were rarely met. A review of 44 studies examining the use of clonidine in hypertension revealed a 1.5% incidence of depression (Paykel et al., 1982). This suggests that depression, if it occurs, is rare during clonidine treatment.

While depression is mentioned as a possible side-effect of calcium channel blockers and angiotensin converting enzyme inhibitors, this view is based on a relatively low number of case reports. Indeed, there is suggestive evidence that calcium channel blockers may be beneficial in the treatment of affective disorders. There is no evidence that diuretic medications directly cause depression although they may lead to electrolyte imbalance that could masquerade as depression, especially in the elderly. Depressed mood has been reported to be associated with other antihypertensive agents such as bretylium, disopyramide, and procainamide, although no systematic studies exist (Levenson, 1993).

Antiarrhythmic drugs

Psychiatric side-effects of digitalis treatment were originally described by William Withering who introduced this drug into medical practice. The association between the digitalis and depression is made plausible by observations that this drug inhibits synthesis and reuptake of norepinephrine. Depressive-like features including depressed mood, fatigue, agitation, insomnia, and nightmares have been described during treatment with digoxin even though the more typical complication of this treatment is delirium and visual hallucinations including scotomas. A well-controlled study demonstrated an association between digoxin and depressive disorders (Schleifer *et al.*, 1991). However, more patients had depressive disorders at baseline than at follow up, making the findings difficult to interpret. Depressive symptoms during digoxin treatment could be seen at therapeutic or at supratherapeutic levels (Eisendrath and Sweeny, 1987).

Anticholesterol drugs

Interest in the possible association between depression and anticholesterol drugs has been triggered by observations from controlled clinical trials that show that cholesterol reductions may increase mortality from suicide and violence (Muldoon *et al.*, 1990; Law *et al.*, 1994). Engelberg (1992) has proposed that lowered serum cholesterol might be associated with decreased brain membrane lipid viscosity causing a decrease in the exposure of surface serotonin receptors. Depressive symptoms have been observed during treatment with the anticholesterol agents pravastatine, lovastatine, and cholestyramine (Lechleitner *et al.*, 1992).

Hormonal agents

Corticosteroids are hormones needed by man to adapt to stress and sustain life. Psychiatric disturbance, especially depression, is often associated with abnormal cortisol metabolism. Abnormal cortisol metabolism, in turn, is known to cause changes in mood, thinking, and behaviour. It is not surprising, therefore, that the use of corticosteroid treatment is associated with depression. The manic syndrome, however, is more common. Women may be somewhat more frequently affected (Rundell and Wise, 1989); those with systemic lupus erythematosus and those receiving high doses of corticosteroids may be at increased risk (Lewis and Smith, 1983). Depressive symptoms often occur early in the course of treatment and mood changes may occur either after the beginning or discontinuation of treatment (Lewis and Smith, 1983). Approaches to management include slowing the rate of change in dosage, since the symptoms are frequently associated with increasing or tapering of the medication. It has been suggested that an alternate day steroid regime may be preferable to a daily regime (Cordess *et al.*, 1981). Tricyclic antidepressants have been reported to exacerbate psychosis in patients being treated with corticosteroids and are, therefore, preferably avoided.

Several reports have documented the occurrence of both depressive and manic syndromes accompanying the use of anabolic steroids. These drugs may be prescribed for treatment of disorders such as myotonic dystrophy and hypogonadism. However, these drugs are abused much more commonly by weightlifters and other athletes; recent estimates suggest that there may be over one million users in the USA alone. The prevalence of mood disorders has been found to be substantially increased during periods of use over periods of non-use and may be highly dose dependent. The full affective syndrome is seen in about 22% of individuals taking these drugs (Pope and Katz, 1988). Discontinuation of anabolic steroids has also been reported to be associated with depressed mood; these symptoms appear to respond well to serotonin reuptake inhibitors (SSRI) (Malone and Dimeff, 1992).

Oral contraceptives have been reported to be associated with depression and have received considerable attention since the 1960s. It has been suggested that the use of oral contraceptives with lower doses of oestrogen and progesterone may be associated with lower frequency of depressive symptoms. Twin studies have suggested that the propensity to develop depression during oral contraceptive use may be at least in part based on hereditary factors (Kendler *et al.*, 1988). Controlled double-blind studies, however, reveal inadequate evidence to establish a causal association between depression and oral contraceptives (Patten and Love, 1993; Long and Kathol, 1993).

Cancer chemotherapeutic agents

Several drugs used in the treatment of cancer including methotrexate, alkylating agents such as decarbazine, vinblastine, asparaginase, and procarbazine have been associated with depressive symptoms. Interferon, used in the treatment of leukaemia, has also been associated with dose-dependent fatigue-asthenic symptoms resembling depressive disorder (Adams *et al.*, 1984). Depressive symptoms may also be associated with the use of metoclopramide, a drug often used to treat gastrointestinal symptoms accompanying chemotherapy. Depressive symptoms may be seen in as many as 40% of patients undergoing chemotherapy (Middleboe *et al.*, 1994). However, depression is quite common in cancer patients, with prevalence ranging from 6% to 42% (Middleboe *et al.*, 1994). It is, therefore, difficult to tease apart the effects of illness from those due to the treatment. Clearly, more systematic research is needed. It is an intriguing possibility that treatment of depression may have a favourable impact on the outcome of malignancy; this question deserves further investigation.

Anticonvulsants

Depressive symptoms have been reported to be associated with the use of anticonvulsants such as phenytoin, carbamazepine, phenobarbitone, and felbamate. Unfortunately, however, "depression" reported in several studies is usually attributed to sedation and psychomotor slowing related to these medications. Few controlled studies exist, however; in a careful study, Robertson *et al.* (1987) reported that 40% of the 64 patients on anticonvulsants had major depressive features (34% had a family history of affective disorder). Phenobarbitone was more frequently associated with depression while carbamazepine was associated with less depression and anxiety. Discontinuation of anticonvulsants may also be associated with anxiety and depression (Ketter *et al.*, 1994). Brent *et al.* (1990) followed up a cohort of 39 epileptic patients for a median of 26.5 months. Treatment with phenobarbitone was associated more frequently with depression than carbamazepine or no treatment. Depression associated with phenobarbitone treatment was continued and tended to decline after switching to carbamazepine or no medication. Thus patients on phenobarbitone, in particular those with a family history of depression, need to be closely monitored for emergence of depressive features. Carbamazepine may be an effective, possibly safer anticonvulsant for use in patients at risk for anticonvulsant-induced mood disorders (Depression Guideline Panel, 1993).

Antibiotic drugs

The observation of the antidepressant effect of the monoamine oxidase inhibitor, iproniazid, used in the treatment of tuberculosis in the early 1950s, was a landmark in the introduction of the early antidepressant medications. Paradoxically, however, depression has been associated with the use of several antituberculous medications. In particular, depression is frequently associated with the use of cycloserine as well as ethionamide. The symptoms appear to be dose dependent and psychotic features appear to be common (Holdiness, 1987). Unfortunately, however, these drugs are not used alone in the treatment of tuberculosis; it is, therefore, difficult to be certain about the causative role of this drug in the reported depressive syndromes (Wallach and Gershon, 1972).

Few controlled studies have appeared in the literature in relation to the association between other antibiotics and depression. Dapsone has been described to be associated with depression and anger. Amphotericin B is reported to be associated with depression as well as delirium.

Histamine (H$_2$) blockers

H$_2$ blockers such as cimetidine, famotidine, and ranitidine are frequently associated with delirium especially when used intravenously in medically ill or elderly patients. While several case reports describe the occurrence of depressive syndromes with cimetidine, no systematic studies have been conducted.

Controlled studies of oral ranitidine show no increase in depression due to treatment with this drug (Robins *et al.*, 1984).

Sympathomimetic agents

The occurrence of depressive syndromes in patients withdrawing from sympathomimetic agents such as fenfluramine, methylphenidate, and pemoline has been reported in a number of case reports and uncontrolled studies (Oswald *et al.*, 1971). Levodopa, a drug commonly used in the treatment of parkinsonism, has also been associated with depression. It is, however, difficult to disentangle the depressive syndrome that may be intrinsic to Parkinson's disease from the symptoms caused by the medications. Depression occurs at a higher than expected frequency in 21–47% of patients with Parkinson's disease (Dooneief *et al.*, 1992; Starkstein *et al.*, 1990). In one study, Parkinson patients treated with levodopa had more depressive symptoms than a group of patients treated with anticholinergic drugs and amantidine (Mindham *et al.*, 1976).

Antipsychotic drugs

A substantial number of studies have reported occurrences of depression during treatment of schizophrenia with antipsychotic drugs. The co-occurrence of depression-like features with extrapyramidal symptoms was termed "akinetic depression" by Van Putten and May (1978). The occurrence of depression along with extrapyramidal symptoms (EPS) has been interpreted as being induced by antipsychotic drugs; on the other hand, this association may be viewed as symptoms occurring as part of the Parkinson's syndrome and, therefore, being a "pseudo" depression. This view is supported by the fact that these so-called depressive symptoms disappear after cessation of the antipsychotic drug treatment. However, clozapine, which is free of EPS, is not associated with depression and even an antidepressant affect has been described. Thus, the depression that appears during antipsychotic drug treatment is more likely to be a Parkinson's syndrome that may be mistaken for depression. Indeed, several studies actually show an antidepressant effect of the antipsychotic drugs. Thus, antipsychotic drugs play little role in the causation of the depressive syndrome in chronic or acute schizophrenic patients (Angst, 1992).

Sedative–hypnotic drugs

It is often believed that sedative–hypnotic drugs can trigger or perpetuate depressive symptoms. However, few systematic studies have been conducted that establish the causal association. The reports of depression-like symptoms observed during high dose benzodiazepine treatment may be related to sedation (Pascualy and Vieth, 1989). An association has been reported between depression and the use of methaqualone, a hypnotic drug used rarely these days (Buckner and Mandell, 1990). Several reports describe an association between depression and benzodiazepine withdrawal (Keshavan *et al.*, 1988; Ashton, 1995). Depressive symptoms occurring with benzodiazepine withdrawal appear to respond to treatment with the benzodiazepine antagonist flumazenil (Lader and Morton, 1992). It remains unclear whether depressive and/or anxiety symptoms that emerge after discontinuation of anxiolytic/hypnotic drugs represent relapse of the primary disorder, rebound, or true withdrawal phenomena (Lader, 1994).

Psychotropic drug withdrawal

Withdrawal symptoms are associated with virtually all antidepressant drugs, and may include depressive features. Typical symptoms of withdrawal syndrome from SSRIs include decreased energy, insomnia, nightmares, anorexia, headaches, confusion, lightheadedness and paraesthesia. Hypomanic features are also seen. These symptoms have been reported following discontinuation of the SSRI, paroxetine (Koopowitz and Berk, 1995; Block *et al.*, 1995). Similar symptoms may be seen after discontinuation of monoamine oxidase inhibitors such as tranylcypromine as well (Halle and Dilsaver, 1993). Withdrawal from tricyclic antidepressants is associated with a flu-like syndrome including several features of depression (Ceccherini-Nelli *et al.*, 1993).

Mood disturbances are seen after withdrawal from other psychotropic drugs. Depressive symptoms are consistently seen following discontinuation of amphetamines (Abramovitz and Aaron, 1984). Discontinuation of anticholinergic drugs have been found to be associated with a depression-like syndrome (Keshavan *et al.*, 1985). Discontinuation of lithium is associated with mood disturbances, especially mania, although this is debated (Schou, 1993).

PATIENT EVALUATION AND DIFFERENTIAL DIAGNOSIS

When faced with a patient who may have an iatrogenic depressive syndrome, a complete medical and psychiatric history with emphasis on recent drug ingestion and complete physical and neurological examinations should be completed. Iatrogenic depression needs to be distinguished from major depressive disorders that may be identical but related to a primary affective disorder or an organic affective disorder due to some other cause. As discussed earlier, the emergence of depression in most clinical settings is related to multiple aetiological factors; it is important to clarify the extent to which one or more drugs contribute to the syndrome in interaction with other factors. The following general guidelines are likely to help the physician in the diagnosis and treatment of the patient who presents with the features of depression during treatment with medications.

1. Obtain a detailed medication history. Inquire into prior episodes of iatrogenic depression. It is critical to clarify any recently introduced new medications as well as any recent change in dose. Some patients may neglect to mention certain medications which they consider as unimportant such as eye drops or contraceptive pills, etc.
2. Conduct a thorough medical assessment. As discussed earlier, several medical conditions, (i.e. hypothyroidism) may result in signs and symptoms resembling depression; often delirium may be mistaken for depression. Laboratory evaluation including blood levels of drugs for which levels are available would be valuable as well.
3. Conduct a thorough psychiatric assessment to examine the presence or absence of the specific symptoms and signs of major depression as per DSM-IV. It is also important to determine the presence of another concurrent nonaffective psychiatric condition that may contribute to the depression-like symptoms. The history should also include inquiry into the presence of other risk factors such as a personal and/or family history of affective illness.
4. Certain other medication side-effects may mimic depression. An example is the parkinsonism caused by antipsychotic drugs or metoclopramide, or oversedation due to sedative–hypnotic drugs.
5. Establish the temporal relationship between the depressive symptoms and the introduction, discontinuation, or change in the dosage of a medication.

GUIDELINES TO MANAGEMENT

Discontinuation of the medications that caused the depressive syndrome may be sufficient to resolve many cases of iatrogenic depression. The decision to discontinue the medication should be made on an individual basis weighing the clinical benefits of continuing the medication against the potential risks of continuation and toxicity. These decisions require an awareness of the potential efficacy and complications of alternative treatments. If the depression resolves after the discontinuation of the drug, the next question that will frequently pose itself is about appropriate alternative treatment of the primary medical condition. If the alternatives are clearly inferior to the original drug, a re-challenge of the original drug may be indicated in some cases. If a change of medication is not practical because an effective alternative is not available or not feasible, one should consider prescribing antidepressant medication. The choice of the antidepressant may be influenced by the patient's medical condition and the concomitant medications. It should be borne in mind that

Table 2. Drug interactions between antidepressants and other medications.

Drug	Mechanism	Clinical outcome
A. Interactions with heterocyclic antidepressants		
MAOI	Increaed synaptic availability of neurotransmitters	Hypertensive reactions
Cimetidine	Inhibition of metabolism	Increased heterocyclic levels, increased adverse effects
Antipsychotics	Additive anticholinergic and antiadrenergic effects; mutual inhibition of metabolism	Increased anticholinergic and orthostatic side-effects
Stimulants	Inhibition of heterocyclic metabolism	Increased heterocyclic blood levels, increased side-effects
Phenytoin	Reduced blood level	Increased risk of seizures
Pressor agents	Increased central adrenergic transmission	Hypertension
B. Interactions with SSRIs		
Heterocyclic antidepressants	Inhibition of metabolism	Increased heterocyclic blood levels, increased toxicity
MAOI	Synergistic serotonergic enhancement	Hypertensive hyperthermic reaction
Theophylline	Inhibition of microsomal liver enzymes	Increased side-effects
Antipsychotic drugs	Antidopamine effect of SSRIs, inhibition of microsomal liver enzymes	Increased side-effects
Beta-blocking agents	Possibly serotonergic effect	Increased risk of cardiac conduction defects
C. Interactions with MAOIs		
Heterocyclic antidepressants	Synergistic "neurotransmitter" enhancement	Hypertensive reaction
Tyramine-rich foods	Increased synaptic tyramine	Hypertensive reaction
Pressor agents, stimulants, sympathomimetics	Increased synaptic availability of catecholamines	Hypertensive reaction
Narcotics	Possibly increased serotonergic transmission	Hypertensive–hyperthermic reaction

For further details, see Kapur and Kambhampati (1992) and Maxmen (1991).

antidepressant medications may have potentially significant interactions with several medications that are concomitantly prescribed for medical illnesses. Table 2 lists some drug interactions commonly associated with tricyclic antidepressants.

CONCLUSIONS

While a wide variety of drugs has been reported to cause depression in psychiatric and medical practice, the cause–effect association between these drugs and depression is still to be considered inadequately established in most situations. For certain drugs such as reserpine, amphetamine withdrawal, and steroids, some clinical evidence exists of association with depression; for other drugs the literature must be considered quite inconclusive. When depressive symptoms do occur in clinical practice for the majority of situations the differential diagnosis is relatively straightforward and in most cases the symptoms remit with the discontinuation of the offending agent. Depression could potentially have an adverse impact on the prognosis of the underlying medical disorder(s); recognition and appropriate management of the disorder is therefore critical. Further research is needed to establish the causal association between a variety of drugs and depressive symptoms.

REFERENCES

Abramovitz M and Aaron H (eds) (1984) *The Medical Letter on Drugs and Therapeutics*. The Medical Letter, Inc, 26, 75–78.

Adams F, Quesada JR and Gutterman JV (1984) Neuropsychiatric manifestations of human leukocyte interferon therapy in patients with cancer. *JAMA*, **252**, 9338–9341.

American Psychiatric Association (1994) *Diagnostic and Statistical Manual of Mental Disorder 4th revision*, Washington, DC: American Psychiatric Association.

Angst F (1992). In: MS Keshavan and J Kennedy (eds) *Drug Induced Dysfunction in Psychiatry*. Hemisphere Publishing Corporation, 181–188.

Ashton H (1995) Protracted withdrawal from benzodiazepines: the post-withdrawal syndrome. *Psychiatr Ann*, **25(3)**, 174–179.

Avorn J, Everitte DE and Weiss S (1986) Increased antidepressant use in patients prescribed β-Blockers. *JAMA*, **255**, 357–360.

Block M, Stager SV, Braun AR and Ruinow DR (1995) Severe psychiatric symptoms associated with paroxetine withdrawal. *Lancet*, **346**, 57.

Brent DA, Crumrine PK, Varma R, Brown AV and Allan MJ (1990) Phenobarbitone treatment and major depressive disorder in children with epilepsy: A naturalistic follow up: *Pediatrics*, **85**, 1086–1091.

Bright LA and Everitt DE (1992) β-Blockers and depression. Evidence against an association. *JAMA*, **267(13)**, 1783–1787.

Buckner JC and Mandell W (1990) Risk factors for depressive symptomatology in a drug using population. *Am J Public Health*, **80**, 580–585.

Ceccherini-Nelli A, Bardellini L, Cur A *et al.* (1993) Antidepressant withdrawal: prospective findings. *Am J Psychiatry*, **150(1)**, 165.

Cordess C, Folstein M and Drachman D (1981) Psychiatric side effects of alternate day steroid therapy. *Br J Psychiatry*, **138**, 504–506.

Demuth GW and Ackerman SH (1983) Alphamethyldopa and depression: a clinical study and review of literature. *Am J Psychiatry*, **140**, 534–538.

Depression Guideline Panel (1993) Depression in primary care: Volume I. Detection and

Diagnosis. *Clinical Practice Guideline No. 5*. Rockville, MD: US Department of Health and Human Services. 67–71.

Dhondt ADT and Hooijer C (1995) Is medication a significant aetiologic factor in geriatric depression? Considerations and a preliminary approach. *Int J Geriatric Psychiatry*, **10**, 1–8.

Dooneief G, Mirabello E, Bell K, Marder K, Stern Y and Mayeux A (1992) An estimate of the incidence of depression in idiopathic Parkinson's disease. *Arch Neurol*, **49**, 305–307.

Edwards GJ (1989) Drug related depression. In: KR Herbst and ES Paykel (eds) *Depression*. Oxford: Heinemann, 81–108.

Eisendrath SG and Sweeney MA (1987) Toxic neuropsychiatric effects of digoxin at the therapeutic serum concentrations. *Am J Psychiatry*, **144**, 506–507.

Engelberg H (1992) Low serum cholesterol and suicide. *Lancet*, **339**, 727–729.

Goodwin FK and Bunney WE (1971) Depression following reserpine: A reevaluation. *Semin Psychiatry*, **3**, 435–448.

Goodwin FK, Ebert MH and Bunney WE (1972) Mental effects of reserpine in man: review: In: R Shader (ed) *Psychiatric Complications of Medical Drugs*. New York: Raven Press, 73–102.

Halle MT and Dilsaver SC (1993) Tranylcypromine withdrawal phenomena. *J Psychiatry Neurosci*, **18(1)**, 49–50.

Holdiness MR (1987) Neurobiological manifestations and toxicities of the antituberculosis drugs: a review. *Med Toxicol*, **2(1)**, 33–51.

Kapur S and Kambhampati RK (1992) Drug interactions. In: MS Keshavan and J Kennedy (ed) *Drug Induced Dysfunction in Psychiatry*. Hemisphere Publishing Corporation, 21–37.

Kendler KS, Martin NG, Heath AC, Handelsman D and Eaves LJ (1988) A twin study of the psychiatric side effects of oral contraceptives. *J Nerv Ment Dis*, **176(3)**, 153–160.

Keshavan MS, Moodely P, Eales M, Joyce E and Yeragani VK (1988) Delusional depression following benzodiazepine withdrawal. *Can J Psychiatry*, **33**, 626–627.

Keshavan MS, Burton S, Murphy M, Checkley SA and Crammer JL (1985) Benzhexol withdrawal and cholinergic mechanisms in depression. *Br J Psychiatry*, **147**, 560–563.

Ketter TA, Malow BA, Flamini R *et al.* (1994) Anticonvulsant withdrawal emergent psychopathology. *Neurology*, **44(1)** 55–61.

Koopowitz LF and Berk M (1995) Paroxetine induced withdrawal effects. *Hum Psychopharmacol*, **10**, 147–148.

Lader MH (1994) Anxiety of depression during withdrawal of hypnotic treatments. *J Psychosom Res*, **38**, 113–123.

Lader MH and Morton SV (1992) A pilot study of the effects of flumazenil on symptoms persisting after benzodiazepine withdrawal. *J Psychopharm*, **6(3)**, 357–363.

Law MR, Thompson SG and Wald NJ (1994) Assessing possible hazards of reducing serum cholesterol. *Br Med. J*, **308**, 373–379.

Lechleitner M, Hoppichler F, Konwalinka G, Patsch JR and Braunsteiner H (1992) Depressive symptoms in hypercholesterolemic patients treated with pravastatin. *Lancet*, **340**, 910.

Levenson JL (1993) Cardiovascular disease. In: A Stoudemire and BS Fogel (eds) *Psychiatric Care of the Medical Patient*. New York: Oxford University Press, 539–555.

Lewis DS and Smith RE (1983) Steroid-induced psychiatric syndromes: A report of 14 cases and a review of the literature. *J Affect Disord*, **5**, 319–332.

Long TD and Kathol RG (1993) Critical review of data supporting affective disorder caused by nonpsychotropic medication. *Ann Clin Psychiatry*, **5**, 259–270.

Malone DA and Dimeff RJ (1992) Use of fluoxetine in depression associated with anabolic steroid withdrawal: A case series. *Am J Psychiatry*, **53**, 130–132.

Maxmen JS (1991) *Psychotropic Drugs: Fast Facts*. New York, London: WW Norton.

Metzger ER and Friedman RS (1994) Treatment-related depression: Medications from virtually every class of drug have been implicated in causing depression. *Psychiatry Ann*, **24(10)**, 540–544.

Middleboe TO, Mortensen EL and Bech P (1994) Depressive symptoms in cancer patients undergoing chemotherapy: A psychometric analysis. *Psychother Psychosom*, **61**, 171–177.

Mindham RHS, Marsden CD and Parkes JD (1976) Psychiatric symptoms during L-dopa therapy for Parkinson's disease and their relationship to physical disability. *Psychol Med*, **6**, 23–33.

Muldoon MF, Manuck SB and Matthews KA (1990) Lowering cholesterol concentrations and mortality: A quantitative review of primary prevention trials. *Br Med J*, **301**, 309–314.

Oswald I, Lewis SA, Dunleavy DLF, Brezinova V and Briggs M (1971) Drugs of dependence though not of abuse: Fenfluramine and imipramine. *Br Med J*, **3**, 70–73.

Pascualy M and Vieth RL (1989) Depression as an adverse drug reaction. In: RG Robinson and PV Rabin (eds) *Depression and Coexisting Disease*. New York: Igaku-Shoin, 132–151.

Patten SB and Love EJ (1993) Can drugs cause depression? A review of the evidence. *J Psychiatr Neurosci*, **18(3)**, 92–102.

Paykel ES, Fleminger R and Watson JP (1982) Psychiatric effects of antihypertensive drugs other than reserpine. *J Clin Psychopharmacol*, **2**, 14–39.

Pope HG and Katz DL (1988) Affective psychotic symptoms associated with anabolic steroid use. *Am J Psychiatry*, **145**, 487–490.

Robertson MM, Trimble MR and Townsend HR (1987) Phenomenology of depression in epilepsy. *Epilepsia*, **28**, 364–372.

Robins AH, McFadyen AL, Lucke W and Wright JP (1984) Effect of the H_2-receptor antagonist ranitidine on depression and anxiety in duodenal ulcer patients *Postgrad Med J*, **60**, 353–355.

Rundell JR and Wise MG (1989) Causes of organic mood disorder. *J Neuropsychiatry Clin Neurosci*, **1**, 398–400.

Schildkraut JJ and Kety SS (1967) Biogenic amines and emotion. *Science*, **156**, 21–30.

Schleifer SJ, Slater WR, Macari-Hinson MM, Coyle DA, Kahn M, Zucker HD and Gorlin R (1991) Digitalis and β-blocking agents: Effects on depression following myocardial infarction. *Am Heart J*, **121**, 1397–1402.

Schou M (1993) Is there a lithium withdrawal syndrome? An examination of the evidence. *Br J Psychiatry*, **163**, 514–418.

Starkstein SE, Preziosi TJ, Bolduc PL and Robinson RG (1990) Depression in Parkinson's disease. *J Nerv Ment Dis*, **178**, 27–31.

Thiessen BQ, Wallace SM, Blackburn JL, Wilson TW and Bergman U (1990) Increased prescribing of antidepressant subsequent to beta-blocker therapy. *Arch Intern Med*, **150**, 2286–2290.

Van Putten T and May PRA (1978) Akinetic depression in schizophrenia. *Arch Gen Psychiatry*, **38**, 902–907.

Wallach MB and Gershon S (1972) Psychiatric sequelae to tuberculosis chemotherapy. In: RI Shader (ed) *Psychiatric Complications of Medical Drugs*. New York, Raven Press.

Yudofsky SC (1992) β-blockers and depression: The clinician's dilemma. *JAMA*, **267 (13)**, 1826–1827.

Zelnik T (1987) Depressive effects of drugs. In: OG Cameson (ed) *Presentations of Depression*. New York: John Wiley, 355–399.

Index

nb – page numbers in **bold** refer to tables. Page numbers in *italic* refer to figures.

Index compiled by C. Purton